Our Dramatic Heritage

VOLUME 1

Our Dramatic Heritage

VOLUME 1: *Classical Drama
and the Early Renaissance*

Edited by Philip G. Hill

Rutherford ● Madison ● Teaneck
Fairleigh Dickinson University Press
London and Toronto: Associated University Presses

© 1983 by Associated University Presses, Inc.

Associated University Presses, Inc.
440 Forsgate Drive
Cranbury, N.J. 08512

Associated University Presess Ltd
25 Sicilian Avenue
London WC1A 2QH, England

Associated University Presses
2133 Royal Windsor Drive
Unit 1
Mississauga, Ontario
Canada L5J 1K5

Library of Congress Cataloging in Publication Data
Main entry under title:

Our dramatic heritage.

   Contents: v. 1. Classical drama and the early
Renaissance.
   1. European drama.   I. Hill, Philip G. (Philip
George), 1934–
PN6111.087   1983   808.82   81-65294
ISBN 0-8386-3106-1 (v. 1)

Contents

Acknowledgments	7
Introduction	9
The Oresteia (Aeschylus)	
Agamemnon	17
Choephoroe	34
Eumenides	48
Oedipus Rex (Sophocles)	61
Medea (Euripides)	90
Lysistrata (Aristophanes)	117
The Dyskolos (Menander)	154
Miles Gloriosus (Titus Maccus Plautus)	178
The Brothers (Publius Terentius Afer)	223
The Trojan Women (Lucius Annaeus Seneca)	248
Abraham (Hrotsvitha)	276
The Second Shepherds' Play, *Everyman*, and *Pierre Pathelin* (authors unknown)	
The Second Shepherds' Play	289
Everyman	300
Pierre Pathelin	314
The Doubles according to Plautus (a commedia dell'arte scenario)	332
The Mandrake (Niccolò Machiavelli)	338

Acknowledgments

CAUTION: Professionals and amateurs are hereby warned that these plays and translations, being fully protected under the copyright laws of the United States of America, the British Commonwealth, including the Dominion of Canada, and all other countries which are signatories to the Universal Copyright Convention and the International Copyright Union, are subject to royalty. All rights, including professional, amateur, motion picture, recitation, lecturing, public reading, radio broadcasting, and television, are strictly reserved. All inquiries for rights must be addressed to the copyright owners.

ACKNOWLEDGEMENT is made to copyright holders and publishers for permission to reprint the following:

The Oresteia by Aeschylus. Translated by George Thomson. Reprinted by permission of George Thomson.

Oedipus Rex by Sophocles, translated by Dudley Fitts and Robert Fitzgerald, is reprinted by permission of Harcourt Brace Jovanovich, Inc.; copyright 1949 by Harcourt Brace Jovanovich, Inc.; renewed 1977 by Cornelia Fitts and Robert Fitzgerald. CAUTION: All rights, including professional, amateur, motion picture, recitation, lecturing, public reading, radio broadcasting, and television are strictly reserved. Inquiries on all rights should be addressed to Harcourt Brace Jovanovich, Inc., 757 Third Avenue, New York, New York 10017. Distributed in the British Commonwealth, excluding Canada, by permission of Faber and Faber, Ltd.

Medea by Euripides. Translated by Frederic Prokosch. Reprinted by permission of Frederic Prokosch.

Lysistrata by Aristophanes, translated by Douglass Parker. Copyright © 1964 by William Arrowsmith. Reprinted by arrangement with The New American Library, Inc., New York, N.Y.

The Dyskolos from *The Dyskolos* by Menander, translated and with an Introduction, Notes and Bibliography by Carroll Moulton. Copyright © 1977 by Carroll Moulton. Reprinted by arrangement with The New American Library, Inc., New York, N.Y.

Major Bullshot-Gorgeous from *Three Plays by Plautus*, translated by Paul Roche. Paul Roche, whose renditions of the Greek and Latin classics are well known in the United States, is an English poet who frequently visits these shores on campus engagements.

Introduction

This book is the first in a projected four-volume series that will illustrate the development of European drama from its beginning in ancient Greece to the mid-twentieth century. The beginning point is fixed by the fact that no scripts survive by any playwright earlier than Aeschylus, but the ending has arbitrarily been set at World War II because that holocaust not only put a temporary halt to most dramatic activity in Europe, but also marked a philosophical and cultural dividing line that is reflected in the drama as well as in most other areas of human endeavor.

Some 2,400 years of playwriting in more than a dozen major languages can hardly be compressed with complete satisfaction into even so bulky an anthology as this one. Difficult choices have been made, and a great many fine plays have necessarily been omitted. There have been several guiding principles in choosing the works that do appear that, once understood, may guide the reader in forming a judgment about what is here. With only a couple of exceptions, every play in these volumes is first, last, and primarily a blueprint for theatrical production; each was so intended by its creator, and each has been judged on that basis in the selection process. What is being traced, in short, is the development of a tradition of performance, of which little remains in most cases other than the script that was originally prepared for that performance. That one can now read many of these scripts as one would literature prepared chiefly to be read is an exciting extra value for those who are skilled at creating a performance in the mind's eye, but to see that as an end in itself is as narrow as to read the sheet music for a great symphony without yearning to hear it performed. So notable an exception to this rule as Seneca, who is represented here because of the profound influence of his work on Renaissance tragedians, only serves to reinforce its importance with respect to all the others. Since their authors' chief purpose was to create a performance, these scripts must be understood and judged as performances, and every effort has been made to select the most playable scripts (and the most playable translations when choices were open) in order best to represent the tradition that is here under scrutiny.

As the performing tradition developed and flourished in Europe, each playwright found himself working in a milieu heavily influenced by those who had preceded him. This influence should not be exaggerated, but neither should it be ignored. Some of the most significant innovators managed to break in major ways from the tradition that they inherited, but frequently the greatest playwrights were those who worked comfortably within, or brought to fullest fruition, those principles handed to them by their forebears. Thus, it is appropriate to ask, with respect to any playwright, something about the cultural milieu within which he worked, the influences upon him, and how he in turn influenced others. For the most part, the theater is not an iconoclastic or radical institution; it tends to please its public in the "traditional" way as that tradition is then understood. These plays have been selected, then, in part to show the continuity of these influences—even in some cases across centuries.

9

The sticky problem of translation is difficult enough in any literary form, but it is especially vexing in the case of drama. The usual problems of accuracy and poetic beauty are complicated further by the fact that the lines of a drama must be spoken aloud on a stage, and meanings must be intelligible—indeed, fascinating—to an audience in a theater. The problem of the translator may simply be stated as providing the essence of the original in a form compatible with the tastes and understandings of a modern audience speaking another language, but this glib formulation hardly does justice to the acute agony involved in balancing faithfulness to the original against practical theatrical needs. The translations in these volumes have been selected with these problems in mind, and they represent the editor's best judgment of what, among the available translations of a work, might best play on a modern stage and communicate meaningfully with a modern audience. Both excellence in scholarship and high aesthetic sensitivity are needed in a play translator; this is a combination not easily found.

For the most part, the plays appear in these volumes in chronological order; all dates associated with plays are the dates of first production unless they are identified otherwise. Slight variations in strict chronological order have occasionally been introduced in order to keep two works by the same playwright together or to complete the picture of development in a single country. The introduction to each play provides biographical information about the playwright, a list of his major works, some observations on the social and theatrical milieu in which he worked, and a brief critical discussion of the play itself. All footnotes have been provided by the present editor except where specific credit is given otherwise.

This volume traces the European drama through its Greek and Roman origins as well as through its reappearance in Europe in the early Renaissance. Although this dividing point was arbitrarily chosen, it does have the advantage of emphasizing how, despite the chronological remoteness of antiquity, the dramatic forms and characters of the ancient world reappeared as part of a performing heritage after the long "darkness" of the Middle Ages. In fact, however scanty the written records, that performing tradition was maintained throughout that period of cultural revamping, thus not only bridging the ages but also encouraging the reawakening that so profoundly quickened Western civilization. The full flowering of the Renaissance, the "Golden Age," is reserved for volume 2.

Our Dramatic Heritage

VOLUME 1

The Oresteia

Aeschylus

Aeschylus was the first great master of the art of playwriting. Since no complete scripts have survived from writers earlier than he, attempts to credit Aeschylus with a major share in the invention of theatrical art are largely speculative, but most scholars find it reasonable to assume that, before Aeschylus, drama was little more than elaborate choral singing and dancing, with a single actor providing solo counterpoint. Aristotle credits Aeschylus with inventing the notion of two actors onstage exchanging dialogue, and there is reason to believe that Aeschylus also devoted a great deal of attention to the proper staging of his plays, training the chorus, designing costumes and scenery, creating spectacular theatrical effects, and in other ways earning the title of the first play*wright*—a craftsman of plays. To what extent other, unknown artists before Aeschylus should share some of this credit one cannot be sure, but it is certain that, irrespective of the extent to which Aeschylus may have invented these devices, he was surely their first great master. At the dawn of recorded theatrical history, Aeschylus emerges as a consummate artist whose work has rarely been equaled and never exceeded in Occidental drama.

Aeschylus was born around 525 B.C. in the city of Eleusis, near Athens. Little is known of his life, but he fought in the battles of Marathon and Salamis and was proud of his prowess as a warrior and as one of the saviors of Athenian democracy. He competed frequently in the annual playwriting contests that were a highlight of the Athenian year, regularly writing and producing the three tragedies and a satyr play that constituted a day's entertainment. He won first place in this competition between thirteen and twenty-eight times, and he was so greatly respected that he was given the singular honor of having his plays revived in this competition after his death. Aeschylus traveled widely by ancient standards and was both wealthy and well-born enough to be well received wherever he went. He died in Sicily in 456 B.C., and legend maintains that he wrote his own epitaph, which cites his skill as a soldier but never mentions his writing. Of the more than ninety plays that Aeschylus wrote, only seven have survived more or less complete. *The Persians* (472 B.C.) treats Athens's recent war with Persia and is primarily a patriotic and lyrical work; *Seven against Thebes* (467 B.C.) is the third play of a trilogy based on the Oedipus legend; the dates of *The Suppliants* and *Prometheus Bound* are not known, but recently discovered evidence suggests that both are late in Aeschylus's career. If so, no direct evidence survives other than fragments with respect to his early plays. Both *The Suppliants* and *Prometheus Bound* are the first plays of their respective trilogies, with the former the story of the fifty daughters of Danaus, who are fleeing Egypt to escape hated marriages, and the latter the story of Prometheus, who brought the gift of fire to man and whom Zeus chained to a rock in punishment. The last three plays of Aeschylus, *Agamemnon*, *Choephoroe* (The Libation Bearers), and *Eumenides* (The Furies), fit together as the only surviving trilogy from classical times.

The trilogy is usually entitled *The Oresteia*. It is tempting to infer from it that Aeschylus's other trilogies, as well as those of the other Greek playwrights, were similarly built around unifying themes and actions, but it appears that this was not always so. Even in the case of *The Oresteia*, the satyr play that concluded Aeschylus's complete presentation one spring day in 458 B.C. has now been lost; one cannot be sure how its boisterous comedy may have complemented the unquestioned terror and sweeping thematic complexity of the surviving portions. What is worse, no exact information survives regarding the music, the dance, the singing, the acting, and the stagecraft that went into the total success of that day. Legend reports that children screamed and women had miscarriages at the frightening appearance of the Furies; surely any theatrical presentation that offered so much power must have been remarkable indeed. Theater is so ephemeral an art that there is always difficulty in imaginatively reconstructing a performance simply from reading a script, but distance in time and culture from the fifth-century-B.C. Athenians renders this process even more difficult. It is clear that the chorus was the central focus of the event; in reading the script today one must picture a singing and dancing spectacle of compelling beauty and power, within which the lines spoken (or in many cases sung) by the actors were important but by no means preeminent.

Aeschylus was also able to assume in his audience a ready familiarity with Greek legend that is not nearly so widespread today. Tantalus, founder of what is now known as the House of Atreus, was condemned to Hades by the gods for killing his own son; that son, Pelops, was restored to life and had two sons, Atreus and Thyestes. When Thyestes seduced his brother's wife, Atreus killed Thyestes' children and served them up to him in a stew. Thyestes' one surviving son, Aegisthus, is still seeking revenge for these atrocities when *The Oresteia* opens. Atreus, in the meantime, had two sons, Menelaus and Agamemnon, who married half-sisters, Helen and Clytemnestra. When Helen was seduced by Paris and spirited away to Troy, Agamemnon joined forces with his brother in the renowned ten-year siege of Troy. In order to gain a favorable wind so that the fleet might sail to Troy, Agamemnon sacrificed the life of his daughter Iphigenia, a fanatic act for which Clytemnestra can never forgive him. During Agamemnon's ten-year absence at Troy, Aegisthus has partially accomplished his revenge by seducing Clytemnestra, and the two of them have plotted to gain full vengeance by murdering Agamemnon upon his return.

As *Agamemnon*, the first part of the trilogy, opens, a Watchman sees a beacon fire that signals to Argos (Agamemnon's kingdom, ruled in his absence by Clytemnestra) the long-awaited fall of Troy. There ensues a religious celebration and thanksgiving for the great victory, after which (telescoping time in a nonrealistic but theatrically satisfying manner) a Herald enters to report that Agamemnon will soon be home. Shortly, Agamemnon himself appears in the full splendor of a returning hero. Among the spoils of conquest, Agamemnon has brought with him Cassandra, daughter of Priam (king of Troy). Cassandra has been granted by Apollo the gift of seeing the future, but she is damned in that no one will believe her prophecies. Clytemnestra, further outraged by the presence of Agamemnon's paramour, proceeds to kill them both, but not before Cassandra has foreshadowed the rest of the trilogy by forecasting her own and Agamemnon's deaths, Orestes' murder of his mother, and his eventual acquittal. At the climactic moment of the first play, the central doors of the palace swing open to reveal the bloody bodies of Agamemnon and Cassandra, the former enmeshed in a net and hacked to death in his bath, with the triumphant Clytemnestra and Aegisthus standing over them.

In the *Choephoroe*, Electra, Agamemnon's daughter, is praying at his grave some years later. Orestes, her brother, returns from years of banishment, having received orders from Apollo to avenge his father by killing his mother and her lover. After a scene of recognition between brother and sister, the details of their plan of vengeance are worked out and the bloody act is consummated, but no sooner is Clytemnestra dead than Orestes is attacked by the Furies, frightful presences that personify Clytemnestra's revenge and that demand Orestes' life in expiation for his murder of his mother. In the *Eumenides,* the last part of the trilogy, Orestes flees to Apollo's temple at Delphi seeking protection. Apollo has the power to spare Orestes' life, but not to rid him of the Furies, so he is sent to Athena's shrine on the Acropolis—the very hill where this play was performed in 458 B.C. Athena decrees that Orestes shall stand trial at the Areopagus, a large rock (and later a building) at which justice was traditionally administered in Athens. On a narrowly split vote, with Athena casting the deciding ballot, Orestes is acquitted, and the Furies are changed into friendly spirits of justice who will forever inhabit the Areopagus.

Aeschylus's predominant theme throughout this bloody tale is nothing less than the evolution of civilization from barbarism, the substitution of human justice for the ancient code of *dikê* (retribution)—an eye for an eye and a tooth for a tooth. Even as far back as Tantalus, one horrendous crime had led to the next, with the victims in each case seeking vengeance by committing still more crimes. Aeschylus demonstrates what each generation has to learn anew: that there can be no end to such retribution when every victim feels duty-bound to kill the perpetrator of the preceding crime. One of the fundamental tenets of civilization has been the surrendering of blood "rights" in such cases to the state, with the innocent to be freed and the guilty punished without the committing of a further crime. Aeschylus is thus able to end his tragedy on a very positive note, for the imbalance in justice and thus in society that existed at the beginning of the trilogy is finally set right; a new order and a new justice are established which, especially to an Athenian audience, represent the highest and best that corporate man can achieve. The magnificent scope of this concept, and the brilliance with which Aeschylus derives it from one of the widely known legends of his society, are at the root of the greatness of this play.

Aeschylus makes use of an austerity of characterization that may at first strike a reader as foreign or strange. Sophocles and Euripides throughout the fifth century made increasing use of psychological insights to develop human characters whose motivations seem more and more understandable by modern realistic standards. Still, there is a kind of primitive beauty and simplicity to Aeschylus's characters that has caused them rightly to be compared to stiff, archaic statues; they are not entirely of this world, but they show insight into human essence at an extremely valuable primordial level. The pride of the returning Agamemnon, the hate of the vengeful Clytemnestra, the anguish of the driven Orestes, tap areas of human collective subconsciousness so deep and so true that one would not willingly trade them for more three-dimensional characterizations.

The structure of the Greek tragedy was not rigid or invariable, but typically included a *prologue,* which consisted of all that material preceding the entry of the chorus. The choral entry song was called the *parodos;* the bulk of the play consisted of an alternating series of *episodes* and choral *odes.* Each episode might include no more than three speaking actors (two in Aeschylus's earlier plays), though the same actor might return in a later episode as a different character. The standard number of episodes was five, and the last episode, together with the choral exit lines at the end of the play, was known as the *exodos.* The reader may wish to study each of the three plays in *The Oresteia* to find how this pattern is followed and how it is occasionally varied.

The grandeur, the awe, the beauty, and the sheer magnificence of Aeschylus's work make it an admirable beginning point for a study of European drama. It is fortunate that, if only one trilogy was to survive, it was this masterful work of the first great playwright. Across the centuries and across cultural chasms, *The Oresteia* reaches the modern audience not complete, but nevertheless breathtaking. For completeness, one would need not only the missing textual parts, not only the staging conventions now lost in history, but also the beauty of Aeschylus's poetry, which in the original is great indeed. Modern directors continue to seek satisfactory ways of rendering all of this on the modern stage, but everyone agrees that the ideal solution to this problem has not yet been found. The imagination of the reader must work at maximum capacity to leap time, space, and custom and to restage *The Oresteia* in the mind's eye.

George Thomson's excellent translation, here newly emended by him and published for the first time in this form, is based on his edition of the Greek text (2 vols., Prague, 1966).

The Oresteia

Translated by George Thomson

Agamemnon

Characters
Watchman
Chorus of Old Men
Clytemnestra
Herald
Agamemnon
Cassandra
Aegisthus
Captain of the Guard

The scene is the entrance to the palace of the Atreidae. Before the doors stand shrines of the gods. A WATCHMAN *is posted on the roof.*

WATCHMAN. I've prayed God to release me from sentry duty
All through this long year's vigil, like a dog
Couched on the roof of Atreus, where I study
Night after night the pageantry of this vast
Concourse of stars, and moving among them like
Noblemen the constellations that bring
Summer and winter as they rise and fall.
And I am still watching for the beacon signal
All set to flash over the sea the radiant
News of the fall of Troy. So confident
Is a woman's spirit, whose purpose is a man's.

Every night, as I turn in to my stony bed,
Quilted with dew, not visited by dreams,
Not mine—no sleep, fear stands at my pillow
Keeping tired eyes from closing once too often;
And whenever I start to sing or hum a tune,
Mixing from music an antidote to sleep,
It always turns to mourning for the royal house,
Which is not in such good shape as it used to be.
But now at last may the good news in a flash
Scatter the darkness and deliver us!
[*The beacon flashes.*]
O light of joy, whose gleam turns night to day,
O radiant signal for innumerable
Dances of victory! Ho there! I call the queen,
Agamemnon's wife, to raise with all the women
Alleluias of thanksgiving through the palace
Saluting the good news, if it is true
That Troy has fallen, as this blaze portends;
Yes, and I'll dance an overture myself.

17

My master's dice have fallen out well,
and I
Shall score three sixes for this night-
watching. [*A pause.*]
Well, come what will, may it soon be
mine to grasp
In this right hand my master's, home
again! [*Another pause.*]
The rest is secret. A heavy ox has trod-
den
Upon my tongue. These walls would
have tales to tell
If they had mouths. I speak only to
those
Who are in the know; to others—I
know nothing. [*The* WATCHMAN *goes
into the palace. Women's cries are heard.
Enter* CHORUS OF OLD MEN.]

CHORUS. It is ten years since those
armed prosecutors of Justice, Menelaus
and Agamemnon, twin-sceptred in
God-given sovranty, embarked in the
thousand ships crying war, like eagles
with long wings beating the air over a
robbed mountain nest, wheeling and
screaming for their lost children. Yet
above them some god, maybe Apollo or
Zeus, overhears the sky-dweller's cry
and sends after the robber a Fury.
[CLYTEMNESTRA *comes out of the palace
and unseen by the elders places offerings before the shrines.*] Just so the two kings
were sent by the greater king, Zeus, for
the sake of a promiscuous woman to
fight Paris, Greek and Trojan locked
fast together in the dusty betrothals of
battle. And however it stands with them
now, the end is unalterable; no flesh,
no wine can appease God's fixed indig-
nation.
    As for us, with all the able-bodied
men enlisted and gone, we are left here
leaning our strength on a staff; for, just
as in infancy, when the marrow is still
unformed, the War-god is not at his
post, so it is in extreme old age, as the
leaves fall fast, we walk on three feet,
like dreams in the daylight. [*They see*
CLYTEMNESTRA.]
    O Queen, Clytemnestra, what news?
what message sets light to the altars?
All over the town the shrines are ablaze
with unguents drawn from the royal
stores and the flames shoot up into the
night sky. Speak, let us hear all that

may be made public, so healing the anxieties that have gathered thick in our
hearts; let the gleam of good news scatter them! [CLYTEMNESTRA *goes out to tend
the other altars of the city.*]

Strength have I still to recall that sign
which greeted the two kings
Taking the road, for the prowess of
song is not yet spent.
I sing of two kings united in sovranty,
leading
Armies to battle, who saw two eagles
Beside the palace
Wheel into sight, one black, and the
other was white-tailed,
Tearing a hare with her unborn litter.
Ailinon cry, but let good conquer!

Shrewdly the priest took note and com-
pared each eagle with each king,
Then spoke out and prefigured the fu-
ture in these words:
"In time the Greek arms shall demolish
the fortress of Priam;
Only let no jealous God, as they fasten
On Troy the slave's yoke,
Strike them in anger; for Artemis
loathes the rapacious
Beagles of Zeus that have slaughtered
the frail hare.
Ailinon cry, but let good conquer!
O Goddess, gentle to the tender whelp
of fierce lions
As to all young life of the wild,
So now fulfil what is good in the omen
and mend what is faulty.
And I appeal unto the Lord Apollo,
Let not the north wind hold the fleet
storm-bound,
Driving them on to repay that feast
with another,
Inborn builder of strife, feud that fears
no man, it is still there,
Treachery keeping the house, it re-
members, revenges, a child's death!"
Such, as the kings left home, was the
seer's revelation.
Ailinon cry, but let good conquer!
Zeus, whoe'er he be, if so it best
Please his ear to be addressed,
So shall he be named by me.
All things have I measured, yet
None have found save him alone,
Zeus, if a man from a heart heavy-la-
den

Seek to cast his cares aside.

Long since lived a ruler[1] of the world,
Puffed with martial pride, of whom
None shall tell, his day is done;
Also, he who followed him
Met his master and is gone.
Zeus the victorious, gladly acclaim him;
Perfect wisdom shall be yours;

Zeus, who laid it down that man
Must in sorrow learn and through
Pain to wisdom find his way.
When deep slumber falls, remembered
   wrongs
Open old wounds anew, then at last
Wisdom slowly enters in.
Harsh the grace dispensed by powers
   immortal,
Pilots of the human soul.

Even so the elder king,
Marshal of the thousand ships,
Rather than distrust a priest,
Torn with doubt to see his men
Harbor-locked, hunger-pinched, hard-
   oppressed,
Strained beyond endurance, still
Watching, waiting, where the never-tir-
   ing
Tides of Aulis ebb and flow:

And still the storm blew from moun-
   tains far north,
With moorings windswept and hungry
   crews pent
In rotting hulks,
With tackling all torn and seeping tim-
   bers,
Till Time's slow-paced, enforced inac-
   tion
Had all but stripped bare the bloom of
   Greek manhood.
And then was found but one
Cure to allay the tempest—never a blast
   so bitter—
Shrieked in a loud voice by the priest,
   "Artemis!"[2] striking the Atreidae[3]
with dismay, each with his staff smit-
   ing the ground and weeping.

And then the king spoke, the elder,
   saying:
"The choice is hard—hard to disobey
   him,
And harder still

To kill my own child, my palace jewel,
With unclean hands before the altar
Myself, her own father, spill a maid's
   pure blood.
I have no choice but wrong.
How shall I fail my thousand ships and
   betray my comrades?
So shall the storm cease, and the men
   eager for war clamor for that virginal
   blood righteously! So pray for a
   happy outcome!"

And when he bowed down beneath the
   harness
Of cruel coercion, his spirit veering
With sudden sacrilegious change,
He gave his whole mind to evil counsel.
For man is made bold with base-con-
   triving
Impetuous madness, first cause of
   much grief.
And so then he slew his own child
For a war to win a woman
And to speed the storm-bound fleet
   from the shore to battle.

She cried aloud "Father!", yet they
   heard not;
A girl in first flower, yet they cared not,
The lords who gave the word for war.
Her father prayed, then he bade his
   vassals
To seize her where swathed in folds of
   saffron
She lay, and lift her up like a yearling
With bold heart above the altar,
And her lovely lips were bridled
That they might not cry out, cursing
   the House of Atreus,

With gags, her voice sealed with brute
   force and crushed.
And then she let fall her cloak
And cast at each face a glance that
   dumbly craved compassion;
And like a picture she would but could
   not greet
Her father's guests, who at home
Had often sat when the meal was over,
The cups replenished, with all hearts
   enraptured
To hear her sing grace with clear un-
   sullied voice for her loving father.

The end was unseen and unspeakable.
The task of priestcraft was done.

For Justice first chastens, then she
  presses home her lesson.
The morrow must come, its grief will
  soon be here,
So let us not weep today.
It shall be made known as clear as day-
  break.
And so may all this at last end in good
  news,
For which the queen prays, the next of
  kin and stay of the land of Argos.
[CLYTEMNESTRA *appears at the door of
  the palace.*]
Our humble salutations to the queen!
Hers is our homage, while our master's
  throne
Stands empty. We are still longing to
  hear
The meaning of your sacrifice. Is it
  good news?
CLYTEMNESTRA. Good news! With good
  news may the day be born
From mother Night! Good news be-
  yond all hope!
My news is this: The Greeks have taken
  Troy.
CHORUS. What? No, it cannot be true! I
  cannot grasp it.
CLYTEMNESTRA. The Greeks hold
  Troy—is not that plain enough?
CHORUS. Joy steals upon me and fills my
  eyes with tears.
CLYTEMNESTRA. Indeed, your looks be-
  tray your loyalty.
CHORUS. What is the proof? Have you
  any evidence?
CLYTEMNESTRA. Of course I have, or
  else the Gods have cheated me.
CHORUS. You have given ear to some
  beguiling dream.
CLYTEMNESTRA. I would not come
  screaming fancies out of my sleep.
CHORUS. Rumors have wings—on these
  your heart has fed.
CLYTEMNESTRA. You mock my intelli-
  gence as though I were a girl.
CHORUS. When was it? How long is it
  since the city fell?
CLYTEMNESTRA. In the night that gave
  birth to this dawning day.
CHORUS. What messenger could bring
  the news so fast?
CLYTEMNESTRA. The God of Fire, who
  from Ida sent forth light
And beacon by beacon passed the
  flame to me.

From the peak of Ida first to the cliff of
  Hermes[4]
On Lemnos, and from there a third
  great lamp
Was flashed to Athos, the pinnacle of
  Zeus;
Up, up it soared, luring the dancing
  fish
To break surface in rapture at the
  light;
A golden courier, like the sun, it sped
Post-haste its message to Macistus,
  thence
Across Euripus, till the flaming sign
Was marked by the watchers on Mes-
  sapium,
And thence with strength renewed
  from piles of heath
Like moonrise over the valley of
  Asopus,
Relayed in glory to Cithaeron's heights,
And still flashed on, from eager sen-
  tinels,
Leaping across the lake from peak to
  peak,
It passed the word to burn and burn,
  and flung
A comet to the promontory that stands
Over the Gulf of Saron, there it
  swooped
Down to the Spider's Crag above the
  city,
Then found its mark on the roof of this
  house of Atreus,
That beacon fathered by Ida's far-off
  fires.
Such were the stages of our torch relay,
And the last to run is the first to reach
  the goal.
That is my evidence, the testimony
  which
My lord has signaled to me out of
  Troy.
CHORUS. Lady, there will be time later
  to thank the Gods.
Now I ask only to listen: speak on and
  on.
CLYTEMNESTRA. Today the Greeks have
  occupied Troy.
I seem to hear there a very strange
  street-music.
Pour oil and vinegar into one cup, you
  will see
They do not make friends. So there
  two tunes are heard.
Slaves now, the Trojans, brothers and

aged fathers,
Prostrate, sing for their dearest the last
dirge.
The others, tired out and famished
after the night's looting,
Grab what meal chance provides,
lodgers now
In Trojan houses, sheltered from the
night frosts,
From the damp dews delivered, free to
sleep
Off guard, off duty, all night to rest in
peace.
Therefore, provided that they show
due respect
To the altars of the plundered town
and are not
Tempted to lay coarse hands on sanc-
tities,
Remembering that the last lap—the
voyage home—
Lies still ahead of them, then, if they
should return
Guiltless before God, the curses of the
bereaved
Might be placated—barring accidents.
That is my announcement—a message
from my master.
May all end well, and may I reap the
fruit of it!
CHORUS. Lady, you have spoken with a
wise man's judgment.
Now it is time to address the gods once
more
After this happy outcome of our cares.

Thanks be to Zeus and to gracious
Night, housekeeper of heaven's embroidery, who has cast over the towers
of Troy a net so fine as to leave no escape for old or young, all caught in the
snare! All praise to Zeus, who with a
shaft from his outstretched bow has at
last brought down the transgressor!

"By Zeus struck down!" The truth is all
clear
With each step plainly marked. He
said, Be
It so, and so it was. A man denied once
That heaven pays heed to those who
trample
Beneath the feet holy sanctities. He lied
wickedly;
For God's wrath soon or late destroys
all sinners filled

With pride, puffed up with vain pre-
sumption,
And great men's houses stocked with
silver
And gold beyond measure. Far best to
live
Free of want, without grief, rich in the
gift of wisdom.
Glutted with gold, the sinner kicks
Justice out of his sight, yet
She sees *him* and remembers.

As sweet temptation lures him onwards
With childlike smile into the death-
trap,
He cannot help himself. His curse is lit
up
Against the darkness, a bright baleful
light.
And just as false bronze in battle ham-
mered turns black and shows
Its true worth, so the sinner time-tried
stands condemned.
His hopes take wing, and still he gives
chase, with foul crimes branding all
his people.
He cries to deaf heaven, none hear his
prayers.
Justice drags him down to hell as he
calls for succor.
Such was the sinner Paris, who
Rendered thanks to a gracious
Host by stealing a woman.

She left behind her the ports all astir
With throngs of men under arms filing
onto troopships,
She took to Troy in lieu of dowry
death.
A light foot passed through the gates
and fled,
And then a cry of lamentation rose.
The seers, the king's prophets, mut-
tered darkly:
"Bewail the king's house that now is
desolate,
Bewail the bed marked with print of
love that fled!"
Behold, in silence, without praise, with-
out reproach,
He sits upon the ground and weeps.
Beyond the wave lies his love;
Here a ghost seems to rule the palace!
Shapely the grace of statues,
Yet they bring him no comfort,
Eyeless, lifeless and loveless.

Delusive phantoms that float through
   the night
Beguile him, bringing delight sweet but
   unsubstantial;
For, while the eye beholds the heart's
   desire,
The arms clasp empty air, and then
The fleeting vision fades and glides
   away
On silent wing down the paths of slum-
   ber.
The royal hearth is chilled with sorrows
   such as these,
And more; in each house from end to
   end of Greece
That sent its dearest to wage war in
   foreign lands
The stout heart is called to steel itself
In mute endurance against
Blows that strike deep into the heart's
   core:
Those that they sent from home they
Knew, but now they receive back
Only a heap of ashes.

The God of War holds the twin scales
   of strife,
Heartless gold-changer trafficking in
   men,
Consigning homeward from Troy a jar
   of dust fire-refined,
Making up the weight with grief,
Shapely vessels neatly packed
With the ashes of their kin.
They mourn and praise them saying,
   "He
Was practiced well in sword and spear,
And he, who fell so gallantly—
All to avenge another man's wife":
It is muttered in a whisper
And resentment spreads against each
   of the royal warlords.
They lie sleeping, perpetual
Owners each of a small
Holding far from their homeland.

The sullen rumors that pass mouth to
   mouth
Bring the same danger as a people's
   curse,
And brooding hearts wait to hear of
   what the night holds from sight.
Watchful are the Gods of all
Hands with slaughter stained. The
   black
Furies wait, and when a man

Has grown by luck, not justice, great,
With sudden turn of circumstance
He wastes away to nothing, dragged
Down to be food in hell for demons.
For the heights of fame are perilous.
With a jealous bolt the Lord Zeus in a
   flash shall blast them.
Best to pray for a tranquil
Span of life and to be
Neither victor nor vanquished.
—The news has set the whole town
   aflame.
Can it be true? Perhaps it is a trick.
—Only a child would let such fiery
   words
Kindle his hopes, then fade and flicker
   out.
—It is just like a woman
To accept good news without the evi-
   dence.
—An old wives' tale, winged with a
   woman's wishes,
Spreads like wildfire, then sinks and is
   forgotten.

We shall soon know what the beacon
   signifies,
Whether it is true or whether this joy-
   ful daybreak
Is only a dream sent to deceive us all.
Here comes a messenger breathless
   from the shore,
Wearing a garland and covered in a
   cloud
Of dust, which shows that he has news
   to tell,
And not in soaring rhetoric of smoke
   and flame,
But either he brings cause for yet
   greater joy,
Or else,—no, let us abjure the alterna-
   tive.
Glad shone the light, and gladly break
   the day!
[*Enter* HERALD.]
HERALD. O joy! Argos, I greet you, my
   fatherland!
Joy brings me home after ten years of
   war.
Many the shattered hopes, but this has
   held.
Now I can say that when I die my
   bones
Will lie at rest here in my native soil.
I greet you joyfully, I greet the Sun,
Zeus the All-Highest, and the Pythian

King,
Bending no more against us his fatal
shafts,
As he did beside Scamander⁵—that was
enough,
And now defend us, Savior Apollo; all
The Gods I greet, among them
Hermes, too,
Patron of messengers, and the spirits of
our dead,
Who sent their sons forth, may they
now prepare
A joyful welcome for those whom war
has spared.
Joy to the palace and to these images
Whose faces catch the sun, now, as of
old,
With radiant smiles greet your sovran
lord,
Agamemnon, who brings a lamp to
lighten you
And all here present, after having
leveled
Troy with the mattock of just-dealing
Zeus,
Great son of Atreus, master and
monarch, blest
Above all living men. The brigand
Paris
Has lost his booty and brought down
the house of Priam.
CHORUS. Joy to you, Herald, welcome
home again!
HERALD. Let me die, having lived to see
this day!
CHORUS. Your yearning for your coun-
try has worn you out.
HERALD. So much that tears spring to
the eyes for joy.
CHORUS. Well, those you longed for
longed equally for you.
HERALD. Ah yes, our loved ones longed
for our safe return.
CHORUS. We have had many anxieties
here at home.
HERALD. What do you mean? Has there
been disaffection!
CHORUS. Never mind now. Say nothing
and cure all.
HERALD. Is it possible there was trouble
in our absence?
CHORUS. Now, as you said yourself, it
would be a joy to die.
HERALD. Yes, all has ended well. Our
expedition
Has been successfully concluded, even

though in part
The issue may be found wanting. Only
the Gods
Prosper in everything. If I should tell
you all
That we endured on shipboard in the
night watches,
Our lodging the bare benches, and
even worse
Ashore beneath the walls of Troy, the
rains
From heaven and the dews that seeped
Out of the soil into lice-infested blan-
kets;
If I should tell of those winters, when
the birds
Dropped dead and Ida heaped on us
her snows;
Those summers, when unruffled by
wind or wave
The sea slept breathless under the
glare of noon—
But why recall that now? It is all past,
Yes, for the dead past never to stir
again.
Ah, they are all gone. Why count our
losses? Why
Should we vex the living with grievance
for the dead?
Goodbye to all that! For us who have
come back,
Victory has turned the scale, and so be-
fore
This rising sun let the good news be
proclaimed
And carried all over the world on wings
of fame:
"These spoils were brought by the con-
querors of Troy
And dedicated to the Gods of Greece."
And praise to our country and to Zeus
the giver
All thanks be given. That is all my
news. [CLYTEMNESTRA *appears at the
palace door.*]
CHORUS. Thank God that I have lived
to see this day!
This news concerns all, and most of all
the queen.
CLYTEMNESTRA. I raised my alleluia
hours ago,
When the first messenger lit up the
night,
And people mocked me saying, "Has a
beacon
Persuaded you that the Greeks have

captured Troy?
Truly a woman's hopes are lighter than
air."
But I still sacrificed, and at a hundred
Shrines throughout the town the
women chanted
Their endless alleluias on and on.
Singing to sleep the sacramental flames,
And now what confirmation do I need
from you?
I wait to hear all from my lord, for
whom
A welcome is long ready. What day is
so sweet
In a woman's life as when she opens
the door
To her beloved, safe home from war?
Go and tell him
That he will find, guarding his prop-
erty,
A wife as loyal as he left her, one
Who in all these years has kept his
treasuries sealed,
Unkind only to enemies, and knows no
more
Of other men's company than of tem-
pering steel. [*Exit.*]
HERALD. Such a protestation, even
though entirely true,
Is it not unseemly on a lady's lips?
CHORUS. Such is her message, as you
understand,
Full of fine phrases plain to those who
know.
But tell us now, what news have you of
the king's
Co-regent, Menelaus? Is he too home
again?
HERALD. Lies cannot last, even though
sweet to hear.
CHORUS. Can you not make your news
both sweet and true?
HERALD. He and his ships have vanished. They are missing.
CHORUS. Did he sail ahead or the same
storm smite them all?
HERALD. You have told a long disaster
in a word.
CHORUS. Has no one news whether he is
alive or dead?
HERALD. Only the Sun, from whom the
whole earth draws life.
CHORUS. Tell us about the storm. How
did it fall?
HERALD. A day of national rejoicing
must not be marred

By any jarring tongue. A messenger
who comes
With black looks bringing the long
prayed-against
Report of total rout, which both afflicts
The state in general and in every
household leaves
The inmates prostrate under the
scourge of war—
With such a load upon his lips he may
fitly
Sing anthems to the Furies down in
hell;
But when he greets a prospering peo-
ple with
News of the war's victorious end—how
then
Shall I mix foul with fair and find
words to tell you
Of the blow that struck us out of that
angry heaven?
Water and Fire, those age-old
enemies,
Made common cause against the
homebound fleet.
Darkness had fallen, and a northerly
gale
Blew up and in a blinding thunder-
storm
Our ships were tossed and buffeted
hull against hull
In a wild stampede and herded out of
sight;
Then, at daybreak, we saw the Aegean
in blossom
With a waving crop of corpses and scattered timbers.
Our ship came through, saved by some
spirit, it seems,
Who took the helm and piloted her,
until
She slipped under the cliffs into a cove.
There, safe at last, incredulous of our
luck,
We brooded all day, stunned by the
night's disaster.
And so, if any of the others have survived,
They must be speaking of us as dead
and gone.
May all yet end well! Though it is most
to be expected
That Menelaus is in some great distress,
Yet, should some shaft of sunlight spy
him out

Somewhere among the living, rescued by Zeus,
Lest the whole house should perish, there is hope
That he may yet come home. There you have the truth.
CHORUS. Tell us who invented that
Name so deadly accurate?
Was it one who presaging
Things to come divined a word
Deftly tuned to destiny?
Helen—hell indeed she carried
To men, to ships, to a proud city, stealing
From the silk veils of her chamber, sailing seaward
With the Zephyr's breath behind her;
And they set forth in a thousand ships to hunt her
On the path that leaves no imprint,
Bringers of endless bloodshed.

So, as Fate decreed, in Troy,
Turning into keeners kin,
Furies, instruments of God's
Wrath, at last demanded full
Payment for the stolen wife;
And the wedding song that rang out
To greet the bride from beyond the Broad Aegean
Was in time turned into howls of imprecation
From the countless women wailing
For the loved ones they had lost in war for her sake,
And they curse the day they gave that
Welcome to war and bloodshed.

An old story is told of an oxherd, who reared at his hearth a lion-cub as a pet for his children,
Pampered fondly by young and old with morsels begged from the master's table.
But Time showed him up in his true nature after his kind—a beast savaging sheep and oxen,
Mad for the taste of blood, and only then did they learn too late their nursling was a curse from heaven.

And so it seemed then there came to rest in Troy
A sweet-smiling calm, a clear sky, seductive,
A rare pearl set in gold and silver,

Shaft of love from a glancing eye.
She is seen now as an agent
Of death sent from Zeus, a Fury
Demanding a bloody bride-price. [*Enter* CLYTEMNESTRA.]

From ancient times people have believed that when
A man's wealth has come to full growth it breeds
And brings forth tares and tears in plenty.
No, I say, it is only wicked deeds
That increase, fruitful in evil.
The house built on justice always
Is blest with a happy offspring.

And yet the pride bred of wealth often burgeons anew
In evil times, a cloud of deep night,
Spectre of ancient crimes that still
Walks within the palace walls,
True to the dam that bore it.

But where is Justice? She lights up the smoke-darkened hut.
From mansions built by hands polluted
Turning to greet the pure in heart,
Proof against false praise, she guides
All to its consummation. [*Enter* AGAMEMNON *in a chariot followed by another chariot carrying* CASSANDRA *and spoils of war.*]

Agamemnon, conqueror, joy to our king! How shall my greeting neither fall short nor shoot too high? Some men feign rejoicing or sorrow with hearts untouched; but those who can read man's nature in the book of the eyes will not be deceived by dissembled fidelity. I declare that, when you left these shores ten years ago to recover with thousands of lives one woman, who eloped of her own free will, I deemed your judgment misguided; but now in all sincerity I salute you with joy. Toil happily ended brings pleasure at last, and in time you shall learn to distinguish the just from the unjust steward.

AGAMEMNON. First, it is just that I should pay my respects
To the land of Argos and her presiding

Gods,
My partners in this homecoming as also
In the just penalty which I have in-
flicted on
The city of Troy. When the supreme
court of heaven
Adjudicated on our cause, they cast
Their votes unanimously against her,
though not
Immediately, and so on the other side
Hope hovered hesitantly before it van-
ished.
The fires of pillage are still burning
there
Like sacrificial offerings. Her ashes
Redolent with riches breathe their last
and die.
For all this it is our duty to render
thanks
To the celestial powers, with whose as-
sistance
We have exacted payment and struck
down
A city for one woman, forcing our en-
try
Within the Wooden Horse, which at
the setting
Of the Pleiads like a hungry lion leapt
Out and slaked its thirst in royal blood.
As to your sentiments, I take due note
And find that they accord with mine.
Too few
Rejoice at a friend's good fortune. I
have known
Many dissemblers swearing false al-
legiance.
One only, though he joined me against
his will,
Once in the harness, proved himself a
staunch
Support, Odysseus, be he now alive or
dead.
All public questions and such as con-
cern the Gods
I shall discuss in council and take steps
To make this triumph lasting; and if
here or there
Some malady comes to light, appropri-
ate
Remedies will be applied to set it right.
Meanwhile, returning to my royal
palace,
My first duty is to salute the Gods
Who led me overseas and home again
Victory attends me; may she remain
with me!

CLYTEMNESTRA. Citizens of Argos,
councillors and elders,
I shall declare without shame in your
presence
My feelings for my husband. Diffidence
Dies in us all with time. I shall speak of
what
I suffered here, while he was away at
the war,
Sitting at home, with no man's com-
pany,
Waiting for news, listening to one
Messenger after another, each bringing
worse
Disasters. If all his rumored wounds
were real,
His body was in shreds, shot through
and through.
If he had died—the predominant re-
port—
He was a second Geryon,[6] an out-
stretched giant
With three corpses and one death for
each,
While I, distraught, with a noose press-
ing my throat,
Was rescued forcibly, to endure still
more.
   And that is why our child is not pres-
ent here,
As he should be, pledge of our mar-
riage vows,
Orestes. Let me reassure you. He lives
Safe with an old friend, Strophius, who
warned me
Of various dangers—your life at risk in
Troy
And here a restive populace, which
might perhaps
Be roused to kick a man when he is
down.
   As for myself, the fountains of my
tears
Have long ago run dry. My eyes are
sore
After so many nights watching the
lamp
That burnt at my bedside always for
you.
If I should sleep, a gnat's faint whine
would shatter
The dreams that were my only com-
pany.
   But now, all pain endured, all sorrow
past,
I salute this man as the watchdog of the

fold,
The mainstay that saves of the ship, the
  sturdy oak
That holds the roof up, the longed-for
  only child,
The shore despaired-of sighted far out
  at sea.
God keep us from all harm! And now,
  dearest,
Dismount, but not on the bare gound!
  Servants,
Spread out beneath those feet that have
  trampled Troy
A road of royal purple,[7] which shall
  lead him
By the hand of Justice into a home un-
  hoped-for,
And there, when he has entered, our
  vigilant care
Shall dispose of everything as the Gods
  have ordained.
AGAMEMNON. Lady, royal consort and
  guardian of our home,
I thank you for your words of welcome,
  extended
To fit my lengthy absence; but due
  praise
Should rather come from others; and
  besides,
I would not have effeminate graces un-
  man me
With barbarous salaams and beneath
  my feet
Purple embroideries designed for sa-
  cred use.
Honor me as a mortal, not as a god.
Heaven's greatest gift is wisdom. Count
  him blest
Who has brought a long life to a happy
  end.
I shall do as I have said, with a clear
  conscience.
CLYTEMNESTRA. Yet tell me frankly, ac-
  cording to your judgment.
AGAMEMNON. My judgment stands.
  Makes no mistake about that.
CLYTEMNESTRA. Would you not in time
  of danger have vowed such an act?
AGAMEMNON. Yes, if the priests had rec-
  ommended it.
CLYTEMNESTRA. And what would Priam
  have done, if he had won?
AGAMEMNON. Oh, he would have trod
  the purple without a doubt.
CLYTEMNESTRA. Then you have nothing
  to fear from wagging tongues.

AGAMEMNON. Popular censure is a po-
  tent force.
CLYTEMNESTRA. Men must risk envy in
  order to be admired.
AGAMEMNON. A contentious spirit is un-
  seemly in a woman.
CLYTEMNESTRA. Well may the victor
  yield a victory.
AGAMEMNON. Do you set so much store
  by this victory?
CLYTEMNESTRA. Be tempted, freely van-
  quished, victor still!
AGAMEMNON. Well, if you will have it,
  let someone unlace
These shoes, and, as I tread the purple,
  may
No far-off god cast at me an envious
  glance
At the prodigal desecration of all this
  wealth!
Meanwhile, extend your welcome to
  this stranger.[8]
Power tempered with gentleness wins
  God's favor.
No one is glad to be enslaved, and she
Is a princess presented to me by the
  army,
The choicest flower culled from a host
  of captives.
And now, constrained to obey you, set-
  ting foot
On the sacred purple, I pass into my
  home.
CLYTEMNESTRA. The sea is still there,
  nothing can dry it up,
Renewing out of its infinite abundance
Unfailing streams of purple and blood-
  red dyes.
So too this house, the Gods be praised,
  my lord,
Has riches inexhaustible. There is no
  counting
The robes *I* would have vowed to tram-
  ple on,
Had some oracle so instructed, if by
  such means
I could have made good the loss of one
  dear soul.
So now your entry to your hearth and
  home
Is like a warm spell in the long winter's
  cold,
Or when Zeus from the virgin grape at
  last
Draws wine, the coolness that falls on
  the house

(For then from the living root the new
   leaves raise
A welcome shelter against the burning
   Dog-Star)
As man made perfect moves about his
   home. [*Exit* AGAMEMNON.]
Zeus, perfecter of all things, fulfil my
   prayers
And fulfil also your own purposes!
   [*Exit.*]
CHORUS. What is this delirious dread,
Ominous, oracular,
Droning through my brain with unre-
   lenting
Beat, irrepressible prophet of evil?
Why can I not cast it out
Planting good courage firm
On my spirit's empty throne?
In time the day came
When the Greeks with anchors cast
Moored the sloops of war, and troops
Thronged the sandy beach of Troy.

So today my eyes have seen
Safe at last the men come home.
Still I hear the strain of stringless
   music,
Dirge of the Furies, a choir uninvited
Chanting in my heart of hearts.
Mortal souls stirred by God
In tune with fate divine the shape
Of things to come; yet
Grant that these forebodings prove
False and bring my fears to naught.

If a man's health be advanced over the
   due mean,
It will trespass soon upon sickness, who
   stands
Next neighbor, between them a thin
   wall.
So does the vessel of life
Launched with a favoring breeze
Suddenly founder on reefs of destruc-
   tion.
Caution seated at the helm
Casts a portion of the freight
Overboard with measured throw;
So the ship may ride the storm.
Furrows enriched each season with
   showers from heaven
Banish hunger from the door.

But if the red blood of a man spatters
   the ground, dripping and deadly,
   then who

Has the magical power to recall it?
Even the healer[9] who knew
Spells to awaken the dead,
Zeus put an end to his necromancy.
Portions are there preordained,
Each supreme within its own
Province fixed eternally.
That is why my spirit groans
Brooding in fear, and no longer it
   hopes to unravel
Mazes of a fevered mind. [*Enter* CLY-
   TEMNESTRA.]
CLYTEMNESTRA. You, too, Cassandra,
   come inside! The merciful
Zeus gives you the privilege to take part
In our domestic sacrifice and stand
Before his altar among the other slaves
   there.
Put by your pride and step down. Even
   Heracles
Submitted once to slavery, and be con-
   soled
In serving a house whose wealth has
   been inherited
Over so many generations. The harsh-
   est masters
Are those who have snatched their har-
   vest out of hand.
You shall receive here what custom
   prescribes.
CHORUS. She is speaking to you. Caught
   in the net, surrender.
CLYTEMNESTRA. If she knows Greek and
   not some barbarous language,
My mystic words shall fill the soul
   within her.
CHORUS. You have no choice. Step
   down and do her will.
CLYTEMNESTRA. There is no time to
   waste. The victims are
All ready for the knife to render thanks
For this unhoped-for joy. If you wish to
   take part,
Make haste, but, if you lack the sense to
   understand,—[*To the* CHORUS.]
Speak to her with your hands and drag
   her down.
CHORUS. She is like a wild animal just
   trapped.
CLYTEMNESTRA. She is mad, the foolish
   girl. Her city captured,
Brought here a slave, she will be bro-
   ken in.
I'll waste no words on her to demean
   myself. [*Exit.*]
CHORUS. I feel no anger—no, I pity

you.
Unhappy girl, go in! Bow to your fate!
CASSANDRA. Oh! oh! Apollo!
CHORUS. What blasphemy, to wail in
Apollo's name!
CASSANDRA. Oh! oh! Apollo!
CHORUS. Again she cries in grief to the
god of joy!
CASSANDRA. Apollo, my destroyer! a
second time!
CHORUS. Ah, she foresees what is in
store for her.
She is now a slave, and yet God's gift
remains.
CASSANDRA. Apollo, my destroyer!
What house is this?
CHORUS. Do you not know where you
have come, poor girl?
Then let us tell you. This is the House
of Atreus.
CASSANDRA. Yes, for its very walls smell
of iniquity,
A charnel house that drips with chil-
dren's blood.
CHORUS. How keen her scent to seize
upon the trail!
CASSANDRA. Listen to them as they be-
wail the foul
Repast of roast meat for a father's
mouth!
CHORUS. Enough! Reveal no more! We
know it all.
CASSANDRA. What is it plotted next?
Horror unspeakable,
A hard cross for kinsfolk.
The hoped-for savior is far away.
CHORUS. What does she say? This must
be something new.
CASSANDRA. Can it be so—to bathe one
who is travel-tired,
And then smiling stretch out
A hand followed by a stealthy hand!
CHORUS. She speaks in riddles, and I
cannot read them.
CASSANDRA. What do I see? A net!
Yes, it is she, his mate and murderess!
Cry alleluia, cry, angels of hell, rejoice,
Fat with blood, dance and sing!
CHORUS. What is the Fury you have
called upon?
Helpless the heart faints with the sink-
ing sun.
Closer still draws the stroke.
CASSANDRA. Ah, let the bull beware!
It is a robe she wraps him in, and
strikes!

Into the bath he slumps heavily,
drowned in blood.
Such her skilled handicraft.
CHORUS. It is not hard to read her
meaning now.
Why does the prophet's voice never
have good to tell,
Only cry woes to come?
CASSANDRA. Oh, pitiful destiny! Having
lamented his,
Now I lament my own passion to fill the
bowl.
Where have you brought me? Must I
with him die?
CHORUS. You sing your own dirge, like
the red-brown bird
That pours out her grief-stricken soul,
Itys, Itys! she cries, the sad nightingale.
CASSANDRA. It is not so; for she, having
become a bird,
Forgot her tears and sings her happy
lot,
While I must face the stroke of two-
edged steel.
CHORUS. From whence does this cas-
cade of harsh discords
Issue, and where will it at last be
calmed?
Calamity you cry—Oh where must it
end?
CASSANDRA. O wedding day, Paris the
curse of all!
Scamander, beside whose clear waters I
grew
Now I must walk weeping by Acheron.
CHORUS. Even a child could under-
stand.
The heart breaks, as these pitiful cries
Shatter the listening soul.
CASSANDRA. O fall of Troy, city of Troy
destroyed!
The king's rich gifts little availed her so
That she might not have been what she
is now.
CHORUS. What evil spirit has possessed
Your soul, strumming such music upon
your lips
As on a harp in hell?
CASSANDRA. Listen! My prophecy shall
glance no longer
As through a veil like a bride newly-
wed,
But bursting towards the sunrise shall
engulf
The whole world in calamities far
greater

Than these. No more riddles, I shall in-
struct,
While you shall verify each step, as I
Nose out from the beginning this
bloody trail.
Upon this roof—do you see them?—
stands a choir—
It has been there for generations—a
gallery
Of unmelodious minstrels, a merry
troop
Of wassailers drunk with human blood,
reeling
And retching in horror at a brother's
outraged bed.
Well, have I missed? Am I not well-
read in
Your royal family's catalogue of crime?

CHORUS. You come from a far country
and recite
Our ancient annals as though you had
been present.

CASSANDRA. The Lord Apollo bestowed
this gift on me.

CHORUS. Was it because he had fallen in
love with you?

CASSANDRA. I was ashamed to speak of
this till now.

CHORUS. Ah yes, adversity is less fastidious.

CASSANDRA. Oh, but he wrestled strenu-
ously for my love.

CHORUS. Did you come, then, to the act
of getting child?

CASSANDRA. At first I consented, and
then I cheated him.

CHORUS. Already filled with his gift of
prophecy?

CASSANDRA. Yes, I forewarned my people of their destiny.

CHORUS. Did your divine lover show no
displeasure?

CASSANDRA. Yes, the price I paid was
that no one listened to me.

CHORUS. Your prophecies seem credible
enough to us.

CASSANDRA. Oh!
Again the travail of the prophetic
trance
Runs riot in my soul. Do you not see
them
There, on the roof, those apparitions—
children
Murdered by their own kin, in their
hands
The innards of which their father ate—

oh
What a pitiable load they carry! For
that crime
Revenge is plotted by the fainthearted
lion,
The stay-at-home, stretched in my mas-
ter's bed
(Being his slave, I must needs call him
so),
Lying in wait for Troy's great con-
queror.
Little he knows what that foul bitch
with ears
Laid back and rolling tongue intends
for him
With a vicious snap, her husband's
murderess.
What abominable monster shall I call
her—
A two-faced amphisbene[10] or Scylla[11]
that skulks
Among the rocks to waylay mariners,
Infernal sea-squid locked in internecine
Strife—did you not hear her alleluias
Of false rejoicing at his safe return?
Believe me or not, what must be will be,
and then
You will pity me and say, She spoke the
truth.

CHORUS. The feast of Thyestes I recognized, and shuddered,
But for the rest my wits are still astray.

CASSANDRA. Your eyes shall see the
death of Agamemnon.

CHORUS. No, hush those ill-omened
lips, unhappy girl!

CASSANDRA. There is no Apollo present,
and so no cure.

CHORUS. None, if you speak the truth;
yet God forbid!

CASSANDRA. Pray God forbid, while they
close in for the kill!

CHORUS. What man is there who would
plot so foul a crime?

CASSANDRA. Ah, you have altogether
misunderstood.

CHORUS. But how will he do it? That es-
capes me still.

CASSANDRA. And yet I can speak Greek
only too well.

CHORUS. So can Apollo, but his oracles
are obscure.

CASSANDRA. Ah, how it burns me up!
Apollo! Now
That lioness on two feet pours in the
cup

My wages too, and while she whets the
blade
For him promises to repay my passage
money
In my own blood. Why wear these
mockeries,
This staff and wreath? If I must die,
then you
Shall perish first and be damned. Now
we are quits!
Apollo himself has stripped me, look-
ing upon me
A public laughingstock, who has en-
dured
The name of witch, waif, beggar, casta-
way,
So now the god who gave me second
sight
Takes back his gift and dismisses his
servant,
Ready for the slaughter at a dead man's
grave.
Yet we shall be avenged. Now far away,
The exile shall return, called by his
father's
Unburied corpse to come and kill his
mother.
Why weep at all this? Have I not seen
Troy fall,
And those who conquered her are thus
discharged.
I name this door the gate of Hades:
now
I will go and knock, I will take heart to
die.
I only pray that the blow may be mor-
tal,
Closing these eyes in sleep without a
struggle,
While my life blood ebbs quietly away.
CHORUS. O woman, in whose wisdom is
so much grief,
How, if you know the end, can you ap-
proach it
So gently, like an ox that goes to the
slaughter?
CASSANDRA. What help would it be if I
should put if off?
CHORUS. Yet, while there is life there's
hope—so people say.
CASSANDRA. For me no hope, no help.
My hour has come.
CHORUS. You face your end with a cou-
rageous heart.
CASSANDRA. Yes, so they console those
whom life has crossed.

CHORUS. Is there no comfort in an honorable death?
CASSANDRA. O Priam, father, and all
your noble sons! [*She approaches the
door, then draws back.*]
CHORUS. What is it? Why do you turn
back, sick at heart?
CASSANDRA. Inside there is a stench of
dripping blood.
CHORUS. It is only the blood of their
fireside sacrifice.
CASSANDRA. It is the sort of vapor that
issues from a tomb.
CHORUS. No scent, it seems, of Syrian
frankincense.
CASSANDRA. I will go now and finish my
lament
Inside the house. Enough of life! O
friends!
I am not scared. I beg of you only this:
When the day comes for them to die, a
man
For a man, woman for woman, remem-
ber me!
CHORUS. Poor soul condemned to
death, I pity you.
CASSANDRA. Yet one word more, my
own dirge for myself.
I pray the Sun, on whom I now look
my last,
That he may grant to my master's aven-
gers
A fair price for the slave-girl slain at his
side.
O sad mortality! when fortune smiles,
A painted image; and when trouble
comes,
One touch of a wet sponge wipes it
away. [*Exit.*]
CHORUS. And her case is even more pit-
iable than his.

Human prosperity never rests but always craves more, till blown up with
pride it totters and falls. From the opu-
lent mansions pointed at by all passersby none warns it away, none cries,
"Let no more riches enter!" To him was
granted the capture of Troy, and he
has entered his home as a god, but
now, if the blood of the past is on him,
if he must pay with his own death for
the crimes of bygone generations, then
who is assured of a life without sorrow?

AGAMEMNON. Oh me!

CHORUS. Did you hear?

AGAMEMNON. Oh me, again!

CHORUS. It is the King. Let us take counsel!

1. I say, raise a hue and cry!
2. Break in at once!
3. Yes, we must act.
4. *They* spurn delay.
5. They plot a tyranny.
6. Must we live their slaves?
7. Better to die.
8. Old men, what can we do?
9. We cannot raise the dead.
10. His death is not yet proved.
11. We are only guessing.
12. Let us break in and learn the truth!

[*The doors are thrown open and* CLYTEMNESTRA *is seen standing over the bodies of* AGAMEMNON *and* CASSANDRA, *which are laid out on a purple robe.*]

CLYTEMNESTRA. All that I said before to bide my time
Without any shame I shall now unsay. How else
Could I have plotted against an enemy
So near and seeming dear and strung the snare
So high that he could not jump it? Now the feud
On which I have pondered all these years has been
Fought out to its conclusion. Here I stand
Over my work, and it was so contrived
As to leave no loophole. With this vast dragnet
I enveloped him in purple folds, then struck
Twice, and with two groans he stretched his legs,
Then on his outspread body I struck a third blow,
A drink for Zeus the Deliverer of the dead.
There he lay gasping out his soul and drenched me
In these deathly dew-drops, at which I cried
In sheer delight like newly-budding corn
That tastes the first spring showers. And so,
Venerable elders, you see how the matter stands.
Rejoice, if you are so minded. I glory in it.

With bitter tears he filled the household bowl;
Now he has drained it to the dregs and gone.

CHORUS. How can you speak so of your murdered king?

CLYTEMNESTRA. You treat me like an empty-headed woman.
Again, undaunted, to such as understand
I say—commend or censure, as you please—
It makes no difference—here is Agamemnon,
My husband, dead, the work of this right hand,
Which acted justly. There you have the truth.

CHORUS. Woman, what evil brew have you devoured to take
On you a crime that cries out for a public curse?
Yours was the fatal blow, banishment shall be yours,
Hissed and hated of all men.

CLYTEMNESTRA. Your sentence now for me is banishment,
But what did you do then to contravene
His purpose, when, to exorcise the storms,
As though picking a ewe-lamb from his flocks,
Whose wealth of snowy fleeces never fails
To increase and multiply, he killed his own
Child, born to me in pain, my best-beloved?
Why did you not drive *him* from hearth and home?
I bid you cast at me such menaces
As make for mastery in equal combat
With one prepared to meet them, and if, please God,
The issue goes against you, suffering
Shall school those grey hairs in humility.

CHORUS. You are possessed by some spirit of sin that stares
Out of your bloodshot eyes matching your bloody hands.
Dishonored and deserted of your kin, for this
Stroke you too shall be struck down.

CLYTEMNESTRA. Listen! By Justice, who

avenged my child,
By the Fury to whom I vowed this sacrament,
No thought of fear shall enter through this door
So long as the hearth within is kindled by
Aegisthus, faithful to me now as always.
Low lies the man who insulted his wedded wife,
The darling of the Chryseids[12] at Troy,
And stretched beside him this visionary seer,
Whom he fondled on shipboard, both now rewarded,
He as you see, and she swanlike has sung
Her dying ditty, his tasty side dish, for me
A rare spice to add relish to my joy.

CHORUS. Oh, for the gift of death
To bring the long sleep that knows no waking,
Now that my lord and loyal protector
Breathes his last. For woman's sake
Long he fought overseas,
Now at home falls beneath a woman's hand.
  Helen, the folly-beguiled, having
    ravaged the city of Troy,
  She has set on the curse of Atreus
  A crown of blood beyond ablution.

CLYTEMNESTRA. Do not pray for death nor turn your anger against one woman as the slayer of thousands!

CHORUS. Demon of blood and tears
Inbred in two women single-hearted!
Perched on the roof he stands and preens his
Sable wings, a carrion-crow.
Loud he croaks, looking down
Upon the feast spread before him here below.

CLYTEMNESTRA. Ah now you speak truth, naming the thrice-fed demon, who, glutted with blood, craves more, still young in his hunger.

CHORUS. When will the feast be done?
Alas, it is the will of Zeus,
Who caused and brought it all to pass.
Nothing is here but was decreed in heaven.

CLYTEMNESTRA. It was not my doing, nor am I Agamemnon's wife, but a ghost in woman's guise, the shade of the banqueter whom Atreus fed.

CHORUS. How is the guilt not yours?
And yet the crimes of old may well
Have had a hand, and so it drives
On, the trail of internecine murder.

CLYTEMNESTRA. What of *him*? Was the guilt not his, when he killed the child that I bore him? And so by the sword he has fallen.

CHROUS. Alas, the mind strays. The house is falling.
A storm of blood lays the walls in ruins.
Another mortal stroke for Justice' hand
Will soon be sharpened.
  Oh me, who shall bury him, who sing
    the dirge?
  Who shall intone at the tomb of a
    blessed spirit
  A tribute pure in heart and truthful?

CLYTEMNESTRA. No, I'll bury him, but without mourners. By the waters of Acheron Iphigenia is waiting for him with a kiss.

CHORUS. The charge is answered with countercharges.
The sinner must suffer: such is God's will.
The ancient curse is bringing down the house
In self-destruction.

CLYTEMNESTRA. That is the truth, and I would be content that the spirit of vengeance should rest, having absolved the house from its madness.

[*Enter* AEGISTHUS *with a bodyguard.*]

AEGISTHUS. Now I have proof that there are Gods in heaven,
As I gaze on this purple mesh in which
My enemy lies, son of a treacherous father.
His father, Atreus, monarch of this realm,
Was challenged in his sovran rights by mine,
Thyestes, his own brother, and banished him
From hearth and home. Later he returned
A suppliant and found sanctuary, indeed
A welcome; for his brother entertained him
To a feast of his own children's flesh, of which
My father unsuspecting took and ate.
Then, when he knew what he had done, he fell

Back spewing out the slaughtered flesh
and, kicking
The table to the floor, with a loud cry
He cursed the House of Pelops. That is
the crime
For which the son lies here. And fitly
too
The plot was spun by me; for as a child
I was banished with my father, until
Justice
Summoned me home. Now let me die,
for never
Shall I live to see another sight so
sweet.
CHORUS. Aegisthus, if it was you who
planned this murder,
Then be assured, the people will stone
you for it.
AEGISTHUS. Such talk from the lower
benches! Even in dotage
Prison can teach a salutary lesson.
Better submit, or else you shall smart
for it.
CHORUS. You woman, who stayed at
home and wallowed in
His bed, you plotted our great com-
mander's death!
AEGISTHUS. Orpheus[13] led all in rapture
after him.
Your senseless bark will be snuffed out
in prison.
CHORUS. You say the plot was yours, yet
lacked the courage
To raise a hand but left it to a woman!
AEGISTHUS. As his old enemy, I was sus-
pect.
Temptation was the woman's part. But
now
I'll try my hand at monarchy, and all
Who disobey me shall be put in irons

And starved of food and light till they
submit.
CHORUS. Oh, if Orestes yet beholds the
sun,
May he come home and execute them
both!
AEGISTHUS. Ho, my guards, come for-
ward, you have work to do.
CAPTAIN OF THE GUARD. Stand by, draw
your swords!
CHORUS. We are not afraid to die.
AEGISTHUS. Die! We'll take you at your
word.
CLYTEMNESTRA. Peace, my lord, and let
no further wrong be done.
Captain, sheathe your swords. And
you, old men,
Go home quietly. What has been, it had
to be.
Scars enough we bear, now let us rest.
AEGISTHUS. Must I stand and listen to
their threats?
CHORUS. Men of Argos never cringed
before a rogue.
AEGISTHUS. I shall overtake you yet—
the day is near.
CHORUS. Not if Orestes should come
home again.
AEGISTHUS. Vain hope, the only food of
castaways.
CHORUS. Gloat and grow fat, blacken
justice while you dare!
AEGISTHUS. All this foolish talk will cost
you dear.
CHORUS. Flaunt your gaudy plumes and
strut beside your head.
CLYTEMNESTRA. Pay no heed to idle
clamor. You and I,
Masters of the house, shall now direct it
well.

Choephoroe

Characters

Orestes
Pylades
Chorus of Servingwomen
Electra
Household slave
Clytemnestra
Nurse
Aegisthus

The scene as before. Enter ORESTES *and* PY-
LADES.
ORESTES. Hermes, whose home is
underground, whose eyes
Look down on my paternal heritage,
Deliver me, do battle by my side!
*   *   *   *   *
I have come back, restored to my
fatherland.

And standing beside my father's tomb I
  call
On him to hear my prayers.
* * * * *
A lock to Inachus, who nurtured me,
And now another in token of my
  grief.[1]
* * * * *
I was not present, Father, to lament
Your death nor raise a hand in sorrow,
  when
Your body was carried out of the
  house. [*A cry is heard within.* ELECTRA
  and the CHORUS OF SERVINGWOMEN
  come out of the palace.]

What do I see? What is this gathering
Of women clothed in black? Is it some
  new
Affliction, or do they bring perhaps
Drink-offerings to propitiate the dead?
It must be so, for there I think I see
My sister, Electra, walking bowed in
  grief.
O Zeus, defend us! May I avenge my
  father!
Pylades, let us stand aside, until
We have learnt the meaning of this act
  of prayer.
CHORUS. Out of the palace we have
  come
To dedicate these offerings.
My maiden cheek is freshly furrowed.
On shrill cries my sick heart has fed
  continually.
The sundered linen shrieks in tune
  with dirges, while
Raiment torn lays bare
Twin breasts to the beating palm for
  this calamity.

A shriek was heard, it pierced the
  night,
Prophetic terror breathing wrath,
A heavy haunting cry of horror,
It rang out loud and long, where the
  women's chambers are.
And then the prophets, asked the
  meaning of the dream,
Cried out their answer:
Dead souls in the ground below de-
  nounce the murderers.

Now to placate such ills implacable—
O hear, Earth, Mother!—fearful she
  has sent me,

Godless woman! I scarce dare to speak
  the name.
When blood is spilled, it cannot be re-
  deemed.
O house where only sorrows thrive,
O royal roof in ruins laid,
Engulfed anew in shades accursed
Of darkest night, which have been
  drawn
Down by death of the master!

Respect for power unmatched in battle
  once,
In men's ears and hearts public, all-per-
  vasive,
Now is drawn aside, and men fear; for
  fortune is
A god in mortal eyes and more than
  god.
And yet the scale of Justice stands
And watches, swift to visit some
In life, for others pain abides
In twilit realms, while on the rest
Night descends everlasting.

When blood is shed and drunk by
  mother Earth,
the vengeful gore congeals indelibly.
Slow-paced judgment carries the of-
  fender on, till grief
Gluts his greedy appetite.

As he who treads the virgin bower can
  find
No cure, so too, though stream on
  stream should pour
Their sweet cleansing waters on the
  hand of blood, the old
Stain shall not be wiped away.
For me, the Gods drove the engines of
  fate
Against my city, from home they led
  me
A captive here to live in bondage.
And so I must needs endure my mas-
  ters'
Orders right or wrong, and hide
My bitter thoughts; and yet beneath my
  cloak I weep
To see the wanton pride of those set
  over me.
ELECTRA. Bondswomen of the royal
  retinue,
Since you too are participants in this act
Of intercession, give me your advice.
What shall I say to dedicate these gifts,

What words contrive to please my
  father's ear?
That I have brought them from a lov-
  ing wife
To her dear lord, an offering from my
  mother?
No, that would be too shameless—then
  what else,
While I lay on the tomb these holy oils?
Or shall I use the customary prayer,
"Bless those who have sent these gar-
  lands in your honor
And for their good gifts give good re-
  compense"?
Or pour in silence without ceremony,
Just as he died, a draught for the
  thirsty earth
As though to cast out scourings, then
  turn and fling
The vessel behind me with averted
  eyes?
I beg you to advise me, and, since we
  share
Inside those doors a common enemy,
Do not be afraid to unfold your
  thoughts to me;
For destiny as surely awaits the free
As those who are forced to bow to
  another's will.
CHORUS. Since you desire it, and since I
  worship this
Tomb as an altar, I will speak my mind.
ELECTRA. Yes, speak as a worshipper at
  my father's grave.
CHORUS. Bless in this act all those who
  wish him well.
ELECTRA. Who are there among his
  kinsfolk so disposed?
CHORUS. Yourself, and then those who
  hate Aegisthus.
ELECTRA. You mean the prayer must be
  made for just you and me?
CHORUS. You understand; take thought
  accordingly.
ELECTRA. Who else can we mention be-
  side ourselves?
CHORUS. Have you forgotten far-away
  Orestes?
ELECTRA. Well said—oh, that indeed is
  good advice.
CHORUS. Remember too those guilty of
  his murder.
ELECTRA. What should I say of them?
  What do you mean?
CHORUS. Ask them to grant that God or
  man may come—

ELECTRA. May come to judge them, or
  to execute?
CHORUS. Yes, say quite plainly, to take
  life for life.
ELECTRA. Is that a rightful prayer to ask
  of heaven?
CHORUS. Why not—to pray evil for our
  enemies?
ELECTRA. O mediator between the quick
  and dead,
Hermes, convey my prayer to those
  who from
Below watch over this house, to Earth
  who brings
All creatures forth and after nurturing
  them
Is quickened by them and conceives
  again,
While I pour out these lustral offerings
And call on my dear father to have
  mercy
On me and lead Orestes home to shine
A light for the whole house; who are
  both now
Outcasts, bartered like chattels by our
  mother
For her new bedfellow, Aegisthus, who
Shares her guilt for your murder—I a
  slave,
Orestes banished and disinherited,
While they flaunt the riches usurped
  from you.
Oh, I beseech you, speed Orestes
  home—
That is my prayer—O hear me, Father,
  hear,
And grant to me in heart more chastity,
In hand more cleanness, than my
  mother had.
So much for us, and for our enemies
I beg you to visit a judgment on their
  sins,
From those who took life justly taking
  life.
This evil supplication, made for them,
Is set between my own auspicious pray-
  ers.
To us be giver of good gifts, by the
  grace
Of Heaven and Earth and Justice who
  shall prevail!
So having prayed, I pour these offer-
  ings,
And, while I pour them, sing for the
  dead a dirge.
CHORUS. Come, let fall a plaintive tear,

Fall for our fallen lord,
Before a tomb that shields the good
And holds pollution hence, with these
Propitiations paid.
Hearken to us, O King!
O ghostly sense, wake and hear!
Ah me, may he come, a warrior,
One who shall free the house, bearing a
Scythian bow
To bend afar off, and armed too with
that
Bludgeon of wood to wield in close
fight as well!

ELECTRA. The Earth has drunk the gifts
left for our father.
And now I have strange news to share
with you.

CHORUS. News? What is it? My heart
dances with fear.

ELECTRA. I found laid on the grave this
lock of hair.

CHORUS. Whose can it be? What man or
maid has left it?

ELECTRA. None could have left it there
apart from me.

CHORUS. True, those who should have
are his enemies.

ELECTRA. And yet to look at it is
strangely like—

CHORUS. Like whose? Tell me; I miss
your meaning still.

ELECTRA. My own. In texture it is the
same as mine.

CHORUS. Orestes—can it be? A secret
tribute?

ELECTRA. His hair was of this selfsame
quality.

CHORUS. But how could he have dared
to bring it here?

ELECTRA. Perhaps he sent it to grace his
father's grave.

CHORUS. Why then, this news is greater
cause for tears,
If it means that he will not come home
again.

ELECTRA. I am too stricken to the heart.
The waves
Of sorrow swell and from these eyes
falls drop
By drop the surging tide, as I regard
These curls—whose are they, if they
are not his?
Hers they could never be, the mur-
deress,
My mother, and yet how unmotherly,
The godless woman. I cannot accept it

As a sure gift from him, my best-be-
loved,
Orestes, and yet the hope smiles on me.
If only it had a voice to calm my doubts
That I might have known whether to
reject it
Or with him mourn beside our father's
tomb!
Helpless my spirit drifts; and yet, if
God
Should grant to us to win deliverance,
From a small seed shall spring a mighty
tree.
But look! Footprints—another testi-
mony—
His own, and with him some compan-
ion too.
Two outlines are there here, two tracks
of feet.
And see, the heels of these are shaped
like mine,
Making when measured out a perfect
match.
What agonies are here, what shattered
wits! [ORESTES *comes forward.*]

ORESTES. Thank God for having
granted you your prayer
And ask his blessing for what has yet to
be done.

ELECTRA. For what am I indebted to
him now?

ORESTES. You see the sight for which
you have prayed so long.

ELECTRA. How do you know whom I
have been calling for?

ORESTES. I know that you have idolized
Orestes.

ELECTRA. And how have I been favored
in my prayer?

ORESTES. Here am I, and none dearer
shall you find.

ELECTRA. Stranger, it is a trick you are
playing on me.

ORESTES. If so, I have been conspiring
against myself.

ELECTRA. As being Orestes, then, I say
to you—

ORESTES. You see me and do not know
me; yet just now,
When you found that token and followed up my tracks,
Your heart leapt at the very thought of
me.
Compare that lock with the hair from
which it was cut.
Look at this cloth, your handiwork—

see where
Your batten struck, and the beasts in
  the embroidery.
Ah, calm yourself! We must restrain
  our joy.
Our bitterest enemies are those most
  near.
ELECTRA. O happy presence, in my
  heart endowed
With a fourfold portion: father are you
  to me,
To you is turned a mother's love, for
  she
Is hated utterly, and a sister's,[2] whom
They killed without pity; and last for
  yourself,
My own true brother, yours is all my
  love.
CHORUS. O darling of your father's
  house, O hope
Watered with tears, seed of deliver-
  ance,
Trust in your courage, and you shall
  repossess
Your father's heritage, if only Might
And Right stand by your side, and with
  them third,
Of all the greatest, Zeus Deliverer!
ORESTES. Zeus, Zeus, look down upon
  our plight, regard
The eagle's nestlings orphaned of their
  sire,
Whom the vile serpent folded in her
  coils
And crushed to death; see us standing
  here,
Both faint with hunger, my sister here
  and me,
Whose father was your priest. If you
  destroy
The eagle's brood, what hand so liberal
Shall sacrifice on feast days in your
  honor?
No more this royal stem, this withered
  stump
Of greatness, will avail to grace your al-
  tar.
Oh, cherish it, restore it! Then this
  house,
Which now lies fallen, shall once more
  be great.
CHORUS. Oh children, saviors of your
  father's house,
Silence, lest eavesdroppers should over-
  hear
And make all known to those whom

may I soon see
Burning alive in pools of spluttering
  pitch!
ORESTES. Apollo will not break his faith,
  by whose
Almighty oracle I have been com-
  manded
To undertake this hazard. His
  prophetess
Cried loud and long of chilly blasts to
  turn
The heart's blood cold, if I should fail
  to seek
Those murderers out and put them to
  the death
My father died, their lives for his, in-
  censed
At the loss of my inheritance; for else,
  he said,
On my own soul in punishment would
  fall
A host of horrors let loose by the angry
  dead,
Ravenous ulcers to devour the flesh
And sprouting from them a crop of
  hoary hairs,
And worse, the assault of Furies roused
  to life
Out of a father's blood by dead men's
  prayers,
With sudden fits of madness in the
  night,
Which haunt and harass, so he said,
  and scourge
Beyond the frontiers the execrated sin-
  ner;
For him no part in the mixing of wine
Or offerings at grace; his father's un-
  seen
Spirit shall bar him from the altars, none
Shall give him lodging nor lodge with
  him; so
Forlorn and friendless he shall waste
  away
In solitude to everlasting death.
So spoke the oracle, and shall I not
  trust God?
Many desires all gather to one end—
The God's command, a son's grief for a
  father,
Resentment for the loss of my estate,
And anger that my glorious country-
  men,
Whose bravery brought down the
  towers of Troy,

Should bend the knee to those two
  women; for
His heart is a woman's, as he shall soon
  see.

CHORUS. O Fate, ordain that the end
shall be reached where Justice walks
into battle! For the tongue which curses
let a cursing tongue be rendered, blow
for blow, let the doer be done by as he
did—so it is ordered.

ORESTES. Teach me, O Father, O Father
  dread,
How by speech or action
To speed upward the soul that Earth
Holds so deep in her bosom.
As day is reversed in night, so may a
  dirge of praises
Bring to the dead some comfort.
CHORUS. My son, the flames devour the
  flesh but not the spirit.
The soul of the dead in time shows to
  the quick his anger;
For a dirge to the departed is a lamp
  that lights the sinner,
And the just lament of children for the
  father that begot them
From full hearts shall be sent ahunting.
ELECTRA. Father, attend, attend to this
Dirge so long belated,
As each child in succession pays
Tribute in lamentation.
As suppliant I implore sanctuary, he as
  outcast.
All that is here is evil.
CHORUS. And yet in good time shall
  God of his grace call a happier tune
  for the reunion of friends from the
  loving-cup drinking together.
ORESTES. Would that on Trojan soil,
  Father, struck by a foeman's lance,
In fight laid low, your life had ended!
How proud then your children would
  walk eyed of all men,
With you in a sepulchre far hence, an
  honored
Load for the House of Atreus!
CHORUS. Then loving and beloved of all
  who fell in battle,
A regent among the dead, you would
  have shone in glory
In attendance on the greatest of the
  kings that reign in Hades
(For in life you were a great king) and
  dispense the fate of all souls

With dread sceptre of final judgment.
ELECTRA. No, not a tomb in Troy, laid
  in dust with the rest of those
That War struck down beneath her
  towers!
I wish rather that those who destroyed
  him had died first,
Cut down by their own kith and kin,
  before we
Tasted of tribulation.

CHORUS. For what might have been, as
for pearls beyond price, you may pray,
but in vain. Two blows strike home,
one for the dead, our helper, and one
for the miscreants that still hold power,
the usurpers.

ORESTES. Ah, that is a shot to the heart!
Zeus, Zeus, from under the earth send
Speedy revenge to follow
The foul hand of the mortal sinner,
Even a son that is like his mother!
CHORUS. May this mouth soon be
  moved
To chant gladly the alleluia
Over a man and a woman
Smitten to death! For why still
Hide the hope that is beating
Within me? The heart's front is bat-
  tered
Down by the fierce gust of a long-ran-
  kling spite.
ELECTRA. When will he strike with his
  hand,
O when shall the head be sundered?
Grant that a sign be given!
A just payment I seek from sinners.
Hear us, O Earth and you shades ma-
  jestic!
CHORUS. It is written that blood craves
  blood, that a Fury must spring from
  the slaughtered and crown one vio-
  lent end with another!
ORESTES. O shame, Earth! Shame, in-
  fernal sovranties!
Look on us, look, resentful curses of
  the dead,
The heirs of Atreus, a lonely remnant
  left,
Astray and lost, dispossessed
And homeless—O Zeus, can nothing
  save us?
CHORUS. And yet fear shakes my heart
At these ominous cries of sorrow.
Hopeless awhile, it gathers

Black to the core in deepest
Dread of the destined future;
But then strength returns, armed for
action,
Courage revives faith in a cause all but
lost.
ELECTRA. With what speech shall our
purpose best be won?
Is it the wrongs I suffered at a
motherly hand?
The tongue may speak soft, but those
are unassuaged;
For like the fierce wolf my heart
Is true to hers, deaf to cries of mercy.
CHORUS. I beat the breast and danced
an eastern dirge,
And like a Cissian mourner mad
With clutching hand and rending nail
On breast and cheek I mingled tears
with blood.
ELECTRA. Oh me, hateful heart!
Oh wicked mother, hateful was his
bearing out,
A king, without followers,
With none to mourn over him,
You laid him unwept in unhallowed
soil.
ORESTES. Can it be true? So dishonored!
Why then,
For those dishonors she shall repay
him,
So help me, almighty powers,
To strike with these eager hands—
Let her but die, and then let me be
taken!
CHORUS. His limbs were lopped first—
you must be told all—
Cut off by those hands that so en-
tombed his
Dismembered, maimed, mangled limbs
To brand his son's name with unheard-
of shame.
ELECTRA. Such was our father's death,
and I was kept
In misery, treated with contempt,
Within my chamber kenneled like a
dog.
Remember this and write it in your
heart.
CHORUS. Receive these appeals
With open ear and firm and steady
heart!
For so at present stands the case,
But more we all yearn to hear.
With calm resolve must the lists be en-
tered.

ORESTES. I call to you, Father, fight be-
side your own!
ELECTRA. And I to his join a daughter's
tearful plaint.
CHORUS. And all with one voice to-
gether cry aloud,
O hear us, rise from darkness, wake,
Stand at our side for battle!
ORESTES. With Strife shall Strife join in
combat, Right with Right.
ELECTRA. O heaven, heed, grant our
task a just event!
CHORUS. Misgiving steals through my
soul to hear them pray.
The fatal end has long been fixed,
Now it is near fulfilment.

Evil inborn and bred, terrible stroke of
bloodshed
Chanted with imprecations!
O wrong, wrong that is past appease-
ment!

Cure for the House is none save of it-
self; its own blood
Shed by its own must heal it.
We sing this to the powers of darkness.

Grave lords of the dead, confer upon
these two children the strength that
shall conquer!
ORESTES. Father, who died a most un-
royal death,
Bequeath to us the mastery of your
house!
ELECTRA. And I entreat you, Father, set
me free,
Who now am sold in slavery to Aegisthus!
ORESTES. And so you shall receive the
solemn feasts
Which custom orders, or else be denied
them.
ELECTRA. Out of my dowry I shall bring
you gifts
To grace your tomb upon my wedding
day.
ORESTES. Earth, send my father to look
down on the battle!
ELECTRA. Persephone,[3] release his shining might!
ORESTES. Father, remember the bath
filled with your blood!
ELECTRA. Have you forgotten the net
which they spread for you?
ORESTES. And bound your limbs in fet-

ters of fine thread?

ELECTRA. Helplessly trapped in treacherous coverlets!

ORESTES. Father, are you not stirred by these reproaches?

ELECTRA. Father, lift up to us the face we loved!

ORESTES. Send Justice to defend your kith and kin,
If you would conquer those who conquered you!

ELECTRA. Regard us here, nestlings beside your tomb!

ORESTES. Let not the race of Pelops perish utterly!

ELECTRA. Children are floats that lift the dead to life.

ORESTES. Grant us our prayers and so save yourself!

CHORUS. This intercession has been commensurate
To recompense a long-neglected grave.
Now you must put your fortune to the proof.

ORESTES. It shall be done; but first it is not amiss
To ask what prompted her to dedicate
This tardy penance for a sin past cure?—
Not goodwill to the dead; for such a gift
Could earn no favor nor cancel the offence.
Can you instruct me in what she intended?

CHORUS. I can, for I was there. The wicked woman
Was driven to send these offerings against her will
By a nightmare that racked her guilty soul.

ORESTES. Did she disclose to you what she was dreaming of?

CHORUS. She said she dreamt she gave birth to a snake.

ORESTES. What followed then? How did the vision end?

CHORUS. She nursed it like a babe in swaddling-clothes.

ORESTES. What nourishment did it crave—a newborn serpent?

CHORUS. She dreamt she gave it breast and suckled it.

ORESTES. With paps unwounded by so vile a creature?

CHORUS. It drew from them with the milk a curd of blood.

ORESTES. Ah, this is more than an idle apparition.

CHORUS. Then with a shriek of terror she awoke,
And through the palace at her command the lamps
Flared up, and she sent us with these offerings
To heal the deep affliction of her spirit.

ORESTES. I pray to the Earth and to my father's tomb
That this vision may prove oracular.
As I interpret it, it tallies well.
Since, issuing from where I saw the light
The snake was wrapped in swaddling-clothes and mouthed
The breast that nourished me, with kindly milk
Mingling those drops of blood, which made her shriek
In terror, so, as she gave that monster life,
So she must die a violent death, and I
Shall turn into a dragon and murder her.

CHORUS. I accept your reading of the apparition,
And may it prove true. Now give us your instructions:
What must we do and what forbear to do?

ORESTES. It is soon told. First, *she* must go inside
To see that our enterprise is well concealed,
So that the couple whose cunning killed a king
Be caught by cunning, as Apollo has commanded.
Then I, with my true friend here, Pylades,
Disguised as travelers, shall approach the door
Speaking the Phocian dialect, and if no
Doorkeeper opens to us, since it is a house
Bewitched with sin, we will wait till the passersby
Take stock and say, "Where is Aegisthus? Why
Does he close his doors against these strangers?"—then,
Stepping across the threshold, if I find
That scoundrel seated on my father's

throne,
Or if he should come to greet me, lift-
ing up
To mine those eyes that shall be soon
cast down.
Before he can ask, "Where is the stran-
ger from?"
My steel shall strike, and so a Fury
never
Starved shall drain a third great
draught of blood.
And so to *you* I say, keep a close watch
[*To* ELECTRA.]
Inside the house, and to *you* I com-
mend [*To the* CHORUS.]
Silence in season and timeliness in
speech.
The rest is for my comrade's eyes alone
To guide me in this ordeal of the
sword.
CHORUS. Fearful beasts bringing much
Harm to man breed on earth;
Monsters huge hid from sight lurk be-
neath
Smiling seas; and baleful lights sweep-
ing through the vaulted skies
Swing suspended over all
Creatures that fly and that walk on the
ground; and remember
How they rage, the stormy blasts.

Yet the deeds dared by man's
Forward spirit who shall tell?
Women too, whose perverse loves con-
trive
Crimes of blood provoking blood-
stained revenges, sin for sin.
Once a woman's lawless lust
Gains the supremacy, swiftly it brings
to destruction
Wedded ties in beast and man.

Those who cannot grasp the truth, let
them
Take thought touching that
Flash of torchlit treachery,
Which the black heart of Althaea[4]
plotted,
By whose hand the firebrand was burnt
which
Dated back to the day her child
Cried as he issued from her
Womb, and measured his span of life
On to the death appointed.

No less wicked too was Scylla,[5] whose

False heart foe-beguiled
Dared the death of dearest kin,
All for one necklace rare, wrought of
fine gold,
A gift brought from Crete; hence in se-
cret,
While in slumber her Nisus lay,
Ah, she shore his immortal
Locks—a pitiless heart was hers!
Hermes led him to darkness.

And since I call back to mind the
wicked crimes
Of old . . .—To no purpose! *This* unhal-
lowed, vile
Union, which the world abhors,
A wife's deceit framed against a war-
rior—
Have you no harsh words to censure
that?
I praise the hearth where no fires of
passion burn,
A meek heart such as graces woman.
—Of all the crimes told in tales the
Lemnian[6]
Is chief, a sin cried throughout the
world with such
Horror that, if men relate
Some monstrous outrage, they call it
Lemnian.
Abhorred of man, scorned of God,
Their seed is cast out for evermore;
For none respect what the Gods abomi-
nate.
Is *this* not well and justly spoken?

A sword of piercing steel is poised
To strike well home, which unerring
Justice
Shall thrust to cleave the hearts of all
Those who trample underfoot
The sanctities
Of Zeus, to ungodly deeds inclining.

The tree of Justice shall not fall,
And Fate's strong hand forges steel to
arm her.
There comes to wipe away with fresh
Blood the blood of old a son,
Obeying some
Inscrutable Fury's deadly purpose.
[*Enter* ORESTES *and* PYLADES. *They go
up to the door.*]
ORESTES. Ho there! Ho! I call a third
time: ho!
Let Aegisthus grant us hospitality! [*A*

SERVANT *comes to the door.*]

SERVANT. All right, I hear you. Where is the stranger from?

ORESTES. Announce me to your masters. I bring them news.
Go quickly, for Night's chariot draws on
The hour for travelers to seek repose.
Let someone in authority come out,
A woman, or more properly a man;
For we can speak more freely man to man. [CLYTEMNESTRA *comes to the door, attended by* ELECTRA.]

CLYTEMNESTRA. Strangers, declare your wishes. Here you shall have
A welcome such as the house is noted for—
Warm baths and beds to ease the travel-tired
And the presence of an honest company;
But if you have in mind some graver matter,
That is man's business, and to men we shall impart it.

ORESTES. I am a stranger from Phocis, and I have come
To Argos on an errand of my own;
But as I shod my feet to take the road,
A man came up to me whom I did not know—
Strophius the Phocian[7] was his name, he said,—
"Stranger," he said to me, "if you are bound
For Argos, please inform the parents of
Orestes that their son is dead, and bring
An answer back, whether they wish to fetch
His body or leave it here duly lamented
And laid to rest an exile even in death."
That was the message. Whether I now address
One in authority and near to him
I do not know, but his parents should be told.

ELECTRA. Oh, it is all over, all pitilessly destroyed!
O irresistible curse of our ancestors
So widely ranging! Even that which seemed
Safely disposed beyond the reach of harm
Has been brought down by an arrow from afar,
Leaving me desolate, stripped of all I loved.
And now Orestes—he who wisely resolved
To keep his foot outside the miry clay,
Now that one hope that might at last have purged
The house of wickedness, do not mark it as present.

ORESTES. I could have wished, visiting such a house
On which God smiles, that happier news had made
Me known to you; for nothing brings such delight
As the gentle intercourse of host and stranger.
But I would have deemed it wrong not to fulfil
My solemn promise to those I love so dearly.

CLYTEMNESTRA. You shall be entertained as you deserve.
You are welcome notwithstanding; for, if you
Had not brought the news, others would have come.
Now it is time for you to be attended.
[*To* ELECTRA.] Escort them in and wait upon their needs.
Do this, I tell you, as you shall answer for it.
Meanwhile I shall inform the master of
The house and shall consult all of our friends
What should be done concerning this event. [CLYTEMNESTRA, ELECTRA, ORESTES *and* PYLADES *go into the palace.*]

CHORUS. How soon shall our voices be lifted in praise of Orestes? O Earth, O Tomb, now is the time to strengthen his hand; let Hermes arise out of the darkness to look down on the contest! [*The* NURSE *comes out of the palace.*]

It seems the stranger is already making mischief.
Here is Orestes' old nurse, bathed in tears.
What is it, Cilissa? What brings you to the gates?

NURSE. My mistress has commanded me to bring
Aegisthus to the strangers instantly,

That he may hear their message man
from man.
Before the servants she affects a sor-
rowful
Demeanor, yet with a lurking smile
At news that makes her happy, and he
too
Will now be overjoyed. What years of
grief
Are locked up in this breast, which I
have borne
Within these walls—old, mixed-up
memories—
And now Orestes, who was entrusted to
me
Out of his mother's arms—my dearest
care—
And what a troublesome child he was!
For sure, like a dumb animal, a sense-
less babe
Must needs have a nurse's wits to nour-
ish it.
A child in swaddling clothes cannot de-
clare
His wants, that he would eat or drink
or make
Water, nor will his belly wait upon
Attendance. Nurses must have second
sight,
And even so they may be deceived, and
then
Must wash the linen white—such was
my task
Tending Orestes, his father's son and
heir;
And now he is dead, they tell me, and I
must take
The news to him whose wickedness in-
fects
The house, and watch how it warms his
heart.
CHORUS. With what equipment did she
bid him come?
NURSE. Equipment? How? I do not
understand you.
CHORUS. Attended by his retinue, or
alone?
NURSE. He is told to bring his royal
bodyguard.
CHORUS. Then, as you hate him, not a
word about that!
Tell him to come alone, and come at
once,
Come and fear nothing and feed his
happy heart.
NURSE. Can it be that you see some

good in the report?
CHORUS. Who knows but Zeus may yet
turn an ill wind?
NURSE. How, if our last hope, Orestes,
is gone?
CHORUS. A good prophet would not yet
read it so.
NURSE. Have you reason to doubt that
the news is true?
CHORUS. Go, take your message and do
as you are told.
The Gods will care for what is their
concern.
NURSE. I will go. God grant that all is
for the best!
CHORUS. Hear us, O Father Zeus, hear
our prayer!
Grant that those win the day who
would see
Lawlessness at last dethroned!
Nothing we ask but what is just: O
Zeus, defend us!
Let the champion who has gone in
Be upheld now in the fray. Zeus, who
has made him
Great, shall take at will a twofold re-
compense and threefold.

Think of that lordly sire whose untried
Colt is now yoked and all set to run!
Lay a steady, guiding hand
Upon the rein until the breathless race
is over!

Grant that he may grasp the great
Prize the Gods have kept for him
Here—his ancient heritage.
So with vengeance fresh redeem
The full debt of those ancestral crimes.
Let us rejoice and set a crown on the
palace!
O let it soon be revealed
Gleaming and friendly and free
Out of the veil of encircling dark-
ness!

Hermes[8] too shall lend a hand,
Named the keen and cunning one.
Much at will he can reveal.
Night he draws before the eyes
With voice veiled that none may under-
stand.

Thus, with all done at last,
Music set to breezes fair,
Women's shrill songs of joy

Shall be heard, "All is well!"
Bringing peace to those we love.
And with stout heart, as she cries
"Child!"
Let him cry "Father!" and kill her!

May his heart turn to stone,
Hard as Perseus',[9] merciless!
Make the end bloody, wipe
Clean the old stain, that this
House may win deliverance! [*Enter*
AEGISTHUS.]
AEGISTHUS. I come in answer to the
summons.
Strangers, they say, have brought un-
welcome news,
Orestes' death, another wound to open
Old sores in this sad house. How shall I
judge
Whether it is true or women's idle
rumor?
CHORUS. We have heard it, but go in-
side and ask
The strangers. Make enquiry on the
spot.
AEGISTHUS. I want to see that messen-
ger and ask
If he was present at the death. They
shall
Not hoodwink me. My wits are wide
awake.
[AEGISTHUS *enters the palace.*]

CHORUS. Zeus, what shall I say? The
moment has come, with the fate of the
house on a knife's edge. Is it to fall, or
shall the son be restored to the wealth
of his fathers? That is the issue, and he
faces alone two monsters—may he
prove master! [*A cry is heard within.*]

He is at work. Better stand clear awhile,
in case
It goes against him. The issue has been
decided. [*The* SERVANT *comes to the
door.*]
SERVANT. Oh, oh! My master has been
murdered!
Oh me! A third cry for the dead! Help!
Unbolt the women's chambers! And yet
even
A strong hand is too weak to help the
dead.
Ho!
They must be deaf or sleeping. All my
cries

Are wasted. Where is Clytemnestra?
what
Is she doing? Now, it seems, her own
Head must bend beneath the axe of
Justice. [CLYTEMNESTRA *comes to the
door.*]
CLYTEMNESTRA. What is it? What is the
meaning of that shout?
SERVANT. It means the living are being
killed by the dead.
CLYTEMNESTRA. Ah me, a riddle! yet I
can read its meaning.
Quick, let me have a man-axe, then we
shall see
Who wins, who loses. It has come to
this. [ORESTES *and* PYLADES *come out of
the palace. The body of* AEGISTHUS *lies at
their feet.*]
ORESTES. I have been looking for you.
He is all right.
CLYTEMNESTRA. Aegisthus, dearest love!
Oh, he is dead!
ORESTES. You love him? Well, then you
shall share his grave,
Faithful in everything even to death.
CLYTEMNESTRA. O stay, my son! Dear
child, have pity on
This bosom where in slumber long ago
Your toothless gums drew in the milk
of life!
ORESTES. Pylades, what shall I do? Shall
I spare my mother?
PYLADES. What then hereafter of the
oracles
And solemn declarations of Apollo?
Better that men should hate you than
the Gods.
ORESTES. Your counsel shall prevail.
Come with me. I
Shall kill you by his side. Since you pre-
ferred
Him to my father while he lived, die
with him!
CLYTEMNESTRA. I brought you up—let
me grow old with you!
ORESTES. What, live with you, my
father's murderess!
CLYTEMNESTRA. Fate had a hand, my
son, in your father's end.
ORESTES. Yes, the same fate which now
decrees your own.
CLYTEMNESTRA. Have you no dread of a
mother's curse, my child?
ORESTES. Your child no more, because
you cast me out.
CLYTEMNESTRA. No, not cast out—I sent

you away to friends.

ORESTES. Son of a royal father, foully sold!

CLYTEMNESTRA. What then was the payment that I took for you?

ORESTES. For very shame I cannot answer that.

CLYTEMNESTRA. No, no! Remember too *his* faithlessness!

ORESTES. Do not reproach him. It was for you he toiled abroad.

CLYTEMNESTRA. It is hard for a woman parted from her man.

ORESTES. What but his labor keeps her safe at home?

CLYTEMNESTRA. So then, my son, you mean to kill your mother?

ORESTES. It is not I, it is you who kill yourself.

CLYTEMNESTRA. Beware of the hell-hounds of a mother's curse!

ORESTES. And how, if I spare you, escape from his?

CLYTEMNESTRA. My pleas are fruitless— warm tears at a cold tomb.

ORESTES. My father's destiny has determined yours.

CLYTEMNESTRA. Ah me, I gave birth to a snake and not a son.

ORESTES. That panic-stricken nightmare was prophetic.
Wrong shall be done to you for the wrong you did. [*They go into the palace.*]

CHORUS. I mourn for them both, and yet, since the tale
Of bloodshed is now crowned in brave Orestes,
I choose to have it so, that this great house
May rise again and not perish utterly.

Upon the sons of Priam Justice in time did bring
Heavy and harsh judgment;
To Agamemnon too and to his house it came,
A double lion, double strife.
On to the goal he held his course heaven-sped,
Following well the Lord Apollo's command.
　　Cry Alleluia, lift up in the house a song,
　　Deliverance from evil and the waste of wealth,

From rough, thorny ways.

Yes, he has come, the God who with a sly assault
Ambushes evildoers;
Deftly his hand was guided in the battle by
The child of Zeus the truly-named,
Whom it is right that mortals call Righteousness.
Deadly the blast she breathes on those that shed blood.
Just as Apollo cried out of his holy shrine,
So does his word advance never at fault against
The ingrown disease which in the house is lodged;
For God's will is always stronger than sin.
　　On us the light has shone! Now let the fallen house
　　Out of the shadows rise; for it was long enough
　　The chains of evil held it down.

It shall be purified in the appointed time,
When he has cleansed the hearth of the defiling sin,
And all those who wept shall have their sorrow turned
To joy, greeting man's salvation from wrong. [*The doors are opened and torches lit within, revealing the bodies of* AEGISTHUS *and* CLYTEMNESTRA *laid out in purple robes on a couch, with* ORESTES *standing over them.*]

ORESTES. See here our country's double tyranny!
How stately were they sitting on their thrones,
Both pledged to slay my father and so doomed
To die themselves together—they kept their word.
See here the snare which they contrived to enmesh
My father's hands and feet—what shall I call it?
A pit for wild beasts, or a winding-sheet,
Or a cloak spread by some highwayman to catch
The passing traveler? Come, spread it out,

This skilful masterpiece, that he who is
Father of all creation and looks down
On the whole world, the Sun, having
observed
My mother's wicked handiwork, may
stand
My witness at the judgment which is to
come
And certify that I put her to death
Justly—as for Aegisthus, he has paid
The penalty prescribed for adulterers;
But she, who plotted this horror for
her own
Husband, to whom she bore within her
womb
Children, a load of love which now has
turned
To hate, as they have shown by their
sharp fangs—
What do you think of her? If she had
been
A scorpion or sea-snake, her very touch
Would rot the unbitten hand. Rather
than share
House with such a monster, may the
Gods
Destroy me and my children and chil-
dren's children!
CHORUS. With a fearful death she has
paid for her foul deed, reaping the
crop which she sowed with her own
hand.
ORESTES. The deed was hers, was it not?
I have a witness,
This robe, that here she plunged Aegis-
thus' sword:
See how bloodstains have joined with
time and worn
The dye out of the pattern! I am now
present,
Now only, to praise and lament my
father,
Greeting this web that wove his death
and weeping
For all that has been done and suffered
here,
For the whole race, and for my own
fate too,
Bearing the stains of this grim victory.
CHORUS. All men have been born to
sorrow, which is present for some to-
day and for others is stored up.
ORESTES. So then, to tell you plainly—I
do not know
How it will end—my wits are out of
hand

Like horses that with victory in sight
Shy and dash wildly off the course—so
I feel
Here at the heart a throbbing—but
while I have
My senses, I declare that I killed my
mother
In a just cause, because she killed my
father,
And that I was driven to do it in obedi-
ence
To the oracle of Apollo, who pro-
claimed
That, if I did it, I should be cleared of
guilt,
And that, if not—I will not name the
penalty,
Something beyond imagination; and so,
Garlanded with these sprigs of suppli-
cation,
I make my way to his prophetic shrine
And the glorious light of his undying
fire,
A suppliant stained with blood; for he
commanded me
To seek no hearth but his; and mean-
while I
Call on my fellow-countrymen to give
In time to come their evidence, how all
this
Was brought about, an outcast, leaving
to
Their safekeeping, in life and death,
my name.
CHORUS. You must not bend your lips
to such ill-omened
Talk after delivering your country and
With one swift stroke lopping two
dragon's heads.
ORESTES. Look! Do you see those
women, like Gorgons,
All clothed in black, their heads and
arms entwined
With writhing snakes! How can I es-
cape?
CHORUS. What imaginings are these, O
father's dearest
Son? Stay and fear nothing. You have
won.
ORESTES. Imaginings! They are real
enough to me.
Can you not see them? Hounds of a
mother's curse!
CHORUS. It is the blood still dripping
from your hands
That confuses your wits, but it will pass.

ORESTES. O Lord Apollo! See how thick
    they come,
And from their eyes are oozing gouts
    of blood!
CHORUS. You shall be purified! Apollo's
    touch
Shall save you and from all troubles set
    you free.
ORESTES. You cannot see them, and yet
    how plain they are!
They are coming to hunt me down.

Away, away! [*Exit.*]
CHORUS. Good luck, and may God
    guide you to the end!

This is the third storm to have struck
the house: first, the slaughter of children; next, the fall of the great king
who had conquered Troy; and now—is
it final destruction or deliverance at
last? When shall the curse be laid to
rest?

Eumenides

Characters
Priestess
Apollo
Orestes
Ghost of Clytemnestra
Chorus of Furies
Athena
Escort of Women

*Before the temple of Apollo at Delphi. Enter
    the* PRIESTESS.
PRIESTESS. First among all the gods to
    whom this prayer
Shall be addressed is the first of
    prophets, Earth;
And next her daughter, Themis, who
    received
The oracular shrine from her; third,
    another
Daughter, Phoebe, who having settled
    here
Bestowed it as a birthday gift, together
With her own name, on Phoebus;
    whereupon,
Leaving his native isle of Delos and
    landing
In Attica, he made his way from there
Attended by the sons of Hephaestus,
    who tamed
The wilderness and built a road for
    him;
And here Zeus, having inspired him
    with his art,
Set him, the fourth of prophets, on this
    throne,
His own son and interpreter, Apollo.

Together with these deities I pay
Homage to Athena and to the nymphs
    that dwell
In the Corycian caves on the rugged
    slopes
Of Parnassus, where Dionysus led
His troop of frenzied Bacchants to
    catch and kill
King Pentheus like a mountain-hare;
    and so,
After calling on Poseidon and the
    springs
Of Pleistus, watering this valley, and
    last
On Zeus the All-Highest, who makes all
    things perfect,
I take my seat on the oracular throne,
Ready to be consulted. Let all Greeks
Approach by lot according to custom
And I shall prophesy to them as God
    dictates. [*She enters the temple, utters a
    loud cry, and returns.*]
O horror, horror! I have been driven
    back
Strengthless, speechless, a terror-struck
    old woman,
By such a sight as was never seen be-
    fore.
Entering the shrine I saw at the navel-
    stone
In the posture of a suppliant a man
Who held an olive-branch and an un-
    sheathed sword
In hands dripping with blood; and all
    round him,
Lying fast asleep, a gruesome company

Of women—yet not women—Gorgons rather;
And yet not Gorgons; them I saw once in a picture
Of the feast of Phineus: these are different.
They have no wings, and are all black, and snore,
And drops ooze from their eyes, and the rags they wear
Unutterably filthy. What country could
Have given such creatures birth, I cannot tell.
Apollo is the master of this house,
So let him look to it, healer, interpreter,
Himself of other houses purifier. [*The inside of the temple is revealed, as described, with* APOLLO *and* HERMES *standing beside* ORESTES.]
APOLLO. I will keep faith, at all times vigilant,
Whether at your side or far away, and never
Mild to your enemies, whom you now see
Subdued by sleep, these unloved virgins, these
Children hoary with age, whose company
Is shunned by God and man and beast, being born
For evil, just as the abyss from which they come
Is evil, the bottomless pit of Tartarus.[1]
Yet you must fly before them, hotly pursued,
Past island cities and over distant seas,
Enduring all without faltering, until
You find sanctuary in Athena's citadel,
And there, embracing her primeval image, you
Shall stand trial, and after healing words
From me, who commanded you to kill your mother,
You shall be set free and win your salvation.
ORESTES. O Lord Apollo, you have both wisdom and power,
And, since you have them, use them on my behalf!
APOLLO. Remember, endure and have no fear! And you,
Hermes, go with him, guide him, guard his steps.

An outcast from mankind, yet blest of Zeus. [*Exeunt* HERMES *and* ORESTES. *Enter the ghost of* CLYTEMNESTRA.]
CLYTEMNESTRA. Oho! asleep! What good are you to me asleep?
While I, deserted and humiliated,
Wander, a homeless ghost. I warn you that
Among the other spirits of the dead
(The taunt of murder does not lose its sting
In the dark world below) I am the accused
And not the accuser, with none to defend me,
Brutally slain by matricidal hands.
Look on these scars, and remember all
The wineless offerings which I laid upon
The hearth for you at many a solemn midnight—
All now forgotten, all trampled underfoot!
And *he* is gone! Light as a fawn he skipped
Out of your snare and now he laughs at you.
Oh hear me! I am pleading for my soul!
O goddesses of the underworld, awake!
I, Clytemnestra, call you now in dreams!
CHORUS. Mu!
CLYTEMNESTRA. Ah, you may mew, but he is fled and gone.
He has protectors who are no friends of mine.
CHORUS. Mu!
CLYTEMNESTRA. Still so drowsy, still so pitiless?
Orestes has escaped, the matricide!
CHORUS. Oh, oh!
CLYTEMNESTRA. Still muttering and mumbling in your sleep!
Arise, do evil! is not that your task?
CHORUS. Oh, oh!
CLYTEMNESTRA. How sleep and weariness have made common cause
To disenvenom the foul dragon's rage!
CHORUS. Oh, oh! where is the scent? Let us mark it down!
CLYTEMNESTRA. Yes, you may bay like an unerring hound,
But still you are giving chase only in your dreams.
What are you doing? Rise, slothful

lugabeds,
Stung by the scourge of my rebukes, arise
And blow about his head your bloody breath,
Consume his flesh in bellifuls of fire!
Come on, renew the chase and hunt him down! [*Exit.*]
CHORUS. We have been put to shame! What has befallen us?
The game has leapt out of the snare and gone.
In slumber laid low, we let slip the prey.

Aha, son of Zeus! pilferer, pillager!
A God, to steal away the matricide!
A youth to flout powers fixed long ago!

In dream I felt beneath the heart a swift
Charioteer's sharp lash.
Under the ribs, under the flank
It rankles yet, red and sore,
Like the public scourger's blow.

This is the doing of the younger gods.
Dripping with death, red drops
Cover the heel, cover the head.
Behold the earth's navel-stone
Thick with heavy stains of blood!

His own prophetic cell he has himself defiled,
Honoring mortal claims, reckless of laws divine,
And dealing death to Fates born of old.

He injures us and yet *him* he shall never free,
Not in the depths of hell, never shall he have rest
But suffer lasting torment below.
APOLLO. Out, out! Be off, and clear this holy place
Of your foul presence, or else from my golden bow
Shall spring a snake of silver and bite so deep
That from your swollen bellies you shall spew
The blood which you have sucked! Your place is where
Heads drop beneath the axe, eyes are gouged out,
Throats slit, and men are stoned, limbs

lopped, and boys
Gelded, and a last whimper heard from spines
Spiked writhing in the dust. Such celebrations,
Which fill heaven with loathing, are your delight.
Off with you, I say, and go unshepherded,
A herd shunned with universal horror!
CHORUS. O Lord Apollo, hear us in our turn!
You are not an abettor in this business.
You are the culprit. On you lies the whole guilt.
APOLLO. Explain yourselves. How do you make that out?
CHORUS. It was at your command that he killed his mother.
APOLLO. I commanded him to take vengeance for his father.
CHORUS. So promising the acceptance of fresh blood.
APOLLO. I promised to absolve him from it here.
CHORUS. Why do you insult the band that drove him here?
APOLLO. This mansion is not fit for your company.
CHORUS. But this is the task that has been appointed to us.
APOLLO. What is this privilege that you are so proud of?
CHORUS. To drive all matricides from hearth and home.
APOLLO. And what of a woman who has killed her husband?
CHORUS. That is not manslaughter within the kin.
APOLLO. So then you set at naught the marriage-bond
Sealed by Zeus and Hera, and yet what tie
Is stronger, joined by Fate and watched over
By Justice, than the joy which Aphrodite
Has given to man and woman? If you let those
Who violate that covenant go unpunished,
You have no right to persecute Orestes.
Why anger here, and there passivity?
On this in time Athena shall pass judgment.
CHORUS. We shall give chase and never

let him go.

APOLLO. Pursue him then, and make trouble for yourselves.

CHORUS. No words of yours can circumscribe our powers.

APOLLO. I would not have your powers even as a gift.

CHORUS. Then take your proud stand by the throne of Zeus.
Meanwhile a mother's blood is beckoning to us,
And we must go and follow up the trail.

APOLLO. And I will still safeguard the suppliant.
A wrong unheard-of in heaven and on earth
Would be his protest, if I should beak faith. [*A year passes. Before a shrine of Athena at Athens. Enter* ORESTES.]

ORESTES. O Queen Athena, I have come here in obedience
To the Lord Apollo. Grant me sanctuary,
An outcast, yet with hands no longer sullied, for
The edge of my pollution has been worn
Off on countless paths over land and sea;
And now, in accordance with his word, present
Before your image, I entreat you to
Receive me here and pass the final judgment.

CHORUS. Step where our dumb informer leads the way;
For as the hounds pursue a wounded fawn,
So do we dog the trail of human blood.
How far we have traveled over land and sea,
Faint and footsore but never to be shaken off!
He must be somewhere here, for I smell blood.

—Beware, I say, beware!
Look on all sides for fear he find some escape!
—Ah, here he is, desperate,
Clasping that image awaiting trial.
—It cannot be! The mother's blood
That he has spilt is irrecoverable.
—Ravenous lips shall feed upon his living flesh

And on his blood—a lush pasturage.
—And others shall he see in hell, who wronged
Parents, guests or gods;
For Hades is a stern inquisitor of souls,
Recording all things till the hour of judgment.

ORESTES. Taught by long suffering, I have learnt at what
Times it is right to keep silence and when
To break it, and in this matter a wise
Instructor has charged me to speak. The stain
Of matricide has been washed out in the flow
Of swine's blood[2] by Apollo. I could tell
Of many who have given me lodging and no
Harm has befallen them from my company;
And now with lips made pure I call upon
Athena to protect me and so join
Our peoples as allies for all time to come.
Wherever she may be, on Libyan shores
Or by the stream of Trito, where she came
To birth, or like a captain keeping watch
On the heights of Phlegra against some enemy,
O may she come—far off, she can still hear me—
And from my sufferings deliver me!

CHORUS. Neither Apollo nor Athena can
Save your soul from perdition, a feast for fiends.
Have you no answer? Do you spurn us so,
Fattened for us, our consecrated host?

Let us dance and declare in tune with this grim music the laws which it is ours to enforce on the life of man. It is only those that have blood on their hands who need fear us at all, but from them without fail we exact retribution.

Mother Night, your children cry! Hear, black Night!
It is ours to deal by day and dark night judgment.

The young god Apollo has rescued the
matricide!
Over the blood that has been shed
Maddening dance, melody desperate,
deathly,
Chant to bind the soul in hell,
Spell that parches flesh to dust.

This the Fates who move the whole
world through
Have assigned to us, a task for all fu-
ture ages,
To keep watch on all hands that drip
red with kindred blood.
Over the blood that has been shed
Maddening dance, melody desperate,
deathly,
Chant to bind the soul in hell,
Spell that parches flesh to dust.

Such are the powers appointed us from
the beginning,
None of the Gods of Olympus to eat
with us, while we
Take no part in the wearing of white—
no,
Other pleasures are our choice—
Wrecking the house, hunting the
man,
Hard on his heels ever we run,
And though his feet be swift we
waste and wear him out.

Hence it is thanks to our zealous en-
deavor that from such
Offices Zeus and the Gods are ex-
empted, and yet he
Shuns us because we are covered in
blood, not
Fit to share his majesty.
Wrecking the house, hunting the
man,
Hard on his heels ever we run,
And though his feet be swift we
waste and wear him out.

Glories of men, how bright in the day is
their splendor,
Yet shall they fade in the darkness of
hell,
Faced with our grisly attire and danc-
ing
Feet attuned to sombre melodies.
Nimble the feet leap in the air,
Skip and descend down to the
ground,

Fugitive step suddenly tripped up in
fatal confusion.

Caught without knowing he stumbles,
his wickedness blinds him,
Such is the cloud of pollution that
hangs
Over him and on his house, remem-
bered
Many generations after him.
Nimble the feet leap in the air,
Skip and descend down to the
ground,
Fugitive step suddenly tripped up in
fatal confusion.

Our task is such. With long memories
We keep constant watch on human sin.
What others spurn is what we prize,
Our heaven their hell, a region of
trackless waste,
Both for the quick and dead, for blind
and seeing too.

What wonder then that men bow in
dread
At these commandments assigned to us
By Fate—our ancient privilege?
We are not without our own honors
and dignities,
Though we reside in hell's unfathom-
able gloom. [*Enter* ATHENA.].
ATHENA. I heard a distant cry, as I was
standing
Beside Scamander to take possession of
The lands which the Achaean princes
have
Bestowed on my people in perpetuity;
And thence I have made my way across
the sea
In wingless flight; and now, as I regard
Before my shrine this very strange
company,
I cannot but ask, in wonder, not in
fear,
Who you may be. I address you all in
common,
This stranger here who is seated at my
image,
And you, who are not human in ap-
pearance
Nor yet divine; but rather than speak ill
Without just cause let me receive your
answer.
CHORUS. Daughter of Zeus, your ques-
tion is soon answered.

We are the dismal daughters of dark
  Night,
Called Curses in the palaces of hell.
ATHENA. I know your names then and
  your parentage.
CHORUS. And now let us inform you of
  our powers.
ATHENA. Yes, let me know what office
  you perform.
CHORUS. We drive the matricide from
  hearth and home.
ATHENA. Where? In what place does his
  persecution end?
CHORUS. A place where joy is something
  quite unknown.
ATHENA. Is that your hue and cry
  against this man?
CHORUS. Yes, because he dared to kill
  his mother.
ATHENA. Was he driven to it perhaps
  against his will?
CHORUS. What force could drive a man
  to matricide?
ATHENA. It is clear there are two parties
  to this case.
CHORUS. We challenged him to an
  ordeal by oath.
ATHENA. You seem to seek only the
  semblance of justice.
CHORUS. How so? Explain, since you
  are so rich in wisdom.
ATHENA. Do not use oaths to make the
  wrong prevail.
CHORUS. Then try the case yourself and
  give your judgment.
ATHENA. Will you entrust the verdict to
  my charge?
CHORUS. Yes, a worthy daughter of a
  worthy father.
ATHENA. Stranger, what is your answer?
  Tell us first
Your fatherland and family and what
Misfortune overtook you, and then an-
  swer
The charge against you. If you have
  taken your stand
Here as a suppliant with full confidence
In the justice of your cause, now is the
  time
To render on each count a clear reply.
ORESTES. O Queen Athena, first let me
  remove one doubt.
I am not a suppliant seeking
  purification.
I was already cleansed before I took
This image in my arms, and I can give

Evidence of this. The manslayer is re-
  quired
To keep silent until he has been
  anointed
With sacrificial blood. That has been
  done,
And I have traveled far over land and
  sea
To wear off the pollution. So, having
  set
Your mind at rest, let me tell you who I
  am.
I come from Argos, and my father's
  name—
For asking me that I thank you—was
  Agamemnon,
The great commander, with whom not
  long ago
You wiped out Troy. He died an evil
  death,
Murdered on his return by my black-
  hearted
Mother, who netted him in a bath of
  blood.
And therefore I, restored from banish-
  ment,
In retribution for my father's death,
I killed my mother; and yet not I
  alone—
Apollo too must answer for it, having
Warned me what anguish would afflict
  me if
I should fail to take vengeance on the
  guilty.
Whether it was just or not, do you de-
  cide.
ATHENA. This is too grave a case for
  mortal minds,
Nor is it right that I should judge an
  act
Of blood shed with such bitter conse-
  quences,
Especially since you have come to me
As one already purified, who has done
  no wrong
Against this city. But your opponents
  here
Are not so gentle, and, if their plea
Should be rejected, the poison dripping
  from
Their angry bosoms will devastate my
  country.
The issue is such that, whether I let
  them stay
Or turn them out, it is fraught with in-
  jury.

But be it so. Since it has come to this,
I will appoint judges for homicide,
A court set up in perpetuity.
Do you prepare your proofs and witnesses,
Then I, having selected from my people
The best, will come to pass a final judgment. [*Exit.*]
CHORUS. Now the world shall see the
downfall of old commandments
made
Long ago, if the accurst matricide
should win his case.
Many a bitter blow awaits parents from
their own children in the times to
come.

We who had the task to watch over human life shall now
Cease to act, giving free rein to deeds
of violence.
Crime shall spread from house to
house like a plague, and whole cities
shall be desolate.

Then let no man stricken cry
Out in imprecation, "Oh
Furies!" Thus shall fathers groan,
Thus shall mothers weep in vain,
Since the house of righteousness
Lies in ruins, overthrown.

Times there are when fear is good,
Keeping watch within the soul.
Needful too are penalties.
Who of those that have not nursed
Wholesome dread within them can
Show respect to righteousness?

Choose a life despot-free, yet restrained by rule of law.
God has appointed the mean as the
master in all things.
Wickedness breeds pride, but from wisdom is brought forth
Happiness prayed for by all men.

So, we say, men must bow down before
the shrine of Right.
Those who defy it shall fail; for the ancient commandments
Stand—to respect parents and honor
the stranger.
Only the righteous shall prosper.

The man who does what is right by
choice, not constraint,
Shall prosper always; the seed of just
men shall never perish.
Not so the captain who ships a load of
ill-gotten gains.
Caught in the gathering storm his
proud sail shall be torn from the
masthead.

He cries to deaf ears, no longer able to
ride
The gale, and meanwhile his guardian
spirit is close beside him
And scoffs to see him despair of ever
again making port,
Dashed on the reefs of Justice, un-
looked-on and unlamented. [*Enter*
ATHENA *with the* JUDGES, *followed by
citizens of Athens.*]
ATHENA. Herald, give orders to hold
the people back,
Then sound the trumpet and proclaim
silence.
For while this new tribunal is being en-
rolled,
It is right that all should ponder on its
laws,
Both the litigants here whose case is to
be judged,
And my whole people for all genera-
tions. [*Enter* APOLLO.]
CHORUS. Apollo, what is there here that
concerns you?
We say you have no authority in this
matter.
APOLLO. I come both as a witness, the
accused
Having been a suppliant at my sanc-
tuary
And purified of homicide at my hands,
And also to be tried with him, for I too
Must answer for the murder of his
mother.
Open the case, and judge as you know
how.
ATHENA. The case is open. You shall be
first to speak. [*To the* CHORUS.]
The prosecutors shall take precedence
And first inform us truthfully of the
facts.
CHORUS. Many in number, we shall be
brief in speech.
We beg you to answer our questions
one by one.
First, is it true that you killed your

mother?

ORESTES. I killed her. That is true, and not denied.

CHORUS. So then the first of the three rounds is ours.

ORESTES. You should not boast that you have thrown me yet.

CHORUS. Next, since you killed her, you must tell us how.

ORESTES. Yes, with a drawn sword leveled at the throat.

CHORUS. Who was it who impelled or moved you to it?

ORESTES. The oracle of this God who is my witness.

CHORUS. The God of prophecy ordered matricide?

ORESTES. Yes, and I have not repented it to this day.

CHORUS. You *will* repent it, when you have been condemned.

ORESTES. My father shall defend me from the grave.

CHORUS. Having killed your mother, you may well trust the dead!

ORESTES. She was polluted by a double crime.

CHORUS. How so? Explain your meaning to the judges.

ORESTES. She killed her husband and she killed my father.

CHORUS. She died without bloodguilt, and you still live.

ORESTES. Why did you not hunt her when she was alive?

CHORUS. She was not bound by blood to the man she killed.

ORESTES. And am I then bound by blood to my mother?

CHORUS. Abandoned wretch, how did she nourish you
Within the womb? Do you repudiate
The nearest and dearest tie of motherhood?

ORESTES. Apollo, give your evidence. I confess
That I did this deed as I have said.
Pronounce your judgment: was it justly done?

APOLLO. Athena's appointed judges, I say to you,
Justly, and I, as prophet, cannot lie.
Never from my prophetic shrine have I
Said anything of city, man or woman
But what my father Zeus has commanded me.

This plea of mine must override all others,
Since it accords with our great father's will.

CHORUS. Your argument is, then, that Zeus commanded you
To charge Orestes with this criminal act
Regardless of the bond between son and mother?

APOLLO. It is not the same, to murder a great king,
A woman too to do it, and not in open
Fight like some brave Amazon, but in such
Manner as I shall now inform this court.
On his return from battle, bringing home
A balance for the greater part of good,
She welcomed him with fine words and then, while
He bathed, pavilioned him in a purple robe
And struck him down and killed him—a man and king
Whom the whole world had honored. Such was the crime
For which she paid. Let the judges take note.

CHORUS. According to your argument Zeus gives
Precedence to the father; yet Zeus it was
Who cast into prison his own father Kronos.
Judges, take note, and ask him to explain.

APOLLO. Abominable monsters, loathed by gods
And men, do you not understand that chains
Can be unfastened and prison doors unlocked?
But once the dust has drunk a dead man's blood,
He can never rise again—for that no remedy
Has been appointed by our almighty Father,
Although all else he can overturn at will
Without so much effort as a single breath.

CHORUS. See what your plea for the defendant means.
Is this not what he did—to spill his

mother's

Blood on the ground? And shall he then be allowed

To live on in his father's house? What public

Altar can he approach and where find fellowship?

APOLLO. The mother is not a parent, only the nurse

Of the seed which the true parent, the father,

Commits to her as to a stranger to

Keep it with God's help safe from harm. And I

Have proof of this. There can be a father

Without a mother. We have a witness here,

This daughter of Olympian Zeus, who sprang

Armed from her father's head, a goddess whom

No goddess could have brought to birth. Therefore,

Out of goodwill to your country and your people

I sent this suppliant to seek refuge with you,

That you, Athena, may find in him and his

A faithful ally for all time to come.

ATHENA. Enough has now been spoken. Are you agreed

That I call on the judges to record

Their votes justly according to their conscience?

APOLLO. Our quiver is empty, every arrow spent.

We wait to hear the issue of the trial.

ATHENA. And has my ruling your approval too?

CHORUS. Sirs, you have heard the case, and now declare

Judgment according to your solemn oath.

ATHENA. Citizens of Athens, hear my declaration

At this first trial in the history of man.

This great tribunal shall remain in power

Meeting in solemn session on this hill,[3]

Where long ago the Amazons encamped

When they made war on Theseus, and sacrificed

To Ares—hence its name. Here reverence

For law and inbred fear among my people

Shall hold their hands from evil night and day,

Only let them not tamper with the laws,

But keep the fountain pure and sweet to drink.

I warn you not to banish from your lives

All terror but to seek the mean between

Autocracy and anarchy; and in this way

You shall possess in ages yet unborn

An impregnable fortress of liberty

Such as no people has throughout the world.

With these words I establish this tribunal

Grave, quick to anger, incorruptible,

And always vigilant over those that sleep.

Let the judges now rise and cast their votes.

CHORUS. We charge you to remember that we have

Great power to harm, and vote accordingly.

APOLLO. I charge you to respect the oracles

Sanctioned by Zeus and see that they are fulfilled.

CHORUS. By interfering in what is not your office

You have desecrated your prophetic shrine.

APOLLO. Then was my Father also at fault when he

Absolved Ixion, the first murderer?

CHORUS. Keep up your chatter, but, if our cause should fail,

We shall lay on this people a heavy hand.

APOLLO. Yes, you will lose your case, and then you may

Spit out your poison, but it will do no harm.

CHORUS. Insolent youth mocks venerable age.

We await the verdict, ready to let loose

Against this city our destructive rage.

ATHENA. The final judgment rests with me, and I

Announce that my vote shall be given to Orestes.

No mother gave me birth, and in all things

Save marriage I commend with all my
heart
The masculine, my father's child in-
deed.
Therefore I cannot hold in higher es-
teem
A woman killed because she killed her
husband.
If the votes are equal, Orestes wins.
Let the appointed officers proceed
To empty the urns and count the votes.

ORESTES. O bright Apollo, how shall the
judgment go?

CHORUS. O black mother Night, are you
watching this?

ORESTES. My hour has come—the halter
or the light.

CHORUS. And ours—to exercise our
powers or perish.

APOLLO. Sirs, I adjure you to count
carefully.
If judgment errs, great harm will come
of it,
Whereas one vote may raise a fallen
house.

ATHENA. He stands acquitted on the
charge of bloodshed,
The human votes being equally divided.

ORESTES. Lady Athena, my deliverer,
I was an outcast from my country, now
I can go home again and live once
more
In my paternal heritage, thanks to you
And to Apollo and to the third, the
Savior,
Who governs the whole world. Before I
go
I give my word to you and to your peo-
ple
For all posterity that no commander
Shall lead an Argive army in war
against
This city. If any should violate this
pledge,
Out of the graves which shall then
cover us
We would arise with adverse omens to
Obstruct and turn them back. If, how-
ever,
They keep this covenant and stand by
your side,
They shall always have our blessing.
And so farewell!
May you and your people always pre-
vail

Against the assaults of all your
enemies! [*Exit.*]

CHORUS. Oho, you junior gods, since
you have trod under foot
The laws of old and robbed us of our
powers,
We shall afflict this country
With damp contagion, bleak and bar-
ren, withering up the soil,
Mildew on bud and birth abortive.
Venomous pestilence
Shall sweep your cornlands with infec-
tious death.
To weep?—No! To work? Yes! To
work ill and lay low the people!
So will the maids of Night mourn for
their stolen honors.

ATHENA. Let me persuade you to forget
your grief!
You are not defeated. The issue of the
trial
Has been determined by an equal vote.
It was Zeus himself who plainly testified
That Orestes must not suffer for what
he did.
I beg you, therefore, do not harm my
country,
Blasting her crops with drops of rank
decay
And biting cankers in the early buds.
Rather accept my offer to stay and live
In a cavern on this hill and there re-
ceive
The adoration of my citizens.

CHORUS. Oho, you junior gods, etc.

ATHENA. No, *not* dishonored, and there-
fore spare my people!
I too confide in Zeus—why speak of
that?—
And I alone of all the Olympian gods
Know of the keys which guard the trea-
sury
Of heaven's thunder. But there is no
need of that.
Let my persuasion serve to calm your
rage.
Reside with me and share my majesty;
And when from these wide acres you
enjoy
Year after year the harvest offerings
From couples newly-wed praying for
children,
Then you will thank me for my inter-
cession.

CHORUS. How can you treat us so?
Here to dwell, ever debased, defiled!

Hear our passion, hear, black Night!
For the powers once ours, sealed long,
  long ago
Have by the junior gods been all
  snatched away.
ATHENA. You are my elders, and there-
  fore I indulge
Your passion. And yet, though not so
  wise as you,
To me too Zeus has granted under-
  standing.
If you refuse me and depart, believe
  me,
This country will yet prove your heart's
  desire,
For as the centuries pass so there will
  flow
Such glory to my people as will assure
To all divinities worshipped here by
  men
And women gathered on festive holi-
  days
More honors than could be yours in
  any other
City throughout the world. And so, I
  beg you,
Keep from my citizens the vicious spur
Of internecine strife, which pricks the
  breast
Of manhood flown with passion as with
  wine!
Abroad let battle rage for every heart
That is fired with love of glory—that
  shall be theirs
In plenty. So this is my offer to you—
To give honor and receive it and to
  share
My glory in this country loved by
  heaven.
CHORUS. How can you, etc.
ATHENA. I will not weary in my benedic-
  tions,
Lest it should ever be said that you, so
  ancient
In your divinity, were driven away
By me and by my mortal citizens.
No, if Persuasion's holy majesty,
The sweet enchantment of these lips di-
  vine,
Has power to move you, please, reside
  with me.
But, if you still refuse, then, since we
  have made
This offer to you, it would be wrong to
  lay
Your hands upon us in such bitter

rage.
Again, I tell you, it is in your power to
  own
This land attended with the highest
  honors.
CHORUS. Lady Athena, what do you of-
  fer us?
ATHENA. A dwelling free of sorrow.
  Pray accept.
CHORUS. Say we accept, what privileges
  shall we have?
ATHENA. No family shall prosper with-
  out your grace.
CHORUS. Will you ensure us this pre-
  rogative?
ATHENA. I will, and bless all those that
  worship you.
CHORUS. And pledge that assurance for
  all time to come?
ATHENA. I need not promise what I will
  not perform.
CHORUS. Your charms are working, and
  our rage subsides.
ATHENA. Here make your dwelling,
  where you shall win friends.
CHORUS. What song then shall we chant
  in salutation?
ATHENA. A song of faultless victory—
  from land and sea,
From skies above let gentle breezes
  blow
And breathing sunshine float from
  shore to shore;
Let crops and cattle increase and multi-
  ply
And children grow in health and hap-
  piness,
And let the righteous prosper; for I, as
  one
Who tends flowers in a garden, cherish
  fondly
The seed that bears no sorrow. That is
  your part,
While I in many a battle shall strive un-
  til
This city stands victorious against all
Its enemies and renowned throughout
  the world.
CHORUS. We accept; we agree to dwell
  with you
Here in Athens, which by grace of Zeus
Stands a fortress for the gods,
Jeweled crown of Hellas. So
With you now we join in prayer
That smiling suns and fruitful soils
  unite to yield

Lifelong joy, fortune fair,
Light and darkness reconciled.

ATHENA. For the good of my people I
have given homes in the city to these
deities, whose power is so great and so
slowly appeased; and, whenever a man
falls foul of them, apprehended to answer for the sins of his fathers, he shall
be brought to judgment before them,
and the dust shall stifle his proud boast.

CHORUS. Free from blight may the early
  blossom deck
Budding trees, and may no parching
  drought
Spread across the waving fields.
Rather Pan in season grant
From the flocks and herds a full
Return from year to year, and from the
  rich
Store which these gods vouchsafe
May the Earth repay them well!

ATHENA. Guardians of my city, listen to
the blessings they bring, and remember
that their power is great in heaven and
hell, and on earth too they bring to
some glad music and to some lives
darkened with weeping.

CHORUS. Free from sudden death that
  cuts
Short the prime of manhood, blest
In your daughters too, to whom
Be granted husband and home, and
  may the dread Fates
Keep them safe, present in every
  household,
Praised and magnified in every place!

ATHENA. Fair blessings indeed from
powers that so lately were averted in
anger, and I thank Zeus and the spirit
of persuasion that at last there is no
strife left between us, except that they
vie with me in blessing my people.

CHORUS. Peace to all, free from that
Root of evil, civil strife!
May they live in unity,
And never more may the blood of kin
  be let flow!
Rather may all of them bonded to-
  gether
Feel and act as one in love and hate!

ATHENA. From these dread shapes, so
quick to learn a new music, I foresee
great good for my people, who, if only
they repay their favors with the reverence due, shall surely establish the
reign of justice in a city that will shine
as a light for all mankind. [*Enter* ESCORT
OF WOMEN, *carrying crimson robes and
torches.*]

CHORUS. Joy to you all in your justly ap-
  pointed riches,
Joy to all the people blest
With the Virgin's love, who stands
Next beside her Father's throne!
Wisdom man has learnt at last.
Under her protection this
Land enjoys the grace of Zeus.

ATHENA. Joy to you also, and now let
me lead you in torchlight to your new
dwelling place! Let solemn oblations
speed you in joy to your home beneath
the earth, and there imprison all harm
while still letting flow your blessings!

CHORUS. Joy to you, joy, yet again we
  pronounce our blessing,
Joy to all the citizens,
Gods and mortals both alike.
While you hold this land and pay
Homage to our residence,
You shall have no cause to blame
Chance and change in human life.
ATHENA. I thank you for your gracious
  salutations,
And now you shall be escorted in the
  light
Of torches to your subterranean dwell-
  ing,
Attended by the sacristans of my tem-
  ple
Together with this company of girls
And married women and others bowed
  with years.
Women, let them put on these robes of
  crimson,
And let these blazing torches light the
  way,
That the goodwill of our new co-resi-
  dents
Be shown in the manly prowess of your
  sons! [*The* CHORUS *put on the crimson
  robes and a procession is formed led by
  young men in armor, with the* CHORUS
  and the escort following, and behind them

the citizens of Athens. The rest is sung as the procession moves away.]

CHORUS OF THE ESCORT. Pass on your way, O powers majestic,
Daughters of darkness in happy procession!
People of Athens, hush, speak fair!

Pass to the caverns of earth immemorial
There to be worshipped in honor and glory!
People of Athens, hush, speak fair!

Gracious and kindly of heart to our people,
Come with us, holy ones, hither in gladness,
Follow the lamps that illumine the way!
O sing at the end alleluia!

Peace to you, peace of a happy community,
People of Athens! Zeus who beholds all
Watches, himself with the Fates reconciled.
O sing at the end alleluia!

Notes to *Agamemnon*

1. Uranus, who was overthrown by his son Kronos. The latter was in turn overthrown by his son Zeus, thus establishing the dynasty of gods worshipped by the early Greeks. Zeus's justice is *dikê*, retributive justice, the subject of *The Oresteia*.
2. Daughter of Zeus, goddess of children and childbirth.
3. The sons of Atreus: Agamemnon and Menelaus.
4. The string of beacons that brought the news of the fall of Troy to Clytemnestra has been imaginatively located on a series of peaks, each of which was the scene of some mythological disaster.
5. A river near Troy.
6. A giant with three bodies who had to be killed three times.

7. Cloth dyed purple (with dye extracted from shellfish) was very expensive. To walk upon it was desecration.
8. Cassandra, daughter of Priam and Hecuba.
9. Asclepius, son of Apollo, learned medicine so well that he was able to raise the dead, whereupon he was struck down by Zeus.
10. A monstrous snake with a head at either end.
11. Another monster, this one with six heads and twelve feet.
12. Chryseis was Agamemnon's concubine at Troy. By pluralizing her name, Clytemnestra implies that there were many such.
13. Noted for his enchanting song—the opposite of what Aegisthus is hearing from the Chorus.

Notes to *Choephoroe*

1. Orestes, following an ancient rite, dedicates a lock of his hair to the river god, then another to his dead father.
2. Iphigenia.
3. The wife of Pluto, and hence a source of power from the dead.
4. Another wicked mother, who caused the death of her son by burning the magic log upon which his life depended.
5. Not the monster of *Agamemnon*, note 11 above, this Scylla killed her father, Nisus, by clipping a lock of his magic hair.
6. The women of Lemnos arose simultaneously and massacred their husbands.
7. The old friend to whom Orestes had been entrusted as a child.
8. The messenger of the dead and of trickery, here invoked because of the deceptive message just sent to Aegisthus.
9. A heroic son of Zeus who slew the Gorgon Medusa.

Notes to *Eumenides*

1. The underworld.
2. Swine's blood was used in a purifying rite to absolve a murderer of guilt.
3. The Areopagus, a rocky hill (at the entrance to the Acropolis) where Orestes' trial was taking place.

Oedipus Rex

Sophocles

While Aeschylus was still in his prime and very active as a playwright, Sophocles appeared on the scene. Some thirty years Aeschylus's junior, Sophocles was born about 496 B.C. in the village of Colonus just outside Athens. Very little is known about his life, but a combination of legend and early documentation suggests that he belonged to a fairly well-to-do family, that he received a good education, and that he may have studied under Aeschylus. How he became interested in the theater or what sort of apprenticeship he may have served is not known, but in 468 B.C. he won his first victory in the annual playwriting competition; Aeschylus won second place that year. In a long and active life, Sophocles won this competition at least eighteen times, and one source asserts that he never finished below second place. It appears that, in some sixty years of playwriting, he completed about thirty of the four-play combinations which a dramatist was required to submit for the competition. None of these survives in its entirety, and only seven of the single tragedies are extant, in addition to one satyr play.

In a lifetime that spanned almost the entire fifth century B.C. (a century which encompassed the peak of Athenian civilization), Sophocles was active in public life, although he was chiefly devoted to the arts rather than to politics. He was elected to several public offices and served as ambassador to other governments, as well as founding an organization devoted to the development of the arts and humanities. All the extant evidence suggests that he was a pleasant, congenial, and popular person whose intellectual insights and cultivated manners enriched and vivified the lives of those about him. He died in his native Colonus in 406 B.C., shortly before the final defeat of Athens in the Peloponnesian War put an end to the ancient Greek democracy.

Sophocles played a major role in developing basic dramatic form and structure beyond Aeschylus's important innovations. Sophocles is said by some ancient sources to have invented several important scenic devices; some even credit him with inventing scene painting. Most authorities agree, however, that his most important contribution was the notion of the third actor; that is, where Aeschylus in his earlier plays had never used more than two speaking characters per episode, Sophocles introduced the idea of three. The advantages of this arrangement in terms of enriched human interplay were evidently apparent immediately, for Aeschylus adopted it for his late plays (see *The Oresteia*) and later playwrights used it regularly. Three remained the limit throughout classical times, though of course the same actors reappeared in later episodes in other roles. Although none of Sophocles' complete trilogies survives, there is evidence to suggest that the three tragedies which comprised such a trilogy were less closely linked in plot or theme in Sophocles' work than they were in Aeschylus's. Apparently each of Sophocles' separate plays could stand on its own as an independent work of theatrical art; still, without the other scripts one cannot be sure what cumulative theatrical effects they may have offered.

61

The seven tragedies that survive were collected by a scholar some two centuries after Sophocles' death. Upon what basis he selected them, or for what purpose, is unknown, although they may have been for school use. In any case, they appear to derive from the last forty years or so of the playwright's career, and certainly come from separate and unrelated trilogies. *Ajax* may have been written around 447; it concerns a warrior hero who falls through pride to crime and suicide. *Antigone* appeared around 441, and tells the story of Oedipus's daughter—though it was written on a separate occasion and was not a part of the same trilogy as *Oedipus Rex*. *The Trachinian Maidens*, probably dated not long after *Antigone*, tells of the death of Heracles and his wife following upon the former's crimes and overweening pride. *Electra* was written perhaps between 430 and 415, and is Sophocles' treatment of the same story Aeschylus told in *Choephoroe*. (Since Euripides later treated the Electra story too, it is especially interesting and instructive to compare these three works of the three great Greek tragedians.) *Philoctetes* was written in 409, and tradition holds that *Oedipus at Colonus* is also a product of Sophocles' old age; he may well have been nearly ninety when he wrote it. *Philoctetes* is the story of the persecution, by Greek hero figures, of a young man already stigmatized by a wound that never healed, whereas *Oedipus at Colonus* tells of the death of Oedipus, who, as an old man, became an object of religious veneration who was taken directly into heaven by the gods. *The Searching Satyrs*, although incomplete, is the nearest thing to a complete satyr play that has survived. It may date from early in Sophocles' career. It revolves around a group of satyrs looking for some cattle stolen by Hermes from Apollo and is a mild parody of the tragic style of Sophocles' other plays.

Oedipus Rex may be dated around the same time as *Electra*. It is widely regarded as Sophocles' greatest play. The basic Oedipus legend with which the playwright worked was well known to his audience. Laïos, king of Thebes, learned from the oracle at Delphi that a son born to him and his wife Iocastê would kill Laïos and marry Iocastê. Thinking to avoid this fate, Laïos and Iocastê arranged to kill their infant son by spiking his ankles together and leaving him on the mountainside to die. Their agent in this murder, a shepherd, took pity on the child and gave it to another shepherd, who in turn took it to Polybos, king of Corinth, who raised the child as his own. When Oedipus came of age, he learned from the oracle at Delphi that he was fated to kill his father and marry his mother, whereupon he left Corinth to avoid such a possibility. Journeying toward Thebes, Oedipus met an old man at a crossroad and killed him in a quarrel; the old man was Laïos. Continuing toward Thebes, Oedipus encountered the Sphinx, a fabulous monster preying upon the city, and, by successfully answering its riddle, killed it. The citizens of Thebes, in gratitude for this delivery and learning that Laïos was dead, offered Oedipus the crown and an opportunity to marry the widowed queen. He accepted and for many years ruled well. As the play opens, however, a mysterious plague has settled over Thebes, and in the prologue Creon, whom Oedipus has sent to the oracle at Delphi to learn the cause of the plague, reports that the killer of Laïos must be found and punished if the plague is to be lifted. Oedipus immediately swears to do just that, and the play is a careful, step-by-step search for Laïos's killer—who turns out, of course, to be Oedipus himself. Because these details would be familiar to an Athenian audience, the strength of the play does not lie in any surprise discovery of who the killer is. Rather, it lies in the excruciating irony of watching Oedipus move toward the discovery that the audience knows beforehand. This exciting use of dramatic irony (that situation in which the audience knows more about the onstage circumstances than one or more of the characters) as the organizing structural principle of the play has been called Sophoclean irony by some commentators, since Sophocles was apparently the first, and certainly one of the most successful, to use it in this manner. The neat intricacy with which each plot detail dovetails with the next has made *Oedipus Rex* a benchmark of expert plotting by which other plays have ever since been measured.

As the importance of plot in Sophocles' work advances beyond that in Aeschylus's, and as there is corresponding diminution in the importance of the chorus, there is also growth in the complexity of character development. There is still much appeal to the archetypal in Sophocles, and it may be difficult to tell how much of one's horror at Oedipus's fate springs from an instinctive dread of incest and patricide. Still, the very logical motivations that Sophocles sketches for Oedipus, Iocastê, Creon, and even the Shepherd render them believably human and understandable. Oedipus may be guilty of too much pride in his stubborn insistence that he will learn the full truth no matter who gets hurt, but his emotions can readily be shared by all. Creon is neatly depicted as Oedipus's opposite, unwilling to act on any matter until he has carefully considered all sides of the problem. Iocastê, proud of her assurance early in the play that oracles are nonsense, becomes a pitiful figure unable to speak a word when the full horror of her situation becomes apparent to her. The Shepherd and the Messenger are well-intentioned but all-too-human dupes; the Shepherd is often played with comic touches that, at the crucial moment of his entrance, relieve the strain a bit. Only the chorus is left, intentionally, with very little to characterize it, for the chorus represents the middle way among the extremes of the play—the average Greek citizen, intelligent, sensitive, but unwilling to disturb the status quo.

Thematically the play is also very powerful. The final lines of the chorus, "Let none / Presume on his good fortune until he find / Life, at his death, a memory without pain," certainly sum up one important message of the play, but, like all great thematic works, *Oedipus Rex* raises more questions than it answers. Oedipus himself does not suffer from the famous complex that now bears his name, but the nature of his guilt is probed from every side. Is it fair for him to be punished for what he made every conceivable effort to avoid? How, indeed, can one live in a universe where the gods themselves seem to conspire against one? Are some people damned before they are born? These, and related ideas, lead implacably to the ultimate human questions: why are we here, and what is our proper relationship to ourselves, to the universe, and to God?

Sophocles is justly praised for the beauty of his language, and even in translation one can perceive some of the important reasons that this is so. In *Oedipus Rex*, Sophocles makes unusually effective use of imagery, not only in vivid similes and metaphors from moment to moment, but in overall imagistic patterns that profoundly enhance the effectiveness of the play. The predominant pattern is the contrast between light and darkness, between blindness and seeing. At the most obvious level, it is evident that Teiresias, the blind prophet, is the only one at the beginning of the play who "sees" clearly. Oedipus, by the end of the play, has blinded himself because he cannot bear what he has forced himself to see. Only in blindness can Oedipus see himself clearly. Supporting this obvious level of symbolic meaning are the similes and metaphors used throughout the play, from the moment when Oedipus first resolves to "bring what is dark to light." His great quarrel with Teiresias is full of light/dark imagery, as is the final scene of the play in which Oedipus is already blind. Significantly, the god whose oracle informs the play is Phoibos Apollo, the god of light. Such imagistic patterns are usually not overtly apparent to an audience in the theater, but they subliminally enrich the fabric of the play in such a way that they have importance as theatrical devices and not simply as objects for scholarly study.

Curiously enough, the tetralogy of which *Oedipus Rex* was a part won only second prize when it was first produced in the Theater of Dionysus, but since the other three plays are now lost (as are the tetralogies with which Sophocles' was competing), one cannot evaluate the appropriateness of the judges' decision that day. Aristotle makes frequent reference to *Oedipus Rex* in the *Poetics* in contexts which make it clear that he regarded the play with the utmost esteem. Critics throughout the intervening centuries have treated it, without serious challenge, as one of the two or three finest tragedies of all time. It has been performed repeatedly in every major language and in nearly every country in the world, and will no doubt continue to be performed and reinterpreted as long as man aspires to tragic insights.

Oedipus Rex

An English Version
by Dudley Fitts and Robert
Fitzgerald

Characters
Oedipus, King of Thebes
A Priest
Creon, brother of Iocastê
Teiresias, a blind seer
Iocastê, the Queen, wife of Oedipus
Messenger
Shepherd of Laïos
Second Messenger
Chorus of Theban Elders

SCENE. *Before the palace of Oedipus,*
King of Thebes. A central door and two
lateral doors open onto a platform which
runs the length of the façade. On the plat-
form, right and left, are altars; and three
steps lead down into the orchestra, *or*
chorus-ground. At the beginning of the ac-
tion these steps are crowded by suppliants
who have brought branches and chaplets of
olive leaves and who lie in various attitudes
of despair. OEDIPUS *enters.*

OEDIPUS. My children, generations of
   the living
In the line of Kadmos,[1] nursed at his
   ancient hearth:
Why have you strewn yourselves before
   these altars
In supplication, with your boughs and
   garlands?
The breath of incense rises from the
   city
With a sound of prayer and lamentation. Children,
I would not have you speak through
   messengers,
And therefore I have come myself to

hear you—
I, Oedipus, who bear the famous
   name.[2] [*To a* PRIEST.]
You, there, since you are eldest in the
   company,
Speak for them all, tell me what preys
   upon you,
Whether you come in dread, or crave
   some blessing:
Tell me, and never doubt that I will
   help you
In every way I can; I should be heart-
   less
Were I not moved to find you suppliant
   here.
PRIEST. Great Oedipus, O powerful
   King of Thebes!
You see how all the ages of our people
Cling to your altar steps: here are boys
Who can barely stand alone, and here
   are priests
By weight of age, as I am a priest of
   God,
And young men chosen from those yet
   unmarried;
As for the others, all that multitude,
They wait with olive chaplets in the
   squares,
At the two shrines of Pallas,[3] and
   where Apollo
Speaks in the glowing embers. Your
   own eyes
Must tell you: Thebes is in her extrem-
   ity
And can not lift her head from the
   surge of death.
A rust consumes the buds and fruits of
   the earth;

64

The herds are sick; children die un-
    born,
And labor is vain. The god of plague
    and pyre
Raids like detestable lightning through
    the city,
And all the house of Kadmos is laid
    waste,
All emptied, and all darkened: Death
    alone
Battens upon the misery of Thebes.

You are not one of the immortal gods,
    we know;
Yet we have come to you to make our
    prayer
As to the man of all men best in adver-
    sity
And wisest in the ways of God. You
    saved us
From the Sphinx, that flinty singer, and
    the tribute
We paid to her so long; yet you were
    never
Better informed than we, nor could we
    teach you:
It was some god breathed in you to set
    us free.

Therefore, O mighty King, we turn to
    you:
Find us our safety, find us a remedy,
Whether by counsel of the gods or
    men.
A king of wisdom tested in the past
Can act in a time of troubles, and act
    well.
Noblest of men, restore
Life to your city! Think how all men
    call you
Liberator for your triumph long ago;
Ah, when your years of kingship are
    remembered,
Let them not say *We rose, but later fell*—
Keep the State from going down in the
    storm!
Once, years ago, with happy augury,
You brought us fortune; be the same
    again!
No man questions your power to rule
    the land:
But rule over men, not over a dead
    city!
Ships are only hulls, citadels are noth-
    ing,
When no life moves in the empty pas-
    sageways.
OEDIPUS. Poor children! You may be
    sure I know
All that you longed for in your coming
    here.
I know that you are deathly sick; and
    yet,
Sick as you are, not one is as sick as I.
Each of you suffers in himself alone
His anguish, not another's; but my
    spirit
Groans for the city, for myself, for you.

I was not sleeping, you are not waking
    me.
No, I have been in tears for a long
    while
And in my restless thought walked
    many ways.
In all my search, I found one helpful
    course,
And that I have taken: I have sent
    Creon,
Son of Menoikeus, brother of the
    Queen,
To Delphi, Apollo's place of revelation,
To learn there, if he can,
What act or pledge of mine may save
    the city.
I have counted the days, and now, this
    very day,
I am troubled, for he has overstayed
    his time.
What is he doing? He has been gone
    too long.
Yet whenever he comes back, I should
    do ill
To scant whatever hint the god may
    give.
PRIEST. It is a timely promise. At this
    instant
They tell me Creon is here.
OEDIPUS. O Lord Apollo!
May his news be fair as his face is
    radiant!
PRIEST. It could not be otherwise: he is
    crowned with bay,[4]
The chaplet is thick with berries.
OEDIPUS. We shall soon know;
He is near enough to hear us now.
    [*Enter* CREON.] O Prince:
Brother: son of Menoikeus:
What answer do you bring us from the
    god?
CREON. It is favorable, I can tell you,
    great afflictions

Will turn out well, if they are taken
  well.
OEDIPUS. What was the oracle? These
  vague words
Leave me still hanging between hope
  and fear.
CREON. Is it your pleasure to hear me
  with all these
Gathered around us? I am prepared to
  speak,
But should we not go in?
OEDIPUS. Let them all hear it.
It is for them I suffer, more than for
  myself.
CREON. Then I will tell you what I
  heard at Delphi.

In plain words
The god commands us to expel from
  the land of Thebes
An old defilement that it seems we shel-
  ter.
It is a deathly thing, beyond expiation.
We must not let it feed upon us longer.
OEDIPUS. What defilement? How shall
  we rid ourselves of it?
CREON. By exile or death, blood for
  blood. It was
Murder that brought the plague-wind
  on the city.
OEDIPUS. Murder of whom? Surely the
  god has named him?
CREON. My lord: long ago Laïos was our
  king,
Before you came to govern us.
OEDIPUS. I know;
I learned of him from others; I never
  saw him.
CREON. He was murdered; and Apollo
  commands us now
To take revenge upon whoever killed
  him.
OEDIPUS. Upon whom? Where are they?
  Where shall we find a clue
To solve that crime, after so many
  years?
CREON. Here in this land, he said. If we
  make enquiry,
We may touch things that otherwise es-
  cape us.
OEDIPUS. Tell me: Was Laïos murdered
  in his house,
Or in the fields, or in some foreign
  country?
CREON. He said he planned to make a
  pilgrimage.

He did not come home again.
OEDIPUS. And was there no one,
No witness, no companion, to tell what
  happened?
CREON. They were all killed but one,
  and he got away
So frightened that he could remember
  one thing only.
OEDIPUS. What was that one thing? One
  may be the key
To everything, if we resolve to use it.
CREON. He said that a band of highway-
  men attacked them,
Outnumbered them, and overwhelmed
  the King.
OEDIPUS. Strange, that a highwayman
  should be so daring—
Unless some faction here bribed him to
  do it.
CREON. We thought of that. But after
  Laïos' death
New troubles arose and we had no
  avenger.
OEDIPUS. What troubles could prevent
  your hunting down the killers?
CREON. The riddling Sphinx's song
Made us deaf to all mysteries but her
  own.
OEDIPUS. Then once more I must bring
  what is dark to light.
It is most fitting that Apollo shows,
As you do, this compunction for the
  dead.
You shall see how I stand by you, as I
  should,
To avenge the city and the city's god,
And not as though it were for some dis-
  tant friend,
But for my own sake, to be rid of evil.
Whoever killed King Laïos might—who
  knows?—
Decide at any moment to kill me as
  well.
By avenging the murdered king I pro-
  tect myself.

Come, then, my children: leave the al-
  tar steps,
Lift up your olive boughs! One of you
  go
And summon the people of Kadmos to
  gather here.
I will do all that I can; you may tell
  them that. [*Exit a* PAGE.]
So, with the help of God,
We shall be saved—or else indeed we

are lost.

PRIEST. Let us rise, children. It was for this we came,
And now the King has promised it himself.
Phoibos⁵ has sent us an oracle; may he descend
Himself to save us and drive out the plague. [*Exeunt* OEDIPUS *and* CREON *into the palace by the central door. The* PRIEST *and the* SUPPLIANTS *disperse R. and L. After a short pause the* CHORUS *enters the orchestra.*]

Strophe 1

CHORUS. What is the god singing in his profound
Delphi of gold and shadow?
What oracle for Thebes, the sun-whipped city?

Fear unjoints me, the roots of my heart tremble.
Now I remember, O Healer,⁶ your power, and wonder:
Will you send doom like a sudden cloud, or weave it
Like nightfall of the past?

Ah no: be merciful, issue of holy sound:
Dearest to our expectancy: be tender!

Antistrophe 1

Let me pray to Athenê, the immortal daughter of Zeus,
And to Artemis her sister
Who keeps her famous throne in the market ring,
And to Apollo, bowman at the far butts of heaven—

O gods, descend! Like three streams leap against
The fires of our grief, the fires of darkness;
Be swift to bring us rest!

As in the old time from the brilliant house
Of air you stepped to save us, come again!

Strophe 2

Now our afflictions have no end.
Now all our stricken host lies down
And no man fights off death with his mind;

The noble plowland bears no grain,
And groaning mothers can not bear—
See, how our lives like birds take wing,
Like sparks that fly when a fire soars,
To the shore of the god of evening.

Antistrophe 2

The plague burns on, it is pitiless,
Though pallid children laden with death
Lie unwept in the stony ways,

And old gray women by every path
Flock to the strand about the altars

There to strike their breasts and cry
Worship of Zeus in wailing prayers:
Be kind, God's golden child!⁷

Strophe 3

There are no swords in this attack by fire,
No shields, but we are ringed with cries.

Send the besieger plunging from our homes
Into the vast sea-room of the Atlantic
Or into the waves that foam eastward of Thrace—

For the day ravages what the night spares—

Destroy our enemy, lord of the thunder!
Let him be riven by lightning from heaven!

Antistrophe 3

Phoibos Apollo, stretch the sun's bow-string,
That golden cord, until it sing for us,
Flashing arrows in heaven! Artemis, Huntress,
Race with flaring lights upon our mountains!

O scarlet god, O golden-banded brow,
O Theban Bacchos in a storm of Maenads, [*Enter* OEDIPUS, *center.*]
Whirl upon Death, that all the Undying hate!

Come with blinding cressets, come in joy!

OEDIPUS. Is this your prayer? It may be answered. Come,
Listen to me, act as the crisis demands,
And you shall have relief from all these evils.

Until now I was a stranger to this tale,
As I had been a stranger to the crime.
Could I track down the murderer without a clue?
But now, friends,
As one who became a citizen after the murder,
I make this proclamation to all Thebans:
If any man knows by whose hands Laïos, son of Labdakos,
Met his death, I direct that man to tell me everything,
No matter what he fears for having so long withheld it.
Let it stand as promised that no further trouble
Will come to him, but he may leave the land in safety.

Moreover: If anyone knows the murderer to be foreign,
Let him not keep silent: he shall have his reward from me.
However, if he does conceal it, if any man
Fearing for his friend or for himself disobeys this edict,
Hear what I propose to do:

I solemnly forbid the people of this country,
Where power and throne are mine, ever to receive that man
Or speak to him, no matter who he is, or let him
Join in sacrifice, lustration, or in prayer.
I decree that he be driven from every house,
Being, as he is, corruption itself to us: the Delphic
Voice of Zeus has pronounced this revelation.
Thus I associate myself with the oracle
And take the side of the murdered king.

As for the criminal, I pray to God—
Whether it be a lurking thief, or one of a number—
I pray that that man's life be consumed in evil and wretchedness.
And as for me, this curse applies no less
If it should turn out that the culprit is my guest here,
Sharing my hearth. You have heard the penalty.
I lay it on you now to attend to this
For my sake, for Apollo's, for the sick
Sterile city that heaven has abandoned.
Suppose the oracle had given you no command:
Should this defilement go uncleansed for ever?
You should have found the murderer: your king,
A noble king, had been destroyed! Now I,
Having the power that he held before me,
Having his bed, begetting children there
Upon his wife, as he would have, had he lived—
Their son would have been my children's brother,
If Laïos had had luck in fatherhood!
(But surely ill luck rushed upon his reign)—
I say I take the son's part, just as though
I were his son, to press the fight for him
And see it won! I'll find the hand that brought
Death to Labdakos' and Polydoros' child,
Heir of Kadmos' and Agenor's line.
And as for those who fail me,
May the gods deny them the fruit of the earth,
Fruit of the womb, and may they rot utterly!
Let them be wretched as we are wretched, and worse!

For you, for loyal Thebans, and for all
Who find my actions right, I pray the favor
Of justice, and of all the immortal gods.

LEADER OF THE CHORUS. Since I am under oath, my lord, I swear

I did not do the murder, I can not name
The murderer. Might not the oracle
That has ordained the search tell where to find him?

OEDIPUS. An honest question. But no man in the world
Can make the gods do more than the gods will.

LEADER. There is one last expedient—

OEDIPUS. Tell me what it is. Though it seem slight, you must not hold it back.

LEADER. A lord clairvoyant to the lord Apollo,
As we all know, is the skilled Teiresias.
One might learn much about this from him, Oedipus.

OEDIPUS. I am not wasting time:
Creon spoke of this and I have sent for him—
Twice, in fact; it is strange that he is not here.

LEADER. The other matter—that old report—seems useless.

OEDIPUS. Tell me. I am interested in all reports.

LEADER. The King was said to have been killed by highwaymen.

OEDIPUS. I know. But we have no witnesses to that.

LEADER. If the killer can feel a particle of dread,
Your curse will bring him out of hiding!

OEDIPUS. No.
The man who dared that act will fear no curse. [*Enter the blind seer* TEIRESIAS *led by a* PAGE.]

LEADER. But there is one man who may detect the criminal.
This is Teiresias, this is the holy prophet
In whom, alone of all men, truth was born.

OEDIPUS. Teiresias: seer: student of mysteries,
Of all that's taught and all that no man tells,
Secrets of Heaven and secrets of the earth:
Blind though you are, you know the city lies
Sick with plague; and from this plague, my lord,
We find that you alone can guard or save us.

Possibly you did not hear the messengers?
Apollo, when we sent to him,
Sent us back word that this great pestilence
Would lift, but only if we established clearly
The identity of those who murdered Laïos.
They must be killed or exiled. Can you use
Birdflight or any art of divination
To purify yourself, and Thebes, and me
From this contagion? We are in your hands.
There is no fairer duty
Than that of helping others in distress.

TEIRESIAS. How dreadful knowledge of the truth can be
When there's no help in truth! I knew this well,
But did not act on it: else I should not have come.

OEDIPUS. What is troubling you? Why are your eyes so cold?

TEIRESIAS. Let me go home. Bear your own fate, and I'll
Bear mine. It is better so: trust what I say.

OEDIPUS. What you say is ungracious and unhelpful
To your native country. Do not refuse to speak.

TEIRESIAS. When it comes to speech, your own is neither temperate
Nor opportune. I wish to be more prudent.

OEDIPUS. In God's name, we all beg you—

TEIRESIAS. You are all ignorant.
No; I will never tell you what I know.
Now it is my misery; then, it would be yours.

OEDIPUS. What! You do know something, and will not tell us?
You would betray us all and wreck the State?

TEIRESIAS. I do not intend to torture myself, or you.
Why persist in asking? You will not persuade me.

OEDIPUS. What a wicked old man you are! You'd try a stone's

Patience! Out with it! Have you no feeling at all?

TEIRESIAS. You call me unfeeling. If
you could only see
The nature of your own feelings . . .

OEDIPUS. Why,
Who would not feel as I do? Who could
endure
Your arrogance toward the city?

TEIRESIAS. What does it matter!
Whether I speak or not, it is bound to
come.

OEDIPUS. Then, if "it" is bound to come,
you are bound to tell me.

TEIRESIAS. No, I will not go on. Rage as
you please.

OEDIPUS. Rage? Why not! And I'll tell
you what I think:
You planned it, you had it done, you all
but
Killed him with your own hands: if you
had eyes,
I'd say the crime was yours, and yours
alone.

TEIRESIAS. So? I charge you, then,
Abide by the proclamation you have
made:
From this day forth
Never speak again to these men or to
me;
You yourself are the pollution of this
country.

OEDIPUS. You dare say that! Can you
possibly think you have
Some way of going free, after such insolence?

TERESIAS. I have gone free. It is the
truth sustains me.

OEDIPUS. Who taught you shamelessness? It was not your craft.

TEEIRESIAS. You did. You made me
speak. I did not want to.

OEDIPUS. Speak what? Let me hear it
again more clearly.

TEIRESIAS. Was it not clear before? Are
you tempting me?

OEDIPUS. I did not understand it. Say it
again.

TEIRESIAS. I say that you are the murderer whom you seek.

OEDIPUS. Now twice you have spat out
infamy. You'll pay for it!

TEIRESIAS. Would you care for more?
Do you wish to be really angry?

OEDIPUS. Say what you will. Whatever
you say is worthless.

TEIRESIAS. I say that you live in hideous
love with her
Who is nearest you in blood. You are
blind to the evil.

OEDIPUS. It seems you can go on
mouthing like this for ever.

TRESIAS. I can, if there is power in
truth.

OEDIPUS. There is:
But not for you, not for you,
You sightless, witless, senseless, mad
old man!

TEIRESIAS. You are the madman. There
is no one here
Who will not curse you soon, as you
curse me.

OEDIPUS. You child of endless night!
You can not hurt me
Or any other man who sees the sun.

TEIRESIUS. True: it is not from me your
fate will come.
That lies within Apollo's competence,
As it is his concern.

OEDIPUS. Tell me:
Are you speaking for Creon, or for
yourself?

TEIRESIUS. Creon is no threat. You
weave your own doom.

OEDIPUS. Wealth, power, craft of states-
manship!
Kingly position, everywhere admired!
What savage envy is stored up against
these,
If Creon, whom I trusted, Creon my
friend,
For this great office which the city once
Put in my hands unsought—if for this
power
Creon desires in secret to destroy me!

He has brought this decrepit fortune-
teller, this
Collector of dirty pennies, this prophet
fraud—
Why, he is no more clairvoyant than I
am! Tell us:
Has your mystic mummery ever ap-
proached the truth?
When that hellcat the Sphinx was per-
forming here,
What help were you to these people?
Her magic was not for the first man
who came along:
It demanded a real exorcist. Your
birds—
What good are they? or the gods, for

the matter of that?
But I came by,
Oedipus, the simple man, who knows
nothing—
I thought it out for myself, no birds
helped me!
And this is the man you think you can
destroy,
That you may be close to Creon when
he's king!
Well, you and your friend Creon, it
seems to me,
Will suffer most. If you were not an old
man,
You would have paid already for your
plot.

LEADER OF THE CHORUS. We can not see
that his words or yours
Have been spoken except in anger,
Oedipus,
And of anger we have no need. How
can God's will
Be accomplished best? That is what
most concerns us.

TEIRESIAS. You are a king. But where
argument's concerned
I am your man, as much a king as you.
I am not your servant, but Apollo's.
I have no need of Creon to speak for
me.

Listen to me. You mock my blindness,
do you?
But I say that you, with both your eyes,
are blind:
You can not see the wretchedness of
your life,
Nor in whose house you live, no, nor
with whom.
Who are your father and mother? Can
you tell me?
You do not even know the blind
wrongs
That you have done them, on earth
and in the world below.
But the double lash of your parents'
curse will whip you
Out of this land some day, with only
night
Upon your precious eyes.
Your cries then—where will they not be
heard?
What fastness of Kithairon[8] will not
echo them?
And that bridal-descant of yours—
you'll know it then,

The song they sang when you came
here to Thebes
And found your misguided berthing.
All this, and more, that you can not
guess at now,
Will bring you to yourself among your
children.

Be angry then. Curse Creon. Curse my
words.
I tell you, no man that walks upon the
earth
Shall be rooted out more horribly than
you.

OEDIPUS. Am I to bear this from him?—
Damnation
Take you! Out of this place! Out of my
sight!

TEIRESIAS. I would not have come at all
if you had not asked me.

OEDIPUS. Could I have told that you'd
talk nonsense, that
You'd come here to make a fool of
yourself, and of me?

TEIRESIAS. A fool? Your parents
thought me sane enough.

OEDIPUS. My parents again!—Wait: who
were my parents?

TEIRESIAS. This day will give you a
father, and break your heart.

OEDIPUS. Your infantile riddles! Your
damned abracadabra!

TEIRESIAS. You were a great man once
at solving riddles.

OEDIPUS. Mock me with that if you like;
you will find it true.

TEIRESIAS. It was true enough. It
brought about your ruin.

OEDIPUS. But if it saved this town?

TEIRESIAS [*to the* PAGE] Boy, give me
your hand.

OEDIPUS. Yes, boy; lead him away.—
While you are here
We can do nothing. Go; leave us in
peace.

TEIRESIAS. I will go when I have said
what I have to say.
How can you hurt me? And I tell you
again:
The man you have been looking for all
this time,
The damned man, the murderer of
Laïos,
That man is in Thebes. To your mind
he is foreign-born,
But it will soon be shown that he is a

Theban,
A revelation that will fail to please. A
blind man,
Who has his eyes now; a penniless man,
who is rich now;
And he will go tapping the strange
earth with his staff.
To the children with whom he lives
now he will be
Brother and father—the very same; to
her
Who bore him, son and husband—the
very same.
Who came to his father's bed, wet with
his father's blood.

Enough. Go think that over.
If later you find error in what I have
said,
You may say that I have no skill in
prophecy. [*Exit* TEIRESIAS, *led by his*
PAGE. OEDIPUS *goes into the palace.*]

Strophe 1
CHORUS. The Delphic stone of
prophecies
Remembers ancient regicide
And a still bloody hand.
That killer's hour of flight has come.
He must be stronger than riderless
Coursers of untiring wind,
For the son of Zeus[9] armed with his
father's thunder
Leaps in lightning after him;
And the Furies follow him, the sad
Furies.

Antistrophe 1
Holy Parnassos'[10] peak of snow
Flashes and blinds that secret man,
That all shall hunt him down:
Though he may roam the forest shade
Like a bull gone wild from pasture
To rage through glooms of stone.
Doom comes down on him; flight will
not avail him;
For the world's heart calls him desolate,
And the immortal Furies follow, for
ever follow.

Strophe 2
But now a wilder thing is heard
From the old man skilled at hearing
Fate in the wingbeat of a bird.
Bewildered as a blown bird, my soul
hovers and can not find

Foothold in this debate, or any reason
or rest of mind.
But no man ever brought—none can
bring
Proof of strife between Thebes' royal
house,
Labdakos' line, and the son of Polybos;[11]
And never until now has any man
brought word
Of Laïos' dark death staining Oedipus
the King.

Antistrophe 2
Divine Zeus and Apollo hold
Perfect intelligence alone of all tales
ever told;
And well though this diviner works, he
works in his own night;
No man can judge that rough unknown
or trust in second sight,
For wisdom changes hands among the
wise.
Shall I believe my great lord criminal
At a raging word that a blind old man
let fall?
I saw him, when the carrion woman[12]
faced him of old,
Prove his heroic mind! These evil
words are lies. [*Enter* CREON.]
CREON. Men of Thebes:
I am told that heavy accusations
Have been brought against me by King
Oedipus.

I am not the kind of man to bear this
tamely.

If in these present difficulties
He holds me accountable for any harm
to him
Through anything I have said or
done—why, then,
I do not value life in this dishonor.
It is not as though this rumor touched
upon
Some private indiscretion. The matter
is grave.
The fact is that I am being called dis-
loyal
To the State, to my fellow citizens, to
my friends.
LEADER OF THE CHORUS. He may have
spoken in anger, not from his mind.
CREON. But did you hear him say I was
the one

Who seduced the old prophet into ly-
ing?
LEADER. The thing was said; I do not
know how seriously.
CREON. But you were watching him!
Were his eyes steady?
Did he look like a man in his right
mind?
LEADER. I do not know.
I can not judge the behavior of great
men.
But here is the King himself. [*Enter*
OEDIPUS.]
OEDIPUS. So you dared come back.
Why? How brazen of you to come to
my house,
You murderer! Do you think I do not
know
That you plotted to kill me, plotted to
steal my throne?
Tell me, in God's name: am I coward, a
fool,
That you should dream you could ac-
complish this?
A fool who could not see your slippery
game?
A coward, not to fight back when I saw
it?
You are the fool, Creon, are you not?
hoping
Without support or friends to get a
throne?
Thrones may be won or bought: you
could do neither.
CREON. Now listen to me. You have
talked; let me talk, too.
You can not judge unless you know the
facts.
OEDIPUS. You speak well: there is one
fact; but I find it hard
To learn from the deadliest enemy I
have.
CREON. That above all I must dispute
with you.
OEDIPUS. That above all I will not hear
you deny.
CREON. If you think there is anything
good in being stubborn
Against all reason, then I say you are
wrong.
OEDIPUS. If you think a man can sin
against his own kind
And not be punished for it, I say you
are mad.
CREON. I agree. But tell me: what have
I done to you?

OEDIPUS. You advised me to send for
that wizard, did you not?
CREON. I did. I should do it again.
OEDIPUS. Very well. Now tell me:
How long has it been since Laïos—
CREON. What of Laïos?
OEDIPUS. Since he vanished in that on-
set by the road?
CREON. It was long ago, a long time.
OEDIPUS. And this prophet,
Was he practicing here then?
CREON. He was; and with honor, as
now.
OEDIPUS. Did he speak of me at that
time?
CREON. He never did;
At least, not when I was present.
OEDIPUS. But . . . the enquiry?
I suppose you held one?
CREON. We did, but we learned noth-
ing.
OEDIPUS. Why did the prophet not
speak against me then?
CREON. I do not know; and I am the
kind of man
Who holds his tongue when he has no
facts to go on.
OEDIPUS. There's one fact that you
know, and you could tell it.
CREON. What fact is that? If I know it,
you shall have it.
OEDIPUS. If he were not involved with
you, he could not say
That it was I who murdered Laïos.
CREON. If he says that, you are the one
that knows it!—
But now it is my turn to question you.
OEDIPUS. Put your questions. I am no
murderer.
CREON. First, then: You married my sis-
ter?
OEDIPUS. I married your sister.
CREON. And you rule the kingdom
equally with her?
OEDIPUS. Everything that she wants she
has from me.
CREON. And I am the third, equal to
both of you?
OEDIPUS. That is why I call you a bad
friend.
CREON. No. Reason it out, as I have
done.
Think of this first: would any sane man
prefer
Power, with all a king's anxieties,
To that same power and the grace of

sleep?
Certainly not I.
I have never longed for the king's
power—only his rights.
Would any wise man differ from me in
this?
As matters stand, I have my way in
everything
With your consent, and no respon-
sibilities.
If I were king, I should be a slave to
policy.

How could I desire a scepter more
Than what is now mine—untroubled
influence?
No, I have not gone mad; I need no
honors,
Except those with the perquisites I have
now.
I am welcome everywhere; every man
salutes me,
And those who want your favor seek
my ear,
Since I know how to manage what they
ask,
Should I exchange this ease for that
anxiety?
Besides, no sober mind is treasonable.
I hate anarchy
And never would deal with any man
who likes it.

Test what I have said. Go to the
priestess
At Delphi, ask if I quoted her correctly.
And as for this other thing: if I am
found
Guilty of treason with Teiresias,
Than sentence me to death! You have
my word
It is a sentence I shall cast my vote
for—
But not without evidence! You do
wrong
When you take good men for bad, bad
men for good.
A true friend thrown aside—why, life
itself
Is not more precious! In time you will
know this well:
For time, and time alone, will show the
just man,
Though scoundrels are discovered in a
day.
LEADER. This is well said, and a prudent
man would ponder it.

Judgments too quickly formed are
dangerous.
OEDIPUS. But is he not quick in his
duplicity?
And shall I not be quick to parry him?
Would you have me stand still, hold my
peace, and let
This man win everything, through my
inaction?
CREON. And you want—what is it, then?
To banish me?
OEDIPUS. No, not exile. It is your death
I want,
So that all the world may see what
treason means.
CREON. You will persist, then? You will
not believe me?
OEDIPUS. How can I believe you?
CREON. Then you are a fool.
OEDIPUS. To save myself?
CREON. In justice, think of me.
OEDIPUS. You are evil incarnate.
CREON. But suppose that you are
wrong?
OEDIPUS. Still I must rule.
CREON. But not if you rule badly.
OEDIPUS. O city, city!
CREON. It is my city, too!
LEADER. Now, my lords, be still. I see
the Queen,
Iocastê, coming from her palace cham-
bers;
And it is time she came, for the sake of
you both.
This dreadful quarrel can be resolved
through her. [*Enter* IOCASTÊ.]
IOCASTÊ. Poor foolish men, what wicked
din is this?
With Thebes sick to death, is it not
shameful
That you should rake some private
quarrel up? [*To* OEDIPUS.]
Come into the house—And you, Creon,
go now:
Let us have no more of this tumult over
nothing.
CREON. Nothing? No, sister: what your
husband plans for me
Is one of two great evils: exile or death.
OEDIPUS. He is right. Why woman, I
have caught him squarely
Plotting against my life.
CREON. No! Let me die.
Accurst if ever I have wished you
harm!
IOCASTÊ. Ah, believe it, Oedipus!
In the name of the gods, respect this

oath of his
For my sake, for the sake of these people here!

Strophe 1

LEADER. Open your mind to her, my
lord. Be ruled by her, I beg you!
OEDIPUS. What would you have me do?
LEADER. Respect Creon's word. He has
never spoken like a fool,
And now he has sworn an oath.
OEDIPUS. You know what you ask?
LEADER. I do.
OEDIPUS. Speak on, then.
LEADER. A friend so sworn should not
be baited so,
In blind malice, and without final
proof.
OEDIPUS. You are aware, I hope, that
what you say
Means death for me, or exile at the
least.

Strophe 2

LEADER. No, I swear by Helios,[13] first in
Heaven!
May I die friendless and accurst,
The worst of deaths, if ever I meant
that!
It is the withering fields
That hurt my sick heart:
Must we bear all these ills,
And now your bad blood as well?
OEDIPUS. Then let him go. And let me
die, if I must,
Or be driven by him in shame from the
land of Thebes.
It is your unhappiness, and not his talk,
That touches me. As for him—
Wherever he is, I will hate him as long
as I live.
CREON. Ugly in yielding, as you were
ugly in rage!
Natures like yours chiefly torment
themselves.
OEDIPUS. Can you not go? Can you not
leave me?
CREON. I can.
You do not know me; but the city
knows me,
And in its eyes I am just, if not in
yours. [*Exit* CREON].

Antistrophe 1

LEADER. Lady Iocastê, did you not ask
the King to go to his chambers?
IOCASTÊ. First tell me what has hap-

pened.
LEADER. There was suspicion without
evidence; yet it rankled
As even false charges will.
IOCASTÊ. On both sides?
LEADER. On both.
IOCASTÊ. But what was said?
LEADER. Oh let it rest, let it be done
with!
Have we not suffered enough?
OEDIPUS. You see to what your decency
has brought you:
You have made difficulties where my
heart saw none.

Antistrophe 2

LEADER. Oedipus, it is not once only I
have told you—
You must know I should count myself
unwise
To the point of madness, should I now
forsake you—
You, under whose hand,
In the storm of another time,
Our dear land sailed out free.
But now stand fast at the helm!
IOCASTÊ. In God's name, Oedipus, in-
form your wife as well:
Why are you so set in this hard anger?
OEDIPUS. I will tell you, for none of
these men deserves
My confidence as you do. It is Creon's
work,
His treachery, his plotting against me.
IOCASTÊ. Go on, if you can make this
clear to me.
OEDIPUS. He charges me with the mur-
der of Laïos.
IOCASTÊ. Has he some knowledge? Or
does he speak from hearsay?
OEDIPUS. He would not commit himself
to such a charge,
But he has brought in that damnable
soothsayer
To tell his story.
IOCASTÊ. Set your mind at rest.
If it is a question of soothsayers, I tell
you
That you will find no man whose craft
gives knowledge
Of the unknowable. Here is my proof:

An oracle was reported to Laïos once
(I will not say from Phoibos himself,
but from
His appointed ministers, at any rate)
That his doom would be death at the

hands of his own son—
His son, born of his flesh and of mine!
Now, you remember the story: Laïos
  was killed
By marauding strangers where three
  highways meet;
But his child had not been three days
  in this world
Before the King had pierced the baby's
  ankles
And had him left to die on a lonely
  mountain.

Thus, Apollo never caused that child
To kill his father, and it was not Laïos'
  fate
To die at the hands of his son, as he
  had feared.
This is what prophets and prophecies
  are worth!
Have no dread of them. It is God him-
  self
Who can show us what he wills, in his
  own way.
OEDIPUS. How strange a shadowy mem-
  ory crossed my mind,
Just now while you were speaking; it
  chilled my heart.
IOCASTÊ. What do you mean? What
  memory do you speak of?
OEDIPUS. If I understand you, Laïos was
  killed
At a place where three roads meet.
IOCASTÊ. So it was said;
We have no later story.
OEDIPUS. Where did it happen?
IOCASTÊ. Phokis, it is called: at a place
  where the Theban Way
Divides into the roads toward Delphi
  and Daulia.
OEDIPUS. When?
IOCASTÊ. We had the news not long be-
  fore you came
And proved the right to your succes-
  sion here.
OEDIPUS. Ah, what net has God been
  weaving for me?
IOCASTÊ. Oedipus! Why does this
  trouble you?
OEDIPUS. Do not ask me yet.
First, tell me how Laïos looked, and tell
  me
How old he was.
IOCASTÊ. He was tall, his hair just
  touched
With white; his form was not unlike
  your own.

OEDIPUS. I think that I myself may be
  accurst
By my own ignorant edict.
IOCASTÊ. You speak strangely.
It makes me tremble to look at you, my
  King.
OEDIPUS. I am not sure that the blind
  man can not see.
But I should know better if you were to
  tell me—
IOCASTÊ. Anything—though I dread to
  hear you ask it.
OEDIPUS. Was the King lightly escorted,
  or did he ride
With a large company, as a ruler
  should?
IOCASTÊ. There were five men with him
  in all: one was a herald;
and a single chariot, which he was driv-
  ing.
OEDIPUS. Alas, that makes it plain
  enough! But who—
Who told you how it happened?
IOCASTÊ. A household servant,
The only one to escape.
OEDIPUS. And is he still
A servant of ours?
IOCASTÊ. No; for when he came back at
  last
And found you enthroned in the place
  of the dead king,
He came to me, touched my hand with
  his, and begged
That I would send him away to the
  frontier district
Where only the shepherds go—
As far away from the city as I could
  send him.
I granted his prayer; for although the
  man was a slave,
He had earned more than this favor at
  my hands.
OEDIPUS. Can he be called back quickly?
IOCASTÊ. Easily.
But why?
OEDIPUS. I have taken too much upon
  myself
Without enquiry; therefore I wish to
  consult him.
IOCASTÊ. Then he shall come. But am I
  not one also
To whom you might confide these fears
  of yours?
OEDIPUS. That is your right; it will not
  be denied you,
Now least of all; for I have reached a
  pitch

Of wild foreboding. Is there anyone
To whom I should sooner speak?

Polybos of Corinth is my father.
My mother is a Dorian: Meropê.
I grew up chief among the men of
  Corinth
Until a strange thing happened—
Not worth my passion, it may be, but
  strange.

At a feast, a drunken man maundering
  in his cups
Cries out that I am not my father's son!

I contained myself that night, though I
  felt anger
And a sinking heart. The next day I
  visited
My father and mother, and questioned
  them. They stormed,
Calling it all the slanderous rant of a
  fool;
And this relieved me. Yet the suspicion
Remained always aching in my mind;
I knew there was talk; I could not rest;
And finally, saying nothing to my par-
  ents,
I went to the shrine of Delphi.

The god dismissed my question without
  reply;
He spoke of other things. Some were
  clear,
Full of wretchedness, dreadful, unbearable:
As, that I should lie with my own
  mother, breed
Children from whom all men would
  turn their eyes;
And that I should be my father's murderer.

I heard all this, and fled. And from
  that day
Corinth to me was only in the stars
Descending in that quarter of the sky,
As I wandered farther and farther on
  my way
To a land where I should never see the
  evil
Sung by the oracle. And I came to this
  country
Where, so you say, King Laïos was
  killed.

I will tell you all that happened there,
  my lady.

There were three highways
Coming together at a place I passed;
And there a herald came towards me,
  and a chariot
Drawn by horses, with a man such as
  you describe
Seated in it. The groom leading the
  horses
Forced me off the road at his lord's
  command;
But as this charioteer lurched over to-
  wards me
I struck him in my rage. The old man
  saw me
And brought his double goad down
  upon my head
As I came abreast. He was paid back,
  and more!
Swinging my club in this right hand I
  knocked him
Out of his car, and he rolled on the
  ground. I killed him.

I killed them all.
Now if that stranger and Laïos were—
  kin,
Where is a man more miserable than I?
More hated by the gods? Citizen and
  alien alike
Must never shelter me or speak to
  me—
I must be shunned by all. And I myself
Pronounced this malediction upon my-
  self!
Think of it: I have touched you with
  these hands,
These hands that killed your husband.
  What defilement!

Am I all evil, then? It must be so,
Since I must flee from Thebes, yet
  never again
See my own countrymen, my own
  country,
For fear of joining my mother in mar-
  riage
and killing Polybos, my father. Ah,
If I was created so, born to this fate,
Who could deny the savagery of God?

O holy majesty of heavenly powers!
May I never see that day! Never!
Rather let me vanish from the race of

men
Than know the abomination destined
me!
LEADER. We too, my lord, have felt dis-
may at this.
But there is hope: you have yet to hear
the shepherd.
OEDIPUS. Indeed, I fear no other hope
is left me.
IOCASTÊ. What do you hope from him
when he comes?
OEDIPUS. This much:
If his account of the murder tallies with
yours,
Then I am cleared.
IOCASTÊ. What was it that I said
Of such importance?
OEDIPUS. Why, "marauders," you said,
Killed the king, according to this man's
story.
If he maintains that still, if there were
several,
Clearly the guilt is not mine: I was
alone.
But if he says one man, singlehanded,
did it,
Then the evidence all points to me.
IOCASTÊ. You may be sure that he said
there were several;
And can he call back that story now?
He can not.
The whole city heard it as plainly as I.
But suppose he alters some detail of it:
He can not ever show that Laïos' death
Fulfilled the oracle: for Apollo said
My child was doomed to kill him; and
my child—
Poor baby!—it was my child that died
first.
No. From now on, where oracles are
concerned,
I would not waste a second thought on
any.
OEDIPUS. You may be right. But come:
let someone go
For the shepherd at once. This matter
must be settled.
IOCASTÊ. I will send for him.
I would not wish to cross you in any-
thing,
And surely not in this.—Let us go in.
[*Exeunt into the palace.*]

Strophe 1
CHORUS. Let me be reverent in the ways
of right,

Lowly the paths I journey on;
Let all my words and actions keep
The laws of the pure universe
From highest Heaven handed down.
For Heaven is their bright nurse,
Those generations of the realms of
light;
Ah, never of mortal kind were they be-
got,
Nor are they slaves of memory, lost in
sleep:
Their Father is greater than Time, and
ages not.

Antistrophe 1
The tyrant is a child of Pride
Who drinks from his great sickening
cup
Recklessness and vanity,
Until from his high crest headlong
He plummets to the dust of hope.
That strong man is not strong.
But let no fair ambition be denied;
May God protect the wrestler for the
State
In government, in comely policy,
Who will fear God, and on His ordi-
nance wait.

Strophe 2
Haughtiness and the high hand of dis-
dain
Tempt and outrage God's holy law;
And any mortal who dares hold
No immortal Power in awe
Will be caught up in a net of pain:
The price for which his levity is sold.
Let each man take due earnings, then,
And keep his hands from holy things,
And from blasphemy stand apart—
Else the crackling blast of heaven
Blows on his head, and on his desper-
ate heart;
Though fools will honor impious men,
In their cities no tragic poet sings.

Antistrophe 2
Shall we lose faith in Delphi's ob-
scurities,
We who have heard the world's core
Discredited, and the sacred wood
Of Zeus at Elis praised no more?
The deeds and the strange prophecies
Must make a pattern yet to be under-
stood.
Zeus, if indeed you are lord of all,

Throned in light over night and day,
Mirror this in your endless mind:
Our masters call the oracle
Words on the wind, and the Delphic vi-
sion blind!
Their hearts no longer know Apollo,
And reverence for the gods has died
away. [*Enter* IOCASTÊ.]
IOCASTÊ. Princes of Thebes, it has oc-
curred to me
To visit the altars of the gods, bearing
These branches as a suppliant, and this
incense.
Our King is not himself: his noble soul
Is overwrought with fantasies of dread,
Else he would consider
The new prophecies in the light of the
old.
He will listen to any voice that speaks
disaster,
And my advice goes for nothing. [*She
approaches the altar, R.*] To you, then,
Apollo,
Lycean[14] lord, since you are nearest, I
turn in prayer.
Receive these offerings, and grant us
deliverance
From defilement. Our hearts are heavy
with fear
When we see our leader distracted, as
helpless sailors
Are terrified by the confusion of their
helmsman. [*Enter* MESSENGER.]
MESSENGER. Friends, no doubt you can
direct me:
Where shall I find the house of
Oedipus,
Or, better still, where is the King him-
self?
LEADER. It is this very place, stranger;
he is inside.
This is his wife and mother of his chil-
dren.
MESSENGER. I wish her happiness in a
happy house,
Blest in all the fulfillment of her mar-
riage.
IOCASTÊ. I wish as much for you: your
courtesy
Deserves a like good fortune. But now,
tell me:
Why have you come? What have you to
say to us?
MESSENGER. Good news, my lady, for
your house and your husband.
IOCASTÊ. What news? Who sent you
here?
MESSENGER. I am from Corinth.
The news I bring ought to mean joy for
you,
Though it may be you will find some
grief in it.
IOCASTÊ. What is it? How can it touch
us in both ways?
MESSENGER. The people of Corinth,
they say,
Intend to call Oedipus to be their king.
IOCASTÊ. But old Polybos—is he not
reigning still?
MESSENGER. No. Death holds him in his
sepulchre.
IOCASTÊ. What are you saying? Polybos
is dead?
MESSENGER. If I am not telling the
truth, may I die myself.
IOCASTÊ [*to a* MAID-SERVANT]. Go in, go
quickly; tell this to your master.

O riddlers of God's will, where are you
now!
This was the man whom Oedipus, long
ago,
Feared so, fled so, in dread of destroying him—
But it was another fate by which he
died. [*Enter* OEDIPUS, *center.*]
OEDIPUS. Dearest Iocastê, why have you
sent for me?
IOCASTÊ. Listen to what this man says,
and then tell me
What has become of the solemn
prophecies.
OEDIPUS. Who is this man? What is his
news for me?
IOCASTÊ. He has come from Corinth to
announce your father's death!
OEDIPUS. Is it true, stranger? Tell me in
your own words.
MESSENGER. I can not say it more
clearly: the King is dead.
OEDIPUS. Was it by treason? Or by an
attack of illness?
MESSENGER. A little thing brings old
men to their rest.
OEDIPUS. It was sickness, then?
MESSENGER. Yes, and his many years.
OEDIPUS. Ah!
Why should a man respect the Pythian
hearth,[15] or
Give heed to the birds that jangle above
his head?
They prophesied that I should kill

Polybos,
Kill my own father; but he is dead and
buried,
And I am here—I never touched him,
never,
Unless he died of grief for my depar-
ture,
And thus, in a sense, through me. No.
Polybos
Has packed the oracles off with him
underground.
They are empty words.

IOCASTÊ. Had I not told you so?

OEDIPUS. You had; it was my faint heart
that betrayed me.

IOCASTÊ. From now on never think of
those things again.

OEDIPUS. And yet—must I not fear my
mother's bed?

IOCASTÊ. Why should anyone in this
world be afraid,
Since Fate rules us and nothing can be
foreseen?
A man should live only for the present
day.

Have no more fear of sleeping with
your mother:
How many men, in dreams, have lain
with their mothers!
No reasonable man is troubled by such
things.

OEDIPUS. That is true; only—
If only my mother were not still alive!
But she is alive. I can not help my
dread.

IOCASTÊ. Yet this news of your father's
death is wonderful.

OEDIPUS. Wonderful. But I fear the living woman.

MESSENGER. Tell me, who is this woman
that you fear?

OEDIPUS. It is Meropê, man; the wife of
King Polybos.

MESSENGER. Meropê? Why should you
be afraid of her?

OEDIPUS. An oracle of the gods, a
dreadful saying.

MESSENGER. Can you tell me about it or
are you sworn to silence?

OEDIPUS. I can tell you, and I will.
Apollo said through his prophet that I
was the man
Who should marry his own mother,
shed his father's blood
With his own hands. And so, for all

these years
I have kept clear of Corinth, and no
harm has come—
Though it would have been sweet to
see my parents again.

MESSENGER. And is this the fear that
drove you out of Corinth?

OEDIPUS. Would you have me kill my
father?

MESSENGER. As for that
You must be reassured by the news I
gave you.

OEDIPUS. If you could reassure me, I
would reward you.

MESSENGER. I had that in mind, I will
confess: I thought
I could count on you when you returned to Corinth.

OEDIPUS. No: I will never go near my
parents again.

MESSENGER. Ah, son, you still do not
know what you are doing—

OEDIPUS. What do you mean? In the
name of God tell me!

MESSENGER.—If these are your reasons
for not going home.

OEDIPUS. I tell you, I fear the oracle
may come true.

MESSENGER. And guilt may come upon
you through your parents?

OEDIPUS. That is the dread that is always in my heart.

MESSENGER. Can you not see that all
your fears are groundless?

OEDIPUS. How can you say that? They
are my parents, surely?

MESSENGER. Polybos was not your
father.

OEDIPUS. Not my father?

MESSENGER. No more your father than
the man speaking to you.

OEDIPUS. But you are nothing to me!

MESSENGER. Neither was he.

OEDIPUS. Then why did he call me son?

MESSENGER. I will tell you:
Long ago he had you from my hands,
as a gift.

OEDIPUS. Then how could he love me
so, if I was not his?

MESSENGER. He had no children, and
his heart turned to you.

OEDIPUS. What of you? Did you buy
me? Did you find me by chance?

MESSENGER. I came upon you in the
crooked pass of Kithairon.

OEDIPUS. And what were you doing

there?
MESSENGER. Tending my flocks.
OEDIPUS. A wandering shepherd?
MESSENGER. But your savior, son, that
day.
OEDIPUS. From what did you save me?
MESSENGER. Your ankles should tell you
that.
OEDIPUS. Ah, stranger, why do you
speak of that childhood pain?
MESSENGER. I cut the bonds that tied
your ankles together.
OEDIPUS. I have had the mark as long as
I can remember.
MESSENGER. That was why you were
given the name you bear.[16]
OEDIPUS. God! Was it my father or my
mother who did it?
Tell me!
MESSENGER. I do not know. The man
who gave you to me
Can tell you better than I.
OEDIPUS. It was not you that found me,
but another?
MESSENGER. It was another shepherd
gave you to me.
OEDIPUS. Who was he? Can you tell me
who he was?
MESSENGER. I think he was said to be
one of Laïos' people.
OEDIPUS. You mean the Laïos who was
king here years ago?
MESSENGER. Yes; King Laïos, and the
man was one of his herdsmen.
OEDIPUS. Is he still alive? Can I see him?
MESSENGER. These men here
Know best about such things.
OEDIPUS. Does anyone here
Know this shepherd that he is talking
about?
Have you seen him in the fields, or in
the town?
If you have, tell me. It is time things
were made plain.
LEADER. I think the man he means is
that same shepherd
You have already asked to see. Iocastê
perhaps
Could tell you something.
OEDIPUS. Do you know anything
About him, Lady? Is he the man we
have summoned?
Is that the man this shepherd means?
IOCASTÊ. Why think of him?
Forget this herdsman. Forget it all.
This talk is a waste of time.

OEDIPUS. How can you say that,
When the clues to my true birth are in
my hands?
IOCASTÊ. For God's love, let us have no
more questioning!
Is your life nothing to you?
My own is pain enough for me to bear.
OEDIPUS. You need not worry. Suppose
my mother a slave,
And born of slaves: no baseness can
touch you.
IOCASTÊ. Listen to me, I beg you: do
not do this thing!
OEDIPUS. I will not listen; the truth
must be made known.
IOCASTÊ. Everything that I say is for
your own good!
OEDIPUS. My own good
Snaps my patience, then; I want none
of it.
IOCASTÊ. You are fatally wrong! May
you never learn who you are!
OEDIPUS. Go, one of you, and bring the
shepherd here.
Let us leave this woman to brag of her
royal name.
IOCASTÊ. Ah, miserable!
That is the only word I have for you
now.
That is the only word I can ever have.
[*Exit into the palace.*]
LEADER. Why has she left us, Oedipus?
Why has she gone
In such a passion of sorrow? I fear this
silence:
Something dreadful may come of it.
OEDIPUS. Let it come!
However base my birth, I must know
about it.
The Queen, like a woman, is perhaps
ashamed
To think of my low origin. But I
Am a child of Luck; I cannot be dis-
honored.
Luck is my mother; the passing
months, my brothers,
Have seen me rich and poor. If this is
so,
How could I wish that I were someone
else?
How could I not be glad to know my
birth?

Strophe
CHORUS. If ever the coming time were
known to my heart's pondering,

Kithairon, now by Heaven I see the
   torches
At the festival of the next full moon,
And see the dance, and hear the choir
   sing
A grace to your gentle shade:
Mountain where Oedipus was found,
O mountain guard of a noble race!
May the god who heals us lend his aid,
And let that glory come to pass
For our king's cradling-ground.

Antistrophe

Of the nymphs that flower beyond the
   years,
Who bore you, royal child,
To Pan of the hills or the timberline
   Apollo,
Cold in delight where the upland
   clears,
Or Hermês for whom Kyllenê's[17]
   heights are piled?
Or flushed as evening cloud,
Great Dionysos, roamer of mountains,
He—was it he who found you there,
And caught you up in his own proud
Arms from the sweet god-ravisher
Who laughed by the Muses' foun-
   tains?[18]

OEDIPUS. Sirs: though I do not know
   the man,
I think I see him coming, this shepherd
   we want:
He is old, like our friend here, and the
   men
Bringing him seem to be servants of my
   house.
But you can tell, if you have ever seen
   him.

[*Enter* SHEPHERD *escorted by servants.*]

LEADER. I know him, he was Laïos' man.
   You can trust him.

OEDIPUS. Tell me first, you from
   Corinth: is this the shepherd
We were discussing?

MESSENGER. This is the very man.

OEDIPUS. [*to* SHEPHERD]. Come here.
   No, look at me. You must answer
Everything I ask.—You belonged to
   Laïos?

SHEPHERD. Yes: born his slave, brought
   up in his house.

OEDIPUS. Tell me: what kind of work
   did you do for him?

SHEPHERD. I was a shepherd of his,
   most of my life.

OEDIPUS. Where mainly did you go for
   pasturage?

SHEPHERD. Sometimes Kithairon, sometimes the hills near-by.

OEDIPUS. Do you remember ever seeing
   this man out there?

SHEPHERD. What would he be doing
   there?

OEDIPUS. This man standing here. Have
   you ever seen him before?

SHEPHERD. No. At least, not to my recollection.

MESSENGER. And that is not strange, my
   lord. But I'll refresh
His memory: he must remember when
   we two
Spent three whole seasons together,
   March to September,
On Kithairon or thereabouts. He had
   two flocks;
I had one. Each autumn I'd drive mine
   home
and he would go back with his to Laïos'
   sheepfold.—
Is this not true, just as I have described
   it?

SHEPHERD. True, yes; but it was all so
   long ago.

MESSENGER. Well, then: do you remember back in those days,
That you gave me a baby boy to bring
   up as my own?

SHEPHERD. What if I did? What are you
   trying to say?

MESSENGER. Kind Oedipus was once
   that little child.

SHEPHERD. Damn you, hold your
   tongue!

OEDIPUS. No more of that!
It is your tongue needs watching, not
   this man's.

SHEPHERD. My King, my Master, what is
   it I have done wrong?

OEDIPUS. You have not answered his
   question about the boy.

SHEPHERD. He does not know . . . He is
   only making trouble . . .

OEDIPUS. Come, speak plainly, or it will
   go hard with you.

SHEPHERD. In God's name, do not torture an old man!

OEDIPUS. Come here, one of you; bind
   his arms behind him.

SHEPHERD. Unhappy king! What more
   do you wish to learn?

OEDIPUS. Did you give this man the

child he speaks of?
SHEPHERD. I did.
And I would to God I had died that
very day.
OEDIPUS. You will die now unless you
speak the truth.
SHEPHERD. Yet if I speak the truth; I
am worse than dead.
OEDIPUS. Very well; since you insist
upon delaying—
SHEPHERD. No! I have told you already
that I gave him the boy.
OEDIPUS. Where did you get him? From
your house? From somewhere else?
SHEPHERD. Not from mine, no. A man
gave him to me.
OEDIPUS. Is that man here? Do you
know whose slave he was?
SHEPHERD. For God's love, my King, do
not ask me any more!
OEDIPUS. You are a dead man if I have
to ask you again.
SHEPHERD. Then . . . Then the child
was from the palace of Laïos.
OEDIPUS. A slave child? or a child of his
own line?
SHEPHERD. Ah, I am on the brink of
dreadful speech!
OEDIPUS. And I of dreadful hearing.
Yet I must hear.
SHEPHERD. If you must be told, then . . .
They say it was Laïos' child;
But it is your wife who can tell you
about that.
OEDIPUS. My wife!—Did she give it to
you?
SHEPHERD. My lord, she did.
OEDIPUS. Do you know why?
SHEPHERD. I was told to get rid of it.
OEDIPUS. An unspeakable mother!
SHEPHERD. There had been prophe-
cies . . .
OEDIPUS. Tell me.
SHEPHERD. It was said that the boy
would kill his own father.
OEDIPUS. Then why did you give him
over to this old man?
SHEPHERD. I pitied the baby, my King,
And I thought that this man would
take him far away
To his own country. He saved him—
but for what a fate!
For if you are what this man says you
are,
No man living is more wretched than
Oedipus.

OEDIPUS. Ah God!
It was true! All the prophecies!—Now,
O Light, may I look on you for the last
time!
I, Oedipus,
Oedipus, damned in his birth, in his
marriage damned,
Damned in the blood he shed with his
own hand! [*He rushes into the palace.*]

Strophe 1
CHORUS. Alas for the seed of men.

What measure shall I give these gener-
ations
That breathe on the void and are void
And exist and do not exist?

Who bears more weight of joy
Than mass of sunlight shifting in im-
ages,
Or who shall make his thought stay on
That down time drifts away?
Your splendor is all fallen.

O naked brow of wrath and tears,
O change of Oedipus!
I who saw your days call no man blest—
Your great days like ghosts gone.

Antistrophe 1
That mind was a strong bow.
Deep, how deep you drew it then, hard
archer,
At a dim fearful range,
And brought dear glory down!

You overcame the stranger—
The virgin with her hooking lion
claws—
And though death sang, stood like a
tower
To make pale Thebes take heart.

Fortress against our sorrow!

Divine king, giver of laws,
Majestic Oedipus!
No prince in Thebes had ever such re-
nown,
No prince won such grace of power.

Strophe 2
And now of all men ever known
Most pitiful is this man's story:
His fortunes are most changed, his

state
Fallen to a low slave's
Ground under bitter fate.

O Oedipus, most royal one!
The great door that expelled you to the light
Gave at night—ah, gave night to your glory:
As to the father, to the fathering son.

All understood too late.

How could that queen whom Laïos won,
The garden that he harrowed at his height,
Be silent when that act was done?

Antistrophe 2
But all eyes fail before time's eye,
All actions come to justice there.
Though never willed, though far down the deep past,
Your bed, your dread sirings,
Are brought to book at last.

Child by Laïos doomed to die,
Then doomed to lose that fortunate little death,
Would God you never took breath in this air
That with my wailing lips I take to cry:

For I weep the world's outcast.

Blind I was, and cannot tell why;
Asleep, for you had given ease of breath;
A fool, while the false years went by.
[*Enter, from the palace,* SECOND MESSENGER.]
SECOND MESSENGER. Elders of Thebes, most honored in this land,
What horrors are yours to see and hear, what weight
Of sorrow to be endured, if, true to your birth,
You venerate the line of Labdakos!
I think neither Istros nor Phasis, those great rivers,
Could purify this place of the corruption
It shelters now, or soon must bring to light—
Evil not done unconsciously, but willed.

The greatest griefs are those we cause ourselves.
LEADER. Surely, friend, we have grief enough already;
What new sorrow do you mean?
SECOND MESSENGER. The Queen is dead.
LEADER. Iocastê? Dead? But at whose hand?
SECOND MESSENGER. Her own.
The full horror of what happened you cannot know,
For you did not see it: but I, who did, will tell you
As clearly as I can how she met her death.

When she had left us,
In passionate silence, passing through the court,
She ran to her apartment in the house,
Her hair clutched by the fingers of both hands.
She closed the doors behind her; then, by that bed
Where long ago the fatal son was conceived—
That son who should bring about his father's death—
We heard her call upon Laïos, dead so many years,
And heard her wail for the double fruit of her marriage,
A husband by her husband, children by her child.
Exactly how she died I do not know:
For Oedipus burst in moaning and would not let us
Keep vigil to the end: it was by him
As he stormed about the room that our eyes were caught.
From one to another of us he went, begging a sword,
Cursing the wife who was not his wife, the mother
Whose womb had carried his own children and himself.
I do not know: it was none of us aided him,
But surely one of the gods was in control!
For with a dreadful cry
he hurled his weight, as though wrenched out of himself,
At the twin doors: the bolts gave, and he rushed in.
And there we saw her hanging, her

body swaying
From the cruel cord she had noosed
  about her neck.
A great sob broke from him,
  heartbreaking to hear,
As he loosed the rope and lowered her
  to the ground.

I would blot out from my mind what
  happened next!
For the King ripped from her gown the
  golden brooches
That were her ornament, and raised
  them, and plunged them down
Straight into his own eyeballs, crying,
  "No more,
No more shall you look on the misery
  about me,
The horrors of my own doing! Too
  long you have known
The faces of those whom I should
  never have seen,
Too long been blind to those for whom
  I was searching!
From this hour, go in darkness!" And
  as he spoke,
He struck at his eyes—not once, but
  many times;
And the blood spattered his beard,
Bursting from his ruined sockets like
  red hail.
So from the unhappiness of two this
  evil has sprung,
A curse on the man and woman alike.
  The old
Happiness of the house of Labdakos
Was happiness enough: where is it to-
  day?
It is all wailing and ruin, disgrace,
  death—all
The misery of mankind that has a
  name—
And it is wholly and for ever theirs.
LEADER. Is he in agony still? Is there no
  rest for him?
SECOND MESSENGER. He is calling for
  someone to lead him to the gates
So that all the children of Kadmos may
  look upon
His father's murderer, his mother's—
  no,
I can not say it! And then he will leave
  Thebes,
Self-exiled, in order that the curse
Which he himself pronounced may de-
  part from the house.

He is weak, and there is none to lead
  him.
So terrible is his suffering. But you will
  see:
Look, the doors are opening; in a moment
You will see a thing that would crush a
  heart of stone. [*The central door is
  opened;* OEDIPUS, *blinded, is led in.*]
LEADER.Dreadful indeed for men to
  see.
Never have my own eyes
Looked on a sight so full of fear.

Oedipus!
What madness came upon you, what
  daemon
Leaped on your life with heavier
Punishment than a mortal man can
  bear?
No: I cannot even
Look at you, poor ruined one.
And I would speak, question, ponder,
If I were able. No.
You make me shudder.
OEDIPUS. God. God.
Is there a sorrow greater?
Where shall I find harbor in this world?
My voice is hurled far on a dark wind.
What had God done to me?
LEADER. Too terrible to think of, or to
  see.

Strophe 1
OEDIPUS. O cloud of night,
Never to be turned away: night coming
  on,
I can not tell how: night like a shroud!

My fair winds brought me here. O
  God. Again
The pain of the spikes where I had
  sight,
The flooding pain
Of memory, never to be gouged out.
LEADER. This is not strange.
You suffer it all twice over, remorse in
  pain,
Pain in remorse.

Antistrophe 1
OEDIPUS. Ah dear friend
Are you faithful even yet, you alone?
Are you still standing near me, will you
  stay here,
Patient, to care for the blind? The blind

man!
Yet even blind I know who it is attends
    me,
By the voice's tone—
Though my new darkness hide the
    comforter.
LEADER. Oh fearful act!
What god was it drove you to rake
    black
Night across your eyes?

Strophe 2

OEDIPUS. Apollo. Apollo. Dear
Children, the god was Apollo.
He brought my sick, sick fate upon me.
But the blinding hand was my own!
How could I bear to see
When all my sight was horror
    everywhere?
LEADER. Everywhere; that is true.
OEDIPUS. And now what is left?
Images? Love? A greeting even,
Sweet to the senses? Is there anything?
Ah, no, friends: lead me away.
Lead me away from Thebes. Lead the
    great wreck
And hell of Oedipus, whom the gods
    hate.
LEADER. Your fate is clear, you are not
    blind to that.
Would God you had never found it
    out!

Antistrophe 2

OEDIPUS. Death take the man who un-
    bound
My feet on that hillside
And delivered me from death to life!
    What life?
If only I had died,
This weight of monstrous doom
Could not have dragged me and my
    darlings down.
LEADER. I would have wished the same.
OEDIPUS. Oh never to have come here
With my father's blood upon me!
    Never
To have been the man they call his
    mother's husband!
Oh accurst! Oh child of evil,
To have entered that wretched bed—
    the selfsame one!
More primal than sin itself, this fell to
    me.
LEADER. I do not know how I can an-
    swer you.

You were better dead than alive and
    blind.
OEDIPUS. Do not counsel me any more.
    This punishment
That I have laid upon myself is just.
If I had eyes,
I do not know how I could bear the
    sight
Of my father, when I came to the
    house of Death,
Or my mother: for I have sinned
    against them both
So vilely that I could not make my
    peace
By strangling my own life. Or do you
    think my children,
Born as they were born, would be sweet
    to my eyes?
Ah never, never! Nor this town with its
    high walls,
Nor the holy images of the gods. For I,
Thrice miserable!—Oedipus, noblest of
    all the line
Of Kadmos, have condemned myself to
    enjoy
These things no more, by my own
    malediction
Expelling that man whom the gods de-
    clared
To be a defilement in the house of
    Laïos.
After exposing the rankness of my own
    guilt,
How could I look men frankly in the
    eyes?
No, I swear it,
If I could have stifled my hearing at its
    source,
I would have done it and made all this
    body
A tight cell of misery, blank to light and
    sound:
So I should have been safe in a dark
    agony
Beyond all recollection. Ah Kithairon!
Why did you shelter me? When I was
    cast upon you,
Why did I not die? Then I should
    never
Have shown the world my execrable
    birth.

Ah Polybos! Corinth, city that I be-
    lieved
The ancient seat of my ancestors: how
    fair

I seemed, your child! And all the while
  this evil
Was cancerous within me! For I am sick
In my daily life, sick in my origin.

O three roads, dark ravine, woodland
  and way
Where three roads met: you, drinking
  my father's blood,
My own blood, spilled by my own
  hand: can you remember
The unspeakable things I did there,
  and the things
I went on from there to do? O mar-
  riage, marriage!
The act that engendered me, and again
  the act
Performed by the son in the same
  bed—Ah, the net
Of incest, mingling fathers, brothers,
  sons,
With brides, wives, mothers: the last
  evil
That can be known by men: no tongue
  can say
How evil! No. For the love of God, con-
  ceal me
Somewhere far from Thebes; or kill
  me; or hurl me
Into the sea, away from men's eyes for
  ever.
Come, lead me. You need not fear to
  touch me.
Of all men, I alone can bear this guilt.
  [*Enter* CREON.]
LEADER. We are not the ones to decide;
  but Creon here
May fitly judge of what you ask. He
  only
Is left to protect the city in your place.
OEDIPUS. Alas, how can I speak to him?
  What right have I
To beg his courtesy whom I have
  deeply wronged?
CREON. I have not come to mock you,
  Oedipus,
Or to reproach you, either. [*To* ATTEND-
  ANTS.]—You, standing there:
If you have lost all respect for man's
  dignity,
At least respect the flame of Lord
  Helios:
Do not allow this pollution to show it-
  self
Openly here, an affront to the earth
And Heaven's rain and the light of day.

No, take him
Into the house as quickly as you can
For it is proper
That only the close kindred see his
  grief.
OEDIPUS. I pray you in God's name,
  since your courtesy
Ignores my dark expectation, visiting
With mercy this man of all men most
  execrable:
Give me what I ask—for your good, not
  for mine.
CREON: And what is it that you would
  have me do?
OEDIPUS. Drive me out of this country
  as quickly as may be
To a place where no human voice can
  ever greet me.
CREON. I should have done that before
  now—only,
God's will had not been wholly revealed
  to me.
OEDIPUS. But his command is plain: the
  parricide
Must be destroyed. I am that evil man.
CREON. That is the sense of it, yes; but
  as things are,
We had best discover clearly what is to
  be done.
OEDIPUS. You would learn more about a
  man like me?
CREON. You are ready now to listen to
  the god.
OEDIPUS. I will listen. But it is to you
That I must turn for help. I beg you,
  hear me.

The woman in there—
Give her whatever funeral you think
  proper:
She is your sister.—But let me go,
  Creon!
Let me purge my father's Thebes of
  the pollution
Of my living here, and go out to the
  wild hills,
To Kithairon, that has won such fame
  with me,
The tomb my mother and father ap-
  pointed for me,
And let me die there, as they willed I
  should.
And yet I know
Death will not ever come to me
  through sickness
Or in any natural way: I have been pre-

served
For some unthinkable fate[19] But let
    that be.
As for my sons, you need not care for
    them.
They are men, they will find some way
    to live.
But my poor daughters, who have
    shared my table,
Who never before have been parted
    from their father—
Take care of them, Creon; do this for
    me.
And will you let me touch them with
    my hands
A last time, and let us weep together?
Be kind, my lord,
Great prince, be kind! Could I but
    touch them,
They would be mine again, as when I
    had my eyes. [*Enter* ANTIGONE *and* IS-
    MENE, *attended.*]
Ah, God!
Is it my dearest children I hear weep-
    ing?
Has Creon pitied me and sent my
    daughters?
CREON. Yes, Oedipus: I knew that they
    were dear to you
In the old days, and know you must
    love them still.
OEDIPUS. May God bless you for this—
    and be a friendlier
Guardian to you than he has been to
    me!

Children, where are you?
Come quickly to my hands; they are
    your brother's—
Hands that have brought your father's
    once clear eyes
To this way of seeing—Ah dearest
    ones,
I had neither sight nor knowledge
    then, your father
By the woman who was the source of
    his own life!
And I weep for you—having no
    strength to see you—,
I weep for you when I think of the bit-
    terness
That men will visit upon you all your
    lives.
What homes, what festivals can you at-
    tend
Without being forced to depart again

in tears?
And when you come to marriageable
    age,
Where is the man, my daughters, who
    would dare
Risk the bane that lies on all my chil-
    dren?
Is there any evil wanting? Your father
    killed
His father; sowed the womb of her who
    bore him;
Engendered you at the fount of his
    own existence!

That is what they will say of you.

Then, whom
Can you ever marry? There are no
    bridegrooms for you,
And your lives must wither away in
    sterile dreaming.

O Creon, son of Menoikeus!
You are the only father my daughters
    have,
Since we, their parents, are both of us
    gone forever.
They are your own blood: you will not
    let them
Fall into beggary and loneliness;
You will keep them from the miseries
    that are mine!
Take pity on them; see, they are only
    children,
Friendless except for you. Promise me
    this,
Great Prince, and give me your hand in
    token of it. [CREON *clasps his right
    hand.*]
Children:
I could say much, if you could under-
    stand me,
But as it is, I have only this prayer for
    you:
Live where you can, be as happy as you
    can—
Happier, please God, than God has
    made your father!
CREON. Enough. You have wept
    enough. Now go within.
OEDIPUS. I must; but it is hard.
CREON. Time eases all things.
OEDIPUS. But you must promise—
CREON. Say what you desire.
OEDIPUS. Send me from Thebes!
CREON. God grant that I may!

OEDIPUS. But since God hates me . . .
CREON. No, he will grant your wish.
OEDIPUS. You promise?
CREON. I can not speak beyond my
   knowledge.
OEDIPUS. Then lead me in.
CREON. Come now, and leave your chil-
   dren.
OEDIPUS. No! Do not take them from
   me!
CREON. Think no longer
That you are in command here, but
   rather think
How, when you were, you served your
   own destruction. [*Exeunt into the house
   all but the* CHORUS; *the* LEADER *chants
   directly to the audience.*]
LEADER. Men of Thebes: look upon
   Oedipus.
This is the king who solved the famous
   riddle
And towered up, most powerful of
   men.
No mortal eyes but looked on him with
   envy,
Yet in the end ruin swept over him.

Let every man in mankind's frailty
Consider his last day; and let none
Presume on his good fortune until he
   find
Life, at his death, a memory without
   pain.

1. The legendary founder of Thebes.
2. Famous because he had killed the Sphinx
and thus saved the city.
3. Pallas Athene was the special protector of
Athens; Athens and Thebes are often compared
throughout the play.
4. A wreath of bay leaves was emblematic of
victory.
5. Another name for Apollo.
6. Apollo.
7. Athene, Zeus's daughter.
8. The mountain near Thebes upon which the
infant Oedipus was put out to die.
9. Apollo.
10. A mountain near Delphi, sacred to Apollo.
11. Polybos had raised Oedipus as his own son.
12. The Sphinx.
13. The sun god, sometimes associated with
Apollo.
14. Light bringing.
15. The oracle at Delphi.
16. "Oedipus" means swollen foot.
17. A mountain sacred to Hermes.
18. The chorus is speculating that Oedipus may
be the son of a nymph who seduced one of the
gods.
19. Oedipus became a holy man, and was taken
up by the gods at the end of his life; he did not
suffer an ordinary death.

Medea

Euripides

Euripides, the youngest of the three great Greek tragedians, was born in approximately 485 B.C., but died in 407, a few months before Sophocles. As is true of so many figures of antiquity, there are few really dependable facts known regarding his life, but from a combination of history and legend there emerges a general picture of Euripides as a rebel and a malcontent, especially as compared with Sophocles, who was apparently well liked and fitted comfortably into Athenian society. Euripides' religious, political, and social attitudes were iconoclastic, and his plays reveal a great deal of doubt in such matters as the moral worth of the traditional gods or the degree to which man's intelligence is adequate to guide his life. Such questions were stirringly debated in fifth-century-B.C. Athens, and Euripides was thus reflecting an important segment of his society in raising them through his plays, but the impression remains that his more radical views disquieted many of those about him. Still, when Euripides died, Sophocles is reported to have dressed the chorus of his next play in mourning as a mark of special respect.

Euripides appears to have written about twenty-two of the four-play groups that were entered in the annual Athenian competition, but he won first prize only five times (one of them posthumously). Still, nineteen of his separate plays (but no complete trilogy) survive, and this relatively high number apparently reflects the especially high esteem in which his works were held during the centuries immediately following his death. His ideas were widely quoted, and his influence both on Roman drama and later on Renaissance European drama was greater than that of either of his contemporaries. Even Euripides' ideas of what constituted tragedy were revolutionary, and many of his works would, by modern standards, be termed melodramas or, in some cases, satiric comedies. The psychological insight with which he presented his characters has had a profound influence on the development of drama of all types to the present day.

It is impractical to deal with as many as nineteen plays here, but a few of those which are most frequently produced in the twentieth century can be mentioned. *Hippolytus,* which dates from 428 B.C., is the story of the overwhelming sexual passion of Phaedra for her stepson, Hippolytus, who remains indifferent to her. Both die disastrously, and the terrible consequences of passion beyond the control of human reason have been the subject of many other treatments of the same story by later dramatists. *The Trojan Women,* produced in 415, is a tremendously moving antiwar play depicting the misery of the women of Troy following the fall of that city. It is the more remarkable that Euripides wrote such a play at a time when Athens was at war, and had just sacked an enemy city in much the manner that Troy was devastated; it is no wonder that Euripides often aroused antagonism with his views. *Electra,* dating from 413, is especially interesting in allowing one to compare Euripides' version of that story with Aeschylus's in *Choephoroe* and

Sophocles' in his *Electra*. *The Bacchae,* produced posthumously in 405, tells an especially bloody story of a group of women so gripped by religious frenzy that they literally tear to pieces the son of one of them; the clash of human reason with uncontrollable passion has been found to have special relevance to many twentieth-century horrors.

Medea dates from rather early in Euripides' career (431). The plot is based, as were those of almost all Greek tragedies, on a myth well known to the Athenian audience, but knowledge of that myth is far less important to *Medea* than it has been to the earlier plays in this volume. Indeed, if one did not already know them, one could learn the salient facts from the play itself, many from the Nurse's opening speech, which is simply direct address to the audience. Medea was a barbarian princess with celestial connections who assisted Jason in his quest for the Golden Fleece. Out of love for Jason, Medea committed crimes of monstrous dimensions, and for some years the two of them were passionately loyal to each other. As the play opens in Corinth, however, Jason has decided to abandon Medea and their children in order to marry the daughter of Kreon, king of Corinth. Medea, in her grief and rage, seeks revenge, and she achieves it not only by killing Kreon and his daughter, but also by killing Jason's sons in order to hurt him even at the sacrifice of her own happiness. Only at the end of the play is a supernatural element introduced, as Medea is borne out of Corinth in a fiery chariot drawn by dragons while prophesying the next events in her story.

This *deus ex machina* ending is typical of many of Euripides' plays and is reflective of the fact that by this time the Greek theater had, among its scenic devices, a cranelike machine by which a god could be lowered into the scene to resolve whatever problems remained at the end of a play. That such a contrived ending rings hollow today is not simply a peculiarity of modern taste, for Aristotle condemned it too in the *Poetics*. Whether Euripides couldn't think of a better ending or whether he responded to the taste of a spectacle-loving audience cannot be known, but it is noteworthy that *Medea* actually does not need anything that the *deus ex machina* provides. All the principal problems of the plot are already solved before the supernatural elements enter it, and only in a thematic sense might there be some real need to show that the gods are supporting the justice of Medea's cause.

Medea is full of interesting structural features that suggest both Euripides' mastery of certain elements of playwriting and his cavalier disregard of those aspects which apparently didn't interest him. Although *Oedipus Rex* demonstrates how the prologue had developed into a fully dramatic confrontation among two or three characters, Euripides makes use of direct address to the audience to get across the basic facts that need to be communicated. The latter part of the prologue does introduce a second character, but the exchange of information between them is still rather contrived. Euripides' use of the chorus continues the trend already noted toward further diminution of its importance in the entire procedings. The chorus in *Medea* has some beautiful poetry, but it provides little more than interludes between the episodes, with the latter carrying almost all the interest. Within these episodes, the presence of the chorus is almost ignored at times, and one wonders why they don't do something to stop Medea's horrible plans—until one realizes that the chorus is meant simply as a group of commentators, and not as active participants in the action in any theatrical way. This is a convention that can be made perfectly clear in production, although in reading it may seem a bit disquieting. Euripides makes use of a third character in episodes when he needs one, but much of the time he uses just two: Medea and whoever is to argue with her. There is much use of nonspeaking extras to fill plot needs, but nothing is done to develop their characters. Time is compressed out of all realistic proportion, a technique which pervades nearly all drama but which is especially evident here when Medea sends for Jason and almost instantly he enters. All of these devices are characteristic of plot structuring which establishes its own theatrical conventions, free of the limitations that more conservative artists tend to thrust upon themselves. Whether these conventions work with an audience or not is very much a function of how effectively they are carried out on the stage; Euripides' use of them has proved both a source of inspiration and a stumbling block to generations of directors.

Probably the greatest single area of interest in most of Euripides' plays is his development of character, and nowhere is this truer than in the case of Medea herself. That she is an evil, vengeful murderess is evident, and yet Euripides invests her with such sympathetic and humanly understandable motives and attitudes that one identifies deeply with her even in all her evil. Euripides probed the human psyche as did neither of his famous peers, bringing psychological insight and detail to the problem of why human beings behaved as they did. In a sense, this very process contributed to the antireligious bias of which Euripides is often accused, for to explain behavior in human terms is to remove the necessity for superhuman explanation, and to explain the behavior of gods in human terms is to remove them from godlike status altogether. Even when gods appear in Euripides' plays, as they often do, it is usually as personifications of human passions and as a symbolic way of explaining human behavior. The suffering of Jason, Kreon, Aegeus, and even the Nurse in *Medea* is convincingly presented in humanly understandable ways, but the great fascination is with Medea herself. Her crimes are so monstrous that one cannot imagine committing them, yet her motivations are those which one recognizes in oneself, perhaps to such an extent that one begins to wonder under what circumstances one might indeed be capable of such violence. Euripides had a special facility, too, for portraying the feelings of the defeated, the underdog, or the minority, especially when they rise suddenly to defend themselves, and Medea can readily become a symbol for the wronged marriage partner, for women in general, or for almost any who think of themselves as oppressed. This, no doubt, is one of the key factors in her continued appeal across the centuries.

The central theme of *Medea* is the clash of reason and passion, raised in this case to titanic proportion because of the monstrous passions involved. In an age when many philosophers were arguing that man's reason was his supreme faculty, and that through reason man was infinitely perfectible, Euripides and others maintained that the sweep of passion was so strong that reason frequently could not resist it; *Medea* certainly illustrates such a situation. Medea reasons with herself about the enormity of her proposed crime, even hesitating finally to kill her children because she loves them so much. Finally, however, even while she hesitates, the sheer force of her passionate hatred and need for revenge sweeps her into her ultimate bloody act. That few mortals would actually do anything so monstrous is somewhat beside the point. Some would, and the fundamental emotion touches the depths of human understanding, reminding one that there is almost no evil to which mankind will not stoop when sufficiently emotionally stimulated, no matter how unreasoning such an action may seem. So bald a statement of Euripides' theme should not betray one into believing that the play is written in support of a single thesis, however. The issues raised when extreme emotion sweeps a human being into unreasoning acts are complex enough for many plays, and they have indeed been the central focus of a great many. Euripides explores many of their ramifications here, by no means exhausting the subject but holding audience interest through a series of interconnecting questions. That the play continues to elicit these results in a great many modern productions is notable proof of Euripides' success.

Although Euripides reduced the significance of the chorus a good deal, he was nevertheless able to write poetry of great beauty; the chorus's hymn to Athens that follows the Aegeus episode is justly famed as one of the most beautiful choral odes in all Greek drama. Thus, beauty of poetry, acuteness of psychological insight in character development, and gory—at times even sensational—action were all key features of Euripides' work that were to influence the development of drama for more than a thousand years. In the modern era, Aeschylus and Sophocles have been returned to a position of even greater critical admiration, but the work of Euripides continues to fascinate and to sound notes that are tellingly modern.

Medea

Translated by Frederic Prokosch

Characters

Medea
Jason
Kreon
Medea's children
Attendant
Nurse
Aegeus
A Messenger
Chorus of Corinthian Women

SCENE: *Corinth before the house of Medea. The* NURSE *enters from the house.*

NURSE. Oh how I wish that famous ship,
The Argo, had never made its way through
The blue Symplegades[1] to the land of Colchis![2]
How I wish the pine tree had never been felled
In the glades of Pelion,[3] and never
Been hewn into oars for the heroes
Who went to fetch the Golden Fleece
For Pelias![4] For then my mistress, Medea,
Would never have sailed to the towers
Of the land of Iolcos, her heart on fire
With love for Jason! Nor would she
Ever have beguiled the daughters
Of Pelias into slaying their father,
Nor have come to live in Corinth with her
Husband and children. For a long time
She found favor with the people here
In the land of exile; and she did
All things in complete accord with Jason;
And indeed it is this—when a woman
Stands loyally by a man—which brings
To men the only sure salvation. But now
Their love has fallen into decay; and
There's hatred everywhere. For Jason
Has betrayed his children and my mistress;
He has taken a royal bride to his bed,
The daughter of Kreon, who is the ruler
Of this land. And poor Medea, scorned
And deserted, can do nothing but appeal
To the vows they made to one another,[5]
And remind him of the eternal pledge
They made with their right hands clasped.
And she calls upon the gods to witness
How Jason is repaying her for her love.
She lies half famished; her body is bowed
Utterly with grief, wasting away the whole
Day long. So it has been since she
Learned that he has betrayed her.
Never stirring an eye, never lifting
Her gaze from the ground; and when her friends
Speak to her in warning she no more listens
Than a rock listens, or the surging sea wave.
Only now and then she turns her snowy neck
And quietly laments, and utters her father's
Name, and the name of her land and home,
Which she deserted when she followed
The man who now brings her such dishonor.

93

Pitiful woman! She has learned at last
Through all her sufferings how lucky
Are those who have never lost their
Native land. She has come to feel
A hatred for her children, and no
longer
Wants to see them. Indeed, I fear
She may be moving toward some
dreadful
Plan; for her heart is violent.
She will never submit to this cruel
Treatment. I know her well: her anger
Is great; and I know that any man
Who makes an enemy of her
Will have it hard . . . Look;
Here come the children; they have
been playing.
Little they know of their mother's mis-
ery; little
The hearts of the young can guess of
sorrow! [*The* ATTENDANT *brings in*
MEDEA's *children.*]
ATTENDANT. Why are you standing
here, in front of the gates?
You've been maid for so many years to
my mistress;
Why have you left her alone, then,
Only to stand outside the gates and la-
ment?
NURSE. Listen, old man, who watch over
Jason's
Sons! It's a sad, sad thing for faithful
Servants like us to see our master's
Fortunes meet with disaster; it stirs
Us to the heart. I am so lost in grief,
Now, that a longing came over me to
step
Outside the gates, and tell the whole
wide
World and the heavens of my mistress's
sorrows!
ATTENDANT. Poor lady! Hasn't she
ceased her weeping yet?
NURSE. Ceased? Far from it! This is
only
The beginning; there is far more to
come.
ATTENDANT. Poor, foolish lady; though
I shouldn't call her that;
But how little she knows of this latest
trouble!
NURSE. What do you mean, old man?
Come! Don't be afraid to tell me!
ATTENDANT. Nothing at all; I should
never have mentioned it.
NURSE. No, no; by your wise old beard I

beg you,
Don't hide anything from your fellow
servant!
Tell me; and, if you wish, I'll keep it
secret.
ATTENDANT. Well, as I was passing the
usual place
Where the old men sit playing
draughts,
Down by the holy fountain of Pirene,[6]
I happened to overhear one of them
saying
That Kreon, king of the land, intends
to send
These children, and their mother from
Corinth,
Far away into exile. But whether it was
The truth he was speaking, I do not
know;
I hope and pray it wasn't the truth.
NURSE. And will Jason allow this thing
to happen to his sons,
Even though he is on bad terms with
their mother?
ATTENDANT. Old ties give way to new
ones; and his
Love for this family of ours is dying
away.
NURSE. Oh, it looks dark indeed for us;
New sorrows are being added to old
ones,
Even before the old ones have faded!
ATTENDANT. Be still, be still; don't whis-
per a word of it.
This isn't the proper time to tell our
mistress.
NURSE. O little children,
Do you hear how your father feels to-
ward you?
May evil befall him!
But no; he is still my master. Yet how
cruelly
He has betrayed his dear ones!
ATTENDANT. And which of us has not
done the same?
Haven't you learned long ago, my dear,
How each man loves himself far more
Than his neighbor? Some, perhaps,
From honest motives; some for private
gain.
So you see how Jason deserts his chil-
dren
For the pleasure of his new bride.
NURSE. Go back into the house, chil-
dren;
All will be well. Try to keep them

Out of the way, old man; keep them far
From their mother as long as she feels
This desperate anger. I have already
    seen
The fire in her eyes as she watched
Them, almost as though she were wish-
    ing
Them harm. I am sure her anger
Won't end till she has found a victim.
Let's hope the victim will be
An enemy, and not a friend! [*Within the
    house.*]
MEDEA. Lost, oh lost! I am lost
In my sufferings. I wish, oh I wish
That I could die. . . .
NURSE. My dear children, what did I tell
    you?
Your mother's mind is filled with the
    wildest
Fancies; her heart is wild with anger!
Run quickly back into the house.
Keep out of her sight. Do not
Go near her. Beware of the wildness
And bitterness of her heart!
Go, quickly, quickly!
I can feel that her fury will rise
And redouble! I can hear
In that cry the rising thunderstorm,
I can feel the approach of thunder and
    lightning!
Oh what will she do, in the pride
And torment of her soul? What
Evil thing will she do? [*The* ATTENDANT
takes the children into the house.]
MEDEA. [*Within.*] Oh, I have suffered
And suffered enough for all these
    tears!
I call destruction upon you, all, all of
    you,
Sons of a doomed mother, and the
    father too!
May ruin fall on the entire house!
NURSE. I am full of pity,
Full of deep pity for you! Yet why
Do the children share their father's
    crime?
Why should you hate them? O my poor
    children,
I fear some outrage will befall you!
Yes, strange and terrible is the temper
    of princes.
There is none they need to obey;
There is none that can check them:
There is nothing to control
The madness of their mood.
How much better off are the rest of us

Who've been taught to live equally with
    our neighbors! All I wish
Is to grow old quietly, not in pride,
But only in humble security.
It's the moderate thing that always
    sounds
Best to our ears; and indeed it is
The moderate thing that is best in prac-
    tice.
For power grows beyond control;
Power brings comfort to no man.
And I say, the greater the power, the
    greater
The ruin when it finally falls. [*Enter the*
CHORUS *of Corinthian women. The fol-
lowing lines are chanted.*]
CHORUS. I heard the voice,
I heard the loud lament
Of the pitiful lady from Colchis:
Oh tell me, mother, is she still
Unquiet? As I stood
By the house with the double gates
I heard the sound of weeping from
    within.
I grieve for the sorrow of this family
Which I have come to love.
NURSE. There is no family left; it has
    gone,
It has gone forever. The master now
Has a royal bride in the bed beside
    him,
And our mistress is withering away
In her chamber, and finds no solace
Or warmth in words
That friends can utter.
MEDEA. [*Within.*] Oh how I wish that a
    stroke of lightning
Would fall from heaven and shatter my
    head!
Why should I live any longer?
Death would bring release; in death
I could leave behind me the horror of
    living.
CHORUS. Did you hear, almighty Zeus?
O earth, O heaven, did you hear
The cry of woe this woman has ut-
    tered?
Oh why, poor lady, should you long
For that unutterable haven of rest?
Death only can bring it; and death
    comes only too soon!
No, no, there is no need to pray for
    death.
And if your man is drawn
To a new love, remember,
Such things occur often; do not feel

hurt.
For God will be your ultimate friend
  the judge
In this as in all matters.
So do not mourn too much,
Do not waste away in sorrow
For the loss of the one you loved!
MEDEA. [*Within.*] Great Themis, O lady
  Artemis, look down
On all I am suffering; and suffering in
  spite
Of all the vows my husband made me.
I pray that I may some day see
Him and his bride brought down to
  ruin.
And their palace ruined for all the
  wrong
They dared to do me without cause.
O my own father, my own country,
Shameful it was of me to leave you,
And to have killed my brother before I
  left you!
NURSE. Do you hear what she says? Do
  you hear
How loudly she cries to Themis, the
  goddess of promises,
And to Zeus, whom men think of as the
  Emperor of Vows?
One thing I know. It is no small thing
That draws such anger from our mis-
  tress!
CHORUS. Let her come forth and see us,
Let her listen to our words of warning,
Let her lay aside the rage and violence
  of her heart;
Never shall I refuse to help my friends,
Never shall they turn to me in vain.
Go, go, and bring her from the house
That we may see her; speak kindly to
  her!
Hurry, before she does some violent
  thing.
I feel her passion rising to a new pitch.
NURSE. Yes; I shall go; but I deeply
  doubt
Whether I can persuade my mistress.
Still, I shall gladly go and try;
Though she glares upon her servants,
  those
That approach and dare to speak to
  her,
With the fiery look of a lioness with
  cubs!
You would be right, I think
If you called both ignorant
And trivial those poets of old who

wrote
Their songs for festivities and ban-
  quets,
Graceful and pleasant sounds for men
Who lived in gaiety and leisure.
For none of them learned a way
For the song or the musicians
To still man's suffering. And suffering
  it is
From which all killing springs, and all
  calamity
Which falls on the homes of men.
Yet it would be a blessing, surely,
If songs could heal the wounds which
  sorrow
Inflicts on men! What good is music
And singing at an idle banquet? It
  seems to me
That men who are sitting at the ban-
  quet table
Have pleasure enough already. . . . [*The
  NURSE goes into the house.*]
CHORUS. I heard a cry that was heavy
  and sick with sorrow.
Loud in her bitterness she cries
On the man who betrayed her mar-
  riage bed!
Full of her wrongs she cries
To the gods, to Themis, to the bride of
  Zeus,
To the Keeper of Vows, who brought
  her away
To the shores of Greece which face the
  shores of Asia,
Through the straits at night to the gate-
  way opening
On the unlimited salty sea. [*Toward the
  end of this song, MEDEA enters from the
  house.*]
MEDEA. Ladies of Corinth, I have come
  forth
From my house, lest you should feel
Bitterness toward me; for I know that
  men
Often acquire a bad name for their
  pride—
Not only the pride they show in public,
But also the pride of retirement; those
  who
Live in solitude, as I do, are frequently
Thought to be proud. For there is no
  justice
In the view one man takes of another,
Often hating him before he has suf-
  fered
Wrong, hating him even before he has

seen
His true character. Therefore a foreig-
ner
Above all should fit into the ways of a
city.
Not even a native citizen, I think,
should risk
Offending his neighbors by rudeness
or pride.
But this new thing has fallen upon me
So unexpectedly, my strength is bro-
ken.
O my friends, my life is shattered;
My heart no longer longs for the bless-
ings
Of life but only for death! There was
One man through whom I came to see
The world's whole beauty; and that
Was my husband; and he has turned
out
Utterly evil. O women, of all creatures
That live and reflect, certainly it is we
Who are the most luckless. First of all,
We pay a great price to purchase a hus-
band;
And thus submit our bodies to a per-
petual
Tyrant. And everything depends on
whether
Our choice is good or bad—for divorce
Is not an honorable thing, and we may
not
Refuse to be married. And then a wife
is
Plunged into a way of life and behavior
Entirely new to her, and must learn
What she never learned at home—
She must learn by a kind of subtle
Intuition how to manage the man who
Lies beside her. and if we have the luck
To handle all these things with tact
And success, and if the husband is will-
ing
To live at our side without resentment,
Then life can become happy indeed.
But if not, I'd rather be dead.
A man who is disgusted with what he
Finds at home, goes forth to put an end
To his boredom, and turns to a friend
Or companion of his own age; while we
At home continue to think of him,
And of him only. And yet people
Say that we live in security at home,
While the men go forth to war.
How wrong they are! Listen:
I'd rather be sent three times over

To the battlefront than give
Birth to a single child. Still,
My friends, I realize that all this applies
Not to you but to me; you after all
Have a city of your own, and a family
Home, and a certain pleasure in life,
And the company of your friends. But
I am utterly lonely, an exile, cast off
By my own husband—nothing but a
captive
Brought here from a foreign land—
without
A mother or brother, without a single
Kinsman who can give me refuge in
this sea
Of disaster. Therefore, my ladies, I ask
Only one thing of you: promise me
Silence. If I can find some way, some
Cunning scheme of revenge against my
Husband for all that he has done to
me,
And against the man who gave away his
Daughter, and against the daughter
who
Is now my husband's wife; then please
Be silent. For though a woman is
Timid in everything else, and weak,
and
Terrified at the sight of a sword: still,
When things go wrong in this thing of
love,
No heart is so fearless as a woman's;
No heart it so filled with the thought of
blood.
CHORAGUS. Yes; I promise you this.
You will be right,
Medea, in avenging yourself on
Your husband. It does not surprise
Me to see you lost in despair . . . But
look!
I see Kreon, our king, approaching:
He will have some news to tell us. [*Enter*
KREON, *with his following.*]
KREON. Listen to me, Medea! You, with
your angry looks
And all that bitterness against your
husband;
I order you to leave my kingdom! I or-
der you
To go with both your children into ex-
ile,
And immediately, this is my decree.
And I
Will not return to my house until I
have
Hurled you beyond the borders of my

kingdom.

MEDEA. Oh, now I am lost indeed! This is the end
Of all things for me! Now my enemies
Are bearing down on me in all their force;
And I have no refuge left in this hour of ruin.
And yet, let me ask you this one thing, Kreon:
Why is it, Kreon, you are sending me away?

KREON. I am afraid of you. I need no longer pretend
Otherwise. I am afraid you will do my daughter
Some mortal harm. And I have many reasons
For being afraid of this. You are a cunning
Woman, Medea, expert in all kinds of magic,
So I hear. And you are enraged by the loss
Of your husband's love. I have also heard
Them say that you are planning some kind
Of mischief against Jason and the bride,
And the bride's father, myself, as well.
It is against these things I take precautions.
I tell you, Medea, I'd rather incur your hatred now
Than be soft-hearted and later learn to regret it.

MEDEA. This is not the first time, Kreon!
Many times before has this strange reputation
Done me harm. A sensible man should
Never nowadays bring up his children
To be too clever or exceptional. For one thing,
These talents never bring them profit;
For another, they end by bringing envy
And hatred from others. If you present
New ideas to a group of fools, they'll think you
Ignorant as well as idle. And if your fame
Should come to exceed the established reputations,
They'll hate you for it. This has been
My own experience. Some think me

clever,
And resent it; some think me not
So very clever after all, and disapprove.
And you, Kreon, are somehow afraid
That I may do something to harm you.
But you need not worry. It isn't for someone
Like me to quarrel with kings. After all,
Why should I? You haven't harmed me.
You've allowed your daughter to marry
As you saw fit. I hate my husband, certainly;
But as for you, I feel you have acted
Reasonably enough. I don't grudge you
Your good fortune. I wish you luck
With your daughter's marriage, Kreon,
But beg you only, let me live on in this
Land. I have been wronged, but I shall remain
Quiet, and submit to those above me.

KREON. Your words are gentle enough, Medea.
Yet in my heart I can't help dreading
That you are planning some evil;
And I trust you now even less than before.
It is easier to deal with a quick-tempered
Man or woman than with one who is subtle
And soft-spoken. No. You must go at once.
Make no more speeches. It is settled.
You are my enemy, and there is nothing
You can do to prolong your stay in my country.

MEDEA. I implore you! By your knees, by your newly wed daughter!

KREON. You are wasting your words. You will never persuade me.

MEDEA. Then you'll drive me out without listening to my prayers?

KREON. I shall; for I love my own family more than you.

MEDEA. O my country! How my heart goes back to you now!

KREON. I, too, love my country above all things, except my children.

MEDEA. How cruelly passionate love can deal with men!

KREON. And yet, it all depends on the luck men have.

MEDEA. O Zeus, never forget the man who caused this!

KREON. Go now; go. Spare me this useless trouble.

MEDEA. No trouble, no pain, nothing has been spared me!

KREON. Soon one of my men shall lead you away by force.

MEDEA. Not that, Kreon, not that! I beg you, Kreon.

KREON. It seems you insist on creating a disturbance.

MEDEA. I will go. I will go. That is not what I intended.

KREON. Why all this commotion, then? What is it you want?

MEDEA. Let me stay here just a single day longer,
Kreon. Let me stay and think over where
I shall go in exile, and how I shall find
A living for my children, for whom their father
Has completely failed to provide. Take pity
On them, Kreon! You too have children
Of your own; you too must have a soft place
In your heart for them. What happens to me now
No longer matters; I only grieve
For the suffering that will come to my children.

KREON. I am not a cruel man, Medea. I have often made
Blunders, out of sheer compassion. Even now
I feel I am making a mistake. All the same,
Have it your own way. But let me warn you! If
Tomorrow at sunrise still finds you and your
Children within the frontiers of my land,
You shall die for it. That is my verdict;
It is final. So stay this one day
Longer, if you must. One day is
Not enough to bring disaster. [*Exit* KREON *with his following.*]

CHORAGUS. Pitiful woman! Oh we pity
The sorrows you suffer!
Where will you turn now? Who can help you?
What home remains, what land
Is left to save you from destruction?
O Medea, you have been hurled by
heaven
Into an ocean of despair.

MEDEA. Everything has gone wrong. None can deny it.
But not quite everything is lost; don't
Give up hope, my friends! There still are
Troubles in store for the young bride,
And for the bridegroom too. Do you think
I would have fawned on that old man without
Some plan and purpose? Certainly not.
I would never have touched him
With my hands. But now, although he
Could have crushed all my plans by instant
Exile, he has made a fatal error;
He has given me one day's reprieve.
One day in which I can bring death
To the three creatures that I loathe:
The father, the bride, my husband.
There are many manners of death
Which I might use; I don't quite know yet
Which to try. Shall I set fire
To the bridal mansion? Or shall I sharpen
A sword and steal into the chamber
To the wedding bed and plunge it
Into their hearts? One thing
Stands in my way. If I am caught
Making my way into the bridal room
On such an errand, I shall surely
Be put to death, and my foes will end
By triumphing over me. Better to take
The shortest way, the way I am best trained in:
Better to bring them down with poison.
That I will do, then. And after that?
Suppose them dead. What city will take me in then?
What friend will offer me shelter in his land,
And safety, and a home? None.
Then best to wait a little longer;
Perhaps some sure defense will appear,
And I can set about this murder
In stealth and stillness. And if no help
Should come from fate, and even if death
Is certain, still I can take at last
The sword in my own hand and go forth
Boldly to the crime, and kill. Yes,
By that dark Queen whom I revere

above
All others, and whom I now invoke
To help me, by Hecate[7] who dwells
In my most secret chamber: I swear
No man shall injure me and not regret
it.
I will turn their marriage into sorrow
And anguish! Go now, go forward to
this
Dangerous deed! The time has come
for courage.
Remember the suffering they caused
you! Never
Shall you be mocked because of this
wedding
Of Jason's, you who sprung from a no-
ble
Father and whose grandfather was the
Sun-God
Himself! You have the skill; what is
more,
You are a woman: and it's always a
woman
Who is capable of a noble deed,
Yet expert in every kind of mischief!

Strophe 1
CHORUS. The sacred rivers are flowing
back to their sources!
The order of the world is being re-
versed!
Now it is men who have grown deceit-
ful,
Men who have broken their sacred
vows,
The name of woman shall rise to favor
Again; and women once again
Shall rise and regain their honor: never
Again shall ill be said of women!

Antistrophe 1
Those poets of old shall cease at last
To sing of our faithlessness. Never
On us did Phoebus, the god of music,
Lavish the talents of the lyre,
Else I should long ago have sung
A song of rebuttal to the race
Of men: for the years have many
things
To tell of them as well as of us!

Strophe 2
You sailed away from your father's
dwelling
With your heart on fire, Medea! And
you passed

Between the rocky gates of the seas;
And now you sleep on a foreign shore,
In a lonely bed: now you are driven
Forth, and far away from the land
Once more you go in exile and dis-
honor!

Antistrophe 2
Gone is the dignity of vows,
Gone from great Hellas the sense of
honor.
It has flown and vanished in the skies.
And now no father's dwelling house
Stands as a refuge from this storm!
Now another princess lies
In the bed which once was yours, and
rules your home! [*As the* CHORUS *ap-
proaches the end of the song,* JASON *en-
ters.*]
JASON. This is not the first time I have
noticed
How difficult it is to deal with a violent
temper.
Ah, Medea, if you had patiently ac-
cepted
The will of our ruler, you might have
stayed on
Quietly in this land and this house.
But now your pointless complaints
Are driving you into exile. Not that I
Minded them myself; I didn't mind it
at all
When you called Jason an evil man.
But,
Considering your references to the
King
Himself, you may count yourself lucky
That your punishment is exile. Person-
ally,
I have always done my best to calm
The King's anger, and would have
liked
To see you stay on here. But you re-
fused
To give up this sort of folly, and kept
on
Slandering him; with the result that
you
Are facing banishment. Nevertheless,
In spite of your behavior, I feel in-
clined
To do you a favor; I have come to
make
Some sort of provision for you and the
children,
My dear, so that you won't be penniless

When you are in exile; for I know that
exile
Will not be easy. And even though
you hate me,
Medea, my thoughts of you will con-
tinue
To be friendly as always.
MEDEA. You filthy coward!
That is the only name I can find for
you,
You and your utter lack of manliness!
And now you, who are the worst of my
enemies,
Now you too have chosen to come to
me! No!
It isn't courage which brings you,
Nor recklessness in facing the friends
You have injured; it is worse than that,
It is the worst of all human vices:
Shamelessness. Still, you did well to
come to me,
For now I can ease my heart by reviling
you:
And perhaps you too will suffer as you
listen.
Let me begin, then, at the very begin-
ning.
I saved your life; every Greek who
Sailed with you on the Argo knows
I saved you, when you were sent to
tame
The fire-breathing bulls and to yoke
them,
And to sow the deadly fields. Yes,
And I killed the many-folded serpent
Who lay guarding the Golden Fleece,
Forever wakeful, coil upon coil.
And I raised a beacon of light
To bring you to safety. Freely
I deserted my own father and my own
home;
And followed you to Iolcos, to the hills
Of Pelion: and all this time my love
Was stronger than my reason. And I
brought
Death to Pelias by his own daughters'
Hands; I utterly destroyed the house-
hold.
All of these things I did for you,
Traitor! And you forsook me, and took
Another wife, even though I had borne
Your children. Had you been childless,
One might have pardoned your wish
For a second wedding. But now
All my faith in your vows has vanished.
I do not know whether you imagine

That the gods by whom you swore
Have disappeared or that new rules
Are now in vogue in such matters;
For you must be aware that you have
Broken your vows to me. Oh this poor
Right hand, which you so often
pressed!
These knees, which you so often
Used to embrace! And all in vain,
For it was an evil man
That touched me! How wildly
all my hopes have fallen through! . . .
Come, Jason, I shall speak to you quite
frankly,
As though we still were friends. Can I
possibly
Expect any kindness from someone like
you?
Still, let us assume that I can:
It will only make you appear
Still more ignoble. Very well.
Where shall I go? Home to my father?
Home to him and the land I betrayed
When I followed you? Or back
To the pitiful daughters of Pelias?
What a fine welcome they would give
me,
Who arranged the death of their own
father!
So this is how it now stands with me.
I am loathed by my friends at home;
And for your sake I made enemies
Of others whom I need never have
Harmed. And now, to reward me
For all this, look, look,
How doubly happy you've made me
Among the women of Hellas! Look
What a fine, trustworthy husband
I have had in you! And now
I am to be cast forth into exile,
In utter misery, alone with my children
And without a single friend! Oh,
This will be a shameful shadow upon
you,
As you lie in your wedding bed! That
Your own children, and their mother,
Who saved your life, should go
Wandering around the world like beg-
gars! . . .
O Zeus, why have you given us a way to
tell
True gold from the counterfeit, but no
way,
No emblem branded on a man's body
whereby
We can tell the true man from the

false?

CHORAGUS. Dreadful is the anger,
And past all healing,
When lovers in fury
Turn against each other!
JASON. The time has come, it seems,
When I must speak, and speak well,
And like a good helmsman
Reef up my sail and weather
The tempest of your tongue. . . .
And since you dwell so heavily
On all the favors you did me,
Medea, I am certain that I owe
The safety of my voyage to Aphrodite[8]
Alone among gods and men. Not that I
Doubt your skill; but all the same,
I prefer not to dwell on this notion
That love, with all its irresistible
Power, compelled you to save my life.
I don't think we need go into details.
I admit that you meant well,
And did your best. But when it comes
to this matter of my safety, let me
Point out that you got rather more
Than you gave. First of all,
Instead of living in a barbaric land,
You've come to Greece and enjoyed
Contact with a country where justice
And law prevail, and not brute force;
And what is more, the Greeks thought
Rather highly of you. You even
Acquired a certain fame here.
　Whereas,
If you had stayed on in that outer
Fringe of the world, your name
Would now be quite unknown. Frankly,
I'd rather have real fame and distinc-
tion
Than mighty stores of gold in my halls
Or the talent to sing more sweetly
Than Orpheus.[9] That is my answer
To your version of all my labors; re-
member,
It was you who brought up this matter.
As for your bitter attack on my mar-
riage
With the princess, I think I can prove
First of all that it was a shrewd move;
Secondly, a thoroughly sober one;
And finally, that I did it in your interest
And that of your children . . . Wait!
Please remain calm . . . Since I had
come
From Iolcos involved in every kind of
trouble,
And an exile, what could be luckier

For me than marriage with the king's
Own daughter? It was not—since it is
This that seems to rankle in you—
It was not that I grew weary
Of going to bed with you, and began
To look around for a new wife. Nor
Was it that I was anxious
To have more children. The two
We have are quite enough;
I don't complain. No, it was this,
First of all: that we might live
In comfort, and not in poverty.
Believe me, I have learned how
A man's friends desert him
The moment he is penniless . . . And
then
I wanted to bring up my sons
In a manner worthy of my position; I
Even hoped that by having more sons,
Who would live as brothers to yours,
We might draw the entire family
Into harmony, and all be happy. You
Yourself need no more children;
But I would do well to help
The sons I have through the sons
I hope to have. Do you disagree
With all this? You would agree
If it weren't for this matter of love
Which rankles in you. But you women
Have developed such curious notions:
You think that all is well
As long as your life at night
Runs smoothly. But if something
Happens which upsets your way of
love,
Then all that you once found lovely
And desirable you now find hateful.
Believe me, it would have been better
Far if men could have thought up
Some other way of producing children,
And done away with women; then
No evil would ever have come to men.
CHORAGUS. O Jason, you have given this
speech
Of yours a convincing enough air; and
yet I somehow feel, though perhaps I
Shouldn't say so, that you have acted
Wickedly in betraying your wife.
MEDEA. I suppose I am different in
many
Ways from most people, for I feel
That the worst punishment should
Fall on the man who speaks
Brilliantly for an evil cause,
The man who knows he can make
An evil thing sound plausible

And who dares to do so. And still,
Such a man isn't really so very wise
After all. Listen, Jason. You need
Not bring forth these clever phrases
And specious arguments; for a single
Word from me will destroy you. Con-
sider:
Had you not been a coward, Jason, you
Would have spoken frankly to me
First, and not concealed your wedding
Plans from the one who loved you.
JASON. And you, no doubt, would have
Done all you could to help
Me, if I had spoken of this
Matter: you, who even now cannot
Control the rage in your heart.
MEDEA. It wasn't this that restrained
    you.
No. It was that you thought it might
Not be altogether proper, as you grew
Older, to have a foreign wife.
JASON. You may be quite sure of one
    thing,
Medea. It was not because of any
Woman that I made this royal
Marriage. It was as I said before:
Because I wanted security for you,
And also to be the father
Of royal children bound by blood
To our two children: a thing which
Would have brought welfare to all of
    us.
MEDEA. I don't want the kind of welfare
That is brought by suffering. I
Don't want the kind of safety
Which ends in sorrow.
JASON. Reflect on that opinion, Medea;
It will make you wiser. Don't
Search for sorrow in prosperity.
Don't keep looking for pain
In a piece of good luck.
MEDEA. Go on; mock me. You at least
Have a home to turn to. But I
Am going into exile, and alone.
JASON. It was you who made this choice;
There is no one else to blame.
MEDEA. How so? By marrying and de-
    serting you?
JASON. You called down an evil curse on
    the royal house.
MEDEA. I have brought a curse to your
    own house too, I think.
JASON. Well, I don't propose to go
Into this any further. But if
You'd like to take along some
Of my money into exile, please

Say so. I am prepared to be
Generous on this point, and even
To give you letters to friends of mine
Abroad who will treat you well. It
    would
Be madness for you to refuse this offer.
It will be to your own gain,
Medea, if you give up your anger.
MEDEA. I will never accept favors
From friends of yours; and I'll
Accept nothing from you, so please
Don't offer it. Gifts from a coward
Bring luck to no one.
JASON. Very well then. I call upon
The gods to witness that I
Have tried in every way to help
You and the children. It is
You who refuse my offers. It
Is you who are stubbornly rejecting
Your friends. And for this,
Medea, you will surely suffer.
MEDEA. Please go! I can see you are
Longing to be with your new
Sweetheart. Aren't you lingering
Too long outside her bedroom? Go,
And taste the joys of your wedding.
Go, and God help you; you may end
By regretting this kind of wedding!
    [JASON *goes out.*]

Strophe 1

CHORUS. When love has passed its limits
It brings no longer good:
It brings no peace or comfort to any
    soul.
Yet while she still moves mildly there is
    no fire
So sweet as that which is lit by the god-
    dess of love.
Oh never, upon me, Cypris,[10]
Send forth from your golden bow
The unerring arrow poisoned with de-
    sire!

Antistrophe 1

Let my heart be temperate: for that
Is the wisest gift of the gods.
Let not that terrible goddess drive
Me to jealousy or rage! Oh let me never
Be one of those who incessantly are
    driven
To some new, forbidden longing!
Let her guide us gently toward the man
    we choose;
Let her bless our beds with repose.

Strophe 2

O my country, my own home
Let me never leave my city,
Let me never lose my way
In the dark and pitiless life
Where each new day brings sorrow!
O, let me first succumb
To death, yes, let me die
Before I suffer the hopeless
Grief of the loss of a home!

Antistrophe 2

I have seen it with my own eyes,
I have heard my own heart tell me:
There is no city, no,
No friend who will give you pity
In the hour of your deepest woe.
O, let him perish in darkness
Who is faithless to his friends
And lets his heart stay frozen!
Let no such man be my friend! [MEDEA
*has been sitting in despair on the stairway
during this song.* AEGEUS *enters.*]

AEGEUS. Joy to you, Medea! This is the
best
Kind of greeting between old friends!
MEDEA. And joy to you, Aegeus, son
Of Pandion, king of Athens!
How does it happen that you
Have set foot in this country?
AEGEUS. I have come from the ancient
oracles of Phoebus.
MEDEA. And why did you visit that great
center of prophecy?
AEGEUS. I went to ask how I might
bring fertility to my seed.
MEDEA. Tell me, has your life been
childless hitherto?
AEGEUS. Some divine visitation, I think,
has made me childless.
MEDEA. Have you a wife, or not?
AEGEUS. I have, Medea.
MEDEA. And what did Phoebus tell you
about begetting children?
AEGEUS. Words far too subtle for any
man to understand.
MEDEA. Is it proper for you to tell me
what he said?
AEGEUS. Certainly; what I need is
cleverness like yours.
MEDEA. Then what were the God's
words? Tell me, if I may hear them.
AEGEUS. That I shouldn't loosen the
hanging neck of the wine skin . . .
MEDEA. Till when? What must you do
first? Where must you go?

AEGEUS. Till I have returned again to
my native home.
MEDEA. Then why have you come sailing to this land?
AEGEUS. There is a man called Pittheus,
who is King of Troezen.
MEDEA. A son of Pelops, so they say,
and a man of piety.
AEGEUS. I want to discuss this oracle of
the God with him.
MEDEA. He is a man full of skill and experience in these matters.
AEGEUS. As well as the dearest of my
old spear-bearing friends.
MEDEA. Good luck to you then! And
success to your wishes!
AEGEUS. But why do you look so pale
and woebegone?
MEDEA. O Aegeus, my husband has
turned out to be the vilest of men!
AEGEUS. What do you mean? Tell me
what has made you so unhappy.
MEDEA. Jason is wronging me, and utterly without provocation.
AEGEUS. What has he done? Tell me
more clearly, Medea.
MEDEA. He has taken another wife to
take my place.
AEGEUS. Does he really dare to do such
a cruel thing!
MEDEA. He does indeed! He loved me
once, but no longer.
AEGEUS. Has he fallen in love? Has he
wearied of your bed?
MEDEA. Ah, he's a great lover! But
never true to his love. . . .
AEGEUS. Let him go, then, if he is really
as bad as you say.
MEDEA. He's in love with the idea of
marrying royalty.
AEGEUS. And who is the father of this
princess? Please go on.
MEDEA. Her father is Kreon, King of
Corinth.
AEGEUS. Indeed, Medea, I understand
your grief.
MEDEA. I am lost. And there is more: I
am being banished!
AEGEUS. Banished? By whom? This is
something new you tell me.
MEDEA. Kreon is driving me from
Corinth into banishment.
AEGEUS. Does Jason consent? This is a
contemptible thing.
MEDEA. Not in so many words, but he
Has not really opposed it.

O Aegeus, I beg you, I
Implore you, by your beard
And by your knees, I beseech you,
Have pity on me! Have pity
On a friend who is in trouble!
Don't let me wander about
In exile! Let me come
To your land of Athens, let me
Find refuge in your halls! And there,
With heaven's consent, you may find
Your love grow fertile and be
Blessed with children, and your life
At last end happily. You don't
Know, Aegeus, how good your luck
Has been, for I shall end
Your sterility; I shall bring
Power to your seed; for I know
Of drugs that can do this.
AEGEUS. There are many reasons, my
  dear
Lady, why I should like to do
This for you: first, for the sake
Of the children you promise me
(For in that matter, frankly,
I'm at my wits' end). But
Let me state my position. If
You arrive in Athens, I shall
Stand by you as I am bound
To do. But I must warn you
First, my friend: I won't agree
To take you with me. If you
Arrive at my halls of our own
Accord, you shall live there in safety;
I shan't surrender you to anyone.
But you yourself must manage
Your escape from this land, for
I have no wish to incur ill
Will among my friends here.
MEDEA. Very well. So be it. Make me a
  formal
Pledge on this, and I shall be satisfied.
AEGEUS. Do you distrust me? What is it
  that troubles you?
MEDEA. I trust you, yes. But the house
Of Pelias and Kreon as well
Both detest me. If you are bound
To me by an oath, then,
When they come to drag me
Away from your country, I know
You will remain true to your
Vow and stand by me. Whereas,
If it's only a promise, you might
Not be in a position to resist
Their demands; for I am weak,
And they have both money and
A royal house to help them.

AEGEUS. You show considerable
  foresight
In these matters, I must say. Still,
If you insist, I shan't refuse you.
From my own point of view, too,
It might be just as well to have
An excuse like this oath to present
To your enemies. . . . Now name your
  gods.
MEDEA. Swear by the plain of Earth.
And by my father's father Helios,
The Sun God, and in one sweeping
Phrase by the whole host of the gods
  . . .
AEGEUS. Swear to do what or not to do
  what?
Tell me.
MEDEA. Swear that you will never cast
Me from your land, nor ever
As long as you live, allow
An enemy of mine to carry me away.
AEGEUS. I swear by the Earth,
And by the holy light of Helios.
The Sun God, and by the entire
Host of the gods, that I will
Abide by the terms you have just made.
MEDEA. Very well. And if you should
  fail,
What curse are you willing to incur?
AEGEUS. Whatever happens to such as
  disregard the gods.
MEDEA. Go in peace, Aegeus. All is well,
Now; I shall arrive in your city
As soon as I possibly can—after
I have done what I must do,
And accomplished what I desire.
  [AEGEUS *goes out.*]
CHORAGUS. May Hermes, the God of
  Travelers,
Go with you on your way, Aegeus,
And bring you safely home!
And may you find the thing you have
  been seeking
For so long; you seem to be a generous
  man.
MEDEA. O Zeus, and Justice who are
The child of Zeus, and light
Of the Sun God! Now, my friends,
Has come the hour of my triumph.
Now I have started on the road;
Now I know that I shall bring
Revenge on the ones I hate. For
At the very moment that my doom
Looked darkest of all, this man
Aegeus appeared, like a harbor for all
My hopes; and to him I can

Fasten the cable of my ship
When I come to the town and fortress
Of Pallas Athene.[11] And now let me
Tell you of all my plans. Listen;
They will not be idle words,
Or pleasant. I shall send
A servant to Jason and ask
For an interview, and when he
Comes, I shall be soft and conciliatory;
I shall tell him that I've thought
Better of it; that I agree; that
Even the treacherous marriage
With the princess, which he is
Celebrating, strikes me as sensible,
And all for the best. However,
I shall beg him to let the children
Stay on here: not that I'd dream
Of leaving my babies to be
Insulted in a land that loathes
Me; but purely as a stratagem;
And I shall kill the king's
Own daughter. For I shall
Send them gifts in their
Little hands, to be offered
To the bride to preserve
Them from banishment; a finely
Woven dress and a golden diadem.
And if she takes these things and
Wears them on her body, she,
And whoever touches her, will
Die in anguish; for I shall
Rub these things with deadly
Poison. That will be that;
But it is the next thing I
Must do which sets me weeping.
For I will kill my own
Children! My own dear children,
Whom none shall take from me.
And when I have brought ruin
On the house of Jason, I shall
Flee from the land and flee
From the murder of my children;
For it will be a terrible deed
To do! It isn't easy, my friends,
To bear the insults of one's
Enemies. And so it shall be.
For what have I left in life?
I have no land, no home,
No harbor to protect me.
What a fool I was to leave
My father's house, to put
My faith in the words
Of a Greek! And for this
He will pay the penalty,
So help me God. Never
Again will he see his sons

Alive; never will he have a son
By this new bride. For she
Is doomed to die, and die
Hideously from the power
Of my poison. Let no man
Think I am a feeble, frail-hearted
Woman who sits with folded
Hands: no, let them know me
For the opposite of that—one
Who knows how to hurt her
Enemies and help her friends.
It is lives like that that
Are longest remembered!
CHORAGUS. Since you have told us all
    your plans,
Let me say this to you:
Do not do this thing!
MEDEA. There is nothing else I can do.
It is forgivable that you should
Say this: but remember, you
Have not suffered as I have!
CHORAGUS. Woman, can you really
    bring yourself
To destroy your own flesh and blood?
MEDEA. I can; for in that way
I can hurt my husband most cruelly.
CHORAGUS. And yourself as well! You
    will be
The most miserable of women.
MEDEA. Then I will; no matter.
No word of warning now can stop me!
[*The* NURSE *enters;* MEDEA *turns to her.*]
Go and tell Jason to come to me.
And remember, I send you
On a mission of great secrecy. Say
Nothing of the plans I have
Prepared; don't say a word, if
You are loyal to your mistress
And loyal to the race of women!

Strophe 1
CHORUS. Oh listen! We know of a
    land[12]
Where dwell the sons of Erechtheus,
Fed on the food of wisdom, and blessed
    with the blood of gods,
Raised on a soil still holy and still un-
    conquered; and there
Moving amid that glittering air where
    the legends
Say that lovely Harmonia,[13] the golden-
    haired,
Brought forth the Sacred Nine, the Pie-
    rian Muses!

Antistrophe 1
And where they say that Cypris

The divine one, sailed to draw the
Water out of the wandering stream of
  Cephisus, and the gentle
Winds passed over the land: and over
  her glittering
Head the long, sweet-scented rose
  wreaths
Were wound by the Loves, who sit by
  Wisdom's side
And in all virtuous deeds are the
  friends of mortals.

Strophe 2
Then how can this city, O how
Can these sacred streams which wel-
  come
Only the ones they love,
O tell, how can they welcome
You who are evil? You
Who are killing your sons? O think
Of the sons you plan to slay,
Of the blood you plan to shed!
We beg, we implore you, Medea:
Do not murder your sons!

Antistrophe 2
Oh where can your hand or your heart,
Medea, find the hardness
To do this frightful thing
Against your sons? O how
Can you look on them and yet
Not weep, Medea? How
Can you still resolve to slay them?
Ah, when they fall at your feet
For mercy, you will not be able
To dip your hands in their blood!
  [JASON *enters.*]
JASON. I have come at your bidding,
Medea. For although you are
Full of hatred for me, this small
Favor I will grant you; I will
Listen to you, my lady, and hear
What new favor you are asking.
MEDEA. Jason, I beg your forgiveness
  for what
I have said! Surely you can afford
To forgive my bad temper; after all,
There has been much love between us!
I have reasoned with myself and
Reproached myself. "Poor fool," I said,
"Why am I so distraught? Why am I
So bitter against all good advice,
Why am I so angry at the rulers
Of this country, and my husband
As well, who does the best he can
For me in marrying a royal princess,

And in having royal children, who
Will be brothers to my own? Why not
Stop complaining? What is wrong
With me, when the gods are being
So generous? Don't I have my
Children to consider? Don't I realize
That we are exiles after all, and in need
Of friends?" . . . And when I had
Thought all this over, Jason, I saw
How foolish I'd been, and how silly
My anger. So now I agree with you.
I think you are well advised in
Taking this new wife; and I was mad.
I should have helped you in your plans,
  I
Should have helped arrange the wed-
  ding.
I should have stood by the wedding
Bed and been happy to wait
On your bride. But we women are—
Well, I shan't say entirely
Worthless; but we are what we
Are. And you men shouldn't stoop
To our level; you shouldn't reply
To our folly with folly. I give in.
I admit I was wrong.
I have thought better of it all. . . . [*She
  turns toward the house.*]
Come, come, my children, come
Out from the house, come
And greet your father and then
Say goodbye to him. Give up
Your anger, as your mother does;
Be friends with him again,
Be reconciled! [*The* ATTENDANT *enters
  with the children.*]
We have made peace now,
Our bitterness is gone. Take
His right hand. . . . O God:
I can't help thinking of the things
That lie dark and hidden
In the future! . . . My children,
Hold out your arms—the way
One holds them in farewell after
A long, long life. . . . I am close
To tears, my children! I am
Full of fear! I have ended
My quarrel with your father at last,
And look! My eyes are full of tears.
CHORAGUS. And our eyes too
Are filling with tears. O,
Do not let disasters worse
Than the present descend on you!
JASON. I approve of your conduct,
Medea; not that I blame you
For anything in the past. It is

Natural for a woman to be
Furious with her husband when he
Begins to have other affairs. But
Now your heart has grown more sen-
sible,
And your mind is changed for the bet-
ter;
You are behaving like a woman
Of sense. And of you, my sons,
Your father will take good care,
And make full provision,
With the help of God. And I
Trust that in due time you
With your brothers will be among
The leading men in Corinth. All
You need to do is grow up,
My sons; and as for your future,
You may leave it safely
In the hands of your father,
And of those among the gods
Who love him. I want to see
You when you've grown to be
Men, tall and strong, towering
Over my enemies! . . . Medea, why
Are your eyes wet with tears?
Why are your cheeks so pale? Why
Are you turning away? Don't these
Happy words of mine make you
happy?
MEDEA. It is nothing. I was only think-
ing about these children.
JASON. Take heart, then. I shall look
after them well.
MEDEA. I will, Jason. It is not that I
don't trust you.
Women are weak; and tears come easily
to them.
JASON. But why should you feel dis-
turbed about the children?
MEDEA. I gave birth to them, Jason.
And when
You prayed that they might live long,
My heart filled with sorrow to think
That all these things must happen.
Well now; I have told you some of the
things
I called you here to tell you; now
Let me tell you the rest. Since
The ruler of this land has resolved
To banish me, and since I am
Considered an enemy, I know
It will be best for me not to stand
In your way, or in the way of the king,
By living here. I am going forth
From this land into exile. But these
Children—Oh let them feel that you

Are protecting them, and beg
Of Kreon not to banish them!
JASON. I doubt whether I can persuade
him; still, I will try.
MEDEA. Or at least ask your wife
To beg her father to do this,
And give the children reprieve from
exile.
JASON. I will try; and with her I think I
shall succeed.
MEDEA. She's a woman, after all;
And like all other women.
And I will help you in this matter;
I will send the children to her
With gifts far more exquisite,
I am sure, than any now to be
Found among men—a finely woven
Dress and a diadem of chased gold.
There; let one of the servants
Go and bring me these lovely orna-
ments. [*One of the* ATTENDANTS *goes
into the house.*]
And she'll be happy not in one way,
But a thousand! With so splendid
A man as you to share her bed,
And with this marvelous gown
As well, which once the Sun-God
Helios
Himself, my father's father, gave his
descendants. [*The* ATTENDANT *returns
with the poisoned dress and diadem.*]
There, my children, take these wed-
ding
Presents in your hands and take
Them as an offering to the royal
Princess, the lucky bride;
Give them to her; they are
Not gifts to be scorned.
JASON. But why do you give them away
So rashly, Medea? Do you think
The royal palace is lacking
In dresses, or in gold? Keep them.
Don't give them away. If my wife
Really loves me, I am sure she
Values me more highly than gold.
MEDEA. No, don't say that, Jason.
For I have heard it said
That gifts can persuade even
The gods; and men are governed
More by gold than by words! Luck
Has fallen on your bride, and
The gods have blessed her fortune.
She is young: she's a princess.
Yet I'd give not only gold
But my life to save my children
From exile. Enter that rich palace

Together, children, and pray
To your father's new bride; pray
To my mistress, and beg her
To save you from banishment. Present
This garment to her; and above
All let her take the gift from you
With her own hands. Go; don't linger.
And may you succeed, and bring
Back to your mother the good
News for which she longs! [*Exit* JASON,
the ATTENDANT, *and the children bearing
the poisoned gifts.*]

Strophe 1
CHORUS. No hope now remains for the
   children's lives!
No, none. Even now they are moving
   toward death;
The luckless bride will accept the gown
   that will kill her,
And take the golden crown, and hold it
In her hand, and over her golden head
   will
Lift the garment of Hell!

Antistrophe 1
The grace and glitter of gold will en-
   chant her:
She will put on the golden robe and
   wear
The golden crown: and deck herself as
   the bride
Of death. And thus, pitiful girl,
Will fall in the trap; will fall and perish.
She will never escape!

Strope 2
You likewise, O miserable groom,
Who planned a royal wedding cere-
   mony,
Do not see the doom you are bringing
Upon your sons; and the terrible death
Now lying in wait for your bride. Pity
Upon you! O, how you are fallen!

Antistrophe 2
And I weep for you too, Medea,
O mother who are killing your sons,
Killing in revenge for the loss
Of your love: you whom your lover Ja-
   son
Now has deserted and betrayed
To love and marry another mistress!
   [*Enter* ATTENDANT *with the children.*]
ATTENDANT. My lady, your children are
   reprieved

From exile. The royal bride was
Delighted to receive your gifts
With her own hands. And there
Is peace between her and your chil-
   dren. . . .
Medea! Why are you so distraught
At this lucky moment? Why are you
Turning your head away? Are you not
Happy to hear this news, my lady?
MEDEA. Oh, I am lost!
ATTENDANT. That cry does not suit the
   news I have brought you, surely!
MEDEA. I am lost! I am lost!
ATTENDANT. Have I told you of some
   disaster, without knowing it?
Was I wrong in thinking that my news
   was good?
MEDEA. You have said what you have
   said:
I do not wish to blame you.
ATTENDANT. Then why are you so dis-
   turbed? Why are you weeping?
MEDEA. Oh, my old friend, I can't help
   weeping.
It was I, it was I and the gods,
Who planned these things so badly.
ATTENDANT. Take heart, Medea. Your
   sons will bring
You back to your home some day.
MEDEA. And I'll bring others back to
   their homes,
Long before that happens!
ATTENDANT. And often before this,
   mothers have been
Parted from their sons. Bear your
   troubles,
Medea, as all mortals must bear them.
MEDEA. I will, I will. Go back into the
   house;
And plan your daily work for the chil-
   dren. [*The* ATTENDANT *goes into the
   house, and* MEDEA *turns to her children.*]
MEDEA. O my children, my children,
You will still have a city,
You will still have a home
Where you can dwell forever, far
Away from me, far forever
From your mother! But I am
Doomed to go in exile to another
Land, before I can see you
Grow up and be happy, before
I can take pride in you, before
I can wait on your brides and
Make your marriage beds, or hold
The torch at your wedding
Ceremony! What a victim I am

Of my own self-will! It was
All in vain, my children, that I
Reared you! It was all in vain
That I grew weary and worn,
And suffered the anguish and pangs
Of childbirth! Oh pity me! Once
I had great hopes for you; I
Had hopes that you'd look after
Me in my old age, and that you'd
Lovingly deck my body with your own
    hands
When I died, as all men hope
And desire. But now my lovely
Dreams are over. I shall love
You both. I shall spend my life
In grief and solitude. And never
Again will you see your mother
With your own dear eyes; now
You will pass into another
Kind of life. Ah, my dear children,
Why do you look at me like this?
Why are you smiling your sweet
Little smiles at me? O children,
What can I do? My heart gives
Way when I see the joy
Shining in my children's eyes.
O women, I cannot do it! . . .
Farewell to all my plans!
I will take my babies away with me
From this land. Why should I hurt
Their father by hurting them? Why
Should I hurt myself doubly? No:
I cannot do it. I shall say
Good-bye to my plans. . . . And yet—
Oh, what is wrong with me? Am I
Willing to see my enemies go
Unpunished? Am I willing to be
Insulted and laughed at? I shall
Follow this thing to the end.
How weak I am! How weak to let
My heart be touched by these soft
Sentiments! Go back into the house.
My children. . . . And if anyone
Prefers not to witness my sacrifice,
Let him do as he wishes! My poor
Heart, have pity on them, let them
Go, the little children! They'll bring
Cheer to you, if you let them
Live with you in exile! . . . No,
By all the avenging Furies,
This shall not be! Never shall I
Surrender my children to the insolence
and mockery of my enemies! It is
Settled. I have made my decision.
And since they must die, it is
Their mother who must kill them.

Now there is no escape for the young
Bride! Already the crown is on
Her head; already the dress is
Hanging from her body; the royal
Bride, the princess is dying! This
I know. And now—since I
Am about to follow a dreadful
Path, and am sending them
On a path still more terrible—
I will simply say this:
I want to speak to my children. [*She
calls and the children come back; she takes
them in her arms.*]
Come, come, give me your hands,
My babies, let your mother kiss
You both. O dear little hands,
Dear little lips: how I have
Loved them! How fresh and young
Your eyes look! How straight
You stand! I wish you joy
With all my heart; but not here;
Not in this land. All that you
Had here your father has stolen
From you. . . . How good it is
To hold you, to feel your soft
Young cheeks, the warm young
Sweetness of your breath. . . . Go now;
Leave me. I cannot look at you
Any longer. . . . I am overcome. . . .
    [*The children go into the house again.*]
Now at last I understand the full
Evil of what I have planned.
At last I see how my passion
Is stronger than my reason: passion,
Which brings the worst of woes to mor-
    tal man. [*She goes out at the right, to-
    ward the palace.*]
CHORAGUS. Many a time before
I have gone through subtler reasoning,
Many times I have faced graver ques-
    tioning
Than any woman should ever have to
    face:
But we women have a goddess to help
    us, too,
And lead us into wisdom.
Not all of us; perhaps not many;
But some women there are who are ca-
    pable of wisdom.
And I say this: that those who have
    never
Known the fullness of life and never
    had children,
Are happier far than those who are
    parents.
For the childless, who never discover

whether
Their children grow up to be a cause
for joy or for pain,
Are spared many troubles:
While those who know in their houses
The sweet presence of children—
We have seen how their lives are
wasted by worry.
First they fret about how they shall
raise them
Properly; and then how to leave them
enough
Money to live on; and then they con-
tinue
To worry about whether all this labor
Has gone into children that will turn
out well
Or turn out ill: and the question re-
mains unanswered.
And let me tell of one more trouble,
The last of all, and common to all mor-
tals:
For suppose you have found enough
For them to live on, and suppose
You have seen them grow up and turn
out well;
Still, if fate so decrees it, Death
Will come and tear away your children!
What use is it, then, that the gods
For the sake of children
Should pile on us mortals,
After all other griefs,
This grief for lost children? This grief
Greater by far than any? [MEDEA *comes
out of the house.*]
MEDEA. I have been waiting in suspense,
Ladies; I have waited long to learn
How things will happen. . . . Look!
I see one of Jason's
Servants coming toward us; he is
Panting; and the bearer of news,
I think; of bad news. . . . [*A* MESSENGER
rushes in.]
MESSENGER. Fly, Medea, fly!
You have done a terrible thing, a thing
Breaking all human laws: fly,
Take a ship for the seas,
Or a chariot for the plains!
MEDEA. Why? What reason have you for
asking me to fly?
MESSENGER. She lies dead! The royal
princess
And her father Kreon too!
They have died: they have
Been slain by your poisons!
MEDEA. You bring me blessed news!

Now
And from now on I count you
Among my friends, my benefactors!
MESSENGER. What! Are you insane? Are
you mad,
Medea? You have done an outrage
To the royal house: Does it make you
Happy to hear it? Can you hear
Of this dreadful thing without horror?
MEDEA. I too have words to say in reply
To yours. Do not be impatient,
My friend. Tell me: how did
They die? You will make me doubly
Happy if you say they died in anguish!
MESSENGER. When those two children,
your own babies.
Medea, came with their father and en-
tered
The palace of the bride, it gave
Joy to all of us, the servants
Who have suffered with you; for in-
stantly
All through the house we whispered
That you had made up your quarrel
With your husband. One of us kissed
Your children's hands, and another
Their golden hair, and I myself was so
Overjoyed that I followed them in per-
son
To the women's chambers. And there
stood
Our mistress, whom we now serve
Instead of you; and she kept her eyes
fixed
Longingly on Jason. When she caught
Sight of your children, she covered up
Her eyes, and her face grew pale, and
she
Turned away, filled with petulance
At their coming. But your husband
tried
To soothe the bride's ill humor,
And said: "Do not look so unkindly
At your friends! Do not feel angry:
Turn your head to me once more, and
Think of your husband's friends
As your own friends! Accept these
gifts,
And do this for my sake: beg
Of your father not to let these children
Be exiled!" And then, when she saw
The dress, she grew mild and yielded,
And gave in to her husband. And be-
fore
The father and the children had gone
Far from her rooms, she took

The gorgeous robe and put it on;
And she put the golden crown on her curly
Head, and arranged her hair in the shining
Mirror, smiling as she saw herself reflected.
And then she rose from her chair
And walked across the room, stepping
Softly and delicately on her small
White feet, filled with delight at the gift,
And glancing again and again at the delicate
Turn of her ankles. And after that
It was a thing of horror we saw.
For suddenly her face changed its color,
And she staggered back, and began
To tremble as she ran, and reached
A chair just as she was about
To fall to the ground. An old
Woman servant, thinking no doubt that this
Was some kind of seizure, a fit
Sent by Pan, or some other god,
Cried out a prayer: and then, as she
Prayed, she saw the flakes of foam
Flow from her mouth, and her eyeballs
Rolling, and the blood fade from her face.
And then it was a different prayer
She uttered, a terrible scream, and one
Of the women ran to the house
Of the King, and another to the newly
Wedded groom to tell him what had
Happened to the bride; and the whole
House echoed as they ran to and fro.
Let me tell you, time enough for a man
To walk two hundred yards passed
Before the poor lady awoke from her trance,
With a dreadful scream and opened
Her eyes again. A twofold torment was
Creeping over her. The golden diadem
On her head was sending forth a violent
Stream of flame, and the finely
Woven dress which your children gave
Her was beginning to eat into the poor
Girl's snowy soft flesh. And she
Leapt from her chair, all on fire,
And started to run, shaking her head
To and fro, trying to shake off
The diadem; but the gold still
Clung firmly, and as she shook her hair

The fire blazed forth with double fury.
And then she sank to the ground, helpless.
Overcome; and past all recognition
Except to the eye of a father—
For her eyes had lost their normal
Expression, and the familiar look
Had fled from her face, and from the top
Of her head a mingled stream
Of blood and fire was pouring. And
It was like the drops
Falling from the bark of a pine
Tree when the flesh dropped away
From her bones, torn loose
By the secret fangs of the poison.
And terror kept all of us
From touching the corpse; for we
Were warned by what had happened.
But then her poor father who knew
Nothing of her death, came suddenly
Into the house and stumbled over
Her body, and cried out as he folded
His arms about her and kissed her,
And said: "O my child, my poor child,
Which of the gods has so cruelly
Killed you? Who has robbed me of you,
Who am old and close to the grave? O
My child let me die with you!" And he
Grew silent and tried to rise to his
Feet again, but found himself
Fastened to the finely spun dress,
Like vine clinging to a laurel
Bough, and there was a fearful
Struggle. And still he tried to lift
His knees, and she writhed and clung
To him; and as he tugged, he
Tore the withered flesh from
His bones. And at last he could
No longer master the pain, and
Surrendered, and gave up the ghost.
So there they are lying together:
And it is a sight to send us weeping. . . .
As for you, Medea, I will say
Nothing of your own problems: you
Yourself must discover an escape
From punishment. I think, and I have
Always thought, the life of men
Is a shadow; and I say without
Fear that those who are wisest among
All men, and probe most deeply
Into the cause of things—they are
The ones who suffer most deeply! For,
Believe me, no man among mortals is happy;
If wealth comes to a man, he may be

Luckier than the rest; but happy—
never. [*Exit* MESSENGER.]
CHORAGUS. It seems that heaven has
sent, today,
A heavy load of evils upon Jason;
And he deserves them. Alas, poor girl,
Poor daughter of Kreon! I pity you
And your anguish; and now you are
Gone, all because of your wedding with
Jason:
Gone away to the halls of Hades!
MEDEA. Women, the deed shall be
done! Swiftly
I will go and kill my children,
And then leave the land: and not
Delay nor let them be killed by
A crueler hand. For die they
Must in any case: and if
They must be slain, it is I,
Their mother who gave them life,
Who must slay them! O my heart,
My heart, arm yourself in steel!
Do not shrink back from this hideous
Thing which has to be done! Come,
My hand, and seize the sword, take it
And step forward to the place where
My life's true sorrow begins! Do not
Be a coward . . . do not think
Of the children, and how dear
They are to you who are their mother!
For one brief day, Medea, forget
Your children; and then forever
After you may mourn; for though
You will kill them, they were dear to
you,
Very dear. . . . I am a miserable
woman! [*With a cry* MEDEA *rushes into
the house.*]

Strophe
CHORUS. O Earth, and the all-brighten-
ing
Beam of the Sun, look, look
Upon this lost one, shine upon
This pitiful woman before she raises
Her hand in murder against her sons!
For lo! these are the offspring
Of thine own golden seed, and I fear
That divine blood may now be shed by
men!
O Light flung forth by Zeus,
O heavenly Light,
Hold back her hand,
Restrain her, and drive out
This dark demoniac fury from the
house!

Antistrophe
Was it all in vain, Medea,
What you suffered in bearing your
sons?
Was it utterly in vain
You bore the babes you loved, after
you left
Beyond you that dark passage through
the straits
And past the perilous rocks, the blue
Symplegades?
Wretched woman, how has it happened
That your soul is torn by anger
And darkened by the shadow of death?
Heavy will be the price
To pay for kindred blood staining the
earth!
Heavy the woe sent down by heaven
On the house of the killer for such a
crime! [*A cry is heard from the children
within.*]
CHORAGUS. Listen! Do you hear? Do
you hear the children crying?
Hate-hardened heart! O woman born
for evil!
FIRST SON. [*Crying within.*] What can I
do? How can I run from mother's
hands?
SECOND SON. [*Crying within.*] I don't
know! We are lost, we are lost,
brother!
CHORAGUS. Shall I enter the house? Oh
surely
I must help! I must save these children
from murder!
FIRST SON. [*Within.*] Help, in the name
of heaven! We need your help!
SECOND SON. [*Within.*] Now, now it's
coming closer! The sword is falling!
CHORAGUS. Oh, you must be made of
stone or steel,
To kill the fruit of your womb
With your own hands, unhappy
woman!
I have heard of only one,
Of all the women who ever lived, who
laid
Her hand upon her children: it was
Ino,
Who was driven insane by the Gods
When the wife of Zeus sent her wan-
dering from her home.
And wild with grief at killing her chil-
dren,
She flung herself from the sea-battered
cliff

And plunged into the sea, and in the
sea
Rejoined her two dead children.
Can anything so dreadful ever happen
again?
Woe flows forth from the bed of a
woman
Whom fate has touched with trouble!
Great is the grief that they have
brought on men! [*Enter* JASON *with his
attendants.*]
JASON. Ladies, you have been sitting
near
This house! Tell me! Is Medea, is
The woman who did this frightful
Thing, still in the house? Or has she
Fled already? Oh believe me, she'll
have
To hide deep under the earth, or fly
On wings through the sky, if she
Hopes to escape the vengeance
Of the royal house! Does she dream,
After killing the ruler of the land, that
She herself can escape from these halls
Unpunished? But I am thinking of her
Far less than of her children; for she
Herself will duly suffer at the hands
Of those she wronged. Ladies, I have
Come to save the lives of my
Boys, lest the royal house should
Harm them in revenge for this
Vile thing done by their mother.
CHORAGUS. O Jason, you do not yet
know
The full depth of your misery, or
You would not have spoken those
words!
JASON. What do you mean? Is she plan-
ning to kill me also?
CHORAGUS. Your boys are dead; dead at
their mother's hand.
JASON. What have you said, woman?
You are destroying me!
CHORAGUS. You may be sure of this:
your children are dead.
JASON. Oh where did she kill them?
Was it here, or in the house?
CHORAGUS. Open the doors, and you
will see their murdered bodies!
JASON. Open the doors! Unlock the
bolts! Undo
The fastenings! And let me see this
twofold
Horror! Let me see my murdered boys!
Let me look on her whom I shall kill in
vengeance! [*His attendants rush to the*

door. MEDEA *appears above the house in a
chariot drawn by dragons. The dead chil-
dren are at her side.*],
MEDEA. Why do you batter at the doors?
Why do you shake these bolts,
In quest of the dead and their
Murderess? You may cease your
trouble,
Jason; and if there is anything you
Want to say, then say it! Never
Again shall you lay your hand on me;
So swift is the chariot which my
Father's father gave me, the Sun God
Helios, to save me from my foes!
JASON. Horrible woman! Now you are
utterly
Loathed by the gods, and by me, and
By all mankind. You had the heart
To stab your children; you,
Their own mother, and to leave me
Childless; you have done these fearful
Things, and still you dare to gaze
As ever at the sun and the earth! Oh
I wish you were dead! Now at last
I see clearly what I did not see
On the day I brought you, loaded
With doom, from your barbarous home
To live in Hellas—a traitress
To your father and your native land.
On me too the gods have hurled
The curse which has haunted you. For
You killed your own brother at his
Fireside, and them came aboard our
Beautiful ship the Argo. And that
Was how it started. And then you
Married me, and slept with me, and
Out of your passion bore me children;
And now, out of your passion, you
have
Killed them. There are no women in all
Of Greece who would dare to do this.
And
Yet I passed them over, and chose you
Instead; and chose to marry my own
Doom! I married not a woman,
But a monster, wilder of heart than
Scylla[14] in the Tyrrhenian Sea!
But even if I hurled a thousand
Insults at you, Medea, I know
I could not wound you: your heart
Is so hard, so utterly hard. Go,
You wicked sorceress; I see
The stains of your children's blood
Upon you! Go; all that is left
To me now is to mourn. I shall never
Lie beside my newly wedded love;

I shall never have my sons, whom
I bred and brought up, alive
Beside me to say a last farewell!
I have lost them forever,
And my life is ended.

MEDEA. O Jason, to these words of
   yours
I could make a long reply; but
Zeus, the father, himself well knows
All that I did for you, and what
You did to me. Destiny has
Refused to let you scorn my love,
And lead a life of pleasure,
And mock at me; nor were the royal
Princess and the matchmaker
Kreon destined to drive me into exile,
And then go untormented! Call me
A monster if you wish; call me
The Scylla in the Tyrrhenian Sea.
For now I have torn your heart:
And this indeed was destined, Jason!

JASON. You too must feel the pain; you
   will share my grief, Medea.

MEDEA. Yes; but the pain is milder,
   since you cannot mock me!

JASON. O my sons, it was an unspeakable mother who bore you!

MEDEA. O my sons, it was really your
   father who destroyed you!

JASON. But I tell you: it was not my
   hand that slew them!

MEDEA. No; but your insolence, and
   your new wedding slew them!

JASON. And you thought this wedding
   cause enough to kill them?

MEDEA. And you think the anguish of
   love is trifling for a woman?

JASON. Yes, if her heart is sound: but
   yours makes all things evil.

MEDEA. Your sons are dead, Jason!
   Does it hurt you when I say this?

JASON. They will live on, Medea, by
   bringing suffering on you.

MEDEA. The gods are well aware who
   caused all this suffering.

JASON. Yes, the gods are well aware.
   They know your brutal heart.

MEDEA. You too are brutal. And I am
   sick of your bitter words!

JASON. And I am sick of yours. Oh
   Medea, it will be easy to leave you.

MEDEA. Easy! Yes! And for me too!
   What, then, do you want?

JASON. Give me those bodies to bury,
   and to mourn.

MEDEA. Never! I will bury them myself.

I will take them myself to Hera's
Temple, which hangs over the Cape,
Where none of their enemies can
Insult them, and where none can defile
Their graves! And in this land
Of Corinth I shall ordain a holy
Feast and sacrifice, forever after,
To atone for this guilt of killing.
And I shall go myself to Athens.
To live in the House of Aegeus,
The son of Pandion. And I predict
That you, as you deserve, will die
Without honor; and your head crushed
By a beam of the shattered *Argo*[15];
And then you will know the bitter
End of all my love for you!

JASON. May the avenging fury of our
   sons
Destroy you! May Justice destroy
You, and repay blood with blood!

MEDEA. What god, what heavenly power
Would listen to you? To a breaker
Of oaths? To a betrayer of love?

JASON. Oh, you are vile! You sorceress!
   Murderess!

MEDEA. Go to your house. Go, and bury
   your bride.

JASON. Yes, I shall go; and mourn for
   my murdered sons.

MEDEA. Wait; do not weep yet, Jason!
   Wait till age has sharpened your
   grief!

JASON. Oh my sons, whom I loved! My
   sons!

MEDEA. It was I, not you, who truly
   loved them.

JASON. You say you loved them; yet you
   killed them.

MEDEA. Yes. I killed them to make you
   suffer.

JASON. Medea, I only long to kiss them
   one last time.

MEDEA. Now, now, you long to kiss
   them!
Now you long to say farewell:
But before, you cast them from you!

JASON. Medea, I beg you, let me touch
   the little bodies of my boys!

MEDEA. No. Never. You speak in vain.

JASON. O Zeus, high in your heaven,
Have you heard these words?
Have you heard this unutterable
Cruelty? Have you heard this
Woman, this monster, this murderess?
And now I shall do the only
Thing I still can do! Yes!

I shall cry, I shall cry
Aloud to heaven, and call on
The gods to witness how you
Killed my sons, and refused
To let me kiss them farewell,
Or touch them, or give them burial!
Oh, I'd rather never have seen them
    live,
Than have seen them slaughtered so!
    [*The chariot carries* MEDEA *away.*]
CHORAGUS. Many, many are the things
That Zeus determines, high on the
    Olympian throne;
Many the things beyond men's under-
    standing
That the gods achieve, and bring to
    pass.
Many the things we think will happen,
Yet never happen.
And many the things we thought could
    never be,
Yet the gods contrive.
Such things have happened on this day,
And in this place!

1. The rocks at the entrance to the Black Sea.
2. Medea's homeland.
3. A mountain in Thessaly.
4. Jason's uncle, who usurped the throne of Iolcos from Jason, then sent the latter to find the Golden Fleece.
5. Jason was not regarded as legally married to Medea because she was a foreigner.
6. A famous fountain in Corinth.
7. The goddess invoked by sorcerers and witches.
8. Jason argues that he owes his safety to the goddess of love, not to Medea.
9. A mythical poet and musician who accompanied Jason on the *Argo*.
10. Another name for Aphrodite.
11. I.e., to Athens.
12. This is a hymn to the beauty of Athens.
13. Aphrodite's daughter.
14. After Scylla betrayed her father for love of a foreigner, the gods turned her into a sea monster living in a cave on the straits dividing Italy from Sicily.
15. This is indeed the ignoble death that Jason suffered.

Lysistrata

Aristophanes

At the same time that tragedy developed in classical Greece, there also flourished another, separate dramatic form: comedy. The origins of this form are even more obscure than those of tragedy, the rules or guidelines under which it operated less clearly known, and the surviving commentary from ancient writers far less complete and less enlightening. Of the scripts themselves, only the works of one playwright in the genre known as Old Comedy survive, but his plays are among the greatest comedies ever created by man. That writer is Aristophanes.

Aristophanes was born around 450 B.C. and died around 388. He was a citizen of Athens and a property owner on the nearby island of Aegina. It is not clear what conditions he found in the comic drama when he first began working in that form around 430 B.C., but what he made of it is well demonstrated in the eleven scripts that have survived (out of approximately forty that he is reported to have written). He took a lively interest in both the politics and the philosophical pursuits of fifth-century-B.C. Athens, railing against the series of warlike policies that led eventually to the destruction of Athenian society. By the time of his death, Aristophanes found himself in a far more repressive society, with censorship and political subjugation forcing him to modify his theatrical approaches a great deal. His last play is the only surviving example of what is known to scholars as Middle Comedy, a domestic form far different from Aristophanes' early work but which led directly to the comic standards that have dominated Occidental theater for more than two millennia.

Old Comedy, at least as exemplified by Aristophanes' earlier ten plays, was a truly exuberant form. It loosely resembled the tragedies, at least in that it used a chorus and a limited number of principal speaking actors, began the play with a prologue followed by a parodos, and ended it with an exodos, while the portion between consisted of alternating choral songs and acted episodes. In tone and style, however, comedy and tragedy were utter opposites, for the comic choruses were often animals or extremely foolish human beings cavorting wildly, the characters were usually fools and buffoons even if they represented great leaders or gods, and the plots were based rather simply on a "happy idea" that was a complete inversion of ordinary human behavior but that was so presented as to point up the foolishness of that behavior. The entire proceedings were conducted in an atmosphere reminiscent of the fertility rites out of which comedy may well have evolved, with obscene language and gesture, frank and open representation of sexual activity and excretion, and especially the prominent display of oversized phalluses, the symbols as well as the source of fertility in so many early cultures. The conclusion of most of these plays is a joyous celebration, with feasting, drinking, and a ritual marriage or pairing off of lovers.

Aristophanes' plays make such extensive use of political satire and topical jokes that could be understood only by an audience thoroughly familiar with life in fifth-century-B.C. Athens that many of the surviving eleven have been enjoyed more in the study than in the theater. Those which have been staged with some frequency in modern times, however, include *The Birds* (144 B.C.), in which an ideal society is established (and ridiculed) by a group of birds in Cloudcuckooland, and *The Frogs* (405), in which, after the death of Euripides and Sophocles, Dionysus journeys into Hades to bring at least one great tragic poet back to earth. There is a contest in Hades between Euripides and Aeschylus, and the latter is finally chosen to return. Full appreciation of even this play, however, depends on an audience's intimate knowledge of many of the tragedies of each author, for the work of each is parodied with cutting effectiveness. *The Clouds* (423) is noteworthy especially for the fact that Socrates is lowered to the stage in a basket to solve the play's problems, a trenchant parody of the *deus ex machina* device used so frequently by Euripides; the style and tone of the play are fascinatingly preserved in the tradition that, at the first performance, Socrates rose to his feet in the audience so that the spectators might compare his features with the mask of the actor portraying him. *Plutus* (388) is chiefly interesting because it was Aristophanes' last surviving play and illustrates the change in form to Middle Comedy. It is far more domestic in its outlook and subject matter, and the use of a chorus has dwindled simply to dancing interludes (no words are provided in the text) between episodes.

By far the most popular of Aristophanes' plays with modern audiences has been *Lysistrata*, first produced in 411 B.C., when Athens's long war with its neighbors seemed as though it would never end, but when any real peace could have been achieved only by a total Athenian surrender. It is another tribute to the breadth of taste and vision of Athenian audiences that Aristophanes could successfully produce an antiwar play under those circumstances. The universality of the antiwar theme is part of the explanation for the play's success with later generations, but the chief explanation undoubtedly lies in the "happy idea" that Aristophanes conceived around which to build the plot—that wars could be ended if the women on both sides went on a sex strike. Sex as a central subject of humor is as old as recorded history and as new as the latest locker-room joke, and no one has used it more effectively in the theater than Aristophanes. The openly sexual nature of *Lysistrata*'s plot is frank, free, healthy, and unfettered in a style completely opposite to the sniggering and leering of most modern sex comedies, wherein the underlying assumption is that open discussion of such matters is funny only because it is dirty. Lysistrata's sex strike is as natural as a hunger strike, as its participants deny themselves and others one of the basic necessities of their lives and then suffer grotesquely until an accommodation has been reached. The plot of *Lysistrata* is episodic in the modern sense of that word, for, once the "happy idea" has been stated in the prologue, the bulk of the play consists of laughing at the way various individuals and groups react to the strain it places upon them. As soon as these comic possibilities have been explored, there is a resolution scene in which Lysistrata's purposes are realized, peace is concluded, and there can ensue the final scene of revelry and merrymaking that generally characterized the happy outcome of Old Comedy. The chorus consists of half-choruses that debate with each other the merits of the "happy idea"; this structural device may be a remnant of prehistoric phallic worship rather than an innovative idea on Aristophanes' part. Another structural feature with more historic than theatrical justification is the *parabasis*, a scene in which the comic chorus traditionally dropped character and addressed the audience directly, expressing the playwright's ideas on why he should win the competition or on political issues of the day. This concept, although modified, is preserved in *Lysistrata* in two places, but it had disappeared completely by the time of *Plutus*. More and more it was evidently found to be an unacceptable interruption in the flow of dramatic action. The choral sections in *Lysistrata*, including the two parabases, are nevertheless important in this play, and one must remember that singing and dancing of a particularly exuberant and unrestrained nature provided a chief part of their theatrical effectiveness.

Characterization is not one of Aristophanes' strong points. Later comic writers, as they moved away from the social and political concerns of Aristophanes into more domestic problems, developed to a fine art the portrayal of comic characters with depth and finesse, but Aristophanes seems to have been satisfied to create caricatures. Lysistrata is a dynamic leader; Kleonike, Myrrhine, and Lampito are one-dimensional figures used to explore the comic possibilities of the plot (even their names, in Greek, are ribald clues to their essential nature, a practice that English Restoration drama later developed to a high art); and all of the men are fools. One feels no particular sense of loss respecting the lack of development of these characters, for Aristophanes' interest clearly lay elsewhere, and his efforts there more than compensate for what might otherwise have been done with characterization; still, the difference between Old Comedy and everything that came after it is notable in this respect as in others.

Lysistrata is much more than an antiwar play, although it is certainly that. Aristophanes made it plain in a number of his plays that he considered war a stupid pursuit, but he does not indulge in the usual pathos or moral outrage that characterizes most antiwar literature. The basic impracticability of his plot idea only serves to sharpen the satire with which he attacks the governmental policies that have led to war in the first place. Since men have created these governmental policies, Aristophanes soon finds himself writing a feminist polemic as well, in which the fundamental good sense of Lysistrata and her women colleagues is measured against the foolishness of male pride and ego which has led to war. Ultimately, Aristophanes seems to be suggesting, as did Giraudoux more than two thousand years later, that "nothing is ever so wrong in the world that a sensible woman can't set it right in the course of an afternoon." Although comic exaggeration is obviously a factor, Aristophanes makes some telling points in the battle of the sexes, all of them on the side of greater equality. In addition to these political and social issues, Aristophanes indulges in literary satire as well, poking fun at the works of other playwrights and poets. Furthermore, his play is full of personal digs at individuals, usually governmental and social leaders, that would surely lead to libel suits if he were writing today. Modern political cartoons go further than do most media in treating public figures like fools or madmen, but the theater cannot usually go so far. Evidently, for Aristophanes and his audiences no subject was too sacred, and no idea escaped his probing wit. Only with a rather full set of footnotes can one fully appreciate today the range of Aristophanes' ideas; it is fortunate that *Lysistrata* has enough material for universal humor so that audiences are willing to let the more obscure references go by.

Aristophanes' language is so earthy that only in recent years has it become legal to print a fairly accurate translation of his work. Although this earthiness was certainly funny to an Athenian audience, it was not scandalous, and the same play contains beautiful poetry as well. Thus, Aristophanes' mastery of language may be expressed with equal felicity either in a well-turned metaphor or in a particularly neat *double entendre*. *Lysistrata* presents an additional problem in the need to render into English the Spartan accent as opposed to the Athenian, a problem of a sort that is always the despair of translators; in the original these accents were rendered both with satirical accuracy and with theatrically effective humor.

Since the work of the other writers of Old Comedy has not survived, it is accurate in one sense to say that Aristophanes has no peers with whom he might be compared. The high esteem in which his work was held in the ancient world strongly suggests that the very best of Old Comedy does, indeed, survive, but of course there is no way to be sure. In a broader sense, however, one may certainly compare Aristophanes' work with that of any other comic dramatist anywhere, and most critics would rank him with the handful of greatest such writers of all time. Ultimately the finest of comic playwriting is measured not by numbers of laugh lines, not by witty plots, not even by comic characters, but by the inherent comic genius of a play's central images. A sex strike to end wars is so brilliant a comic notion in and of itself that the excellence of Aristophanes' work was assured almost before he began it. Socrates in a basket and a debate between Aeschylus and Euripides in Hades are similarly rich images, and few other writers beyond Molière and Shakespeare have produced similarly effective central comic notions for their plays. The range and exuberance of Aristophanes' work, the very special society in which he lived and the special way in which he was able to interact with it, put him in a comic class by himself. Old Comedy has never been duplicated in nearly 2,500 years, and it seems unlikely ever to recur.

N.B. The footnotes for *Lysistrata* were written by the translator and have been somewhat abridged by the present editor (who has added one note of his own, appropriately labeled). Professor Parker's complete notes, as well as his Introduction and Glossary, may be found in *Lysistrata,* translated by Douglass Parker (Mentor, 1964).

Lysistrata

Translated by Douglass Parker

Characters

Lysistrata ⎫
Kleonike ⎬ Athenian women
Myrrhine ⎭
Lampito, a Spartan woman
Ismenia, a Boiotian girl
Korinthian girl
Policewoman
Koryphaios of the men
Chorus of old men of Athens
Koryphaios of the women
Chorus of old women of Athens
Commissioner of Public Safety
Four Policemen
Kinesias, Myrrhine's husband
Child of Kinesias and Myrrhine
Slave
Spartan herald
Spartan ambassador
Flute-player
Athenian women
Peloponnesian women
Peloponnesian men
Athenian men

SCENE: *A street in Athens. In the background, the Akropolis; center, its gateway, the Propylaia. The time is early morning.*[1] *Lysistrata is discovered alone, pacing back and forth in furious impatience.*

LYSISTRATA. *Women!*
Announce a debauch in honor of Bacchos,
a spree for Pan, some footling fertility fieldday,
and traffic stops—these streets are absolutely clogged
with frantic females banging on tambourines. No urging
for an orgy! But *today*—there's not one woman here. [*Enter* KLEONIKE.]

Correction: one. Here comes my next-door neighbor.
—Hello, Kleonike.[2]
KLEONIKE. Hello to *you*, Lysistrata.
—But what's the fuss? Don't look so barbarous, baby;
knitted brows just aren't your style.
LYSISTRATA. It doesn't
matter, Kleonike—I'm on fire right down to the bone.
I'm positively ashamed to be a woman—a member
of a sex which can't even live up to male slanders!
To hear our husbands talk, we're *sly:* deceitful,
always plotting, monsters of intrigue . . .
KLEONIKE [*Proudly.*] That's us!
LYSISTRATA. And so we agreed to meet today and plot
an intrigue that really deserves the name of monstrous . . .
and WHERE are the women? Slyly asleep at home—
they won't get up for anything!
KLEONIKE. Relax, honey.
They'll be here. You know a woman's way is hard—[*Aside.*] (mainly the way out of the house): fuss over hubby,
wake the maid up, put the baby down, bathe him,
feed him . . .
LYSISTRATA. Trivia. They have more fundamental business
to engage in.
KLEONIKE. Incidentally, Lysistrata, just why are you
calling this meeting? Nothing teeny, I trust?
LYSISTRATA. Immense.
KLEONIKE. Hmmm. And pressing?

121

LYSISTRATA. Unthinkably tense.

KLEONIKE. Then where IS everybody?

LYSISTRATA. Nothing like that. If it were,
we'd already be in session. Seconding motions.
—No, *this* came to hand some time ago. I've spent
my nights kneading it, mulling it, filing it down. . . .

KLEONIKE. Too bad. There can't be very much left.

LYSISTRATA. Only this:
the hope and salvation of Hellas lies with the WOMEN!

KLEONIKE. Lies with the women? Now *there's* a last resort.

LYSISTRATA. It lies with us to decide affairs of state
and foreign policy. The Spartan Question: Peace
or Extirpation?

KLEONIKE. How *fun!* I cast an Aye for Extirpation!

LYSISTRATA. The Utter Annihilation of every last Boiotian?

KLEONIKE. AYE!—I mean Nay. Clemency, please, for those scrumptious eels.[3]

LYSISTRATA. And as for Athens . . . I'd rather not put
the thought into words. Just fill in the blanks, if you will.
—To the point: If we can meet and reach agreement
here and now with the girls from Thebes and the Peloponnese,
we'll form an alliance and save the States of Greece!

KLEONIKE. Us? Be practical. Wisdom from women? There's nothing
cosmic about cosmetics—and Glamor is our only talent.
All we can do is *sit,* primped and painted,
made up and dressed up, [*Getting carried away in spite of her argument.*] ravishing in saffron wrappers,
peekaboo peignoirs, exquisite negligees, those chic,
expensive little slippers that come from the East. . . .

LYSISTRATA. Exactly. You've hit it. I see our way to salvation
in just such ornamentation—in slippers and slips, rouge
and perfumes, negligees and decolletage. . . .

KLEONIKE. How so?

LYSISTRATA. So effectively that not one husband will take up his spear
against another . . .

KLEONIKE. Peachy! I'll have that kimono dyed . . .

LYSISTRATA. . . . or shoulder his shield . . .

KLEONIKE. . . . squeeze into that daring negligee . . .

LYSISTRATA. . . . or unsheathe his sword!

KLEONIKE. . . . and buy those slippers!

LYSISTRATA. Well, now. Don't you think the girls should be here?

KLEONIKE. *Be* here? Ages ago—they should have flown! [*She stops.*]
But no. You'll find out. These are authentic Athenians:
no matter what they do, they do it late.

LYSISTRATA. But what about the out-of-town delegations? There isn't
a woman here from the Shore; none from Salamis . . .

KLEONIKE. *That's* quite a trip. They usually get on board
at sunup. Probably riding at anchor now.

LYSISTRATA. I thought the girls from Acharnai would be here first.
I'm especially counting on them. And they're not here.

KLEONIKE. I think Theogenes' wife is under way.
When I went by, she was hoisting her sandals. . . . [*Looking off right.*] But look!
Some of the girls are coming! [*Women enter from the right.* LYSISTRATA *looks off to the left where more—a ragged lot—are straggling in.*]

LYSISTRATA. And more over here!

KLEONIKE. Where did you find *that* group?

LYSISTRATA. They're from the outskirts.[4]

KLEONIKE. Well, that's something. If you haven't done anything else,
you've really ruffled up the outskirts.
[MYRRHINE *enters guiltily from the right.*]

MYRRHINE. Oh, Lysistrata,
we aren't late, are we? Well, *are* we? Speak to me!

LYSISTRATA. What is it, Myrrhine? Do

you want a medal for tardiness?
Honestly, such behavior, with so much
  at stake . . .
MYRRHINE. I'm sorry. I couldn't find my
  girdle in the dark.
And anyway, we're here now. So tell us
  all about it,
whatever it is.
KLEONIKE. No, wait a minute. Don't
begin just yet. Let's wait for those girls
  from Thebes
and the Peloponnese.
LYSISTRATA. Now *there* speaks the
  proper attitude. [LAMPITO, *a strapping
  Spartan woman, enters left, leading a
  pretty Boiotian girl* (ISMENIA) *and a
  huge, steatopygous* KORINTHIAN.]
And here's our lovely Spartan. Hel*lo*,
  Lampito
dear. Why, darling, you're simply ravishing! Such
a blemishless complexion—so clean, so
  out-of-doors!
And will you look at that figure—the
  pink of perfection!
KLEONIKE. I'll bet you could strangle a
  bull.
LAMPITO. I calklate so.[5]
Hit's fitness whut done it, fitness and
  dancin'. You know
the step? [*Demonstrating.*] Foot it out
  back'ards an' toe yore twitchet. [*The
  women crowd around* LAMPITO.]
KLEONIKE. What unbelievably beautiful
  bosoms!
LAMPITO. Shuckins,
whut fer you tweedlin' me up so? I feel
  like a heifer
come fair-time.
LYSISTRATA. [*Turning to* ISMENIA.] And
  who is this young lady here?
LAMPITO. Her kin's purt-near the blue-
  bloodiest folk in Thebes—
the First Fam'lies of Boiotia.
LYSISTRATA. [*As they inspect* ISMENIA.]
  Ah, picturesque Boiotia:
her verdant meadows, her fruited
  plain . . .
KLEONIKE. [*Peering more closely.*] Her
  sunken
garden where no grass grows.[6] A cultivated country.
LYSISTRATA. [*Gaping at the gawking
  Korinthian.*]
And who is *this*—er—little thing?
LAMPITO. She hails

from over by Korinth, but her kinfolk's
  quality—mighty
big back there.
KLEONIKE. [*On her tour of inspection.*]
  She's mighty big back *here*.
LAMPITO. The womenfolk's all assemb-
  lied. Who-all's notion
was this-hyer confabulation?
LYSISTRATA. Mine.
LAMPITO. Git on with the give-out.
I'm hankerin to hear.
MYRRHINE. Me, too! I can't imagine
what could be so important. Tell us
  about it!
LYSISTRATA. Right away.—But first, a
  question. It's not
an involved one. Answer yes or no. [*A
  pause.*]
MYRRHINE. Well, ASK it!
LYSISTRATA. It concerns the fathers of
  your children—your husbands, ab-
  sent
on active service. I know you all have
  men
abroad.—Wouldn't you like to have
  them home?
KLEONIKE. My husband's been gone for
  the last five months! Way up
to Thrace, watchdogging military
  waste.[7] It's horrible!
MYRRHINE. Mine's been posted to Pylos
  for seven whole months!
LAMPITO. My man's no sooner rotated
  out of the line
than he's plugged back in. Hain't no
  discharge in this war!
KLEONIKE. And lovers can't be had for
  love or money,
not even synthetics. Why, since those
  beastly Milesians
revolted and cut off the leather trade,
  that handy
do-it-yourself kit's *vanished* from the
  open market!
LYSISTRATA. If I can devise a scheme
  for ending the war,
I gather I have your support?
KLEONIKE. You can count on me!
If you need money, I'll pawn the shift
  off my back—

[*Aside.*] (and drink up the cash before
  the sun goes down.)
MYRRHINE. Me, too! I'm ready to split
  myself right up
the middle like a mackerel, and give

you half!

LAMPITO. Me, too! I'd climb Taygetos Mountain plumb to the top to git the leastes' peek at Peace!

LYSISTRATA. Very well, I'll tell you. No reason to keep a secret. [*Importantly, as the women cluster around her.*]

We can force our husbands to negotiate Peace,

Ladies, by exercising steadfast Self-Control—

By Total Abstinence . . . [*A pause.*]

KLEONIKE. From WHAT?

MYRRHINE. Yes, what?

LYSISTRATA. You'll do it?

KLEONIKE. Of course we'll do it! We'd even *die!*

LYSISTRATA. Very well,

then here's the program: Total Abstinence from SEX! [*The cluster of women dissolves.*]

—Why are you turning away? Where are you going? [*Moving among the women.*]

—What's this? Such stricken expressions! Such gloomy gestures!

—Why so pale? —Whence these tears? —What IS this?

Will you do it or won't you? Cat got your tongue?

KLEONIKE. Afraid I can't make it. Sorry. *On with the War!*

MYRRHINE. Me neither. Sorry. *On with the War!*

LYSISTRATA. *This* from my little mackerel? The girl who was ready, a minute

ago, to split herself right up the middle?

KLEONIKE. [*Breaking in between* LYSISTRATA *and* MYRRHINE.]

Try something else. Try anything. If you say so,

I'm willing to walk through fire barefoot. But not

to give up SEX—there's nothing like it, Lysistrata!

LYSISTRATA [*To* MYRRHINE.]

And you?

MYRRHINE. Me, too! I'll walk through fire.

LYSISTRATA. *Women!*

Utter sluts, the entire sex! Will-power, nil. We're perfect raw material for Tragedy,

the stuff of heroic lays. "Go to bed with

a god

and then get rid of the baby"—that sums us up! [*Turning to* LAMPITO.]

—Oh, Spartan, be a dear. If *you* stick by me,

just you, we still may have a chance to win.

Give me your vote.

LAMPITO. Hit's right onsettlin' fer gals to sleep all lonely-like, withouten no humpin'.

But I'm on yore side. We shore need Peace, too.

LYSISTRATA. You're a darling—the only woman here

worthy of the name!

KLEONIKE. Well, just suppose we *did*

as much as possible, abstain from . . . what you said,

you know—not that we *would*—could something like that

bring Peace any sooner?

LYSISTRATA. Certainly. Here's how it works:

We'll paint, powder, and pluck ourselves to the last

detail, and stay inside, wearing those filmy

tunics that set off everything we *have*—and then

slink up the men. They'll snap to attention, go absolutely

mad to love us—but we won't let them. We'll Abstain.

—I imagine they'll conclude a treaty rather quickly.

LAMPITO. [*Nodding.*]

Menelaos he tuck one squint at Helen's bubbies

all nekkid, and plumb throwed up. [*Pause for thought.*] Throwed up his sword.

KLEONIKE. Suppose the men just leave us flat?

LYSISTRATA. In that case,

we'll have to take things into our own hands.

KLEONIKE. There simply isn't any reasonable facsimile!

—Suppose they take us by force and drag us off

to the bedroom against our wills?

LYSISTRATA. Hang on to the door.

KLEONIKE. Suppose they beat us?

LYSISTRATA. Give in—but be bad sports. Be nasty about it—they don't enjoy

these forced
affairs. So make them suffer. Don't
worry; they'll stop
soon enough. A married man wants
harmony—
cooperation, not rape.
KLEONIKE. Well, I suppose so. . . .
[*Looking from* LYSISTRATA *to* LAMPITO.]
If *both* of you approve this, then so do
we.
LAMPITO. Hain't worried over our menfolk none. We'll bring 'em
round to makin' a fair, straightfor'ard
Peace
withouten no nonsense about it. But
take this rackety
passel in Athens: I misdoubt no one
could make 'em
give over thet blabber of theirn.
LYSISTRATA. They're our concern.
Don't worry. We'll bring them around.
LAMPITO. Not likely.
Not long as they got ships kin still sail
straight,
an' thet fountain of money up thar in
Athene's temple.[8]
LYSISTRATA. That point is quite well
covered: We're taking over
the Akropolis, including Athene's temple, today.
It's set: Our oldest women have their
orders.
They're up there now, pretending to
sacrifice, waiting
for us to reach an agreement. As soon
as we do,
they seize the Akropolis.
LAMPITO. The way you put them
thengs,
I swear I can't see how we kin possibly
lose!
LYSISTRATA. Well, now that it's settled,
Lampito, let's not lose
any time. Let's take the Oath to make
this binding.
LAMPITO. Just trot out thet-thar Oath.
We'll swear it.
LYSISTRATA. Excellent.
—Where's the policewoman? [*A huge*
GIRL, *dressed as a Skythian archer (the
Athenian police) with bow and circular
shield, lumbers up and gawks.*]—What
are *you* looking for? [*Pointing to a spot
in front of the women.*]
Put your shield down here. [*The girl
obeys.*] No, hollow *up!* [*The girl reverses*

the shield. Lysistrata looks about brightly.]
—Someone give me the entrails. [*A
dubious silence.*]
KLEONIKE. Lysistrata, what kind
of an Oath are we supposed to swear?
LYSISTRATA. The Standard.
Aischylos used it in a play, they say—
the one where
you slaughter a sheep and swear on a
shield.
KLEONIKE. Lysistrata, you *do not* swear
an Oath for *Peace* on a *shield!*
LYSISTRATA. What Oath do you want?
[*Exasperated.*] Something bizarre and
expensive?
A fancier victim—"Take one white
horse and disembowel"?
KLEONIKE. *White horse?* The symbolism's
too obscure.[9]
LYSISTRATA. *Then how do we swear this
oath?*
KLEONIKE. Oh, *I* can tell you
that, if you'll let me. First, we put an
enormous
black cup right here—hollow up, of
course.
Next, into the cup we slaughter a jar of
Thasian
wine, and swear a mighty Oath that we
won't . . .
dilute it with water.
LAMPITO. [*To Kleonike.*] Let me
corngratulate you—
that were the beatenes' Oath I ever
heerd on!
LYSISTRATA. [*Calling inside.*]
Bring out a cup and a jug of wine!
[TWO WOMEN *emerge, the first staggering
under the weight of a huge black cup, the
second even more burdened with a tremendous wine jar.* KLEONIKE *addresses
them.*]
KLEONIKE. You darlings!
What a tremendous display of pottery!
[*Fingering the cup.*] A girl
could get a glow just *holding* a cup like
this! [*She grabs it away from the first
woman, who exits.*]
LYSISTRATA. [*Taking the wine jar from the
second* SERVING WOMAN *(who exits), she
barks at* KLEONIKE.]
Put that down and help me butcher this
boar! [KLEONIKE *puts down the cup,
over which she and* LYSISTRATA *together
hold the jar of wine (the "boar").* LYSIS-
TRATA *prays.*]

O Mistress Persuasion,
O Cup of Devotion,
Attend our invocation:
Accept this oblation,
Grant our petition,
Favor our mission.

[LYSISTRATA *and* KLEONIKE *tip up the jar and pour the gurgling wine into the cup.* MYRRHINE, LAMPITO, *and the others watch closely.*]

MYRRHINE. Such an attractive shade of blood. And the spurt—
pure Art!

LAMPITO. Hit shore do smell mighty purty! [LYSISTRATA *and* KLEONIKE *put down the empty wine jar.*]

KLEONIKE. Girls, let me be the first [*Launching herself at the cup.*] to take the Oath!

LYSISTRATA [*Hauling* KLEONIKE *back.*]
You'll have to wait your turn like everyone else.
—Lampito, how do we manage with this mob? Cumbersome.
—Everyone places her right hand on the cup. [*The women surround the cup and obey.*]
I need a spokeswoman. One of you to take
the Oath in behalf of the rest. [*The women edge away from* KLEONIKE, *who reluctantly finds herself elected.*] The rite will conclude
with a General Pledge of Assent by all of you, thus confirming the Oath. Understood? [*Nods from the women.* LYSISTRATA *addresses* KLEONIKE.] Repeat after me:
I will withhold all rights of access or entrance

KLEONIKE. I will withhold all rights of access or entrance

LYSISTRATA. From every husband, lover, or casual acquaintance

KLEONIKE. from every husband, lover, or casual acquaintance

LYSISTRATA. Who moves in my direction in erection.—Go on.

KLEONIKE. who m-moves in my direction in erection. Ohhhhh!
—Lysistrata, my knees are shaky. Maybe I'd better . . .

LYSISTRATA. I will create, imperforate in cloistered chastity,

KLEONIKE. I will create, imperforate in cloistered chastity,

LYSISTRATA. A newer, more glamorous, supremely seductive me

KLEONIKE. a newer, more glamorous, supremely seductive me

LYSISTRATA. And fire my husband's desire with my molten allure—

KLEONIKE. and fire my husband's desire with my molten allure—

LYSISTRATA. But remain, to his panting advances, icily pure.

KLEONIKE. but remain, to his panting advances, icily pure.

LYSISTRATA. If he should force me to share the connubial couch,

KLEONIKE. If he should force me to share the connubial couch,

LYSISTRATA. I refuse to return his stroke with the teeniest twitch.

KLEONIKE. I refuse to return his stroke with the teeniest twitch.

LYSISTRATA. I will not lift my slippers to touch the thatch

KLEONIKE. I will not lift my slippers to touch the thatch

LYSISTRATA. Or submit sloping prone in a hangdog crouch.

KLEONIKE. or submit sloping prone in a hangdog crouch.

LYSISTRATA. If I this oath maintain, may I drink this glorious wine.

KLEONIKE. If I this oath maintain, may I drink this glorious wine.

LYSISTRATA. But if I slip or falter, let me drink water.

KLEONIKE. But if I slip or falter, let me drink water.

LYSISTRATA. —And now the General Pledge of Assent:

WOMEN. A-MEN!

LYSISTRATA. Good. I'll dedicate the oblation. [*She drinks deeply.*]

KLEONIKE. Not too much,
darling. You know how anxious we are to become
allies and friends. Not to mention *staying* friends. [*She pushes* LYSISTRATA *away and drinks. As the women take their turns at the cup, loud cries and alarums are heard offstage.*]

LAMPITO. What-all's that bodacious ruckus?

LYSISTRATA. Just what I told you:
It means the women have taken the Akropolis. Athene's
Citadel is ours! It's time for you to go, Lampito, and set your affairs in order

in Sparta. [*Indicating the other women in Lampito's group.*]
Leave these girls here as hostages.
[LAMPITO *exits left.* LYSISTRATA *turns to the others.*] Let's hurry inside
the Akropolis and help the others shoot the bolts.
KLEONIKE. Don't you think the men will send reinforcements
against us as soon as they can?
LYSISTRATA. So where's the worry?
The men can't burn their way in or frighten us out.
The Gates are ours—they're proof against fire and fear—
and they open only on our conditions.
KLEONIKE. Yes!
That's the spirit—let's deserve our reputations: [*As the women hurry off into the Akropolis.*]
UP THE SLUTS! WAY FOR THE OLD IMPREGNABLES! [*The door shuts behind the women, and the stage is empty. A pause, and the* CHORUS OF MEN *shuffles on from the left in two groups, led by their* KORYPHAIOS. *They are incredibly aged Athenians; though they may acquire spryness later in the play, at this point they are sheer decrepitude. Their normally shaky progress is impeded by their burdens: each man not only staggers under a load of wood across his shoulders, but has his hands full as well—in one, an earthen pot containing fire (which is in constant danger of going out); in the other, a dried vinewood torch, not yet lit. Their progress toward the Akropolis is very slow.*]
KORYPHAIOS OF MEN. [*To the right guide of the* FIRST SEMICHORUS, *who is stumbling along in mild agony.*]
Forward, Swifty, keep 'em in step!
Forget your shoulder.
I know these logs are green and heavy—but duty, boy, duty!
SWIFTY. [*Somewhat inspired, he quavers into slow song to set a pace for his group.*]
I'm never surprised. At my age, life is just one damned thing after another.
And yet, I never thought my wife was anything more than a home-grown bother.
But now, dadblast her, she's a National Disaster!
FIRST SEMICHORUS OF MEN. What a catastrophe—
MATRIARCHY!

They've brought Athene's statue[10] to heel,
they've put the Akropolis under a seal,
they've copped the whole damned commonweal. . . .
What is there left for them to steal?

KORYPHAIOS OF MEN. [*To the right guide of the* SECOND SEMICHORUS—*a slower soul, if possible, than Swifty.*]
Now, Chipper, speed's the word. The Akropolis, on the double!
Once we're there, we'll pile these logs around them, and convene
a circuit court for a truncated trial. Strictly impartial:
With a show of hands, we'll light a spark of justice under
every woman who brewed this scheme. We'll burn them all
on the first ballot—and the first to go is Ly . . . [*Pause for thought.*] is Ly . . . [*Remembering and pointing at a spot in the audience.*] is *Lykon's* wife—and there she is, right over there![11]
CHIPPER. [*Taking up the song again.*]
I won't be twitted, I won't be guyed,
I'll teach these women not to trouble us!
Kleomenes the Spartan tried expropriating our Akropolis[12]
some time ago—
ninety-five years or so—
SECOND SEMICHORUS OF MEN.
but he suffered damaging losses when he ran across US!
He breathed defiance—and more as well:
No bath for six years—you could tell.
We fished him out of the Citadel
and quelled his spirit—but not his smell.
KORYPHAIOS OF MEN. That's how I took him. A savage siege: Seventeen ranks
of shields were massed at that gate, with blanket infantry cover
I slept like a baby. So when mere women (who gall the gods
and make Euripides sick) try the same trick, should I
sit idly by? Then demolish the monument I won at Marathon!
FIRST SEMICHORUS OF MEN. [*Singly.*]
—The last lap of our journey!
—I greet it with some dismay.
—The danger doesn't deter me,—but

it's uphill—all the way.
—Please, somebody,—find a jackass
to drag these logs—to the top.
—I ache to join the fracas,—but
my shoulder's aching—to stop.
SWIFTY. Backward there's no turning.
Upward and onward, men!
And keep those firepots burning, or
we make this trip again.
CHORUS OF MEN. [*Blowing into their
firepots, which promptly send forth clouds
of smoke.*]
With a puff (pfffff) . . .
and a cough (hhhhhh) . . .
The smoke! I'll choke! Turn it off!
SECOND SEMICHORUS OF MEN. [*Singly.*]
—Damned embers.—Should be
muzzled.
—There oughta be a law.
—They jumped me—when I whistled—
and then
they gnawed my eyeballs—raw.
—There's lava in my lashes.
—My lids are oxidized.
—My brows are braised.—These ashes
are
volcanoes—in disguise.
CHIPPER. This way, men. And remem-
ber,
the Goddess needs our aid.
So don't be stopped by cinders. Let's
press on to the stockade!
CHORUS OF MEN. [*Blowing again into their
firepots, which erupt as before.*]
With a huff (hfffff) . . .
and a chuff (chffff) . . .
Drat that smoke. Enough is enough!
KORYPHAIOS OF MEN. [*Signalling the
CHORUS, which has now tottered into position before the Akropolis gate, to stop,
and peering into his firepot.*]
Praise be to the gods, it's awake.
There's fire in the old fire yet.
—Now the directions. See how they
strike you: First, we deposit
these logs at the entrance and light our
torches. Next, we crash
the gate. When that doesn't work, we
request admission. Politely.
When *that* doesn't work, we burn the
damned door down, and smoke
these women into submission. That
seem acceptable? Good.
Down with the load . . . ouch, that
smoke! Sonofabitch! [*A horrible tangle
results as the CHORUS attempts to deposit

the logs. The KORYPHAIOS turns to the
audience.*]
Is there a general in the house? We
have a logistical problem. . . . [*No answer. He shrugs.*]
Same old story. Still at loggerheads
over in Samos.[13] [*With great confusion,
the logs are placed somehow.*]
That's better. The pressure's off. I've
got my backbone back. [*To his firepot.*]
What, pot? You forgot your part in the
plot? Urge that smudge
to be hot on the dot and scorch my
torch. Got it, pot? [*Praying.*]
Queen Athene, let these strumpets
crumple before our attack.
Grant us victory, male supremacy . . .
and a testimonial plaque. [*The men
plunge their torches into firepots and arrange themselves purposefully before the
gate. Engaged in their preparations, they
do not see the sudden entrance, from the
right, of the CHORUS OF WOMEN, led by
their KORYPHAIOS. These wear long
cloaks and carry pitchers of water. They
are very old—though not so old as the
men—but quite spry. In their turn, they
do not perceive the CHORUS OF MEN.*]
KORYPHAIOS OF WOMEN. [*Stopping suddenly.*]
What's this—soot? And smoke as well?
I may be all wet,
but this might mean fire. Things look
dark, girls; we'll have to dash. [*They
move ahead, at a considerably faster pace
than the men.*]
FIRST SEMICHORUS OF WOMEN. [*Singly.*]

Speed! Celerity!	Save our sorority
from arson. Com-	And heat exhaus-
bustion.	tion.
Don't let our sis-	shrivel to blister-
terhood	hood.

Fanned into slag by hoary typhoons.
By flatulent, nasty, gusty baboons.
We're late! Run!
The girls might be done!

[*Tutte.*]

Filling my pitcher	was absolute tor- ture:
The fountains in town	are so *crowded* at dawn,
glutted with masses	of the lower classes
blatting and bat- tering,	shoving, and shat- tering

jugs. But I juggled. my burden, and wriggled
away to extinguish the igneous anguish
of neighbor, and sister, and daughter—
Here's Water!

SECOND SEMICHORUS OF WOMEN. [*Singly.*]
Get wind of the news? The gaffers are loose.
The blowhards are off with fuel enough
to furnish a bathhouse. But the finish is pathos:
They're scaling the heights with a horrid proposal.
They're menacing women with rubbish disposal!
How ghastly—how gauche!
burned up with the trash!

[*Tutte.*]
Preserve me, Athene, from gazing on any
matron or maid auto-da-fé'd.
Cover with grace these redeemers of Greece
from battles, insanity, Man's inhumanity.
Gold-browed goddess, hither to aid us!
Fight as our ally, join in our sally
against pyromaniac slaughter—Haul Water!

KORYPHAIOS OF WOMEN. [*Noticing for the first time the* CHORUS OF MEN, *still busy at their firepots, she cuts off a member of her Chorus who seems about to continue the song.*]
Hold it, What have we here? You don't catch true-blue patriots
red-handed. These are authentic degenerates, male, taken
in flagrante.

KORYPHAIOS OF MEN. Oops. Female troops. This could be upsetting.
I didn't expect such a flood of reserves.

KORYPHAIOS OF WOMEN. Merely a spearhead.
If our numbers stun you, watch that yellow streak spread. We
represent just one percent of one percent of This Woman's Army.

KORYPHAIOS OF MEN. Never been confronted with such backtalk. Can't allow it. Somebody
pick up a log and pulverize that brass.

Any volunteers? [*There are none among the male chorus.*]

KORYPHAIOS OF WOMEN. Put down the pitchers, girls. If they start waving that lumber,
we don't want to be encumbered.

KORYPHAIOS OF MEN. Look, men, a few sharp jabs
will stop that jawing. It never fails. The poet Hipponax
swears by it.[14] [*Still no volunteers. The* KORYPHAIOS OF WOMEN *advances.*]

KORYPHAIOS OF WOMEN. Then step right up. Have a jab at me.
Free shot.

KORYPHAIOS OF MEN. [*Advancing reluctantly to meet her.*] Shut up! I'll peel your pelt. I'll pit your pod.

KORYPHAIOS OF WOMEN. The name is Stratyllis. I dare you to lay one finger on me.

KORYPHAIOS OF MEN. I'll lay on you with a fistful. Er—any specific threats?

KORYPHAIOS OF WOMEN. [*Earnestly.*]
I'll crop your lungs and reap your bowels, bite by bite,
and leave no balls on the body for other bitches to gnaw.

KORYPHAIOS OF MEN. [*Retreating hurriedly.*]
Can't beat Euripides for insight. And I quote: *No creature's found
so lost to shame as Woman.*[15] Talk about realist playwrights!

KORYPHAIOS OF WOMEN. Up with the water, ladies. Pitchers at the ready, place!

KORYPHAIOS OF MEN. Why the water, you sink of iniquity? More sedition?

KORYPHAIOS OF WOMEN. Why the fire, you walking boneyard? Self-cremation?

KORYPHAIOS OF MEN. I brought this fire to ignite a pyre and fricassee your friends.

KORYPHAIOS OF WOMEN. I brought this water to douse your pyre. Tit for tat.

KORYPHAIOS OF MEN. *You'll* douse my fire? Nonsense!

KORYPHAIOS OF WOMEN. You'll see, when the facts soak in.

KORYPHAIOS OF MEN. I have the torch right here. Perhaps I should barbecue *you.*

KORYPHAIOS OF WOMEN. If you have any soap, I could give you a bath.

KORYPHAIOS OF MEN. A bath from those polluted hands?

KORYPHAIOS OF WOMEN. Pure enough for a blushing young bridegroom.

KORYPHAIOS OF MEN. Enough of that insolent lip.

KORYPHAIOS OF WOMEN. It's merely freedom of speech.

KORYPHAIOS OF MEN. I'll stop that screeching!

KORYPHAIOS OF WOMEN. You're helpless outside of the jury-box.

KORYPHAIOS OF MEN. [*Urging his men, torches at the ready, into a charge.*] Burn, fire, burn!

KORYPHAIOS OF WOMEN. [*As the women empty their pitchers over the men.*] And cauldron bubble.

KORYPHAIOS OF MEN. [*Like his troops, soaked and routed.*] Arrrgh!

KORYPHAIOS OF WOMEN. Goodness. What seems to be the trouble? Too hot?

KORYPHAIOS OF MEN. Hot, hell! Stop it! What do you think you're doing?

KORYPHAIOS OF WOMEN. If you must know, I'm gardening. Perhaps you'll bloom.

KORYPHAIOS OF MEN. Perhaps I'll fall right off the vine! I'm withered, frozen, shaking . . .

KORYPHAIOS OF WOMEN. Of course. But providentially, you brought along your smudgepot. The sap should rise eventually. [*Shivering, the* CHORUS OF MEN *retreats in utter defeat. A* COMMISSIONER OF PUBLIC SAFETY[16] *enters from the left, followed quite reluctantly by a squad of police—four Skythian archers. He surveys the situation with disapproval.*]

COMMISSIONER. Fire, eh? Females again—spontaneous combustion of lust. Suspected as much. Rubadub-dubbing, incessant incontinent keening for wine, damnable funeral foofaraw for Adonis resounding from roof to roof— heard it all before . . . [*Savagely, as the* KORYPHAIOS OF MEN *tries to interpose a remark.*] and WHERE? The ASSEMBLY! Recall, if you can, the debate on the Sicilian Question: That bullbrained demagogue Demostratos (who will rot, I trust)

rose to propose a naval task force. His wife, writhing with religion on a handy roof, bleated a dirge: "BEREFT! OH WOE OH WOE FOR ADONIS!" And so of course Demostratos, taking his cue, outblatted her: "A DRAFT! ENROLL THE WHOLE OF ZAKYNTHOS!" His wife, a smidgin stewed, renewed her yowling: "OH GNASH YOUR TEETH AND BEAT YOUR BREASTS FOR ADONIS!" And so of course Demostratos (that god-detested blot, that foul-lunged son of an ulcer) gnashed tooth and nail and voice, and bashed and rammed his program through. And THERE is the Gift of Women: MORAL CHAOS!

KORYPHAIOS OF MEN. Save your breath for actual felonies, Commissioner; see what's happened to us! Insolence, insults, these we pass over, but not lese-majesty: We're flooded with indignity from those bitches' pitchers—like a bunch of weak-bladdered brats. Our cloaks are sopped. We'll sue!

COMMISSIONER. Useless. Your suit won't hold water. Right's on their side. For female depravity, gentlemen, WE stand guilty— we, their teachers, preceptors of prurience, accomplices before the fact of fornication. We sowed them in sexual license, and now we reap rebellion. The proof? Consider. Off we trip to the goldsmith's to leave an order: "That bangle you fashioned last spring for my wife is sprung. She was thrashing around last night, and the prong popped out of the bracket. I'll be tied up all day—I'm boarding the ferry right now—but my wife'll be home. If you get the time, please stop by the house in a bit

and see if you can't do something—
anything—to fit
a new prong into the bracket of her
bangle." And bang.
Another one ups to a cobbler—young,
but no apprentice,
full kit of tools, ready to give his awl—
and delivers this gem: "My wife's new
sandals are tight.
The cinch pinches her pinkie right
where she's sensitive.
Drop in at noon with something to
stretch her cinch
and give it a little play." And a cinch it
is.
Such hanky-panky we have to thank for
today's
Utter Anarchy: I, a Commissioner of
Public
Safety, duly invested with extraordinary powers
to protect the State in the Present
Emergency, have secured
a source of timber to outfit our fleet
and solve
the shortage of oarage. I need the
money immediately . . .
and WOMEN, no less, have locked me
out of the Treasury! [*Pulling himself
together.*]
—Well, no profit in standing around.
[*To one of the archers.*] Bring
the crowbars. I'll jack these women
back on their pedestals!
—WELL, you slack-jawed jackass?
What's the attraction?
Wipe that thirst off your face. I said
*crow*bar, not saloon!
—All right, men, all together. Shove
those bars
underneath the gate and HEAVE!
[*Grabbing up a crowbar.*] I'll take this
side.
And now let's root them out, men,
ROOT them out.
One, Two . . . [*The gates to the Akropolis
burst open suddenly, disclosing* LYSIS-
TRATA. *She is perfectly composed and
bears a large spindle. The* COMMIS-
SIONER *and the* POLICE *fall back in con-
sternation.*]
LYSISTRATA. Why the moving equip-
ment?
I'm quite well motivated, thank you,
and here I am.
Frankly, you don't need crowbars

nearly so much as brains.
COMMISSIONER. Brains? O name of infamy! Where's a policeman? [*He grabs
wildly for the* FIRST ARCHER *and shoves
him toward* LYSISTRATA.]
Arrest that woman! Better tie her
hands behind her.
LYSISTRATA. By Artemis, goddess of the
hunt, if he lays a finger
on me, he'll rue the day he joined the
force! [*She jabs the spindle viciously at
the* FIRST ARCHER, *who leaps, terrified,
back to his comrades.*]
COMMISSIONER. What's this—retreat?
Never! Take her on the flank. [*The*
FIRST ARCHER *hangs back. The* COMMIS-
SIONER *grabs the* SECOND ARCHER.]
—Help him.—Will the two of you
kindly TIE HER UP? [*He shoves them
toward* LYSISTRATA. KLEONIKE, *carrying
a large chamber pot, springs out of the entrance and advances on the* SECOND
ARCHER.]
KLEONIKE. By Artemis, goddess of the
dew, if you so much
as touch her, I'll stomp the shit right
out of you! [*The two* ARCHERS *run back
to their group.*]
COMMISSIONER. *Shit?* Shameless!
Where's another policeman? [*He
grabs the* THIRD ARCHER *and propels him
toward* KLEONIKE.]
Handcuff *her* first. Can't stand a foul-
mouthed female. [MYRRHINE, *carrying
a large, blazing lamp, appears at the entrance and advances on the* THIRD
ARCHER.]
MYRRHINE. By Artemis, bringer of light,
if you lay a finger
on her, you won't be able to stop the
swelling! [*The* THIRD ARCHER *dodges
her swing and runs back to the group.*]
COMMISSIONER. *Now* what? Where's an
officer? [*Pushing the* FOURTH ARCHER
toward MYRRHINE.] Apprehend that
woman!
I'll see that *somebody stays to take the
blame!* [ISMENIA *the Boiotian, carrying a
huge pair of pincers, appears at the entrance and advances on the* FOURTH AR-
CHER.]
ISMENIA. By Artemis, goddess of
Tauris, if you go near
that girl, I'll rip the hair right out of
your head! [*The* FOURTH ARCHER *retreats hurriedly.*]

COMMISSIONER. What a colossal mess: Athens' Finest—
finished! [*Arranging the* ARCHERS.] — Now, men, a little *esprit de corps.* Worsted
by women? Drubbed by drabs? *Never!* Regroup,
reform that thin red line. Ready? CHARGE! [*He pushes them ahead of him.*]
LYSISTRATA. I warn you. We have four battalions behind us—
full-armed combat infantrywomen, trained
from the cradle. . . .
COMMISSIONER. Disarm them, Officers! Go for the hands!
LYSISTRATA. [*Calling inside the Akropolis.*] MOBILIZE THE RESERVES! [*A horde of* WOMEN, *armed with household articles, begins to pour from the Akropolis.*] Onward, you ladies from hell!
Forward, you market militia, you battle-hardened
bargain hunters, old sales campaigners, grocery
grenadiers, veterans never bested by an overcharge!
You troops of the breadline, dough-girls—
Show them no mercy! Push! Jostle! Shove!
Call them nasty names! [*Aside.*] Don't be ladylike. [*The* WOMEN *charge and rout the Archers in short order.*]
Fall back—don't strip the enemy! The day is ours! [*The* WOMEN *obey, and the* ARCHERS *run off left. The* COMMISSIONER, *dazed, is left muttering to himself.*]
COMMISSIONER. Gross ineptitude. A sorry day for the Force.
LYSISTRATA. Of course. What did you expect? We're not slaves;
we're freeborn Women, and when we're scorned, we're full
of fury. Never Underestimate the Power of a Woman.
COMMISSIONER. Power? You mean Capacity. I should have remembered
the proverb: *The lower the tavern, the higher the dudgeon.*
KORYPHAIOS OF MEN. Why cast your pearls before swine, Commissioner? I know you've a civil

servant, but don't overdo it. Have you forgotten the bath
they gave us—in public, fully dressed, totally soapless?
Keep rational discourse for *people!* [*He aims a blow at the* KORYPHAIOS OF WOMEN, *who dodges and raises her pitcher.*]
KORYPHAIOS OF WOMEN. I might point out that lifting
one's hand against a neighbor is scarcely civilized behavior—
and entails, for the lifter, a black eye. I'm really peaceful by nature,
compulsively inoffensive—a perfect doll. My ideal is a well-bred
repose that doesn't even stir up dust . . . [*Swinging at the* KORYPHAIOS OF MEN *with the pitcher.*] unless some no-good lowlife
tries to rifle my hive and gets my dander up! [*The* KORYPHAIOS OF MEN *backs hurriedly away, and the* CHORUS OF MEN *goes into a worried dance.*]
CHORUS OF MEN. [*Singly.*]
O Zeus, what's the use of this constant abuse?
How do we deal with this female zoo?
Is there no solution to Total Immersion?
What can a poor man DO? [*Tutti.*]

Query the Adversary!
Ferret out their story!
What end did they have in view,
to seize the city's sanctuary,
snatch its legendary eyrie,
snare an area so very
terribly taboo?
KORYPHAIOS OF MEN [*To the* COMMISSIONER.] Scrutinize those women!
Scour their depositions—assess their rebuttals!
Masculine honor demands this affair be probed to the bottom!
COMMISSIONER. [*Turning to the* WOMEN *from the Akropolis.*]
All right, you. Kindly inform me, dammit, in your own words:
What possible object could you have had in blockading the Treasury?
LYSISTRATA. We thought we'd deposit the money in escrow and withdraw you men
from the war.
COMMISSIONER. The money's the cause

of the war?

LYSISTRATA. And all our internal disorders—the Body Politic's chronic bellyaches: What causes Peisandros' frantic rantings, or the raucous caucuses of the Friends of Oligarchy?[17] The chance for graft. But now, with the money up there, they can't upset the City's equilibrium—or lower its balance.

COMMISSIONER. And what's your next step?

LYSISTRATA. Stupid question. We'll budget the money.

COMMISSIONER. *You'll budget the money?*

LYSISTRATA. Why should you find that so shocking?
We budget the household accounts, and you don't object at all.

COMMISSIONER. That's different.

LYSISTRATA. Different? How?

COMMISSIONER. The War Effort needs this money!

LYSISTRATA. Who needs the War Effort?

COMMISSIONER. Every patriot who pulses to save all that Athens holds near and dear . . .

LYSISTRATA. Oh, *that.* Don't worry. We'll save you.

COMMISSIONERS. *You* will save us?

LYSISTRATA. Who else?

COMMISSIONER. But this is unscrupulous!

LYSISTRATA. We'll save you. You can't deter us.

COMMISSIONER. Scurrilous!

LYSISTRATA. You seem disturbed. This makes it difficult. But, still—we'll save you.

COMMISSIONER. Doubtless illegal!

LYSISTRATA. We deem it a duty. For friendship's sake.

COMMISSIONER. Well, forsake this friend:
I DO NOT WANT TO BE SAVED, DAMMIT!

LYSISTRATA. All the more reason. It's not only Sparta; now we'll have to save you from *you.*

COMMISSIONER. Might I ask where you women conceived this concern about War and Peace?

LYSISTRATA. [*Loftily.*] We shall explain.

COMMISSIONER. [*Making a fist.*] Hurry up, and you won't get hurt.

LYSISTRATA. Then *listen.* And do try to keep your hands to yourself.

COMMISSIONER [*Moving threateningly toward her.*]
I can't. Righteous anger forbids restraint, and decrees . . .

KLEONIKE. [*Brandishing her chamber pot.*]
Multiple fractures?

COMMISSIONER. [*Retreating.*] Keep those croaks for yourself, you old crow! [*To* LYSISTRATA.]
All right, lady, I'm ready. Speak.

LYSISTRATA. I shall proceed:
When the War began, like the prudent, dutiful wives that we are,
we tolerated you men, and endured your actions in silence. (Small wonder—
you wouldn't let us say boo.) You were not precisely the answer
to a matron's prayer—we knew you too well, and found out more.
Too many times, as we sat in the house, we'd hear that you'd done it
again—manhandled another affair of state with your usual
staggering incompetence. Then, masking our worry with a nervous laugh,
we'd ask you, brightly, "How was the Assembly today, dear? Anything
in the minutes about Peace?" And my husband would give
his stock reply.
"What's that to you? Shut up!" And I did.

KLEONIKE. [*Proudly.*] *I* never shut up!

COMMISSIONER. I trust you were shut up. Soundly.

LYSISTRATA. Regardless, *I* shut up.
And then we'd learn that you'd passed another decree, fouler
than the first, and we'd ask again: "Darling, how *did* you manage
anything so idiotic?" And my husband, with his customary glare,
would tell me to spin my thread, or else get a clout on the head.
And of course he'd quote from Homer:
Y^e menne must see to ye warre.[18]

COMMISSIONER. Apt and irrefutably right.

LYSISTRATA. *Right,* you miserable misfit?
To keep us from giving advice while you fumbled the City away

in the Senate? Right, indeed! But this time was really too much:

Wherever we went, we'd hear you engaged in the same conversation: "What Athens needs is a Man."[19] "But there isn't a Man in the country." "You can say that again." There was obviously no time to lose.

We women met in immediate convention and passed a unanimous resolution: To work in concert for safety and Peace in Greece.

We have valuable advice to impart, and if you can possibly deign to emulate our silence, and take your turn as audience, we'll rectify you—we'll straighten you out and set you right.

COMMISSIONER. *You'll* set *us* right? You go too far. I cannot permit such a statement to . . .

LYSISTRATA. Shush.

COMMISSIONER. I categorically decline to shush for some confounded woman, who wears—as a constant reminder of congenital inferiority, an injunction to public silence—a veil! Death before such dishonor!

LYSISTRATA. [*Removing her veil.*] If that's the only obstacle . . .

I feel you need a new panache, so take the veil, my dear Commissioner, and drape it thus—and SHUSH!

[*As she winds the veil around the startled* COMMISSIONER's *head,* KLEONIKE *and* MYRRHINE, *with carding-comb and wool-basket, rush forward and assist in transforming him into a woman.*]

KLEONIKE. Accept, I pray, this humble comb.

MYRRHINE. Receive this basket of fleece as well.

LYSISTRATA. Hike up your skirts, and card your wool, and gnaw your beans—and stay at home!

While we rewrite Homer:

Yᵉ WOMEN must see to yᵉ warre! [*To the* CHORUS OF WOMEN, *as the* COMMISSIONER *struggles to remove his new outfit.*]

Women, weaker vessels, arise! Put down your pitchers.

It's our turn, now. Let's supply our friends with some moral support.

[*The* CHORUS OF WOMEN *dances to the same tune as the* MEN, *but with much more confidence.*]

CHORUS OF WOMEN. [*Singly.*]

Oh, yes! I'll dance to bless their success.

Fatigue won't weaken my will. Or my knees.

I'm ready to join in any jeopardy, with girls as good as *these!* [*Tutte.*]

A tally of their talents convinces me they're giants of excellence. To commence: there's Beauty, Duty, Prudence, Science, Self-Reliance, Compliance, Defiance, and Love of Athens in balanced alliance with Common Sense!

KORYPHAIOS OF WOMEN. [*To the women from the Akropolis.*]

Autochthonous daughters of Attika, sprung from the soil that bore your mothers, the spiniest, spikiest nettles known to man, prove your mettle and attack! Now is no time to dilute your anger. You're running ahead of the wind!

LYSISTRATA. We'll wait for the wind from heaven. The gentle breath of Love and his Kyprian mother will imbue our bodies with desire, and raise a storm to tense and tauten these blasted men until they crack. And soon we'll be on every tongue in Greece—the *Pacifiers.*[20]

COMMISSIONER. That's quite a mouthful. How will you win it?

LYSISTRATA. First, we intend to withdraw that crazy Army of Occupation from the downtown shopping section.

KLEONIKE. Aphrodite be praised!

LYSISTRATA. The pottery shop and the grocery stall are overstocked with soldiers, clanking around like those maniac Korybants, armed to the teeth for a battle.

COMMISSIONER. A Hero is Always Prepared!

LYSISTRATA. I suppose he is. But it does look silly to shop for sardines from behind a shield.

KLEONIKE. I'll second that. I saw a cavalry captain buy vegetable soup on

horseback. He carried
the whole mess home in his helmet.
   And then that fellow from Thrace,
shaking his buckler and spear—a
   menace straight from the stage.
The saleslady was stiff with fright. He
   was hogging her ripe figs—free.
COMMISSIONER. I admit, for the moment, that Hellas' affairs are in one
   hell of
a snarl. But how can you set them
   straight?
LYSISTRATA. Simplicity itself.
COMMISSIONER. Pray demonstrate.
LYSISTRATA. It's rather like yarn. When
   a hank's in a tangle,
we lift it—*so*—and work out the snarls
   by winding it up
on spindles, now this way, now that
   way. That's how we'll wind up the
   War,
if allowed: We'll work out the snarls by
   sending Special Commissions—
back and forth, now this way, now that
   way—to ravel these tense
international kinks.
COMMISSIONER. I lost your thread, but I
   know there's a hitch.
Spruce up the world's disasters with
   spindles—typically woolly
female logic.
LYSISTRATA. If *you* had a scrap of logic,
   you'd adopt
our wool as a master plan for Athens.
COMMISSIONER. What course of action
does the wool advise?
LYSISTRATA. Consider the City as fleece,
   recently
shorn. The first step is Cleansing:
   Scrub it in a public bath,
and remove all corruption, offal, and
   sheepdip. Next, to the couch
for Scutching and Plucking: Cudgel the
   leeches and similar vermin
loose with a club, then pick the prickles
   and cockleburs out.
As for the clots—those lumps that
   clump and cluster in knots
and snarls to snag important posts[21]—
   you comb these out,
twist off their heads, and discard. Next,
   to raise the City's
nap, you card the citizens together in a
   single basket
of common weal and general welfare.
   Fold in our loyal

Resident Aliens, all Foreigners of
   proven and tested friendship,
and any Disenfranchised Debtors.
   Combine these closely with the rest.
Lastly, cull the colonies settled by our
   own people:
these are nothing but flocks of wool
   from the City's fleece,
scattered throughout the world. So
   gather home these far-flung
flocks, amalgamate them with the
   others. Then, drawing this blend
of stable fibers into one fine staple, you
   spin a mighty
bobbin of yarn—and weave, without
   bias or seam, a cloak
to clothe the City of Athens!
COMMISSIONER. This is too much! The
   City's
died in the wool, worsted by the distaff
   side—by women
who bore no share in the War. . . .
LYSISTRATA. None, you hopeless hypocrite?
The quota we bear is double. First, we
   delivered our sons
to fill out the front lines in Sicily . . .
COMMISSIONER. Don't tax me with that
   memory.
LYSISTRATA. Next, the best years of our
   lives were levied. Top-level strategy
attached our joy, and we sleep alone.
   But it's not the matrons
like us who matter. I mourn for the virgins, bedded in single
blessedness, with nothing to do but
   grow old.
COMMISSIONER. Men *have* been known
to age, as well as women.
LYSISTRATA. No, not as well as—better.
A man, an absolute antique, comes
   back from the war, and he's barely
doddered into town before he's married the veriest nymphet.
But a woman's season is brief; it slips,
   and she'll have no husband,
but sit out her life groping at omens—
   and finding no men.
COMMISSIONER. Lamentable state of affairs. Perhaps we can rectify matters:
[*To the audience.*] TO EVERY MAN
   JACK, A CHALLENGE: ARISE!
Provided you can . . .
LYSISTRATA. Instead, Commissioner,
   why not simply curl up and *die?*
Just buy a coffin; here's the place.

[*Banging him on the head with her spindle.*[22]]
I'll knead you a cake for the wake—and these [*Winding the threads from the spindle around him.*]
make excellent wreaths. So Rest In Peace.

KLEONIKE. [*Emptying the chamber pot over him.*] Accept these tokens of deepest grief.

MYRRHINE. [*Breaking her lamp over his head.*]
A final garland for the dear deceased.

LYSISTRATA. May I supply any last request?
Then run along. You're due at the wharf:
Charon's anxious to sail—
you're holding up the boat for Hell!

COMMISSIONER. This is monstrous—maltreatment of a public official—maltreatment of ME! I must repair directly
to the Board of Commissioners, and present my colleagues concrete evidence of the sorry specifics of this shocking attack!

[*He staggers off left.* LYSISTRATA *calls after him.*]

LYSISTRATA. You won't haul us into court on a charge of neglecting
the dead, will you? (How like a man to insist
on his rights—even his last ones.) Two days between death
and funeral, that's the rule. Come back here early
day after tomorrow, Commissioner:
We'll lay you out. [LYSISTRATA *and her* WOMEN *reenter the Akropolis. The* KORYPHAIOS OF MEN *advances to address the audience.*]

KORYPHAIOS OF MEN. Wake up, Athens! Preserve your freedom—the time is Now! [*To the* CHORUS OF MEN.]
Strip for action, men. Let's cope with the current mess. [*The* MEN *put off their long mantles, disclosing short tunics underneath, and advance toward the audience.*]

CHORUS OF MEN. This trouble may be terminal; it has a loaded odor, an ominous aroma of constitutional rot.
My nose gives a prognosis of radical disorder—it's just the first installment of an absolutist plot!

The Spartans are behind it:
they must have masterminded
some morbid local contacts (engineered by Kleisthenes).
Predictably infected,
these women straightway acted
to commandeer the City's cash. They're feverish to freeze
my be-all,
my end-all.
my *payroll!*[23]

KORYPHAIOS OF MEN. The symptoms are clear. Our birthright's already nibbled. And oh, so
daintily: WOMEN ticking off troops for improper etiquette.
WOMEN propounding their featherweight views on the fashionable use
and abuse of the shield. And (if any more proof were needed) WOMEN
nagging us to trust the Nice Laconian, and put our heads
in his toothy maw—to make a dessert and call it Peace.
They've woven the City a seamless shroud, bedecked with the legend
DICTATORSHIP. But I won't be hemmed in. I'll use their weapon
against them, and uphold the right by sneakiness. With knyf under cloke,
gauntlet in glove, sword in olivebranch, [*Slipping slowly toward the* KORYPHAIOS OF WOMEN.] I'll take up my post
in Statuary Row, beside our honored National Heroes,
the natural foes of tyranny: Harmodios, Aristogeiton, and Me.[24]
[*Next to her.*] Striking an epic pose, so, with the full approval
of the immortal gods, I'll bash this loathesome hag in the jaw! [*He does, and runs cackling back to the* MEN. *She shakes a fist after him.*]

KORYPHAIOS OF WOMEN. Mama won't know her little boy when he gets home! [*To the* WOMEN, *who are eager to launch a full-scale attack.*]
Let's not be hasty, fellow . . . hags. Cloaks off first. [*The* WOMEN, *remove their mantles, disclosing tunics very like those of the men, and advance toward the audience.*

CHORUS OF WOMEN. We'll address you, citizens, in beneficial, candid, patriotic accents, as our breeding says we must,

since, from the age of seven, Athens
  graced me with a splendid
string of civic triumphs to signalize her
  trust:
I was Relic-Girl quite early,
then advanced to Maid of Barley;
in Artemis' "Pageant of the Bear" I
  played the lead.
To cap this proud progression,[25]
I led the whole procession
at Athene's Celebration, certified and
  pedigreed
—that cachet
so distingué—
a *Lady!*
KORYPHAIOS OF WOMEN. [*To the audience.*]
I trust this establishes my qualifications.
  I may, I take it, address
the City to its profit? Thank you. I admit to being a woman—
but don't sell my contribution short on
  that account. It's better
than the present panic. And my word is
  as good as my bond,
because I hold stock in Athens—stock I
  paid for in sons. [*To the* CHORUS OF
  MEN.]
—But you, you doddering bankrupts,
  where are your shares in the State?
[*Slipping slowly toward the* KORYPHAIOS
  OF MEN.]
Your grandfathers willed you the
  Mutual Funds from the Persian
  War[26]—
and where are they? [*Nearer.*] You
  dipped into capital, then lost interest
  . . .
and now a pool of your assets won't fill
  a hole in the ground.
All that remains is one last potential
  killing—Athens.
Is there any rebuttal? [*The* KORYPHAIOS
  OF MEN *gestures menacingly. She ducks
  down, as if to ward off a blow, and re-
  moves a slipper.*]
Force is a footling resort. I'll take
my very sensible shoe, and paste you in
  the jaw! [*She does so, and runs back to
  the* WOMEN.]
CHORUS OF MEN. Their native respect
  for our manhood is small,
and keeps getting smaller. Let's bottle
  their gall.
The man who won't battle has no balls
  at all!

KORYPHAIOS OF MEN. All right, men,
  skin out of the skivvies. Let's give
  them a whiff
of Man, full strength. No point in muf-
  fling the essential Us. [*The* MEN *remove
  their tunics.*]
CHORUS OF MEN. A century back, we
  soared to the Heights[27] and beat
  down Tyranny there.
Now's the time to shed our moults and
  fledge our wings once more,
to rise to the skies in our reborn force,
  and beat back Tyranny here!
KORYPHAIOS OF MEN. No fancy grappling with these grannies;
  straightforward strength. The tiniest
toehold, and those nimble, fiddling
  fingers will have their foot
in the door, and we're done for. *No
  amount of know-how can lick
a woman's knack.* They'll want to build
  ships . . . next thing we know,
we're all at sea, fending off female
  boarding parties.
(Artemisia fought us at Salamis. Tell
  me, has anyone caught her
yet?) But we're *really* sunk if they take
  up horses. Scratch
the Cavalry: A woman is an easy rider
  with a natural seat.
Take her over the jumps bareback, and
  she'll never slip
her mount. (That's how the Amazons
  nearly took Athens. On horseback.
Check on Mikon's mural down in the
  Stoa.) Anyway,
the solution is obvious. Put every
  woman in her place—stick her
in the stocks. To do this, first snare
  your woman around the neck. [*He attempts to demonstrate on the* KORYPHAIOS
  OF WOMEN. *After a brief tussle, she works
  loose and chases him back to the* MEN.]
CHORUS OF WOMEN. The beast in me's
  eager and fit for a brawl.
Just rile me a bit and she'll kick down
  the wall.
You'll bawl to your friends that you've
  no balls at all.
KORYPHAIOS OF WOMEN. All right, ladies,
  strip for action. Let's give them a
  whiff
of *Femme Enragée*—piercing and pun-
  gent, but not at all tart. [*The women
  remove their tunics.*]
CHORUS OF WOMEN. We're angry. The

brainless bird who tangles with *us* has
gummed his last mush.
In fact, the coot who even heckles is being daringly rash.
So look to your nests, you reclaimed
eagles—whatever you lay, we'll
squash!
KORYPHAIOS OF WOMEN. Frankly, you
don't faze me. *For* me, I have my
friends—
Lampito from Sparta; that genteel girl
from Thebes, Ismenia—
committed to me forever. *Against* me,
you—permanently
out of commission. So do your
damnedest. Pass a law.
Pass seven. Continue the winning ways
that have made your name
a short and ugly household word. Like
yesterday:
I was giving a little party, nothing
fussy, to honor
the goddess Hekate. Simply to please
my daughters, I'd invited
a sweet little thing from the neighborhood—flawless pedigree, perfect
taste, a credit to any gathering—a Boiotian eel.
But she had to decline. Couldn't pass
the border. You'd passed a law.
Not that you care for my party. You'll
overwork your right of passage
till your august body is overturned, and
you break your silly neck! [*She deftly
grabs the* KORYPHAIOS OF MEN *by the
ankle and upsets him. He scuttles back to
the* MEN, *who retire in confusion.* LYSIS-
TRATA *emerges from the citadel, obviously
distraught.*]
KORYPHAIOS OF WOMEN. [*Mock-tragic.*]
*Mistress, queen of this our subtle scheme,
why burst you from the hall with brangled
brow?*
LYSISTRATA. *Oh, wickedness of woman!
The female mind
does sap my soul and set my wits a-totter.*
KORYPHAIOS OF WOMEN. *What drear accents are these?*
LYSISTRATA. *The merest truth.*
KORYPHAIOS OF WOMEN. *Be nothing loath
to tell the tale to friends.*
LYSISTRATA. *'Twere shame to utter, pain to
hold unsaid.*
KORYPHAIOS OF WOMEN. *Hide not from me
affliction which we share.*
LYSISTRATA. *In briefest compass,* [*Dropping

the paratragedy.*] we want to get laid.
KORYPHAIOS OF WOMEN. By Zeus!
LYSISTRATA. No, no, not HIM! Well,
that's the way things are.
I've lost my grip on the girls—they're
mad for men!
But sly—they slip out in droves. A minute ago,
I caught one scooping out the little hole
that breaks through just below Pan's
grotto.[28] One
had jerry-rigged some block-and-tackle
business
and was wriggling away on a rope.
Another just flat
deserted. Last night I spied one mount-
ing a sparrow,
all set to take off for the nearest bawdy-
house. I hauled
her back by the hair. And excuses, pretexts for overnight
passes? I've heard them all. Here comes
one. Watch. [*To the* FIRST WOMAN, *as
she runs out of the Akropolis.*]
—You there! What's your hurry?
FIRST WOMAN. I have to get home.
I've got all this lovely Milesian wool in
the house,
and the moths will simply batter it to
bits!
LYSISTRATA. I'll bet.
Get back inside.
FIRST WOMAN. I swear I'll hurry right
back!
—Just time enough to spread it out on
the couch?
LYSISTRATA. Your wool will stay un-
spread. And you'll stay here.
FIRST WOMAN. Do I have to let my
piecework *rot*?
LYSISTRATA. Possibly. [*The* SECOND
WOMAN *runs on.*]
SECOND WOMAN. Oh dear, oh goodness,
what shall I do—my flax!
I left and forgot to peel it!
LYSISTRATA. Another one.
She suffers from unpeeled flax.—Get
back inside!
SECOND WOMAN. I'll be right back. I just
have to pluck the fibers.
LYSISTRATA. No. No plucking. You start
it, and everyone else
will want to go and do their plucking,
too. [*The* THIRD WOMAN, *swelling con-
spicuously, hurries on, praying loudly.*]
THIRD WOMAN. *O Goddess of Childbirth,*

grant that I not deliver
until I get me from out this sacred precinct!
LYSISTRATA. What sort of nonsense is
this?
THIRD WOMAN. I'm due—any second!
LYSISTRATA. You weren't pregnant yesterday.
THIRD WOMAN. Today I am—
a miracle! Let me go home for a mid-
wife, *please!*
I may not make it!
LYSISTRATA [*Restraining her.*] You can
do better than that. [*Tapping the*
woman's stomach and receiving a metallic
clang.]
What's this? It's hard.
THIRD WOMAN. I'm going to have a boy.
LYSISTRATA. Not unless he's made of
bronze. Let's see. [*She throws open the*
THIRD WOMAN's *cloak, exposing a huge*
bronze helmet.]
Of all the brazen . . . You've stolen the
helmet from Athene's
statue! Pregnant, indeed!
THIRD WOMAN. I am *so* pregnant!
LYSISTRATA. Then why the helmet?
THIRD WOMAN. I thought my time
might come
while I was still on forbidden ground.
If it did,
I could climb inside Athene's helmet
and have
my baby there. The pigeons do it all
the time.
LYSISTRATA. Nothing but excuses!
[*Taking the helmet.*] This is your baby.
I'm afraid
you'll have to stay until we give it a
name.
THIRD WOMAN. But the Akropolis is *aw-*
ful. I can't even sleep! I saw
the snake that guards the temple.
LYSISTRATA. That snake's a fabrica-
tion.[29]
THIRD WOMAN. I don't care *what* kind it
is—I'm *scared!* [*The other* WOMEN, *who*
have emerged from the citadel, crowd
around.]
KLEONIKE. And those goddamned holy
owls! All night long,
tu-wit, tu-wu—they're hooting me into
my grave!
LYSISTRATA. Darlings, let's call a halt to
this hocus-pocus.
You miss your men—now isn't that the
trouble? [*Shame-faced nods from the*

group.]
Don't you think they miss you just as
much?
I can assure you, their nights are every
bit
as hard as yours. So be good girls; endure!
Persist a few days more, and Victory is
ours.
It's fated: a current prophecy declares
that the men
will go down to defeat before us, provided that *we*
maintain a United Front. [*Producing a*
scroll.] I happen to have
a copy of the prophecy.
KLEONIKE. Read it!
LYSISTRATA. Silence, *please:* [*Reading*
from the scroll.]
But when the swallows, in flight from
the hoopoes, have flocked to a hole
on high, and stoutly eschew their accustomed perch on the pole,
yea, then shall Thunderer Zeus to their
suff'ring establish a stop,
by making the lower the upper . . .
KLEONIKE. Then *we'll* be lying on top?
LYSISTRATA. But should these swallows,
indulging their lust for the perch,
lose heart,
dissolve their flocks in winged dissen-
sion, and singly depart
the sacred stronghold, breaking the
bands that bind them together—
then know them as lewd, the perverted-
est birds that ever wore feather.
KLEONIKE. There's nothing obscure
about *that* oracle. Ye gods!
LYSISTRATA. Sorely beset as we are, we
must not flag
or falter. So back to the citadel! [*As the*
women troop inside.] And if we fail
that oracle, darlings, our image is absolutely *mud!* [*She follows them in. A*
pause, and the CHORUSES *assemble.*]
CHORUS OF MEN. I have a simple
tale to relate you,
a sterling example
of masculine virtue:

The huntsman bold Melanion was once
a harried quarry.
The women in town tracked him down
and badgered him to marry.

Melanion knew the cornered male

eventually cohabits.
Assessing the odds, he took to the
woods and lived by trapping rabbits.

He stuck to the virgin stand, sustained
by rabbit meat and hate,
and never returned, but ever remained
an alfresco celibate.

Melanion is our ideal;
his loathing makes us free.
Our dearest aim is the gemlike flame of
his misogyny.

OLD MAN. Let me kiss that wizened
cheek . . .
OLD WOMAN. [*Threatening with a fist.*]
A wish too rash for that withered flesh.
OLD MAN. and lay you low with a high-
flying kick. [*He tries one and misses.*]
OLD WOMAN. Exposing an overgrown
underbrush.
OLD MAN. A hairy behind, historically
means masculine force: Myronides
harassed the foe with his mighty mane,
and furry Phormion swept the seas
of enemy ships, never meeting his
match—such was the nature of his
thatch.
CHORUS OF WOMEN. I offer an anecdote
for your opinion,
an adequate antidote
for your Melanion:

Timon, the noted local grouch,
put rusticating hermits
out of style by building his wilds inside
the city limits.

He shooed away society
with natural battlements:
his tongue was edgèd; his shoulder,
frigid; his beard, a picket fence.

When random contacts overtaxed him,
he didn't stop to pack,
but loaded curses on the male of the
species, left town, and never came
back.

Timon, you see, was a misanthrope
in a properly narrow sense:
his spleen was vented only on men . . .
we were his dearest friends.
OLD WOMAN. [*Making a fist.*] Enjoy a
chop to that juiceless chin?
OLD MAN. [*Backing away.*] I'm jolted al-

ready. Thank you, no.
OLD WOMAN. Perhaps a trip from a well-
turned shin? [*She tries a kick and
misses.*]
OLD MAN. Brazenly baring the mantrap
below.
OLD WOMAN. At least it's neat. I'm not
too sorry to have you see my dain-
tiness.
My habits are still depilatory; age hasn't
made me a bristly mess. Secure in my
smoothness, I'm never in doubt—
though even down is out.
[LYSISTRATA *mounts the platform and
scans the horizon. When her gaze reaches
the left, she stops suddenly.*]
LYSISTRATA. Ladies, attention! Battle
stations, please!
And quickly! [*A general rush of* WOMEN *to
the battlements.*]
KLEONIKE. What is it?
MYRRHINE. What's all the shouting for?
LYSISTRATA. A MAN! [*Consternation.*]
Yes, it's a man. And he's coming this
way!
Hmm. Seems to have suffered a seizure. Broken out with a nasty attack
of love. [*Prayer, aside.*]
O Aphrodite,
Mistress all-victorious,
mysterious, voluptuous,
you who make the crooked straight . . .
don't let this happen to US!
KLEONIKE. I don't care who he is—*where
is he?*
LYSISTRATA. [*Pointing.*] Down there—
just flanking that temple—Demeter the
Fruitful.
KLEONIKE. My. Definitely a man.
MYRRHINE. [*Craning for a look.*] I wonder
who it can be?
LYSISTRATA. See for yourselves.—Can
anyone identify him?
MYRRHINE. Oh lord, I can. *That* is my
husband—Kinesias.[30]
LYSISTRATA. [*To* MYRRHINE.] Your duty
is clear. Pop him on the griddle, twist
the spit, braize him, baste him, stew
him in his own
juice, do him to a turn. Sear him with
kisses,
coyness, caresses, *everything*—but stop
where Our Oath
begins.
MYRRHINE. Relax. I can take care of
this.

LYSISTRATA. Of course
you can, dear. Still, a little help can't
hurt, now
can it? I'll just stay around for a bit
and—er—poke up the fire.—Everyone
else inside! [*Exit all the* WOMEN *but* LY-
SISTRATA, *on the platform, and* MYR-
RHINE, *who stands near the Akropolis en-
trance, hidden from her husband's view.*
KINESIAS *staggers on, in erection and
considerable pain, followed by a male*
SLAVE *who carries a baby boy.*]
KINESIAS. OMIGOD OUCH!
Hypertension, twinges . . . I can't hold
out much more.
I'd rather be dismembered. *How long,
ye gods, how long?*
LYSISTRATA. [*Officially.*] WHO GOES
THERE? WHO PENETRATES
OUR POSITIONS?
KINESIAS. Me.
LYSISTRATA. A Man?
KINESIAS. Every inch.
LYSISTRATA. Then inch yourself out
of here. Off Limits to Men.
KINESIAS. This *is* the limit.
Just who are *you* to throw me out?
LYSISTRATA. The Lookout.
KINESIAS. Well, look here, Lookout. I'd
like to see Myrrhine.
How's the outlook?
LYSISTRATA. Unlikely. Bring Myrrhine
to you? The idea! Just by the by, who
are you?
KINESIAS. A private citizen. Her hus-
band, Kinesias.
LYSISTRATA. No!
Meeting you—I'm overcome! Your
name, you know,
is not without its fame among us girls.
[*Aside.*]—Matter of fact, we have a
name for *it*.—
I swear, you're never out of Myrrhine's
mouth.
She won't even nibble a quince, or swal-
low an egg,
without reciting, "Here's to Kinesias!"
KINESIAS. For god's sake,
will you . . .
LYSISTRATA. [*Sweeping on over his agony.*]
Word of honor, it's true. Why, when
we discuss our husbands (you know
how women are),
Myrrhine refuses to argue. She simply
insists:
"Compared with Kinesias, the rest have

nothing!" Imagine!
KINESIAS. *Bring her out here!*
LYSISTRATA. Really? And what would I
get out of this?
KINESIAS. You see my situation. I'll raise
whatever I can. This can all be yours.
LYSISTRATA. Goodness.
It's really her place. I'll go and get her.
[*She descends from the platform and
moves to* MYRRHINE, *out of Kinesias'
sight.*]
KINESIAS. Speed!
—Life is a husk. She left our home, and
happiness
went with her. Now pain is the tenant.
Oh, to enter
that wifeless house, to sense that awful
emptiness,
to eat that tasteless, joyless food—it
makes
it hard, I tell you. Harder all the time.
MYRRHINE. [*Still out of his sight, in a voice
to be overheard.*]
Oh, I *do* love him! I'm mad about him!
But he
doesn't want my love. Please don't
make me see him.
KINESIAS. Myrrhine darling, why do you
act this way?
Come down here!
MYRRHINE. [*Appearing at the wall.*] Down
there? Certainly not!
KINESIAS. It's me, Myrrhine. I'm begging you. Please come down.
MYRRHINE. I don't see why you're begging me. You don't need me.
KINESIAS. I don't need you? I'm at the
end of my rope!
MYRRHINE. I'm leaving. [*She turns.*
KINESIAS *grabs the boy from the* SLAVE.]
KINESIAS. No! Wait! At least you'll have
to listen
to the voice of your child. [*To the boy, in
a fierce undertone.*]—Call your mother!
[*Silence.*] . . . to the voice
of your very own child . . . —(Call your
mother, brat!)
CHILD. MOMMYMOMMYMOMMY!
KINESIAS. Where's your maternal in-
stinct? He hasn't been washed or fed
for a week. How can you be so
pitiless?
MYRRHINE. *Him* I pity. Of all the pitiful
excuses
for a father. . . .
KINESIAS. Come down here, dear. For

the baby's sake.

MYRRHINE. Motherhood! I'll have to come. I've got no choice.

KINESIAS. [*Soliloquizing as she descends.*] It may be me, but I'll swear she looks years younger—
and gentler—her eyes caress me. And then they flash:
that anger, that verve, that high-and-mighty air!
She's fire, she's ice—and I'm caught right in the middle.

MYRRHINE. [*Taking the baby.*] Sweet babykins with such a nasty daddy!
Here, let Mummy kissums. Mummy's little darling.

KINESIAS. [*The injured husband.*] You should be ashamed of yourself, letting those women
lead you around. Why do you DO these things?
You only make me suffer and hurt your poor, sweet self.

MYRRHINE. Keep your hands away from me!

KINESIAS. But the house, the furniture, everything we own—you're letting it go to hell!

MYRRHINE. Frankly, I couldn't care less.

KINESIAS. But your weaving's unraveled—the loom is full of chickens! You couldn't care less about *that?*

MYRRHINE. I certainly couldn't.

KINESIAS. And the holy rites of Aphrodite? Think how long
that's been. Come on, darling, let's go home.

MYRRHINE. I absolutely refuse! Unless you agree to a truce
to stop the war.

KINESIAS. Well, then, if that's your decision,
we'll STOP the war!

MYRRHINE. Well, then, if that's your decision,
I'll come back—*after* it's done. But for the present,
I've sworn off.

KINESIAS. At least lie down for a minute.
We'll talk.

MYRRHINE. I know what you're up to—NO!
—And yet. . . . I really can't say I don't love you . . .

KINESIAS. You love me?
So what's the trouble? *Lie down.*

MYRRHINE. Don't be disgusting.
In front of the baby?

KINESIAS. Er . . . no, Heaven Forfend. [*Taking the baby and pushing it at the* SLAVE.]
—Take this home. [*The slave obeys.*] —
Well, darling, we're rid of the kid . . .
let's go to bed!

MYRRHINE. Poor dear. But where does one do
this sort of thing?

KINESIAS. Where? All we need is a little nook. . . . We'll try Pan's grotto. Excellent spot.

MYRRHINE. [*With a nod at the Akropolis.*] I'll have to be pure to get back in *there.*
How can I expunge my pollution?

KINESIAS. Sponge off in the pool next door.

MYRRHINE. I did swear an Oath. I'm supposed to perjure myself?

KINESIAS. Bother the Oath. Forget it—I'll take the blame. [*A pause.*]

MYRRHINE. Now I'll go get us a cot.

KINESIAS. No! Not a cot!
The ground's enough for us.

MYRRHINE. *I'll get the cot.*
For all your faults, I refuse to put you to bed
in the dirt. [*She exits into the Akropolis.*]

KINESIAS. She certainly loves me. That's nice to know.

MYRRHINE. [*Returning with a rope-tied cot.*]
Here. You hurry to bed while I undress. [KINESIAS *lies down.*]
Gracious me—I forgot. We need a mattress.

KINESIAS. Who wants a mattress? Not me!

MYRRHINE. Oh, yes, you do.
It's perfectly squalid on the ropes.

KINESIAS. Well, give me a kiss
to tide me over.

MYRRHINE. *Voilà.* [*She pecks at him and leaves.*]

KINESIAS. OoolaLAlala!
—Make it a quick trip, dear.

MYRRHINE. [*Entering with the mattress, she waves* KINESIAS *off the cot and lays the mattress on it.*] Here we are.
Our mattress. Now hurry to bed while I undress. [KINESIAS *lies down again.*]
Gracious me—I forgot. You don't have

a pillow.

KINESIAS. I do *not* need a pillow.

MYRRHINE. I know, but *I* do. [*She leaves.*]

KINESIAS. What a lovefeast! Only the table gets laid.[31]

MYRRHINE. [*Returning with a pillow.*] Rise and shine! [KINESIAS *jumps up. She places the pillow.*] And now I have everything I need.

KINESIAS. [*Lying down again.*] You certainly do. Come here, my little jewelbox!

MYRRHINE. Just taking off my bra. Don't break your promise: no cheating about the Peace.

KINESIAS. I swear to god, I'll die first!

MYRRHINE. [*Coming to him.*] Just look. You don't have a blanket.

KINESIAS. I didn't plan to go camping— I want to make love!

MYRRHINE. Relax. You'll get your love. I'll be right back. [*She leaves.*]

KINESIAS. Relax? I'm dying a slow death by dry goods!

MYRRHINE. [*Returning with the blanket.*] Get up!

KINESIAS. [*Getting out of bed.*] I've been up for hours. I was up before I was up. [MYRRHINE *spreads the blanket on the mattress, and he lies down again.*]

MYRRHINE. I presume you want perfume?

KINESIAS. Positively NO!

MYRRHINE. Absolutely *yes*—whether you want it or not. [*She leaves.*]

KINESIAS. Dear Zeus, I don't ask for much—but please let her spill it.

MYRRHINE. [*Returning with a bottle.*] Hold out your hand like a good boy. Now rub it in.

KINESIAS. [*Obeying and sniffing.*] This is to quicken desire? Too strong. It grabs your nose and bawls out: *Try again tomorrow.*

MYRRHINE. I'm *awful!* I brought you that rancid Rhodian brand. [*She starts off with the bottle.*]

KINESIAS. This is just *lovely.* Leave it, woman!

MYRRHINE. Silly! [*She leaves.*]

KINESIAS. God damn the clod who first concocted perfume!

MYRRHINE. [*Returning with another bottle.*] Here, try this flask.

KINESIAS. Thanks—but you try mine. Come to bed, you witch—*and please stop bringing things!*

MYRRHINE. *That* is exactly what I'll do. There go my shoes. Incidentally, darling, you *will* remember to vote for the truce?

KINESIAS. I'LL THINK IT OVER! [MYRRHINE *runs off for good.*] That woman's laid me waste—destroyed me, root and branch! I'm scuttled, gutted, up the spout! And Myrrhine's gone! [*In a parody of a tragic kommos.*] Out upon't! But how? But where? Now I have lost the fairest fair, how stick my courage to yet another screwing-place? Aye, there's the rub— And yet, this wagging, wanton babe must soon be laid to rest, or else . . . Ho, Pandar! Pandar! I'd hire a nurse.

KORYPHAIOS OF MEN. Grievous your bereavement, cruel the slow tabescence of your soul. I bid my liquid pity mingle.

Oh, where the soul, and where, alack! the cod to stand the taut attack of swollen prides, the scorching tensions that ravine up the lumbar regions? His morning lay has gone astray.

KINESIAS. [*In agony.*] O Zeus, reduce the throbs, the throes!

KORYPHAIOS OF MEN. I turn my tongue to curse the cause of your affliction—that jade, that slut, that hag, that ogress . . .

KINESIAS. No! Slight not my light-o'-love, my dove, my sweet!

KORYPHAIOS OF MEN. Sweet! O Zeus who rul'st the sky, snatch that slattern up on high, crack thy winds, unleash thy thunder, tumble her over, trundle her under, juggle her from hand to hand; twirl her ever near the ground— drop her in a well-aimed fall on our tortured comrade's tool!

[KINESIAS *exits left. A* SPARTAN HERALD *enters from the right, holding his cloak together in a futile attempt to conceal his condition.*]

HERALD. This Athens? Where-all kin I find the Council of Elders
or else the Executive Board? I brung some news. [*The* COMMISSIONER,[32] *swathed in his cloak, enters from the left.*]

COMMISSIONER. And what are you—a man? a signpost? a joint-stock
company?

HERALD. A herald, sonny, a honest-to-Kastor
herald. I come to chat 'bout thet-there truce.

COMMISSIONER. . . . . carrying a concealed weapon? Pretty underhanded.

HERALD. [*Twisting to avoid the* COMMISSIONER's *direct gaze.*]
Hain't done no sech a thang!

COMMISSIONER. Very well, stand still. Your cloak's out of crease—hernia? Are the roads that bad?

SPARTAN. I swear this feller's plumb tetched in the haid!

COMMISSIONER. [*Throwing open the Spartan's cloak, exposing the phallus.*] You clown,
you've got an erection!

SPARTAN. [*Wildly embarrassed.*] Hain't got no sech a thang!
You stop this-hyer foolishment!

COMMISSIONER. What *have* you got there, then?

SPARTAN. Thet-thur's a Spartan *epistle.*[33] In code.

COMMISSIONER. I have the key.
[*Throwing open his cloak.*]
Behold another Spartan *epistle.* In code. [*Tired of teasing.*]
Let's get down to cases. I know the score,
so tell me the truth. How are things with you in Sparta?

HERALD. Thangs is up in the air. The whole Alliance
is purt-near 'bout to explode. We-uns'll need buckets,
'stead of women.

COMMISSIONER. What was the cause of this outburst?
The great god Pan?

HERALD. Nope. I'll lay 'twere Lampito, most likely. She begun, and then they was off
and runnin' at the post in a bunch, every last little gal
in Sparta, drivin' their menfolk away

from the winner's
circle.

COMMISSIONER. How are you taking this?

HERALD. Painful-like.
Everyone's doubled up worse as a midget nursin'
a wick in a midnight wind come moon-dark time.
Cain't even tetch them little old gals on the moosey
without we all agree to a Greece-wide Peace.

COMMISSIONER. Of course! A universal female plot—all Hellas
risen in rebellion—I should have known! Return
to Sparta with this request: Have them despatch us
a Plenipotentiary Commission, fully empowered
to conclude an armistice. I have full confidence
that I can persuade our Senate to do the same,
without extending myself. The evidence is at hand.

HERALD. I'm a-flyin', Sir! I hev never heered your equal! [*Exeunt hurriedly, the* COMMISSIONER *to the left, the* HERALD *to the right.*]

KORYPHAIOS OF MEN. The most unnerving work of nature,[34]
the pride of applied immorality,
is the common female human.
No fire can match, no beast can best her.
O Unsurmountability,
thy name—worse luck—is Woman.

KORYPHAIOS OF WOMEN. After such knowledge, why persist
in wearing out this feckless war between the sexes?
When can I apply for the post
of all, partner, and general friend?

KORYPHAIOS OF MEN. I won't be ployed to revise, re-do,
amend, extend, or bring to an end
my irreversible credo:
Misogyny Forever!
—The answer's never.

KORYPHAIOS OF WOMEN. All right. Whenever you choose.
But, for the present, I refuse
to let you look your absolute worst,
parading around like an unfrocked

freak:

I'm coming over and get you dressed. [*She dresses him in his tunic, an action (like others in this scene) imitated by the members of the* CHORUS OF WOMEN *toward their opposite numbers in the* CHORUS OF MEN.]

KORYPHAIOS OF MEN. This seems sincere. It's not a trick.

Recalling the rancor with which I
  stripped,
I'm overlaid with chagrin.

KORYPHAIOS OF WOMEN. Now you resemble a man,

not some ghastly practical joke.
And if you show me a little respect
(and promise not to kick), I'll extract
the beast in you.

KORYPHAIOS OF MEN. [*Searching himself.*]
  What beast in me?

KORYPHAIOS OF WOMEN. That insect.
  There. The bug that's stuck
in your eye.

KORYPHAIOS OF MEN. [*Playing along dubiously.*] This gnat?

KORYPHAIOS OF WOMEN. Yes, nitwit!

KORYPHAIOS OF MEN. Of course.
That steady, festering agony. . . .
You've put your finger on the source
of all my lousy troubles. Please
roll back the lid and scoop it out.
I'd like to see it.

KORYPHAIOS OF WOMEN. All right, I'll do
  it. [*Removing the imaginary insect.*]
Although, of all the impossible
  cranks. . .
Do you sleep in a swamp? Just look at
  this.
I've never seen a bigger chigger.

KORYPHAIOS OF MEN. Thanks.
Your kindness touches me deeply. For
  years,
that thing's been sinking wells in my
  eye.
Now you've unplugged me. Here come
  the tears.

KORYPHAIOS OF WOMEN. I'll dry your
  tears, though I can't say why. [*Wiping away the tears.*] Of all the irresponsible boys. . . .
And I'll kiss you.

KORYPHAIOS OF MEN. Don't you kiss me!

KORYPHAIOS OF WOMEN. What made you
  think you had a choice? [*She kisses him.*]

KORYPHAIOS OF MEN. All right, damn

you, that's enough of that ingrained
  palaver.
I can't dispute the truth or logic of the
  pithy old proverb:
Life with women is hell.
Life without women is hell, too.
And so we conclude a truce with you,
  on the following terms:
in future, a mutual moratorium on mischief in all its forms.
Agreed?—Let's make a single chorus
  and start our song. [*The two* CHORUSES *unite and face the audience.*]

CHORUS OF MEN. We're not about to introduce
the standard personal abuse—the
  Choral Smear
Of Present Persons (usually,
in every well-made comedy, inserted
  here.)
Instead, in deed and utterance, we
shall now indulge in philanthropy because we feel
that members of the audience
endure, in the course of current events,
  sufficient hell.
Therefore, friends, be rich! Be flush!
Apply to us, and borrow cash in large
  amounts.
The Treasury stands behind us—
  there—
and we can personally take care of
  small accounts.
Drop up today. Your credit's good.
Your loan won't have to be repaid in
  full until
the war is over. And then, your debt
is only the money you actually get—
  nothing at all.

CHORUS OF WOMEN. Just when we meant
  to entertain
some madcap Karystian men-about-
  town—such flawless taste!—
the present unpleasantness intervened,
and now we fear the feast we planned
  will go to waste.
The soup is waiting, rich and thick;
I've sacrificed a suckling pig—the pièce
  de résistance—
whose toothsome cracklings should
  amaze
the most fastidious gourmets—you, for
  instance.
To everybody here, I say
take potluck at my house today with me
  and mine.

Bathe and change as fast as you can,
bring the children, hurry down, and
  walk right in.
Don't bother to knock. No need at all.
My house is yours. Liberty Hall. What
  are friends for?
Act self-possessed when you come over;
it may help out when you discover I've
  locked the door. [*A delegation of* SPAR-
  TANS *enters from the right, with difficulty.*
  They have removed the cloaks, but hold
  them before themselves in an effort to con-
  ceal their condition.]
KORYPHAIOS OF MEN. What's this? Behold the Spartan ambassadors, dragging their beards,
pussy-footing along. It appears they've
  developed a hitch in the crotch.
  [*Advancing to greet them.*]
Men of Sparta, I bid you welcome! And
  now
to the point: What predicament brings
  you among us?
SPARTAN. We-uns is up a stump. Hain't
  fit fer chatter. [*Flipping aside his cloak.*]
Here's our predicament. Take a look
  for yourselfs.
KORYPHAIOS OF MEN. Well, I'll be
  damned—a regular disaster area.
Inflamed. I imagine the temperature's
  rather intense?
SPARTAN. Hit ain't the heat, hit's the
  tumidity. But words
won't help what ails us. We-uns come
  after Peace.
Peace from any person, any price.
  [*Enter the* ATHENIAN DELEGATION *from*
  the left, led by KINESIAS. *They are wear-*
  ing cloaks, but are obviously in as much
  travail as the SPARTANS.]
KORYPHAIOS OF MEN. Behold our local
  Sons of the Soil, stretching
their garments away from their groins,
  like wrestlers. Grappling
with their plight. Some sort of athlete's
  disease, no doubt.
An outbreak of epic proportions. Athlete's foot?
No. Could it be athlete's . . .?
KINESIAS. [*Breaking in.*] Who can tell us
how to get hold of Lysistrata? We've
  come as delegates
to the Sexual Congress. [*Opening his*
  cloak.] Here are our credentials.
KORYPHAIOS OF MEN. [*Ever the scientist,*
  looking from the ATHENIANS *to the* SPAR-

TANS *and back again.*]
The words are different, but the
  malady seems the same. [*To*
  KINESIAS.]
Dreadful disease. When the crisis
  reaches its height,
what do you take for it?
KINESIAS. Whatever comes to hand.
But now we've reached the bitter end.
  It's Peace
or we fall back on Kleisthenes.[35] And
  he's got a waiting list.
KORYPHAIOS OF MEN. [*To the* SPARTANS.]
Take my advice and put your clothes
  on. If someone
from that self-appointed Purity League
  comes by, you may
be docked. That's what they did to the
  statues of Hermes.[36]
KINESIAS. [*Since he has not yet noticed the*
  SPARTANS, *he interprets the warning as*
  meant for him, and hurriedly pulls his
  cloak together, as do the other ATHE-
  NIANS.]
Thank you. That's excellent advice.
SPARTAN. Hit shorely is.
Hain't nothing to argue after. Let's git
  dressed. [*As they put on their cloaks, the*
  SPARTANS *are finally noticed by*
  KINESIAS.]
KINESIAS. Welcome, men of Sparta!
  This is a shameful
disgrace to masculine honor.
SPARTAN. Hit could be worser.
Ef them Herm-choppers seed us all
  fired up,
they'd *really* take us down a peg or two.
KINESIAS. Gentlemen, let's descend to
  details. Specifically,
why are you here?
SPARTAN. Ambassadors. We come to
  dicker
'bout thet-thur Peace.
KINESIAS. Perfect! Precisely our purpose.
Let's send for Lysistrata. Only she can
  reconcile
our differences. There'll be no Peace
  for us without her.
SPARTAN. We-uns ain't fussy. Call Lysis-
  tratos, too, if you want. [*The gates to*
  the Akropolis open, and LYSISTRATA
  emerges, accompanied by her handmaid,
  PEACE—*a beautiful girl without a stitch*
  on. PEACE *remains out of sight by the*
  gates until summoned.]

KORYPHAIOS OF MEN. Hail, most virile of women! Summon up all your experience:
Be terrible and tender, lofty and lowbrow, severe and demure.
Here stand the Leaders of Greece, enthralled by your charm.
They yield the floor to you and submit their claims for your arbitration.
LYSISTRATA.
Really, it shouldn't be difficult, if I can catch them
all bothered, before they start to solicit each other.
I'll find out soon enough. Where's Peace?—Come here. [PEACE *moves from her place by the gates to* LYSISTRATA. *The delegations goggle at her.*]
Now, dear, first get those Spartans and bring them to me.
Take them by the hand, but don't be pushy about it,
not like our husbands (no savoir-faire at all!).
Be a lady, be proper, do just what you'd do at home:
if hands are refused, conduct them by the handle. [PEACE *leads the* SPARTANS *to a position near* LYSISTRATA.]
And now a hand to the Athenians—it doesn't matter
where; accept any offer—and bring *them* over. [PEACE *conducts the* ATHENIANS *to a position near* LYSISTRATA, *opposite the* SPARTANS.]
You Spartans move up closer—right here— [*To the* ATHENIANS.] and you
stand over here.—And now attend my speech. [*This the delegations do with some difficulty, because of the conflicting attractions of* PEACE, *who is standing beside her mistress.*]
I am a woman—but not without some wisdom:
my native wit is not completely negligible,
and I've listened long and hard to the discourse of my elders—
my education is not entirely despicable. Well,
now that I've got you, I intend to give you hell,
and I'm perfectly right. Consider your actions: At festivals,
in Pan-Hellenic harmony, like true blood-brothers, you share

the selfsame basin of holy water, and sprinkle
altars all over Greece—Olympia, Delphoi,
Thermopylai . . . (I could go on and on, if length were my only object.) But now, when the Persians sit by
and wait, in the very presence of your enemies, you fight
each other, destroy *Greek* men, destroy *Greek* cities!
—Point One of my address is now concluded.
KINESIAS. [*Gazing at* PEACE.]
I'm destroyed, if this is drawn out much longer!
LYSISTRATA. [*Serenely unconscious of the interruption.*]
—Men of Sparta, I direct these remarks to you.
Have you forgotten that a Spartan suppliant once came
to beg assistance from Athens? Recall Perikleidas:
Fifty years ago, he clung to our altar
his face dead-white above his crimson robe, and pleaded
for an army. Messene was pressing you hard in revolt,
and to this upheaval, Poseidon, the Earthshaker, added
another. But Kimon took four thousand troops
from Athens—an army which saved the state of Sparta.
Such treatment have you received at the hands of Athens,
you who devastate the country that came to your aid!
KINESIAS. [*Stoutly; the condemnation of his enemy has made him forget the girl momentarily.*]
You're right, Lysistrata. The Spartans are clearly in the wrong!
SPARTAN. [*Guiltily backing away from* PEACE, *whom he has attempted to pat.*]
Hit's wrong, I reckon, but that's the purtiest behind . . .
LYSISTRATA. [*Turning to the* ATHENIANS.]
—Men of Athens, do you think I'll let *you* off?
Have you forgotten the Tyrant's days,[37] when you wore
the smock of slavery, when the Spartans turned to the spear,
cut down the pride of Thessaly, des-

patched the friends
of tyranny, and dispossessed your op-
pressors? Recall:
On that great day, your only allies were
Spartans;
your liberty came at their hands, which
stripped away
your servile garb and clothed you again
in Freedom!
SPARTAN. [*Indicating* LYSISTRATA.]
Hain't never seed no higher type of
woman.
KINESIAS. [*Indicating* PEACE.]
Never saw one I wanted so much to
top.
LYSISTRATA. [*Oblivious to the byplay, ad-
dressing both groups.*]
With such a history of mutual benefits
conferred
and received, why are you fighting?
Stop this wickedness!
Come to terms with each other! What
prevents you?
SPARTAN. We'd a heap sight druther
make Peace, if we was indemnified
with a plumb strategic location.
[*Pointing at* PEACE's *rear.*] We'll take
thet butte.
LYSISTRATA. Butte?
SPARTAN. The Promontory of Pylos—
Sparta's Back Door.
We've missed it fer a turrible spell.
[*Reaching.*] Hev to keep our
hand in.
KINESIAS. [*Pushing him away.*] The price
is too high—you'll never take that!
LYSISTRATA. Oh, let them have it.
KINESIAS. What room will we have left
for maneuvers?
LYSISTRATA. Demand another spot in
exchange.
KINESIAS. [*Surveying* PEACE *like a map as
he addresses the* SPARTAN.]
Then you hand over to us—uh, let me
see—
let's try Thessaly[38]— [*Indicating the rele-
vant portions of* PEACE.] First of all,
Easy Mountain . . .
then the Maniac Gulf behind it . . . and
down to Megara
for the legs . . .
SPARTAN. You cain't take all of thet!
Yore plumb
out of yore mind!
LYSISTRATA. [*To* KINESIAS.] Don't argue.
Let the legs go. [KINESIAS *nods. A*

pause. General smiles of agreement.]
KINESIAS. [*Doffing his cloak.*]
I feel an urgent desire to plow a few
furrows.
SPARTAN. [*Doffing his cloak.*]
Hit's time to work a few loads of fer-
tilizer in.
LYSISTRATA. Conclude the treaty and
the simple life is yours.
If such is your decision, convene your
councils,
and then deliberate the matter with
your allies.
KINESIAS. *Deliberate? Allies?* We're over-
extended now!
Wouldn't every ally approve of our po-
sition—
Union Now?
SPARTAN. I know I kin speak for ourn.
KINESIAS. And I for ours. Even the
Karystian gigolos.
LYSISTRATA. I heartily approve. Now
first attend to your purification,
then we, the women, will welcome you
to the Citadel
and treat you to all the delights of a
home-cooked banquet.
Then you'll exchange your oaths and
pledge your faith,
and every man of you will take his wife
and depart for home. [LYSISTRATA *and*
PEACE *enter the Akropolis.*]
KINESIAS. Let's hurry!
SPARTAN. Lead on, everwhich
way's yore pleasure.
KINESIAS. This way, then—and
HURRY! [*The delegation exeunt at a
run.*]
CHORUS OF WOMEN. I'd never stint on
anybody.
And now I include, in my boundless
bounty, the younger set.
Attention, you parents of teenage girls
about to debut in the social whirl.
Here's what you get:
Embroidered linens, lush brocades,
a huge assortment of ready-mades,
from mantles to shifts;
plus bracelets and bangles of solid
gold—
every item my wardrobe holds—absolute gifts!
Don't miss this offer. Come to my
place,
barge right in, and make your choice.
You can't refuse.

Everything there must go today.
Finders keepers—cart it away! How can
  you lose?
Don't spare me. Open all the locks.
Break every seal. Empty every box.
  Keep ferreting—
And your sight's considerably better
  than mine
if you should possibly chance to find a
  single thing.
CHORUS OF MEN. Troubles, friend? Too
  many mouths
to feed, and not a scrap in the house to
  see you through?
Faced with starvation? Don't give it a
  thought.
Pay attention; I'll tell you what I'm
  gonna do.
I overbought. I'm overstocked.
Every room in my house is clogged
  with flour (best ever),
glutted with luscious loaves whose size
you wouldn't believe. I need the space;
  do me a favor:
Bring gripsacks, knapsacks, duffle bags,
pitchers, cisterns, buckets, and kegs
  around to me.
A courteous servant will see to your
  needs;
he'll fill them up with A-1 wheat—and
  all for free!
—Oh. Just one final word before
you turn your steps to my front door: I
  happen to own
a dog. Tremendous animal. Can't stand
  a leash. And bites like hell—better
  stay home. [*The united* CHORUS *flocks to
  the door of the Akropolis.*]
KORYPHAIOS OF MEN. [*Banging at the
  door.*] Hey, open up in there! [*The
  door opens, and the* COMMISSIONER *appears. He wears a wreath, carries a torch,
  and is slightly drunk. He addresses the
  KORYPHAIOS.*]
COMMISSIONER. You know the Regula-
  tions.
Move along! [*He sees the entire
  CHORUS.*]—And why are YOU loung-
  ing around?
I'll wield my trusty torch and scorch the
  lot! [*The CHORUS backs away in mock
  horror. He stops and looks at his torch.*]
—*This* is the bottom of the barrel. A
  cheap burlesque bit.
I refuse to do it. I have my pride. [*With
  a start, he looks at the audience, as though

hearing a protest. He shrugs and ad-
  dresses the audience.*]—No choice, eh?
Well, if that's the way it is, we'll take the
  trouble.
Anything to keep you happy. [*The
  CHORUS advances eagerly.*]
KORYPHAIOS OF MEN. Don't forget us!
We're in this, too. Your trouble is ours!
COMMISSIONER. [*Resuming his character
  and jabbing with his torch at the
  CHORUS.*] Keep moving!
Last man out of the way goes home
  without hair!
Don't block the exit. Give the Spartans
  some room.
They've dined in comfort; let them go
  home in peace. [*The CHORUS shrinks
  back from the door.* KINESIAS, *wreathed
  and quite drunk, appears at the door. He
  speaks his first speech in Spartan.*]
KINESIAS. Hain't never seed sech a
  spread! Hit were splendiferous!
COMMISSIONER. I gather the Spartans
  won friends and influenced people?
KINESIAS. And *we've* never been so brilliant. It was the wine.
COMMISSIONER. Precisely. The reason?
  A sober Athenian is just
non compos. If I can carry a little proposal
I have in mind, our Foreign Service will
  flourish,
guided by this rational rule: *No Ambassador
Without a Skinful.* Reflect on our past
  performance:
Down to a Spartan parley we troop, in
  a state
of disgusting sobriety, looking for
  trouble. It muddles
our senses: we read between the lines;
  we hear,
not what the Spartans say, but what we
  suspect
they might have been about to be going
  to say.
We bring back paranoid reports—
  cheap fiction, the fruit
of temperance. Cold-water diplomacy,
  pah! Contrast
this evening's total pleasure, the free-
  and-easy
give-and-take of friendship: If we were
  singing,
*Just Kleitagora and me,
Alone in Thessaly,*

and someone missed his cue and cut in
 loudly,
Ajax, son of Telamon,
He was one hell of a man—
no one took it amiss, or started a war;
we clapped him on the back and gave
 three cheers. [*During this recital, the*
 CHORUS *has sidled up to the door.*]
—Dammit, are you back here again?
 [*Waving his torch.*] Scatter!
Get out of the road, you gallowsbait!
KINESIAS. Yes, everyone out of the way.
 They're coming out. [*Through the door
 emerge the* SPARTAN DELEGATION, *a flutist, the* ATHENIAN DELEGATION, LYSIS-
 TRATA, KLEONIKE, MYRRHINE, *and the
 rest of the women from the citadel, both
 Athenian and Peloponnesian. The*
 CHORUS *splits into its male and female
 components and draws to the side to give
 the procession room.*]
SPARTAN. [*To the* FLUTIST.] Friend and
 kinsman, take up them pipes a
 yourn.
I'd like fer to shuffle a bit and sing a
 right sweet song in honor of Athens
 and us'uns, too.
COMMISSIONER. [*To the* FLUTIST.] Marvelous, marvelous—come, take up your
 pipes! [*To the* SPARTAN.]
I certainly love to see you Spartans
 dance. [*The* FLUTIST *plays, and the*
 SPARTAN *begins a slow dance.*]
SPARTAN. Memory,
  send me
  your Muse,
  who knows
  our glory,
  knows Athens'—
 Tell the story:
 At Artemision
like gods, they stampeded
the hulks of the Medes, and
  beat them.

 And Leonidas
 leading us—
 the wild boars
 And the foam flowered,
 flowered and flowed,
 down our cheeks
 to our knees below.
 The Persians there
 like the sands of the sea—

 Hither, huntress,

virgin, goddess,
tracker, slayer,
to our truce!
Hold us ever
fast together;
bring our pledges
love and increase;
wean us from the
fox's wiles—

Hither, huntress!
Virgin, hither!
LYSISTRATA. [*Surveying the assemblage
 with a proprietary air.*] Well, the pre-
 liminaries are over—very nicely, too.
So, Spartans, [*Indicating the* PELOPONNE-
 SIAN WOMEN *who have been hostages.*]
 take these girls back home. And *you*
 [*To the* ATHENIAN DELEGATION, *indicating the women from the Akropolis.*]
take *these* girls. Each man stand by his
 wife, each wife
by her husband. Dance to the gods'
 glory, and thank them
for the happy ending. And from now
 on, please be careful.
Let's not make the same mistakes again.
 [*The delegations obey; the men and
 women of the* CHORUS *join again for a
 rapid ode.*]
CHORUS. Start the chorus dancing,
 Summon all the Graces,
Send a shout to Artemis in invocation.
 Call upon her brother,
 healer, chorus master,
Call the blazing Bacchus, with his mad-
 dened muster.

Call the flashing, fiery Zeus, and
call his mighty, blessed spouse, and
call the gods, call all the gods,
to witness now and not forget
our gentle, blissful Peace—the gift,
 the deed of Aphrodite.
  Ai!
 Alalai! Paion!
 Leap you! Paion!
 Victory! Alalai!
Hail! Hail! Hail!
LYSISTRATA. Spartan, let's have another
 song from you, a new one.
SPARTAN. Leave darlin' Taygetos,
 Spartan Muse! Come to us
 once more, flyin'
 and glorifyin'
 Spartan themes:

the god an Amyklai,
Tyndaros' twins,
the valiant ones,
playing still by Eurotas' streams.

Up! Advance!
Leap to the dance!

Help us hymn Sparta,
lover of dancin'
lover of foot-pats,
where girls go prancin'
like fillies along Eurotas' banks,
whirlin' the dust, twinklin' their shanks,
shakin' their hair
like Maenads playin'
and jugglin' the thyrsis,
in frenzy obeyin'
Leda's daughter, the fair, the pure
Helen, the mistress of the choir.

Here, Muse, here!
Bind up your hair!

Stamp like a deer! Pound your feet!
Clap your hands! Give us a beat!

Sing the greatest,
sing the mightiest,
sing the conqueror,
sing to honor her—
Athene of the Bronze House!
　　Sing Athene! [*Exeunt omnes, dancing and singing.*]

1. The play's two time scales should be noted. By one, its action encompasses a day, beginning at dawn and lasting until after sundown; by the other, its events logically occupy a period of weeks, if not months—not that this sort of logic has much to do with the case. At no point is the play stopped to indicate the passage of time.
2. Kleonike's actions approach those of the stock bibulous old woman too closely to indicate a sweet young thing. She is older than Lysistrata, who fits comfortably in the vague borderline between "young matron" and "matron." Quite a bit younger are Myrrhine and Lampito.
3. The constant Athenian gustatory passion, rendered sharper by the War's embargo: eels from Lake Kopaïs in Boiotia.
4. Literally, "from Anagyrous," a rural deme of Attika which took its name from the plant *anagyros*, "the stinking bean-trefoil." Kleonike's riposte puns on this by reference to an old proverb: "Well, the *anagyros* certainly seems to have been disturbed" = "you've really stirred up a stink" = "the fat's in the fire." Here, as often when

geographical names are involved, it is more important to render the fact of a pun than the specifics of the original.
5. In employing a somewhat debased American mountain dialect to render the Laconic Greek of Lampito and her countrymen, I have tried to evoke something like the Athenian attitude toward their perennial enemies. They regarded the Spartans as formidably old-fashioned bumpkins, imperfectly civilized, possessed of a determined indifference to more modern value systems.
6. There are frequent references throughout the play to the fact that Athenian women, for cosmetic reasons, plucked out all their pubic hair. [P.H.]
7. Or perhaps treason. The Greek refers to a General Eukrates, who may be the brother of the illustrious and ill-starred Nikias. If so, he was put to death by the Thirty Tyrants in 404.
8. In the Opisthodomos, at the back of the Parthenon, was kept the reserve fund of one thousand silver talents established at the beginning of the War twenty years before. Since the fund had been dipped into during the previous year, Lampito's expression constitutes more than a normal exaggeration.
9. This sentence may seem a startling expansion of the word *poi* (literally, "Whither?"; here, "What is the point of . . . ?"), but is in a good cause—an attempt to explain and motivate the darkest white horse in literature. The sequence is this: Lysistrata, annoyed at the interruption, sarcastically proposed a gaudy sacrifice; Kleonike, whose mind is proof against sarcasm, points out that it has nothing to do with the matter at hand.
10. Not one of Pheidias' colossal statues, but the old wooden figure of Athene Polias ("Guardian of the City") in the Erechtheion.
11. I have given the Koryphaios a bad memory and placed the object of his anger in the audience to point up what is happening. Rhodia, wife of the demagogue Lykon, was a real person, frequently lampooned for her morals. In a not unusual breaking of the dramatic illusion, her name occurs here as a surprise for the expected "Lysistrata." Some commentators, disliking surprises, have decided that Lysistrata is the wife of someone named Lykon—thus managing to ruin a joke and import an obscurity without the change of a word.
12. Kleomenes' occupation of the Akropolis in 508, high point of his unsuccessful bid to help establish the Athenian aristocrats, lasted rather less than the six years which the Chorus seems to remember. The actual time was two days.
13. Most of the Athenian fleet was at the moment based in Samos, practically the only Ionian ally left to Athens, in order to make ready moves against those states who had defected to Sparta in 412 after the Sicilian fiasco.
14. The Greek refers to one Boupalos, a Chian sculptor mercilessly lampooned by the testy poet until, as a doubtful tradition has it, he hanged

himself. The only surviving verse of Hipponax which bears on the subject ("Hold my clothes; I'll sock Boupalos in the jaw") does little to establish the tradition—or, indeed, to dispel the feeling that Hipponax was about as effective a boxer as the Koryphaios.

15. The observation is clearly offered as an illustrative quotation, and the sentiment is certainly Euripidean. But the extant tragic line nearest it in expression is Sophokles *Elektra* 622.

16. That is, a *proboulos,* one of the ten extraordinary Athenian officials appointed in 413 after the Sicilian catastrophe as a check on legislative excesses. Chiefly responsible for drafting the agenda of Senate and Assembly, the commissioners were drawn from men over forty years of age. The two whose names we know were well along: Hagnon was over sixty, Sophokles (if the poet is meant, a matter not absolutely settled) eighty-two. But these instances scarcely prove Wilamowitz' contention that decrepitude was a necessary qualification for the office; and Aristophanes' Commissioner, for all his choleric conservatism, is marked by vigor and intellectual curiosity.

17. This expansion makes more explicit a reference to the political clubs, or *synōmosiai,* who caucussed and combined their votes to gain verdicts and offices, thus paving the road for the oligarchic upheaval in May of 411.

18. *Iliad* 6.492 (Hektor to Andromache).

19. Traditionally interpreted (perhaps with too much enthusiasm) as a reference to the longing of the Athenian commonality for the return of glory-and-shame Alkibiades, who obliged the following summer.

20. In the Greek, *Lysimachas,* "Battle-settlers," a pun on the name of the heroine; also, if D. M. Lewis is right, a reference to her real-life model Lysimache—in 411, priestess of Athene.

21. Most of this rather torturous allegory is self-explanatory, but the "clumps" are the political clubs, or "Friends of Oligarchy," mentioned earlier. See above, note 17.

22. Here and earlier, the women are certainly armed, but with what? The pronouns supplied by the Greek are tantalizingly specific in gender, but in nothing else; solutions usually bring out the worst in interpreters. I have tried to assign appropriate weapons early, and continue them to this denouement—but visualizers (or producers, if any there be) are at liberty, as elsewhere, to use their imaginations. One caveat: the Greek will not bear a direct repetition of the bath given earlier to the Old Men by the Old Women.

23. The *triobolon,* the three-obol per diem wage for jury duty, which often constituted the only income of elderly men. It would naturally be stored inside the Citadel in the Treasury.

24. The reference, to a famous statuary group by the sculptor Kritios in the Athenian Agora, picks up an earlier quotation from a popular *skolion,* or drinking-song, on the assassination of the tyrant Hipparchos: "I'll carry my sword concealed in a myrtle bough. . . ." The translation expands on the idea, but hides the quotation in the familiar "sword in olive branch."

25. Since this passage is frequently cited as primary evidence for the *cursus honorum* of a high-born young girl in fifth-century Athens, here are the steps set forth a bit more explicitly: (1) *arrêphoros* ("relic-bearer") to Athene, one of four little girls who carried the Goddess' sacred objects in Her semi-annual festival of the *Arrêphoria;* (2) *aletris* ("mill-girl") to the Founding Mother (doubtless Athene), one of the girls who ground the meal to be made into sacrificial cakes; (3) *arktos* ("she-bear") at the *Brauronia,* a festival of Artemis held every fifth year at Brauron in Attika, centering on a myth which told of the killing of a tame bear sacred to that goddess; and (4) *kanêphoros* ("basket-bearer"), the maiden who bore the sacrificial cake and led the procession at Athens' most important festivals, such as the City Dionysia and the Great Panathenaia.

26. This money originally made up the treasury of the Delian League, an alliance of Greek states against Persia formed by the Athenian Aristeides in 477; following its transfer, for safety's sake, from the island of Delos to Athens in 454, it became for all practical purposes Athenian property, supported by tribute from the Allies. Athens' heavy expenses in Sicily, followed by the Allies' nonpayment and defection, made this question all too pointed in early 411.

27. To Leipsydrion, in the mountains north of Athens, where the besieged Alkmaionid exiles held out for a time against the forces of the tyrant Hippias. Since this siege, ever after symbolic of the Noble Lost Cause, took place in 513, commentators find it necessary to point out that the Chorus of Men couldn't *really* have fought in a battle 102 years before; that they are pretending, or speaking by extension for the Athenian Fighting Spirit, or whatever. Seemingly, this goes without saying; actually, it is dead wrong. Dramaturgy has little to do with geriatrics; Aristophanes needed a Chorus of Men old enough to be hidebound, decrepit, so old that they would first see the Women's Revolt, not in terms of sex, but of politics—the recrudescence of a personally experienced tyranny. He was cheerfully prepared to have them average 120 years of age, if anyone cared to count. The critical attitude gives one pause: A modern American playwright who composed a fantastic comedy, set in the present, featuring a Chorus of GAR members—would he be greeted with a flourish of actuarial tables?

28. A cave on the Akropolis containing a shrine to the god, outside the Citadel wall, which it adjoined on the northwest.

29. By inserting this speech (and the reply to it) I do not wish to make Lysistrata a religious skeptic, but to point out the joke. No one had ever seen the snake; even its most famous action, that

of assisting Themistokles to persuade the Athenians to abandon the city before the battle of Salamis, had been accomplished by its nonappearance.

30. A perfectly good Greek name, but in this context it evokes a pun on a common sexual application of the verb *kinein*, "move."

31. In the Greek, Kinesias compares his phallos to "Herakles at table"—a stock comedy bit wherein the glutton hero, raving with hunger, is systematically diddled of his dinner by his hosts.

32. I maintain the Commissioner as Athens' representative in this scene, not primarily because of the testimony of the manuscripts (shaky support at best), but from the logic and structure of the speeches themselves.

33. Correctly, a *skytalê*, a tapered rod which was Sparta's contribution to cryptography. A strip of leather was wound around the rod, inscribed with the described message, and unwound for transmission. A messenger then delivered the strip to the qualified recipient, who deciphered it by winding it around a rod uniform in size and shape with the first. Any interceptor found a meaningless string of letters.

34. The ensuing reconciliation scene, with its surrogate sexuality, is one of the most curious in Aristophanes. It is not lyric; yet both its diction, oddly diffuse and redundant, and its meter, a paeonic variation on a common trochaic dialogue measure which paradoxically makes it much more regular, seem to call for extensive choreography. I have tried to hedge my bet by stilting the English and employing an irregular scheme depending heavily on off-rhymes.

35. A notorious homosexual; on that account, one of Aristophanes' favorite targets for at least twenty years.

36. God of messengers and thieves; in Athens in every doorway stood a statue of Hermes (i.e., a *herm*, usually a bust of the god surmounting an ithyphallic pillar), protector of the door and guardian against thieves—it takes one to know one. The wholesale mutilation of these statues by persons unknown, just before the sailing of the Sicilian expedition in 415, led to the recall of Alkibiades—and thus, perhaps, to the loss of the expedition and ultimately of the war.

37. The reign of Hippias, expelled by the Athenians in 510 with the aid of Kleomenes and his Spartans, who defeated the tyrant's Thessalian allies.

38. Puns on proper names, particularly geographical ones, rarely transfer well, as the following bits of sexual cartography will show. "Easy Mountain": an impossible pun on Mt. Oita, replacing the Greek's *Echinous*, a town in Thessaly whose name recalls *echinos* "hedgehog"—slang for the female genitalia. "Maniac Gulf": for Maliac Gulf, with less dimension than the Greek's *Mêlia kolpon*, which puns both on bosom and pudendum. The "legs of Megara" are the walls that connected that city with her seaport, Nisaia.

The Dyskolos

Menander

The distinctions between Old, Middle, and New Comedy were purely arbitrary conveniences of ancient critics. It has already been mentioned that only one example of Middle Comedy survives (Aristophanes' last extant play, *Plutus*), and exactly what characteristics Middle Comedy in general may have had must therefore remain conjectural. It is clear, however, that New Comedy was substantially different from Old, though it began little more than half a century after Aristophanes' death. These differences remain of tremendous importance, since New Comedy has formed the basis for the mainstream of Western comic drama to the present day.

The acknowledged master of New Comedy was Menander, who was born around 342 B.C. and died around 292. Although comedy continued to be written and produced in Athens from the time of Aristophanes to the time of Menander and beyond, none of the scripts of other authors have survived, and modern knowledge of these works is therefore necessarily limited. A great deal of critical commentary has survived, however, which establishes not only Menander's preeminence but also many of the characteristics of his plays and those of his contemporaries. In fact, only small fragments of Menander's works were known until the twentieth century; in 1905, the major portions of three Menandrian plays were found in Egyptian papyri, and only in 1958 was the first virtually complete play of Menander printed from an Egyptian papyrus codex. It is perhaps indicative of the dependability of the earlier critical tradition that these important discoveries have not resulted in significant reassessments of Menander's achievements.

Menander appears to have come from a family of considerable means and to have grown up in an Athens which, although dominated by the Macedonians, was still one of the major cultural centers of the Western world. He maintained personal friendships with the leading political and philosophical figures of his day and may very well have known Aristotle, who left Athens when Menander was nearly twenty years old. Tradition reports that Menander's uncle was Alexis of Thuriei, a comic poet responsible for Menander's education. In any case, he produced his first play shortly after his twentieth birthday, and five years later won his first victory in the annual comic playwriting competition with *The Dyskolos*. He is said to have completed some one hundred plays in his lifetime, and to have drowned in a swimming accident shortly past the age of fifty.

The sole play of Menander's that survives virtually complete is *The Dyskolos*. In it one can see the many changes in structure and in content that separate Old Comedy from New. The play retains a vestigial chorus, but this is not integral to the plot in any way. Menander provides a line or two by way of introducing one choral interlude, but for all practical purposes the only function of the chorus is to provide entertainment between the episodes; the five episodes have evolved into the five acts which were to be the standard form for playwriting for some fifteen hundred years. The script provides no lines for the chorus at all, but simply indicates when a choral interlude is to be performed. The plot is a purely domestic and fictional one, revolving around the overwhelming love of a young man for a nubile young girl, and the obstacles presented to the fulfillment of this love by her obstreperous father. There is no reason to suppose that Menander did not invent these plot devices himself, but they were to become the stock devices of domestic comedy to the present day. These devices were strung together by Menander into a clear, simple, and direct story line, with a single central action in the best Aristotelian sense. Gone were Aristophanes' looser plot structures based on a "happy idea," but gone too was the sense of exuberance and celebration that had elevated these earlier forms into the highest expression of comic art. The plot of *The Dyskolos* may be assumed to be typical of Menander's work: Sostratos, an attractive and well-bred young man from the city, goes hunting in the country and meets a beautiful young girl with whom he instantly falls in love. At the opening of the play, however, he learns that the girl's father is a curmudgeon and misanthrope with whom it is virtually impossible to deal. Thus, Sostratos devotes himself throughout the play, with the help of sundry friends and acquaintances, to winning the irascible old man's assent to a marriage. Each subsequent event in the play contributes to completing this central action, until Knemon capitulates in the climactic speech beginning, "Not one of you could make me change my mind." Evidently Menander could not resist exposing his title character to one further round of harassment, however, and act 5 forms something of a coda in which Knemon is reduced to total acquiescence with the general merrymaking. It may be noted that a domestic plot such as this, based on romantic love, is in one sense more universal than the plots of Aristophanes: it touches common notes in the lives of virtually all human beings rather than gaining its comic effects from specific political and philosophical problems then current in Athens. On the other hand, it may also be said that Aristophanes transcended the particularity of his topical jokes to offer central comic ideas that were universal (stopping wars has been a concern of virtually all societies everywhere), whereas Menander's domestic concerns allow an audience to laugh without having to think much.

Menander's real interest appears to lie more in character development than in thought content. The late work of Euripides may have been more influential in Menander's development than most of Aristophanes' plays, and one can see Euripides' interest in exploring the human psyche at work in much of what Menander has done. Again, there is no way to know how many of the characters in Menander's plays were created by him and how many were a part of his comic heritage when he began to work, but it is certain that these characters have become the stock figures of comedy in the centuries since his time. The young lovers, the irascible parent, the clever servant, the scheming parasite, and the authoritarian cook are stock comic characters who reappear in Roman, Renaissance, and modern drama, always recognizable "types" and yet, when drawn by the best comic playwrights, individualized and human as well. Menander took the masks which had been a standard feature of Greek stagecraft from earliest known times and converted them to individualized use, so that, far from the grotesqueries of Aristophanes' animal masks and giant phalluses, Menander's masks helped the audience to recognize which of the many human stock types each actor was at that moment representing. Masks serving this function were to persist in the comic theater well into the Renaissance. Menander's importance in originating, or at least institutionalizing, these stock characters can hardly be overstated, and in *The Dyskolos* they are typically portrayed, fully developed, and at the same time individualized. Knemon is more than just a typical old curmudgeon, for Menander supplies a great many touches that help to explain his behavior in understandable psychological terms. Sostratos is more than a silly city slicker in love with a country girl; he is rendered warmly human and understandable, for example, not only by his willingness to work the soil, but even more by his inability to do so for very long. This approach to character development, refined from Euripides but especially adapted to comedy by Menander, has provided the basis for much Western drama (and almost all Western comedy) for over two thousand years.

The Dyskolos is not without thematic interest as well. It explores country mores and city mores, contrasting the people and the interests of each life-style. It explores appropriate reaction to the ill behavior of others, both in the extreme misanthropy of Knemon and in the milder, nobler rejection of dishonorable conduct by Sostratos and Gorgias. It explores the matter of how marriage contracts may best be worked out, with both love and business convenience as factors to be considered. It can hardly be argued that any of these issues is investigated with a great deal of profundity; it seems unlikely that, even without the heritage of over two millennia of dramatic tradition, Menander's audiences found these insights especially new or challenging. Menander's poetry may similarly be described as workmanlike and effective, but hardly of the beauty and impressiveness of the great writers of the preceding century. Plot and characterization were the great achievements of Menander's art, and these achievements were considerable indeed.

One ancient critic is quoted as having exclaimed, "O Menander! O life! Which of you imitated the other?" Of course, this alleged "realism" is a long way from what would be described as realism in today's theater, but it points to Menander's very considerable achievements that set the pattern for the future development of drama. For underlying both the intricacies of his human characters and the logical development of his domestic plots is a commitment to portraying the loves and concerns of ordinary people, a commitment which the fifth-century-B.C. Greeks seem not to have shared, but which has furnished a rationale for most later innovations in dramatic technique at least up to the nineteenth century. The notion that an audience in a theater wishes to identify with people and situations much like its own may be said to have originated in New Comedy. Furthermore, the workmanlike notion that there are definite playwriting techniques and strategies which one may master and which will lead toward these goals is illustrated by another anecdote surviving from Menander's work. A friend is supposed to have asked him whether his play was ready for the approaching festival, and Menander is reported to have replied, "Yes, I have the structure worked out; I need only set the lines to it." This insight into Menander's working methods may not be documentable, but it rings with truth across the centuries.

N.B. All footnotes for The Dyskolos were written by the translator.

The Dyskolos

Translated by Carroll Moulton

Characters
Pan, god of the woodlands
Chaireas, parasite of Sostratos
Sostratos, son of Kallippides
Pyrrhias, young slave of Sostratos
Knemon, the dyskolos, *an old farmer,*
*   father of Myrrhine*
Myrrhine, daughter of Knemon, beloved of
*   Sostratos*
Daos, Gorgias' servant
Gorgias, Knemon's stepson
Sikon, a cook
Geta, slave of Sostratos' family
Simiche, old servant of Knemon
Mother of Sostratos
Kallippides, father of Sostratos

SCENE. *Phyle, a country district near
Athens. In the center of the stage is the en-
trance to a cave, where a shrine, sacred to*
PAN *and the Nymphs, is located. Two houses
are at either side: stage right is the house of*
KNEMON, *stage left the house of* GORGIAS.
*The exit stage right leads to the fields, the
exit stage left leads to the road to town.*

Prologue

[*Enter* PAN.]
PAN. Our scene's the countryside, in Attica,
where farmers till the rocks for bread.
   This place
is Phyle. The Nymphs are famous here:
their sacred cave is right behind me.
On my right, the farm is owned by
   Knemon,
a man self-exiled from the human race:
an utter grouch and not gregarious.
That understates the case! He's over
   sixty
and refuses to enjoy a chat with anyone.
Because we're neighbors, he consents
   to greet me,
though this is an exception to his rule.
I'm sure he's promptly sorry he's been
   civil.
All the same, despite this temperament,
he got married to a widow. Her first
   husband
had just died and left behind a son:
the child was very young then.
The marriage was more like suing for
   divorce,
with sessions held all day and half the
   night.
Knemon nagged and was unhappy.
   When a little girl
was born, things went from bad to
   worse. When nothing else
could change her bitter, dreary way of
   life,
his wife renounced the grouch, sought
   out her son
again, and lived with him. He owns a
   little
piece of land here, barely big enough
to feed himself, his mother, and a single
servant, faithful to the family.
The lad's turned out a fine young man,
who boasts a fund of sense beyond his
   years:
maturity comes easily when life goes
   hard.
Old Knemon grouches on, his solitude
intact but for his daughter and a servant hag.

157

He carries logs, and digs, and sweats,
and hates the world in order: starting
  here
with wife and neighbors, and going on
  for miles
down the road. A lonely childhood,
  though,
has kept his daughter innocent: piously
she tends this shrine. Her care of us in-
  clines
my Nymphs and me to keep a special
  watch
on her. So, when a young man from
  the town,
whose father is extremely rich and
  owns
some large estates, came out to hunt
  here with
a friend, he chanced upon our neighborhood
and fell in love with Knemon's daughter. (You
might say a god had had a hand in it.)
These are the highlights: if you wish to
  `see
the details (as I hope you do), you will.
Because I think I see the youthful lover
coming toward us with his fellow
  huntsman.
Their words will pick up just where I've
left off. [Exit.]

Act 1

Enter SOSTRATOS and CHAIREAS.
CHAIREAS. What, Sostratos? You saw a
  free-born girl who crowned
these statues of the Nymphs with flowers, and you fell
for her like that?
SOSTRATOS. At once.
CHAIREAS. Fast work. I'll bet
you left the house to fall in love on purpose!
SOSTRATOS. You're joking, Chaireas.
  I'm the one who's suffering.
CHAIREAS. [Sarcastically.] Oh, I believe
  it!
SOSTRATOS. I've brought you here with
  me
so you can help me. You're a friend,

and very
practical.
CHAIREAS. Well, in such cases, Sostratos,
my strategies are these. A friend of
  mine
is horny for a whore: my plan's abduction.
I get loaded, burn her door down, am
  totally
irrational. I get him laid before
they're introduced. Delay can only swell
his love; a swift relief cures swift
  amours.
But say a friend plans marriage to a
  maiden,
I change my tack and do his homework
  for him.
I learn the background, income, personal details.
The way I fix things, any friend of
  mine
remembers me forever.
SOSTRATOS. Sure he does—
[Aside.] but all this may not suit me.
CHAIREAS. [Continuing right on.] Now the
  first
requirement is for you to fill me in.
SOSTRATOS. I sent my hunting servant
  Pyrrhias out early . . .
CHAIREAS. Where to?
SOSTRATOS. To meet the father of the
  girl,
or else to find her guardian,
whoever he may be.
CHAIREAS. [Taken aback.] Good God,
  you're kidding!
SOSTRATOS. [Sheepishly.] I guess you're
  right. I shouldn't
have used a servant for that kind of
  thing.
But men in love don't often think so
  clearly.
I've been wondering for some time at
  his delay.
I told him to investigate things here
and then report directly back at home.
[Enter PYRRHIAS, at a dead run.]
PYRRHIAS. Let me pass! Watch out! Get
  out of the way!
The madman's after me!
SOSTRATOS. What's this, boy?
PYRRHIAS. Clear out!
SOSTRATOS. What is it?
PYRRHIAS. He's throwing stones and
  mud at me!
I've had it!

SOSTRATOS. What? Where are you running, idiot?
PYRRHIAS. [*Stops short.*]
You mean he's stopped?
SOSTRATOS. Of course!
PYRRHIAS. But I thought . . .
SOSTRATOS. [*Exasperated.*] What on earth
are you trying to say?
PYRRHIAS. Let's get out of here!
SOSTRATOS. *Where?*
PYRRHIAS. [*Shuddering, and pointing to*
KNEMON's *house.*]
As far away as possible from that door!
Oh, he's the son of Woe! The man who lives
in there, the man you sent me to—he's crazy!
He's cracked! The devil's in him, he's
. . . [*Breaks off with a grimace.*]
OHHHH! My *toes!!* I think I've broken almost
all of them! I fell and . . .
SOSTRATOS. [*To* CHAIREAS, *with a gesture*
toward PYRRHIAS.] Has he
gone mad, or done something he shouldn't?
CHAIREAS. He's obviously berserk.
PYRRHIAS. [*Still panting from his run.*]
No, no!!
Believe me, Sostratos! You must look out!
I ran so fast from him I'm out of breath.
[*Collecting himself.*]
I knocked and said that I was looking for
the master. An old and bitchy servant came
to meet me, and she pointed out the place
he was—a little hill, where he was crawling around
where his wild pears grow, gathering
bits of wood . . .[1]
CHAIREAS. How upset he is!
Do tell us what's the matter.
PYRRHIAS. I walked along
and came up near to him. I had in mind
to be extremely suave and tactful when
I spoke to him. "I beg your pardon, sir,"
I said, "I've come to see you on some business
which concerns you." He shot back,
"You bastard,

you've come to trespass on my farm. What's
the idea? You have some nerve!" With that,
he threw a load of dirt right in my face!
CHAIREAS.
The hell with him!
PYRRHIAS. I blinked and cursed him.
But then the old guy grabbed a stick and started
beating me. He shouted angrily,
"What business could we have together? Don't
you know the public road?"
CHAIREAS. This farmer
has to be completely nuts!
PYRRHIAS. Then he
began to chase me, round the hill at first,
and then right down here through the brush, damn near
two miles. He pelted me with mud
and stones and, when all else had failed, with pears!
The job was a disaster—and the man's
a monster! I'm begging you, clear out!
SOSTRATOS. Coward!
PYRRHIAS. You don't know what you're
up against. He'll eat us alive!
CHAIREAS. Perhaps the fellow is upset today.
Which leads me to believe it better
to postpone our visit, Sostratos.
My general rule for business is to wait
for the right moment.
PYRRHIAS. [*To both of them.*] Be sensible.
CHAIREAS. A nasty
disposition's common to poor farmers:
he's typical. Tomorrow morning early
I'll come out and see him by myself
now that I know the place. For now, relax:
come home with me. I'll handle this for you.
[*Without waiting for* SOSTRATOS' *reaction,*
CHAIREAS *exits.*]
PYRRHIAS. [*Eagerly.*] Let's follow him.
SOSTRATOS. [*Bursts out.*] That faker?
Why, he leaped
at an excuse to leave. Quite plainly
from the start
he disapproved of marriage plans
and came with me reluctantly. But—
YOU!
I'm damned if you don't get a whipping!

PYRRHIAS. [*Shocked.*] Why, what have I
done wrong, Sostratos?
SOSTRATOS. You clearly broke some law
here. . . .
PYRRHIAS. [*Thinking he means theft.*] I
swear I didn't take a thing.
SOSTRATOS. If that's
the truth, would he have beaten you?
PYRRHIAS. [*Staring offstage.*] He's here,
in person! I'm retreating, chief! You
talk
to him. [PYRRHIAS *exits in a panic.*][2]
SOSTRATOS. I couldn't do that! I'm no
good
at speeches. What am I to say to him?
He hardly looks the friendly sort.
He's bent on business. I'll
retreat a little from his door. That's
better.
He's all alone, and shouting: perhaps
he's mad?
By heaven, he's beginning to frighten
me!
I'd be a liar if I didn't admit it. [*Enter
KNEMON, in a towering rage.*]
KNEMON. Old Perseus was divinely
favored—*twice!*
He had his wings and didn't have to
meet
a single passerby. He also had
that thing to change the men who
bothered him
to stone.[3] What a fine possession! I
wish I had it now—I'd convert
this place into a sculpture garden!
Life is unendurable, by heaven,
when chattering strangers trespass on
your land!
You'd think, by God, I *liked* to waste my
time
along the highway! Well, I've given up
working
on this section of the farm. Too many
people
bother me. Just now they've chased
right up the hill
to get at me! God damn these wretched
mobs!!
[*Sees SOSTRATOS.*]
Someone's here again—standing right
at my front door!
SOSTRATOS [*To himself.*] I wonder if he'll
hit me.
KNEMON. The situation's desperate: a
man
can't even be alone to hang himself!

SOSTRATOS. [*Addressing him.*] Please
don't be angry at me, sir. I'm waiting
for a friend here.
KNEMON.]*Rhetorically.*] You see what I
was saying?
[*To SOSTRATOS.*] You think this property's the public square?
[*Ironically.*] If you've arranged appoint-
ments at my house,
you should provide for greater comfort. [*His voice rising.*] Why not
install a chair here? [*Shouts.*] Or, even
better, build
a *meeting room?* [*Desperate.*] This confounded insolence!
It plagues my life! My life's a living
hell!
[*Exits into his house.*]
SOSTRATOS. It's pretty clear that this affair is not
to be a casual effort; it's going to need
some nerve. I think I'll go see Geta,
Father's
slave. The very man I need, in fact:
he's got imagination, and he's most
experienced in every sort of planning.
I know he'll have a way to change the
old
man's mood. [*Pauses, then to himself.*]
Let's not lose time!
A lot might come of this, just in
a single day. [*A noise is heard at the door
of KNEMON'shouse.*] But someone's
coming out. [*Enter KNEMON's daughter.*][4]
MYRRHINE. Oh, heavens, what an awful
thing has happened!
What will I do? The nurse has gone
and dropped
our bucket down the well!
SOSTRATOS. [*Transfixed.*] Gods above,
Apollo, Castor, Pollux! Heal me—save
me!
What beauty!
MYRRHINE. [*Still to herself.*] When he
went out, my father
told me to heat some water. . . .
SOSTRATOS. [*To the audience.*] She's marvelous!
MYRRHINE. [*Distracted.*] He'll beat her to
a pulp if he should learn
what's happened. I've got no time to
waste—
dearest Nymphs, I must borrow water
from you.
[*Hesitates.*] I'd be ashamed, though, to

disturb the prayers
of anyone inside the shrine. . . .
SOSTRATOS. [*Addressing her.*] If I may,
I'd be delighted to fetch the water for
you.
MYRRHINE. [*Eagerly.*] Oh, yes—please
do! [*She gives him a jug.*]
SOSTRATOS. [*To himself, as he moves toward the cave.*] She's from the country, but
she's so well mannered! Can any of the
honored gods
save me now from love? [*He exits into the
shrine just as a noise is heard.*]
MYRRHINE. Oh, Lord,
what was that noise? Is Father coming
out?
I'll catch a beating if he finds me here
outside. [DAOS *enters from* GORGIAS'
house. He is speaking to GORGIAS'
mother, inside.]
DAOS. I can't keep sitting here with you
while Gorgias has to dig alone.
I'll have to help him.
[*He turns away from the door, and says to
himself.*] Damn you, poverty!
Why is it that we're always poor?
Our bad luck's like a guest who comes
to visit
and who won't go away.
[*Sostratos reenters from the shrine, bearing
the water.*]
SOSTRATOS. [*To* MYRRHINE.] I've
brought the water back
for you.
MYRRHINE. [*Motioning him toward* KNE-
MON'S *door.*] Please, over here.
DAOS. [*To himself.*] What can this man
be up to?
SOSTRATOS. [*To* MYRRHINE.] Good-bye!
Look after your father. [*Exit* MYR-
RHINE, *into* KNEMON'S *house.* SOS-
TRATOS *looks after her, and says to him-
self.*]
Oh, lord, I'm miserable! [*He gathers
himself together.*] Stop moaning, Sos-
tratos.
It's going to be all right.
DAOS. [*Eavesdropping, to himself.*] How's
that?
SOSTRATOS. [*Still to himself.*] Don't
worry.
Return with Geta, as you planned just
now—
and tell him everything that's hap-
pened here. [*Exit* SOSTRATOS.]

DAOS. [*Suspiciously.*] I'm ill-at-ease about
this business.
In fact, I don't approve of it at all!
This lad is doing favors for a girl—suspicious!
Knemon should rot in hell for this!
He leaves his little girl here all alone
and takes no proper care to guard her.
It's likely that the young man heard of
this
and sneaked up here to take advantage
of
a windfall. Clearly I will have to tell her
brother,
as quickly as I can, in order that
we both may see about protecting her.
I think I'd better go right now,
because I see a group of somewhat
drunken
worshipers of Pan carousing toward us.
I'd just as soon avoid their revelry.
[*Exit.*]

[*Choral Interlude.*][5]

Act 2

Enter GORGIAS *and* DAOS, *in the middle of
a conversation.*
GORGIAS. From what you've said of this
affair, Daos,
you handled it too casually.
DAOS. How's that?
GORGIAS. By God, you should have
pinned the man right on
the spot, whoever he was, and warned
him not
to try a thing like that again! But, as it
is,
you backed away from everything, just
like
a stranger. You can't just shuck off
family
obligations, Daos. My sister's still
our obligation, though her father keeps
avoiding us. But let's not imitate
his grumpiness. Besides, if shame
should come
upon my sister, the blame is also mine.
Outside the family, gossips never know
who did it. All they know is that it's

done.

DAOS.[6] But Master Gorgias, I'm absolutely scared
to death of the old man. He'll string me up
directly if he finds me at
his door.

GORGIAS. [*Reflectively.*] He is a problem,
I admit.
Converting him to better ways is
difficult:
we can't convince him by reproaching
him.
The law's on his side if we force him,
and
his grouchy temper turns aside persuasion.

DAOS. [*Staring offstage.*] Hold on a bit.
We haven't come in vain.
As I predicted, our man's come back.
[*Enter* SOSTRATOS.]

GORGIAS. You mean that one who's
wearing fancy clothes?

DAOS. That's him!

GORGIAS. A rascal, judging by his looks.

SOSTRATOS. [*To himself.*] I couldn't locate Geta at my house.
My mother's getting ready for a
sacrifice—
I don't know which—she's always at her
prayers,
parading round the town performing
them.
She's sent our servant out to hire some
chef.
I wasn't going to get involved in that
affair. I thought it best to come back
here
The time has to come to speak out for
myself.
No more pacing back and forth. I'll
knock.
Once I do that, my second thoughts
won't count.

GORGIAS. [*Steps up to him.*] I have a
pretty serious thing to say
to you, my friend. Please listen.

SOSTRATOS. Gladly. What's the matter?

GORGIAS. It's my opinion that the luck
of every
man is bound to change, no matter if
he's doing well or just the opposite;
and if a man is lucky, he'll only stay
that way as long as he can manage his
affairs without unjustly harming
others.

When his fortunate position leads
him to injustice, then he can expect
some changes in his fortune for the
worse.
A man who's doing badly, though, may
find
a better share in life, if in his plight
he lives uprightly, bears his fate with
simple
courage, and is admired for his integrity.
What's all this mean? I wouldn't feel
too smug
about your wealth, if I were you. Don't
come
and injure us, the poor. But rather
show
to others you deserve the wealth you
have.

SOSTRATOS. [*Puzzled.*] You think I'm doing something wrong right now?

GORGIAS. [*Bluntly.*] You thought you'd
get away with something cheap.
You planned to lure a free-born girl to
sin,
or watch for opportunity to do a thing
you'd pay for with your life!

SOSTRATOS. [*Shocked.*] My God!

GORGIAS. [*Sententiously.*] It's hardly
fair for you to use your leisure
to trouble those who have to work. Remember:
an injured man who's poor is hard to
handle.
The public's on his side, and he believes
that you've assaulted him, not simply
pushed him.

SOSTRATOS. [*Earnestly.*] I wish your lot
were better, friend! But now
please hear my side. . . .

DAOS. [*Interrupting.*] Master, that was
quite
a speech. Well done![7]

SOSTRATOS. [*Reprovingly.*] You too, you
chatterer!
I saw a certain girl here. I'm in love
with her. If this is wrong, I guess I'm
guilty.
What else am I to say? Except that I
have come here not to her, but so that I
may meet her father. Since I'm free by
birth
and have enough to live on, I'm prepared
to ask her hand without a dowry,

pledging

eternal love. [*Solemnly.*] If I came here intent

on evil, or to do to you some secret

harm, my friend, may Pan here and his Nymphs

avenge the deed by striking me right down

beside this house. I'm terribly upset

that you believed me less than honorable.

GORGIAS. [*Impressed.*] Well, if for my part I was more abrupt

than necessary, I apologize.

Your words convince me. You have me as your friend.

My man, I spoke to you not as a stranger:

I'm kin to her. The girl is my half-sister.

SOSTRATOS. [*Brightly.*] That's great! You'll be a help in what I plan!

GORGIAS. How so?

SOSTRATOS. You seem to be a generous man.

GORGIAS. I hardly want to put you off with vain

excuses, but I'll tell you how things are.

She's got a father like no other human

being who ever lived.

SOSTRATOS. [*Ironically.*] I think I know his temper.

GORGIAS. Trouble's not the word for it.

This farm he has would sell for quite a sum,

I think. But he refuses to employ a soul,

and works it all alone. He won't take on

a servant in the house, or hire a man:

he has no neighbor to disturb his solitude.

For him the nicest thing is seeing nobody.

He works most often with his daughter at

his side; he'll talk to her, but only her.

He finds it hard to chat with other people.

He says he'll marry her to any man

he finds who's like himself.

SOSTRATOS. [*Gloomily.*] But that's never!

GORGIAS. Friend, I wish you wouldn't get

involved. It's useless. Leave us be. We are

the ones who have to deal with this bad luck.

SOSTRATOS. But tell me, man, have you ever been in love?

GORGIAS. I can't imagine it.

SOSTRATOS. Why not? Who's stopping you?

GORGIAS. A realistic look

at hardship, which is all I have in life.

SOSTRATOS. You certainly don't sound as if you've been

in love. You tell me to give up. But that's

no longer in my power.

GORGIAS. We don't resent you, but your carrying on is useless.

SOSTRATOS. Not if I win the girl.

GORGIAS. But you can't win.[8]

I'll prove that to you if you follow me

to where he's working. It's a valley near to us.

SOSTRATOS. What are you going to do?

GORGIAS. I'll just

drop in a word about his daughter's wedding;

I'd gladly witness the event myself.

Right off he'll raise objections to a match,

reviling one and all. The sight of you,

a gentleman of leisure, will revolt him.

SOSTRATOS. He's there right now?

GORGIAS. Oh, no. He'll go

a little later by his same old route.

SOSTRATOS. He'll take the girl, you think?

GORGIAS. It's hard to say.

Maybe.

SOSTRATOS. I'm ready! Bring me to the place.

And, I entreat you, take my side.

GORGIAS. How so?

SOSTRATOS. How so? Let's go there and you'll see.

DAOS. [*Interrupting.*] Hold on!

You're going to stand around in fancy clothes

while we're at work?

SOSTRATOS. Why not?

DAOS. He'll start at once

to throw mud at you and curse you out

as idle. You'll have to dig with us. Perhaps

he'll venture then to hear a word from you,

believing you're a poor, small farmer, hard

at work.

SOSTRATOS. I'll do what you suggest. Lead on. [*He starts taking off his cloak.*]

GORGIAS. [*Half to himself.*] Why force yourself to suffer?

DAOS. [*Slyly, aside to* GORGIAS.] I've a plan:
we'll work today as hard as possible.
This guy will sprain his back, and then we won't
be bothered in the future with his visits.

SOSTRATOS. [*Turning back to them.*] Bring out a mattock for me.

DAOS. Here—take mine.
I've got to see to building up the fence.
It needs some work.

SOSTRATOS. Fine. Give it here to me. [*To* GORGIAS.] You've saved me.

DAOS. [*To* GORGIAS.] Master, see you there. I'm off. [*Exit* DAOS.]

SOSTRATOS. [*Continuing.*] You see, I'm going to marry her, or else
I'll die!

GORGIAS. If that's the way you really feel,
I wish you luck. [*Exit.*]

SOSTRATOS. [*Euphorically.*] Oh, honored gods! Friend,
the very things which you supposed would turn
me back have doubly spurred me on to act.
To get the girl would be stupendous,
if she's been raised outside the company
of women, and if she's innocent of evil.
She's not been terrified by any aunt
or nurse, but rather nurtured nobly in
the country by her father, who's a man that loathes
life's evil ways. [*Pauses.*] This mattock weighs a ton.
It's going to kill me—but I'll have to see
this through, now that I've started on the way. [*Exit.*]

[*Enter* SIKON, *dragging a sheep for the sacrifice.*]

SIKON. This sheep's no ordinary beauty! Devil
take it. If I pick it up, it grabs
a tree branch in its mouth and starts to eat
the leaves; that way it pulls itself right off
my shoulder. If it's on the ground, it won't

move on. A paradox! The *sheep* is chopping me,
the cook, to pieces. I'd rather drag a sailboat
down the road.[9] Thank God, we've come at last
to where we've to sacrifice. [*Nods toward the shrine.*] Greetings,
Pan. [*Sees* GETA, *offstage, and calls to him.*] So far behind? [*Enter* GETA, *staggering under a heavy load of baggage.*]

GETA. Those blasted women
piled me with a load to carry that
would make four donkeys sweat.

SIKON. It looks as if
a large-ish crowd is coming. You've a raft
of rugs for them to sit on!

GETA. [*Inquiring where he is to put his load.*]
What . . . ?[10]

SIKON. [*Gesturing.*] Right here.

GETA. Done. [*He drops the baggage.*] I'm certain, if she had a dream
of Pan in Paiania,[11] we'd be off
at once to sacrifice.

SIKON. [*Curious.*] Who had a dream?

GETA. [*Wearily.*] Don't bug me.

SIKON. Oh come on, Geta, tell.
Who had it?

GETA. Mistress had it.

SIKON. What'd she see?

GETA. [*Impatient.*] You'll kill me. Well, she saw the god . . .

SIKON. You mean Pan here?

GETA. . . . that's right . . .

SIKON. Do what?

GETA. . . . take Master Sostratos . . .

SIKON. A fine young man . . .

GETA. . . . and clap him into chains . . .

SIKON. Good God!

GETA. . . . and then equip him with a farmer's
cloak and mattock, and order him to work
the neighbor's land.

SIKON. [*Amazed.*] How strange!

GETA. We're sacrificing
because of this bad omen.

SIKON. I understand. [*All business now.*] Grab up this stuff again
and take it in. Let's get the couches ready
and make the other preparations. We'll be all set whenever they come. I hope
it all goes well. Cheer up, you pessimist!

I'll fill you up with gourmet food today.

GETA. I've always liked you and admired your skill—[*Aside.*] But I'll believe the food when it's in front of
me. [*They exit into the shrine.*]

[*Choral Interlude*]

Act 3

Enter KNEMON, *talking to* SIMICHE *the
maid as he comes out the door.*

KNEMON. Old woman, shut the door
and lock it tight
till I get back again. I don't think that
will be until it's after dark. [*Enter* SOS-
TRATOS' *mother, with a large party of servants and guests*]

MOTHER.[12] [*Addressing* SOSTRATOS' *sister,*
PLANGON.]
Move on quickly, Plangon. We should
have done
the sacrifice by now.

KNEMON. [*Staring at them.*] What's going
on?
A crowd! To hell with them!

MOTHER. [*To a maid.*] Parthenis, pipe
the song of Pan. They say one
shouldn't pray
in silence to this god. [*Enter* GETA, *from
the shrine.*]

GETA. You got here safely!

KNEMON. By God, they really nauseate
me!

GETA. We've been waiting here for you
some time.

MOTHER. Is all in order for the
sacrifice?

GETA. Oh, yes. All set.

MOTHER. That sheep, at least, won't
wait around much longer.
Poor thing, it's almost dead. Well, go
inside.
Prepare the baskets, holy water, and
the sacred cakes. [*They all start to make
their way into the cave.*]

GETA. [*As he leaves, seeing* KNEMON.]
What are you gaping at? [*Exit.*]

KNEMON. [*Outraged.*] God damn you all!
They're making me fall idle!
I can't be off and leave the house with

them
around. These Nymphs are nuisances
as neighbors.
I'll have to tear the house down—build
again
some other place. These people
sacrifice like thieves!
They bring their picnic baskets, bot-
tles—not for
the gods, but for themselves. A proper
gift
for gods is holy incense and a cake:
the god gets all the offering when it's
burned.
But these men give the gods
a sheep's tail and a bladder, parts which
they
can't eat, and then they gobble up the
rest. [*Moves to his front door.*]
Woman, open up the door at once.
I think we'll have to work inside today.
[*Exit.*] [*Enter* GETA *from the shrine.*]

GETA. [*To the servants inside.*] You say
you left the stewing pot behind?
You must all be hung over. Now what
do we do? [*Moves toward* KNEMON'S
house.]
I guess I'll have to bother the god's
neighbors. [*Knocks at* KNEMON'S *door.*]
Hey, there, inside: boy! [*Mutters to himself.*] By heavens, I'm sure
there's nothing worse than those repul-
sive slave
girls in the cave. [*Turns back to the door
and knocks.*] Servants—hey! [*As before.*]
Getting laid is all
they think about . . . Hey, there, inside,
come out!! . . .
and slandering all who catch them at
it. . . . Boy!
What's going on here? Slaves! There's
not a soul
inside. [*Listens at the door.*] Ah, now
there's someone coming out. [*Enter*
KNEMON, *furious.*]

KNEMON. You thrice accursed being,
why's your hand
upon my door? Speak up!

GETA. [*Stepping back.*] Don't bite!

KNEMON. I'll bite
and eat you too, God damn it!

GETA. Good lord, calm down!

KNEMON. You wretch, have you and I
got business with
each other?

GETA. Oh, no, no business. Look—I

haven't
brought a witness: I'm not collecting
  debts.[13]
I've come to ask you for a stewing pot.
KNEMON. [*Incredulous.*] A stewing pot?
GETA. A pot.
KNEMON. You ought to get a whipping!
You think I've got an ox to sacrifice,
the way you people do?
GETA. [*Aside.*] You probably
don't have a snail. [*Hastily.*] Good-bye,
  good sir. The girls
inside the shrine requested me to
  knock
upon your door and ask. I did. You
  have no pots.
I'll tell them that when I get back.
  [*Muttering, as he leaves.*] Gods above!
The old man bites just like a snake!
  [*Exit.*]
KNEMON. Wild animals, they are! They
  come right up
and knock as if you were a friend.
  [*Turns toward the shrine.*] If I
catch any man come to my door, and
  don't
make an example out of him, then
count me as a nobody. I don't
know how this guy got off so well just
  now. [*Exit.*] [*Enter* SIKON *from the
  shrine; he is speaking over his shoulder to
  GETA, inside.*]
SIKON. The hell with you! You say he
  swore at you?
You probably were rude to him. [*Turns
  away from the cave.*] It's clear
that most men cannot handle things
  like this.
I've got some skill at them. My custom-
  ers in town
are legion, and I borrow stuff from
  neighbors
all the time. It takes a little buttering
  up.
For instance, if an older chap
comes to the door, at once I say, "Dear
  sir."
An old hag gets "Madame." In middle
age they're called "Priestess." A servant
  should
be flattered thus: "Good man," or "My
  dear boy."
The people in the shrine are crude;
  they should be whipped. [*Knocks at
  KNEMON's door.*] Hey, boys! [KNEMON
  appears at his doorway.]

Come out, dear sir, I'd like to speak
  with you.
KNEMON. [*If anything, angrier than before.*]
You're back? Again?
SIKON. [*Taken aback.*] Oh boy, what's
  this?
KNEMON. It seems
you're riling me on purpose. Didn't I
  say
to you to keep away? [*Calls inside.*] Old
  woman, bring the whip! [KNEMON
  grabs hold of SIKON.]
SIKON. [*Struggling.*] Let go of me!
KNEMON. [*Sarcastically.*] Let go?
SIKON. Please, sir, stop! [SIKON *breaks
  free.*]
KNEMON. [*Snarling at him.*] Come back
  for more!
SIKON. [*Starting to swear.*] May God . . .
KNEMON. [*Interrupting.*] You're jabber-
  ing still?
SIKON. [*Calming down a little.*] I came to
  ask you for a casserole.
KNEMON. [*Enraged.*] I haven't *got* a cas-
  serole—or knife,
or salt, or vinegar, or anything.
I've *told* you all to keep away from me.
SIKON. You didn't tell *me.*
KNEMON. I'm telling you now!
SIKON. [*Aside.*] Worse luck for you. [*To
  KNEMON.*] Well, couldn't you tell me
  where
I'd find someone to lend it to me?
KNEMON. I knew it!
Still chattering at me?
SIKON. Many thanks! Good-bye.
KNEMON. I don't need any farewell
  words from you!
SIKON. I take them back then!
KNEMON. [*Grumbling as he turns to go back
  into his house.*] Insufferable! [*Exit.*]
SIKON. He's pounded
me to bits—and I was so polite!
A lot of difference *that* makes. Do I try
again? It won't be easy if all the people
  here
are going to use me as a punching bag.
  [*Pondering.*] Why don't I roast the
  meat? I will. I've got
a broiling pan. Meanwhile, so long to
  the Phylasians!
I don't need them. I'll make do with
  what I have. [*Exit.*] [*Enter* SOSTRATOS,
  weary and disheveled.]
SOSTRATOS.[14] Whoever needs more
  problems, let him come

to hunt in Phyle! Oh! I'm done for:
my lower back, my shoulders, and my
  neck—
all over! Right away I fell to work,
being young and strong. I swung the
  mattock way
up high and struck in deep, like any
  pro.
The work went well, but not for very
  long.
I started turning round a bit to see
if the old man was coming up, together
with his daughter. I rubbed my back a
  little,
while the others weren't looking. But
  when
the work dragged on, I started stretching backwards:
I was as stiff as wood. Still no one came.
The sun beat down. And finally
I looked just like a crane—was scarcely
bending up and then, with my whole
  body,
going down again. When he saw me,
Gorgias said, "It doesn't look as if
he'll come today, my friend." "what
  then?" I said
at once. "Shall we leave off—come back
  tomorrow?"
Daos took over for me. That's the story
  of
my first attempt. I cannot tell you why
on earth I've come back here, but I am
  drawn
back to this place like some automaton.
  [*Enter* GETA *from the shrine; he speaks
  over his shoulder to* SIKON, *inside.*]
GETA. Come on, now, man! You think
  I'm blessed with sixty hands?
I light the grill for you, I take
the innards of the sheep . . . do carrying, washing,
chopping . . .[15] I knead the cakes, bring
  round the pots. . . .
The smoke in there is blinding me!
  [*Sarcastically.*] I'm having a real holi-
  day!
SOSTRATOS. Hey, Geta!
GETA. [*Still not seeing him.*] Who's call-
  ing?
SOSTRATOS. I am.
GETA. Who?
SOSTRATOS. You see me?
GETA. Yes!
It's Master.
SOSTRATOS. Tell me what you're doing

here.
GETA. You're asking "What?" We've
  done the sacrifice and are preparing
  lunch for you.
SOSTRATOS. My mother's here?
GETA. Oh, yes.
SOSTRATOS. And father?
GETA. He's expected. Go inside.
SOSTRATOS. I've got an errand first.
  [*Thinking out loud.*] It's lucky that
the sacrifice took place here. I'll invite
the farmer Gorgias without delay,
and also Daos. When they've joined
  with us
in celebrating, they'll be even better
allies. They'll help me win the girl.
GETA. [*Overhearing.*] What's that? You're
  off to bring some more to lunch?
  [*Ironically.*] Well, go ahead! As far as
  I'm concerned,
invite three thousand! I was well aware
I'd not get anything to eat. How could
  I?
Go on, invite the world! You've just
  killed off
a beauty of a sheep. You think those
  charming
women would share a thing with me inside? Not on
your life. They wouldn't part with
  grains of salt!
SOSTRATOS. Don't worry. Geta. Today
  will turn out fine. [*Turns toward the
  shrine.*]
I'll prophesy that by myself, O Pan.
Of course, I always greet you, and respect you.[16] [*Exit.*] [*Enter from* KNE-
  MON's *house* SIMICHE, *the maid; she is
  distraught.*]
SIMICHE. Oh trouble, trouble, triple
  trouble's mine.[17]
GETA. Oh, devil take it! Some old
  woman's come out the grouch's door.
SIMICHE. [*As before.*] What will I have to
  suffer?
I tried to get the bucket from the well
without my master's knowing. . . .
I tied his mattock to a little rope. . . .
It was too weak and rotten—and
it broke on me!!
GETA. [*Ironically.*] Good show!
SIMICHE. So now—poor me!
I've let the bucket *and* the mattock
  drop!
GETA. There's one thing left to do:
  jump in yourself!

SIMICHE. And Knemon wants the mattock, just by chance,
to move some dung in the yard.[18] He's
running round
looking for it and shouting. . . . [*A noise
is heard at the door;* SIMICHE *freezes in
terror.*] God, that's him!
GETA. Run for your life, you wetched
woman! Run! [*Enter* KNEMON.]
Too late! Defend yourself!
KNEMON. [*Enraged.*] Where is that thief?
SIMICHE. [*Cowering.*] Oh, master! It was
an accident!
KNEMON. Go on inside!
SIMICHE. Oh, tell me what you're going
to do?
KNEMON. [*Savagely.*] DO? I'm going to
tie you up . . .
SIMICHE. [*Shrieks.*] Oh, no!
KNEMON. And use that same old rope to
drop you down!
GETA. Bravo! If the rope is really rot-
ten.
SIMICHE. Shall I call Daos from next
door to help?
KNEMON. Call Daos, wretch, now that
you've ruined me?
I told you once. Get in the house! Go
on! [*Exit* SIMICHE, KNEMON *sighs to
himself.*]
Oh, dear. I'm utterly forsaken now.[19]
Like no one else! I shall go down the
well:
what else is there to do?
GETA. [*Addressing him.*] We'll give you a
rope
and hook.
KNEMON. [*Turning on him.*] May all the
gods give *you* damnation,
if you talk nonsense to me like that!
[*Exit.*]
GETA. I'd deserve it, too. He's rushed
inside
again, the wretched fellow. What a life!
The quintessential Attic countryman:
he fights the rocks, which bear him
thyme and sage.
Hardship's his lot, and he gets nothing
for it. [*Looking offstage, he sees* SOS-
TRATOS *approaching.*] But here's the
master coming toward us with
his guests in tow. [*Looking more closely, he
is amazed.*] They're laborers from
round
the district here! How out of place this
is.

Why bring them over now? Where *did*
he get to know them? [*Exit into the
cave.*][20] [*Enter* SOSTRATOS, GORGIAS,
and DAOS.]
SOSTRATOS. I wouldn't hear of a refusal.
We've
got quite enough to go around. By
God,
who in the world can say he will not
come
to lunch when his friend's just made a
sacrifice?
For, I assure you, long before we met
I was your friend. [*He turns to the servant.*] Take in these tools, Daos,
and then come back.
GORGIAS. [*To* DAOS.] You can't leave
Mother all alone.
Go in and see to what she needs.
I'll come right back myself in just a
minute. [*Exit* DAOS *to* GORGIAS' *house.*
SOSTRATOS *and* GORGIAS *go into the
shrine.*]

[*Choral Interlude*]

Act 4

Enter SIMICHE *from* KNEMON'S *house; she
is distraught.*
SIMICHE. Oh God, what misery! Can
someone help us?
Oh, please help! [*Enter* SIKON *from the
shrine.*]
SIKON. Damn it! Will you,
by all that's holy, let us pour our
drinks[21]
in peace? You shout at us, you beat us,
now
you wail at us. Your household's downright weird!
SIMICHE. The master's down the well!
SIKON. What's that?
SIMICHE. I'm telling you—
he went to get the mattock and the
bucket,
and then he slipped, and now he's
fallen in!
Right down the well!
SIKON. You don't mean him—
the grouch? By God, that's good! I'm

glad.
My dear old lady, now it's up to you.
SIMICHE. What should I do?
SIKON. Go find a rock, a heavy bowl,
or anything like that, and throw it
down on him!
SIMICHE. Oh, please, go down and save
him!
SIKON. Go fight a rabid dog inside a
well?[22] Not me.
SIMICHE. [*Desperately.*] Oh, Gorgias,
wherever are you? [*Enter* GORGIAS,
from the shrine.]
GORGIAS. Here!
What's the matter, Simiche?
SIMICHE. I've just
been telling him. My master's down the
well!
GORGIAS. [*Shouting inside.*] Come out
here, Sostratos! [*To* SIMICHE.] Quick!
Show the way. [SOSTRATOS *rushes out
from the cave, and follows* GORGIAS *and*
SIMICHE *into* KNEMON's *house.*]
SIKON. [*Gleefully.*] The gods are really
up there, after all! [*Shakes his fist at*
KNEMON's *door.*]
So you begrudge a stewing pot to those
who sacrifice, you rogue! You've fallen
in now:
drink up your water, then, so you don't
have
to share it with a soul! [*Turns back.*] The
Nymphs have punished him
just now for me, and justly. You can't
insult a chef and get away with it!
There's something sanctified about our
art.
Of course, a waiter's less important.
You
can treat him any way you want. [*Listens
at* KNEMON's *door.*] He can't be dead.
There's someone crying "Daddy!" . . .[23]
. . . What a sight
do you think he'll be, by God!
Drenched from his dip,
all shivering. A pretty picture! [*To the
audience.*] I'll
just love to see it, friends! [*He calls into
the shrine.*]
Start pouring out an offering, girls, but
change the prayer to this:
"May the old man be rescued, as a cripple
with mutilated legs!" That way he won't
be able to annoy the god his neighbor,
or bother those who sacrifice. If I get

hired
again to cook, I'll want him out of action. [*Exit into the shrine. Enter* SOS-
TRATOS *from* KNEMON's *house.*]
SOSTRATOS. By all the gods, men, I have
never seen
before a man who just missed drown-
ing at
a more attractive time!
I've had a marvelous adventure there!
When we rushed in, young Gorgias at
once
sprang down the well, while Knemon's
girl
remained with me around the top.
What else
were we to do? Except that she began
to tear her hair, to moan, to strike her
breast.
And I, the golden boy, stood by her,
just
as if I were her nurse, and begged her
not
to grieve like that. I looked at her as on
a splendid work of art. I couldn't have
cared
about the injured man below, except
I had to keep on hauling at the rope.
I nearly was the death of him, in fact.
While looking at her, I let go the rope,
about three times! But Gorgias was
splendid.
He really outdid Atlas! He held, and
got
him up at last. With Knemon safe, I
came
out here. I really couldn't keep a hold
on my emotions any longer.
I nearly went and kissed her: that's the
way
I feel! Right now, I'm going to . . . [*A
noice is heard at* KNEMON's *door.*] Here
they are! [*Enter* KNEMON, MYRRHINE,
and GORGIAS.[24] SOSTRATOS *stares at*
MYRRHINE.]
Oh, Zeus, deliver me! What a sight![25]
GORGIAS. [*Kindly.*] Tell me, Knemon, if
you want anything.
KNEMON. [*Weakly.*] What's that? I'm ill.
GORGIAS. Take heart.
KNEMON. Oh, it's all right.
Old Knemon won't annoy you any
more
in the future.
GORGIAS. Such misfortune is the price
of being alone, you know. You nearly

died
just now. A man your age has got to
    live
with a companion.
KNEMON. Gorgias, I'm not
too well, I know. Go quickly, call your
    mother. [*Exit* GORGIAS *to his own
    house.*]
It seems we only learn our lessons
    when
we suffer some bad accident. [*To* MYR-
    RHINE.] Little girl, please hold me up.
SOSTRATOS. [*Enviously.*] Oh, lucky man!
KNEMON. [*Irked, seeing* SOSTRATOS.] You
    wretch, why are you standing
    there?[26] . . . Not one of you
could make me change my mind. You'll
    have to let me have
my way. I think I've made just one mis-
    take. That was
to feel that I alone was self-sufficient
    and
would need no one. Now that I see how
    death can be
so swift and sudden, I know that I was
    wrong in this.
A man needs someone standing by to
    help him out.
I hadn't admitted that before, because I
    thought
that every man around cared only for
    his own
profit. By God, I thought there wasn't
    one of them
who was concerned for other men.
    That was what blinded me.
One man has just now proved the op-
    posite:
Gorgias, who's done a deed that's
    worthy of
the finest gentleman. I never let him
    near
my door, or gave him help in anything,
or greeted or conversed with him, and
    still he saved me.
Another man might well have said:
    "You don't allow
me in—well, I won't come. You've
    never helped us out—
I won't help you." [*Catches sight of* GOR-
    GIAS, *who has now returned, and looks
    embarrassed.*] What's the matter, boy?
    If I
should die—I think that's likely, seeing
    as how I feel—
or whether I live, I'm making you my

legal son,
and heir to what I own. It's yours. And
    take the girl:
she's in your care. Find her a man. For
    even if
I live, I won't be able to. Not a single
    one
will ever please me. If I survive,
    though, let
me live the way I want. Do all else as
    you wish.
Thank God, you're sensible. You're just
    the man to be
your sister's guardian. Give half of my
    estate
as dowry for her; the rest can feed me
    and your mother. [*To* MYRRHINE.]
Help me lie down, my girl. I think it's
    not a man's
job to say more than he has to. [*He sits
    up again.*] But, child, I
want to add a bit about myself and how
I lived. If everyone lived so, there'd be
    no courts,
men wouldn't drag each other off to
    prison, war
would vanish—all would be content
    with modest lives. [*To the audience.*]
But your ways suit you better, doubt-
    less. So, live on. [*Almost to himself, with
    some self-pity.*]
The difficult old *dyskolos* won't hinder
    you.
GORGIAS. I'll see to everything. If you
    agree, though, you
must help us quickly find a bridegroom
    for the girl.
KNEMON. [*Very much his old self.*] Look
    here! I've said what I intended! Can't
    you leave me?
GORGIAS. [*Gesturing toward* SOSTRATOS.]
    This man would like to meet you . . .
KNEMON. [*Sharply.*] Absolutely not!
GORGIAS. He helped to save you.
KNEMON. [*Pausing*] Oh. Who's that?
GORGIAS. Right here. [*He beckons to* SOS-
    TRATOS.] Come on!
KNEMON. [*Looking* SOSTRATOS *over.*] He's
    sunburned. . . . he's a farmer, eh?
GORGIAS. [*Eagerly.*] Oh yes, Father.
He's not a wealthy idler, wasting time
    all day. . . .[27]
KNEMON. Wheel me in now. [*Exeunt
    KNEMON and his family.*][28]
SOSTRATOS. [*To* GORGIAS.] My father
    won't object to this.

GORGIAS. Then, Sostratos,
I give her to you in betrothal, here
before the gods as witnesses. You deserve her.[29]
You came to us with no put-on emotion, but
sincerely, and you've thought it right to
go all out
to marry her. Brought up in luxury,
you willingly
worked on the farm. It's this way most
of all that true
men are revealed: if someone rich
should undertake
to imitate the poor. A man like this will
bear
a change in fortune bravely. You have
proved your worth.
May you maintain it.
SOSTRATOS. [*Rather pleased with himself.*]
I'll be even better yet! [*Pauses.*] I
guess to praise oneself is somewhat
vulgar, though. [*He looks offstage.*] But
here's my father! What luck!
GORGIAS. [*Looking off in the same direction.*] Kallippides?
Is *he* your father?
SOSTRATOS. Sure.
GORGIAS. [*Impressed.*] By heaven, he's
awfully rich!
And he deserves it—quite a farmer!
[*Enter* KALLIPPIDES.]
KALLIPPIDES. I appear
to be too late. They've surely eaten up
the sheep
by now and gone back to the farm.
GORGIAS. [*To* SOSTRATOS] He looks as if
he's starving. Shall we approach him
now?
SOSTRATOS. No let him eat.
He'll be in better spirits.
KALLIPPIDES. [*Seeing* SOSTRATOS.] Sos-
tratos, you've eaten?
SOSTRATOS. [*Nodding.*] But there's some
left for you. Go in.
KALLIPPIDES. I will indeed. [*He exits into
the shrine.*]
GORGIAS. You'll want to talk to him in
private now. Go on inside.
SOSTRATOS. [*Pointing at* KNEMON's *house.*]
You'll wait for me in there, all right?
GORGIAS. I won't go out.
SOSTRATOS. I'll call you right away.
[GORGIAS *exits to* KNEMON's *house,* SOS-
TRATOS *to the shrine.*]

[*Choral Interlude*]

Act 5

Enter SOSTRATOS *and* KALLIPPIDES *from
the shrine.*
SOSTRATOS. [*Upset.*] You're not behaving, Father, in the way
I wanted. I expected more from you!
KALLIPPIDES. How's that? Didn't I consent? You *ought* to have
the girl you love! I'm willing.
SOSTRATOS. [*Reprovingly.*] Not completely.
KALLIPPIDES. By the gods, I am! I know
that marriage
for youngsters is the most secure this
way—
when it is entered into based on love.
SOSTRATOS. So I'm to marry Gorgias'
sister, since
he's worthy of relationship with us.
But how then can you say you won't
betroth
my sister to him in return?
KALLIPPIDES. That's bad?
[*Jokingly.*] I'm not about to get two
paupers in
the family at once! One's quite enough.
SOSTRATOS. [*Solemnly.*] You talk of
money now. It comes and goes.
If you are sure it's going to always stay
with you, why go ahead—don't share a
thing
you have with anyone. But if you're not
secure, and trust to luck for all you
have,
you shouldn't be stingy with it, Father.
Luck
will take away your cash and give it all
to someone else, perhaps to someone
undeserving.
That's why I say you must yourself, as
long
as you have money, use it generously,
Father. Be a help to all, and make
as many as you can lead better lives.
This is remembered always, even if
your luck should fail. Your friends will
help you then.
A friend in sight is far more valuable
than hidden wealth, which you keep
hoarded up.
KALLIPPIDES. [*Taken aback.*] You know
me, Sostratos. I'm not about
to bury what I have with me. How
could I?

It's yours. You think this man is
 worthy, and
you want him as a friend. All right.
 Good luck.
Why quote me proverbs? Go ahead,
 I'm willing.[30]
Be generous and share. I'm utterly
convinced by you.
SOSTRATOS. Convinced?
KALLIPPIDES. Yes, absolutely.
Don't let it worry you.
SOSTRATOS. I'll call him, then. [Enter
 GORGIAS from KNEMON's house.]
GORGIAS. I heard the whole of what you
 said
as I was coming out the door. Well . . .
I look upon you, Sostratos, as friendly,
and I am very fond of you myself.
But I don't want to get involved with
 things
too grand for me. I'm not cut out for
 them.
SOSTRATOS. What do you mean?
GORGIAS. I'm giving you my sister
as your wife. But as for marrying
 yours—
well, I'm reluctant.
SOSTRATOS. You're refusing?
GORGIAS. I don't believe a man should
live on others' money.
SOSTRATOS. That's nonsense, Gorgias.
 You just don't think
you're worth enough to marry her.
GORGIAS. I think I'm worthy of her. But
 to take
a lot when I have little isn't right.
KALLIPPIDES.[31] By God, I think that
 while you're noble, you're
a trifle inconsistent.
GORGIAS. How?
KALLIPPIDES. You'd like to seem
content, although you're poor. Since
 I'm agreed,
why not give in?
GORGIAS. All right. I'd certainly be
 poor,
both in my wallet and my wits,
if I rejected my one chance to live.
SOSTRATOS. Well done![32] Let's see to
 the betrothal now.
KALLIPPIDES. [To GORGIAS.] My boy, I
 give to you my daughter for
your marriage, and to bear you children. And
as dowry, I bestow three talents.[33]
GORGIAS. [Proudly.] And I

have one to give as dowry for my sister.
KALLIPPIDES. Don't do too much, now.
GORGIAS. But I have the land.
KALLIPPIDES. [Grandly.] Keep all of it,
 my son. Now go and bring
your mother and your sister here to
 meet
the women in our clan.
GORGIAS. [Bowled over.] Oh, yes! Of
 course.
SOSTRATOS.[34] We'll stay here for the
 night, nearby the shrine,
and in the morning celebrate the wed-
 dings,
Gorgias. And bring along the old man
here. With us he'll be assured of getting
what he needs.
GORGIAS. He won't come willingly.
SOSTRATOS. Persuade him.
GORGIAS. If I can. [Exit into KNEMON's
 house.]
SOSTRATOS. We ought to have
a fine drinking party now, Father,
and all-night vigils for the women.[35]
KALLIPPIDES. [Ironically.] They'll
be at the drinking, and it's we, I'm sure,
who'll watch all night. I'll go inside and
 get
things ready for you. [Exit into the
 shrine.]
SOSTRATOS. Good idea. [Exuberant.] A
 man
who's sensible should not despair of
 anything
at all. Hard work and care can get
you everything. Just now I've proof of
 this:
I've managed to arrange a match which
 no one
would have thought I could in just one
 day!
[Enter GORGIAS, with his mother and sister.]
GORGIAS. [To the women.] Let's go. A little faster.
SOSTRATOS. [Seeing them.] Over here!
 [SOSTRATOS leads them to the entrance to
 the shrine and
calls to his mother inside.]
Receive these ladies, Mother! [They go
 in. SOSTRATOS turns back to GORGIAS.]
 Knemon's not
come yet?
GORGIAS. [Shaking his head.] Why, he
 begged me to take away
old Simiche, so he would be alone
completely.

SOSTRATOS. What a man!

GORGIAS. Yes.

SOSTRATOS. Let him be.
We should go in.

GORGIAS. [*Hesitating.*] I'm pretty shy to
be
with ladies, Sostratos. . . .

SOSTRATOS. Oh, nonsense. Come!
You've got to think of them as "family"
   now. [*Exeunt into the cave. Enter*
SIMICHE *from* KNEMON'*s house.*]

SIMICHE. All right, all right, all right! I'll
   leave you too.
You'll lie there all alone. I pity you.
They wanted you to come, but you refused.
You're going to have a shock again, by
   God, and it'll be worse than what you
   had just now. [*Enter* GETA *from the
   shrine.*]

GETA. I'll just come out and see. . . . [*He
   is interrupted by the noise of a flute, playing
at the party.*][36]
Why pipe at me, you wretched man? I
   can't enjoy it.
They've sent me out to check the invalid. [*He shouts inside.*] Quit it! [*The
   flute music stops momentarily, but is heard
throughout the following scene.*]

SIMICHE. [*Addressing* GETA.] Let someone else go in and sit with him, I say.
I want to go and chat with mistress, say
   farewell
to her and hug her.

GETA. That's sensible. Go on inside.
Meanwhile I'll take care of him. [*Exit*
   SIMICHE.] [GETA *rubs his hands.*] I've
   waited ages
for this chance, but couldn't leave my
   work in there. . . .[37] [*He peeps into*
   KNEMON'*s house, and then walks over
   and calls into the cave.*]
. . . Sikon, come out here on the double! [*Turns back.*] Boy, we've got
some fun here! [*Enter* SIKON *from the
   cave, a bit drunk.*]

SIKON. You called?

GETA. I did indeed!
You want revenge for what you took
   back there?

SIKON. [*Indignant.*] I take it in the rear?
Why don't you go and blow. . . .[38]

GETA. [*Persisting, conspiratorially.*] The
   grouch is in there sleeping, all alone.

SIKON. [*Calming down and suddenly interested.*] And how's
he doing?

GETA. Oh, not that bad.

SIKON. [*Catches his meaning, but is a bit
   hesitant.*] He couldn't get up and hit
   us?

GETA. [*Ironically.*] I don't think he'll be
   doing any getting up.

SIKON. How sweet it is! I'll go in there
   and ask to borrow
something. He'll go berserk!

GETA. [*Suddenly.*] Why don't we first
   drag him out here and set him down,
and *then* start knocking on the door for
   favors? Oh,
we'll burn him! It will be fantastic!

SIKON. I'm scared we might
be caught by Gorgias and beaten.

GETA. No one will ever
hear us, with all the partying in there.
   [*Seriously.*] We surely
have to tame this reprobate. He's our
   relation
now, and he's a care to us. He'll be a
   burden
if he always acts like this.

SIKON. [*Cautiously.*] Just try to get him
out here without anyone seeing.

SIKON. [*Gesturing toward the house.*] Go
on, you first!

SIKON. [*At the door, he turns.*] Wait just a
   minute, please! Don't go off and
   leave me!

GETA. [*In a stage whisper.*] Shhh! Don't
   make a sound!

SIKON. [*Whispering back.*] *I'm* not making
   noise! [*Together they exit into* KNEMON'*s
   house, and return in a few seconds carrying the old man fast asleep on his bed.*][39]

GETA. [*Leading the way.*] To the right.

SIKON. Okay.

GETA. Right here. [*They set down their
   burden.*] We're ready!

SIKON. Fine!
I'll be the first. [*To the flutist inside.*] Be
   sure you keep time to my music!
   [SIKON *starts beating on* KNEMON'*s door
   and shouting to imaginary slaves inside.*]
Slave! Little slave! Oh, fine slaves! Boy!
   Slaves!

KNEMON. [*Horrified, now that he is awake.*]
   I'm done for!

SIKON. [*Turns around to see* KNEMON,
   feigns surprise.*]
Hello! You live in here?

KNEMON. [*Angrily.*] Of course I do!

What do you want?

SIKON. To borrow pots from you. I'd also like a bowl.

KNEMON. [*Furiously trying to stand up.*] Who'll help me up?

SIKON. [*Turns back to the door and shouts inside.*]

I know you've got them—I just know it. And also seven tripods and a dozen tables!

Be quick now, slaves! I'm in a hurry!

KNEMON. We haven't got them.

SIKON. [*Turning back to* KNEMON.] You haven't got them?

KNEMON. You heard me!

SIKON. [*Lightly.*] Oh! I'll run along then.

KNEMON. [*Moans.*] Oh, God! How miserable! How was I brought out here? Who set me down in front here? [*Sees* GETA.] You get away from me!

GETA. All right. [*He goes to the door of the house and starts pounding and shouting.*] Slave! Slave! Women! Men! Porter!

KNEMON. You madman, you're about to break the door!

GETA. [*Disregarding him.*] We need nine mats from you!

KNEMON. From who?

GETA. And an Oriental rug—a hundred-foot one!

KNEMON. [*Gnashing his teeth.*] Oh, I wish I had my whip! [*Calling.*] Simiche!!! Where is she?

GETA. [*As before.*] Am I to go to someone else for them?

KNEMON. [*Shouting.*] Oh! Stop!! SIMICHE!!! [*He sees* SIKON, *who has walked over to him.*] May God take care you rot in hell! What do you want?

SIKON. [*Slowly and tormentingly.*] I'd like to have a large, bronze mixing bowl!

KNEMON. [*Purple with rage.*] Who'll help me up?

GETA. [*Comes over and, with* SIKON, *stands over the old man.*] I'm sure you've got that Oriental, Pop— I'm positive!

KNEMON. I haven't got it! Nor the bowl! I'll kill that Simiche!

SIKON. [*Sternly.*] Sit still, and don't you grumble! You're antisocial. You hate women. You won't come to where we sacrifice. You'll have to

bear all this, then. There's no one here to help you. Go on and bite your tongue. . . .[40]

. . . Your wife and daughter first were welcomed with a kiss and now they're having a most pleasant time in there.

The party stories started. I prepared for the men's drinking.

And also . . . [*He breaks off.*] Are you listening? Don't doze off!

GETA. No, indeed!

KNEMON. [*Groans.*] Ohhhh!

SIKON. So you wish you'd gone! I'll finish. We offered wine. The couch was spread. I laid the tables— for that's my job, you see—[*Breaks off.*]—you're listening, eh! [*Portentously.*]

Remember—I'm a master chef!

GETA. [*Believing he sees* KNEMON *weaken.*] He's coming round.

SIKON. [*Continuing his description, and waxing eloquent.*]

Another man decanted old and noble wine into a vessel, mixing in a stream drawn from the water of the Nymphs. He toasted all the men.

Another did it for the women. The drinking went on, and on, and on.[41] You're listening? A tipsy girl, a maid, who veiled her youthful face, stepped out to dance. The flower blushed as she began the rhythm. She trembled, shyly— but another joined her hand in hers and waltzed!

GETA. [*To* KNEMON.] You've been through hell. Now dance: come, get up on your feet.

KNEMON. Whatever do you want, you wretches?

GETA. Come on, get up! You're boorish.

KNEMON. Damn it. No!

GETA. Are we to take you in, then?

KNEMON. [*Desperately.*] What shall I do?

GEAT. [*Picking up on his question.*] Why, dance, of course!

KNEMON. [*Assenting wearily.*] Oh, take me, then.

Perhaps I'll bear things better inside.

GETA. That's wise. We win![42]
Oh, victory! [*Calls for a slave into the
shrine.*] Come, Donax! You, too, Sikon.
Lift this man up and take him in. [*To*
KNEMON.] And you
beware, because if we should catch you
making
more trouble, we won't let you off as
well
as we did this time. [*Shouts into the
shrine.*] Ho! Bring out some crowns
for us, and bring a torch! [*Hands* KNE-
MON *a garland.*] Here, take this.
That's fine. [*He turns to the audience.*]
   Well, now, if you enjoyed our fight
with this old troublemaker, kindly give
us your applause—men, youths, and
children: all!
May Victory, the noble maiden, friend
of laughter, stay our patron to the
end![43] [*Donax and Sikon carry* KNEMON
into the shrine; GETA *follows.*]

1. *bits of wood.* Pyrrhias' phrase in the Greek is
strange, and there is much disagreement about
what it means. The word he uses for "wood" literally means a wooden instrument of torture, placed
like a yoke on the victim's neck so that he is forced
to stoop. Possibly Knemon's posture as he prowls
in the pear patch, and Pyrrhias' feeling that he is
some sort of monster, prompt the use of the word.
But possibly the word was used colloquially as a
term of abuse, and Pyrrhias breaks off for a moment to curse Knemon.
   2. Exit of Pyrrhias. I agree with Sandbach's argument that this is the last we see of this character.
Others hold that he does not exit stage left (and
thus back to town), but rather to the cave, whence
he reenters later to console Sostratos. The text
there, however, is perfectly intelligible with just
Sostratos and Daos on stage; and a reappearance
by Pyrrhias would create a severe strain if, as
seems likely, Menander was restricted to three
speaking actors who shared all the roles in the
play.
   3. *to stone.* The "thing" that Perseus possessed
is, of course, the head of the Gorgon Medusa. Sent
by the evil king Polydectes to to kill Medusa, Perseus was aided in his mission by Athena; he acquired some winged sandals, slew Medusa, and
returned to avenge himself by petrifying Polydectes. As Sandbach notes, the extended reference to mythology is an unusual and highly dis-
tinctive opening for Knemon. It is the last thing
we would expect from an enraged farmer, and
serves immediately to focus our interest on this
character "type."
   4. Knemon's daughter. The list of *dramatis per-*

sonae in the papyrus does not assign Knemon's
daughter a name, and both Sandbach and Handley believe that the Myrrhine referred to in a
lacunose passage in act 4 (see note 26) is Knemon's
divorced wife, the mother of Gorgias. The wife is
a nonspeaking character. No argument appears to
me decisive here: whereas the name Myrrhine always belongs in New Comedy to an older, married
woman, the authority of the list itself is reduced by
its failure to include the mother of Sostratos, who
probably speaks at the beginning of act 3 (see note
12). I assign the daughter the name Myrrhine,
and prefer to leave Gorgias' mother nameless,
purely for dramatic convenience.
   5. *Choral Interlude.* The nature of the choral
performances in New Comedy cannot be determined. It is conjectured that the papyrus presents
us with an abbreviation for the phrase "song of the
chorus." But we have no idea what the song was,
how it was related to the episodes of the play (if it
was so related), whether it was accompanied by
dancing, etc. Indeed, we are not even sure of the
size of the chorus at this period, though some have
inferred from a reference in Aristotle's *Politics*
that the Aristophanic chorus of twenty-four had
by the fourth century been reduced to fifteen. It
seems likely that by Menander's time the choral
interludes had little relation to the play's action
and merely served as light entertainments between the acts. On the other hand, we should note
how skillfully the chorus is introduced in Daos's
concluding lines: similar motivation for the
chorus's first appearance is found in three other
Menandrian comedies.
   6. The speech of Daos. The text is in bad condition here. We have lost the preceding line, in
which Gorgias may have commanded Daos to
knock at Knemon's door. An unusual amount of
supplementation is necessary through this and the
following speech of Gorgias, due to the bad condition of the papyrus.
   7. I follow Handley's interpretation of Daos's
remark here, and of Sostratos' reproof. The latter's abruptness seems better directed at Daos,
who has interrupted him, than at Gorgias, whom
he wishes to convince.
   8. *you can't win.* The sentence after these words
is guesswork, due to the state of the text. I follow
Sandbach's reconstruction.
   9. *down the road.* The Greek is more compressed
than the English here, and is a fine example of
Sikon's highly individual manner of speech. In
one sentence he is made to combine two
metaphors: he is being ground to mincemeat by
the sheep, which is in turn compared to a large
boat that is dragged along over land.
   10. *what . . . ?* The text of this line is both
mutilated and corrupt; the stage direction for
Geta, his question, and Sikon's answer are all conjectural.
   11. *Paiania.* Another district of Attica, about
twenty miles from Phyle, where there was a shrine

dedicated to Pan. The journey would be a considerable project.

12. *Sostratos' mother.* I follow Sandbach here in assigning a speaking part for Sostratos' mother, and in supposing that Sostratos' sister is here identified by name.

13. *debts.* Athenians were accompanied by witnesses when they visited debtors and demanded payment: cf. Aristophanes, *Clouds* 1214ff.

14. *Sostratos' speech.* The situation of Sostratos is strikingly similiar to that of Ferdinand in *The Tempest.* Both young men must undergo the trial of physical labor to prove their worth to their beloved's father. In Shakespeare, of course, Prospero directly imposes the trial on Ferdinand, and he regards his situation somewhat differently (cf. III.i.1ff).

15. *chopping.* The text is mutilated here: I follow Sandbach's interpretation and adopt with him the supplement of Arnott, *ta keramia.*

16. *and respect you.* Sostratos probably means to guard against leaving the impression of presumptuousness. He prophesies all on his own that everything will turn out all right; he then remembers the presence of Pan and hastens to reassure the god of his devotion. At least, so I understand his afterthought. Sandbach believes that Sostratos declares his *philanthropia* for Gorgias and Daos.

17. *triple trouble's mine.* The diction is para-tragic in Greek as in English. One may compare the punning salutation to the dead at Aristophanes, *Frogs* 184.

18. *dung in the yard.* The Greek simply says "inside." It would not, in fact, be surprising if Knemon and his animals lived under the same roof.

19. *forsaken now.* Para-tragic self-pity: I follow Handley and Winnington-Ingram on these lines. Sandbach objects that it is inconsistent of Knemon to bewail his isolation; a lonely life, after all, was what he chose. Yet inconsistency is part of the characterization, and the humor is all the greater in that this solemn reflection is prompted by the loss of a mattock.

20. *into the cave.* I assume that Geta exits here in disgust and does not wait to hear the ensuing dialogue.

21. *drinks.* The Greek here refers to libations, offerings to the gods that were made at various points during a party.

22. *a rabid dog inside a well.* This appears to be a proverbial expression. A fable of Aesop describes a gardener who tries to rescue his dog from a well, only to be bitten by the dog. I have added the word "rabid."

23. *"Daddy!"* The text is lacunose here, and restoration is impossible.

24. *Enter Knemon, Myrrhine, and Gorgias.* How, precisely, is Knemon brought out? Some believe that he is on a rolling couch or chair. Sandbach argues that the *ekkyklema*, or rolling machine, was used to reveal the interior of Knemon's house. I am not entirely convinced. The most sensible solu-

tion for production is to place Knemon on some sort of rolling bed.

25. *What a sight!* Handley believes that Sostratos is referring to Knemon here. But more consistent with his character is an expression of admiration for Myrrhine, and it is more amusing if he pays no attention to Knemon: after all, he has just told us of his indifference to the old man.

26. *standing there.* Eight verses and part of a ninth are lost here. Gorgias must be presumed to return with his mother during the beginning of Knemon's great speech. It is notable that with this speech the meter of the Greek changes from iambic trimeter to trochaic tetrameter. I have tried to reflect the change in the translation by employing generally longer lines. Handley speculates that the change of meter is intended "to underline the special nature of the occasion"; it is true that this is the structural climax of the play. The meter reverts to the standard iambic trimeter at the beginning of the fifth act, but changes once again, to iambic tetrameter, for the next scene.

27. *wasting time all day.* Two verses are lost here.

28. *Exeunt Knemon and his family.* Knemon must have agreed to the marriage, or simply told Gorgias to arrange things as he sees fit. I consider that the various supplements offered for the these two and one-half verses are most uncertain, so have left a gap here.

29. *you deserve her.* The text is corrupt here. I have translated the line as sense would seem to demand: cf. Sandbach's note in *Commentary,* pp. 250–51.

30. *I'm willing.* A conjecture, since the last part of the line is corrupt.

31. I adopt Sandbach's reconstruction for the next four speeches.

32. *well done.* I adopt the supplement of Barigazzi and Blake.

33. *three talents.* I have not substituted a modern equivalent, since to do so would be artificial. The ancient evidence suggests that Kallippides' offer is extremely generous; wealthy families in Athens appear to have been satisfied with far less.

34. I adopt Sandbach's suggestion for the first two lines of this speech; cf. *Commentary,* p. 263.

35. *all-night vigils for the women.* Both men and women are to be included in the party; Kallippides drags out an old chestnut in the joke repertory of Greek comedy when he suggests that the women will do more than their fair share of drinking.

36. Here the meter changes once again, to iambic tetrameter. The music of the flutist maintains the audience's awareness of the party inside the shrine, even as Knemon is being tormented on stage.

37. *my work in there*... Two lines are lost here.

38. Sikon, drunk, misunderstands Geta's words (capable of a double meaning in Greek) and imposes a sexual sense on the question. He responds with a vulgar outburst, comparatively rare in New

Comedy.

39. I infer that Knemon is carried out on his bed, though such is not mentioned.

40. *bite your tongue.* Two lines are lost here. Sikon presumably begins his account of the party. His original objective, to spark envy and regret in Knemon, soon gives way to a lyrical, exuberant pleasure in the account for its own sake.

41. *the drinking went on* . . . The Greek here is uncertain. It is likely, however, that Sikon is more imaginative in the original than he is in translation: one possibility is that he conveys the soddenness of the occasion by comparing it to "watering a beach."

42. *We win!* This exclamation, and that of the following line (where the meter changes back to iambic trimeter), may also be related to Geta's explicit hope for the victory of Menander's play in the competition: see note 43.

43. *to the end.* The request for applause, and for first prize in the dramatic competition, is a conventional element in New Comedy. The final couplet, whose formulaic quality I have tried to suggest by the rhyme in English, was used by Menander for the end of at least two other plays (cf. *Misoumenos* 465–66, *Sikyonios* 422–23).

Miles Gloriosus

Titus Maccus Plautus

The decline of Greek drama from the brilliance of the fifth-century-B.C. tragedians to eventual oblivion coincides with the decline of Greece as a Mediterranean power. Rome was rising in its place, and Roman drama must next occupy attention, but the overriding fact is that Rome did not display the keen interest in the art of the theater that had inspired Greece. The pattern often followed by the Roman conquerors as they expanded over the then-known Western world was first to seize control of a society militarily, then to absorb its culture. Nowhere was this pattern more evident than in the development of the Roman theater, and no playwright's works more clearly illustrate the pattern than do those of Plautus.

Plautus was born in Umbria, north of Rome, in around 254 B.C. Since he was a commoner (perhaps even a slave) and not a Roman citizen, even less is known of his life than is known regarding other important Roman writers. Even his real name is in some doubt, but when, as a successful playwright, he achieved Roman citizenship, he seems to have chosen for himself the name Titus Maccus Plautus; "Maccus" was the name of the clown in the popular folk farces of the region, and "Plautus" means "splayfoot." These clues, in addition to the play scripts themselves, have led to the legend that Plautus was an itinerant actor in the folk farces in his youth, that he was of a clownish appearance with big feet, that he went into business for himself as a merchant and a miller, but failed, and that he finally turned to playwriting rather late in life, the theater being what he knew best. He became so popular as a playwright that his works were widely performed for centuries after his death, and the legends grew to the point of crediting him with writing some 130 plays. The Roman scholar Varro, writing in the first century B.C., discredited most of these claims and accepted only 21 plays as genuinely Plautian. Since 21 have survived to today (one as only a fragment), it is widely assumed that these are the same ones Varro mentioned. Thus, the modern world may have the body of Plautus's work very nearly complete. According to Cicero, Plautus died in 184 B.C.

Plautus's work as a playwright was to "translate" the plays of Menander and the other Greek writers of New Comedy. Since none of Plautus's source plays survives, one cannot know with certainty just what this translating involved, but there is every reason to suppose that he made significant changes such that the resulting plays might with some justice be termed Roman rather than Greek plays. Evidently in some cases the plots of two or more Greek plays were combined into one Plautian work; character and place names, as well as topical references, were regularly changed from Greek to Roman (although many Greek references remain as well); perhaps most significantly, the tone and style of Plautus's plays are far more vigorously farcical than anything now known of Menander's. Yet the plays remain fundamentally Greek. The chorus has disappeared, but the New Comedy division into five acts is still evident and the plots and characters are the standard ones known from Menander and his contemporaries (the fragments and critical commentary

tell much, even where complete plays have not survived). Even the standard out-
door setting remains the same, with two or three houses as well as a stage right exit
to the harbor or the country and a stage left exit to the town. Governmental
censorship was a real problem in Plautus's day, and it may be that keeping the plays
ostensible translations of Greek works while nevertheless expressing Roman insights and sensibilities gave Plautus a kind of theatrical freedom that he could not
achieve otherwise. In fact, all surviving Roman drama owes a similar debt to Greek
models, and the exact reasons that artists of Plautus's undoubted talents chose to
work in this way can probably never be known.

Plautus's plays are glorious, rough-and-tumble farces that reveal a remarkably
acute sense of what is playable in a theater. The large and impressive Roman
theaters that have survived to today in Europe were the sites of gladitorial combats,
circuses, and even naval battles, but were built perhaps two centuries after Plautus
lived and were not the theaters for which he wrote. In his day, theatrical presentation was a matter of a rough wooden platform, perhaps set up in a city square on
market day, and a need to compete with many other distractions for an audience's
attention. This spirit pervades his plays, as one regularly finds situations carefully
set up, explained over and over to an audience, then the joke quickly worked out
with the maximum in physical humor. Subtleties of characterization are rare, and
plots frequently turn on dramatic irony—an understanding shared with the audience but withheld from one or more of the characters. Much of the dialog is written
to be sung, or perhaps done in a "patter" routine with musical accompaniment. It is
not known with certainty whether Plautus's actors used masks, but later Roman
actors certainly did. Perhaps Plautus's greatest gift was in his use of language, for
he turned street-corner Latin into a poetic instrument of marvelous flexibility, with
a steady stream of puns, alliteration, and created words of his own that have been
the despair of translators. His metrical structures are so artistically effective, and at
the same time so eminently playable when spoken aloud in the theater, that
Plautus's works were read as great literature for many centuries after the fall of
Rome and then revived as great stage pieces in the Renaissance and modern times.

Among the twenty complete plays of Plautus that survive, four may be mentioned (in addition to *Miles Gloriosus*) that have been more widely imitated than the
others, though all of Plautus's surviving plays are surely of major importance in the
development of European comedy. *Amphitruo* is the story of Jupiter's seduction of a
faithful wife by disguising himself as her husband; the story has captivated the
attention of later writers to such an extent that, when Jean Giraudoux wrote *Am-
phitryon 38* in 1929, he claimed to have counted thirty-seven earlier versions of the
story. *Aulularia* (The Pot of Gold) contains the original "miser" character whom
Molière immortalized in *L'Avare* (The Miser). *Captivi* (The Captives) is perhaps a
little more carefully plotted and less farcical than most Plautian comedies; it is the
story of a man who, in buying up slaves to exchange for his son, who is in enemy
slavery, unknowingly buys his own second son, who had been stolen years before.
The play becomes quite warmly human in its insight into the stresses of those in
captivity. *The Menaechmi* is madcap confusion as long-lost twin brothers are
reunited after multiple rounds of mistaken identity; Shakespeare redoubled the
confusion with two sets of twins in *The Comedy of Errors*.

"*Miles Gloriosus*" has been translated as "the braggart warrior"; the term is now so
widely used in that sense that it can be found in most English dictionaries as a
common noun. Plautus named his characters in ways that tried to reflect their
principal qualities, and thus his miles gloriosus with the tongue-twisting Latin
name of Pyrgopolinices has here been translated as Major Bullshot-Gorgeous. Perhaps nothing can fully capture in English the cleverness of Plautus's wordplay, but
the hint at obscenity together with the insight into what makes this man tick has
been cleverly captured by the translator. The character has been so popular that he
has appeared over and over in European drama, most notably developed by Shakespeare as Falstaff. Other characters in *Miles Gloriosus* will be immediately recogniz-

able from *The Dyskolos:* the clever servant who controls the situation, the honest but not-too-bright young lovers, the parasite, the cook. Even the foolish old man, though much kinder than Knemon, is not far removed from him in other respects. The sexy harlot has no parallel in *The Dyskolos,* but is also one of the standard characters used endlessly in later drama. Yet, though all of these characters are stock figures, Plautus has used them in such a way as to make them live as comic caricatures; in the absence of his New Comedy models, one must credit Plautus with finding, as a good cartoonist does today, just the right bold strokes with which to implant these comic exaggerations of human beings in audience memory. It is these same strokes that have made Plautus's roles so eminently "actable," giving actors just the kind of help they need to create masterly farcical portraits in the theater.

The basic plot of *Miles Gloriosus* is really very simple: Halcyon is in love with Goldilocks, who is being held in semicaptivity by the Major; Halcyon's servant, Dodger, arranges an elaborate trick to win her for his master, and they all escape together. The trick itself is complicated because so many people are fooling others as to their proper identities, and Plautus goes to great lengths to make sure that his audience understands at each step just what is taking place. In the reading, these elaborate explanations seem to slow the play down, but in performance they are necessary to insure that everyone can share in the dramatic irony on which the comic success of the play depends. It is also true, however, that there are other long segments of the play which do not advance the plot at all (such as the first 200 lines of act 3), but that evidently exist primarily to allow a good comic actor (in this case, Prolix) to get laughs at the expense of his own character. It is the presence of scenes such as these that lead one to conclude that Plautus cared a lot more about getting some good laughs from his audience than he did about structural tightness or close adherence to a central action. One may fault Plautus for this kind of structural laxness, but it seems certain that he knew what he was doing with respect to allowing a successful actor to get laughs in a tried and tested way. Clearly the plotting here is less carefully articulated than in what has survived of Menander's work, but Plautus's apparent carelessness is very likely explained in terms of the immediate theatrical needs that he faced. A modern director might very well make some judicious cuts.

The language of the translation reprinted here is a very interesting attempt to find modern equivalents for the linguistic gymnastics that Plautus performed. Though occasionally it may cloy in reading, the translator has asked that his work be judged by the way it sounds when spoken aloud. In taking this position, he aligns himself squarely with Plautus, who probably did not think of himself as writing literature at all. As did most great playwrights of every age, Plautus kept performance uppermost in his mind. Time has tested Plautus's choices in this respect and found him right, for Plautus's works have been both adapted and performed more frequently than have those of any other ancient playwright.

N.B. All footnotes in the ensuing text are those of the translator.

Major
Bullshot-Gorgeous
(Miles Gloriosus)

Translated by Paul Roche

Characters

*Major Bullshot-Gorgeous (Pyrgopolynices),
   a soldier*
Shabby Suckpot (Artotrogus), his hanger-on
*Dodger (Palaestrio), servant[1] of Halcyon
   but temporarily in the household of the
   Major*
*Mr. Prolix (Periplectomenus), an old gentle-
   man of Ephesus*
Pox (Sceledrus), servant of the Major
*Goldilocks (Philocomasium), girlfriend of
   Halcyon and abducted by the Major*
*Halcyon (Pleusicles), young Athenian in
   love with Goldilocks*
Penny (Lucrio), servant of the Major
*Madam Love-a-duck (Acroteleutium), a
   merry widow[2]*
Milphidippa (Milphidippa), her maid
*Small boy (Puer), in the household of Mr.
   Prolix*
Cario (Cario), cook of Mr. Prolix
(also orderlies and porters)

TIME AND SETTING. *A street in Ephesus, a
Greek town in Asia Minor. Two large
houses next to each other:* MAJOR
BULLSHOT-GORGEOUS's *and* MR. PROLIX's.
*The exit on stage left leads into town; that
on the right to the port. The time is about ten
o'clock in the morning.*

Act 1

Enter MAJOR BULLSHOT-GORGEOUS *from
his house, followed by* SHABBY SUCKPOT.

*Orderlies carry in a shield that would fit a
giant of six foot three. The Major is far from
that but his self-satisfied face wears a look of
almost militant glory as he struts up and
down with dangling sword. He swishes his
black-and-scarlet military great-cloak about
him as he turns.* SHABBY SUCKPOT, *small,
scruffy, sycophantic but intelligent, dodges
in and out of the Major's legs, mimicking
him at his heels.*

MAJOR. Make sure my damn shield's
   bright.
Give it a sheen like the sun in a cloud-
   less sky:
A light that in the hurly-burly of the
   fight
Shoots into the faces of my foes—
Straight in the eye. . . .
Right? [*Everybody bows and nods. The* MA-
   JOR *smiles, pulls out his sword and strokes
   it.*]
Right!
This good steel of mine,
I mean to cheer him up.
He mustn't fret and pine
Dangling here all day long
Without a goddam thing
To do. . . . Poor Bladey!
All you want
Is to make good mincemeat
Of . . . [*Wheeling around with a flourish.*]
Where is Shabby Suckpot?
. . . of the enemy. [*Lunges at the air as
   SHABBY SUCKPOT scuttles from behind.*]
SUCKPOT. He's right behind you, sir:
Right next to this strong successful man
   with his stamp of a prince,
I mean you, sir:

181

This hero Mars himself isn't a match for.

MAJOR. [*Sheathing his sword with sublime self-absorption.*]
Who was that fellow I saved at the battle of Maggoty Meadows?
Where the commander-in-chief was Bigbangbonides Allmixedupides—
The grandson of Neptune.

SUCKPOT. [*Instantly inventing.*] I remember.
You mean the one with the solid gold armor.
Ha! You just puffed away his battalions with a breath:
Like a gust of wind among leaves and roof-straws.

MAJOR. [*With a lofty wave of his hand.*] Hell, that was nothing! . . .
Not really.

SUCKPOT. Hell's bells—absolutely nothing!
Not to those other exploits I could tell of
Which . . . [*Aside.*] you never did.
[*Turns to the audience with a grimace as* MAJOR BULLSHOT-GORGEOUS *stalks upstage with his back turned.*]
If anyone
Ever saw a louder-mouthed more stupendous liar,
He can have *me* for a present:
Self-sold into slavery lock-stock-and-barrel . . .
Ahem! Yes—if it weren't for one thing:
[*Licks his lips.*]
I'm crazy about his pickled olives.

MAJOR. [*Wheeling around again.*] Where've you got to?

SUCKPOT. [*Popping up behind him.*] Right here, sir . . .
Take that elephant in India, by Jiminy!
The way you pounded its front paw to pieces with one punch.

MAJOR. [*Eyeing him narrowly.*] Front paw—eh, what?

SUCKPOT. [*Quickly.*] Front backside, I meant to say.

MAJOR. [*Loftily.*] It was the merest tap.

SUCKPOT. Don't I know it! If you'd really tried
You'd have gone through its hide, its inside, its whole skeleton:
You'd have put your arm clean through the elephant.

MAJOR. [*With disarming modesty.*] I'd rather not talk of it now.

SUCKPOT. [*Ponderously ironic.*] I'd rather not talk of it now.
To talk to little *me* of all your wonder-work,
I know it well. [*To the audience with a sour grin.*] It's my tummy lands me in for all this tommyrot:
I've got to let the stuff seep into my ears
Or my teeth'll have nothing in which to steep.
I've got to back him up in every goddam lie he tells.

MAJOR. [*Importantly.*] What was I saying?

SUCKPOT. Aha! I know exactly—as if you'd said it. [*Racks his brains.*]
Dammit, so you did, sir! . . .
I remember you *did.*

MAJOR. Did what?

SUCKPOT. [*Desperately.*] Well . . . whatever it was you did.

MAJOR. Do you . . .

SUCKPOT. [*Leaping in.*] Have a writing pad? Yes, and a pen. [*Hurriedly produces a waxed tablet and stylus from the folds of his tunic.*]

MAJOR. You're a genius at putting soul and soul together:
Yours to mine.

SUCKPOT. [*Looking him straight in the eye.*] Well, it's only right, sir.
I've got you studied through and through,
And I take the trouble to sniff out your wishes
Even before you've wished them.
[*Begins jotting things down.*]

MAJOR. [*Fishing for more tall stories.*] And you remember things, eh?

SUCKPOT. Yes sir! I remember things.
[*Totting up his list.*] A hundred in Cilicia—add fifty.
A hundred in Go-in-and-grabia,
Thirty Sardinians, sixty Macedonians—
That's the list of human beings
You've polished off in a single day.

MAJOR. [*Dryly.*] Which makes the grand total of human beings . . . ?

SUCKPOT. [*Rapidly totting up on his fingers.*] Seven thousand.

MAJOR. [*Smugly.*] Yes, it ought to come to about that.
Your sum's correct.

SUCKPOT. [*Ingratiatingly.*] And nothing recorded, either:
It's all kept in the head.
MAJOR. [*Approvingly.*] You've certainly got a good memory.
SUCKPOT. [*To the audience with a sigh.*] It's fodder prodded.
MAJOR. [*Patting him on the back.*] Well, just go on as you are
And you can stuff yourself:
You can always share my table.
SUCKPOT. [*Rubbing his hands.*] Ah! What about that time in Cappodocia
When you would have slain five hundred men at once—
In a single blow—
If your damn sword hadn't gone dead.
MAJOR. [*With a toss of the head.*] Oh, those—
They were measly footsloggers,
So I let them live.
SUCKPOT. [*Hand on his heart.*] Why should I tell you
What is known to the whole race of man:
You are the one and only Major Bullshot-Gorgeous on earth—
Unbeatable for bravery, beauty and big deeds,
And loved by all the ladies. [*Flutters his eyes.*]
And how can they be blamed?
You're so darned good-looking.
Those girls for instance yesterday
Who jerked me by the sleeves . . .
MAJOR. [*Halting in his stride.*] Ah! What did they say to you?
SUCKPOT. They kept quizzing me.
"Surely that's Achilles?" says one of them.
"No, it's his brother," says I.
"No wonder he's so beautiful!" says t'other:
"And such a gentleman.
Just look at that hair—it's ravishing. . . .
Aren't they lucky, the girls that go to bed with him?"
MAJOR. They really said that, eh?
SUCKPOT. [*Deadpan.*] Well, didn't they both beseech me
To bring you past them today as if you were on parade?
MAJOR. [*Trying to yawn.*] Oh what a bore it is to be so beautiful!
SUCKPOT. [*Nodding vigorously.*] You can say that again.

They're an absolute pest, the women:
Teasing and wheedling and almost screaming
To be allowed to see you.
They send for me so mercilessly
I can hardly attend to your affairs.
MAJOR. [*Pompously.*]
I think it's time for us to go toward the forum.
I want to pay those tyros I enlisted yesterday.
King Seleucus, you know, pressed me earnestly
To raise and enlist recruits for him.
I've decided to devote my day entirely to the King.
SUCKPOT. [*With a tortured grin.*] Well, let's go.
MAJOR. Orderlies, fall-in and follow.
[*The* MAJOR *sweeps off, with* SHABBY SUCKPOT *and the orderlies prancing and gesticulating in his wake.*]

Act 2

Prologue

DODGER *enters the street from the house of* MAJOR BULLSHOT-GORGEOUS. *He is a pleasant-looking young fellow, neatly dressed, quick witted, well-educated—as slaves often were—and brimming with self-confidence. He is as devoted to his real master as he finds his present master—the* MA-JOR—*ridiculous. What he most enjoys is organizing people and events. Now he steps downstage, faces the audience, and smilingly makes a formal bow.*
DODGER. Mine is the pleasure of unfolding to you this plot; yours to do me the kindness of listening. If anyone would rather not, I hope he'll get up and go, so leave a seat for somebody who does. [*Waits, while fixing his audience with a gimlet eye.*] Well, I'll tell you why you're sitting in this place of mirth. Here's the title and the plot of the comedy we are putting on. In Greek it is called "Alazon," which in Latin we translate as "Gloriosus": "Bullshot-Gorgeous." [*Waves a hand backstage.*]

This town is Ephesus. That military Major who just went off to the forum, is my master: a hard-on swaggering impudent stinker, chock-full of lies and lechery. He says all women instinctively run after him; but actually wherever he goes they all think him quite absurd. In fact, most of the demoiselles here—as you'll observe—have crooked mouths through trying to keep a straight face. [*Chuckles at his own joke.*]

Now I've not served this man very long and I'd like you to know how I came to him and left my former master. So, your attention, please: this is the plot. [*Shakes his head sadly.*]

My master was a fine young man in Athens—Athens in Attica, that is— where he was head-over-heels in love with a certain girl[13] and she with him— which is the nicest way to be in love [*winks*]. Well, he was sent on a government mission of public importance to Naupactus. Meanwhile this Major [*grimaces*] comes by chance to Athens and worms his way into a meeting with my master's sweetheart. He proceeds with gifts of wine, trinkets, and extravagant titbits to get round her mother— the old bawd—and onto the most intimate footing. Then one day he sees his chance, does this fine military Major: [*Gives a little spit into the wings.*] hoodwinks the disgraceful old baggage, this—this mother of my master's loved-one: claps the girl on shipboard without the mother knowing a thing, and abducts her off to Ephesus much against her will. [*Shakes his head at this dastardly action.*]

Naturally, as soon as I hear my master's sweetheart has been snatched away to Athens, I streak off, book a passage, and get myself on a ship to bring the news at Naupactus. But when we'd put out to sea, the gods thought fit to let pirates capture the ship, with me on board. So there I was, stymied in my voyage to my master before I'd even started. [*Sighs, bends toward the audience with the air and tone of "you won't believe what follows."*]

The pirate who got hold of me gives me as a present to this very same soldier, the Major. And when *he* takes me home to his house whom should I light my eyes on but my master's girl from Athens. [*Waits for this to sink in.*]

As we come face to face she signals me with her eyes not to recognize her. Later, when the chance arises, she speaks to me bitterly of her fate and says she longs to get away from this house and escape to Athens, where, she says, she is deeply in love with my master. She adds that there's nobody on earth who so wholeheartedly abominates this same soldier. [*Shakes his head.*]

When I saw where the girl's feelings really lay, I grabbed myself a writing-pad, sealed up a letter and slipped it to a certain businessman to take to that love-lorn master of mine in Athens— telling him to come here. [*His face lights up.*]

Well, he hasn't ignored my message. In fact he's here, right next door, staying with a friend of his father's: a delightful old boy who's aiding and abetting his guest in this affair of the heart. Oh, yes, he's giving us every possible encouragement in word and deed. [*With a slow smile.*]

As a result, I've fixed up a splendid device inside the house [*jerks his head toward the* MAJOR's *house*] which makes it possible for the lovers to meet and spend some time together. . . . You see, the Major gave this girl one particular room into which nobody was to set foot but himself. In the wall of this room, this boudoir, I've scooped out a hole. It opens up a secret way for the girl to get from the Major's house to that one. [*Points toward* MR. PROLIX's *house.*] The old gentleman knows about it of course. In fact he suggested it. [*Leaning forward and taking the audience into his confidence.*]

Now the man the Major's chosen to keep watch on the girl—a fellow servant of mine—is a pretty worthless sort of fellow. We're going to give him a very curious disease of the eyes—oh, so cunningly, so consummate and ambidexterously!—which will make him *not* see what he really sees. [*Does a little dance.*]

Just to keep *you* from getting mixed up, however: this one girl [*indicates the* MAJOR's *house*] is going to play the part of two: coming and going from each

house. She's the same girl, of course,
but she'll pretend to be another. That's
how we're going to fool her sentry. [*His
attention is caught.*]

Excuse me, there's our neighbor's
door. It's the old gentleman coming
out—the nice old boy I told you of.
[DODGER *steps to one side.*]

[*Enter* MR. PROLIX *from his house. He is a
spry old body of about seventy, quietly but
perfectly dressed. His freshly shampooed
curly hair and beard look as crisp as lamb's
wool. Though one would expect his lively
black eyes to be often twinkling, they register
at the moment nothing but outrage. The old
man really seems to be worked up: brandishing an embossed silver-headed cane, he
shouts at the servants standing in the doorway.*]

PROLIX. And after this, I swear to god,
If you don't break the legs of any in-
    truder spotted on our roof,
I'm going to rip the rawhide off your
    backs.
Now all our neighbors know exactly
    what goes on inside my house. . . .
Looking through the skylight. . . .
    Really!
Can you beat it?
Well, I'm giving orders here and now,
To the whole bang lot of you,
If you see anyone whatsoever
Getting onto our roof from that sol-
    dier's house,
Unless it be Dodger,
You're to pitch him headlong into the
    street.
I don't care
If he says he's chasing a chicken or a
    pigeon or a pet monkey—
You're all dead men if you don't batter
    him to bits:
And I want no bones left either.
You'll have to use something else for
    counters
When they break the Gambling Act at
    the next party. [*Shakes his cane and
    mutters.*]
DODGER. [*Leaning toward the audience and
    jerking a finger in the direction of the* MA-
    JOR'*s house.*] Strikes *me*
Someone *chez nous* has gone and put his
    foot in it.
Bones to be broken!

So that's the old codger's edict, eh?
But *I'm* excepted . . . well, that's nice:
I don't give a damn for what he does to
    the rest.
Let me go up to him. [*Takes a step for-
    ward.*]
PROLIX. Isn't that Dodger coming to-
    ward me?
DODGER. [*Cheerily.*] Mr. Prolix, sir, how
    are you doing?
PROLIX. [*Glumly.*] Oh, Dodger, there
    isn't anyone in the world I'd rather
    see and talk to.
DODGER. What's going on, sir?
Why are you in such a tizzy about *our*
    household?
PROLIX. [*Grimly.*] We're finished.
DODGER. Why, what's up?
PROLIX. The thing's out.
DODGER. What thing's out?
PROLIX. [*Shaking his cane again.*] Some
    goddam wretch from your house
Has just gone and seen my guest and
    Goldilocks kissing,
Through the skylight—our skylight.
DODGER. Who did the seeing?
PROLIX. It was one of your colleagues.
DODGER. But which one?
PROLIX. [*Helplessly.*] I don't know. He
    darted off like a streak.
DODGER. [*Coolly.*] I have a suspicion—
    I'm done for.
PROLIX. I bawled at him as he went.
    "Hey, you there," I says,
"What are you doing on our roof?"
"I'm chasing an ape," he says, and dis-
    appears.
DODGER. [*Gritting his teeth.*] God, how it
    riles me to be done for
Just because of a worthless baboon!
But how's Goldilocks? Is she still inside
    here? [*Nods toward* MR. PROLIX'*s
    house.*]
PROLIX. She was when I came out.
DODGER. Then for heaven's sake go and
    tell her
To get herself over to our house
Just about as quickly as she can.
The whole household's got to see her
    there, at home. . . .
Unless of course she wants us slaves
To be martyrs to her love affair
And all join the Club-of-the-strung-up.
PROLIX. [*With new hope.*] As good as
    told. Anything else?
DODGER. Yes, impress this on her:

She's not to budge an inch from
woman's wiles,
But apply the book of rules right up to
the hilt.
PROLIX. How do you mean?
DODGER. Bamboozle him who said he
saw her
Into seeing that he didn't.
And even if she's been
Spotted here a hundred times
She's still to say she wasn't.
She's got a mouth and plenty of lip,
She's full of brass and full of tricks:
She's shrewd and sure.
She's got self-confidence and stamina.
And she can sham.
If anyone accuses her
She turns right round on solemn oath
Outswears him flat.
She's chockablock with double-think
And double-talk and solemn double-
deals
She's chockablock with stocks of sweet
Seduction and deceit.
Her shelves are stuffed with humbug.
No woman, sir,
Needs to ask a barrow-boy for deviled
apples[4]:
She's got a gardenful at home and all
the spices
For concocting every deviled dish there
is.
PROLIX. [*With a smile.*] All this
I shall unfold to her if she is here.
But what are you churning over in
your mind?
DODGER. [*With an admonitory finger.*]
Sh-h! Quiet, sir, a second.
I'm calling a committee meeting with
my soul
To consider what's to do,
What campaign of trickery pursue
To out-trick that slave who had a view
Of her kissing through your skylight.
How make unseen
A certain sight
That certainly has been?
PROLIX. Go ahead and think.
Meanwhile I'll leave you on your own.
[*The old man steps to one side and with
an amused quizzical look watches him,
while running on in an undertone com-
mentary.*]
Just look at him now, with a frown on
his brow,
Standing there dreaming up ways out:

With his knuckles he taps his bosom,[5]
perhaps
He intends to summon his brains
out.
Now his head's gone awry; left hand on
left thigh,
Right hand is computing on fingers.
Right thigh gets a smack—a terrible
whack—
Oh, he's stuck: his solution malin-
gers.
He's snapping his digits, he's getting
the fidgets,
What a tussle! He's shaking his head:
That idea won't work. But he's not go-
ing to shirk
And offer us half-baked bread.
[DODGER *has been sitting on the curb.
Now he puts his chin on his hand.*]
Ah—very solemn![6] He's building a col-
umn:
He's resting his chin upon *that*.
Thanks very much! But I don't care for
such
An erection—oh no, not a scrap.
For I happen to know it . . . a foreigner
poet[7]
Was pillaried up on a pillar
While by day and by night
He was kept pretty tight
By chains that would guard a gorilla
[DODGER *shifts again.*]
My god, what a pose! As graceful as
those
Which slaves take up sweetly[8] in
comedies.
He's not going to rest today till he's
guessed
What he's searching for so, and the
remedies. [DODGER *jumps up.*]
He's got it at last, I believe. . . . Oh no,
blast! [DODGER *has sat down again.*]
Now don't go and have a siesta!
Do what you do, or you'll be black and
blue
From mooning around—indeed *yes*, sir!
[DODGER *seems to have gone into a day-
dream.*]
Dodger, I say! Were you drunk yester-
day?
Hi there! I'm talking to *you*.
Wake up if you can, break out of it,
man:
It's morning I tell you—it's true.
DODGER. [*In a trance.*] I know. I heard
you.

PROLIX. [*Executing a little dance in front of him, brandishing his silver-headed cane.*]
See the attack?
The foe's at your back.
Think double-quick,
Get help in the nick.
It's high time to sweep
On and not sleep.
Steal a march round
If a way can be found
For your army, and then
Rally our men.
Block off the foe
With ambush and so
Cut their supply line;
But make sure that our line
Is open and lies
Intact for supplies.
Get on! Go ahead!
Be quick or be dead.[9]
Just say you'll direct
The campaign. I expect
We'll certainly win:
Do the enemy in.
DODGER. [*Springing up with melodramatic readiness.*] I do say it: I shall direct.
PROLIX. [*Shakes him by the hand.*] And I say you'll force the issue and win.
DODGER. [*Hands still clasped.*] Jove bless you for that.
PROLIX. [*Still in the stilted phrases of melodrama.*] Pray, will you not make me privy to your plan?
DODGER. [*Imperiously.*] Silence, if you please!
I shall usher you into the purlieus of my strategy.
You shall know my plans as well as *I* do.
PROLIX. Plans I'll give you back—intact.
DODGER. [*Bending toward* PROLIX *as if he were going to impart amazing news to him.*] The soul of my master is encompassed
By the hide of an elephant,
And he has not more sense than a stone.
PROLIX. [*Dryly.*] This was not unknown to me.
DODGER. Wait! My purpose—my grand strategy—is this:
There has arrived from Athens here—
or so I'll have it—
Goldilocks's own twin sister,
Bringing a lover of hers.
The girls are as much alike as two
drops of milk.
And the visitors
Are being lodged and entertained here
at your house—
Or so I'll say.
PROLIX. [*Claps him on the back.*] Perfect!
Splendid. Congratulations!
DODGER. [*Grinning with self-satisfaction.*]
Then when that slave, my colleague.
Goes off to the Major to accuse her
with what he saw—
Kissing a strange young men here—
I'll turn right round and prove to him
That what he saw was Goldilocks's sister
Kissing her own young man.
PROLIX. Why, it's terrific!
That's the story I'll keep to if the Major questions me.
DODGER. [*Cautiously.*] But be sure to say:
They're absolutely the dead spit of one another.
And Goldilocks must be warned about this too—
Or the Major'll question her and trip her up.
PROLIX. Very neat! . . .
But what if he wants to see them together—then what?
DODGER. [*with a wave of the hand.*] Simple. Three hundred pretexts can be found:
"She's not at home, she's gone for a walk,
She's asleep, she's dressing,
She's having a bath,
She's at dinner, at a party,
Busy . . . not convenient . . . quite impossible."
Anything you like to put him off:
Provided only he gets started right
And believes our lies.
PROLIX. [*Nodding.*] Seems fine to me.
DODGER. Then go inside and if the girl's there
Tell her to pop back home *toute de suite.*
Explain and unfold to her
This whole concept of the twin sister—
Then she'll be able to keep to our wonderful plan.
PROLIX. [*Beaming.*] I'll prepare you a girl fit for a degree.
Anything else?
DODGER. No. Just go in.
PROLIX. I'm going. [MR. PROLIX *enters his house, humming happily to himself.*]

DODGER. [*Quietly walking toward the* MA-
JOR'*s house.*]
I'll go inside as well and advance him
by a point
By discovering craftily what flunky
from our joint
Had a monkey-hunt today; for he
surely has let out
To some buddy on the staff all his news
about
The mistress of my master: how he saw
her here next door,
With a fellow, kissing. . . . *I* know what
they are: [*Mimicks.*]
"I just can't keep a secret—that's how I
am."
If I find the chap who saw her, I'll
ready with my ram
And engines of assau .—I'm mobilized
in full.
I'll take the man by force; oh yes, I will,
And if I *don't* discover him that way,
I'll go sniffing like a hound and track
my fox at bay [*His attention is caught.*]
Aha! It's our door opening. . . . Shh! I
mustn't shout.
Look, it's Goldilocks's guard, my colleague, coming out. [*Enter* POX *from
the* MAJOR'*s house. He is a small weedy
fellow, well known for a whiner and
sucker-up to his master. He can hardly
wait to find someone to unload his latest
gossip onto.*]
POX. [*Muttering as he hurries along.*] Yes
. . . yes,
Unless I was sleepwalking on the tiles
today,
What I saw next door and no mistake
Was Master's mademoiselle herself—
Goldilocks—but up to no good.
DODGER. [*To himself.*] So *he's* the fellow
who saw her kissing.
He's given himself away.
POX. [*Nervously.*] Who's that?
DODGER. [*Stepping forward.*] Your fellow
servant. . . . How are you doing, Pox?
POX. [*Rubbing his hands.*] Ah! You,
Dodger. . . . I'm glad.
DODGER. Why? Is something wrong?
Out with it.
POX. [*Wheedling.*] I'm afraid . . .
DODGER. Afraid of what?
POX. That we slaves—oh dear!—today
Are heading for such a slaughtering
and stringing up.
DODGER. Head for it on your own, then.

That's not the kind of heading-for or
heading-from I cultivate.
POX. [*Rubbing his hands again.*] I don't
suppose you know . . .
A perfectly frightful piece of news
That's fallen on our house.
DODGER. [*Coldly.*] What kind of frightful
piece of news?
POX. [*Clicking.*] Tch! Tch! A disgrace.
DODGER. [*Turning away.*] Keep it to
yourself then.
Don't tell *me.* I don't want to know.
POX. [*Following him.*] Well, I can't stop
you knowing:
i chased our monkey today over their
roof.
DODGER. [*Unconcernedly.*] Which simply
means, Pox,
That an idiotic man chased an idiotic
animal.
POX. [*Nettled.*] Damn your eyes!
DODGER. [*Blandly.*] You'd do better . . . to
go on with your story—
Now that you've begun.
POX. [*Sniveling.*] Well, over the house
next door, just by chance
I chanced to look down through the
skylight,
And what do I clap eyes on
But Goldilocks there kissing . . . some-
one else . . .
A quite unknown young man.
DODGER. [*Holding up his hands in pre-
tended horror.*] What, Pox? I'm
shocked.
Absolutely shocked!
POX. [*Gloating.*] Oh, I saw her all right.
DODGER. You? . . . Really?
POX. Me. Really . . . with these two eyes
of mine.
DODGER. [*Shaking his head.*] Get along
with you! You're kidding. . . .
You never saw a thing.
POX. [*Leering up at him.*] Do you notice
anything wrong with these two eyes?
DODGER. That's something you'd better
ask a doctor.
But [*wagging a finger at him*]
For the love of heaven,
Don't be in a rush to spread that story
round,
Or you'll go crashing into catas-
trophe—
Yes, head-over-heels and of your own
creating.
You'd better stop this stupidity at once

Or you've damned yourself twice over.

POX. Twice? Really! . . . How?

DODGER. Well, just let me tell you.
In the first place,
If you accuse Goldilocks falsely—
That'll finish you;
and in the second, if it's true,
You're finished just the same,
Because *you* were the one put on to
  guard her.

POX. [*Shaken but pigheaded.*] I can't
  vouch for what's in store for me.
But I certainly can for what I saw.

DODGER. Sticking to it, eh? You poor
  mutt!

POX. Well, what the deuce d'you want
  me to say
Except what I saw?
As a matter of fact she's there right
  now:
Next door.

DODGER. [*Clapping his hand to his head.*]
  Hey, d'you mean she's not at *home*?

POX. [*Shrugging.*] Go and see for yourself. . . .
I don't ask anyone to believe what *I* say.

DODGER. That's exactly what I'm going
  to do. [*Hurries into the* MAJOR'*s house.*]

POX. [*Calling after him.*] I'll wait here for
  you meanwhile
And keep a crafty watch
To see when that young heifer
Comes back from her pastures to her
  stall. [*Placing himself fairly and squarely
  on the neighboring doorstep—*MR. PRO-
  LIX'*s—*POX *begins a series of gloomy
  reflections.*]
But what shall I do? For the Major
Especially chose me to guard her.
So *if* I let on,
I *am* a dead man;
But if I keep mum
And the facts become known:
I'm a dead man again.
What a cursed affront is a woman!
I go on the roof and she's gone
From her own room:
My god, what a girl! And what gall!
  [*Whines and sighs.*]
If this gets to the ears of the Major
He'll string us all up—that I wager:
Including yours truly.
By heaven, I'd rather,
Whatever the story,
Keep my mouth shut
Than *be* offered up

Oh, so cruelly! [*Shakes his head glumly.*]
No, I simply can't look after a woman
  who's out for sale.
[DODGER *returns, pretending to be over-
  whelmed with apprehension on behalf of*
  POX.]

DODGER. Pox, oh, Pox!
Is there a man on earth who can give
  and bear
Such appalling shocks?
Is there anyone born
Under a more
Angry and lorn
Star
Than you are?

POX. [*Nervously.*] What's up?

DODGER. Will you just tell someone to
  gouge out your eyes,
Because they see the nonexistent.

POX. What's nonexistent?

DODGER. I wouldn't give an empty
  filbert for your life.

POX. [*With a pinched look.*] What's
  wrong?

DODGER. You ask *me* what's wrong?

POX. [*Truculently.*] And why shouldn't I
  ask?

DODGER. [*Gravely.*] Aren't you going to
  give instructions
For the clipping of that twaddling
  tongue?

POX. Why should I give instructions?

DODGER. [*At the top of his lungs.*] Be-
  cause, you nit, Goldilocks is at home
And you insisted that you saw her
Kissing and hugging a man next door.

POX. [*Unmoved.*] Fancy eating bird-
  seed[10] when wheat is so cheap!

DODGER. Meaning what?

POX. That you're blear-eyed.

DODGER. [*Snorting.*] Blear-eyed—you
  block? You're blind.
She's at home all right.

POX. What d'you mean—at home?

DODGER. I mean, goddammit, *at home.*

POX. [*Uneasily.*] Go on, Dodger, you're
  playing with me.

DODGER. Then I've gone and got my
  hands dirty.

POX. Oh?

DODGER. Yes—playing with filth.

POX. Go to hell!

DODGER. No, that's where you're going
  to go, Pox,
If you don't change your eyesight and
  your talk. [*Listens.*]

There's the door. Ours. [MAJOR
BULLSHOT-GORGEOUS's *front door opens
and reveals* GOLDILOCKS *standing there.
She is an exquisitely shaped young lady,
in the latest fashion and with her beautiful hair shining in ringlets on her shoul-
ders. She flashes* DODGER *an exultant
smile.* POX, *suspecting a trick, refuses to
turn around and does not see her.*]
POX. [*Doggedly.*] I'm keeping my eyes
glued to this one.
There's no way of getting from this
house to the next
Except through this door. [*He pats* MR.
PROLIX's *front door fondly.*]
DODGER. [*Winking at* GOLDILOCKS.] But
look, she's *there!*
You're poxed, Pox.
POX. [*Unmoved.*] I see for myself, I
think for myself,
And most of all—I believe for myself.
No man alive's going to bluff me into
thinking
She's not in this house.
I'm plumping myself right here:
She hasn't a chance of sneaking past
me. [*True to his words,* POX *plants him-
self even more fairly and squarely on* MR.
PROLIX's *doorstep.* GOLDILOCKS, *still
standing in the other doorway, exchanges
signs—and smiles—with* DODGER, *who
signals her back into the* MAJOR's *house.*]
DODGER. [*Jubilantly to himself.*] I've got
him.
Now for hurling him from the ram-
parts.
[*Sweetly to* POX.] Would you like me to
get you to admit
That you're completely cockeyed?
POX. [*Defiant.*] Go on, do it.
DODGER. And that you're as brainless as
you're blind?
POX. I'd love it.
DODGER. [*As if he were in court.*] You say
Master's young lady is in this house,
eh? [*Pointing to* PROLIX's *house.*]
POX. Yes and I insist I saw her—right
there inside—
Kissing another man.
DODGER. You know there's no connec-
tion
Between this house and ours?
POX. I know that.
DODGER. And not a sundeck, garden, or
any communication
Except through the skylight?

POX. I know.
DODGER. Well then:
If she's at home
And I actually make you see her com-
ing out of the house
Do you deserve a thorough thrashing?
POX. I do.
DODGER. [*Sarcastically.*] Watch that door
So that she doesn't slip from under you
And cross over to our house.
POX. [*Fervently.*] My intention exactly.
DODGER. [*Stepping briskly to the* MAJOR's
front door.] I'll have her here in a
jiffy:
Standing here in the street right in
front of you.
POX. [*Over his shoulders.*] Fine! Go and
do it. [DODGER *slips into the* MAJOR's
house, leaving POX *standing where he is,
his eyes still glued to the other front door.*]
POX. [*Becoming uneasy at* DODGER's *cock-
sureness, shifts impatiently.*] I am some-
what anxious to know
If I really saw what I saw,
And of course also
If he does what he said he can do:
Prove her at home. I'm sure
I've got eyes in my head
And don't need to beg
For anyone else's instead. [*Grimaces.*]
But this fellow's a terrible fawner.
He's always forever all over her:
First to be called for his dinner,
First to be given his fodder.
And he's only been about three[11]
Years in all
In my master's servants' hall.
Yet nobody has such a ball—
As *he.* [*Breaks off.*]
But I'd better mind what I'm doing and
watch this door.
I'll block it off completely—like this.
[POX *plasters himself against the door
with his arms and legs spread-eagled. The*
MAJOR's *front door opens quietly and*
DODGER *and* GOLDILOCKS *stand in the
doorway. They cannot move for laughter.
He signals her to caution.*]
DODGER. Sh-h! Don't forget instruc-
tions.
GOLDILOCKS. [*Archly.*] You *do* go on
about it.
DODGER. I'm scared stiff you won't be
sufficiently subtle.
GOLDILOCKS. [*Laughing quietly.*] Just give
me half a score of guileless girls

And I'll make them consummate mis-
tresses of guile
Simply from what I throw away.
DODGER. [*Pointedly.*] Well, now's the
time to work your wiles.
I'll drop back a little. [*Hangs back and
calls out.*]
Pox, now what do you say?
POX. [*Still glued.*] I'm fixed on *this*. . . .
But I've got a pair of ears:
Say what you want.
DODGER. I'd say it won't be long now
Before you're absolutely fixed . . . in
that position:
Right outside the town gate—
Arms pronged and all, on a gibbet.
POX. Now what d'you say that for?
DODGER. [*Snapping his fingers.*] Here,
man, look to your left.
Who's that young lady?
POX. [*Forces himself to turn—gasps.*] God
in heaven! . . . Master's
mademoiselle!
DODGER. [*With heavy sarcasm.*] I rather
think so too. . . .
Come on, now—whenever you're
ready.
POX. [*Turning pale.*] For what? What am
I going to do?
DODGER. Die—with dispatch.
GOLDILOCKS. [*Sweeping forward.*] Where
is that model servant
Who so monstrously slandered
A perfectly innocent woman!
DODGER. [*Pointing derisively.*] He's all
yours, ma'am. There he is:
The man who told me all I told you.
GOLDILOCKS. [*Advancing upon him.*] So,
you criminal,
It was *me* you say you saw, was it,
Kissing here next door?
DODGER. And with an unknown young
man, he said.
POX. [*Glaring.*] By god, I spoke the
truth.
GOLDILOCKS. [*Louder.*] Me? . . . You saw
me?
POX. Yes, with these eyes of mine.
GOLDILOCKS. [*Icily.*] Which I have a feel-
ing you're going to lose
By-and-by:
They see more than meets the eye.
POX. [*Shouting.*] I swear I'm not going
to be
Scared out of seeing what I saw.
GOLDILOCKS. [*Tossing her head.*] It's fatu-

ous and I'm a fool
To go on bandying words with this
lunatic:
I've got him by the hair.
POX. Give over threatening me.
I'm well aware my tomb will be a gib-
bet.
It's where my ancestors already lie:
Father, grandfather, and great-grand-
father—
Yes, and great-great-grandfather . . .
You won't dig out these eyes of mine
with threats. [*Clutches hold of
DODGER.*]
For love and kisses, tell me:
Where did she come from?
DODGER. [*Stiffly.*] Where else but home?
POX. Home?
DODGER. [*Waving a hand before POX.*]
Can you see me?
POX. [*Indignantly.*] Of course I can see
you. . . . [*Thinks aloud.*]
But it's sinister, it's queer,
The way she got from here to there.
We have no balcony at all
And no garden anywhere
All the windows are grated . . . all.
[*Swings his eyes on GOLDILOCKS.*]
And yet without a doubt I saw
You—inside—next door.
DODGER. Scum! Still accusing her?
You won't give up, will you?
GOLDILOCKS. [*Ingenuously.*] Good
heavens! Then the dream I had last
night
Has all come true.
DODGER. [*With well-prepared excitement.*]
Oh! What did you dream?
GOLDILOCKS. [*Breathlessly.*] Let me tell
you;
And you can both put your minds to it.
Last night I dreamt I saw my own twin
sister
Arrive in Ephesus from Athens with
her lover.
It seemed they were on a visit here to-
gether,
Lodging in the house next door.
DODGER. [*With a wink at the audience.*]
That's Dodger's dream. . . . [*As one
riveted.*] Go on, go on!
GOLDILOCKS. It seemed I was overjoyed
my sister had come,
But because of her I was caught up, it
seemed,
In a ghastly scandal.

For in my dream my own servant
  charged me—[*Flashes her eyes at* POX.]
Just as you are doing now—
With having kissed a strange young
  man,
When actually it was that twin sister of
  mine
Kissing her own lover.
And so I dreamt I was wronged: dread-
  fully slandered.
DODGER. [*Slapping his thighs.*] Why, this
  whole dream's being worked out in
  fact.
Dammit, it all fits! [*With an urgent look at*
  GOLDILOCKS.]
Get inside, ma'am, and say your pray-
  ers.
I think you ought to tell the Major.
GOLDILOCKS. [*Moving toward the door.*]
  Naturally.
I have no intention of being slandered
  with impunity. [*Throws another look at*
  POX *as she sweeps off into the* MAJOR'S
  house.]
POX. I fear I've gone and done it.
My back's already smarting.
DODGER. I suppose you know you're a
  goner?
POX. [*With a sickly grin.*] Anyway, she's
  certainly at home *now.*
That's absolutely certain. . . .
And I'm going to keep her fixed:
I'm going to watch our own front door.
  [POX *shuffles over to the* MAJOR'S *front
  door and spread-eagles himself as before.*]
DODGER. [*Sowing further doubt.*] It's ex-
  traordinary—isn't it, Pox!—
The way her dream fitted in
With your imagining:
Your belief you saw her kissing.
POX. *Now* I don't know what to believe.
For what I thought I saw,
Now I think I didn't see.
DODGER. [*Mercilessly.*] There isn't a
  chance, I'd say,
Of your snapping out of this in time.
Once the thing gets to Master's ears,
You've cooked your goose.
POX. [*Hopelessly.*] I realize now: a fog
  befogged my eyes.
DODGER. That's as plain as a pikestaff.
She was in here all the time.
POX. [*Scratching his head, then immediately
  remembered he is spread-eagled.*] I don't
  know what to say for sure:
I didn't see her . . . yet I did.

DODGER. Hell! Your stupidity
Very nearly sent us all to the
  bottom. . . .
Trying to be the boss's blue-eyed boy!
Why, you nearly ruined yourself! [*Cocks
  an ear.*]
Excuse me, there goes our neighbor's
  door. [GOLDILOCKS, *pretending to be
  her twin sister, comes out of* MR. PRO-
  LIX'S *house. She has slipped on a different
  dress and put a rose in her hair. Using an
  artificial—somewhat "fruity"—voice, she
  stands giving directions to a slave inside.*]
GOLDILOCKS. Enkindle the fire on the
  altar:
I'm full of glory and gladness
Toward Diana of Ephesus.
I'll sweeten her nose with the odor
Of incense grains from Arabia.
In the places of Neptune she saved me;
In the boisterous halls of his palace
When ravaged I was by the waves' race.
POX. [*Without changing his position, slowly
  turns his head.*] Oh Dodger! Dodger!
DODGER. [*Mimicking.*] Oh Pox! Pox!
  [*Switching to severity.*] What do you
  want?
POX. [*Gulping and pointing.*] The
  woman—the one who just came
  out—
It's Master's lady—Goldilocks—
Or isn't it?
DODGER. [*Rubbing his eyes.*] Damned if it
  isn't! Looks like her.
But it's a miracle if she's passed from
  here to there.
POX. [*Blinking.*] Can you have the slight-
  est doubt it's her?
DODGER. Seems like it.
POX. [*Jumping off his doorstep.*] Come on,
  let's call her. [*Brazenly walks up to her.*]
Hi there! What are you doing, Goldi-
  locks?
What business have you here?
I mean, what are you up to in that
  house? [GOLDILOCKS *looks straight past
  him.*]
Got nothing to say? . . . I'm talking to
  you.
DODGER. [*Grinning.*] You darn well
  aren't.
You're talking to yourself.
She's not answering.
POX. [*At the top of his lungs.*] Hey, you—
  you stuffed strumpet,
Wandering abroad among the neigh-

bors—
I'm addressing *you.*

GOLDILOCKS. [*Giving him a cold, hard look.*] To whom, sir, are you babbling?

POX. [*Red in the face.*] To whom? To *you.*

GOLDILOCKS. [*Unruffled.*] And who *are* you?
What business do you presume with me?

POX. [*Stammering.*] Y-you ask me who I *am?*

GOLDILOCKS. And why should I not ask what I do not know?

DODGER. [*Stepping in front of her with a wink.*] Then who am *I*, ma'am, if you don't know *him?*

GOLDILOCKS. A great nuisance to me, whoever you are: both of you.

POX. [*Quailing.*] You don't know us?

GOLDILOCKS. [*Turning her back.*] Certainly not. Neither of you.

POX. [*Nervously to* DODGER.] I'm fearfully afraid . . .

DODGER. Of what?

POX. That we've gone and lost our identities.
She said she didn't know either one of us.

DODGER. [*Deadpan.*] My dear Pox,
This is something I must follow up:
Are we ourselves or someone else?
Perhaps some neighbor on the sly
Has gone and swapped us for some others.

POX. [*Pinching himself.*] Well, I'm all *me.*

DODGER. [*Tapping himself.*] And so—by god!—am I. [*With a sidelong look at* GOLDILOCKS.]
Woman, you're looking for trouble.
[*She pretends to ignore him.*]
I'm talking to you. . . . Hi there! Goldilocks!

GOLDILOCKS. [*Trying not to giggle.*] You must be off your head
To give me such a crazy name.

DODGER. Hoity-toity! . . . By what name, then?

GOLDILOCKS. [*Pouting.*] Honéstia.

POX. Ha! Ha! Ha! Goldilocks, you little cheat—
Trying to get yourself another name!
It's Humbuggia, not Honéstia:
You cheater of my master!

GOLDILOCKS. [*With big wide open eyes.*] *I?*

POX. Yes, you.

GOLDILOCKS. But I only arrived yesterday in Ephesus:
Last evening from Athens,
With a young Athenian gentleman, my fiancé.

DODGER. [*Impressed.*] Well, madam,
Tell me what your business is here in Ephesus.

GOLDILOCKS. [*Looking him straight in the eye.*] I heard my own twin sister was here,
And I came to find her.

POX. [*Between his teeth.*] You're a bad one!

GOLDILOCKS. No, just incredibly silly—
To be chatting to you two. . . . I'm going. [*Turns on her heel.*]

POX. [*Grabbing her.*] I won't let you go.

GOLDILOCKS. [*Struggling.*] Let me loose.

POX. You're caught redhanded, my girl.
I won't let you loose.

GOLDILOCKS. [*In ringing tones.*] If you don't let go of me this instant,
My hand and *your* face are coming into collision.

POX. [*Angrily to* DODGER.] You're just standing by, you bastard!
Why don't you nab her from your side?
[GOLDILOCKS *swings and catches* POX *a solid blow on the cheek.*]

DODGER. [*Folding his arms and watching.*]
I've no desire to get a battering.
How do I know she's really Goldilocks
And not someone the dead spit of her?

GOLDILOCKS. [*In a wrestler's lock with* POX.] Are you going to let me go or not?

POX [*Panting.*] Let you go?
I'm going to drag you home all the way . . .
Willy-nilly if you don't come willingly.

GOLDILOCKS. [*Tossing her head toward* MR. PROLIX's *house.*] This is where I live, and I'm a guest.
My home's in Athens.
What *you* call home I want no part of.
And as to you two men—
I don't know you and I don't want to.

POX. [*Snorting.*] Take it to court, then.
I'm not for the life of me going to let you go:
Not unless I have your word of honor
That if I do
You'll get yourself over into the Major's house here.

GOLDILOCKS. [*Struggling.*] You're forcing me, you, you—who? [*After several more seconds of tussle,* GOLDILOCKS *gives way.*]

All right: I give you my word—
Let me go and I'll disappear
Into whatever house you say.

POX. [*Releasing her.*] There! I've let you go.

GOLDILOCKS. [*Shakes out her tresses and with a mocking laugh darts into* PROLIX'*s house.*] Yes, you've let me go. . . . And I'm gone! [*She slams the door in their faces.*]

POX. [*Red with fury.*] Kept her word like a woman!

DODGER. [*Dryly.*] Pox, you let the quarry slip through your fingers.
She's our master's girl all right. [*Bends toward him.*]
Do you want to show real verve?

POX. How?

DODGER. [*Between his teeth.*] Go into your house and fetch me a sword.

POX. What'll you do with it?

DODGER. [*Fiercely.*] I'm going to break into that house
And whomsoever I see inside kissing Goldilocks,
I shall quarter him on the spot.

POX. [*Hesitant.*] So you think it was she?

DODGER. Good heavens, man! I'm certain.

POX. [*Wiping his forehead.*] God! What a show she put on.

DODGER. Off with you now and bring me the sword.

POX. [*Disappearing into the* MAJOR'*s house.*] Yes, yes—I'll have it here in a jiffy.

DODGER. [*To the audience, chuckling.*]
No one, not even a brigade of dragoons
Or column of men,
Can match the confident action and cool
Nerve of a woman.
Oh, the precision with which she has studied
And acted both parts!
The way she's bamboozled my colleague, that prig
Of a scrupulous guard . . .
The hole I cut through the wall is a sheer
Marvel of genius.

POX. [*Running out of the house.*] Hey, Dodger, we don't need a sword.

DODGER. Well, what now?

POX. [*Breathless.*] Master's mistress is here—right at home.

DODGER. At home? . . . N-no?

POX. Lying back on her couch.

DODGER. [*Grimly.*] Then you're predicting your personal doom.

POX. What do you mean?

DODGER. Well, you've gone and manhandled
The lady from next door.

POX. [*Going pale.*] O god! I'm afraid I have.

DODGER. And no one on earth can alter the fact
That's she's our girl's twin sister:
Precisely the one you saw kissing through the skylight.

POX. [*Going weak at the knees.*] Y-yes: it's all obvious now. . . .
She was the one—as you say.
Lord, what a near shave!
What if I'd told the m-master?

DODGER. [*Stiffly.*] If you've got any sense you'll keep your mouth shut.
A servant should say much less than he savvies.
In any case I am leaving you now:
I want no part of your maneuvers.
I'm going in here to see my neighbor.
Your muddles upset me. If the master comes
And asks for me, here I'll be—
And here you can come and get me.
[DODGER *wanders off, nose in air, into* MR. PROLIX'*s house.*]

POX. [*Resentfully.*] So he's gone, has he?
Takes about as much interest in his master
As if he were as free as a goddam freedman.
At any rate, the girl is now inside the house:
I saw her there just now stretched out at home.
I'm going to keep my eye on her—and that's for sure. [POX *takes up his stance on the* MAJOR'*s front doorstep.*]

[*Shouts and recriminations burst from the other house, and in a moment* MR. PROLIX *stomps out, brandishing his silver cane and making an excellent show of rage.*]

PROLIX. Hell and damnation! These fellows here next door,

The cursed servants of the soldier,
Take me for a female—not a man at
all.
They're simply laughing up their
sleeves at me.
Is my invited guest, the lady
Who came from Athens yesterday with
her friend,
To be coerced and bandied about like a
bauble?
And she a full and freeborn citizen!
[*Marches toward the* MAJOR's *house.*]
POX. [*Trying to make himself small.*] Lord
help me—now I'm done for!
He's making a beeline for me. Oh!
I've landed myself in a mess, I fear.
This old tyke's tirade makes that clear.
PROLIX. [*Still advancing.*] I'll show him!
Look here, Pox—
You absolute cesspool, Pox!
Are you the man who made a game of
my guest just now—
In front of my house?
POX. [*Cringing.*] Dear sweet neighbor,
listen.
PROLIX. [*Thundering.*] Listen? Me? To
you!
POX. I—I can explain.
PROLIX. Explain? . . . *That* outrage? *That*
irrevocable misconduct?
Do you think you freebooters have the
right
To do anything you like—you, you
ruffian?
POX. [*Whining.*] Oh, please, sir.
PROLIX. So help me every god and god-
dess that there is,
If you're not handed over to me now
For one long-drawn-out and bloody
birching
Lasting from the morning till the night.
You smashed my gutters and my tiles,
You chased an ape no better than your-
self;
You spied upon my guest from there
As she hugged and kissed her heart's
desire.
You had the gall to impute immodesty
To that decent girl next door—
The mistress of your master—
And me with grossest infamy.
Then you trifled with my guest outside
my house. . . .
Oh, if you're not handed to me now
As a holocaust to lash,
I'll heap your master with more shame

Than the sea has combers in a hur-
ricane. [*Raises his stick.*]
POX. [*Crumpled before him.*] Oh Mr. Pro-
lix, sir, I'm so hard pressed
I've no idea what to tackle first:
Make excuses to you now?
Or if you think it best,
And *that* girl isn't *this*
And this girl isn't that:
Apologize and take the blame. . . .
I mean I don't know even now
What I really saw:
That girl of yours is so like ours,
If indeed she's not the same.
PROLIX. Then go inside my house and
look: You'll soon know.
POX. May I?
PROLIX. May you? I *command* you.
Study her at leisure.
POX. [*Walking backwards and bowing.*]
Yes, sir, yes sir! I'll do that. [*As* POX
disappears into MR. PROLIX's *house, the
latter hurries over to the front door of the*
MAJOR *and shouts through the grat-
ing.*]
PROLIX. Hi there, Goldilocks! Quick!
Race over to my house. It's imperative.
Then when Pox has gone, quick,
Race back home again. [PROLIX *twiddles
his thumbs anxiously on the doorstep.*]
Oh dear!
I'm so afraid she's going to mess it up.
If he doesn't see the girl in there . . .
Ah!
The door's opening. [POX *staggers out.*]
POX. By all the immortal powers! The
gods themselves I claim
Could not make two different women
more the same.
PROLIX. [*Severely.*] And so?
POX. [*Humbly.*] And so I deserve a clob-
bering.
PROLIX. And so she isn't this one?
[*Indicating the* MAJOR's *house.*]
POX. [*Still dazed.*] Even if she is, she
isn't.
PROLIX. But you saw that one?
POX. That one and her guest:
Hugging and kissing.
PROLIX. And is that one this one?
POX. I don't know.
PROLIX. [*Magnanimously.*] Would you
like to know—for certain?
POX. Very much.
PROLIX. Then go straight into your
house and see

If this one—yours—is there inside.

POX. [*Full of gratitude.*] Oh yes, sir! It's a
wonderful suggestion.

I'll come straight back to you outside.
[POX *runs into the* MAJOR'*s house.*]

PROLIX. [*Holding his sides with laughter.*] I
swear I've never seen a human being

More twisted inside out—

More beautifully bamboozled. [*Freezing
his laughter.*] But here he is again.
[POX *shuffles out of the* MAJOR'*s house
and throws himself at* MR. PROLIX'*s feet.*]

POX. Mr. Prolix, I beseech you,

By all the gods and men, by my own
stupidity,

By these your knees . . .

PROLIX. [*Impatiently.*] Yes, yes—beseech
me for what?

POX. To forgive

My senseless insensitivity.

I realize now I've been a stupid, sightless sod.

For Goldilocks is *there*—inside.

PROLIX. So, you've seen them both, you
stinker?

POX. [*With bowed head.*] I've seen them
both, sir.

PROLIX. [*Tight-lipped.*] Will you please
bring your master out here.

POX. Oh sir, I do admit

I deserve a dreadful drubbing

And I assert I've deeply wronged

Your lady guest. . . .

I thought she really was

My master's woman.

And anyway, my master

Had appointed me to watch her.

But—ah!—two drops of water from
one well

Could not be as much alike

As that guest of yours is like this girl.

Furthermore I do confess

That through the skylight

I peeped into your house.

PROLIX. [*Snorting.*] You do confess! I
saw you do it.

No doubt you also saw

My two guests kissing there?

POX. Yes, I saw them—why deny it?—

But what I saw was Goldilocks, I
thought.

PROLIX. What! You'd rate me with the
very scum?

Make me knowingly condoner of an
outrage done

Against my neighbor in my home?

POX. [*Pathetically.*] I do realize now at
last,

Now that I see the whole thing whole,

That I acted like a blooming fool.

But, sir, I didn't act from spite.

PROLIX. [*Tartly.*] No, you acted from
presumption.

A man in the servant state should aim

To keep his eyes, hands and tongue

Well tamed.

POX. [*Still kneeling and looking up.*] Sir, if
I mutter a word again

From this day on—

Even what I know for certain—

Have me hamstrung.

I'll hand myself right over to you.

But this time, sir,

Please give your pardon.

PROLIX. [*Strokes his beard, surveying* POX
with distaste. Finally he growls:] I'll
force myself to think

You meant no harm;

And for this once, I'll pardon.

POX. [*Still groveling.*] Oh, sir—god bless
you!

PROLIX. [*Gruffly.*] And if you want the
gods to bless you too,

You'll damn well hold your tongue in
future:

Not know even what you know,

See past even what you see.

POX. [*Kissing* PROLIX'*s feet.*] Oh, that's
beautiful advice, sir!

I'll go and do it. . . .

But have I apologized enough?

PROLIX. Just go.

POX. [*Staggers to his feet, bowing.*] Is there
nothing else you'd like?

PROLIX. Yes—not to know you.

POX. [*Begins to move off, mumbling to himself.*]

He gave me his word *here*. . . .

Nice of him to be so kind

And stop being angry,

But *I* know better.

The moment the Major comes in from
the forum

I'm to be grabbed—at home.

He and that Dodger are making ar-
rangements

To sell me—I feel it—I've known it
some time.

Thanks very much! . . . I'll not fall for
that.

I'll scuttle away to some little hole

And there lie low for a day or two

Till all this fuss and fury is over.
God knows! I've earned enough ret-
ribution
To do for a whole impious nation. [POX
slinks off in the direction of the country.]
PROLIX. [*Gazes after him and chuckles.*]
So the fellow's decamped!
And I'm darn-well sure
A stuck pig's sense
Is a good deal more.
To be diddled like that—
Ha ha ha!—
From seeing what he saw.

Why his eyes and his ears,
Even his brain,
Have collapsed in our favor:
We're doing fine,
Oh fine—so far!

The way that girl
Romped through her part!
Now I'll return
To the parliament,
For Dodger's back
With me at home
And Pox has gone
Off to roam.
The Senate now
Can sit full house,
So I must go—
I mustn't miss
The sorting out of parts. [MR. PROLIX,
humming a ditty, goes into his house.]

Act 3

*Half an hour later. A council of war has
been held in* MR. PROLIX's *house. The time
has come for the conspirators to meet outside
and clinch their plans.* DODGER *creeps out
furtively and calls to the others.*
DODGER. [*In a loud whisper, holding up a
cautionary hand.*] Hey! Halcyon, keep
the rest of them inside a minute till I
take a good look around. We don't
want our little meeting to be surprised.
We've got to make sure the spot is safe
from the enemy intelligence. . . . Can't
risk our plans. . . . [*Mutters to himself as
he looks around warily.*] A plan's worse

than useless if the enemy gets hold of
it:[12] nothing but a pitfall. Once let the
enemy get whiff of your strategy and
you've bound yourself hand and foot—
yes, and tongue. They'll do to you exactly what you'd planned for *them*. So
I'm going to make darn sure there isn't
a big-ears about—left or right—lying in
wait for us. [*Tiptoes behind a pillar and
gazes down the street.*] Good! A strictly
vacuous view right to the bottom. I'll
call them: Hey there! Prolix and Halcyon—come on out! [*Enter MR. PROLIX
and HALCYON. The latter is a good-looking
young man in his early twenties. His carefully tailored clothes of excellent weave show
that he comes from the well-to-do professional classes. Though usually of a sunny
disposition (and generous to the point of
naiveté) his preoccupied look speaks of the
problems of love. He is also worried about
being a burden to his friend PROLIX.*]

PROLIX. Here we are—at your disposal.
DODGER. [*Surveying them with approval.*]
Good troops are easy to command.
What I want to know is this:
Are we to go ahead with the plans we
made inside?
PROLIX. Of course! They're perfect for
our purposes.
DODGER. And you, Halcyon?
HALCYON. If it pleases you two,
How could it displease *me*? [*Turns to
DODGER.*]
What man more than you
Is mine entirely?
DODGER. Nicely and becomingly said,
sir!
PROLIX. [*With a twinkle in his eye.*] As well
it ought to be!
HALCYON. [*Turning to PROLIX with a
sigh.*] Seriously, sir, this enterprise
Makes me miserable as hell:
Bothers me body and soul.
PROLIX. [*Putting a hand on his arm.*]
Come on! What's bothering you?
HALCYON. That I should thrust on you,
A man of reverend years,
These stripling's cares.
They do not suit your soul
Or character at all.
That I should see you strain
Just for love of me
To further my love affairs,
And do such things as age

Like yours would leave alone . . .
I blush to cast on you
Such worries when you're old.
DODGER. [*Pretending to be shocked.*] Man,
What new love is this:
Blushing for what you do?
Halcyon, you're no lover,
You're the shadow
Of what a lover is.
HALCYON. But to harry
Such an elder
With a lover's worry!
PROLIX. [*With sudden fire.*] What are you
saying, my boy?
Do I seem such a dreary old death's-
head to you?
Such a tottering, terrible old mummy?
Why, I wasn't born more than fifty-
four years ago! [*Winks at the audience
at this patent untruth.*]
I'm a keen-eyed, quick-handed, neat-
footed youngster.
DODGER. [*Shaking a finger at* HALCYON.]
His hair is silver perhaps
But there isn't the tiniest trace
Of age in his heart: the same
Beautiful spirit is still
Inside him as when he was born.
HALCYON. [*Promptly.*] Dodger, that's
perfectly true;
Just as I'm finding out too.
The way he is kind is the way
A very young man might do.
PROLIX. [*Preening himself.*] What's more,
you'll find, my boy,
The harder the task you ask
The more one with you I am
In furthering your lover's aim.
HALCYON. No need to tell me that, sir.
PROLIX. Ah! But I want you to know it
direct,
Not at second hand.
For unless one has fallen in love oneself
One can hardly understand
The passionate heart.
And my old body still has
Some love and some juice;
And for the finer delights of life
I still have a use:
I can crack a good joke,
I'm a gracious guest.
At table I don't contradict,
At dinners I watch my manners:
I don't talk more than my share,
Shut up when somebody else
Has the floor.

I'm no spitter and hawker—
No sniveling boor. No sir!
My birthplace is Ephesus—not Apulia.
I'm not an animal from Animulia.[13]
DODGER. [*To* HALCYON, *tongue-in-cheek.*]
What a lovely old man he is
If this inventory is his!
He must have been reared—oh
surely!—
In Venus's nursery.
PROLIX. [*Puffing up with pleasure.*] Oh,
you'll find I'm better at doing than
saying!
I never steal another man's girl at a
party.
No! And I don't go grabbing the caviar
Or cornering the cocktails or
Starting a quarrel over the wine.
If anyone gets difficult
I just go home and cut the cackle.
To be gracious, loving, affable
Is what I aim for at the table.
DODGER. [*Beginning to fidget.*] My dear
sir,
Everything you do is strictly charming.
Show me three such men
And I'll pay the weight of them in gold.
HALCYON. [*Sincerely.*] And *I* say you
won't find another
Man of his age so delightful
Or such a friend to a friend.
PROLIX. [*Basking in their eulogies.*]
Well, Halcyon, I'll make you admit
I'm still a youngster at heart,
Bursting with ways to proffer you help.
Do you need a lawyer grave and fierce?
[*Knits his brow and pulls down the cor-
ners of his mouth.*]
Here I am! . . . Or one that's suave?
[*Demonstrates with an oily smile.*]
You'll find me suaver than the sea,
More silent and calm, more meltingly
Genial than a western breeze. [*With
hand to his heart.*] And from this same
resourceful seat
I'll produce the liveliest guest for you at
dinner,
The nicest buddy when you eat,
And wizard of a caterer.
But when it comes to dancing girls[14]—
oh my!—
I've got the most curvaceous cutey beat.
[*Executes a little belly-dance*]
DODGER. [*Stifling a yawn, to* HALCYON.]
With such a mass of talent, sir,
What would you wish—

If a wish could add a single jot?
HALCYON. [*Earnestly.*] The ability to
   match
His kindnesses with thanks:
Yes, and yours—I know how much
Worry I am causing both of you.
Oh, and the expense, [*Turns to* PROLIX.]
I am putting you to
Bothers me a lot.
PROLIX. [*Clapping him on the back.*] Fool-
   ish boy!
When one pays out money for a shrew-
   ish wife
Or for an enemy,
That is cost.
But money spent on an honest guest
Or on a friend, is money made—
As money spent on things divine,
For a wise man, is—sheer gain.
   [DODGER *looks in despair at* HALCYON
   but gets no sympathy from that quarter.
   Meanwhile PROLIX *goes on.*]
By the grace of god I have the means
To entertain you gracefully.
So eat, drink and enjoy yourself with
   me:
Put on the trappings of hilarity.
It's an open house and I am open too,
Living the life I wish to do.
By the grace of god, as I say, I'm rich
And could have taken a wife of means
   and parts.
But how could I induce
Myself to introduce
Into the house a woman that barks?
DODGER. [*Unable to resist giving* HALCYON
   a sharp nudge.]
Why not, sir? Having children is a very
   happy business.
PROLIX. [*Vigorously shaking his head.*] Be-
   lieve you me: having your own free-
   dom[15] is infinitely happier.
DODGER. [*With a polite sigh.*] You're an
   all-round genius, sir, at giving good
   advice.
PROLIX. [*Off again.*] Oh, I know it's all
   very nice
To marry a tractable wife;
But where in the world is she
To be found? . . . Now take me:
Am I really to bring home
A dame who'll never dream
Of saying to me this:
"Buy me some wool, my darling, to
   weave
You a beautiful soft warm coat to have

For the winter to keep you from cold,
   and some
Nice thick vests"?
Not on your life!
That's not the sort of thing a wife
Ever suggests.
But before the crow of the cock
She'd wake me with a shock
And say:
"Darling, give me some money for
   Mother's Day[16]
To buy me a present for Mother.
Give me some money to make
Preserves, and some money to take
The woman who predicts
On Minerva's Day, and the priest,
And some for the analyst
Of dreams, and the herbalist.
And wouldn't it be a shame
If we left out the madame
Who tells your future fate
From your eyebrows' state?
Then there's the modiste,
We can't afford to miss.
And the cateress is cross
Because of course
It's been some time
Since she had a dime.
And the midwife's made a fuss
Because she hasn't had enough. . . .
And oh! There's nothing worse
Than not to tip the nurse
Who looks after
The young slaves
Under your own rafter." [MR. PROLIX
   fetches a sigh, from the depths.]
This is the kind of expense galore
And a great deal more
That stops me taking a wife
Who'd boss me out of my life.

DODGER. [*Distantly.*] Ah, sir: the gods
are certainly kind to you. Once you let
go of that liberty of yours, you won't so
easily put it back in its goddam place
again.
HALCYON. [*Somewhat shaken.*] But it *is* an
asset, surely, for a man of great wealth
and considerable station to bring up
children to perpetuate his name and
family.
PROLIX. What do I want with children
when I have so many relatives? As
things are, I lead a peaceful, happy life:
please my fancy as I want to. On my
demise my property gets shared out

among my relatives. [DODGER *is about to
interrupt but* PROLIX *with a sly smile waves
him away.*]

Before daylight they're there:
Asking if I've passed a peaceful night.
They offer sacrifice—
Give me a bigger part than they give
    themselves.
I am escorted to the sacrificial banquet.
They ask me home for lunch, and
    clamor
For me to come to dinner.
The least happy of them
Is the one that's sent me least:
They fight to give me presents.
Meanwhile I just murmur to myself:
"It's my goods they're gaping after
But it's *me* their competition nurtures
    and supports."
DODGER. [*Offhandedly.*] All beautifully
    thought out, sir!
Your life arranged around you to a tee!
You enjoy yourself—
And that's as good as twins or triplets.
PROLIX. [*Taking him up.*] By god! If I
    had children,
Then the troubles would begin.
I'd worry myself silly right away.
My son has a temperature—
I think he's dying.
He's fallen down drunk
Or been chucked off his horse—
I'm terrified he's broken his legs
Or snapped his neck.
DODGER. [*With perfunctory politeness as he
    twiddles his thumbs, rocks on his heels
    with impatience.*] Here's a man who's
    got a right to be rich and have a long
    life:
He looks after his own and has a good
    time,
And he sees to his friends.
HALCYON. [*Bursting out with youthful ad-
    miration.*] Oh, what a lovely man!
So help me heaven—but I wish the
    gods
Didn't lump together all our human
    lives
In one indiscriminate lot,
Instead of doing what a decent sales-
    man does:
Marking up the price of perfect goods
To sell as they deserve,
And cutting down the price
Of items that are soiled.

So should the gods have allotted hu-
    man life:
To the man of charming character,
Sweet longevity;
To the nasty criminal,
A quick dispatch.
If they'd arranged things so,
Bad men would be less abundant
And do their dirty deeds with less
    abandon.
What is more:
The cost of living would—for the
    good—
Drop through the floor.
PROLIX. [*Holding up his hands in avuncu-
    lar reproof.*] No, it's shallow and it's
    silly
To criticize the gods and to abuse
    them. . . .
But it's time we stopped all this.
I must do some marketing for you,
    dear guest,
To entertain you in my house
As well as you and I could wish
With a slap-up time
And every bang-up special dish.
HALCYON. [*With a gesture of reproval.*]
    But, sir, I'm quite embarrassed
At the cost I've put you to already.
Such hospitality from a friend
No guest can revel in
And not become a nuisance after a
    three days' stay.
After *ten* days he becomes an Iliad of
    disasters.
Even if the master
Is not unwilling to put up with it,
The servants grumble. [*Meanwhile
    DODGER in a state of restlessness has gone
    and sat down on the doorstep, from where
    during the remainder of this conversation
    he amuses the audience with a series of
    gestures of impatience and despair.*]
PROLIX. Ah! My friend,
My servants have been trained to serve
    and not to boss me
Or try to keep me under their thumbs.
If what *I* want gripes them—well,
I'm the stroke in this rowing outfit:
They've got to do it just the same
Even if they hate it, or get a hiding. . . .
Now for that shopping I spoke about.
HALCYON. [*As* PROLIX *begins to go* HAL-
    CYON *puts a hand on his arm.*] If you
    really must, sir,
But please don't buy a lot,

Don't be extravagant:
Just anything will do for me.
PROLIX. [*Turns on him sharply.*] Oh, stop
that now!
Stop these clichés of such stilted non-
sense.
Now you're pulling that lower-class
cant on me
Which makes guests say the moment
they've sat down
And dinner's on the table:
"Oh, my host! Was it really necessary
To go to this expense—just for us?
You must have been mad. Why, this
Would do for ten!"
They blame you for what you've
bought
But they dig in just the same.
DODGER. [*With a combination of admira-
tion and desperate irony.*] By god!
That's exactly what they do.
How shrewd of him and how observ-
ant!
PROLIX. [*Underlining his remarks with cane
in hand.*] And none of these same
people,
No matter how you pile the food on
them,
Ever say:
"Oh, please, stop!
Have this dish removed;
Take away the ham, I'd rather not.
This eel, cold, would be superb:
Remove it, to the side with it."
You won't hear suchlike sentiments
From any one of them.
No, they just tumble and topple across
the table, grabbing and guzzling.
DODGER. [*With a sigh.*] A good descrip-
tion from a gentleman
Of bad manners, sir!
PROLIX. Oh, I haven't told you the hun-
dredth part.
If only there were time, how I could
dissertate!
DODGER. [*Leaping up from the doorstep.*]
But since there's not, sir,
Let's get on with the plot, sir.
I'd like you both to fix
Your attention on the matter.
I'll need your service, Mr. Prolix.
I've hit on an idea
That's absolutely dapper
Of shearing our long-haired soldier
And giving Goldilock's lover
The hope

To elope
And have her. [DODGER *beckons the other
two to his side and clears his throat. The
conversation begins in mock committee-
meeting style.*]
PROLIX. I should like to be given the
scheme of this idea.
DODGER. And I should like to be given
the ring you wear.
PROLIX. What use will you put it to?
DODGER. When I have it, I'll unfold my
scheme to you.
PROLIX. Here you are sir, use it. [*Hands
over ring.*]
DODGER. And here's my grand idea,
peruse it. . . .
HALYCON. And here are our ears, ready
to infuse it.

DODGER. [*Getting down to brass tacks.*]
Now my master is the most pertina-
cious pursuer of female flesh that ever
there was, or I believe ever will be.
HALCYON. [*Vigorously interrupting.*] Hear!
Hear! to that!
DODGER. And he asseverates that the
beauty of Paris is as nothing to his; in
fact, he says, lays it down on record,
that all the women of Ephesus can't
stop from running after him.
PROLIX. [*Cynically.*] A good many husbands, *I* can tell you, heartily wish that
what you say were true. . . . But I know
exactly what you mean. So, come to the
point, will you, Dodger!
DODGER. Well sir, can you find me some
perfectly irresistible "femme fatale"
whose brains and bosom are equally re-
plete with wiles and strategies?
PROLIX. Freeborn or freegrown?
DODGER. I don't mind which; but give
me one who's on the make—embodies
her livelihood in her body—and has
some common sense. Intelligence I
don't expect. None of them has that.
PROLIX. [*Doing a little diagram in the air
with his cane.*] Do you want her to be
sumptuous or only scrumptious?
DODGER. [*Slightly altering the diagram in
the air with a finger.*] You know . . . suc-
culent: just about as young and irresistible a dish as possible.
PROLIX. [*After a little more thought.*] Aha!
The very thing: one of my own
clients—a real swinging doll. . . . But
what do you want her for?

DODGER. You are to take her home to your house, then bring her here all got up like a married woman: hair piled high in a braided coiffure . . . and she's to pretend she's your wife. That's what she'll be told.

HALCYON. *I* don't see where this is getting you.

DODGER. [*Grinning.*] You *will*. . . . Does she have a maid?

PROLIX. A minx of the first water.

DODGER. *She'll* be needed too. This is what you tell the girl and her maid: the chick's to pretend she's your wife but dying for the Major. She gave this ring to her little nymphet—maid—who turned it over to me to pass on to the Major . . . I being the go-between in this affair. [DODGER *is getting louder and louder.*]

PROLIX. [*Testily.*] I can hear you, thank you. I'm not deaf. I've got a pair of very good ears.[18]

DODGER. [*Sobered.*] I'll give the ring to him, saying it was sent as a present by your wife through me in order to bring the two of them together. . . . That's the sort of man he is: the poor wretch will be simply slavering for her. Whoring is the stinker's only hobby.

PROLIX. [*Beaming.*] If you'd sent the great god Sun to do the searching for you, you'd not uncover two more perfect wenches for this job. Be full of optimism.

DODGER. [*Waving him on.*] Fine! On with the job. It presses hard. [*Turns to* HALCYON *as* PROLIX *disappears down the street.*] And now, Halcyon: your turn to listen, please.

HALCYON. At your command.

DODGER. Make quite sure that when the Major comes back home you'll not go calling Goldilocks by her proper name.

HALCYON. [*Mystified.*] By what name, then?

DODGER. [*Shocked that he has forgotten it already.*] Honéstia.

HALCYON. [*Apologetic.*] Oh yes, of course! The name we settled on.

DODGER. [*With a brisk slap on the back.*] Good! Off with you.

HALCYON. [*Reluctant to move.*] I'll remember, but what use—I'd like to know—is remembering?

DODGER. [*Giving him a shove.*] I'll tell you when the time comes. Meanwhile keep your mouth shut. *He's* doing his stuff now: in due course *you'll* have your part to play.

HALCYON. All right! I go inside.

[HALCYON *enters* MR. PROLIX's *house.*]

DODGER. Make sure you keep strictly to what I say. [DODGER *saunters a few steps toward the* MAJOR's *house, delighted with the intrigue he has set in motion and whistling a little tune.*]

What things I'm stirring up!
Oh, what machines of war
I'm moving forward fast!
Today I'm going to tear
The Major's girl from him
When my troops fall in.
But I'll call that fellow, Pox, out here.

[*Shouts through the* MAJOR's *door.*]

Hey, Pox! If you're not too boxed:
Step outside. . . . It's Dodger calling.

[*Enter* PENNY *from the* MAJOR's *house. He is a fat youth in his middle teens, very much at home in the world and well aware on which side his bread is buttered. He lurches into the street unsteadily.*]

PENNY. [*Thickly.*] Poxsh? . . . He'sh . . . engaged.

DODGER. [*Eyeing him with disapproval.*] At what?

PENNY. Absorbing . . . in his sleep.

DODGER. Absorbing?

PENNY. Yeah! . . . I mean he's snoring. And snoring is absorbing—of a sorts.

DODGER. [*Impatiently.*] So Pox is inside asleep, is he?

PENNY. [*Grinning.*] Asleep? Not his nose. That's snorting—like a trumpet. You see, he looks after the cellar. . . . He was just putting some spice into a barrel when he touched a cup and took a nip—privately.

DODGER. Fancy that now! And you were just—helping him. Louse!

PENNY. What are you after?

DODGER. What gave him the nerve to fall asleep?

PENNY. [*Shrugging.*] His eyes—I presume.

DODGER. That's not what I asked. Tosspot! . . . Come over here. [PENNY *crawls toward him.*]
You're a dead duck if I don't have the truth.

Did you draw the wine for him?

PENNY. [*Insolently.*] No, I didn't.

DODGER. You deny it?

PENNY. You're damned right, I do. He said I mustn't say I did. So I didn't really draw off eight halfpints into a jug, and he didn't really gulp the hot stuff off for lunch.

DODGER. And *you* didn't really take a swig either?

PENNY. A swig? So help me heaven! I couldn't swig a thing.

DODGER. Why not?

PENNY. Because I just sopped it up. The darn stuff was so peppered it burnt my throat off.

DODGER. [*With a deep sigh.*] It is given to some to get gloriously drunk, and to others—to get vinegar and water. . . . A fine cellarer and under-cellarer the cellar's got!

PENNY. You'd damn well do the same if *you* had got it. You're only jealous because you can't follow suit.

DODGER. Well well well! . . . Did he ever draw wine before this? [*A pause.*] Answer me, you little thief. And, just for your benefit, I'm telling you, Master Penny, if you let out a lie—I'm going to murder you.

PENNY. [*Sticking his tongue out.*] Oh yeah! So *you* can go and tattle all I've told, and when I get flung out of my nice cellar stoned, you can get another under-cellarer and make yourself the cellarer.

DODGER. [*Holding up his hands in deprecation.*] No no! I wouldn't do that. . . . Come along, make a clean breast of it.

PENNY. Honestly, I never saw him draw any. [*Grinning slyly.*] But it went like this: he'd give *me* orders and then *I'd* draw it.

DODGER. That's why the wine-jars were always standing on their heads?

PENNY. God, no, mister! That's not why the wine-jars were always . . . jiggling about. There was a little section of the cellar that was very slippery, and propped up there like this . . . [*gives a demonstration, lolling drunkenly against a pillar*] was a two-quart jug, and ever so often this two-quart jug would fill itself up. . . . Oh, ten times over I've seen it full and empty—mostly full. And when

the jug got jolly the wine-jars got jiggling.

DODGER [*With a growl and a shove.*] Off with you—into the house. The jolly jiggling things in the cellar are *you:* holding downright bacchanals there. Wait till I fetch the boss from the forum!

PENNY. [*Gulping.*] Then I'm finished. If the boss comes home and hears of this, he'll string me up—because I never reported it. [*Fixes the audience with a moony look.*] I'm going to get the hell out of here. Put off the reckoning till another day. . . . You won't tell him, will you? Promise me! [*Begins to stagger away from the house.*]

DODGER. [*Blocking him.*] Where are you off to?

PENNY. [*Blankly.*] I've been sent . . . somewhere. I'll be right back.

DODGER. [*Sternly.*] Who sent you?

PENNY. Miss Goldilocks.

DODGER. Go on, then. But come straight back.

PENNY. [*Darting down the street with an unexpected burst of speed and calling over his shoulder.*]You bet! And in my absence—when the disaster's all divided out—do take my share, will you? [*Disappears.*]

DODGER. [*With a slow smile.*] Now I understand what the girl is up to. Pox is taking a nap and she's got rid of her underguard so she can skip across to this house here. . . . Fine! [*His attention is caught by the sight of a striking pair coming down the street.*] Aha! Mr. Prolix with the girl I commissioned him to bring. . . . My, what a lovely eyeful! The gods are with us— *I* should say! . . . Holds herself and dresses like a real lady—no mere piece of baggage. What a shapely deal it's shaping into—under *me!*

[*Enter* MR. PROLIX *with* MADAM LOVE-A-DUCK *and her maid,* MILPHIDIPPA. LOVE-A-DUCK *is a tall girl in her early twenties, with the body and carriage of a fashion-model, and a deep purring voice.* MIL-PHIDIPPA *is younger, a mere sixteen: small, dark and lively, with a husky voice and the liquid come-hither look of the genuine sex-kitten*]

PROLIX. [*In an expansive gesture.*] And so, Love-a-duck, my dear,

And you too, Milphidippa,
At your house I explained the whole
　thing to you from A to Z;
But if you haven't grasped our game
　completely—
Our little gambit, ha ha ha!—
I'm going to give you one more lesson.
If you do understand it on the other
　hand,
We can talk of something else.
LOVE-A-DUCK. [*Laughs sarcastically.*] Oh,
　of course! patron,
I *would* be a witless boob, wouldn't I,
If I took on work for someone under
　contract
And once inside the workshop
Let all my tricks of the trade fly out the
　window!
PROLIX. [*Apologetically.*] But it's a good
　thing to caution you.
LOVE-A-DUCK. [*Sarcastically.*] Oh, of
　course!
The whole world knows how much it
　means
To caution a merry widow.[19]
In point of fact, my ears had barely be-
　gun
To drink in your dissertation
When I told you myself exactly
How the Major could be cut down to
　size.
PROLIX. [*With dogged diplomacy.*] Still, no
　one on his own knows quite enough;
Though many a time I've seen
People flee from the territory of good
　advice
Long before they'd got there or got
　any.
LOVE-A-DUCK. Ah! But if a woman
Has something shocking and spiteful
　up her sleeve
She remembers it with a memory
Irremovable, unremitting and immor-
　tal.
That same woman faced with some-
　thing honest and deserving
Is oblivious at once:
She simply can't remember.
PROLIX. [*Pointedly.*] That's why I'm
　afraid of *your* forgetting.
You see, you're going to have the
　chance—you two—
Of doing both:
What you do helps me but hurts the
　Major.
LOVE-A-DUCK. [*Winking at* MILPHIDIPPA.]

So long as we're unaware of doing
　good,
You needn't fear.
PROLIX. [*Sighing.*] Oh, what a worthless
　ware is woman!
LOVE-A-DUCK. Don't worry! Her com-
　plement is even worse.
PROLIX. She deserves no better. . . .
　Come along now. [*The move toward his
　house.*]
DODGER [*Adjusting the folds of his tunic,
　smoothing down his hair, and generally
　straightening himself.*] Shall I go and
　meet them? [*They are upon him before
　he considers himself ready to be seen by the
　gorgeous* LOVE-A-DUCK. *He bows.*]
Glad to see you safely back, sir.
And so—oh by god!—so stunningly
Decked out for your stroll. [*Waves a
　hand delicately toward the two girls.*]
PROLIX. [*With obvious pride.*] Hm, hm! A
　good and timely meeting, Dodger.
I present you with the girls you com-
　missioned me to bring:
All suitably bedizened for the business.
DODGER. [*His eyes shining.*] Magnificent!
　You're my man! [*Jauntily toward the
　girls.*] I'm Dodger. How-do-you-do,
　Love-a-duck!
LOVE-A-DUCK. [*Chillingly to* PROLIX.]
　Who is this character who calls me by
　my name?
PROLIX. [*Chuckling.*] Aha! This is our
　master-planner.
LOVE-A-DUCK. [*Unchilling slightly and
　holding out a hand.*] How-do-you-do,
　master-planner!
DODGER. [*Deferentially.*] How-do-you-do,
　ma'am. . . . Please tell me this:
Has he freighted you with full instruc-
　tions?
PROLIX. The two girls I bring are
　primed up to the hilt.
DODGER. Let's see how thoroughly.
I don't want the tiniest slip.
PROLIX. I've added nothing of my own,
Nothing new, to your instructions.
LOVE-A-DUCK. [*Cutting in.*] In short, you
　want your master, the Major,
Made a fool of—don't you?
DODGER. You've said it.
LOVE-A-DUCK. It's all arranged:
With charm, shrewdness, neatness and
　finesse.
DODGER. And I want you to pretend
You're the wife of Mr. Prolix.

LOVE-A-DUCK. His wife I'll be.

DODGER. And pretend you're head-over-heels in love with the Major.

LOVE-A-DUCK. I shall be head-over-heels.

DODGER. And that I and your maid are the go-betweens
Handling this affair for him.

LOVE-A-DUCK. What a fortuneteller you'd have made!
Everything you say is coming true.

DODGER. And that little minx of a maid of yours
Passed on this ring from you to me for him with love.

LOVE-A-DUCK. Completely correct!

PROLIX. [*With resentment.*] What's the earthly use of all this repetition
Of things they know by heart?

LOVE-A-DUCK. [*Laying a hand on his arm.*] No, it's better.
Think, dear sugar-daddy,
How a decent shipwright
Lays the keel down true and straight,
Then the ship comes easy
Once the framework's ready.
So this keel of ours
Is straight and set and steady.
And our master-builder
Has workmen not unskilled, sir;
So if our timber-dealer
Doesn't dilly-dally—
I know that willy-nilly.
Our ship will soon be ready.

DODGER. No doubt you also know the boss, my Major?

LOVE-A-DUCK. [*Throwing up her hands.*] What a question!
How could I escape knowing
Such a public nuisance:
With his pomades and his permanent waves,
And his scent-drenched, wench-bent, lecherous ways?

DODGER. [*Anxiously.*] But he doesn't know *you*, does he?

LOVE-A-DUCK. [*Impatiently.*] How could he know me, never having seen me?

DODGER. [*Rubbing his hands.*] How prettily you talk!
When we've finished with him
He won't be sitting pretty.

LOVE-A-DUCK. [*A little tartly.*] Why don't you leave the man to me.
And stop your worrying?
If *I* don't make a pretty ass of him

You can blame me for everything.

DODGER. Go on, then, go inside:
And get to work with all your wits.

LOVE-A-DUCK. [*With a reassuring smile.*] Leave it to us.

DODGER. Come, Prolix, get the girls inside, sir.
I'll meet the Major in the forum,
Give him this ring and tell him
It comes to me by your wife,
Who's sighing away her life for him.
When he and I get back from the forum
Send Milphidippa to us—the moment we're back—
As though she comes on a secret mission.

PROLIX. [*Ushering the girls to the front door.*] We will.
Don't give it a thought.

DODGER. If you'll look after that,
I'll see to it he comes here—ha ha!—
With his goose already stuffed. [*Goes off in the direction of the forum.*]

PROLIX. [*Calling after him.*] A pleasant walk and pleasant work!
Let me tell you: if I make a real success of this
And my young guest gets the Major's girl today
And carries her away to Athens—
If we pull this off, I say,
I've got something—something special—for you. [*The sound of* DODGER's *jubilant shout in the distance.*]

LOVE-A-DUCK. [*With a nod toward the* MAJOR's *house.*] Is the girl lending a hand?

PROLIX. Oh, in the neatest, prettiest way!

LOVE-A-DUCK. Then the future is secure.
With all our talents for subversion added up,
I feel quite sure
We'll never be outclassed in gamesmanship.

PROLIX. [*Lending an arm to* LOVE-A-DUCK.] Very well, then, let's go in and there review
Our parts, so when the Major comes we'll carry them through
With precision and finesse,
And do
The job without a mess.

LOVE-A-DUCK. [*Taking his arm with a*

laugh.] Yes.
We wait for *you!* [*The three of them go into*
MR. PROLIX's *house.*]

Act 4

MAJOR BULLSHOT-GORGEOUS *and* DODGER
walk slowly down the street on their way
back from the forum. The MAJOR *seems to*
swell as he walks, sniffing with self-satisfac-
tion.

MAJOR. It gives one such a rosy feeling
To have things going so rosily—all ac-
cording to plan.
Today I sent my agent to King
Seleucus
With the recruits I've mustered for
him.
They'll police his kingdom for him
While *I* take a rest.
DODGER. Ha ha ha ha ha!
Stop worrying about King Seleucus.
I've got something much nearer at
home. [*Winks.*]
She's new, she's dazzling. . . .
There's a proposition which I'm au-
thorized to bring.
MAJOR. [*Halting in his tracks.*] Aha! Then
everything takes second place.
I'm with you, speak—
I'm all ears, and all yours.
DODGER. [*Drawing him into the shadows.*]
Shh! Look round and see
There's no one about to overhear us.
I'm under strictest orders—shhh!—
To handle this with secrecy.
MAJOR. [*Majestically surveying the neigh-*
borhood.] There's no one about.
DODGER. [*Feverishly undoing a knot in his*
handkerchief and taking out PROLIX's
ring.] Here . . . the first intallment, sir
. . . of her passion.
MAJOR. [*Reaching out a trembling palm.*]
What is it? Where's it from?
DODGER. [*Holding up the ring.*] From a
dazzling and delectable lady
Who is in love with you and pines
After your excruciatingly handsome—
mm, mm—
Handsomeness.

And now her maid has brought this
ring
From her to me to give you.
MAJOR. [*Snatching the ring.*] And she?
Is she freeborn or a slave set free?
DODGER. [*Shocked.*]. Tut tut, sir!
Do you think I'd have the nerve
To act as go-between
For you and a woman once a slave—
When you can't even take care of
All the freeborn ladies after you?
MAJOR. [*Smugly.*] Married or unmar-
ried?
DODGER. [*Archly.*] Married *and* unmar-
ried.
MAJOR. [*Ponderously.*] One and the same
woman!
Married and unmarried—how?
DODGER. Girl bride—groom a grand-
dad.
MAJOR. Haaa! . . . Great!
DODGER. Oh, she's lovely! Every inch a
lady.
MAJOR. [*Swinging his eyes on him.*] I warn
you— no lies!
DODGER. The only girl in the world to
touch you.
MAJOR. [*With an incredulous whistle.*] Go
on? . . . She *must* be a beauty.
Who is she?
DODGER. The wife of old Prolix here—
Right next door.
She's simply dying for you, sir:
Wants to get away from him—
Can't stand the old geezer any more.
She's sent me to you begging and be-
seeching
You'd let her have the permit and the
privilege
Of being yours.
MAJOR. *Her* wish? By God, *I'm* willing.
[*Slips on the ring.*]
DODGER. [*Whistling.*] And is *she!*
MAJOR. [*Clutches* DODGER *by the shoulder.*]
What are we going to do with the
other one—
The bird inside the house?
DODGER. [*Shrugging.*] Oh, just go and
tell her to buzz off—
Wherever she wants to.
As a matter of fact, her twin sister's
here,
And the mother:
They want to fetch her.
MAJOR. [*Panting with excitement.*] Eh,
d'you mean it?

Her mother's come to Ephesus?

DODGER. [*Casually.*] That's what they say: those who ought to know.

MAJOR. [*Slapping his thighs.*] God, what a chance to get the girl out of the house!
It's perfect.

DODGER. [*Lowering his voice.*] And of course you want to do it—er—*perfectly?*

MAJOR. Of course! Just you tell me how.

DODGER. Well, you'd like to shift her straight away,
Wouldn't you?
But you'd also like her to go—gratefully, yes?

MAJOR. [*Nodding vigorously.*] That's what I'd like.

DODGER. Then this is what you do.
You're pretty rich. . . .
Tell her to keep all the jewels and trinketry you fitted her out with,
Keep them as a present—and go. . . .
Remove herself to wherever she wants to.

MAJOR. [*Slowly.*] An excellent suggestion—y-yes,
But make darn sure
I don't go and lose *her*
And then have the other one change her mind.

DODGER. Pooh! Such scruples!
She adores you. You're the apple of her eye.

MAJOR. [*Puffing himself up.*] Venus—adores me.

DODGER. [*Cocking his head.*] Sh-h, quiet!
It's the door.
Over here, sir. Out of sight. [*He pulls him into deeper shadow as* MILPHIDIPPA *steps into the street out of* MR. PROLIX's *front door.*]
It's her packet-boat coming out: her go-between,[20]
The one who brought me the ring I handed you.

MAJOR. [*Looking her up and down with a subdued wolf-whistle.*] Hm! A pretty little baggage.

DODGER. [*With a wave of his hand.*] Why man, compared to her mistress
She's nothing but a baby baboon—
The chick of a pterodactyl.[21] [*They watch* MILPHIDIPPA *darting her head about.*]
Just look at the way

She chases about with her eyes
And bird-catches with her ears!

MILPHIDIPPA. [*To herself as she spots them.*]
So here's the circus—in front of the house—
Where I do my tricks.
I shall pretend I do not see them
Or even know they've got here.

MAJOR. [*Cocking his head.*] Quiet!
We'll strain our ears and see if she mentions *me.*

MILPHIDIPPA. [*Looking about in every direction except where they are.*] I hope there's no one lurking near
Minding someone else's business,
Not his own . . . and spying:
Somebody who never
Has to sing for supper.
They're the sort I'm most afraid of.
Such could block me, such could balk me
Somehow, somewhere,
As my mistress leaves the house
On her way here
Full of passion for this hero
Who's so dashing, who's so darling. . . .
Oh, the handsome Major!

MAJOR. [*Digging* DODGER *in the ribs.*] So this one's dying for me too?
Lauds my looks. . . . I'll be damned!
Her admiration needs no elbow grease.

DODGER. [*Distractedly.*] I don't follow.

MAJOR. [*Smothering guffaws at his own joke.*] It's already scoured, highly polished.

DODGER. [*Pulling himself together.*] Can you wonder when it's focused all on you:
Such a highly polished subject!

MAJOR. Ah yes! And her mistress herself
Is pretty well groomed—pretty elegant.
I swear to you, Dodger,
I begin to fancy her a bit already.

DODGER. What! Before you've even clapped eyes on her?

MAJOR. [*Thumping him on the back.*] Believing you is good as seeing.
Besides, this little packet-boat
Sets me on a course of loving—
Even *in absentia.*

DODGER. Oh not her, sir!
Not for love and kisses!
She's engaged to *me.*
If the mistress marries you today,
The packet-boat and I get spliced at

once.

MAJOR. [*With a grunt of satisfaction.*]
Then what are you waiting for?
Go up and speak to her.

DODGER. [*Preparing to step forward.*] Just
you follow me, sir.

MAJOR. I'm right behind you.

MILPHIDIPPA [*Sighing.*] Oh, how I wish I
could meet the man
I came out here to see!

DODGER. [*Pushes the* MAJOR *back into the
shadows and, out of sight, addresses* MIL-
PHIDIPPA.] So you shall.
Your wish will be fulfilled.
Be full of confidence and have no fear:
There is a certain man who knows
Where the man you're searching is.

MILPHIDIPPA. [*Pretending to be mystified.*]
Whom do I hear so close?

DODGER. [*Mysteriously.*] A comrade in
your councils
And a partner in your plans.

MILPHIDIPPA. [*Clapping her hand to her
mouth.*] Good heavens, then!
What I'm hiding is not hid.

DODGER. Is not hidden, yet is hid.

MILPHIDIPPA. How can *that* be?

DODGER. Hidden from the falsely
friendly
Safely with your faithful friend.

MILPHIDIPPA. What's the watchword—
If you're one of our Bacchantes?

DODGER. A certain woman is in love
with . . .
A certain man.

MILPHIDIPPA. [*Giggling.*] Silly!
Quite a lot of women are.

DODGER. Are, but don't send presents
from their fingers.

MILPHIDIPPA. Ah! Now I understand
you:
The rough places you make plain. . . .
But is anyone about?

DODGER. [*Shoving the* MAJOR *further into
the shadows and stepping out.*] Yes and
no . . . if you want him. [*Bows.*]

MILPHIDIPPA. [*Fluttering her eyes.*] Oh!
. . . Can I have you to myself?

DODGER. For a short or long—
Intercourse?

MILPHIDIPPA. Just a sentence.

DODGER. [*To the* MAJOR.] I'll be back.

MAJOR. [*Peevishly.*] What about *me?*
Have I got to stand about
So dashing and damn handsome all for
nothing?

DODGER. Stand by, sir, and be patient:
It's your affair I'm working on.

MAJOR. [*Agonized.*] Hurry! I'm on tenterhooks.

DODGER. One must tread carefully—
don't you know?—
Handling merchandise like this.

MAJOR. [*Sinking back into the shadows.*] All
right! All right!
Whatever you think'll get results.

DODGER. [*To* MILPHIDIPPA.] The man's
as stupid as a stone. . . .
I'm with you again—what would you
like?

MILPHIDIPPA. Some advice.
How's this Troy to be attacked?

DODGER. Pretend she's dying for him.

MILPHIDIPPA. I know that.

DODGER. Go into raptures
Over his face and figure—
His fantastic actions.

MILPHIDIPPA. [*Pouting.*] That's all orga-
nized—
I showed you just a while ago.

DODGER. [*Lamely.*] For the rest then,
keep alert:
Take your cue from me.

MAJOR. [*With a hiss from the shadows.*]
Hey, there!
Suppose *I* could have a share
In what's going on? [DODGER *slips back to
him.*]
Good! Back at last!

DODGER. Right here, sir. At your service.

MAJOR. [*Jealously.*] What's the woman
telling you?

DODGER. [*Pulling a long face.*] Her poor
mistress, she says,
Is moaning and groaning—completely
distraught:
Worn out with weeping;
Because she needs you,
Because she doesn't have you,
So she's sent her maid to you.

MAJOR. [*Smugly.*] Tell the girl to come
here.

DODGER. [*Holding up an admonitory
finger.*] Now you know what you're
about, sir?
Be superior.
You don't care for the idea.
Bawl me out for making you so vulgar.

MAJOR. [*With a knowing grin.*] Yes, I've
got it.
I'll keep to that exactly.

DODGER. [*Loud and peremptorily.*] So you
  want me to call
The woman who wants you?
MAJOR. [*Working his face into a picture of
  disdain.*] If she's got anything to ask—
Let her approach.
DODGER. Approach, woman—
If you've got anything to ask.
MILPHIDIPPA. [*Fluttering with awe as she
  steps forward and curtsies.*]
O-oh!—Oh! Prince Charming!
MAJOR. So she knows my surname!
Heaven grant your wishes, woman.
MILPHIDIPPA. [*Almost incoherent with pal-
  pitation.*]
T-the permission t-to—to
Pass a lifetime with you, sir.
MAJOR. [*Looking down his nose.*] You ask
  too much.
MILPHIDIPPA. Oh, it's not for *me*, sir!
For my mistress—she's languishing.
MAJOR. [*Distantly.*] Many another
  woman,
To whom it is not given,
Craves precisely *that*.
MILPHIDIPPA. [*Her eyes swimming with ad-
  miration.*] And no wonder!
No wonder you're so dear, sir:
A man so handsome, such a hero,
Such a priceless specimen
Of bravery and beauty.
Was there ever man
So fit for deity?
DODGER. [*Hand on his heart.*] By Her-
cules! In point of fact,
He's hardly human. [*Between his teeth.*] I
  bet there's more humanity
In a goddam vulture!
MAJOR. [*Apologetically to* DODGER.] She's
  in such raptures
I must extol myself a little. [*Puffs himself
  up and begins to stride about.*]
DODGER. [*To* MILPHIDIPPA, *who can
  hardly contain herself.*]
Just look at how the jackass struts! [*To
  the* MAJOR.] Sir, won't you answer
  her?
She's the woman from the woman I just
  mentioned.
MAJOR. [*Managing to yawn.*] Which one?
I recall so many.
I really can't remember.
MILPHIDIPPA [*Pathetically.*] From her
  who plunders
Her own fingers
Just to robe

Yours with riches. [*Pointing to the ring
  on the* MAJOR's *hand.*]
Yes, that's the ring I brought to
  Dodger.
He passed it on to *you*, sir.
From the lady who so loves you.
MAJOR. Well, what now, girl?
Why don't you tell me?
MILPHIDIPPA. [*Melodramatically, as she
  wrings her hands.*]
Spurn not the heart that craves you:
And has no life except in yours.
To be or not to be hence onwards
Lies in him that she adores.
MAJOR. [*Striking a pose of magnanimous
  sternness.*] Well, what does she want?
MILPHIDIPPA. To address you, to em-
  brace you,
Oh, sir, to caress you.
Yes, yes, yes!
For unless you
Bring her help, her heart is broken.
  [*Snatches his hand.*]
Great Achilles, grant my prayer.
Handsome hero help a lady.
Show your noble nature—
Oh, king-killer! Oh town-taker!
  [DODGER, *on the point of collapsing,
  shakes his head at the* MAJOR *in signal to
  stand firm.*]
MAJOR. [*Pushing her away.*] God, how
  tedious all this is! [*With mock sternness
  at* DODGER.] I've told you often
  enough, you bum,
Not to commit me to the common run.
DODGER. Woman, do you hear?
I've told you before and I tell you now:
Without a fee commensurate
This prize boar
Does not inseminate
Every little sow.
MILPHIDIPPA. [*On her knees.*] He can
  have any sum he asks.
DODGER. Three hundred golden
  sovereigns, then.
He won't take less from anyone.
MILPHIDIPPA. Good gracious! That's
  scandalously cheap.
MAJOR. Greed never was a vice of mine.
I'm rich enough and I've got more—
A whole bushelful of golden
  sovereigns.
DODGER. [*Making absurd gestures behind
  the* MAJOR's *back.*]
Not to mention treasure. . . . Oh, and
  silver!

Not just mounds of it, but mountains.
Why, not even Aetna's higher.
MILPHIDIPPA. [*With huge eyes.*] O-oh,
  how exciting! [*Under her breath.*] What
  a liar!
DODGER. [*In an undertone to* MIL-
  PHIDIPPA.] Good sport, eh?
MILPHIDIPPA. How'm I doing?
Playing up to you all right? [*Returns to
  the* MAJOR.]
For the love of mercy, sir,
Send me back to her.
DODGER. [*Nudging him.*] Why don't you
  give her an answer?
Either you will or you won't.
MILPHIDIPPA. [*Dabbing her eyes.*] Yes,
  why would you torture
A poor desperate soul
Who's never done you any harm?
MAJOR. [*Melting.*] Tell her to come out
  to us herself.
Say I'll do all she asks. [*He begins to strut
  again.*]
MILPHIDIPPA. Oh sir!
Now you're acting as you ought to:
She wants you and you want her.
DODGER. [*To himself.*] No flies on that
  girl, by Jove!
MILPHIDIPPA. And you haven't spurned
  my prayer
But granted what I asked for. [*Aside to
  DODGER.*] Doing all right, eh?
DODGER. [*Exploding.*] Lord! I just can't
  keep from laughing.
MILPHIDIPPA. [*Almost doubled up.*] That's
  why I had to turn my back on you.
MAJOR. [*Striding into their orbit again.*] My
  girl, you haven't an inkling
What an honor I'm paying your mis-
  tress.
MILPHIDIPPA. Oh sir, I do have an ink-
  ling—
And I'll tell her so.
DODGER. He could sell this service to
  another woman
For his weight in gold.
MILPHIDIPPA. [*Struggling to keep a straight
  face.*] Good heavens, yes! I believe
  you.
DODGER. Great warriors—nothing but—
Are born from the women he makes
  pregnant.
His sons live eight hundred years.
MILPHIDIPPA. [*To DODGER under her
  breath.*] Get on with you—you liar!
MAJOR. [*Striking a monumental pose.*] As a

matter of fact,
They live a good straight thousand:
From epoch to epoch.
DODGER. [*Apologetically.*] I kept the
  figures down, sir,
In case she thought I might be lying.
MILPHIDIPPA. [*Hand on mouth to simulate
  wonder—and hide her laughs.*] God
  have mercy!
How may years will he live himself
If his sons live so long?
MAJOR. My girl, I was born on the day
  after
Jove was born to Ops.[22]
DODGER. If he'd only been born the day
  before Jove
It's *he* who'd now be reigning in
  heaven.
MILPHIDIPPA. [*Almost hysterical.*] Enough,
  enough, I entreat you!
Let me leave you alive—
If it's still possible.
DODGER. Why don't you go, then,
Now that you've got your answer?
MILPHIDIPPA. [*Hanging back, entranced.*]
  Y-yes . . . I shall go and bring the lady,
  sir.
On whose behalf I am acting . . .
Is there . . . anything else . . . you wish?
MAJOR. Just not to be more handsome
  than I am:
My looks are such a bore to me.
DODGER. [*To MILPHIDIPPA, sharply.*] Well,
  what are you waiting for?
Aren't you going?
MILPHIDIPPA. [*Tearing her eyes away.*]
  Yes . . . going.
DODGER. [*Behind her as she goes to the
  door.*] And there's this, too—are you
  listening?—
Tell her with consummate art
And give her a galloping heart. [*Lowers
  his voice.*]
Tell Goldilocks, if she's there,
To cross to us over here—
The Major's waiting.
MILPHIDIPPA. [*To DODGER, whispering.*]
  She's here with my mistress: [*Nods to-
  ward PROLIX's house.*]
They've been listening to our talk.
DODGER. [*Whispering back.*] Splendid!
Our little chat'll help them
Steer a cleverer course.
MILPHIDIPPA. [*Loudly.*] You're holding
  me—I'm off.
DODGER. I'm not even touching you,

Let alone . . . I'd better not say!
[MILPHIDIPPA, *with an encouraging
glance at* DODGER *over her shoulder, goes
into* PROLIX's *house.*]
MAJOR [*Shouts after her.*] Tell her to get a
move on and come out.
We'll make this matter a priority.
[*Turns to* DODGER.]
And now, Dodger, what am I going to
do?
We can't let this girl in
Till we get the other out.
DODGER. [*Assuming indifference.*] Why
ask *me*?
I've already told you the way to do it:
The jewelry and the costumes you
equipped her with—
Let her have them. . . .
Let her snaffle the lot.
Tell her it's time she went back home.
Say her twin sister's here with her
mother
And it's a very good thing for her
To go back home with them.
MAJOR. How do you know they're here?
DODGER. Because I saw that sister of
hers
With my very own eyes.
MAJOR. Have they met, those two?
DODGER. They have.
MAJOR. [*Suddenly leering.*] A fine strap-
ping lass, eh what?
DODGER. [*With disgust.*] Oh, *you* want to
corner everything!
MAJOR. [*Still leering.*] And where did the
sister say the *mother* was?
DODGER. [*Coolly.*] Lying on board ship
with sore and swollen eyes.
So the captain says who brought them
here. . . .
This captain's staying with our next
door neighbor.
MAJOR. And *he*? A lovely lusty lad, eh?
DODGER. [*With a curl of the lip.*] Come
off it, sir!
A fine stallion for the mares you are:
Running after everything—male and
female. . . .
Let's get down to business.
MAJOR. [*Beginning to fidget.*] Now about
that advice you were giving me—
I'd like *you* to talk it over with her.
You and she get along so well together.
DODGER. Oh, no no, sir! Surely you, sir,
Must do that little job yourself?
Say you've simply *got* to have a wife:

Relatives are pushing, friends are
pressing.
MAJOR. [*Nervously.*] You really think
that?
DODGER. How could I *not*?
MAJOR. [*Bracing himself.*] Very well, I go
inside.
Meanwhile, you keep watch before the
house
And call me when the other one comes
out.
DODGER. Just look after your own per-
formance, sir.
MAJOR. [*Attempting a swagger.*] I'll look
after it all right.
If she won't go quietly, I'll—I'll
Kick her out.
DODGER. [*With force.*] Oh, don't do that,
sir:
Much better have her leave
Happily and grateful.
Give her those things I told you to.
Let her carry away
All that jewelry and stuff you fixed her
up with.
MAJOR. God, I hope she does!
DODGER. You'll persuade her quite eas-
ily, I think.
But go on in. Don't keep standing here.
MAJOR. [*Dithering.*] I'm yours to com-
mand. [*Walks uncertainly into his
house.*]
DODGER. [*Grinning at the audience.*] Ha!
Ha!
This womanizing Major,
Does he differ in one jot
From the picture that I gave you—
Eh what?
Now for Love-a-duck to join me here
Or her minx of a maid or Halcyon. . . .
[*As the door of* PROLIX's *house opens.*]
Jumping Jupiter! What timing
everywhere!
The very ones I wanted here,
Coming out *en bloc*
Next door. [MADAM LOVE-A-DUCK, MIL-
PHIDIPPA *and* HALCYON, *with the air of
conspirators, step cautiously into the
street.*]
LOVE-A-DUCK. [*Beckoning her accomplices.*]
Come on, look about and be alert:
There may be someone watching us.
MILPHIDIPPA. No one around that I can
see
Except the very one we want.
DODGER. [*Stepping forward.*] As I do you.

MILPHIDIPPA. Hi! Master-planner—
what are you doing?

DODGER. *I* master-planner? Bah!

MILPHIDIPPA. What on earth?

DODGER. Next to you I'm hardly fit
To plug a peg in a wall.

MILPHIDIPPA. [*Coyly.*] Oh go on!

DODGER. Yes, you're the smoothest little
vixen ever. [*Turning to* LOVE-A-DUCK.]
The way she trimmed down the Major—
It was a treat!

MILPHIDIPPA. [*Pleased.*] I'd hardly
started.

DODGER. Never mind! The whole
thing's shaping nicely.
Just go on as you are—you're wonderful.
The Major, if you please,
Has gone to beg his mistress to abandon him
And—ha ha ha!—depart with mother
and sister for Athens.

HALCYON. [*Throwing his cap into the air.*]
Hip hip! . . . Magnificent!

DODGER. What's more,
All the dress and jewelry he heaped on
her—
He's giving her the lot . . . a present—
Just to get rid of her.
I told him to.

HALCYON. [*Beaming.*] Then the thing's a
dead certainty:
She wants to go and he wants to have
her gone.

DODGER. [*Wagging a finger gravely.*] Ah
ah! Don't you know
That when one's almost out of a steep
well,
Right at the top,
That's when the danger's at its height—
Of falling right to the bottom again?
We've got our little operation to the
top,
But one whiff of suspicion from the
Major
And we don't get it out.
Now is the moment for the greatest
guile. [*Surveys them all grandly.*]
I see we have enough material for the
purpose:
Three women, you for a fourth, me
fifth,
And the old gentleman making six.
With all our chicanery lumped together—

The whole six of us—
I'm pretty sure we could undermine
and take by storm
any goddam city on this earth. . . .
So go and put your minds to it.

LOVE-A-DUCK. [*Pointedly.*]
That's why we're here—
Entirely at your disposition—

DODGER. Charming of you.
These, then, are your instructions,
madam.

LOVE-A-DUCK. Thank you, General.
I'll follow them to the letter—
As far as in me lies.

DODGER. I want the Major sunk—
Hook, line and sinker.

LOVE-A-DUCK. An order, sir which is to
me
Sheer self-indulgence.

DODGER. And you know how, don't
you?

LOVE-A-DUCK. [*Clasping her bosom.*] Oh
yes!
I pretend I'm torn in two by my passion.

DODGER. Right.

LOVE-A-DUCK. And because of this passion
I've divorced my husband—[*Tosses her
head in the direction of* PROLIX's *house.*]
Just to marry him.

DODGER. Correct.
But there's one thing more:
Say that this house [*jerking a thumb at*
PROLIX's *house.*]
Is part of your own dowry
and that after you divorced him
The old man left you here. . . .
We can't have the Major
Scared to enter another man's house
later.

LOVE-A-DUCK. [*Nodding.*] A sound precaution.

DODGER. And when he comes out of his
house
I want you to stand a little way off,
Pretending you're no match for his
crushing good looks:
You're overwhelmed by the sheer style
of him,
And of course in ecstasy
Over his figure, his face, his charm, his
beauty. . . .
Got it straight?

LOVE-A-DUCK. [*Laughing.*] Completely.
Will you be satisfied with a perform-

ance so finished
That it's flawless?
DODGER. Absolutely. [*Turns to* HAL-
CYON.]
Your turn for instructions now, sir.
The moment all this is done
and Love-a-duck's gone inside—
You hurry over to us here in a sea captain's togs.
You'll wear a broad-brimmed hat—
navy blue[23]—a woolen eye-patch, and a
navy-blue cloak (that's the seaman's
color you know) fastened at the left
shoulder with a free arm dangling.
You're all tackle-and-trim: hell yes!
You're a skipper. . . . The old man, by
the way, has all the props you need—
some of his slaves are fishermen.
HALCYON. [*Scratching his head.*] Fine! I'm
all togged up. But you don't tell me
what to do.
DODGER. You come here to fetch Goldilocks in her mother's name, saying that
if she's going to Athens she must hurry
with you to the harbor and give instructions for the things she wants on board,
to be carried to the ship. If she's not
coming, you say you're going to cast off
immediately since there's a fair wind.
HALCYON. A pretty pleasing picture.
Proceed.
DODGER. The Major'll promptly urge
her to get a move on and go, so as not
to keep her mother waiting.
HALCYON. Ha! You're a crafty one!
DODGER. [*With a broad grin.*] And I'll tell
her to ask for me as her assistant in carrying her luggage down to the harbor.
. . . Ha ha! To the harbor, naturally,
he'll order me to go with her. . . . And
after that, I don't need to tell you, sir:
I'm off to Athens with you, straight.[24]

HALCYON. [*Grasping his hand.*] And
when you get there,
I shan't let you be a slave three days
Before I set you free.
DODGER [*Spontaneously embraces* HAL-
CYON. *Then, briskly:*]
Off with you now, sir,
And put on your togs.
HALCYON. [*Beginning to go.*] Anything
else?
DODGER. [*Winking.*] Yes. Remember
everything.
HALCYON. [*Blithely.*] I'm off. [*He disap-*

pears into PROLIX's *house.*]
DODGER. [*Turning to the two girls.*] And
you get going inside too.
I'm pretty sure the Major's
On the point of coming out.
LOVE-A-DUCK. [*Dropping him an ironic
curtsy.*] Your commands, my Com-
mandant,
Are posted in our hearts.
DODGER. In which case, away with you,
scram!
Look, the door's opening. Perfect tim-
ing! [*The two girls scuttle away into* PRO-
LIX's *house.*]
DODGER. [*Smiling to himself.*] Out he
comes in fine fettle: he's got his
wish—
Gaping, poor fool, in his paradise. [*The*
MAJOR *strides out and straight up to*
DODGER. *He bursts out exultingly.*]
MAJOR. She's agreed.
Goldilocks has agreed. . . .
My heart's desires—just what I
wanted—
And all nice and friendly.
DODGER. What on earth kept you in
there so long?
MAJOR. [*Smugly.*] I'd no idea till this mo-
ment
How much that woman loved me.
DODGER. You mean it?
MAJOR. [*Wiping his brow.*] Why, I had to
argue and argue—
She's as stubborn as a log—
But finally I got what I wanted.
And I granted her, handed her,
Everything she wished for, everything
she asked for:
I even handed her *you.*
DODGER. [*Leaping to attention.*] Even me?
. . . What! [*Quickly pulls a long face.*]
How can I live without you?
MAJOR. [*Patting him on the back.*] Come,
man, don't be downcast!
I'll see you're freed from her.
I tried every way I could
To make her agree to go without you,
But she kept right on.
DODGER. [*In a small crushed voice.*] Ah
well!
I'll leave it to the gods—and you.
It's a bitter pill . . . losing such a won-
derful master,
But at least I'll have the happiness of
knowing
That *your* beauty and *my* efforts

Landed you the girl next door:
Whom now I bring you.
MAJOR. [*Moved.*] Say no more
I'll give you liberty and riches
If you bring it off.
DODGER. Bring it off! It's done.
MAJOR. [*Holding his side.*] Oh, how I
    ache for her!
DODGER. [*In his best bedside manner.*]
    Gently does it, sir.
Relax; not so eager. . . .
But here she is, coming out. [DODGER
    and the MAJOR *step to the side as* MADAM
    LOVE-A-DUCK *and* MILPHIDIPPA
    emerge.]
MILPHIDIPPA. [*In a whisper, as she catches
    sight of them.*]
There's the Major, ma'am,
All ready for you.
LOVE-A-DUCK. [*Also whispering.*] Where?
MILPHIDIPPA. On the left.
LOVE-A-DUCK. [*Making a grimace.*] I see
    him.
MILPHIDIPPA. Look at him sideways
So he won't know we see him.
LOVE-A-DUCK. Yes, I see him.
Ah! Milphidippa—
Now's the time for two bad girls
To become much worse.
MILPHIDIPPA. [*Giggling.*] You begin.
LOVE-A-DUCK. [*Gathering herself together
    and launching herself melodramatically.*]
    No-o?
You don't mean you actually met him?
    [*Aside to* MILPHIDIPPA.] Don't spare
    your voice: make him hear.
MILPHIDIPPA. [*Cockily.*] Why, I spoke to
    him face to face—
Calmly—took my own time—
Quite at home—just as I felt like.
MAJOR [*Aside to* DODGER.] D'you hear
    what she says?
DODGER. [*Nodding.*] I do.
The girl's in transports because she met
    you.
LOVE-A-DUCK. O you fortunate girl!
MAJOR. [*Aside.*] How they seem to fall
    for me!
DODGER. Naturally!
LOVE-A-DUCK. But it's a miracle, what
    you tell me.
You actually went up to him and
    asked?
Why, they say he has to be approached
By letters and ambassadors—
Just like a king.

MILPHIDIPPA. I dare say.
I had a terrible time getting near him
And winning him over.
DODGER. [*Nudging the* MAJOR.] What
    glory, sir, you have among the ladies!
MAJOR. [*Shrugging.*] I put up with it—
    since Venus wishes.
LOVE-A-DUCK. [*Piously lifting up her
    hands.*]
I offer the Lady Venus thanks
Exceedingly,
And pray and beseech her
Pleadingly:
To let me have
The man I love
The man I yearn for.
Make him kind to me,
Not turn from me:
For whom I burn.
MILPHIDIPPA. I piously hope so,
    madam,
Though lots of women yearn for him
And he scorns them—spurns them
    all—
You're the exception, madam.
LOVE-A-DUCK. [*Wringing her hands.*]
    That's what so worries me: his dis-
    dain.
His eyes may change his mind for him
Once he sees me.
His superior taste will turn him away
From the very sight of me.
MILPHIDIPPA. [*Laying a hand on her arm.*]
    No, it won't. Be more cheerful,
    ma'am.
MAJOR. [*Aside.*] She doesn't think much
    of herself, eh what!
LOVE-A-DUCK. [*Sorrowfully.*] I fear you
    painted me in too glowing colors.
MILPHIDIPPA. Not at all,
I made you out less pretty than you
    are.
LOVE-A-DUCK. [*Almost hysterical.*] But if
    . . . if
He will not marry me . . .
I'll hug him by the knees, I'll—I'll
Beg him to—or else . . .
Or else if I fail to win him,
I'll commit suicide.
I can't live without him. I realize *that.*
MAJOR [*Starting forward.*] I've got to stop
    her committing suicide, surely?
Shall I go to her?
DODGER. [*Holding him back.*] Far from it.
You'll make yourself cheap
Lavishing yourself like that.

Let her come to *you*.
Let *her* do the seeking and pining and
waiting.
You don't want to go and ruin your
reputation, do you?
Then, for god's sake be careful.
It's never been given to mortal man—
I shouldn't think—except to two:
You and Sappho's Phaon,[25]
To be so blessed by love of woman.
LOVE-A-DUCK. [*As if throwing reserve to the
winds.*] I'm going to him if you don't
call him out:
Please—my little Milphidippa!
MILPHIDIPPA. [*Holding her back.*] No no!
Let's wait till somebody comes out.
LOVE-A-DUCK. [*Tossing from left to right.*] I
can't stand it.
I'm going to him.
MILPHIDIPPA. The doors are shut.
LOVE-A-DUCK. I'll break them open.
MILPHIDIPPA. You're out of your senses.
LOVE-A-DUCK. [*Blindly advancing.*] If he
has ever been in love,
If his wisdom match his beauty,
Whatever I may do in passion—
He will forgive me.
DODGER. [*Holding the* MAJOR *in check.*]
Fancy that, sir!
She's gone quite dotty over you, poor
thing.
MAJOR. [*At breaking point.*] It's—it's . . .
mutual.
DODGER. [*Shocked.*] Sh-h! You don't
want her to hear.
MILPHIDIPPA. [*Making a sign of encour-
agement to her mistress.*] Why do you
stand there, in a trance?
Why don't you knock?
LOVE-A-DUCK. Because the desire of my
heart is not within.
MILPHIDIPPA. How do you know?
LOVE-A-DUCK. [*Sniffing wildly.*] Oh, I
know it! Without a doubt,
If he were inside—
My nose would smell him out.
DODGER. [*With a hiss in the* MAJOR's *ear.*]
She's a crystal-sniffer, sir.
MAJOR. [*Sublimely.*] Venus rewards her
for being in love with me
With preternatural powers.
LOVE-A-DUCK. [*Sniffing her way along.*]
Somewhere . . . quite near,
Is the one I desire. . . .
I smell him—yes—I swear.
MAJOR. Strike me,

If she doesn't see better with her nose
than her eyes!
DODGER. Blinded with love, sir.
LOVE-A-DUCK. [*Finally decides to see the*
MAJOR *and is about to swoon.*] A-ah!
Hold me up . . . please.
MILPHIDIPPA. [*Supporting her.*] What is
it?
LOVE-A-DUCK. Keep me . . . from falling.
MILPHIDIPPA. Whatever for?
LOVE-A-DUCK. Because I can't stand.
My spirit swoons . . . at the vision.
MILPHIDIPPA. [*With ponderous alertness.*]
Oh, I get it:
You've spotted the soldier?
LOVE-A-DUCK. [*Tragically.*] Ye-es.
MILPHIDIPPA. [*Playing dumb.*] I don't see
him. Where is he?
LOVE-A-DUCK. [*Clutching her bosom.*]
You would see him, you *would*
If you loved him.
MILPHIDIPPA. [*Pertly.*] I'd love him all
right—
Not a whit less than you—
With your permission, Ma'am.
DODGER. [*Nudging the* MAJOR.] You see,
sir, how the ladies
Fall for you to a woman—
At first sight!
MAJOR. [*Dryly.*] Perhaps I never told
you:
I'm the grandson of Venus.
LOVE-A-DUCK. [*Pushing* MILPHIDIPPA *to-
ward them with trembling hands.*] My lit-
tle Milphidippa, please,
Go up to him and speak.
MAJOR. [*Fervently.*] How she adores me!
DODGER. [*With a sign to the* MAJOR.] The
maid's making for us.
MILPHIDIPPA. [*Curtsying and pretending to
fumble.*] S-sirs, I want you to . . .
MAJOR. [*Ogling her.*] And *we* want you.
MILPHIDIPPA. [*Panting.*] Sir . . . I've
brought my mistress out—
As you told me.
MAJOR. [*Coldly, as he controls himself.*]
So I see.
MILPHIDIPPA. Then do tell her to ap-
proach.
MAJOR. I've persuaded myself . . . [*Long
pause.*]
Not to detest her like the others—
Seeing you've begged me.
MILPHIDIPPA. [*With a gesture toward the
tottering* LOVE-A-DUCK.]
But she won't be able to find words

If she comes near you.
Her eyes have popped out of her head
And lopped off her tongue.
MAJOR. [*Pompously.*] Something's got to
  be done,
It seems to me,
About this woman's malady.
MILPHIDIPPA. [*Doing her eye-flutter.*] The
  moment she spotted you
She was taken with quivering and quak-
  ing.
MAJOR. [*Sublimely.*] Even armed soldiers
  do the same;
Don't be surprised at a mere
  woman. . . .
But what does she want me to do?
MILPHIDIPPA. Go to her house, sir.
She wants to live with you—
Spend her life with you.
MAJOR. [*Alarmed.*] What! *I* go to her
  house—
A married woman's?
Her husband would catch me there.
MILPHIDIPPA. Her husband? She's
  thrown him out—
And because of you.
MAJOR. But how could she do that?
DODGER. [*Quickly.*] Because the house
  belongs to *her*—
Her dowry.
MAJOR. [*Pricking up his ears.*] Is that so?
DODGER. It certainly is.
MAJOR. [*Decisively.*] Tell her to go home.
I'll join her there.
MILPHIDIPPA. [*Her eyes liquid with so-
licitation.*] *Please* don't keep her wait-
  ing.
Her whole soul's on tenterhooks.
MAJOR. [*With ill-suppressed excitement.*] No
  no, I won't.
Off with you.
MILPHIDIPPA. [*Taking the dazed* LOVE-A-
DUCK *by the hand.*]
We're going, sir. [MILPHIDIPPA *leads*
LOVE-A-DUCK *into* PROLIX's *house, her
eyes riveted on the* MAJOR *in a state of
shock.*]
MAJOR. [*His attention caught by someone
coming down the street.*] But what do I
  see?
DODGER. What *do* you see?
MAJOR. [*Pointing.*] Look: all got up like a
  sea-green sailor.
DODGER. And making for our house
  too:
Wants you, that's plain. . . .

Why, it's the skipper.
MAJOR. Coming to fetch the girl, I ex-
  pect.
DODGER. Oh yes, of course! [*They step
back and watch, as* HALCYON, *thinking
he is alone, stands poised to knock on the*
MAJOR's *front door.*]
HALCYON.
If I weren't so well aware
That love has had a share
In every kind of dirty trick—
I'd certainly think again
Before my own campaign
For loving let me sally forth like this.
But since I know it's true
That men have done and do
For love a lot of shabby things
And things which are not nice
From Achilles'[26] sacrifice
Of friends without a twinge
For slaughtering (a binge!)
And . . . [*Breaks off as he sees* DODGER *and
the* MAJOR.]
Oh-oh! There's Dodger,
Standing with the Major.
I've got to change my tune. [*Loudly and
impatiently.*]
Damn it all! I say
The daughter of delay
Is surely woman.
And when she makes you wait,
The time it seems to take
Is twice as long
As any time the same.
I really think their game
Is one of habit.
Here I've come to get
Goldilocks, and yet . . . [*Strides to the
door disgustedly.*]
Oh, I'll bang on the door. [*Does so.*]
Hullo, hullo! Is anyone there?
DODGER. [*Stepping up to him.*] What is it,
  young man?
What do you want? Why are you
  knocking?
HALCYON. [*Brusquely.*] I'm looking for
  Goldilocks.
I come from her mother. If she's going
She's got to go. She's holding us up.
We want to sail.
MAJOR. [*Bustles forward.*] It's all ready.
Eh! . . . Dodger . . . the trinkets and
  clothes,
All her baubles and valuables—
Get someone to help you carry the lot
Down to the ship.

It's all packed—everything I gave her.
Let her remove it.
DODGER. Right, sir. [DODGER *goes out,
winking at* HALCYON *as he passes.*]
HALCYON. [*With a voice like a ship's
megaphone.*] Hell's bells, get a move
on!
MAJOR. He won't keep you. [*Surveys
HALCYON's eye-patch with curiosity.*]
What's it for? What have you done to
your eye?
HALCYON. [*Curtly.*] Dammit—I've got
one good eye!
MAJOR. I mean the left one.
HALCYON. [*Spitting.*] If you want to
know, it's because of the sea.
That's why I don't see so well in that
one. . . .
The sea and love.[27] Oh, it's bitter!
If I'd kept away from the sea and love
I'd be seeing with it as well as the
other. . . . [*Stamps impatiently.*]
They're late. They're holding me back.
MAJOR. Look, here they come. [DODGER
appears in the doorway of the MAJOR's
house, leading and supporting GOLDI-
LOCKS, *who dabs her eyes with a handker-
chief.*]
DODGER. [*Severely.*] For love and kisses,
ma'am,
Aren't you *ever* going to stop crying?
GOLDILOCKS. [*Bursting out again.*] H-how
can I help c-crying?
I've had such a lovely life here. . . .
And n-now I'm leaving.
DODGER. [*Giving her arm a secret squeeze.*]
See? Your man there . . .
He's come from your mother and sis-
ter.
GOLDILOCKS. [*Glowing but managing a
glance of supreme indifference.*] I see
him.
MAJOR. [*Fussily.*] Hey there, Dodger!
DODGER. [*Hurrying over.*] What, sir?
MAJOR. [*With a knowing look.*] Why aren't
you giving orders
For all that stuff I gave her
To be carried out? [DODGER *goes to the
door and shouts to the porters inside.*]
HALCYON. [*Stomping up to* GOLDILOCKS.]
Goldilocks, ma'am, good morning.
GOLDILOCKS. [*Almost collapsing with mirth
at the sight of him, but managing a sob.*]
A-and good morning to you, s-sir.
HALCYON. [*Hardly able to keep from fling-
ing his arms around her.*]

Your mother and sister asked me
To give you their best wishes.
GOLDILOCKS. And they have mine.
HALCYON. They're waiting to sail.
They beg you to come while the wind's
still fair.
Of course they would have come along
with me
If your mother's eyes had been a little
better.
GOLDILOCKS. [*After a pause, fixing her eyes
on the* MAJOR *as if she is about to be torn
in two*]
I'm going. . . . I must force myself. . . .
It would be wrong not to go.
HALCYON. I understand.
MAJOR. She'd still be a little simpleton
If she hadn't lived with me.
GOLDILOCKS. [*Between sobs.*] That's
what's so p-painful. . . .
To be wrenched away from such a
man. [*Turns a tear-stained face to the*
MAJOR.]
You could make anyone—just any-
one—
Brim with culture.
My being with you gave me character.
And now I see I've got to . . . t-to give it
all up . . .
The distinction and the . . . [*Breaks
down completely.*]
MAJOR. Don't cry.
GOLDILOCKS. I can't help it . . . when I
look at you.
MAJOR. Come, my dear, bear up.
GOLDILOCKS. Only *I* know how much it
hurts.
DODGER. [*Pulling a long face.*] I know,
Goldilocks,
I'm not surprised you were so happy
here with him;
I'm not surprised his bravery and
beauty
And all his winning ways
Hold your heart back here.
I'm only a slave
But when I look at him [*Takes out a
handkerchief.*]
I too begin to cry . . . at being torn
away. [*Turns away his face to hide his
laughter.*]
GOLDILOCKS. [*Flinging out her arms.*] One
last embrace, please—
Oh may I?—before I go.
MAJOR. You may.
GOLDILOCKS. [*Throwing herself against*

him.] O light of my eyes! Life of my soul!

DODGER. [*Draws her away and directs her tottering steps to* HALCYON.] For god's sake hold the woman up
Or she'll dash herself to pieces. [*She faints into* HALCYON's *too-eager arms.*]

MAJOR. [*Eyeing them.*] Hey, hey! What's going on?

DODGER. The poor girl!
It's given her a turn, sir:
The thought of leaving you.

MAJOR. Run inside and fetch some water.

DODGER. [*Glancing apprehensively at* HALCYON.] Don't waste your time on water.
All she needs, I'd say, is quiet. [*In alarm as the* MAJOR *goes toward her.*] Oh, no no, sir! Don't interfere:
She's coming to.

MAJOR. [*Eyeing* HALCYON *and* GOLDILOCKS *doubtfully.*]
Their two heads are too darn close:
I don't like it. [HALCYON, *unable to restrain himself, gives her what looks very much like a kiss.*] [*Shouting.*] Hey, sailor, unlip your lips:
You're asking for trouble.

HALCYON. [*Coming to his senses.*] I was only trying to see . . .
If she was breathing.

MAJOR. Then you should have used your ear.

HALCYON. [*Shrugging.*] If you'd rather—
I'll let her go.

MAJOR. [*Dithering.*] No no! Hang on to her.

DODGER. [*As a hint to the lovers.*] I'm a little uneasy.

MAJOR. [*Trying to speed up the departure, to the porters.*]
Hurry out with all that stuff of hers:
The stuff I gave her. [*Porters emerge, carrying trunks and cases.*]

DODGER. [*Attempting to distract the* MAJOR *from the lovers.*]
And now before I go,
Dear household god,
One last goodbye!
And you, my fellow slaves, goodbye!
God bless you men and women.
In your conversations, please,
Speak well of me,
Though I'll be far away. [*Sobs up his sleeve.*]

MAJOR. [*Patting him on the shoulder.*]
Come, come, Dodger, cheer up!

DODGER. [*Breaking into sobs.*] B-b-but I can't help w-w-weeping
Because I'm leaving you.

MAJOR. There, there! Bear up.

DODGER. [*Still sobbing.*] Only *I* know th-the p-pain.

GOLDILOCKS. [*Opening her eyes.*] A-ah! What's this? What's happening?
What do I see? . . . Good morning, Morning!

DODGER. [*To her between his teeth.*] So you've come to?

GOLDILOCKS. [*Horrified.*] Good heavens! Who's this strange man I've embraced? I'm ruined. . . . Oh, am I sane? [*Sinks back into* HALCYON's *arms.*]

HALCYON. [*Whispering into her ear.*] Have no fear, my heart's desire.

MAJOR. [*Hearing something.*] What was that?

DODGER. [*Hurriedly.*] She's lost consciousness again, sir. [*Into the lovers' ears, with a hiss,*] I'm afraid, I'm terrified
The whole thing's going to burst wide open. [GOLDILOCKS *quickly revives.*]

MAJOR. [*Overhearing.*] What did you say?

DODGER. [*Wildly extemporizing.*] Just that all that stuff, sir, [*Jerks a finger at* GOLDILOCKS's *luggage.*]
Carted along behind us through the town,
Won't it tend to make certain people
Turn against you?

MAJOR. [*Snorting.*] I gave away what's mine, not theirs.
I don't care a rap for "certain people" . . .
God speed you now—get going.

DODGER. I only say it for your sake, sir.

MAJOR. [*Waving them on impatiently.*] And I believe you.

DODGER. [*With a wan smile.*] So it's goodbye, sir.

MAJOR. [*Holding out his hand.*] All the best to you, my man.

DODGER. [*Bustling the others off.*] Get a move on, quick!
I'll follow in a minute.
I want a last word with my master. [*The procession of* GOLDILOCKS, HALCYON (*holding her up*) *and porters moves away down the street in the direction of the harbor.* GOLDILOCKS *throws back long wist-*

ful glances.]

DODGER. [*Choking out the words.*] Sir,
you've always thought your other
Servants much more loyal than *I* was;
But now I want to thank you deeply
For everything. And if you wished it
I'd rather be a slave of yours
Than someone else's freedman. [*Gives a
sob.*]

MAJOR. Tut tut, my man! Cheer up!

DODGER. [*Gulping.*] And when I think of
how I've got to
Change my ways to ways of women—
Forget about the ways of soldiers . . .

MAJOR. Come on, be a man!

DODGER. I can't, sir, I've lost all inclina-
tion.

MAJOR. Go, follow them, don't hang
back.

DODGER. [*Making a supreme effort.*] Then
. . . goodbye, sir.

MAJOR. Goodbye, my man.

DODGER. [*Stopping.*] And please remem-
ber, sir,
If ever I can free myself
I'll send you a message. . . .
You won't abandon me?

MAJOR. That's not in me.

DODGER. [*Looking him straight in the face.*]
Ponder sometimes on how loyal to
you
I always was. And if you do, sir,
One day you'll discover who
Your friends and enemies really are.

MAJOR. Oh, I do know.
Many a time I've pondered it.

DODGER. Even so, sir, though you've
known it,
Today you'll know it thoroughly.
Indeed, you'll even go so far as
Say I've proved my worth today.

MAJOR. [*Touched.*] I can hardly keep
from telling you to stay.

DODGER. [*In panic.*] Oh, don't do that,
sir!
People'll say that you're a liar:
Untruthful, break your promises,
That of all your servants here
I'm the only faithful one. . . .
Oh, if I thought it could be done
Decently, I'd press you to it.
But no, it can't be . . . so don't do it.

MAJOR. Well then, off with you.

DODGER. I'll put up with . . . the future.

MAJOR. So, it's goodbye.

DODGER. [*Abruptly turning away to prevent
a collapse.*] I'd better just . . . break
away. [*Shaking with emotion, he dashes
off in the direction of the port.*]

MAJOR. [*Fondly calling after him.*] Once
more, goodbye. [*Reflectively stroking
his chin.*] Before this affair I always
thought him
The very worst of servants. Now I find
him
Quite devoted to me. . . .
When I come to think of it,
I was a fool to let him go. [*Turns toward
PROLIX's front door.*]
Now to announce myself to my heart's
desire.
But wait—there goes the door. [*He steps
back as a SMALL BOY of about twelve
skips out of the front door, shouting to
those inside.*]

BOY. Oh, don't go on so! I know my
job.
I'll discover him, wherever on earth he
is.
Yes, I'll follow him up. . . .
Nothing'll be too much trouble.

MAJOR. [*To himself.*] He's obviously
looking for *me*. I'll approach the lad.
[*Goes up to the BOY and strikes a noble
pose.*]
Ahem!

BOY. [*With exaggerated excitement.*] Oh,
sir, I was looking for you:
Most magnificent, most champion,
Most manly man—
Looked after amongst men
By two deities.

MAJOR. [*Avuncularly.*] Which two?

BOY. Mars and Venus.

MAJOR. Clever boy!

BOY. [*Breathlessly.*] The lady . . . she begs
you to go inside, sir.
She wants you, asks for you, waits for
you:
She's full of yearns, sir.
Do help the lovesick lady. [*A pause.*]
Why do you stand there?
Why don't you go inside, sir?

MAJOR. [*Taking a deep breath.*] I go. [*The
MAJOR pushes through PROLIX's front
door.*]

BOY. [*Grinning from ear to ear.*]
He's in the meshes good and proper:
The trap is set, the old man ready
To jump on him—this ruttish, cocky,
Ribald, coxcomb, strutting rotter:
Who thinks that every lady can

Fall at sight for such a man—When really
They think he's awful—everybody—
Women just as much as men. . . .
But now to leap into the riot:
Inside I hear them . . . far from quiet.
[*The* SMALL BOY *is swept aside when, to the sound of pandemonium, the door opens and* MR. PROLIX *bursts out, brandishing his silver cane and shouting to the slaves, who drag out the struggling* MAJOR. *The cook,* CARIO—*a big fat man with a one-tooth grin—stands over him with a carving-knife.*]
PROLIX. Haul him along
And if he won't come
Pick him up bodily:
Chuck him out high
Anywhere under
The earth and sky:
Rend him asunder.
MAJOR. [*Shorn of sword and cloak, and his underwear.*]
Oh, for the love of heaven, Prolix, please!
PROLIX. [*Mimicking him.*] Oh, for the love of heaven . . . you're wasting your breath! [*To* CARIO *grimly.*] Cario, see your knife's good and sharp.
CARIO. [*Grinning as he tests it on one of his own hairs.*] Lor' bless you sir, it's just champing
To be let loose to lop him—ahem! ahem!—
In the randy region of his lower parts,
And string his trinkets round his neck,
Ahem! ahem! Like a baby's rattle.
[*Pretends to take a swipe at the* MAJOR.]
MAJOR. [*With a shriek.*] It's murder!
PROLIX. Not quite . . . it's premature.
CARIO. [*With a flourish of his knife.*] Shall I let fly now, sir?
PROLIX. [*Casually.*] I think I'd like him clobbered first.
CARIO. We'll let him have it.[28] [*Several people close in on the* MAJOR.]
PROLIX. [*An inch from his face.*] What gave you the nerve to seduce another man's wife?
You dirty swine!
MAJOR. [*Rolling his eyes to heaven.*] For the love of all the gods, sir,
She came to me on her own.
PROLIX. [*Snapping his fingers at a couple of slaves.*] That's a lie. . . . Beat him.
[*They raise their cudgels.*]

MAJOR. Wait. I'll explain.
PROLIX. [*Testily to the slaves.*] What's keeping you?
MAJOR. [*Shaking all over.*] Won't you let me speak?
PROLIX. Speak.
MAJOR. I was implored to go to her.
PROLIX. But how did you dare? Take that. [*Strikes him with his cane, and the slaves join in.*]
MAJOR. Ow! Oi! Ow! Please! I've been clobbered enough.
CARIO. [*Running his thumb down the knife.*] Sir, how soon can I cut?
PROLIX. Whenever you like. [*To the slaves who hold him.*] Spread the brute apart—stretch him out. [*The* MAJOR *is pushed onto his back.* CARIO, *still grinning, stands over him with the carving knife.*]
MAJOR. [*In a white panic.*] No! No! Please! Listen
Before he cuts.
PROLIX. [*Grimly.*] Speak out.
MAJOR. [*Hoarse with fright.*] I didn't want to . . . and I didn't
Do anything. . . . God! I though she was a widow.
That's what that little bawd of a maid let on.
PROLIX. [*After a long pause, during which the* MAJOR *sweats, pants and whimpers.*] Swear.
Swear you won't hurt a living soul
Because of this thrashing you've been given here today,
Or because of any future thrashing—
If we let you go alive from here . . .
You horny little grandson of Venus! [*A burst of laughter from all around.*]
MAJOR. [*Abjectly.*] I swear by Jupiter and Mars
That I won't hurt a living soul
For the slugging that I've suffered here today.
Moreover, if I go away from here intact,
Still with my manly testi . . . monials,[29]
I've been let off lightly for my act.
PROLIX. What if you break your word?
MAJOR. Then let me live without
Those, er, testimonials—forever marred.
CARIO. [*Judicially.*] I move we give him one more clobbering
And let him go.

MAJOR. [*In ringing tones.*] Oh, god bless you always
For coming to my rescue!
CARIO. [*Quickly.*] And *you* give us
A hundred pieces of gold.
MAJOR. What for?
CARIO. In evidence of the signal fact
That today we let loose from here,
Together with—ahem—"testimonials"
intact,
The darling little grandson of Venus . . .
Otherwise—and don't imagine you deceive us—
You shall not leave us.
MAJOR. [*Immediately*] You'll get it.
CARIO. That's more sensible.
But your uniform, your soldier's cloak, your sword—
Give up all hope of these—you won't get them back. [*Sees the look of protest in the* MAJOR's *eyes.*]
Shall I clobber him again, sir.
Or will you now undo him?
MAJOR. [*With a sickly smile.*] Have a heart:
I'm so battered I'm undone already.
PROLIX. [*Stiffly.*] Let him loose. [*The servants untie him.*]
MAJOR. [*Staggering to his feet.*] I'm so grateful to you.
PROLIX. If ever I catch you here again,
You'll lose those testimonials. [*Another guffaw from the servants.*]
MAJOR. [*Humbly.*] I don't contest it.
PROLIX. Cario, let's go in. [MR. PROLIX, *followed by* CARIO *with his knife, and the other servants, make a solemn procession back to the house.*]
MAJOR. [*Sits rubbing his bruises, but suddenly brightens at the sound of voices coming down the street.*] Ah, my own servants!
Look, I see them. [*His slaves, headed by* POX,[30] *gather round him—in his underwear as he still is.*]
MAJOR. [*Urgently.*] Goldilocks—has she gone yet, tell me?
POX. Oh, ages ago!
MAJOR. [*Crushed.*] What a catastrophe!
POX. [*Surveying him with interest.*] You'd say something a good deal stronger
If you knew what I know, sir:
That fellow with the woolen eye-patch
Over his left eye—huh!—
Was no sailor.

MAJOR. [*Clutching him.*] Who was he, then?
POX. [*Smugly.*] Goldilocks's lover.
MAJOR. [*Jumping up and shaking him.*] How do you know?
POX. [*Freeing himself.*] I just know.
Right from the time they were outside the city gates
They never stopped kissing and embracing.
MAJOR. [*Sinking back onto the curbstone.*] What a sorry fool I am!
Now I see it:
Led along the garden path . . .
So Dodger was the lousy rat
Who got me tangled in this trap! [*After a pause, the* MAJOR *pulls himself together, rises with dignity, and faces the audience with a faint smile.*]
If other lechers could so fare,
Fewer lechers would be here.
Their nerves would be on keener edge
And they less keen on carnal knowledge. [*Beckons his company of slaves.*]
Let's go back now to my house.
And, Audience, will you clap for us?

---

1. In Latin, *servus:* the English "slave," which carries too many other connotations.

2. In Latin, *meretrix:* the English "courtesan" or "prostitute"—again far too strong a word, usually.

3. Plautus's word is *meretrix,* "prostitute"; but this here, and often elsewhere, carries far too strong a connotation. There is no outlet in our social code for a word which says *meretrix* and at the same time makes you forget it.

4. The play in the Latin is on *mala,* a good word to play with. It means both "apples" and "something bad." If one wants a Freudian connotation, it also means a pole or a mast. A fourth meaning, but possibly not implied here, is "jaw" or "cheek."

5. In antiquity it was often the heart rather than the head which was considered the seat of the intelligence.

6. "Solemn" is not in the Latin. My excuse is that it does catch at least a reflection of the pun between "chin" and "mind" in Plautus' *mento.*

7. It was said in antiquity of the tragic poet Euripides that his aspect was that of "a face on a column." The more direct reference here is to the Roman epic and dramatic poet, Nævius, who was imprisoned (about 206 B.C.) for lampooning the noble family of the Metelli. The ambiguity of these lines has forced me to paraphrase.

8. Plautus's word *dulice*—"in the manner of a slave"—plays with the word "dulce," "sweetly."

9. Paul Nixon in the Loeb Classics, following Leo, omits these lines as doubtful: "Think something up, hit on a plan—whitehot/what's been

seen's got to be unseen, or what's done'll be undone./This man is onto something big: building a big barricade."

10. Plautus uses the word *lolium*. My dictionary translates this as "darnel, cockle, tares." At any rate, it was reputed to be bad for the eyes.

11. Even given the slowness of voyages, this does make the separation of the lovers happen rather a long time ago. Or has Plautus made a slip? It is not the kind of slip that would bother him.

12. I follow Leo in omitting the following two doubtful (and tautologous) lines: "For a well-planned plan is frequently filched/if the conference place is carelessly and incautiously chosen."

13. A small town in Apulia (southern Italy) whose inhabitants typified the country bumpkin.

14. The entry of the dancing girls was an important part of Roman (and sometimes Greek) banquets. They could be naked and were chosen for other talents besides dancing.

15. The play in Latin is between *liberos*, "children," and *liberum*, a "free person."

16. March 1, held in honor of Mars.

17. I omit, with Leo, two preceding lines: "They will be at my house, look after me, come to see how I'm doing, if there's anything I want./I'll have for children those people who send me presents."

18. Leo notes a hopeless gap in the text here.

19. Plautus's actual word is *meretrix,* prostitute. See note 2.

20. I omit, with Leo, the lines: "Packet-boat?" What d'you mean?"/"It's her little maid coming out."

21. A nice problem in anachronisms: Plautus's *spinturnix* (σπινθαείς)—a small ugly extinct bird—is as unknown to *us* as the pterodactyl was (probably) to the ancients.

22. The wife of Saturn and eventually identified with Rhea, the mother of Jupiter. She was the old Italian goddess of fertility.

23. Plautus says: *ferrugineaus*, "the color of iron rust." Or does he mean a sort of gunmetal-blue, or even dark green? We can't be sure. Lucretius, using the word some 129 years later, distinguishes it from green and red.

24. By now it seems obvious that there really will be a ship waiting, bound for Athens.

25. Phaon was the young sailor—according to legend—with whom the poetess Sappho fell in love in middle age and for whose sake she threw herself off the Leucadian cliff when he went to Sicily.

26. Achilles, at Troy, withdrew his forces from the battle to punish Agamemnon for having taken the girl, Briseis, from him.

27. This is the best I can do with Plautus's play on: *Eloquar/maris . . . abstinuissem/amare.* A translator desperately throws in his own pun where there is no way out for the author's.

28. Leo notes a lacuna here.

29. This is the nearest I can get to Plautus's play with the word *intestabilis:* someone without the power to bear witness in court and someone without the genital gland. Castration was, of course, a punishment inflicted by an injured husband.

30. Some editors, worried by the fact that Pox had said he was going to disappear for a few days, give this part to a slave.

The Brothers

Publius Terentius Afer

There is no starker contrast of style, content, and theatrical approach than that between the works of Plautus and those of Publius Terentius Afer, known as Terence. Terence was born in Carthage (in North Africa) within a very few years of the time of Plautus's death; 185 B.C. is a good guess. He was brought to Rome as a slave in the home of a senator who raised him, educated him, and set him free. Terence had good connections and friends in high places, so that he was able to move in the most cultured and educated Roman circles and to bring his work to the attention of those who could do him the most good. He must not have been much past the age of eighteen or twenty when his first play, *Andria* (The Woman of Andros), was produced in 166 B.C., and four more plays followed (their exact order is uncertain) before *Adelphi* (The Brothers) in 160. Shortly thereafter, Terence set sail for Greece, perhaps in search of more of Menander's plays to adapt, and was never heard of again. The circumstances of his death are unknown.

Thus, in a very short life Terence wrote six plays, all of which have been preserved. Like Plautus, Terence translated the plays of the Greek writers of New Comedy, chiefly Menander. Scholarly disputes raged even in ancient times as to how faithfully Terence followed these Greek models in his "translations" and to what extent he reinterpreted them into Roman plays. Lacking the Greek originals, one cannot know in detail what changes Terence introduced, but clearly he arrived at very different results than did Plautus. The boisterous, farcical quality that distinguished Plautus's plays is replaced in those of Terence by a comedy-of-manners atmosphere. Terence concerns himself with carefully articulated plot structure, with complexly developed characterizations (although still based on Menander's stock comic characters), and with thought-provoking thematic issues. He freely admits in his prologues to combining material from two or more Greek plays, and it is known that he changed character names and topical allusions when he saw fit. Beyond that, since none of the Greek plays from which he worked has survived, one cannot be sure how closely his plays reflect their sources. For centuries, before the discovery in recent decades of some Menandrian work, Terence seemed to provide the best insight into what New Comedy once was. Now, though Terence's immediate models are not available, there is at least some of Menander's work to compare to Terence's. Julius Caesar referred to Terence as a "half Menander," intending high praise but at the same time noting that he lacked Menander's comic genius.

The five plays other than *The Brothers* require little discussion here, since all are similar in style and approach. *The Woman of Andros* is the story of young lovers who are united through the discovery that the girl is the long-lost daughter of a respected neighbor. *Hecyra* (The Mother-in-Law) was rewritten and produced in three versions without ever achieving the success for which Terence hoped; it tells of a young married couple separated and then reunited by the discovery of their true identity. *Heautontimorumenos* (The Self-Tormentor) is yet another study of the generation gap, the relationship between fathers and sons. *Eunouchus* (The Eunuch) is a bit more bawdy than Terence's other plays; in it a young man disguises himself as a eunuch in order to gain access to the girl he loves. *Phormio* is the story of a clever servant and a rascally parasite (Phormio) who try to save two young men from their fathers' wrath, as they have married without permission. The commonality of plot devices and character types running through these plays is apparent, and it can best be discussed in connection with Terence's acknowledged masterpiece, *The Brothers.*

Terence based *The Brothers* on a play by Menander, but the prologue states that one scene has been borrowed from a play by another Greek writer of New Comedy, Diphilus. Clearly Terence sticks closer than did Plautus to the tight plot structure so evident in Menander, using a simple central action in the Aristotelian sense and building every incident around furthering that action. Act 1 is devoted entirely to exposition; Aeschinus has abducted a slave girl, and his father and uncle must devote themselves, in their separate ways, to resolving the problems that this creates. Acts 2, 3, and 4 develop the complications in this action, with Aeschinus's own love affair the chief among them. Some critics suggest that *The Brothers* has both a main plot and a subplot, but it appears rather that Terence has so skillfully combined the love problems of the young brothers as to make Aeschinus's troubles function as a major complicating factor in the resolution of the problem of the abducted slave girl. The solution to all these problems is set up by the end of act 4, but actually occurs in act 5 when Demea learns the truth of the situation, accepts it, vows to reform, and uses this "reformation" to prove his point at his brother's expense. Terence's interpolation of a scene by Diphilus (act 2, scene 1) has been judged to be a matter of portraying on the stage the abduction of the slave girl rather than simply reporting it as Menander is assumed to have done. This interpolation may account for the rather late revelation to the audience that Aeschinus stole the girl for his brother Ctesipho rather than for himself; it appears that, had the audience understood this sooner (as Menander may have planned it), they might through dramatic irony have enjoyed much more Demea's self-satisfied assurances that Micio has been raising his son wrong.

Other structural devices in *The Brothers* are standard ones for Terence and probably for the New Comedy writers who preceded him. Exposition is rather obvious and lacking in subtlety, including a soliloquy by Micio that tells the audience everything that is needed before Demea's entrance actually allows the play's action to begin. No doubt the device of one character not seeing or hearing another on stage with him owes much to the size of the Roman stage and the convenience of hiding between the stage houses; it also establishes a theatrical style that, although not fully realistic, was widely imitated for centuries thereafter. The long delays during which one character fails to recognize another who is calling him are part of the same milieu and were apparently sources of great comic effectiveness for the Roman actors.

The play's ending has provoked special critical attention, for many readers find Demea's apparent conversion to a friendly, convivial fellow in act 5 insufficiently motivated, but actors and directors will see at once the theatrical possibilities inherent in this conversion. The actor playing Demea can make clear to the audience in scene 4 that he is not really changing his character at all, but only his tactics; the intent is to punish Micio by giving him a taste of his own medicine, and in his penultimate speech Demea claims that he has succeeded in doing so and has proved his point about overindulgence of children in the bargain. Here again, it is dramatic irony that makes these concluding scenes theatrically effective, for the audience must understand Demea's motives in order to appreciate the effect of his actions on Micio.

Perhaps the most noteworthy aspect of Terence's dramaturgy is his use of Menander's dramatic structure to explore serious thematic issues. Terence is concerned with the generation gap and with the most effective way to raise children. He clearly does not approve of simple authoritarianism, but he sees that permissiveness is not a final answer either. Micio is a much nicer fellow than Demea, and perhaps Aeschinus is more mature than Ctesipho, but both sons are afraid to tell their respective fathers that they have fallen in love, and both need to be chastened before the play is over. Terence wants his audience to think about these matters, to recognize their complexity and to reject simplistic solutions. Terence obviously thinks that the best position lies somewhere between the extremes of authoritarianism and permissiveness, but he does not presume to prescribe exact answers. This use of the comic theater to explore serious social questions has its roots in earlier drama, but it developed to full flower in the plays of Terence. It is a theatrical technique that has been widely employed ever since.

The other main strength of Terence's work is his characterization. He uses the stock characters of Menander, but he humanizes and individualizes them in a way that has set patterns for all future drama. Gone are the bold, deft caricatures of Plautus; Terence's characters are less comic but more human, the sort of people that anyone may find next door or in his own family. They have the bourgeois concerns that motivate most people, and thus it is easy for audiences to identify with them. A scene such as Micio's chastising of Aeschinus by making him think that another man is going to marry Pamphila in act 4, scene 5, is not only gently comic but also wonderfully revealing of the human traits of father and son. The work of character development begun by Menander comes to full fruition in the plays of Terence, and Occidental comedy ever since has tended to emphasize characterization as its chief source of humor.

Terence makes use of a far more refined and gentle style of language than did Plautus, no doubt the result of his better education and more patrician tastes. His plays are written in poetry, but they are not intended for singing, as were Plautus's. Presumably the beauty of his writing was reflected in an elegance of acting style that pronounced the words with full appreciation of their beauty. Twentieth-century translators have not been successful in finding a satisfying English equivalent for Terence's poetic line; the translation reprinted here offers the best approximation available, but necessarily falls short of capturing all that appealed to Roman audiences. The reader must stretch his imagination even more than usual in an attempt to envision the full effectiveness of Terence's play on stage.

Modern audiences have in general felt a greater affinity for Plautus's plays than for Terence's, and in this they reflect the tastes of Roman audiences as well. In both cases, Terence has been more admired by the literary coterie, but Plautus has been far more popular in the theater. In Renaissance Europe this was not so, however, and Terence's plays were widely studied and performed in schools as well as serving as models of incalculable importance for professional playwrights. Thus, with Plautus in comparative disrepute because of his bawdiness, and with Menander's plays lost, Terence's work was the chief medium by which New Comedy became known to the Renaissance and the chief standard by which excellence in comic playwriting was measured. Although one may prefer Plautus today, especially in performance, one cannot fail to appreciate the high level of art attained by Terence as well as his important influence on later generations.

N.B. Certain stage directions, here enclosed in double square brackets, have been added to Professor Carrier's translation by the present editor. The footnotes were written by the translator.

The Brothers
(Adelphoe)

Translated by Constance
Carrier

Characters

Demea ⎱ *old Athenians, brothers*
Micio ⎰
Hegio, old Athenian, a relative of Sostrata
Sostrata, a widow, mother of Pamphila
Aeschinus, son of Demea, adopted by Micio
Ctesipho, son of Demea, brother of Aeschinus
Sannio, a procurer, a slave-dealer in women
Geta, a slave, servant of Sostrata
Syrus ⎱ *slaves, servants of Micio*
Dromo ⎰
Canthara, old nurse in the household of Sostrata

Mute Characters
Pamphila,¹ a young woman loved by Aeschinus
Bacchis,² a courtesan loved by Ctesipho, a lute-girl
Parmeno, a slave, servant of Micio

SCENE: *Athens, in front of the house of Micio and Sostrata.*

Prologue

Because his work's unjustly criticized
And this same play which we're about to act
Has been attacked by his competitors,
The author has decided he'll be witness
And you the judges in this case against him—

Whether his work deserves acclaim or scorn.
Diphilus'³ comedy, *Those Linked in Death,*
(Synapothnescontes) is used by Plautus
For his *Commorientes,* done in Latin.
In the original Greek, there's a young man
Who in the first act carries off a girl
From a slave-monger. Plautus didn't use this,
But our playwright translates it word for word
Into *The Brothers,* which you'll see today.
Whether this is a theft, you must decide,
Or whether the rescue of a long-lost scene.
As to what his ill-wishers say as well—
That he has had as his collaborators
Men of high standing, that they work with him—
Envy considers such a charge disgraceful,
But he himself looks on it as an honor
That he can please men whom the country praises,
Whom you admire, whose skill in carrying out
The management of war and peace you all
Have used unchallenged in your own affairs.

Do not expect a summary of the plot:
The old men who appear first will begin
To clarify the action, and the rest

226

Moves with the play. Keeping an open
   mind,
You'll give the poet further heart for
   writing.

Act 1

Scene 1

[[MICIO *enters from his house.*]]

MICIO: Storax![4] . . . So Aeschinus has
   not come back
From last night's dinner—he nor his es-
   cort-slaves.
People are right who say if you're away
Or late returning, better have happen
   to you
Whatever your wife calls down, or what
   she is thinking,
Angry as she may be, than what par-
   ents fear.
If you're late, your wife is sure you've
   begun an affair,
Or been caught up in one, or else are
   drinking and gaming—
That tho' she can't do without you, you
   can do without her.
When my son stays out, what horrors I
   can imagine,
What trifles worry me!—that he has
   caught cold,
Or fallen down somewhere and broken
   a bone.
Only a fool would take something into
   his heart
And set it up like an idol dearer than
   self—
This isn't even my own son; it's my
   brother's,
And the brother and I as different as
   night and day.
My life's been a good one: all the joys
   of the city,
No profession, no wife—how many
   envy me that!
He's at the opposite pole: he lives in the
   country,
He worships thrift and simplicity, has a
   wife
And a couple of sons. The elder boy I

adopted
As a child, and look on him now as my
   own—indeed,
He's my pride and joy, the thing that I
   hold most dear.
I hope with all my heart I'm as dear to
   him.
I support him, don't often punish, try
   not to nag,
And as a result, while others are pull-
   ing the wool
Over their fathers' eyes, he's honest
   with me.
That's simply the way that I've
   managed to bring him up,
For a boy who's used to lying to his
   father,
Who dares to deceive him, will trick
   other men the more.
Keep a lad in check by teaching him
   what's honor,
What's character—that works much
   better than fear.
My brother doesn't agree; he keeps on
   coming
To me and crying, "What are you up
   to, Micio?
You're losing the boy for us—why?
   And why let him do
And drink as he likes? Why underwrite
   his expenses,
Why give him carte blanche at the
   tailor's? You're out of your mind!"
He can be harsh beyond belief and jus-
   tice,
And to my mind he's wholly wrong in
   his thinking
That an authority based on force is
   stronger
Or longer-lasting than one that springs
   from friendship.
My reasoning is this: I'm quite per-
   suaded
One who behaves from fear of punish-
   ment
Behaves while he's in danger of detec-
   tion—
Or thinks he is; if not, he'll lapse from
   virtue.
You'll find him willing, if kindness
   binds him to you,
Eager to match you, ready to be
   trusted.
A father aims to train his son to choose
The right himself, and not be threats to
   others.

If he can't, he's not fit to be a father.
But isn't that the man I've been speaking of?
He seems a little gloomy; I can expect
The usual arguments. Welcome back, Demea!
[[*Enter* DEMEA *from the country.*]]

Scene 2

DEMEA. A lucky meeting; I've been looking for you.
MICIO. Why such a long face?
DEMEA. Why, with Aeschinus?
You ask me why?
MICIO. I could have told you so.
What has he done?
DEMEA. Done? Why, he has no shame
And no respect—he's even beyond the law.
I won't even mention his earlier escapades.
And what has he done this time?
MICIO. What is it? Tell me.
DEMEA. Breaking and entering; beating up the owner,
Family, slaves, almost to death; kidnapping
A girl he's in love with. The whole town's in an uproar
Over the story. Every man I meet
Tells it—Oh! it's a crying scandal, Micio.
Why, if he needs examples, can't he use
His brother, living quietly in the country?
Nothing like that for him. And when I shout
At him, I shout at you—it's you who've ruined him.
MICIO. The most unjust are the unsophisticated;
Nothing seems right to them but their own actions.
DEMEA. And the point of that remark?
MICIO.—Is that you're quite wrong.
No young man is breaking the law, believe me,
When he's whoring or drunk—no, I swear he isn't, not even
When he's breaking down doors. If we never did these things
It was only that we were too poor; can you credit yourself
With a virtue you owed to poverty alone?

That's not honest: given the wherewithal
We'd have done it ourselves. And if you had any sense,
You'd turn a blind eye, forgive him because he's young,
And not make him wait till he's bundled your corpse to the grave,
To sow his wild oats at a far less suitable age.
DEMEA. Good god, you can drive a man to insanity!
Because the boy's young, you think this isn't a crime?
MICIO. Just listen, don't think that repeating delivers the punch.
You gave your son for adoption; now he is mine,
Whatever offense he commits, Demea, I tell you
Is done against me; I bear the brunt of the business.
The cost of his elegant banquets, his liquor—I pay it;
My money, so long as I have any, goes for his girl;
Perhaps, when it's gone, he'll find her doors shut in his face.
The locks that he forced will be fixed; the clothes that he tore
A tailor can mend; there's money enough, thank God,
For such things still—I haven't been bankrupt yet.
Either give up or call in someone to judge—I can show him, I think, that most of the fault is yours.
DEMEA. Learn fatherhood from those who are truly fathers!
MICIO. Your fatherhood came via nature, mine by design.
DEMEA. You talk of design?
MICIO. Go on like that and I'm leaving.
DEMEA. That's no way to treat me.
MICIO. I'm sick of hearing you talk.
DEMEA. But he's all I think of—
MICIO. And I. But Demea, look:
What we ought to do is share our worries, you taking
One boy, I the other. If you insist on both,
It's as if you wanted back the son that you gave me.
DEMEA. O no, no—
MICIO. *I* think so.
DEMEA. Well, if that's what you want—

Let him go to hell if he wants; it's not
  my doing.
If I hear one word of this later—
MICIO. More temper, Demea?
DEMEA. Do you doubt my word? Have I
  asked that you return him?
I'm worried. I'm not uninvolved. If I
  argue—O well,
You've left me one son to watch out
  for, and he is, thank heaven,
All I could ask for. The other—well,
  he'll find out
Some day—no, I don't want to be too
  harsh—[*Exit.*]
MICIO. There's truth in what he says,
  but not the whole truth.
I don't say I'm not upset; I'd certainly
  rather
He didn't know how much. The way to
  calm him
Is to resist him, face him down, alarm
  him,
However furious he gets. If I fed the
  flames
Or even seemed to him to share the anger,
I'd be crazy as he is. Still, Aeschinus
Can't be let off; no question that he's
  disgraced me.
He's fallen in love with a dozen prosti-
  tutes
And paid them well, then, tired of
  them all,
Claimed he was all for settling down to
  marriage.
That made me hopeful that his blood
  was cooling;
Fine, I thought, fine!—Till it all began
  again.
I need facts. Let me look for him in the
  forum.

Act 2

Scene 1

[[*Enter* AESCHINUS *with* BACCHIS *and* PAR-
  MENO; SANNIO *follows.*]]
SANNIO. Help, help! I'm innocent, I'm
  being cheated— Help me!

AESCHINUS. [*To the girl.*] Be calm; stand
  right there for a minute.
What are you looking back for? There's
  no danger:
With me here he won't touch you.
SANNIO. I don't care who—
AESCHINUS. He's not going to run the
  risk of another beating.
SANNIO. Aeschinus, you know you knew
  what I am: A dealer in slaves—
AESCHINUS: I know.
SANNIO: —but an honest man.
And your "I didn't mean any harm,"
  your apologies—
I'm not having any of those. I'll take
  you to court
Where you'll pay for your insults, and
  pay with more than words.
I can hear you: "Sorry about that; on
  my oath
You didn't deserve any wrong"—when
  I've just been manhandled.
AESCHINUS. [*To* PARMENO] Go on, hurry
  up, open the doors.
SANNIO. Are you deaf?
AESCHINUS. [*To the girl.*] Get in with you
  now.
SANNIO. I won't let her—
AESCHINUS: Parmeno, stand near him—
You're too far away; get closer. Ah,
  that's what I want.
Now don't take your eyes from my face
  for so much as a second.
The minute I nod to you, give him
  your fist in his face
SANNIO. Let him try it—
AESCHINUS. Watch out—take your
  hands off the girl—[[PARMENO *hits*
  SANNIO *in the face.*]]
SANNIO. Dirty pool!
AESCHINUS. He can double it if you're
  not careful. [[PARMENO *hits* SANNIO
  again.]]
SANNIO. Ow! Ow!
AESCHINUS. That came without signal—
  Parmeno, a very wise error.
Go in, girl. [[PARMENO *and* BACCHIS *exit
  into* MICIO'*s house.*]]
SANNIO. What are you, Aeschinus? the
  dictator here?
AESCHINUS. If I were, you'd be wearing
  the emblems your virtues deserve.
SANNIO. What's our tie-up?
AESCHINUS. There is none.
SANNIO. You know what I am?
AESCHINUS. I don't care to.

SANNIO. Have I laid hands on something of yours?

AESCHINUS. If you have you'll regret it.

SANNIO. Then what gives you the right
to make off with a girl that I bought?
Tell me that.

AESCHINUS: You'll do well to stop shouting in front of this house.
If you don't, you are likely to find yourself dragged off inside
And whipped till you're bloody.

SANNIO: A free man whipped?

AESCHINUS: That's what I said.

SANNIO. You devil!—and this is the city
where free men are equal?

AESCHINUS: Slaver, listen to me, if
you've come to the end of your ranting.

SANNIO. Who's doing the ranting?

AESCHINUS. Forget it and come to the
point.

SANNIO. What point?

AESCHINUS. Do you want me to tell you
your business myself?

SANNIO. Why not? A fair deal, though.

AESCHINUS. Fair deals with a dealer in
slaves?

SANNIO. Okay, I'm a pander, then,
dangerous to the young,
Lying, perverting, all that—but I've
done you no harm.

AESCHINUS. That's still in the future, no
doubt.

SANNIO. Let's start this again.

AESCHINUS. The devil take the money
you bought her with—
I'll pay you for her.

SANNIO. Supposing she's not for sale?
You'd force me?

AESCHINUS. No.

SANNIO. I was afraid you might.

AESCHINUS. She shouldn't be sold, she's
free—I so declare her.
You have your choice: the cash, or a
case to plead.
Till I come back, then, pimp, think it
over. [[*Exits into house.*]]

SANNIO. Good God!
No wonder people go crazy from
things like this.
He breaks in, beats me up, makes off
with the girl,
And leaves me bloody and sore in fifty
places.
In return, he'll buy the girl at the price
I paid.

Well, if he's that generous, let him; he's
got his rights.
I want whatever he'll give—but I talk
like a fool:
If I agree to his offer, some witness will
prove
That I sold her, the cash goes in smoke,
and it's "come back tomorrow."
I could even stand that if he'd pay,
though it makes me see red.
But I can face up to the truth; when
you start in my line,
You've got to expect such insults and
learn to take them.
In this case nobody pays, so the talk's
all useless.

Scene 2

[[*Enter* SYRUS *from* MICIO'*s house, speaking
to* AESCHINUS *within.*]]

SYRUS. Say no more, sir; I'll find him
and make him see light
And admit it's all fair. Why, Sannio,
what's this about?
You've been on the mat with my master?

SANNIO. The phoniest match
That I ever saw, or you either—that's
what we had.
He's as worn out with giving the knock-
out as I am with taking.

SYRUS. *Your* fault.

SANNIO. What should I have done?

SYRUS. Let him have his way.

SANNIO. Who better? I let him smash
my teeth.

SYRUS. What I think is
Sometimes it's wise not to seem too hot
for the cash.
Now you were afraid if you gave up
some of your rights,
If you played along—O you fool!—you
wouldn't be getting everything back
with interest.

SANNIO. I buy sure things.

SYRUS. You'll never get rich, you won't;
you don't know the tricks.

SANNIO. Like you do, of course—I've
never been smart enough
To wait for the bird in the bush when
there's one in the hand.

SYRUS. Come on, I know you. What's a
couple of thousand
To do him a favor? Besides, aren't you
off to Cyprus?

SANNIO. [*Aside.*] O damn—

SYRUS. —and so much to take that you've hired a boat.
Hard to decide? Well, settle when you come back.

SANNIO. I won't budge an inch. [*Aside.*] It's this that started it all.

SYRUS. [*Aside.*] He's scared, with that bee in his bonnet.

SANNIO. [*Aside.*] The devil! Now look,
He hits where it hurts. The women and all that I bought
Have got to be sent off to Cyprus, and no time to lose—
If I get to the market too late, they won't leave me my shirt.
If I let this thing go and begin it again when I'm back—
No good; it'll be stone-cold. They'll say, "*Now* you come?
Why did you wait? Where were you?" I might as well
Give up my case as stay here or go to court late.

SYRUS. Well, have you figured out what's coming your way?

SANNIO. Does a gentleman act like this? Did Aeschinus plot
A surprise attack from the first, to get the girl?

SYRUS. [*Aside.*] He's on the skids.
[*Aloud.*] Just this: see if it's okay.
Rather than take the chance of losing it all,
Save yourself such a blow; be happy with half.
Somewhere or other he can scrape that much up.

SANNIO. Am I running the risk, God help me, of losing, then?
Hasn't he any shame? He's shaken my teeth loose,
My head is sore all over from his punching,
And he's going to cheat me as well? I stay here.

SYRUS. As you choose.
Anything else before I leave?

SANNIO. Wait, Syrus—
No matter how I've been treated, rather than sue,
Let me get back what she cost me first, anyway.
Up till now I know we've never been friends.
But you're going to find that I don't

forget a favor.

SYRUS. I'll make it my business—but here's the brother, excited
About his girl.

SANNIO. And what we were speaking of—?

SYRUS. Shortly.

Scene 3

[[*Enter* CTESIPHO, *speaking to himself.*]]

CTESIPHO. A good turn done by anyone is welcome
In a tight spot, but best when the right man does it.
How can I praise a brother like you? I'm certain
There are no words to do you adequate justice.
In this one thing I'm the luckiest man in the world—
Who else has a brother with every possible virtue?

SYRUS. Hello, sir.

CTESIPHO. O, where's Aeschinus?

SYRUS. At home, and waiting.

CTESIPHO. Wonderful!

SYRUS. Sir?

CTESIPHO. Through him I'm still alive.
He puts my interests above his own,
Takes the blame for my foul-mouthed troublemaking—
Who could do more? Who's coming out?

SYRUS. Your brother.

Scene 4

[[*Enter* AESCHINUS.]]

AESCHINUS. Where is that god-forsaken—

SYRUS. It's me he's after.
Is he holding anything? I can't make out.

AESCHINUS. Ctesipho! I've been looking for you. How goes it?
Everything's settled; let's have no more of that gloom.

CTESIPHO. No more of it, not with you for my true blood-brother.
Aeschinus, if I praised you as you deserve
And to your face, you'd think it was flattery.

AESCHINUS. Come, don't be foolish; by

now we know each other—
I'm only sorry we found out almost too late
For anybody, no matter how willing, to help.
CTESIPHO. I was ashamed.
AESCHINUS. Not ashamed, only simple-minded—
To banish yourself for a trifle like that? Absurd!
God forbid—
CTESIPHO. I was wrong.
AESCHINUS. What does Sannio say?
SYRUS. He's calmed down.
AESCHINUS. I'm off to the market to pay him. Go find your girl, brother.
SANNIO. [Aside.] Urge him!
SYRUS. [[To AESCHINUS.]] Come on; any minute he's leaving for Cyprus.
SANNIO. There's not all that rush; I can stay and I will—
SYRUS. O, he'll pay you.
SANNIO. In full?
SYRUS. Yes, in full; keep quiet now, follow him.
SANNIO. Right. [[Exit AESCHINUS and SANNIO.]]
CTESIPHO. Hi, Syrus!
SYRUS. What?
CTESIPHO. Pay off that creature, for heaven's sake—let him
Lose his temper again and my father hear of it, I'm ruined.
SYRUS. O no sir; cheer up and enjoy yourself with the lady.
Have them set the table and get things ready for dinner.
When I've finished my errand I'll come home with the food.
CTESIPHO. That's fine. Things have gone so well we must celebrate.
[[CTESIPHO exits into MICIO's house, while SYRUS hurries after AESCHINUS.]]

Act 3

Scene 1

[[Enter SOSTRATA and CANTHARA.]]
SOSTRATA. Nurse, tell me, how are things going?

CANTHARA. Now, now, don't worry;
Everything's fine. Your pains, poor child, are beginning. [To SOSTRATA.] I swear you're as nervous as though you'd never seen
A birth before this, or borne a child yourself.
SOSTRATA. O dear, we're alone, I've no one, not even Geta,
To send for the midwife, or to go for Aeschinus—
CANTHARA. Don't worry; he'll be here. Never a day goes by
But he comes.
SOSTRATA. He's my only comfort in all my troubles.
CANTHARA. All things considered, ma'am, things could be much worse.
She's been seduced, but think what the young man's like:
Good heart, fine character, well-known family—
SOSTRATA. You're perfectly right; I pray the gods let us keep him.

Scene 2

[[Enter GETA excitedly, talking to himself.]]
GETA. The way things are, no matter what anyone does,
However they try to help, there isn't a thing
Will save my mistress or her daughter or me.
It's as though a wall was around us we can't break through—
Violence, poverty, loneliness, disgrace.
What a world full of wrongs and wrongdoers, and he most of all!
SOSTRATA. [Aside.] Great heavens, why is he rushing so fearfully?
GETA. Nothing of honor, of promise, of pity, has held him back
Or changed his course, though her time is near, poor lady
That he's treated so badly.
SOSTRATA. [Aside.] I can't make out a word
He's saying.
CANTHARA. Let's go a bit closer, ma'am.
GETA. I'm burning with anger, almost out of my mind—
There's nothing I'd like better than to have
That crew where I could pour out my fury on them

While it's still fresh. I'd kill the old man
   first,
That devil's father. Syrus, who led him
   on—
God be my witness, how I'd mangle
   him!—
Catch him around the waist, lift him
   up, then drop him
Head down to split his skull and let his
   brains
And blood spatter the pavement. And
   the young man—
I'd tear his eyes out, throw him over a
   cliff.
Why put off telling this horror to my
   mistress?
SOSTRATA. Call him back! Geta!
GETA. Whoever you are, don't stop me.
SOSTRATA. I'm Sostrata.
GETA. Where are you? It's you I've been
   seeking,
Waiting for. Lucky we met each other.
   But ma'am—
SOSTRATA. What is it? Why are you
   shaking?
GETA. O—
SOSTRATA. Why such a hurry?
Catch your breath.
GETA. We are wholly
SOSTRATA. Wholly—
GETA. Done for.
It's over.
SOSTRATA. Speak out, explain.
GETA. Now—
SOSTRATA. Now what, Geta?
GETA. Aeschinus—
SOSTRATA. What about him?
GETA. He's broken all ties.
SOSTRATA. God help us! You're sure?
GETA. He's fallen in love with some
   woman.
SOSTRATA. O no!
GETA. Doesn't hide it; has kidnapped
   her now from the slaver,
Bold as brass.
SOSTRATA. You know this?
GETA. Sostrata, I saw it myself.
SOSTRATA. O misery—who's to be
   trusted? what can I believe?
Our Aeschinus, dearer than life, our
   hope and our future,
Who swore that he couldn't face life,
   not a day more, without her!
That he'd put the child in his father's
   arms, and in that way
Beg him, persuade him, to let him

marry our girl!
GETA. Don't cry, ma'am. Better plan
   what to do: should we
Just take it, or tell someone?
SOSTRATA. Why, man, are you mad?
You think this ought to be told any-
   where?
GETA. No, I don't.
First off, what he's done shows how lit-
   tle he cares for us.
If we make it public, he'll only deny it
   all;
There'll be a blot on your name and
   your daughter's future.
And even if he confessed, you would
   hardly let her
Marry a man who's announced that he
   loves another.
We had better say nothing.
SOSTRATA. Not for all the world.
I shan't!
GETA. What then?
SOSTRATA. I'll tell.
GETA. Ma'am, think what you're doing.
SOSTRATA. What can be worse than
   things the way they are?
She has no dowry; even the next best
   thing
Is lost—she can't be given as a virgin.
Then what? If he denies it, I'll show
   this ring.
He lost it; I shall make it my witness
   now.
Since in all conscience I haven't been
   involved
In this affair, have given no bribes,
   done nothing wrong,
Nothing to shame her or myself—I'll
   go to court.
GETA. What's left to say? Your argu-
   ment's convinced me.
SOSTRATA. Run then, and tell the facts
   to Hegio,
My husband's kin and friend. He loved
   us all.
GETA. Did he, indeed? Well, no one
   loves us now.
SOSTRATA. See that the midwife is on
   call, Canthara;
Then when she's needed, there'll be no
   delay. [[*Exeunt. Enter* DEMEA *talking to
   himself.*]]

Scene 3

DEMEA. Confound it—now I hear that

Ctesipho
Is as involved in this as Aeschinus.
My luck's gone if so promising a lad
Can be led into evil by his brother.
Where shall I find him? In some filthy
 bar,
No doubt—Aeschinus will have shown
 the way, I'm sure.
O, here comes Syrus: he will give me
 news—
Yet he's one of that crew. If he finds
 out
I'm looking for him, he won't talk, the
 bastard.
I shan't say what I want. [[*Enter* SYRUS
 talking to himself.]]
SYRUS. I've just described
The whole thing to the old man, just as
 it happened.
Nobody ever was more pleased.
DEMEA. [*Aside.*] God, what a fool!
SYRUS. He praised his son, said I'd ad-
 vised him wisely—
DEMEA. [*Aside.*] I could explode!
SYRUS.—And counted out the money.
He even gave me extra for expenses.
(I've made good use of that already.)
DEMEA. [*Aside.*] Ah, see?
Give him an order and the thing's done
 right.
SYRUS. O sir, I hadn't seen you. What's
 the trouble?
DEMEA. Trouble? I marvel at your go-
 ings-on.
SYRUS. They're pretty silly, yes; to put it
 frankly,
Downright ridiculous. [[*Calling to a ser-
 vant within.*]] Dromo, clean these
 fish—
Not the big eel, though; he can enjoy
 the water
A bit till I come back; then he'll be
 boned.
Not now.
DEMEA. Disgraceful!
SYRUS. I don't like it either,
And I make it known. [[*Again calling
 within.*]] Stephanio, be careful
To soak these salt fish well.
DEMEA. Great God in heaven,
Is he doing this with a purpose? Does
 he want praise
For driving the boy to ruin? Trouble,
 trouble!
I see that a day will come when he
 hasn't a penny

And runs away to enlist.
SYRUS. Demea, that's wisdom,
If I may say so, sir—not only to see
What's under your nose but what's in
 the future, too.
DEMEA. Look here, is that lute-playing
 girl at your place still?
SYRUS. That she is.
DEMEA. Will he keep her there?
SYRUS. I suppose so:
He's crazy enough.
DEMEA. Incredible!
SYRUS. It's his father—
Wrongheaded, easy-going, indulgent—
DEMEA. I tell you,
I'm sick of my brother.
SYRUS. O sir, the difference
Between you (and I don't say this just
 to your face)!
Every inch of you is solid wisdom;
He's a fool. You wouldn't have let your
 son
Act so.
DEMEA. Let him? I'd have been on his
 trail
Six months before he'd even so much
 as got involved!
SYRUS. No need to tell *me* of your clear-
 sightedness.
DEMEA. If he'll stay as he is—
SYRUS. You each find your son as you
 want him.
DEMEA. Have you seen mine today?
SYRUS. Your son, sir? (I'll drive the old
 man
To the country.) I think he's been
 working out at the farm.
DEMEA. You're sure about this?
SYRUS. I went with him, sir.
DEMEA. Very well.
I was worried that he might stay here.
SYRUS. And O what a temper!
DEMEA. Over what?
SYRUS. He swore at his brother right
 there in the market
About the lute-girl.
DEMEA. You mean it?
SYRUS. He gave him the works.
The money was being counted when
 who should arrive
But our hero. "Aeschinus!" he shouted.
 "To think
That you would commit such a crime,
 that you would degrade
Our family so!"
DEMEA. O Syrus, I weep for joy!

SYRUS. "It isn't money you're wasting;
  it's your life."
DEMEA. Bless him, he's worthy of all his
  forbears.
SYRUS. Yes.
DEMEA. He's learned their precepts
  well.
SYRUS. I'm not surprised:
He had his teacher right at home.
DEMEA. I work
At it, I never miss a chance, I train him
To look into men's lives as if into
A mirror, and to take example from
  them.
"Do this," I say—
SYRUS. How wise!
DEMEA. "Not that."
SYRUS. How clever!
DEMEA. "Well done," for this—
SYRUS. Great!
DEMEA. "Shame on you!" for that.
SYRUS. A perfect system.
DEMEA. Furthermore—
SYRUS. I'm sorry,
Sir, but I've no more time. I found
  some fish,
Fresh-caught, and I must have them
  see that they're cooked just right.
It's quite as wrong for servants as for
  you, sir,
Not to do what you've just said, and I
  try
To train the other slaves by the same
  rule:
"This is too salty—overdone—not
  clean.
That's just right. Mind you do it so next
  time."
I give the best advice I'm able to:
Tell them to look into each dish as if
Into a mirror, and show them what to
  do.
People may think these acts of ours are
  silly,
But never mind. Give each man what
  he wants.
What's your wish, sir?
DEMEA. A better brain for you.
SYRUS. You're leaving for the country?
DEMEA. Yes.
SYRUS. No good
To stay in town where no one hears
  your teaching. [[*Exit into the house.*]]
DEMEA. The country—yes, I'm leaving;
  that's where he is,
The boy who's both my own and my

concern.
Let Micio, if he will, see to the other.
But who's that in the distance? Is it
  Hegio,
My old compatriot? Can I trust my
  eyes?
It is! My friend from boyhood—why,
  God bless him,
The state has few to equal him these
  days
In good old-fashioned faithfulness and
  courage.
This land will never suffer harm from
  him.
I'm glad to see him, as I'm always glad
To find there's some trace left of that
  old breed.
I'll stop to greet him and to talk a bit.

Scene 4

[[*Enter* HEGIO *and* GETA.]]
HEGIO. By Jove, a nasty business this is,
  Geta;
You're sure it's true?
GETA. Quite true, sir.
HEGIO. Such an act
To come from such a family! Aes-
  chinus,
I swear you're not your father's son!
DEMEA. He's heard, then,
About the girl, and though we're not
  his kin,
He's far more shocked than Micio ever
  was.
If only he'd been here and overheard!
HEGIO. Unless they mend their ways,
  they'll suffer for it.
GETA. Hegio, you're our one and only
  hope:
You must be her defender now, her
  father.
The old man, when he died, made you
  our guardian.
If you leave us, we're lost.
HEGIO. Don't even suggest it:
Of course I will not break my faith with
  him.
DEMEA. I'll speak to him. Hegio, I hope
  you're well.
HEGIO. O, I've been looking for you.
  How do you do?
DEMEA. Looking for me?
HEGIO. Yes, Aeschinus, your son,
Whom you allowed your brother to
  adopt,

Has proved himself a ruffian and a cad.

DEMEA. In what way?

HEGIO. Simulus, our long-time friend—
You knew him?

DEMEA. Yes, of course.

HEGIO. Your son has raped
His daughter.

DEMEA. Heaven forbid!

HEGIO. There's worse to come.

DEMEA. What can you say that could be
worse than that?

HEGIO. Plenty. We might have found
excuses for him—
Darkness, and passion, a young man's
hot blood:
That's human nature. When he knew,
he came
To the girl's mother, freely, wept with
shame,
Begged for their pardon, swore he'd
marry her.
He was forgiven, everything hushed
up,
His word believed. The girl's long over-
due,
And he, this worthy gentleman, has
taken
A lute-player to share his house—the
other,
May the gods punish him, he has deserted.

DEMEA. All this is true past doubt?

HEGIO. The girl's own mother
Is here, the girl (she's proof enough),
and Geta,
A good slave as slaves go; hardworking,
too.
He, no one else, has been their sole
support.
Seize him and chain him up, to get the
truth.

GETA. Torture me if it isn't true, De-
mea.
He won't deny it; question him while
I'm here.

DEMEA. I'm overwhelmed; what can I
do or say?

PAMPHILA. [*From within.*] O, I can't bear
the pain! Juno Lucina,
Who helps in childbirth, help me now,
I pray!

HEGIO. She is in labor?

GETA. Yes, indeed, sir.

HEGIO. Listen:
She begs that you redeem your family's
honor

And do of your free will what law requires.
I pray to heaven you'll do things
properly.
If you do not, I swear I'll stop at nothing
To guard her name and that of her
dead father.
We were kin, he and I, and friends
from childhood;
We shared our lives in war and peace;
we weathered
The bitterness of lean years, side by
side.
I'll work for this cause, struggle, go to
court—
I'd give up life sooner than give them
up.
What do you say, then?

DEMEA. I will see my brother.

HEGIO. Be sure that you consider this,
Demea:
The better you live, and he—the
greater you are
In power and rank and influence and
wealth—
So much the more, then, should you
recognize
Justice, if you would be considered just.

DEMEA. You need not wait. What must
be done will be.

HEGIO. That's like you. Geta, take me to
Sostrata.

DEMEA. This happens as I said it would.
If only
It were all over! Too much freedom
leads
Sooner or later to catastrophe.
I'll go find Micia and pour out the
story. [[*Exit* DEMEA *and* GETA.]]

Scene 5

HEGIO. Courage, Sostrata; do whatever
you can
To comfort her. I'll look for Micio
In town and tell him what's been going
on—
If he is ready to do his duty, let him;
If he has different views, why, let him
tell me
So that I'll know at once how to pro-
ceed. [[*Exit.*]]

Act 4

Scene 1

[[*Enter* CTESIPHO *and* SYRUS.]]
CTESIPHO. My father's gone from town?
SYRUS. Long since.
CTESIPHO. Please tell me—
SYRUS. He's at the farm and hard at
    work, no doubt—
CTESIPHO. I hope he is, I wish he were,
    not ill
But so worn out he'd spend three days
    in bed.
SYRUS. I'd like that too, or anything
    that's better.
CTESIPHO. I want this day to end the
    way it started.
The trouble with the farm is, it's
    nearby;
He couldn't get back, otherwise, by
    nightfall.
Seeing I'm not there, he'll return, I
    know it,
Asking me where I've been—"You're
    gone all day!"—
What shall I say?
SYRUS. No notion?
CTESIPHO. None.
SYRUS. You're hopeless.
Look, you've got friends, dependents,
    sometime-guests?
CTESIPHO. Yes, but—
SYRUS. Say you were with them.
CTESIPHO. When I wasn't?
I can't.
SYRUS. You can.
CTESIPHO. For daytime. Suppose I
    spend the night?
SYRUS. Too bad: no nightly business—
    deals with friends.
O well, relax; I know his way of think-
    ing;
I'll turn that raging bull into a lamb.
CTESIPHO. How?
SYRUS. He loves to hear you praised; I'll
    call you god
And list your virtues.
CTESIPHO. Mine?
SYRUS. He'll weep for joy.
Look there!
CTESIPHO. What is it?
SYRUS. The wolf in the fairy-tale.
CTESIPHO. My father?

SYRUS. Yes.
CTESIPHO. What—
SYRUS. Go inside. I'll manage
CTESIPHO. You haven't seen me, hear?
SYRUS. Go in—keep still!

Scene 2

[[*Enter* DEMEA.]]
DEMEA. No luck at all, and no sign of
    my brother.
Looking for him, I found one of my
    farm boys
Who says my son's not at the farm.
    What next?
CTESIPHO. [*To* SYRUS.] Psst!
SYRUS. What?
CTESIPHO. He's after me?
SYRUS. Yes.
CTESIPHO. Lord!
SYRUS. Chin up.
DEMEA. What's this bad luck? I can't
    make out,
Unless my birthright is to face misfor-
    tune.
I'm first to sense our woes, first to
    define them,
First to warn others—and what's done
    I'm blamed for.
SYRUS. [*Aside.*] Him first? A joke. He'll
    be the last to find out.
DEMEA. I'm back to see if Micio's re-
    turned.
CTESIPHO. Syrus, for heaven's sake
    don't let him in!
SYRUS. I'll work it. Quiet.
CTESIPHO. I've lost faith in you.
I'll lock the girl up with me in some
    room—
That's safe.
SYRUS. I'll get him out.
DEMEA. There's that wretch Syrus.
SYRUS. [[*Pretending not to see* DEMEA.]]
    Who can stand living here unless
    things change?
How many masters have I got? and
    troubles?
DEMEA. What's that he's mumbling? Is
    my brother at home,
My good man?
SYRUS. "Good"? As good as dead.
DEMEA. What's up now?
SYRUS. Only that Ctesipho's given me a
    beating,
And the lute-girl too.
DEMEA. What?

SYRUS. See? He cut my lip.

DEMEA. But why?

SYRUS. He says I made him buy her.

DEMEA. *You* said
You'd gone to the country with him.

SYRUS. He came back crazy,
Stark mad, no shame at beating an old man
Who'd carried him around when he was a baby.

DEMEA. Ctesipho, good for you; you're your father's son.

SYRUS. Good for him? He should keep his fists to himself—

DEMEA. A fine job—

SYRUS. Beating a girl and a slave like me
Who can't hit back: that's a fine job, you think?

DEMEA. None better. Like me, he sees you've caused it all.
Is my brother there?

SYRUS. No.

DEMEA. I wish I knew where he is.

SYRUS. I know, but I'm not telling.

DEMEA. What's that?

SYRUS. That's it.

DEMEA. I'll break your head—

SYRUS. I know the place where he is
But not the name of the man.

DEMEA. Well, tell me the place.

SYRUS. You know the colonnade by the butcher's?

DEMEA. Yes.

SYRUS. Go past that up the street until you find
The hill in front of you; go down that; then
There's a chapel on this side, and next to it an alley.

DEMEA. Which side of the street?

SYRUS. The one with the big wild fig tree.

DEMEA. I know.

SYRUS. Go down there.

DEMEA. That's dead-end.

SYRUS. You're right;
I sound like a fool. Let's start this over again.
There's a quicker way, and one where you won't get lost.
You know where the millionaire Cratinus lives?

DEMEA. Yes.

SYRUS. Go past, turn left, then straight; at Diana's chapel

Go right, near the pool, to a workshop next to the gate,
Across from a mill. He's there.

DEMEA. But what is he doing?

SYRUS. He's ordered some seats with oak legs, for the garden.

DEMEA. [[*Sarcastically.*]] For your drinking-parties? I must hurry to him. [*Exit.*]

SYRUS. It's a workout for you, you gravestone[5]—be on your way.
That Aeschinus is late, and dinner is spoiling,
And Ctesipho's in love, I'll look out for myself—
Go in and pick the tidbits for my plate,
And spend the rest of the day in quiet drinking. [[*Exit.*]]

Scene 3

[[*Enter* MICIO *and* HEGIO.]]

MICIO. But Hegio, I don't deserve this praise;
I must make amends for what was our offense,
Unless you count me a man who feels insulted
When people protest a wrong that he has done,
And so insults them. Don't thank me that I do not.

HEGIO. No, no! I wouldn't want you changed at all.
But when I see the girl's mother, come along,
And tell her the things that you've already told me:
That what she suspects is really Ctesipho's doing.

MICIO. If that's the course we should follow, let's go.

HEGIO. Very well.
We can ease her mind—poor thing, she's wasted away
With worry—and settle your conscience. If you choose,
I'll tell her what you've said.

MICIO. No, no.

HEGIO. All right, then.
A run of bad luck makes us all more likely
To look for insult where there's none intended,
To feel we're being mocked because we're poor.

Apologize in person; that's most calming.

MICIO. Those are true words.

HEGIO. Come inside.

MICIO. That I shall. [[*Exeunt.*]]

Scene 4

[[*Enter* AESCHINUS.]]

AESCHINUS. It's agony to have such
problems thrust
Upon me without warning—What shall
I do,
How shall I deal with them? I'm shak-
ing, shaking,
With fear; my mind won't function; I'm
too chilled
To work up even the outline of a plan.
What can I say? It seems they all sus-
pect me,
And rightly, from the evidence. Sos-
trata
Thinks, the old woman says, I bought
the lute-girl.
(When she went for the midwife, I
rushed up
To ask if Pamphila was near her time,
If the midwife was on call. "Go away,"
she cried.
"You're free with words, but we've no
faith in you now."
"Explain!" I begged, but she only said,
"Goodbye—
And now that you've got the girl you
want, why, keep her!")
What they felt was clear, and yet I held
myself back:
She'd spread the story if I named my
brother.
What then? Say the girl is his? It all
must be
Kept secret. I'll do my part—it may not
get out.
If it did, no one would believe it; too
strong a case.
I kidnapped her and I paid; she's at my
house.
O, I admit it all! If I'd only told my
father
What I had done, he might have let me
marry.
Well, I'm only wasting my time. Come
on, wake up;
Straighten things out with the women.
There's the door—
O Lord, I break out in cold sweat when

I knock!
Hello—it's Aeschinus. Please open the
door—
Wait: Who's coming! I'll hide.

Scene 5

[[MICIO *enters from* SOSTRATA's *house.*]]

MICIO. Sostrata, you both
Must do as I say; I'll tell Aeschinus
what's settled.
Who knocked at the door?

AESCHINUS. [*Aside.*] My father. O Lord!

MICIO. Aeschinus!

AESCHINUS. [*Aside.*] What is all this?

MICIO. You were knocking? [*Aside.*] No
answer.
I'll rib him a little, I think, as he deserves—
A sort of reward for not confiding in
me. [*To* AESCHINUS.] Come, tell me,
son.

AESCHINUS. Not at that door, as far as I
know.

MICIO. So, I wondered what brought
you here. [*Aside.*] He's blushing.
This will work out.

AESCHINUS. But father, I want to know
What business you have in these parts.

MICIO. None, really.
A friend has brought me up from town
just now
To act as witness.

AESCHINUS. Witness?

MICIO. Well, I'll tell you:
Two ladies live here, neither one well
off—
Nobody you would know, I'm sure of
that:
They've come here recently.

AESCHINUS. Yes sir, go on.

MICIO. A girl and her mother—

AESCHINUS. Oh?

MICIO. The father's dead;
My friend is next of kin, and so, by law,
Must marry the girl.

AESCHINUS. My God, no!

MICIO. What's the matter?

AESCHINUS. It's all right; never mind.

MICIO. He's come to take her
Back to Miletus.

AESCHINUS. He's going to carry her off?

MICIO. Yes.

AESCHINUS. To Miletus?

MICIO. Why not?

AESCHINUS. [*Aside.*] This is awful.

What does she say, or her mother?
MICIO. Not a word,
Though the mother tells some story
    that her daughter
Had a child by someone else; she won't
    say who.
But she thinks, because of him, my
    friend shouldn't wed her.
AESCHINUS. And you—good heavens,
    you surely think she's right?
MICIO. I don't.
AESCHINUS. But why? And will he take
    her away?
MICIO. Is there any reason why not?
AESCHINUS. I can only feel
You have acted with neither pity nor
    kindness, father—
Not—though I may sound harsh—like
    a gentleman.
MICIO. In what way, tell me?
AESCHINUS. You ask? How will he feel,
The man who fell in love with her first
    and may
Be still in love with her, for all we
    know,
To stand there, helpless, while she's
    snatched away
And carried off? Why father, it's crimi-
    nal!
MICIO. Explain to me who promised,
    who gave her in marriage,
Who married her? When? And who
    was her guardian?
And why did her fiancé wed somebody
    else?
AESCHINUS. Should a girl—a woman—
    sit at home and wait
Till some distant relative shall end her
    waiting?
Why didn't you bring that up, and ar-
    gue it too?
MICIO. You're silly to think I'd argue
    against the cause
Of a man I was witness for. But all
    these things—
They've nothing to do with us. Come,
    what's the matter?
You're weeping?
AESCHINUS. Father, listen—
MICIO. My son, I've listened;
I know; for I love you; your woes are
    mine.
AESCHINUS. Just as I want to deserve
    that love forever,
So I'm ashamed to have committed this
    act—

Deadly ashamed.
MICIO. I know your sense of honor,
But in this business you've been woe-
    fully careless.
What land, indeed, do you think you're
    living in?
Seducing her, you've broken one of its
    laws:
Your first sin, great, but still a natural
    one
That good men have committed. But
    afterwards
Did you consider your sin, or choose a
    course
And a way to carry it out? How could I
    learn
What shame kept silent till ten months
    had passed?
You've wronged yourself as well as her
    and the child;
Or were the gods to right things while
    you slept?
To waft her to a bridal-chamber here
By magic? Must you be so feckless al-
    ways?
Cheer up. You'll wed her.
AESCHINUS. I?
MICIO. I said "Cheer up."
AESCHINUS. It's not a joke?
MICIO. Why should I joke?
AESCHINUS. Who knows?
I want this so much—I don't dare be-
    lieve it.
MICIO. Go back and pray that you may
    bring her home.
AESCHINUS. Bring home my wife?
MICIO. Now.
AESCHINUS. Now?
MICIO. Quick as you can.
AESCHINUS. Damn it, if I don't love you
    more than life—
MICIO. More than her?
AESCHINUS. Equally.
MICO. Thanks.
AESCHINUS. O—your friend:
Where's he?
MICIO. Gone, vanished, sailed. Get on
    your way!
AESCHINUS. *You* go: the gods hear you;
    you are far better
Than I; your prayers are likelier to suc-
    ceed.
MICIO. I'll go inside and start the prepa-
    ration;
If you are wise, you'll do as I have said.
    [[*Exit.*]]

AESCHINUS. So this is being a father, be-
    ing a son?
Who could do more? No friend, not
    even a brother.
Who wouldn't love him, hold him in his
    heart?
That generosity leaves me afraid
I may, without intending to, displease
    him.
I must watch out. But now I'll go inside
For fear I find that I've delayed my
    wedding. [[*Exit.*]]

Scene 6

[[*Enter* DEMEA.]]
DEMEA. I ache from walking. Damn that
    slave's directions!
I've trudged the town—all over, to the
    gate,
The lake—and no shop, and nobody
    able
To say he'd seen my brother. What I'll
    do
Is sit down here and wait for his re-
    turn.

Scene 7

[[*Enter* MICIO.]]
MICIO. I'll go and tell them that we
    won't delay.
DEMEA. Why, there he is! I've looked
    for you for hours.
MICIO. You have?
DEMEA. To bring you word of other
    crimes
Of your young paragon.
MICIO. Indeed?
DEMEA. Yes, crimes.
MICIO. Absurd.
DEMEA. O, you've misjudged him.
MICIO. I have not.
DEMEA. You think I'm speaking of the
    lute-girl. Well,
It's an Athenian, free-born—
MICIO. I know.
DEMEA. You know it and forgive him?
MICIO. Why not?
DEMEA. Tell me:
Doesn't it drive you crazy?
MICIO. No; I'd rather—
DEMEA. The child's been born.
MICIO. Fine!
DEMEA. She is penniless—
MICIO. I've heard.

DEMEA.—But must be married, even so
MICIO. Of course.
DEMEA. What, then?
MICIO. Whatever suggests itself.
She'll have to be brought over here.
DEMEA. Good Lord,
You think so?
MICIO. There's no more that I can do.
DEMEA. No more? Look: if you're really
    not upset,
At least be man enough to seem that
    way.
MICIO. I've given him the girl; the wed-
    ding's set;
I've calmed their fears. This was my
    major aim.
DEMEA. Do you approve of him, really?
MICO. No. If I could,
I'd change things; since I can't, I'll bear
    them.
Life is a dice-game: if you make a
    throw
That's bad, why, you make up for it
    with skill.
DEMEA. Make up for it? Your skill has
    lost the cash
You paid for the lute-girl—she must be
    sold
For what she'll bring, or at worst given
    away.
MICIO. She isn't to be sold. I'm set
    against it.
DEMEA. Then what—
MICIO. She stays in my house.
DEMEA. Lord preserve us,
Wife and kept woman under the same
    roof?
MICIO. Why not?
DEMEA. The bride learns music too?
MICIO. Of course!
DEMEA. You'll do a rope-dance with
    them both?
MICIO. I shall.
DEMEA. You will?
MICIO. And you shall be the fourth we'll
    need.
DEMEA. Have you no shame?
MICIO. O, that's enough, Demea;
Calm down, calm down; be cheerful,
    show some joy
As men should at the wedding of a son.
I'm going to see them; then I'll come
    back here. [[*Exit.*]]
DEMEA. To lead a life like that—im-
    moral! mad!
Bride with no dowry, lute-girl settled

in;
Household he can't afford; son spoiled
    past saving;
Father a fool. Salus, great Rome's pro-
    tector,
Could never rescue them, though she's
    a goddess.

Act 5

Scene 1

[[*Enter* SYRUS, *drunk.*]]
SYRUS. Syrus, my boy, hooray: you've
    lined your nest
And managed this whole business very
    neatly.
Let's go. I'm stuffed with all those
    goodies.
A walk should do the trick.
DEMEA. Well, look at that!
The way this house is run!
SYRUS. Ho, see who's here!
Our old man. What goes on? Why sad?
DEMEA. You devil—
SYRUS. Shut up! Don't shoot your
    mouth off here, wise guy.
DEMEA. If *I* had hired you—
SYRUS. Think how rich you'd be:
Your fortune would be made.
DEMEA. —You'd serve as warning
To my whole house.
SYRUS. Why? What have I done now?
DEMEA. Done? In this evil-doing, this
    commotion—
Which isn't settled yet—wretch, you get
    drunk
As if it were.
SYRUS. [*Aside.*] I should have stayed in-
    side.

Scene 2

[[*Enter* DROMO.]]
DROMO. Syrus! Hey! Ctesipho wants
    you back!
SYRUS. Go 'way!
DEMEA. Did he speak of my son?
SYRUS. No, No.
DEMEA. You devil,

Is Ctesipho in there?
SYRUS. No.
DEMEA. But that fellow
Mentioned his name.
SYRUS. Not him; some hanger-on.
You know this guy?
DEMEA. I shall.
SYRUS. Don't move!
DEMEA. Let go—
SYRUS. I tell you, don't move.
DEMEA. Take your hands off me—
Or shall I knock your brains out here
    and now? [[*Exit into house.*]]
SYRUS. He's gone. A great addition to a
    party,
Especially Ctesipho's. Now what do I
    do?
Maybe, till things calm down, I'd better
    find
Somewhere to sleep until I sober up.
    [[SYRUS *exists. Enter* DEMEA *from*
    MICIO's *house and* MICIO *from* SOS-
    TRATA's *house.*]]

Scene 3

DEMEA. Lord, what now? Shall I shout
    out my complaints?
Great heaven and earth! Great god of
    all the seas!
MICIO. Oho, he's found out; that is why
    he's yelling—
The case is ready; I must offer help.
DEMEA. Look at him, the corrupter of
    our sons!
MICIO. Master your anger, sir; control
    yourself.
DEMEA. All right. I've got control. No
    further outbursts.
Let's think this over. Didn't we agree
(And you proposed it) we'd not inter-
    fere
In bringing up our sons?
MICIO. I don't deny it.
DEMEA. Why is he drunk, at your
    house? Why do you
Keep him—my boy!—And buy a mis-
    tress for him?
Can't you be fair with me as I with you?
I don't bring up your son; don't bring
    up mine.
MICIO. That's not fair.
DEMEA. Why?
MICIO. Do you forget the proverb,
"The truest friends share everything
    between them"?

DEMEA. You're quite a wit, but it's too
late for speeches.

MICIO. Now listen, if that isn't too de-
manding.
First, if what's bothering you is the
money
The boys spend, think of it this way,
Demea:
You thought you could afford to raise
the two
(Your income seemed enough then for
them both)
And in those days, you were quite cer-
tain, too
That I would marry. Well, try that
again:
Save, scrimp, invest, make every cent
you can
To leave to them. That way you'll earn
your glory.
Let them enjoy the windfall of my
wealth.
You won't lose anything; don't be
alarmed.
My contribution will be profit for you.
Just take your time and think the busi-
ness over—
You'll find you've spared us all a lot of
grief.

DEMEA. Who cares about the money?
It's their morals.

MICIO. Wait. I will come to that. We all
have traits
By which our character can be assessed.
Let two do the same thing, and you
may say,
"One will be harmed, the other go scot-
free."
The deed's the same; only the doers
differ.
The more I see, the more I trust our
boys
To turn out well, for they have com-
mon sense,
Good minds, respect, and fondness for
each other.
Give them free rein—they can be
checked at will.
Are you afraid they may be lax in busi-
ness?
In other matters age can make us
wiser—
The single vice it brings out in all men
Is to grow keener than they should for
gain.
The passing years will sharpen our

lads.

DEMEA. If
Your generalities don't ruin them,
And that permissiveness.

MICIO. Be still; it won't.
Let's have no more such talk; stay here
today;
Stop frowning.

DEMEA. If I must, no doubt I must.
All right, but he and I will leave at
dawn
Tomorrow for the country.

MICIO. Or tonight—
Just for today, be pleasant.

DEMEA. And I'm taking
The lute-girl with me.

MICIO. You'll have won your fight
And won your son besides, no question
there—
Only be sure you keep her.

DEMEA. I'll see to it;
Out there, she'll cook and grind the
meal until
She's full of dust and smoke and ashes.
Likewise
I'll send her out to gather grain at
noon,
I'll get her sunburned till she's coal-
black.

MICIO. Fine!
I'd call that wise. And more: I'd force
the boy
Whether he wants or not, to sleep with
her.

DEMEA. You mock me. Well, I'm glad
that you can take it
So easily. I feel—

MICIO. You've said.

DEMEA. I'm through, then.

MICIO. Come in; let's spend the day the
way we should. [[*Exeunt. There is a
time lapse before* DEMEA *reenters.*]]

Scene 4

DEMEA. Whoever ordered life so well
that time,
Experience, circumstance, did not
change it
And teach him something? You come
out not knowing
The things you thought you knew;
what seemed essential
Loses importance when you test it out.
It's been that way with me, too; I'd re-

ject
The life that I've been living all these
 years,
Now that it's nearly over. Why? I've
 learned
The hard way that there's nothing
 really better
For any man than easy-going kindness.
Compare my brother and me, if you
 need proof.
He's lived in leisure; loved society;
Been calm and kind; hurt no one;
 smiled at all;
Lived for himself, and spared no lux-
 ury—
Everyone loves him and speaks well of
 him.
But I—a farmer, rough and mean, hot-
 headed—
I married—that was misery. We had
 sons:
More worries. So it goes! and in my
 struggles
To save for them, I've ground away
 life.
Now that I'm old, the payment for such
 toil?
Hate—while he lifts no finger and is
 loved.
They worship him, shun me, confide in
 him,
Value him, spend time with him, leave
 me lonely.
They wait my death, but pray he'll live
 forever.
Those whom I worked to raise he's
 made his own,
And at no cost; he reaps what I have
 sown.
Well then, it's about-face, and see if I
Can deal in softer words and acts, so
 challenged.
I want my kin to prize and cherish me.
Does that mean gifts and compliments?
 I'll show them!
What's bankruptcy to me, the elder
 brother?

Scene 5

[[*Enter* SYRUS.]]
SYRUS. O sir, your brother begs you not
 to leave.
DEMEA. What's that? My good man, how
 are things? How goes it?
SYRUS. Fine, sir. Great! [*Aside.*] There!

three unaccustomed phrases
Worked in: *my good man, how are things,
 how goes it?*
DEMEA. Though you're a slave, there's
 nothing mean about you;
I'd like to do you a good turn.
SYRUS. Why, thanks.
DEMEA. And Syrus—
I really mean this, as you'll soon find
 out.

Scene 6

[[*Exit* SYRUS; *enter* GETA.]]
GETA. I thought I'd go see whom
 they're sending for
The bride, ma'am—O hello, sir. Here's
 Demea.
DEMEA. Uh—you are—?
GETA. Geta.
DEMEA. Geta, I've decided
This very day that you're a man to
 prize;
The worthiest of slaves, I'd say, is one
Whose master's interests are his own,
 like you.
And so, if there's an opportunity,
I'll do you a good turn. [*Aside.*] I'm
 learning tact
And very quickly.
GETA. Sir, you're kind indeed
To speak so.
DEMEA. [*Aside.*] One by one I win them
 over.

Scene 7

[[*Enter* AESCHINUS *and* SYRUS.]]
AESCHINUS. I'm bored to death with all
 the fuss they're making
Over a wedding: They've spent all day
 preparing.
DEMEA. Something's wrong, Aeschinus?
AESCHINUS. Is that you, father?
DEMEA. Your father, yes, in blood as
 well as spirit,
Who loves you more than life. But why
 not bring
Your bride home?
AESCHINUS. O, I want to—the musicians
Are late, and those who sing the wed-
 ding-hymn.
DEMEA. Take an old man's advice—
AESCHINUS. Yes, sir?
DEMEA.—Forget them,
Guests, torches, music, hymn singing—

forget them,
And have the garden wall pulled down
  at once.
Then bring her in; make one house out
  of two,
And all her household part of ours.
AESCHINUS. That's genius,
And you're the best of fathers.
DEMEA. Great! I'm "best"—
Micio's house will be an open road
  jammed
With people—and the cost! But I don't
  care:
I am the favorite. I'm "best." Tell
  Croesus
To open up his wallet now for you.
Syrus, get going.
SYRUS. Where, sir?
DEMEA. Break the wall.
Aeschinus, lead them here.
GETA. God bless you, sir;
I see you have the family's best interests
At heart. [[*Exit with* SYRUS.]]
DEMEA. They're worthy of all favors.
Don't you agree?
AESCHINUS. O yes!
DEMEA. Don't have her carried
Up streets and down, a woman fresh
  from childbirth.
AESCHINUS. There couldn't be a better
way than yours, sir.
DEMEA. Leave it to me. But here comes
  Micio.

Scene 8

[[*Enter* MICIO]]
MICIO. My brother's orders? Where is
he? [[*Seeing him.*]] Come, tell me:
You ordered this?
DEMEA. I did, for in every way
I'd make our households one—in
  mutual love,
Support and unity.
AESCHINUS. I beg you, father—
MICIO. I'm not averse.
DEMEA. By heaven, it's our duty.
First off, there's the bride's mother.
MICIO. Yes, What then?
DEMEA. A woman of good repute.
MICIO. I've heard.
DEMEA. Not young.
MICIO. I know.
DEMEA. She's past the age of bearing
  children:
She's all alone—no one for her to turn

to—
MICIO. What's this about?
DEMEA. You've got to marry her,
And [*To* AESCHINUS.] it's your business
  to be sure he does.
MICIO. Marry? I?
DEMEA. You.
MICIO. I? Absurd.
DEMEA. [*To* AESCHINUS.] He'd do it,
If you were a man.
AESCHINUS. Father!
MICIO. You heed him? Idiot!
AESCHINUS. No use: you must.
MICIO. You're mad.
AESCHINUS. Let me beg you—
MICIO. Get out of here, maniac!
AESCHINUS. As a favor, father?
MICIO. Are you out of your mind? I
  marry, at sixty-five,
A doddering old woman? This you
  want?
AESCHINUS. O please—I've promised—
MICIO. Promised? You'd better limit
Your generosity to what belongs to you.
DEMEA. He might ask something
  greater.
MICIO. There isn't any.
DEMEA. Give in.
AESCHINUS. You can't refuse.
DEMEA. Your word?
MICIO. Stop pestering!
AESCHINUS. Not till you yield.
MICIO. You threaten—?
DEMEA. Be generous.
MICIO. It all seems ill-advised, un-
  natural, mad—
Still, if you're so determined—well, I'll
  do it.
AESCHINUS. Splendid!
DEMEA. You're worth my love, but—
MICIO. What?
DEMEA. I'll tell you,
Now that I've won.
MICIO. Go on.
DEMEA. Their nearest kin,
Our relative as well, is Hegio.
He isn't rich; we should do something
  for him.
MICIO. What now?
DEMEA. That bit of land you rent out-
  side of town—
Let's give it to him!
MICIO. *Bit* of land?
DEMEA. Big, small—
We must. He's been a father to her;
  also
He is our relative, a good man. Oh, it's

right
To give it. It's your preaching that I
practise;
I heard you say it not long since: "Our
failing
Is, in old age, to think too much of
money."
Let us try not to; it is sound advice.
AESCHINUS. Please—
MICIO. Very well; you ask it, he shall
have it.
AESCHINUS. Three cheers!
DEMEA. We're brothers in spirit as in
blood. [*Aside.*] I've turned his sword
against him!

Scene 9

[[*Enter* SYRUS.]]
SYRUS. Orders done, sir.
DEMEA. Good man! Today I've come to
the conclusion
That Syrus must be freed.
MICIO. You'll free him?
Why?
DEMEA. Many reasons.
SYRUS. You're a kind man, sir.
I've done my best to bring the two boys
up—
Taught them, and scolded them, and
given the best advice
I could.
DEMEA. That's clear: we trust you to buy
food,
Bring home a whore, make dinner on
short notice—
Not everyone can do the like.
SYRUS. Oh bless you!
DEMEA. Today, take note, he helped to
buy the lute-girl—
His work. Reward him: watch your
slaves improve.
Aeschinus wants you to.
MICIO. You do?
AESCHINUS. Oh yes, sir.
MICIO. Well then, of course. Syrus,
come here. Be free!
SYRUS. Oh thank you, thank you all, but
mostly you.
DEMEA. Delighted.
AESCHINUS. I too—
SYRUS. Yes. To top things off, though.
If my wife Phrygia could be free as
well—
DEMEA. She's a good woman.

SYRUS. And your grandson, sir—
She's his first nurse.
DEMEA. Why then, I give my word,
If she's the first, of course, she must go
free.
MICIO. For that?
DEMEA. For that. I'll pay for her. That
ends it.
SYRUS. May heaven grant you every-
thing you pray for!
MICIO. Syrus, a good day's work.
DEMEA. And likewise, Micio,
If you will do your part and let him
have
A little cash to start on, he'll soon pay
you.
MICIO. Less than a little.
DEMEA. He's honest.
SYRUS. I'll return it—
Just give it.
AESCHINUS. Please do!
MICIO. When I've thought it over.
DEMEA. He will.
SYRUS. What a good man!
AESCHINUS. The best of fathers!
MICIO. What is this? Why have you
changed your ways so sharply?
Is this a whim, this sudden lavishness?
DEMEA. Listen. It is to show that what
they judge
To be your inborn lovable good nature
Comes, not from character or love of
justice,
But from permissiveness, extravagance,
Indulgence. If you scorn my way of life
Since I don't always grant my sons' de-
sires,
Aeschinus, then there's no more I can
say.
Pour money forth; buy, do, all that you
covet.
But if you'd have some voice—when
you are lost
For lack of vision, when your appetite
Is stronger than your wisdom—if a
voice
Can hold you back, correct you, or
agree
If it is right, hear mine.
AESCHINUS. We both bow, father;
You know what's best. But what about
my brother?
DEMEA. I'll let him have his way—but he
must know
It's the last time.
MICIO. Well done.
CANTOR. Applaud, applaud!

1. Pamphila is assigned two lines, offstage cries in childbirth (act 3, scene 4).

2. Bacchis is the name of the lute-girl, referred to in the play only as *puella citharistria*, or a *psaltria*.

3. A poet of the Greek New Comedy, contemporary with Menander.

4. Micio calls back inside to a house servant.

5. Literally *silicernium*, "dry bones" or "funeral feast," that is, fit only to die. The term derives from *silex*, stone, applied to an old man's stooping posture: "he looks at the stones," *silices cernit.*

The Trojan Women

Lucius Annaeus Seneca

Unquestionably, the glory of the Roman theater was its comedy. Some tragedy was performed, and several names of Roman writers of staged tragedy are known, but none of their works has survived except in a few fragments. Apparently most Roman writers of tragedy followed the pattern established by their comic counterparts and copied Greek models. The works of Aeschylus, Sophocles, and Euripides were mined for subject matter, structure, and style (as were those of other Greek playwrights now forgotten), but Euripides was especially popular. His more rhetorical style, together with his tendency toward sensationalism and melodrama, had special appeal for the Romans and is no doubt part of the reason that more Euripidean plays were preserved for the modern age than Aeschylean and Sophoclean plays combined.

One Roman writer of tragedy is of special importance in the development of the European theater even though he didn't write for the stage. This writer is Seneca. Seneca's "plays" are the only Roman tragedies that have been preserved for modern study, but they were not intended by Seneca for stage production. It is possible that he presented them to contemporaries in something akin to public readings, but primarily they were apparently intended as literary pieces. Renaissance enthusiasts, however, thought of Seneca's plays as stage pieces and modeled a great many Renaissance plays after Seneca's supposed practice; in fact, Seneca's plays were occasionally staged in Renaissance theaters and have even been produced (usually as curiosities) in modern times, but Seneca evidently never intended them for such a purpose, and it should therefore come as no surprise that they do not stand up well to analysis as theatrical works.

Lucius Annaeus Seneca (Seneca the Younger, to distinguish him from his father, who attained some fame as a rhetorician and historian) was born in approximately 4 B.C. in Córdoba, Spain, then a part of the Roman Empire. He moved to Rome at an early age, was educated there, and achieved considerable importance as a philosopher and essayist; his works in these areas will not be treated here. He fell in and out of favor with a succession of Roman emperors (at some peril to his life), but eventually became wealthy and powerful as private tutor to the young Nero. When that unbalanced emperor came to power, Seneca was involved in government and political intrigue until inevitably Nero's whim turned against him. Toppled from power, he evaded the emperor's wrath for a short time, but was finally ordered to commit suicide in A.D. 65. Although tainted with opportunism and a thirst for power in his life, Seneca is said to have met death calmly and with the dignity that befitted his Stoic philosophy.

Ten plays by Seneca were thought to be available to Renaissance scholars, but one of these has been judged by later critics to be by another, anonymous hand. The nine Senecan tragedies, then, are *The Trojan Women*, *The Phoenician Women*, *Mad Hercules*, *Medea*, *Phaedra*, *Oedipus*, *Agamemnon*, *Thyestes*, and *Hercules on Oeta*.

The dates of their composition are unknown, but they probably come from late in Seneca's life. All are based on Greek antecedents, but Seneca rewrote plays to suit himself rather than simply translating from the Greek. Although he may have relied in part on other Greek models that do not survive, some of the extant plays of Aeschylus, Sophocles, and Euripides are clearly the sources for some of Seneca's work. Thus, comparisons are easily made, usually to Seneca's detriment. Clearly, the usual standards of plot construction and character development do not apply to Seneca's plays; he is concerned, rather, with long, rhetorical statements of passion, which often become simply bombast. Violence is far more prevalent in Seneca's plays than was considered appropriate by the Greeks, and it is Seneca's standards in this respect that have informed most drama since. Seneca makes use of a five-act structure and of choral odes that separate these acts; the regularity of his poetic rhythms also set a standard for Renaissance playwrights.

The Trojan Women illustrates Seneca's weaknesses, but it also has undeniable power of a sort and is widely regarded as the best of Seneca's plays. Many Greek tragedians dealt with the suffering of the women who survived the fall of Troy, but only Euripides' two plays on the subject, *The Trojan Women* and *Hecuba*, are available today. It is clear that Seneca made use of both of them, but whether he may have made use of additional sources as well cannot be known. A comparison of these two Euripidean scripts with Seneca's play makes clear that Seneca by no means was a mere translator, but that he did make use of the basic stories more or less intact. Hector's son, Astyanax, being hurled from the tower is a key event in Euripides' *The Trojan Women*, whereas Polyxena's sacrifice comes from *Hecuba*, but Seneca has worked these two stories together into a single action that is uniquely his own. Whereas Euripides in his two plays seems chiefly to have been interested in thematic issues, in the misery of war and man's inhumanity to man, Seneca gives little evidence of such overriding concerns. Instead, Seneca is interested primarily in finding effective language with which to externalize the emotions of each of the principal characters. His long set speeches express spectacularly the misery of the speakers, but they do not relate to each other in any but the most casual way, designed to link together the play's events but not to add up to any unified effect. These rhetorical fireworks are truly impressive and occasionally moving, but do not constitute a sufficient basis upon which to structure a satisfying work for the theater.

The play is divided into the standard five acts, with the chorus providing a usually irrelevant interlude between them. At the end of act 1 the chorus interacts with Hecuba in a scene of lamentation, but the other choral interludes have only the flimsiest connection to the rest of the play. Each character makes clear his situation, then expounds at great length on the feelings engendered within him by these circumstances. During these long speeches, it is often unclear where the other characters are supposed to be or whether they are hearing what is being said. Even the site of the action shifts alarmingly, now just outside the tomb of Hector, now at some distance from it, and time passes in ways that go unexplained in terms of the dramatic action. Since early Renaissance writers did not usually have the Greek tragedies available to them, and since they genuinely admired the rhetorical skill that Seneca undeniably exhibits, they adopted a great many of Seneca's practices as though they were the tenets of antiquity. Five-act tragedies in which rhetoric and bombast were highly valued became the Renaissance ideal, and Seneca's penchant for blood and gore (not so evident in *The Trojan Women* as in some of his other plays) became the English Renaissance norm.

To appreciate Seneca's strengths, it is necessary to keep in mind that these long speeches were intended as ends in themselves and not really part of a dramatic action as it is usually employed elsewhere. Most of what happens in Seneca's play is related rather than enacted—a clue in itself to the play's essentially nontheatrical nature. Even the simplest enacted action is veiled in complex rhetoric (for example, Astyanax entering his father's tomb) that would be thoroughly unconvincing in live performance. Often key characters don't speak at all when one would normally expect them to, just disappearing from the scene unaccounted for. On the other hand, the scene between Andromache and Ulysses creates a real measure of suspense, leading one to suppose that Seneca could have written pretty good theatrical works had he chosen to do so. What he did do was to compose some remarkably powerful poetry in which people could express the misery of their immediate situation; this is a long way from tragedy at the heights of which the Greeks were capable, but it is no small achievement either. Many of Andromache's and Hecuba's speeches, especially, are deeply and genuinely moving.

Seneca's chief importance in the theater lies in the impact he had upon other playwrights more than a millennium after his death. Rome is unique among European civilizations in having produced no enduring tragic playwrights and yet had a profound effect upon tragic playwriting.

The Trojan Women
(Troades)

Translated by Frank Justus
Miller

Characters

*Agamemnon, King of the Greek forces in the
    war against Troy*
*Pyrrhus, son of Achilles, one of the active
    leaders in the final events of the war*
*Ulysses, King of Ithaca, one of the most
    powerful and crafty of the Greek chiefs be-
    fore Troy*
*Calchas, a priest and prophet among the
    Greeks*
Talthybius, a Greek messenger
An Old Man, faithful to Andromache
*Astyanax, little son of Hector and An-
    dromache*
*Hecuba, widow of Priam, one of the Trojan
    captives*
*Andromache, widow of Hector, a Trojan
    captive*
*Helena, wife of Menelaüs, king of Sparta,
    and afterward of Paris, a prince of Troy;
    the exciting cause of the Trojan war*
*Polyxena, daughter of Hecuba and Priam
    (persona muta)*
Chorus of captive Trojan women

THE SCENE *is laid on the seashore, with the
smouldering ruins of Troy in the background. The time is the day before the em-
barkation of the Greeks on their homeward
journey.*
    *The long and toilsome siege of Troy is
done. Her stately palaces and massive walls
have been overthrown and lie darkening the
sky with their still smouldering ruins. Her
heroic defenders are either slain or scattered
seeking other homes in distant lands. The
victorious Greeks have gathered the rich
spoils of Troy upon the shore, among these,*
*the Trojan women who have suffered the
usual fate of women when a city is sacked.
They await the lot which shall assign them to
their Grecian lords and scatter them among
the cities of their foes. All things are ready
for the start.*
    *But now the ghost of Achilles has risen
from the tomb, and demanded that Polyxena
be sacrificed to him before the Greeks shall be
allowed to sail away. And Calchas, also, bids
that Astyanax be slain, for only thus can
Greece be safe from any future Trojan war.
And thus the Trojan captives, who have so
long endured the pains of war, must suffer
still this double tragedy.*

Act 1

HECUBA. Whoe'er in royal power has
    put his trust,
And proudly lords it in his princely
    halls;
Who fears no shifting of the winds of
    fate,
But fondly gives his soul to present
    joys:
Let him my lot and thine, O Troy, be-
    hold.
For of a truth did fortune never show
In plainer wise the frailty of the prop
That doth support a king; since by her
    hand
Brought low, behold, proud Asia's
    capitol,
The work of heavenly hands,[1] lies

251

desolate.
From many lands the warring princes came
To aid her cause: from where the Tanaïs
His frigid waves in seven-fold channel pours;
And that far land which greets the newborn day,
Where Tigris mingles with the ruddy sea
His tepid waves; and where the Amazon,
Within the view of wandering Scythia
Arrays her virgin ranks by Pontus' shores.
Yet here, o'erthrown, our ancient city lies,
Herself upon herself in ruins laid;
Her once proud walls in smouldering heaps recline,
Mingling their ashes with our fallen homes,
The palace flames on high, while far and near
The stately city of Assaracus[2]
Is wrapped in gloomy smoke. Yet e'en the flames
Keep not the victor's greedy hands from spoil;
And Troy, though in the grasp of fiery death,
Is pillaged still. The face of heaven is hid
By that dense, wreathing smoke; the shining day,
As if o'erspread by some thick, lowering cloud,
Grows black and foul beneath the ashy storm.
The victor stands with still unsated wrath,
Eyeing that stubborn town of Ilium,
And scarce at last forgives those ten long years
Of bloody strife. Anon, as he beholds
That mighty city, though in ruins laid,
He starts with fear; and though he plainly sees
His foe o'ercome, he scarce can comprehend
That she could be o'ercome. The Dardan spoil
Is heaped on high, a booty vast, which Greece,
In all her thousand ships, can scarce

bestow.
Now witness, ye divinities whose face
Was set against our state, my fatherland
In ashes laid; and thou, proud king of Troy,
Who in thy city's overthrow hast found
A fitting tomb; thou shade of mighty Hector,
In whose proud strength abiding, Ilium stood;
Likewise ye thronging ghosts, my children all,
But lesser shades: whatever ill has come;
Whatever Phoebus' bride[3] with frenzied speech,
Though all discredited, hath prophesied;
I, Hecuba, myself foresaw, what time,
With unborn child[4] o'erweighed, I dreamed a dream
That I had borne a flaming brand. And though,
Cassandra-like, I told my fears, my warnings,
Like our Cassandra's words in after time,
Were all in vain. 'Tis not the Ithacan,[5]
Nor yet his trusty comrade of the night,[6]
Nor that false traitor, Sinon,[7] who has cast
The flaming brands that wrought our overthrow:
Mine is the fire—'tis by my brands ye burn.
But why dost thou bewail the city's fall,
With ancient gossip's prattle? Turn thy mind,
Unhappy one, to nearer woes than these.
Troy's fall, though sad, is ancient story now.
I saw the horrid slaughter of the king,
Defiling the holy altar with its stain,
When bold Aeacides, with savage hand
Entwined in helpless Priam's hoary locks,
Drew back his sacred head, and thrust the sword
Hilt-buried in his unresisting side.
And when he plucked the deep-driven weapon back,
So weak and bloodless was our agèd king,

The deadly blade came almost stainless
 forth.
Whose thirst for blood had not been
 satisfied
By that old man just slipping o'er the
 verge
Of life? Whom would not heavenly wit-
 nesses
Restrain from crime? Who would not
 stay his hand
Before the sacred altar, last resort
Of fallen thrones? Yet he, our noble
 Priam,
The king, and father of so many kings,
Lies like the merest peasant unen-
 tombed;
And, though all Troy's aflame, there's
 not a brand
To light his pyre and give him sepul-
 ture.
And still the heavenly powers are not
 appeased.
Behold the urn; and, subject to its lot,
The maids and matrons of our princely
 line,
Who wait their future lords. To whom
 shall I,
An agèd and unprized allotment, fall?
One Grecian lord has fixed his longing
 eyes
On Hector's queen; another prays the
 lot
To grant to him the bride of Helenus;
Antenor's spouse is object of desire,
And e'en thy hand, Cassandra, hath its
 suitor:
My lot alone they deprecate and fear.
And can ye cease your plaints? O cap-
 tive throng,
Come beat upon your breasts, and let
 the sound
Of your loud lamentations rise anew,
The while we celebrate in fitting wise
Troy's funeral; let fatal Ida,[8] seat
Of that ill-omened judgment, straight
 resound
With echoes of our pitiful refrain.
CHORUS. Not an untrained band, to
 tears unknown,
Thou callest to grief, for our tears have
 rained
In streams unending through the
 years.
Since the time when the Phrygian
 guest[9] arrived
At the friendly court of Tyndarus,

Sailing the sea in his vessel framed
From the sacred pines of Cybele.
Ten winters have whitened Ida's slopes,
So often stripped for our funeral
 pyres;
Ten years have ripened the waving
 grain
Which the trembling reaper has gar-
 nered in
From wide Sigean harvest-fields:
But never a day was without its grief,
Never a night but renewed our woe.
Then on with the wailing and on with
 the blows;
And thou, poor fate-smitten queen, be
 our guide,
Our mistress in mourning; we'll obey
 thy commands,
Well trained in the wild liturgy of de-
 spair.
HECUBA. Then, trusty comrades of our
 fate,
Unbind your tresses and let them flow
Over your shoulders bent with grief,
The while with Troy's slow-cooling dust
Ye sprinkle them. Lay bare your arms,
Strip from your breasts their covering;
Why veil your beauty? Shame itself
Is held in captive bonds. And now
Let your hands wave free to the
 quickening blows
That resound to your wailings. So, now
 are ye ready,
And thus it is well. I behold once more
My old-time Trojan band. Now stoop
And fill your hands; 'tis right to take
Her dust at least from fallen Troy.
Now let the long-pent grief leap forth,
And surpass your accustomed bounds
 of woe.
Oh, weep for Hector, wail and weep.
CHORUS. Our hair, in many a funeral
 torn,
We loose; and o'er our streaming locks
Troy's glowing ashes lie bestrewn.
From our shoulders the veiling gar-
 ments fall,
And our breasts invite the smiting
 hands.
Now, now, O grief, put forth thy
 strength.
Let the distant shores resound with our
 mourning,
And let Echo who dwells in the slopes
 of the mountains
Repeat all our wailings, not, after her

wont,
With curt iteration returning the end.
Let earth hear and heed; let the sea
and the sky
Record all our grief. Then smite, O ye
hands,
With the strength of frenzy batter and
bruise.
With crying and blows and the pain of
the smiting—
Oh, weep for Hector, wail and weep.
HECUBA. Our hero, for thee the blows
are descending,
On arms and shoulders that stream
with our blood;
For thee our brows endure rough
strokes,
And our breasts are mangled with
pitiless hands.
Now flow the old wounds, reopened
anew,
That bled at thy death, the chief cause
of our sorrow.
O prop of our country, delayer of fate,
Our Ilium's bulwark, our mighty de-
fender,
Our strong tower wast thou; secure on
thy shoulders,
Our city stood leaning through ten
weary years.
By thy power supported, with thee has
she fallen,
Our country and Hector united in
doom.
Now turn to another the tide of your
mourning;
Let Priam receive his due meed of your
tears.
CHORUS. Receive our lamentings, O
Phrygia's ruler;
We weep for thy death, who wast twice
overcome.
Naught once did Troy suffer while
thou didst rule o'er her:
Twice fell her proud walls from the
blows of the Grecians,
And twice was she pierced by great
Hercules' darts.
Now all of our Hecuba's offspring have
perished,
And the proud band of kings who
came to our aid;
Thy death is the last—our father, our
ruler—
Struck down as a victim to Jove the Al-
mighty,

All helpless and lone, a mute corpse on
the ground,
HECUBA. Nay, give to another your
tears and your mourning,
And weep not the death of Priam our
king.
But call ye him blessed the rather; for
free,
To the deep world of shadows he
travels, and never
Upon his bowed neck the base yoke
shall he bear.
No proud sons of Atreus shall call him
their captive.
No crafty Ulysses his eyes shall behold;
As boast of their triumphs he shall not
bear onward
In humble submission their prizes of
war.
Those free, royal hands to the scepter
accustomed,
Shall never be bound at his back like a
slave,
As he follows the car of the triumphing
chieftain,
A king led in fetters, the gaze of the
town.
CHORUS. Hail! Priam the blessed we all
do proclaim him;
For himself and his kingdom he rules
yet below;
Now through the still depths of Elysium's shadows
'Midst calm, happy spirits he seeks the
great Hector.
Then hail, happy Priam! Hail all who
in battle
Have lost life and country, but liberty
gained.

Act 2

TALTHYBIUS. Alas, 'tis thus the Greeks
are ever doomed
To lie impatient of the winds' delay,[10]
Whether on war or homeward journey
bent.
CHORUS. Tell thou the cause of this the
Greeks' delay.
What god obstructs the homeward-
leading paths?

TALTHYBIUS. My soul doth quake, and
  all my limbs with fear
Do tremble. Scarce is credence given to
  tales
That do transcend the truth. And yet I
  swear,
With my own eyes I saw what I relate.
Now with his level rays the morning
  sun
Just grazed the summits of the hills,
  and day
Had vanquished night; when suddenly
  the earth,
'Mid rumblings hidden deep and terri-
  ble,
To her profoundest depths convulsive
  rocked.
The tree-tops trembled, and the lofty
  groves
Gave forth a thunderous sound of
  crashing boughs;
While down from Ida's rent and
  rugged slopes
The loosened boulders rolled. And not
  alone
The earth did quake: behold, the swell-
  ing sea[11]
Perceived its own Achilles drawing
  near,
And spread its waves abroad. Then did
  the ground
Asunder yawn, revealing mighty caves,
And gave a path from Erebus to earth.
And then the high-heaped sepulcher
  was rent,
From which there sprang Achilles'
  mighty shade,
In guise as when, in practice for thy
  fates,
O Troy, he prostrate laid the Thracian
  arms,
Or slew the son of Neptune, doomed to
  wear
The swan's white plumes; or when,
  amidst the ranks
In furious battle raging, he the streams
Did choke with corpses of the slain, and
  Xanthus
Crept sluggishly along with bloody
  waves;
Or when he stood as victor in his car,
Plying the reins and dragging in the
  dust
Great Hector's body and the Trojan
  state.
So there he stood and filled the spread-
  ing shore
With wrathful words: "Go, get you
  gone, ye race
Of weaklings, bear away the honors
  due
My manes; loose your thankless ships,
  and sail
Across my seas. By no slight offering
Did ye aforetime stay Achilles' wrath;
And now a greater shall ye pay. Be-
  hold,
Polyxena, once pledged to me in life,
Must by the hand of Pyrrhus to my
  shade
Be led, and with her blood my tomb be-
  dew."
So spake Achilles and the realms of day
He left for night profound, reseeking
  Dis;
And as he plunged within the depths of
  earth,
The yawning chasm closed and left no
  trace.
The sea lies tranquil, motionless; the
  wind
Its boisterous threats abates, and where
  but now
The storm-tossed waters raged in angry
  mood,
The gentle waves lap harmless on the
  shore;
While from afar the band of Tritons[12]
  sounds
The marriage chorus of their kindred
  lord. [*Exit. Enter* PYRRHUS *and*
  AGAMEMNON.]
PYRRHUS. Now that you homeward
  fare, and on the sea
Your joyful sails would spread, my no-
  ble sire
Is quite forgot, though by his single
  hand
Was mighty Troy o'erthrown; for,
  though his death
Some respite granted to the stricken
  town
She stood but as some sorely smitten
  tree,
That sways uncertain, choosing where
  to fall.
Though even now ye seek to make
  amends
For your neglect, and haste to grant the
  thing
He asks, 'tis but a tardy recompense.
Long since, the other chieftains of the

Greeks
Have gained their just reward. What
    lesser prize
Should his great valor claim? Or is it
    naught
That, though his mother bade him
    shun the war,
And spend his life in long, inglorious
    ease,
Surpassing even Pylian Nestor's years,
He cast his mother's shamming gar-
    ments off,
Confessing him the hero that he was?
When Telephus, in pride of royal
    power,
Forbade our progress through his king-
    dom's bounds,
He stained with royal blood the untried
    hand
That young Achilles raised. Yet once
    again
He felt that selfsame hand in mercy
    laid
Upon his wound to heal him of its
    smart.
Then did Eëtion, smitten sore, behold
His city taken and his realm o'er-
    thrown;
By equal fortune fell Lyrnessus' walls,
For safety perched upon a ridgy
    height,
Whence came that captive maid, Briseïs
    fair;
And Chrysa, too, lies low, the destined
    cause
Of royal strife; and Tenedos, and the
    land
Which on its spreading pastures feeds
    the flocks
Of Thracian shepherds, Scyros; Lesbos
    too,
Upon whose rocky shore the sea in
    twain
Is cleft; and Cilla, which Apollo loved.
All these my father took, and eke the
    towns
Whose walls Caÿcus with his vernal
    flood
Doth wash against. This widespread
    overthrow
Of tribes, this fearful and destructive
    scourge,
That swept through many towns with
    whirlwind power—
This had been glory and the height of
    fame

For other chiefs; 'twas but an incident
In great Achilles' journey to the war.
So came my father and such wars he
    waged
While but preparing war. And though
    I pass
In silence all his other merits, still
Would mighty Hector's death be praise
    enough.
My father conquered Troy; the lesser
    task
Of pillage and destruction is your own.
'Tis pleasant thus to laud my noble sire
And all his glorious deeds pass in re-
    view:
Before his father's eyes did Hector lie,
Of life despoiled; and Memnon,
    swarthy son
Of bright Aurora, goddess of the dawn,
For whose untimely death his mother's
    face
Was sicklied o'er with grief, while day
    was veiled
In darkness. When the heaven-born
    Memnon fell,
Achilles trembled at his victory;
For in that fall he learned the bitter
    truth
That even sons of goddesses may die.
Then, 'mongst our latest foes, the Ama-
    zons,
Fierce maidens, felt my father's deadly
    power.
So, if thou rightly estimate his deeds,
Thou ow'st Achilles all that he can ask,
E'en though he seek from Argos or
    Mycenae
Some high-born maid. And dost thou
    hesitate
And haggle now, inventing scruples
    new,
And deem it barbarous to sacrifice
This captive maid of Troy to Peleus'
    son?
But yet for Helen's sake didst thou de-
    vote
Thy daughter to the sacrificial knife.[13]
I make in this no new or strange re-
    quest,
But only urge a customary rite.
AGAMEMNON. 'Tis the common fault of
    youth to have no check
On passion's force; while others feel
    alone
The sweeping rush of this first fire of
    youth,

His father's spirit urges Pyrrhus on.
I once endured unmoved the bluster-
  ing threats
Of proud Achilles, swoll'n with power;
  and now
My patience is sufficient still to bear
His son's abuse. Why do you seek to
  smirch
With cruel murder the illustrious shade
Of that famed chief? 'Tis fitting first to
  learn
Within what bounds the victor may
  command,
The vanquished suffer. Never has for
  long
Unbridled power been able to endure,
But lasting sway the self-controlled en-
  joy.
The higher fortune raises human
  hopes,
The more should fortune's favorite
  control
His vaulting pride, and tremble as he
  views
The changing fates of life, and fear the
  gods
Who have uplifted him above his
  mates.
By my own course of conquest have I
  learned
That mighty kings can straightway
  come to naught.
Should Troy o'erthrown exalt us over-
  much?
Behold, we stand today whence she has
  fallen.
I own that in the past too haughtily
Have I my sway o'er fallen chieftains
  borne;
But thought of fortune's gift has
  checked my pride,
Since she unto another might have
  given
These selfsame gifts. O fallen king of
  Troy,
Thou mak'st me proud of conquest
  over thee,
Thou mak'st me fear that I may share
  thy fate.
Why should I count the scepter any-
  thing
But empty honor and a tinsel show?
This scepter one short hour can take
  away,
Without the aid, perchance, of count-
  less ships

And ten long years of war. The steps of
  fate
Do not for all advance with pace so
  slow.
For me, I will confess ('tis with thy
  grace,
O land of Greece, I speak) I have de-
  sired
To see the pride and power of Troy
  brought low;
But that her walls and homes should be
  o'erthrown
In utter ruin have I never wished.
But a wrathful foe, by greedy passion
  driven,
And heated by the glow of victory,
Within the shrouding darkness of the
  night,
Cannot be held in check. If any act
Upon that fatal night unworthy seemed
Or cruel, 'twas the deed of heedless
  wrath,
And darkness which is ever fury's spur,
And the victorious sword, whose lust
  for blood,
When once in blood imbued, is
  limitless.
Since Troy has lost her all, seek not to
  grasp
The last poor fragments that remain.
  Enough,
And more has she endured of punish-
  ment.
But that a maid of royal birth should
  fall
An offering upon Achilles' tomb,
Bedewing his harsh ashes with her
  blood,
While that foul murder gains the hon-
  ored name
Of wedlock, I shall not permit. On me
The blame of all will come; for he who
  sin
Forbids not when he can, commits the
  sin.
PYRRHUS. Shall no reward Achilles'
  shade obtain?
AGAMEMNON. Yea, truly; all the Greeks
  shall sing his praise,
And unknown lands shall hear his
  mighty name.
But if his shade demand a sacrifice
Of out-poured blood, go take our rich-
  est flocks,
And shed their blood upon thy father's
  tomb;

But let no mother's tears pollute the rite.
What barbarous custom this, that living man
Should to the dead be slain in sacrifice?
Then spare thy father's name the hate and scorn
Which by such cruel worship it must gain.
PYRRHUS. Thou, swoll'n with pride so long as happy fate
Uplifts thy soul, but weak and spent with fear
When fortune frowns; O hateful king of kings,
Is now thy heart once more with sudden love
Of this new maid inflamed? Shalt thou alone
So often bear away my father's spoils?
By this right hand he shall receive his own.
And if thou dost refuse, and keep the maid,
A greater victim will I slay, and one
More worthy Pyrrhus' gift; for all too long
From royal slaughter hath my hand been free,
And Priam asks an equal sacrifice.
AGAMEMNON. Far be it from my wish to dim the praise
That thou dost claim for this most glorious deed—
Old Priam slain by thy barbaric sword,
Thy father's suppliant.
PYRRHUS. I know full well
My father's suppliants—and well I know
His enemies. Yet royal Priam came,
And made his plea before my father's face;
But thou, o'ercome with fear, not brave enough
Thyself to make request, within thy tent
Didst trembling hide, and thy desires consign
To braver men, that they might plead for thee.
AGAMEMNON. But, of a truth, no fear thy father felt;
But while our Greece lay bleeding, and her ships
With hostile fire were threatened, there he lay
Supine and thoughtless of his warlike arms,
And idly strumming on his tuneful lyre.
PYRRHUS. Then mighty Hector, scornful of thy arms,
Yet felt such wholesome fear of that same lyre,
That our Thessalian ships were left in peace.
AGAMEMNON. An equal peace did Hector's father find
When he betook him to Achilles' ships.
PYRRHUS. 'Tis regal thus to spare a kingly life.
AGAMEMNON. Why then didst thou a kingly life despoil?
PYRRHUS. But mercy oft doth offer death for life.
AGAMEMNON. Doth mercy now demand a maiden's blood?
PYRRHUS. Canst *thou* proclaim such sacrifice a sin?
AGAMEMNON. A king must love his country more than child.
PYRRHUS. No law the wretched captive's life doth spare.
AGAMEMNON. What law forbids not, this let shame forbid.
PYRRHUS. 'Tis victor's right to do whate'er he will.
AGAMEMNON. Then should he will the least who most can do.
PYRRHUS. Dost thou boast thus, from whose tyrannic reign
Of ten long years but now the Greeks I freed?
AGAMEMNON. Such airs from Scyros![14]
PYRRHUS. Thence no brother's blood.[15]
AGAMEMNON. Hemmed by the sea!
PYRRHUS. Yet that same sea is ours.
But as for Pelop's house, I know it well.
AGAMEMNON. Thou base-born son of maiden's secret sin,
and young Achilles, scarce of man's estate—
PYRRHUS. Yea, that Achilles who, by right of birth,
Claims equal sovereignty of triple realms:
His mother rules the sea, to Aeacus
The shades submit, to mighty Jove the heavens.
AGAMEMNON. Yet that Achilles lies by Paris slain!
PYRRHUS. But by Apollo's aid, who aimed the dart;
For no god dared to meet him face to

face.

AGAMEMNON. I could have checked thy words, and curbed thy tongue,
Too bold in evil speech; but this my sword
Knows how to spare. But rather let them call
The prophet Calchas, who the will of heaven
Can tell. If fate demands the maid, I yield. [*Enter* CALCHAS.]
Thou who from bonds didst loose the Grecian ships,
And bring to end the slow delays of war;
Who by thy mystic art canst open heaven,
And read with vision clear the awful truths
Which sacrificial viscera proclaim;
To whom the thunder's roll, the long, bright trail
Of stars that flash across the sky, reveal
The hidden things of fate; whose every word
Is uttered at a heavy cost to me:
What is the will of heaven, O Calchas; speak
And rule us with the mastery of fate.
CALCHAS. The Greeks must pay th' accustomed price to death.[16]
Ere on the homeward seas they take their way.
The maiden must be slaughtered on the tomb
Of great Achilles. Thus the rite perform: As Grecian maidens are in marriage led
By other hands unto the bridegroom's home,
So Pyrrhus to his father's shade must lead
His promised bride. But not this cause alone
Delays our ships: a nobler blood than thine,
Polyxena, is due unto the fates;
For from yon lofty tower must Hector's son,
Astyanax, be hurled to certain death.
Than shall our vessels hasten to the sea,
And fill the waters with their thousand sails. [*Exeunt.*]
CHORUS. When in the tomb the dead is laid,
When the last rites of love are paid;
When eyes no more behold the light,
Closed in the sleep of endless night;
Survives there aught, can we believe?
Or does an idle tale deceive?
What boots it, then, to yield the breath
A willing sacrifice to death,
If still we gain no dreamless peace,
And find from living no release?
Say, do we, dying, end all pain?
Does no least part of us remain?
When from this perishable clay
The flitting breath has sped away;
Does then the soul that dissolution share
And vanish into elemental air?
Whate'er the morning sunbeam knows,
Whate'er his setting rays disclose;
Whate'er is bathed by Ocean wide,
In ebbing or in flowing tide:
Time all shall snatch with hungry greed,
With mythic Pegasean speed.
Swift is the course of stars in flight,
Swiftly the moon repairs her light;
Swiftly the changing seasons go,
While time speeds on with endless flow:
But than all these, with speed more swift,
Toward fated nothingness we drift.
For when within the tomb we're laid,
No soul remains, no hov'ring shade.
Like curling smoke, like clouds before the blast,
This animating spirit soon has passed.
Since naught remains, and death is naught
But life's last goal, so swiftly sought;
Let those who cling to life abate
Their fond desires, and yield to fate;
And those who fear death's fabled gloom,
Bury their cares within the tomb.
Soon shall grim time and yawning night
In their vast depths engulf us quite;
Impartial death demands the whole—
The body slays nor spares the soul.
Dark Taenara and Pluto fell,
And Cerberus, grim guard of hell—
All these but empty rumors seem,
The pictures of a troubled dream.
Where then will the departed spirit dwell?
Let those who never came to being tell.

Act 3

Enter ANDROMACHE, *leading the little* AS-
TYANAX.

ANDROMACHE. What do ye here, sad
throng of Phrygian dames?
Why tear your hair and beat your
wretched breasts?
Why stream your cheeks with tears?
Our ills are light
If we endure a grief that tears can
soothe.
You mourn a Troy whose walls but
now have fall'n;
Troy fell for me long since, when that
dread car
Of Peleus' son, urged on at cruel speed,
With doleful groanings 'neath his mas-
sive weight,
Dragged round the walls my Hector's
mangled corse.
Since then, o'erwhelmed and utterly
undone,
With stony resignation do I bear
Whatever ills may come. But for this
child,
Long since would I have saved me
from the Greeks
And followed my dear lord; but
thought of him
Doth check my purpose and forbid my
death.
For his dear sake there still remaineth
cause
To supplicate the gods, an added care.
Through him the richest fruit of woe is
lost—
The fear of naught and now all hope of
rest
From further ills is gone, for cruel fate
Hath still an entrance to my grieving
heart.
Most sad his fear, who fears in
hopelessness.
AN OLD MAN. What sudden cause of fear
hath moved thee so?
ANDROMACHE. Some greater ill from
mighty ills doth rise.
The fate of fallen Troy is not yet
stayed.
OLD MAN. What new disasters can the
fates invent?
ANDROMACHE. The gates of deepest
Styx, those darksome realms
(Lest fear be wanting to our over-

throw),
Are opened wide, and forth from low-
est Dis
The spirit of our buried foeman comes.
(May Greeks alone retrace their steps to
earth?
For death at least doth come to all
alike.)
That terror doth invade the hearts of
all;
But what I now relate is mine alone—
A terrifying vision of the night.
OLD MAN. What was this vision? Speak,
and share thy fears.
ANDROMACHE. Now kindly night had
passed her middle goal,
And their bright zenith had the Bears
o'ercome.
Then came to my afflicted soul a calm
Long since unknown, and o'er my
weary eyes,
For one brief hour did drowsy slumber
steal,
If that be sleep—the stupor of a soul
Forespent with ills: when suddenly I
saw
Before mine eyes the shade of Hector
stand;
Not in such guise as when, with blazing
torch,
He strove in war against the Grecian
ships,
Nor when, all stained with blood, in
battle fierce
Against the Danai, he gained true spoil
From that feigned Peleus' son;[17] not
such his face,
All flaming with the eager battle light;
But weary, downcast, tear-stained, like
my own,
All covered o'er with tangled, bloody
locks.
Still did my joy leap up at sight of him;
And then he sadly shook his head and
said:
"Awake from sleep and save our son
from death,
O faithful wife. In hiding let him lie;
Thus only can he life and safety find.
Away with tears—why dost thou
mourning make
For fallen Troy? I would that all had
fall'n.
Then haste thee, and to safety bear our
son,
The stripling hope of this our van-

quished home,
Wherever safety lies." So did he speak,
And chilling terror roused me from my
    sleep.
Now here, now there I turned my fear-
    ful eyes.
Forgetful of my son, I sought the arms
Of Hector, there to lay my grief. In
    vain:
For that elusive shade, though closely
    pressed,
Did ever mock my clinging, fond em-
    brace.
O son, true offspring of thy mighty
    sire,
Sole hope of Troy, sole comfort of our
    house,
Child of a stock of too illustrious blood,
Too like thy father, thou: such counte-
    nance
My Hector had, with such a tread he
    walked,
With such a motion did he lift his
    hands,
Thus stood he straight with shoulders
    proudly set,
And thus he oft from that high, noble
    brow
Would backward toss his flowing
    locks.—But thou,
O son, who cam'st too late for Phrygia's
    help,
Too soon for me, will that time ever
    come,
That happy day, when thou, the sole
    defense,
And sole avenger of our conquered
    Troy,
Shalt raise again her fallen citadel,
Recall her scattered citizens from flight,
And give to fatherland and Phrygians
Their name and fame again?—Alas, my
    son,
Such hopes consort not with our pres-
    ent state.
Let the humble captive's fitter prayer
    be mine—
The prayer for life. Ah me, what spot
    remote
Can hold thee safe? In what dark lurk-
    ing-place
Can I bestow thee and abate my fears?
Our city, once in pride of wealth se-
    cure,
And stayed on walls the gods them-
    selves had built,

Well known of all, the envy of the
    world,
Now deep in ashes lies, by flames laid
    low;
And from her vast extent of temples,
    walls
And towers, no part, no lurking-place
    remains,
Wherein a child might hide. Where
    shall I choose
A covert safe? Behold the mighty tomb
Wherein his father's sacred ashes lie,
Whose massive pile the enemy has
    spared.
This did old Priam rear in days of
    power,
Whose grief no stinted sepulture be-
    stowed.
Then to his father let me trust the
    child.—
But at the very thought a chilling sweat
Invades my trembling limbs, for much
    I fear
The gruesome omen of the place of
    death.
OLD MAN. In danger, haste to shelter
    where ye may;
In safety, choose.
ANDROMACHE. What hiding-place is safe
From traitor's eyes?
OLD MAN. All witnesses remove.
ANDROMACHE. What if the foe inquire?
OLD MAN. Then answer thus:
"He perished in the city's overthrow."
This cause alone ere now hath safety
    found
For many from the stroke of death—
    belief
That they have died.
ANDROMACHE. But scanty hope is left;
Too huge a weight of race doth press
    him down.
Besides, what can it profit him to hide
Who must his shelter leave and face the
    foe?
OLD MAN. The victor's deadliest pur-
    poses are first.
ANDROMACHE. What trackless region,
    what obscure retreat
Shall hold thee safe? Oh, who will bring
    us aid
In our distress and doubt? Who will de-
    fend?
O thou, who always didst protect thine
    own,
My Hector, guard us still. Accept the

trust
Which I in pious confidence impose;
And in the faithful keeping of thy dust
May he in safety dwell, to live again.
Then son, betake thee hither to the
  tomb.
Why backward strain, and shun that
  safe retreat?
I read thy nature right; thou scornest
  fear.
But curb thy native pride, thy dauntless
  soul,
And bear thee as thine altered fates di-
  rect.
For see what feeble forces now are left:
A sepulcher, a boy, a captive band.
We cannot choose but yield us to our
  woes.
Then come, make bold to enter the
  abode,
The sacred dwelling of thy buried sire.
If fate assist us in our wretchedness,
'Twill be to thee a safe retreat; if life
The fates deny, thou hast a sepulcher.
[*The* BOY *enters the tomb, and the gates
  are closed and barred behind him.*]
OLD MAN. Now do the bolted gates pro-
  tect their charge.
But thou, lest any sign of fear proclaim
Where thou hast hid the boy, come far
  away.
ANDROMACHE. Who fears from near at
  hand, hath less of fear;
But, if thou wilt, take we our steps
  away. [ULYSSES *is seen approaching.*]
OLD MAN. Now check thy words awhile,
  thy mourning cease;
For hither bends the Ithacan his
  course.
ANDROMACHE. [*With a final appealing look
  toward the tomb.*] Yawn deep, O earth,
  and thou, my husband, rend
To even greater depths thy tomb's
  deep cave,
And hide the sacred trust I gave to thee
Within the very bosom of the pit.
Now comes Ulysses, grave and slow of
  tread;
Methinks he plotteth mischief in his
  heart. [*Enter* ULYSSES.]
ULYSSES. As harsh fate's minister, I first
  implore
That, though the words are uttered by
  my lips,
Thou count them not my own. They
  are the voice

Of all the Grecian chiefs, whom Hec-
  tor's son
Doth still prohibit from that homeward
  voyage
So long delayed. And him the fates de-
  mand.
A peace secure the Greeks can never
  feel,
And ever will the backward-glancing
  fear
Compel them on defensive arms to
  lean,
While on thy living son, Andromache,
The conquered Phrygians shall rest
  their hopes.
So doth the augur, Calchas, prophesy.
Yet, even if our Calchas spake no word,
Thy Hector once declared it, and I fear
Lest in his son a second Hector dwell;
For ever doth a noble scion grow
Into the stature of his noble sire.
Behold the little comrade of the herd,
His budding horns still hidden from
  the sight:
Full soon with arching neck and lofty
  front,
He doth command and lead his father's
  flock.
The slender twig, just lopped from par-
  ent bough,
Its mother's height and girth surpasses
  soon,
And casts its shade abroad to earth and
  sky.
So doth a spark within the ashes left,
Leap into flame again before the wind.
Thy grief, I know, must partial judg-
  ment give;
Still, if thou weigh the matter, thou wilt
  grant
That after ten long years of grievous
  war.
A veteran soldier doeth well to fear
Still other years of slaughter, and thy
  Troy,
Still unsubdued. This fear one cause
  alone
Doth raise—another Hector. Free the
  Greeks
From dread of war. For this and this
  alone
Our idle ships still wait along the shore.
And let me not seem cruel in thy sight,
For that, compelled of fate, I seek thy
  son:
I should have sought our chieftain's

son as well.
Then gently suffer what the victor
  bore.[18]
ANDROMACHE. Oh, that thou wert
  within my power to give,
My son, and that I knew what cruel fate
Doth hold thee now, snatched from my
  eager arms—
Where thou dost lie; then, though my
  breast were pierced
With hostile spears, and though my
  hands with chains
Were bound, and scorching flames be-
  girt my sides,
Thy mother's faith would ne'er betray
  her child.
O son, what place, what lot doth hold
  thee now?
Dost thou with wandering footsteps
  roam the fields?
Wast thou consumed amid the raging
  flames?
Hath some rude victor reveled in thy
  blood?
Or, by some ravening beast hast thou
  been slain,
And liest now a prey for savage birds?
ULYSSES. Away with feignéd speech; no
  easy task
For thee to catch Ulysses: 'tis my boast
That mother's snares, and even god-
  desses'
I have o'ercome. Have done with vain
  deceit.
Where is thy son?
ANDROMACHE. And where is Hector
  too?
Where agéd Priam and the Phrygians?
Thou seekest one; *my* quest includes
  them all.
ULYSSES. By stern necessity thou soon
  shalt speak
What thy free will withholds.
ANDROMACHE. But safe is she,
Who can face death, who ought and
  longs to die.
ULYSSES. But death brought near would
  still thy haughty words.
ANDROMACHE. If 'tis thy will, Ulysses, to
  inspire
Andromache with fear, then threaten
  life;
For death has long been object of my
  prayer.
ULYSSES. With stripes, with flames, with
  lingering pains of death

Shalt thou be forced to speak, against
  thy will,
What now thou dost conceal, and from
  thy heart
Its inmost secrets bring. Necessity
Doth often prove more strong than pi-
  ety.
ANDROMACHE. Prepare thy flames, thy
  blows, and all the arts
Devised for cruel punishment: dire
  thirst,
Starvation, every form of suffering;
Come, rend my vitals with the sword's
  deep thrust;
In dungeon, foul and dark, immure;
  do all
A victor, full of wrath and fear, can do
Or dare; still will my mother heart, in-
  spired
With high and dauntless courage, scorn
  thy threats.
ULYSSES. This very love of thine, which
  makes thee bold,
Doth warn the Greeks to counsel for
  their sons.
This strife, from home remote, these
  ten long years
Of war, and all the ills which Calchas
  dreads,
Would slight appear to me, if for my-
  self
I feared: but thou doest threat Tele-
  machus.
ANDROMACHE. Unwillingly, Ulysses, do I
  give
To thee, or any Grecian, cause of joy;
Yet must I give it, and speak out the
  woe,
The secret grief that doth oppress my
  soul.
Rejoice, O sons of Atreus, and do thou,
According to thy wont, glad tidings
  bear
To thy companions: *Hector's son is dead.*
ULYSSES. What proof have we that this
  thy word is true?
ANDROMACHE. May thy proud victor's
  strongest threat befall,
And bring my death with quick and
  easy stroke;
May I be buried in my native soil,
May earth press lightly on my Hector's
  bones:
According as my son, deprived of light,
Amidst the dead doth lie, and, to the
  tomb

Consigned, hath known the funeral
   honors due
To those who live no more.
ULYSSES. [*Joyfully.*] Then are the fates
Indeed fulfilled, since Hector's son is
   dead,
And I with joy unto the Greeks will go,
With grateful tale of peace at last se-
   cure. [*Aside.*]
But stay, Ulysses, this rash joy of thine!
The Greeks will readily believe *thy*
   word;
But what dost thou believe?—his
   mother's oath.
Would then a mother feign her off-
   spring's death,
And fear no baleful omens of that
   word?
They omens fear who have no greater
   dread.
Her truth hath she upheld by straigh-
   test oath.
If that she perjured be, what greater
   fear
Doth vex her soul? Now have I urgent
   need
Of all my skill and cunning, all my arts,
By which so oft Ulysses hath prevailed;
For truth, though long concealed, can
   never die.
Now watch the mother; note her grief,
   her tears,
Her sighs; with restless step, now here,
   now there,
She wanders, and she strains her anx-
   ious ears
To catch some whispered word. 'Tis ev-
   ident,
She more by present fear than grief is
   swayed.
So must I ply her with the subtlest art.
   [*To* ANDROMACHE.]
When others mourn, 'tis fit in sympathy
To speak with kindred grief; but thou,
   poor soul,
I bid rejoice that thou hast lost thy son,
Whom cruel fate awaited; for 'twas
   willed
That from the lofty tower that doth re-
   main
Alone of Troy's proud walls, he should
   be dashed,
And headlong fall to quick and certain
   death.
ANDROMACHE. [*Aside.*] My soul is faint
   within me, and my limbs

Do quake; while chilling fear congeals
   my blood.
ULYSSES. [*Aside.*] She trembles; here
   must I pursue my quest.
Her fear betrayeth her; wherefore this
   fear
Will I redouble.—[*To attendants.*] Go in
   haste, my men,
And find this foe of Greece, the last defense
Of Troy, who by his mother's cunning
   hand
Is safe bestowed, and set him in our
   midst. [*Pretending that the boy is discovered.*]
'Tis well! He's found. Now bring him
   here with haste. [*To* ANDROMACHE.]
Why dost thou start, and tremble? Of a
   truth
Thy son is dead, for so hast thou de-
   clared.
ANDROMACHE. Oh, that I had just cause
   of dread. But now,
My old habitual fear instinctive starts;
The mind does not forget a well-
   learned woe.
ULYSSES. Now since thy boy hath
   shunned the sacrifice
That to the walls was due, and hath escaped
By grace of better fate, our priest de-
   clares
That only can our homeward way be
   won
If Hector's ashes, scattered o'er the
   waves,
Appease the sea, and this his sepulcher
Be leveled with the ground. Since Hec-
   tor's son
Has failed to pay the debt he owed to
   fate,
Then Hector's sacred dust must be de-
   spoiled.
ANDROMACHE. [*Aside.*] Ah me, a double
   fear distracts my soul!
Here calls my son, and here my hus-
   band's dust.
Which shall prevail? Attest, ye heartless
   gods,
And ye, my husband's shades, true
   deities:
Naught else, O Hector, pleased me in
   my son,
Save only thee; then may he still sur-
   vive
To bring thine image back to life and

me.—
Shall then my husband's ashes be
  defiled?
Shall I permit his bones to be the sport
Of waves, and lie unburied in the sea?
Oh, rather, let my only son be slain!—
And canst thou, mother, see thy help-
  less child
To awful death given up? Canst thou
  behold
His body whirling from the battle-
  ments?
I can, I shall endure and suffer this,
Provided only, by his death appeased,
The victor's hand shall spare my Hec-
  tor's bones.—
But he can suffer yet, while kindly fate
Hath placed his sire beyond the reach
  of harm.
Why dost thou hesitate? Thou must de-
  cide
Whom thou wilt designate for punish-
  ment.
What doubts harass thy troubled soul?
  No more
Is Hector here.—Oh say not so; I feel
He is both here and there. But sure am
  I
That this my child is still in life, per-
  chance
To be the avenger of his father's death.
But both I cannot spare. What then? O
  soul,
Save of the two, whom most the Greeks
  do fear.
ULYSSES. [*Aside.*] Now must I force her
  answer. [*To* ANDROMACHE.] From its
  base
Will I this tomb destroy.
ANDROMACHE. The tomb of him
Whose body thou didst ransom for a
  price?
ULYSSES. I will destroy it, and the sepul-
  cher
From its high mound will utterly re-
  move.
ANDROMACHE. The sacred faith of
  heaven do I invoke,
And just Achilles' plighted word: do
  thou,
O Pyrrhus, keep thy father's sacred
  oath.
ULYSSES. This tomb shall soon lie level
  with the plain.
ANDROMACHE. Such sacrilege the
  Greeks, though impious,

Have never dared. 'Tis true the tem-
  ples pure,
E'en of your favoring gods, ye have
  defiled;
But still your wildest rage hath spared
  our tombs.
I will resist, and match your warriors'
  arms
With my weak woman's hands. Despair-
  ing wrath
Will nerve my arm. Like that fierce
  Amazon,[19]
Who wrought dire havoc in the Grecian
  ranks;
Or some wild Maenad[20] by the god
  o'ercome,
Who, thrysus-armed, doth roam the
  trackless glades
With frenzied step, and, clean of sense
  bereft,
Strikes deadly blows but feels no
  counter-stroke:
So will I rush against ye in defense
Of Hector's tomb, and perish, if I must,
An ally of his shade.
ULYSSES. [*To attendants.*] Do ye delay,
And do a woman's tears and empty
  threats
And outcry move you? Speed the task I
  bid.
ANDROMACHE. [*Struggling with attend-
  ants.*] Destroy me first! Oh, take my
  life instead! [*The attendants roughly
  thrust her away.*]
Alas, they thrust me back! O Hector,
  come,
Break through the bands of fate, up-
  heave the earth,
That thou mayst stay Ulysses' lawless
  hand.
Thy spirit will suffice.—Behold he
  comes!
His arms he brandishes, and firebrands
  hurls.
Ye Greeks, do ye behold him, or do I,
With solitary sight, alone behold?
ULYSSES. This tomb and all it holds will
  I destroy.
ANDROMACHE. [*Aside, while the attendants
  begin to demolish the tomb.*] Ah me, can
  I permit the son and sire
To be in common ruin overwhelmed?
Perchance I may prevail upon the
  Greeks
By prayer.—But even now those mas-
  sive stones

Will crush my hidden child.—Oh, let
   him die,
In any other way, and anywhere,
If only father crush not son, and son
No desecration bring to father's dust.
   [*Casts herself at the feet of* ULYSSES.]
A humble suppliant at thy knees I fall,
Ulysses; I, who never yet to man
Have bent the knee in prayer, thy feet
   embrace.
By all the gods, have pity on my woes,
And with a calm and patient heart re-
   ceive
My pious prayers. And as the heavenly
   powers
Have high exalted thee in pride and
   might,
The greater mercy show thy fallen foes.
Whate'er is given to wretched suppliant
Is loaned to fate. So mayst thou see
   again
Thy faithful wife; so may Laërtes live
To greet thee yet again; so may thy son
Behold thy face, and, more than that
   thou canst pray,
Excel his father's valor and the years
Of old Laërtes.[21] Pity my distress:
The only comfort left me in my woe,
Is this my son.
ULYSSES. Produce the boy—and pray.
ANDROMACHE. [*Goes to the tomb and calls
   to* ASTYANAX.] Come forth, my son,
   from the place of thy hiding
Where thy mother bestowed thee with
   weeping and fear. [ASTYANAX *appears
   from the tomb.* ANDROMACHE *presents
   him to* ULYSSES.]
Here, here is the lad, Ulysses, behold
   him;
The fear of thy armies, the dread of
   thy fleet! [*To Astyanax.*]
My son, thy suppliant hands upraise,
And at the feet of this proud lord,
Bend low in prayer, nor think it base
To suffer the lot which our fortune ap-
   points.
Put out of mind thy regal birth,
Thy agéd grandsire's glorious rule
Of wide domain; and think no more
Of Hector, thy illustrious sire.
Be captive alone—bend the suppliant
   knee;
And if thine own fate move thee not,
Then weep by thy mother's woe in-
   spired. [*To* ULYSSES.]
That older Troy beheld the tears

Of its youthful king, and those tears
   prevailed
To stay the fierce threats of the victor's
   wrath,
The mighty Hercules. Yea he,
To whose vast strength all monsters
   had yielded,
Who burst the stubborn gates of hell,
And o'er that murky way returned,
Even he was o'ercome by the tears of a
   boy.
"Take the reins of the state," to the
   prince he said;
"Reign thou on thy father's lofty
   throne,
But reign with the scepter of power—
   and truth."
Thus did that hero subdue his foes.
And thus do thou temper thy wrath
   with forbearance.
And let not the power of great Her-
   cules, only,
Be model to thee. Behold at thy feet,
As noble a prince as Priam of old
Pleads only for life! The kingdom of
   Troy
Let fortune bestow where she will.
ULYSSES. [*Aside.*] This woe-struck
   mother's grief doth move me sore;
But still the Grecian dames must more
   prevail,
Unto whose grief this lad is growing
   up.
ANDROMACHE. [*Hearing him.*] What?
   These vast ruins of our fallen town,
To very ashes brought, shall he uprear?
Shall these poor boyish hands build
   Troy again?
No hopes indeed hath Troy, if such her
   hopes.
So low the Trojans lie, there's none so
   weak
That he need fear our power. Doth
   lofty thought
Of mighty Hector nerve his boyish
   heart?
What valor can a fallen Hector stir?
When this our Troy was lost, his
   father's self
Would then have bowed his lofty
   spirit's pride;
For woe can bend and break the
   proudest soul.
If punishment be sought, some heavier
   fate
Let him endure; upon his royal neck

Let him support the yoke of servitude.
Must princes sue in vain for this poor
   boon?
ULYSSES. Not I, but Calchas doth refuse
   thy prayer.
ANDROMACHE. O man of lies, artificer of
   crime,
By whom in open fight no foe is slain,
But by whose tricks and cunning, evil
   mind
The very chiefs of Greece are over-
   thrown,
Dost thou now seek to hide thy dark in-
   tent
Behind a priest and guiltless gods?
   Nay, nay:
This deed within thy sinful heart was
   born.
Thou midnight prowler, brave to work
   the death
Of this poor boy, dost dare at length
   alone
To do a deed, and that in open day?
ULYSSES. Ulysses' valor do the Grecians
   know
Full well, and all too well the Phrygians.
But we are wasting time with empty
   words.
The impatient ships are tugging at
   their chains.
ANDROMACHE. But grant a brief delay,
   while to my son
I pay the rites of woe, and sate my grief
With tears and last embrace.
ULYSSES. I would 'twere mine
To spare thy tears; but what alone I
   may,
I'll give thee respite and a time for
   grief.
Then weep thy fill, for tears do soften
   woe.
ANDROMACHE. [*To* ASTYANAX.[O darling
   pledge of love, thou only stay
Of our poor fallen house, last pang of
   Troy;
O thou whom Grecians fear, O
   mother's hope,
Alas too vain, for whom, with folly
   blind,
I prayed the war-earned praises of his
   sire,
His royal grandsire's prime of years
   and strength:
But God hath scorned my prayers.
   Thou shalt not live
To wield the scepter in the royal courts

Of ancient Troy, to make thy people's
   laws,
And send beneath thy yoke the con-
   quered tribes;
Thou shalt not fiercely slay the fleeing
   Greeks,
Nor from thy car in retribution drag
Achilles' son; the dart from thy small
   hand
Thou ne'er shalt hurl, nor boldly press
   the chase
Of scattered beasts throughout the for-
   est glades;
And when the sacred lustral day is
   come,
Troy's yearly ritual of festal games,
The charging squadrons of the noble
   youth
Thou shalt not lead, thyself the noblest
   born;
Nor yet among the blazing altar fires,
With nimble feet the ancient sacred
   dance
At some barbaric temple celebrate,
While horns swell forth swift-moving
   melodies.
Oh, mode of death, far worse than
   bloody war!
More tearful sight than mighty Hec-
   tor's end
The walls of Troy must see.
ULYSSES. Now stay thy tears,
For mighty grief no bound or respite
   finds.
ANDROMACHE. Small space for tears,
   Ulysses, do I ask;
Some scanty moments yet, I pray thee,
   grant,
That I may close his eyes though living
   still,
And do a mother's part.
[*To* ASTYANAX.[Lo, thou must die,
For, though a child, thou art too
   greatly feared.
Thy Troy awaits thee; go, in freedom's
   pride,
And see our Trojans, dead yet unen-
   slaved.
ASTYANAX. O mother, mother, pity me
   and save!
ANDROMACHE. My son, why dost thou
   cling upon my robes,
And seek the vain protection of my
   hand?
As when the hungry lion's roar is
   heard,

The frightened calf for safety presses close
Its mother's side; but that remorseless beast,
Thrusting away the mother's timid form,
With ravenous jaws doth grasp the lesser prey,
And, crushing, drag it hence: so shalt thou, too,
Be snatched away from me by heartless foes.
Then take my tears and kisses, O my son,
Take these poor locks, and, full of mother love,
Go speed thee to thy sire; and in his ear
Speak these, thy grieving mother's parting words:
"If still thy manes feel their former cares,
And on the pyre thy love was not consumed,
Why dost thou suffer thy Andromache
To serve a Grecian lord, O cruel Hector?
Why dost thou lie in careless indolence?
Achilles has returned." Take once again
These hairs, these flowing tears, which still remain
From Hector's piteous death; this fond caress
And rain of parting kisses take for him.
But leave this cloak to comfort my distress,
For it, within his tomb and near his shade,
Hath lain enwrapping thee. If to its folds
One tiny mote of his dear ashes clings,
My eager lips shall seek it till they find.
ULYSSES. Thy grief is limitless. Come, break away,
And end our Grecian fleet's too long delay. [*He leads the boy away with him.*]

CHORUS. Where lies the home of our captivity?
On Thessaly's famed mountain heights?
Where Tempe's dusky shade invites?
Or Phthia, sturdy warriors' home,
Or where rough Trachin's cattle roam?
Iolchos, mistress of the main,
Or Crete, whose cities crowd the plain?

Where frequent flow Mothone's rills,
Beneath the shade of Oete's hills,
Whence came Alcides' fatal bow
Twice destined for our overthrow?
But whither shall our alien course be sped?
Perchance to Pleuron's gates we go,
Where Dian's self was counted foe;
Perchance to Troezen's winding shore,
The land which mighty Theseus bore;
Or Pelion, by whose rugged side
Their mad ascent the giants tried.
Here, stretched within his mountain cave,
Once Chiron to Achilles gave
The lyre, whose stirring strains attest
The warlike passions of his breast.
What foreign shore our homeless band invites?
Must we our native country deem
Where bright Carystos' marbles gleam?
Where Chalcis breasts the heaving tide,
And swift Euripus' waters glide?
Perchance unhappy fortune calls
To bleak Gonoëssa's windswept walls;
Perchance our wondering eyes shall see
Eleusin's awful mystery;
Or Elis, where great heroes strove
To win the Olympic crown of Jove.
Then welcome, stranger lands beyond the sea!
Let breezes waft our wretched band,
Where'er they list, to any land;
If only Sparta's cursèd state
(To Greeks and Trojans common fate)
And Argos, never meet our view,
And bloody Pelops' city too;
May we ne'er see Ulysses' isle,
Whose borders share their master's guile.
But thee, O Hecuba, what fate,
What land, what Grecian lord await?

Act 4

Enter HELEN.
HELEN. [*Aside.*] Whatever wedlock, bred of evil fate,
Is full of joyless omens, blood and tears,
Is worthy Helen's baleful auspices.
And now must I still further harm in-

flict
Upon the prostrate Trojans: 'tis my
part
To feign Polyxena, the royal maid,
Is bid to be our Grecian Pyrrhus' wife,
And deck her in the garb of Grecian
brides.
So by my artful words shall she be
snared,
And by my craft shall Paris' sister fall.
But let her be deceived; 'tis better so;
To die without the shrinking fear of
death
Is joy indeed. But why dost thou delay
Thy bidden task? If aught of sin there
be,
'Tis his who doth command thee to the
deed. [*To* POLYXENA.]
O maiden, born of Priam's noble stock,
The gods begin to look upon thy house
In kinder mood, and even now prepare
To grant thee happy marriage; such a
mate
As neither Troy herself in all her
power
Nor royal Priam could have found for
thee.
For lo, the flower of the Pelasgian
lords,
Whose sway Thessalia's far-extending
plains
Acknowledge, seeks thy hand in lawful
wedlock.
Great Tethys waits to claim thee for her
own,
And Thetis, whose majestic deity
Doth rule the swelling sea, and all the
nymphs
Who dwell within its depths. As Pyr-
rhus' bride
Thou shalt be called the child of Peleus
old,
And Nereus the divine. Then change
the garb
Of thy captivity for festal robes,
And straight forget that thou wast e'er
a slave.
Thy wild, disheveled locks confine; per-
mit
That I, with skillful hands, adorn thy
head.
This chance, mayhap, shall place thee
on a throne
More lofty far than ever Priam saw.
The captive's lot full oft a blessing
proves.

ANDROMACHE. This was the one thing
lacking to our woes—
That they should bid us smile when we
would weep.
See there! Our city lies in smouldering
heaps;
A fitting time to talk of marriages!
But who would dare refuse? When
Helen bids,
Who would not hasten to the wedding
rites?
Thou common curse of Greeks and
Trojans too,
Thou fatal scourge, thou wasting pesti-
lence,
Dost thou behold where buried heroes
lie?
And dost thou see these poor unburied
bones
That everywhere lie whitening on the
plain?
This desolation hath thy marriage
wrought.
For thee the blood of Asia flowed; for
thee
Did Europe's heroes bleed, whilst thou,
well pleased,
Didst look abroad upon the warring
kings,
Who perished in thy cause, thou faith-
less jade!
There! get thee gone! prepare thy mar-
riages!
What need of torches for the solemn
rites?
What need of fire? Troy's self shall fur-
nish forth
The ruddy flames to light her latest
bride.
Then come, my sisters, come and celebrate
Lord Pyrrhus' nuptial day in fitting
wise:
With groans and wailing let the scene
resound.
HELEN. Though mighty grief is ne'er by
reason swayed,
And oft the very comrades of its woe,
Unreasoning, hates; yet can I bear to
stand
And plead my cause before a hostile
judge,
For I have suffered heavier ills than
these.
Behold, Andromache doth Hector
mourn,

And Hecuba her Priam; each may claim
The public sympathy; but Helena
Alone must weep for Paris secretly.
Is slavery's yoke so heavy and so hard
To bear? This grievous yoke have I endured,
Ten years a captive. Doth your Ilium lie
In dust, your gods o'erthrown? I know 'tis hard
To lose one's native land, but harder still
To fear the land that gave you birth. Your woes
Are lightened by community of grief;
But friend and foe are foes alike to me.
Long since, the fated lot has hung in doubt
That sorts you to your lords; but I alone,
Without the hand of fate am claimed at once.
Think you that I have been the cause of war,
And Troy's great overthrow? Believe it true
If in a Spartan vessel I approached
Your land; but if, sped on by Phrygian oars,
I came a helpless prey; if to the judge
Of beauty's rival claims I fell the prize
By conquering Venus' gift, then pity me,
The plaything of the fates. An angry judge
Full soon my cause shall have—my Grecian lord.
Then leave to him the question of my guilt,
And judge me not. But now forget thy woes
A little space, Andromache, and bid
This royal maid—but as I think on her
My tears unbidden flow. [*She stops, overcome by emotion.*]
ANDROMACHE. [*In scorn*] Now great indeed
Must be the evil when our Helen weeps!
But dry thy tears, and tell what Ithacus
Is plotting now, what latest deed of shame?
Must this poor maid be hurled from Ida's heights,
Or from the top of Ilium's citadel?
Must she be flung into the cruel sea
That roars beneath this lofty precipice,
Which our Sigeum's rugged crag uprears?
Come, tell what thou dost hide with mimic grief.
In all our ills there's none so great as this,
That any princess of our royal house
Should wed with Pyrrhus. Speak thy dark intent;
What further suffering remains to bear?
To compensate our woes, this grace impart,
That we may know the worst that can befall.
Behold us ready for the stroke of fate.
HELEN. Alas! I would 'twere mine to break the bonds
Which bind me to this life I hate; to die
By Pyrrhus' cruel hand upon the tomb
Of great Achilles, and to share thy fate
O poor Polyxena. For even now,
The ghost doth bid that thou be sacrificed,
And that thy blood be spilt upon his tomb;
That thus thy parting soul may mate with his,
Within the borders of Elysium.
ANDROMACHE. [*Observing the joy with which* POLYXENA *receives these tidings.*]
Behold, her soul leaps up with mighty joy
At thought of death; she seeks the festal robes
Wherewith to deck her for the bridal rites,
And yields her golden locks to Helen's hands.
Who late accounted wedlock worse than death,
Now hails her death with more than bridal joy. [*Observing* HECUBA.]
But see, her mother stands amazed with woe,
Her spirit staggers 'neath the stroke of fate. [*To* HERCUBA.]
Arise, O wretched queen, stand firm in soul,
And gird thy fainting spirit up.
[HECUBA *falls fainting.*] Behold,
By what a slender thread her feeble life
Is held to earth. How slight the barrier now

That doth remove our Hecuba from
  joy.
But no, she breathes, alas! she lives
  again,
For from the wretched, death is first to
  flee.
HECUBA. [*Reviving.*] Still dost thou live,
  Achilles, for our bane?
Dost still prolong the bitter strife? O
  Paris,
Thine arrow should have dealt a dead-
  lier wound.
For see, the very ashes and the tomb
Of that insatiate chieftain still do thirst
For Trojan blood. But lately did a
  throng
Of happy children press me round;
  and I,
With fond endearment and the sweet
  caress
That mother love would shower upon
  them all,
Was oft forespent. But now this child
  alone
Is left, my comrade, comfort of my
  woes,
For whom to pray, in whom to rest my
  soul.
Hers are the only lips still left to me
To call me mother. Poor, unhappy
  soul,
Why dost thou cling so stubbornly to
  life?
Oh, speed thee out, and grant me
  death at last,
The only boon I seek. Behold, I weep;
And from my cheeks, o'erwhelmed
  with sympathy,
A sudden rain of grieving tears de-
  scends.
ANDROMACHE. We, Hecuba, Oh, we
  should most be mourned,
Whom soon the fleet shall scatter o'er
  the sea;
While *she* shall rest beneath the soil she
  loves.
HELEN. Still more wouldst thou be-
  grudge thy sister's lot,
If thou didst know thine own.
ANDROMACHE. Remains there still
Some punishment that I must
  undergo?
HELEN. The whirling urn hath given
  you each her lord.
ANDROMACHE. To whom hath fate al-
  lotted me a slave?

Proclaim the chief whom I must call my
  lord.
HELEN. To Pyrrhus hast thou fallen by
  the lot.
ANDROMACHE. O happy maid, Cas-
  sandra, blest of heaven,
For by thy madness art thou held ex-
  empt
From fate that makes us chattels to the
  Greeks.
HELEN. Not so, for even now the Gre-
  cian king
Doth hold her as his prize.
HECUBA. [*To* POLYXENA.] Rejoice, my
  child.
How gladly would thy sisters change
  their lot
For thy death-dooming marriage. [*To*
  HELEN.] Tell me now,
Does any Greek lay claim to Hecuba?
HELEN. The Ithacan, though much
  against his will,
Hath gained by lot a short-lived prize
  in thee.
HECUBA. What cruel, ruthless provi-
  dence hath given
A royal slave to serve a royal lord?
What hostile god divides our captive
  band?
What heartless arbiter of destiny
So carelessly allots our future lords,
That Hector's mother is assigned to
  him
Who hath by favor gained th' accursed
  arms
Which laid my Hector low? And must I
  then
Obey the Ithacan? Now conquered
  quite,
Alas, and doubly captive do I seem,
And sore beset by all my woes at once.
Now must I blush, not for my slavery,
But for my master's sake. Yet Ithaca,
That barren land by savage seas beset,
Shall not receive my bones. Then up,
  Ulysses,
And lead thy captive home. I'll not re-
  fuse
To follow thee as lord; for well I know
That my untoward fates shall follow
  me.
No gentle winds shall fill thy homeward
  sails,
But stormy blasts shall rage; destructive
  wars,
And fires, and Priam's evil fates and

mine,
Shall haunt thee everywhere. But even
  now,
While yet those ills delay, hast thou re-
  ceived
Some punishment. For I usurped thy
  lot,
And stole thy chance to win a fairer
  prize. [*Enter* PYRRHUS.]
But see, with hurried step and lowering
  brow,
Stern Pyrrhus comes. [*To* PYRRHUS.]
  Why dost thou hesitate?
Come pierce my vitals with thy impious
  sword,
And join the parents of Achilles' bride.
Make haste, thou murderer of agéd
  men,
My blood befits thee too. [*Pointing to*
  POLYXENA.] Away with her;
Defile the face of heaven with murder's
  stain,
Defile the shades.—But why make
  prayer to you?
I'll rather pray the sea whose savage
  rage
Befits these bloody rites; the selfsame
  doom,
Which for my ship I pray and proph-
  esy,
May that befall the thousand ships of
  Greece,
And so may evil fate engulf them all.

CHORUS. 'Tis sweet for one in grief to
  know
That he but feels a common woe;
And lighter falls the stroke of care
Which all with equal sorrow bear;
For selfish and malign is human grief
Which in the tears of others finds re-
  lief.

Remove all men to fortune born,
And none will think himself forlorn;
Remove rich acres spreading wide,
With grazing herds on every side:
Straight will the poor man's drooping
  soul revive,
For none are poor if all in common
  thrive.

The mariner his fate bewails,
Who in a lonely vessel sails,
And, losing all his scanty store,
With life alone attains the shore;

But with a stouter heart the gale he
  braves,
That sinks a thousand ships beneath
  the waves.

When Phrixus fled in days of old
Upon the ram with fleece of gold,
His sister Helle with him fared
And all his exiled wanderings shared;
But when she fell and left him quite
  alone,
Then nothing could for Helle's loss
  atone.

Not so they wept, that fabled pair,
Deucalion and Pyrrha fair,
When 'midst the boundless sea they
  stood
The sole survivors of the flood;
For though their lot was hard and
  desolate,
They shared their sorrow—'twas a com-
  mon fate.

Too soon our grieving company
Shall scatter on the rolling sea,
Where swelling sails and bending oars
Shall speed us on to distant shores.
Oh, then how hard shall be our
  wretched plight,
When far away our country lies,
And round us heaving billows rise,
And lofty Ida's summit sinks from
  sight.

Then mother shall her child embrace,
And point with straining eyes the place
Where Ilium's smouldering ruins lie,
Far off beneath the eastern sky:
"See there, my child, our Trojan ashes
  glow,
Where wreathing smoke in murky
  clouds
The distant, dim horizon shrouds;
And by that sign alone our land we
  know."

Act 5

MESSENGER. [*Entering.*] Oh, cruel fate,
  Oh, piteous, horrible!
What sight so fell and bloody have we
  seen

In ten long years of war? Between thy
  woes,
Andromache, and thine, O Hecuba,
I halt, and know not which to weep the
  more.
HECUBA. Weep whosesoe'er thou wilt—
  thou weepest mine.
While others bow beneath their single
  cares,
I feel the weight of all. All die to me;
Whatever grief there is, is Hecuba's.
MESSENGER.The maid is slain, the boy
  dashed from the walls.
But each has met his death with royal
  soul.
ANDROMACHE. Expound the deed in or-
  der, and display
The twofold crime. My mighty grief is
  fain
To hear the gruesome narrative entire
Begin thy tale, and tell it as it was.
MESSENGER. One lofty tower of fallen
  Troy is left,
Well known to Priam, on whose battle-
  ments
He used to sit and view his warring
  hosts.
Here in his arms his grandson he
  would hold
With kind embrace, and bid the lad ad-
  mire
His father's warlike deeds upon the
  field,
Where Hector, armed with fire and
  sword, pursued
The frightened Greeks. Around this
  lofty tower
Which lately stood, the glory of the
  walls,
But now a lonely crag, the people pour,
A motley, curious throng of high and
  low.
For some, a distant hill gives open view;
While others seek a cliff, upon whose
  edge
The crowd in tiptoed expectation
  stand.
The beech tree, laurel, pine, each has
  its load;
The whole wood bends beneath its hu-
  man fruit.
One climbs a smouldering roof; unto
  another
A crumbling wall precarious footing
  gives;
While others (shameless!) stand on

Hector's tomb.
Now through the thronging crowd with
  stately tread
Ulysses makes his way, and by the hand
He leads the little prince of Ilium.
With equal pace the lad approached
  the wall;
But when he reached the lofty battle-
  ment,
He stood and gazed around with
  dauntless soul.
And as the savage lion's tender young,
Its fangless jaws, all powerless to harm,
Still snaps with helpless wrath and
  swelling heart;
So he, though held in that strong
  foeman's grasp,
Stood firm, defiant. Then the crowd of
  men,
And leaders, and Ulysses' self, were
  moved.
But he alone wept not of all the throng
Who wept for him. And now Ulysses
  spake
In priestly wise the words of fate, and
  prayed,
And summoned to the rite the savage
  gods;
When suddenly, on self-destruction
  bent,
The lad sprang o'er the turret's edge,
  and plunged
Into the depths below.—
ANDROMACHE. What Colchian, what
  wandering Scythian,
What lawless race that dwells by Cas-
  pia's sea
Could do or dare a crime so *hideous*?
No blood of helpless children ever
  stained
Busiris'[22] altars, monster though he
  was;
Nor did the horses of the Thracian
  king[23]
E'er feed on tender limbs. Where is my
  boy?
Who now will take and lay him in the
  tomb?
MESSENGER. Alas, my lady, how can
  aught remain
From such a fall, but broken, scattered
  bones,
Dismembered limbs, and all those no-
  ble signs
In face and feature of his royal birth,
Confused and crushed upon the

ragged ground?
His neck was broken as it struck the
rock;
His brains ejected from his shattered
skull.
Who was thy son lies now a shapeless
corpse.
ANDROMACHE. Thus also is he like his
noble sire.
MESSENGER. When headlong from the
tower the lad had sprung,
And all the Grecian throng bewailed
the crime
Which it had seen and done, the self-
same throng
Returned to witness yet another crime
Upon Achilles' tomb. The seaward side
Is beaten by Rhoeteum's lapping waves;
While on the other sides a level space,
And rounded, gently sloping hills be-
yond,
Encompass it, and make a theater.
Here rush the multitude and fill the
place
With eager throngs. A few rejoice that
now
Their homeward journey's long delay
will end,
And that another prop of fallen Troy
Is stricken down. But all the common
herd
Look on in silence at the crime they
hate.
The Trojans, too, attend the sacrifice,
And wait with quaking hearts the final
scene
Of Ilium's fall. When suddenly there
shone
The gleaming torches of the wedding
march;
And, as the bride's attendant, Helen
came
With drooping head. Whereat the Tro-
jans prayed:
"Oh, may Hermione[24] be wed like this,
With bloody rites; like this may Helena
Return unto her lord." Then numbing
dread
Seized Greeks and Trojans all, as they
beheld
The maid. She walked with downcast,
modest eyes,
But on her face a wondrous beauty
glowed
In flaming splendor, as the setting sun
Lights up the sky with beams more

beautiful,
When day hangs doubtful on the edge
of night.
All gazed in wonder. Some her beauty
moved,
And some her tender age and hapless
fate;
But all, her dauntless courage in the
face
Of death. Behind the maid grim Pyr-
rhus came;
And as they looked, the souls of all
were filled
With quaking terror, pity, and amaze.
But when she reached the summit of
the mound
And stood upon the lofty sepulcher,
Still with unfaltering step the maid ad-
vanced.
And now she turned her to the stroke
of death
With eyes so fierce and fearless that she
smote
The hearts of all, and, wondrous prod-
igy,
E'en Pyrrhus' bloody hand was slow to
strike.
But soon, his right hand lifted to the
stroke,
He drove the weapon deep within her
breast;
And straight from that deep wound the
blood burst forth
In sudden streams. But still the noble
maid
Did not give o'er her bold and haughty
mien,
Though in the act of death. For in her
fall
She smote the earth with angry vio-
lence,
As if to make it heavy for the dead.
Then flowed the tears of all. The Trojans groaned
With secret woe, since fear restrained
their tongues;
But openly the victors voiced their
grief.
And now the savage rite was done. The
blood
Stood not upon the ground, nor flowed
away;
But downward all its ruddy stream was
sucked,
As if the tomb were thirsty for the
draught.

HECUBA. Now go, ye Greeks, and seek
  your homes in peace.
With spreading sails your fleet in safety
  now
May cleave the welcome sea; the maid
  and boy
Are slain, the war is done. Oh, whither
  now
Shall I betake me in my wretchedness?
Where spend this hateful remnant of
  my life?
My daughter or my grandson shall I
  mourn,
My husband, country—or myself
  alone?
O death, my sole desire, for boys and
  maids
Thou com'st with hurried step and sav-
  age mien;
But me alone of mortals dost thou
  fear
And shun; through all that dreadful
  night of Troy,
I sought thee 'midst the swords and
  blazing brands,
But all in vain my search. No cruel
  foe,
Nor crumbling wall, nor blazing fire,
  could give
The death I sought. And yet how near
  I stood
To agèd Priam's side when he was
  slain!
MESSENGER. Ye captives, haste you to
  the winding shore;
The sails are spread, our long delay is
  o'er.

1. The walls of Troy were built by Neptune and Apollo.
2. One of the founders of Troy.
3. Cassandra, whose prophecies were cursed by Apollo never to be believed.
4. Paris, Hecuba's and Priam's son, doomed before birth to destroy his native land.
5. Ulysses.
6. Diomede.
7. The one who deceived the Trojans regarding the wooden horse.
8. Site of the judgment of Paris.
9. Paris, when he abducted Helen.
10. Recalling how the Greek forces were becalmed at Aulis until the gods were appeased by the sacrifice of Iphigenia.
11. Achilles' mother was Thetis, a sea-goddess.
12. Sea-gods.
13. Iphigenia (see note 10) was Agamemnon's daughter.
14. Pyrrhus was the illegitimate son of Achilles and Deidamia, daughter of the king of the island of Scyros.
15. An insulting reference to the bloody vengeance undertaken by Atreus, Agamemnon's father, against his brother Thyestes.
16. A reminder that Iphigenia had been sacrificed in order for the Greeks to get to Troy (see note 10).
17. Patroclus fought in disguise in Achilles' armor and was slain by Hector.
18. Another reference to Agamemnon's sacrifice of Iphigenia.
19. Penthesilea, queen of the Amazons.
20. A female worshiper of Bacchus who, in her religious frenzy, could feel no pain.
21. Ulysses' father.
22. An Egyptian king who practiced human sacrifice.
23. Diomedes, who fed human flesh to his horses.
24. Daughter of Helen and Menelaus.

Abraham

Hrotsvitha

After the time of Seneca, one must leap a thousand years to find the name of the next European playwright whose works are available for modern production. The latter days of the Roman Empire were gaudy with theatrical spectacle, but no drama of enduring merit was written. During the Dark Ages, theatrical activity was severely curtailed in Europe (as were almost all cultural or artistic pursuits), and whatever may have been written by way of drama has not been preserved. In the tenth century, however, in an obscure convent in northern Germany, there dwelt a nun who was interested in playwriting, and whose six plays have been preserved as the earliest known examples of postclassical drama.

Little is known of the life of Hrotsvitha beyond what can be inferred from her prefaces to her poems and plays. It appears that she was born around 935, probably to a family of some means and social position. She entered the Benedictine convent of Gandersheim, a few miles south of Hannover, when she was twenty-three years old, and presumably died there sometime between 970 and 1000. The monasteries and abbeys were the centers of classical learning in the Middle Ages, and Hrotsvitha was well educated under the tutelage of the Abbess Gerberga, who was of royal blood and able to wield great influence in northern Germany. Hrotsvitha prepared, presumably in her own hand, a manuscript containing six plays and a number of poems (including a poetic history of her convent) which was deposited among the convent archives. This document was discovered in 1492 or 1493 by Conrad Celtes, a German poet and scholar who was so charmed by Hrotsvitha's work that he published it in 1501. Hrotsvitha's original manuscript is in a library in Munich; it is the oldest autograph play script in the world.

Latin was the language of educated people throughout Europe in the Middle Ages, and the Latin classics (as well as the Bible in Latin) the textbooks for that education. Thus, Hrotsvitha wrote in Latin, she read the ancients in Latin, and, if her plays were performed, they were performed in Latin. There is no definite record of production, but there is evidence of public performances and declamations at Gandersheim even before Hrotsvitha's time, and internal evidence from her manuscripts certainly makes production altogether likely. She may very well not have been familiar with the works of the Greek playwrights, but with the Romans she was quite enamored. In a preface, she writes specifically of her fascination with Terence and states that she has imitated his forms while attempting to expurgate his content. Pagan subjects and pagan emotions were anathema for Hrotsvitha, but she was not so puritanical as to deny the beauty and skill with which pagan authors could express their ideas.

Hrotsvitha's purposes were determinedly Christian. She wished to glorify God by transmitting stories of martyrs and saints, to edify readers and audiences by the examples of those who overcame temptation, mortified the flesh, and exalted the spirit. For her, chastity was the supreme female virtue, and she had readily at hand the accumulated stories of some 900 years of Christian history upon which to draw for her subject matter. She wrote in a rhythmic prose that approximated Terence's poetic style and followed Terence further in attempting to use her stories to provoke thoughtful consideration of thematic content. That she is far more heavy-handed than Terence in this regard is owing at least as much to the different age in which she lived as it is to her lesser talent. All of her plays are moralizing, simplistic, and austere, but they exhibit a stark medieval beauty that can more than redeem them for some modern audiences. Besides *Abraham*, Hrotsvitha's plays are *Gallicanus*, *Dulcitius*, *Callimachus*, *Paphnutius*, and *Sapientia*. Some of these make more use of humor than does *Abraham*, but *Abraham* exhibits the clearest story line and is widely regarded as her best work. It will serve well to illustrate the others.

Abraham is based on a fourth-century story from the life of Saint Abraham. Although Abraham is the protagonist of the play, it is clearly Mary who generates the most interest and who is a tenderly drawn character. Throughout her work, Hrotsvitha displays an understanding and compassion for fallen women and for the lures of the flesh that may seem somewhat surprising in an author so devoted to their opposites. Even as a seven-year-old child at the opening of the play, Mary is seen to be subject to both spiritual and temporal yearnings, and it is this interplay of forces in her that gives the play special interest. When, after ten years of training, Mary falls to sin and leaves her cell, it is especially noteworthy that Abraham seeks and finally finds her not in a spirit of wrath or chastisement, but of love. His confrontation scene with Mary compares favorably with those written by a great many later writers, who have found the redemption of a fallen woman an appropriate subject for melodrama and bathos. Abraham's appeal, however, is not to authority or to reproach, but simply to love, and Mary's tender repentance rings true even across centuries of cynicism. As the play ends, Mary has returned penitently to the life-style that Hrotsvitha clearly believed was best and truest, and the audience may assume that another soul has been saved.

It is easy to find fault with so naive a drama. The emotions are certainly simplistic, the theology childlike, and the dramatic structure awkward. Ephrem is an uncomfortable foil asking the right questions for easy exposition, and the lesser characters are not developed at all. As the drama reemerged from the roots of religious impulse after a millennium of dormancy, and as classical art and learning first began to mingle with medieval ingenuousness, Hrotsvitha's simple play provides an important landmark. There is no way to know whether other, even earlier scholars may have written and produced plays in a similar vein, but, in the absence of any evidence of such works, Hrotsvitha's plays are the beginning point for a new millennium of theatrical achievement.

Abraham

Translated by Christopher St. John

ARGUMENT: The fall and repentance of Mary, the niece of the hermit Abraham, who, after she has spent twenty years in the religious life as a solitary, abandons it in despair, and, returning to the world, does not shrink from becoming a harlot. But two years later Abraham, in the disguise of a lover, seeks her out and reclaims her. For twenty years she does penance for her sins with many tears, fastings, vigils, and prayers.

Characters
Abraham
Ephrem
Mary
A Friend to Abraham
An Inn-keeper

Scene 1

ABRAHAM. Brother Ephrem, my dear comrade in the hermit life, may I speak to you now, or shall I wait until you have finished your divine praises?

EPHREM. And what can you have to say to me which is not praise of Him Who said: "Where two or three are gathered together in My Name, I am with them"?

ABRAHAM. I have not come to speak of anything which He would not like to hear.

EPHREM. I am sure of it. So speak at once.

ABRAHAM. It concerns a decision I have to make. I long for your approval.

EPHREM. We have one heart and one soul. We ought to agree.

ABRAHAM. I have a little niece of tender years. She has lost both her parents, and my affection for her has been deepened by compassion for her lonely state. I am in constant anxiety on her account.

EPHREM. Ought you who have triumphed over the world to be vexed by its cares!

ABRAHAM. My only care is her radiant beauty! What if it should one day be dimmed by sin.

EPHREM. No one can blame you for being anxious.

ABRAHAM. I hope not.

EPHREM. How old is she?

ABRAHAM. At the end of this year she will be eight.

EPHREM. She is very young.

ABRAHAM. That does not lessen my anxiety.

EPHREM. Where does she live?

ABRAHAM. At my hermitage now; for at the request of her other kinsfolk I have undertaken to bring her up. The fortune left her ought, I think, to be given to the poor.

EPHREM. A mind taught so early to despise temporal things should be fixed on heaven.

ABRAHAM. I desire with all my heart to see her the spouse of Christ and devoted entirely to His service.

EPHREM. A praiseworthy wish.

ABRAHAM. I was inspired by her name.

EPHREM. What is she called?

ABRAHAM. Mary.

EPHREM. Mary! Such a name ought to be adorned with the crown of virginity.

ABRAHAM. I have no fear that she will be unwilling, but we must be gentle.

EPHREM. Come, let us go, and impress on her that no life is so sweet and secure as the religious one.

Scene 2

ABRAHAM. Mary, my child by adoption, whom I love as my own soul! Listen to my advice as to a father's, and to Brother Ephrem's as that of a very wise man. Strive to imitate the chastity of the holy Virgin whose name you bear.

EPHREM. Child, would it not be a shame if you, who through the mystery of your name are called to mount to the stars where Mary the mother of God reigns, chose instead the low pleasures of the earth?

MARY. I know nothing about the mystery of my name, so how can I tell what you mean?

EPHREM. Mary, my child, means "star of the sea"—that star which rules the world and all the peoples in the world.

MARY. Why is it called the star of the sea?

EPHREM. Because it never sets, but shines always in the heavens to show mariners their right course.

MARY. And how can such a poor thing as I am—made out of slime, as my uncle says—shine like my name?

EPHREM. By keeping your body unspotted, and your mind pure and holy.

MARY. It would be too great an honour for any human being to become like the stars.

EPHREM. If you choose you can be as the angels of God, and when at last you cast off the burden of this mortal body they will be near you. With them you will pass through the air, and walk on the sky. With them you will sweep round the zodiac, and never slacken your steps until the Virgin's Son takes you in His arms in His mother's dazzling bridal room!

MARY. Who but an ass would think little of such happiness! So I choose to despise the things of earth, and deny myself now that I may enjoy it!

EPHREM. Out of the mouths of babes and sucklings! A childish heart, but a mature mind!

ABRAHAM. God be thanked for it!

EPHREM. Amen to that.

ABRAHAM. But though by God's grace she has been given the light, at her tender age she must be taught how to use it.

EPHREM. You are right.

ABRAHAM. I will build her a little cell with a narrow entrance near my hermitage. I can visit her there often, and through the window instruct her in the psalter and other pages of the divine law.

EPHREM. That is a good plan.

MARY. I put myself under your direction, Father Ephrem.

EPHREM. My daughter! May the Heavenly Bridegroom to Whom you have given yourself in the tender bud of your youth shield you from the wiles of the devil!

Scene 3

ABRAHAM. Brother Ephrem, Brother Ephrem! When anything happens, good or bad, it is to you I turn. It is your counsel I seek. Do not turn your face away, brother—do not be impatient, but help me.

EPHREM. Abraham, Abraham, what has come to you? What is the cause of this immoderate grief? Ought a hermit to weep and groan after the manner of the world?

ABRAHAM. Was any hermit ever so stricken? I cannot bear my sorrow.

EPHREM. Brother, no more of this. To the point; what has happened?

ABRAHAM. Mary! Mary! my adopted child! Mary, whom I cared for so lovingly and taught with all my skill for ten years! Mary—

EPHREM. Well, what is it?

ABRAHAM. Oh God! She is lost!

EPHREM. Lost? What do you mean?

ABRAHAM. Most miserably. Afterwards she ran away.

EPHREM. But by what wiles did the ancient enemy bring about her undoing?

ABRAHAM. By the wiles of false love. Dressed in a monk's habit, the hypocrite went to see her often. He succeeded in making the poor ignorant child love him. She leapt from the window of her cell for an evil deed.

EPHREM. I shudder as I listen to you.

ABRAHAM. When the unhappy girl knew that she was ruined, she beat her breast and dug her nails into her face. She tore her garments, pulled out her hair. Her despairing cries were terrible to hear.

EPHREM. I am not surprised. For such a fall a whole fountain of tears should rise.

ABRAHAM. She moaned out that she could never be the same—

EPHREM. Poor, miserable girl!

ABRAHAM. And reproached herself for having forgotten our warning.

EPHREM. She might well do so.

ABRAHAM. She cried that all her vigils, prayers, and fasts had been thrown away.

EPHREM. If she perseveres in this penitence she will be saved.

ABRAHAM. She has not persevered. She has added worse to her evil deed.

EPHREM. Oh, this moves me to the depths of my heart!

ABRAHAM. After all these tears and lamentations she was overcome by remorse, and fell headlong into the abyss of despair.

EPHREM. A bitter business!

ABRAHAM. She despaired of being able to win pardon, and resolved to go back to the world and its vanities.

EPHREM. I cannot remember when the devil could boast of such a triumph over the hermits.

ABRAHAM. Now we are at the mercy of the demons.

EPHREM. I marvel that she could have escaped without your knowledge.

ABRAHAM. If I had not been so blind! I ought to have paid more heed to that terrible vision. Yes, I see now that it was sent to warn me.

EPHREM. What vision?

ABRAHAM. I dreamed I was standing at the door of my cell, and that a huge dragon with a loathsome stench rushed violently towards me. I saw that the creature was attracted by a little white dove at my side. It pounced on the dove, devoured it, and vanished.

EPHREM. There is no doubt what this vision meant.

ABRAHAM. When I woke I turned over in my mind what I had seen, and took it as a sign of some persecution threatening the Church, through which many of the faithful would be drawn into error. I prostrated myself in prayer, and implored Him Who knows the future to enlighten me.

EPHREM. You did right.

ABRAHAM. On the third night after the vision, when for weariness I had fallen asleep, I saw the beast again, but now it was lying dead at my feet, and the dove was flying heavenwards safe and unhurt.

EPHREM. I am rejoiced to hear this, for to my thinking it means that some day Mary will return to you.

ABRAHAM. I was trying to get rid of the uneasiness with which the first vision had filled me by thinking of the second, when my little pupil in her cell came to my mind. I remembered, although at the time I was not alarmed, that for two days I had not heard her chanting the divine praises.

EPHREM. You were too tardy in noticing this.

ABRAHAM. I admit it. I went at once to her cell, and, knocking at the window, I called her again and again, "Mary! My child! Mary!"

EPHREM. You called in vain?

ABRAHAM. "Mary," I said. "Mary, my child, what is wrong? Why are you not saying your office?" It was only when I did not hear the faintest sound that I suspected.

EPHREM. What did you do then?

ABRAHAM. When I could no longer doubt that she had gone, I was struck with fear to my very bowels. I trembled in every limb.

EPHREM. I do not wonder, since I, hearing of it, find myself trembling all over.

ABRAHAM. Then I wept and cried out to the empty air, "What wolf has seized my lamb? What thief has stolen my little daughter?"

EPHREM. You had good cause to

weep! To lose her whom you had cherished so tenderly!

ABRAHAM. At last some people came up who knew what had happened. From them I learned that she had gone back to the world.

EPHREM. Where is she now?

ABRAHAM. No one knows.

EPHREM. What is to be done?

ABRAHAM. I have a faithful friend, who is searching all the cities and towns in the country. He says he will never give up until he finds her.

EPHREM. And if he finds her—what then?

ABRAHAM. Then I shall change these clothes, and in the guise of a worldling seek her out. It may be that she will heed what I say, and even after this shipwreck turn again to the harbour of her innocence and peace.

EPHREM. And suppose that in the world they offer you flesh meat and wine?

ABRAHAM. If they do, I shall not refuse; otherwise I might be recognized.

EPHREM. No one will blame you, brother. It will be but praiseworthy discretion on your part to loosen the bridle of strict observance for the sake of bringing back a soul.

ABRAHAM. I am the more eager to try now I know you approve.

EPHREM. He Who knows the secret places of the heart can tell with what motive every action is done. That scrupulous and fair Judge will not condemn a man for relaxing our strict rule for a time and descending to the level of weaker mortals if by so doing he can make more sure of rescuing an errant soul.

ABRAHAM. Help me with your prayers. Pray that I may not be caught in the snares of the devil.

EPHREM. May He Who is supreme good itself, without Whom no good thing can be done, bless your enterprise and bring it to a happy end!

Scene 4

ABRAHAM. Can that be my friend who two years ago went to search for Mary?

Yes, it is he!

FRIEND. Good-day, venerable father.

ABRAHAM. Good-day, dear friend. I have waited so long for you. Of late I had begun to despair.

FRIEND. Forgive me, father. I delayed my return because I did not wish to mock you with doubtful and unreliable news. As soon as I had discovered the truth I lost no time.

ABRAHAM. You have seen Mary?

FRIEND. I have seen her.

ABRAHAM. Where is she? Come, sir, speak! Tell me where.

FRIEND. It goes to my heart to tell you.

ABRAHAM. Speak—I implore you.

FRIEND. She lives in the house of a man who trades in the love of young girls like her. A profitable business, for every day he makes a large sum of money out of her lovers.

ABRAHAM. Her lovers? Mary's lovers?

FRIEND. Yes.

ABRAHAM. Who are they?

FRIEND. There are plenty of them.

ABRAHAM. Good Jesu, what is this monstrous thing I hear? Do they say that she, whom I brought up to be Thy bride, gives herself to strange lovers?

FRIEND. It comes naturally to harlots.

ABRAHAM. If you are my friend, get me a saddlehorse somewhere and a soldier's dress. I am going to get into that place as a lover.

FRIEND. Father, mine are at your service.

ABRAHAM. And I must borrow a felt hat to cover my tonsure.

FRIEND. That is most necessary, if you do not want to be recognized.

ABRAHAM. I have one gold piece. Should I take it to give this man?

FRIEND. You should, for otherwise he will never let you see Mary.

Scene 5

ABRAHAM. Good-day, friend.

INN-KEEPER. Who's there? Good-day, Sir. Come in!

ABRAHAM. Have you a bed for a

traveller who wants to spend a night here?

INN-KEEPER. Why certainly! I never turn anyone away.

ABRAHAM. I am glad of it.

INN-KEEPER. Come in then, and I will order supper for you.

ABRAHAM. I owe you thanks for this kind welcome, but I have a greater favour to ask.

INN-KEEPER. Ask what you like. I will do my best for you.

ABRAHAM. Accept this small present. May the beautiful girl who, I am told, lives here, have supper with me?

INN-KEEPER. Why should *you* wish to see her?

ABRAHAM. It would give me much pleasure. I have heard so much talk of her beauty.

INN-KEEPER. Whoever has spoken to you of her has told only the truth. It would be hard to find a finer wench.

ABRAHAM. I am in love with her already.

INN-KEEPER. It's queer that an old man like you should dangle after a young girl.

ABRAHAM. I swear I came here on purpose to feast my eyes on her.

Scene 6

INN-KEEPER. Mary, come here! Come along now and show off your charms to this young innocent!

MARY. I am coming.

ABRAHAM. Oh, mind, be constant! Tears, do not fall! Must I look on her whom I brought up in the desert, decked out with a harlot's face? Yes, I must hide what is in my heart. I must strive not to weep, and smile though my heart is breaking.

INN-KEEPER. Luck comes your way, Mary! Not only do young gallants of your own age flock to your arms, but even the wise and venerable!

MARY. It is all one to me. It is my business to love those who love me.

ABRAHAM. Come nearer, Mary, and give me a kiss.

MARY. I will give you more than a kiss. I will take your head in my arms and stroke your neck.

ABRAHAM. Yes, like that!

MARY. What does this mean? What is this lovely fragrance. So clean, so sweet. It reminds me of the time when I was good.

ABRAHAM. On with the mask! Chatter, make lewd jests like an idle boy! She must not recognize me, or for very shame she may fly from me.

MARY. Wretch that I am! To what have I fallen! In what pit am I sunk!

ABRAHAM. You forget where you are! Do men come here to see you cry!

INN-KEEPER. What's the matter, Lady Mary? Why are you in the dumps? You have lived here two years, and never before have I seen a tear, never heard a sigh or a word of complaint.

MARY. Oh, that I had died three years ago before I came to this!

ABRAHAM. I came here to make love to you, not to weep with you over your sins.

MARY. A little thing moved me, and I spoke foolishly. It is nothing. Come, let us eat and drink and be merry, for, as you say, this is not the place to think of one's sins.

ABRAHAM. I have eaten and drunk enough, thanks to your good table, Sir. Now by your leave I will go to bed. My tired limbs need a rest.

INN-KEEPER. As you please.

MARY. Get up my lord. I will take you to bed.

ABRAHAM. I hope so. I would not go at all unless you came with me.

Scene 7

MARY. Look! How do you like this room? A handsome bed, isn't it? Those trappings cost a lot of money. Sit down and I will take off your shoes. You seem tired.

ABRAHAM. First bolt the door. Someone may come in.

MARY. Have no fear. I have seen to that.

ABRAHAM. The time has come for me

to show my shaven head, and make myself known! Oh, my daughter! Oh, Mary, you who are part of my soul! Look at me. Do you not know me? Do you not know the old man who cherished you with a father's love, and wedded you to the Son of the King of Heaven?

MARY. God, what shall I do! It is my father and master Abraham!

ABRAHAM. What has come to you, daughter?

MARY. Oh, misery!

ABRAHAM. Who deceived you? Who led you astray?

MARY. Who deceived our first parents?

ABRAHAM. Have you forgotten that once you lived like an angel on earth!

MARY. All that is over.

ABRAHAM. What has become of your virginal modesty? Your beautiful purity?

MARY. Lost. Gone!

ABRAHAM. Oh, Mary, think what you have thrown away! Think what a reward you had earned by your fasting, and prayers, and vigils. What can they avail you now! You have hurled yourself from heavenly heights into the depths of hell!

MARY. Oh God, I know it!

ABRAHAM. Could you not trust me? Why did you desert me? Why did you not tell me of your fall? Then dear brother Ephrem and I could have done a worthy penance.

MARY. Once I had committed that sin, and was defiled, how could I dare come near you who are so holy?

ABRAHAM. Oh, Mary, has anyone ever lived on earth without sin except the Virgin's Son?

MARY. No one, I know.

ABRAHAM. It is human to sin, but it is devilish to remain in sin. Who can be justly condemned? Not those who fall suddenly, but those who refuse to rise quickly.

MARY. Wretched, miserable creature that I am!

ABRAHAM. Why have you thrown yourself down there? Why do you lie on the ground without moving or speaking? Get up, Mary! Get up, my child, and listen to me!

MARY. No! no! I am afraid. I cannot

bear your reproaches.

ABRAHAM. Remember how I love you, and you will not be afraid.

MARY. It is useless. I cannot.

ABRAHAM. What but love for you could have made me leave the desert and relax the strict observance of our rule? What but love could have made me, a true hermit, come into the city and mix with the lascivious crowd? It is for your sake that these lips have learned to utter light, foolish words, so that I might not be known! Oh, Mary, why do you turn away your face from me and gaze upon the ground? Why do you scorn to answer and tell me what is in your mind.

MARY. It is the thought of my sins which crushes me. I dare not look at you; I am not fit to speak to you.

ABRAHAM. My little one, have no fear. Oh, do not despair! Rise from this abyss of desperation and grapple God to your soul!

MARY. No, no! My sins are too great. They weigh me down.

ABRAHAM. The mercy of heaven is greater than you or your sins. Let your sadness be dispersed by its glorious beams. Oh, Mary, do not let apathy prevent your seizing the moment for repentance. It matters not how wickedness has flourished. Divine grace can flourish still more abundantly!

MARY. If there were the smallest hope of forgiveness, surely I should not shrink from doing penance.

ABRAHAM. Have you no pity for me? I have sought you out with so much pain and weariness! Oh shake off this despair which we are taught is the most terrible of all sins. Despair of God's mercy—for that alone there is no forgiveness. Sin can no more embitter His sweet mercy than a spark from a flint can set the ocean on fire.

MARY. I know that God's mercy is great, but when I think how greatly I have sinned, I cannot believe any penance can make amends.

ABRAHAM. I will take your sins on me. Only come back and take up your life again as if you had never left it.

MARY. I do not want to oppose you. What you tell me to do I will do with all my heart.

ABRAHAM. My daughter lives again! I

have found my lost lamb and she is dearer to me than ever.

MARY. I have a few possessions here—a little gold and some clothes. What ought I to do with them?

ABRAHAM. What came to you through sin, with sin must be left behind.

MARY. Could it not be given to the poor, or sold for an offering at the holy altar?

ABRAHAM. The price of sin is not an acceptable offering to God.

MARY. Then I will not trouble any more about my possessions.

ABRAHAM. Look! The dawn! It is growing light. Let us go.

MARY. You go first, dearest father, like the good shepherd leading the lost lamb that has been found. The lamb will follow in your steps.

ABRAHAM. Not so! I am going on foot, but you—you shall have a horse so that the stony road shall not hurt your delicate feet.

MARY. Oh, let me never forget this tenderness! Let me try all my life to thank you! I was not worth pity, yet you have shown me no harshness; you have led me to repent not by threats but by gentleness and love.

ABRAHAM. I ask only one thing, Mary. Be faithful to God for the rest of your life.

MARY. With all my strength I will persevere, and though my flesh may fail, my spirit never will.

ABRAHAM. You must serve God with as much energy as you have served the world.

MARY. If His will is made perfect in me it will be because of your merits.

ABRAHAM. Come, let us hasten on our way.

MARY. Yes, let us set out at once. I would not stay here another moment.

Scene 8

ABRAHAM. Courage, Mary! You see how swiftly we have made the difficult and toilsome journey.

MARY. Everything is easy when we put our hearts into it.

ABRAHAM. There is your deserted little cell.

MARY. God help me! It was the witness of my sin. I dare not go there.

ABRAHAM. It is natural you should dread the place where the enemy triumphed.

MARY. Where, then, am I to do penance?

ABRAHAM. Go into the inner cell. There you will be safe from the wiles of the serpent.

MARY. Most gladly as it is your wish.

ABRAHAM. Now I must go to my good friend Ephrem. He alone mourned with me when you were lost, and he must rejoice with me now that you have been found.

MARY. Of course.

Scene 9

EPHREM. Well, brother! If I am not mistaken, you bring good news.

ABRAHAM. The best in the world.

EPHREM. You have found your lost lamb?

ABRAHAM. I have, and, rejoicing, have brought her back to the fold.

EPHREM. Truly this is the work of divine grace.

ABRAHAM. That is certain.

EPHREM. How is she spending her days? I should like to know how you have ordered her life. What does she do?

ABRAHAM. All that I tell her.

EPHREM. That is well.

ABRAHAM. Nothing is too difficult for her—nothing too hard. She is ready to endure anything.

EPHREM. That is better.

ABRAHAM. She wears a hair shirt, and subdues her flesh with continual vigils and fasts. She is making the poor frail body obey the spirit by the most rigorous discipline.

EPHREM. Only through such a severe penance can the stains left by the pleasures of the flesh be washed away.

ABRAHAM. Those who hear her sobs are cut to the heart, and the tale of her repentance has turned many from their sins.

EPHREM. It is often so.

ABRAHAM. She prays continually for the men who through her were tempted to sin, and begs that she who was their ruin may be their salvation.

EPHREM. It is right that she should do this.

ABRAHAM. She strives to make her life as beautiful as for a time it was hideous.

EPHREM. I rejoice at what you tell me. To the depths of my heart.

ABRAHAM. And with us rejoice phalanxes of angels, praising the Lord for the conversion of a sinner.

EPHREM. Over whom, we are told, there is more joy in heaven than over the just man who needs no penance.

ABRAHAM. The more glory to Him, because there seemed no hope on earth that she could be saved.

EPHREM. Let us sing a song of thanksgiving—let us glorify the only begotten Son of God, Who of His love and mercy will not let them perish whom He redeemed with His holy blood.

ABRAHAM. To Him be honour, glory, and praise through infinite ages. Amen.

The Second Shepherds' Play, Everyman, *and* Pierre Pathelin

Authors Unknown

Notwithstanding the notable work done by Hrotsvitha, the typical pattern of development of the European theater in the Middle Ages was largely uninfluenced by classical forebears. Only as the Renaissance brought the rediscovery of the Greek and Roman authors did their influence begin to mingle in a meaningful way with that of the medieval drama which had emerged from religious worship. It is not within the scope of this volume to trace this emergence in detail, but three examples can serve to illustrate the types of work that were being done. Furthermore, although thousands of such plays were written and hundreds have survived for modern study, the vast majority are only of antiquarian interest. Only a few are of such extraordinary merit that they regularly are produced in modern theatres and demonstrate great appeal for modern audiences. The best among them are offered here.

In the centuries following the fall of the Roman Empire, the Roman Catholic Church gained almost universal acceptance throughout Europe, and the Catholic Mass was itself a vibrantly theatrical celebration. Into the wordless sequences of the Mass, the priests began to insert, as early as the ninth century, additional sections of dialogue, or *tropes*, which dramatized for the largely illiterate congregations the story being told. First in the Easter Mass and then in other services, these dramatizations of the life and works of Jesus, and later of Old Testament stories as well, gradually became of greater and greater interest. Originally in Latin, these short plays were later translated into the vernacular and performed in the sanctuary, then later on the church steps, and finally, as the plays became more elaborate and more secular, in the market squares. In 1210, a papal edict forbade the clergy to perform on a public stage, and, although the plays remained religious in nature, they passed into the control of the laity. In many cases the trade guilds accepted responsibility for producing what soon became vast cycles of these religious plays, with each guild dealing with a single story segment. In performances that might last for several days and cover the entire Bible from creation to the Apocalypse, with hundreds of actors and elaborate technical effects, a single guild's contribution might be the performance of a single episode, either at one "station" around the market square (as was typical on the Continent) or upon a pageant wagon which, in English towns, was moved from street corner to street corner in sequence with dozens of other such wagons.

Several virtually complete cycles and many individual plays of this type have survived in manuscript form. In most cases the authors are unknown, and there is evidence that the plays were written by gradual accrual over a number of years, with many hands involved in the form that is known today. The plays based on biblical stories were known as "mystery" plays, whereas those on nonbiblical religious subjects (primarily the lives of the saints) were called "miracle" plays. Some authorities blur even this distinction and use the terms "mystery" and "miracle" interchangeably. Unquestionably the finest mystery play in English, and perhaps the best in any language, is the one known as the *Second Shepherds' Play*.

The *Second Shepherds' Play* is taken from the so-called Wakefield cycle of mystery plays, a thirty-two play series the manuscript of which dates from the mid-fifteenth century and was apparently written for production in Wakefield, England. Some of these plays were evidently quite old when the manuscript was prepared, others were borrowed from the cycles of nearby towns, and a few were freshly written, or at least revised, by an unknown author of the mid-fifteenth century who is referred to by scholars as the Wakefield Master. The Wakefield cycle contains two plays about the announcement to the shepherds of Jesus' birth; the second of these is known as the *Second Shepherds' Play*, and is one of the plays evidencing the genius of the Wakefield Master.

The play is a wonderfully engaging blend of medieval naiveté and theatrical sophistication. The characters are obviously English medieval countrymen rather than Judean shepherds of a millennium and a half earlier, yet they are so humanly developed as appealing comic rogues that one does not ask for more. Mak and Gill are brilliantly conceived and developed, and even the other three shepherds are given traits that differentiate them from one another. When this extraordinary trio leaves its anachronistic concerns and appears at the manger of the Christ child, the engaging simplicity with which they present themselves, offering the newborn infant a tennis ball and a bob of cherries, is good enough aesthetically to transcend time, distance, and the usual amenities of theatrical structure and to provide the play with a reasonably unified plot almost despite itself. One does not need to take a patronizing attitude toward its primitive qualities to recognize in the *Second Shepherds' Play* a high order of dramatic art.

Although the mystery and miracle plays were religious in nature, they cannot be said to have explored thematic issues particularly. Even so rich a work as the *Second Shepherds' Play* presents its story in a rather straightforward fashion without provoking depth of thought. Perhaps to meet this need, there developed in the late Middle Ages a third type of religious play, the morality. Morality plays did not tell stories about real people at all, but rather presented abstractions in personified form in order to teach a lesson. As was the case with the mystery and miracle plays, there were hundreds of moralities written, but far and away the best of them is *Everyman*. As the title suggests, the play's protagonist represents all of humanity, and as Everyman faces death and finds which of his earthly qualities and pursuits can come to his aid in his moment of final judgment, a definite lesson is taught. One factor that lifts *Everyman* above the general run of morality plays is that the lesson is less simplistic than most. It clearly reflects Roman Catholic doctrine, but does so in a nondogmatic way that raises nearly as many questions as it answers. Despite its surface layer of simplistic medieval theology, *Everyman* is an extraordinarily profound and thought-provoking work.

Everyman has survived in both an English and a Dutch version, and it cannot be said with certainty where the play originated. One widely held theory is that both these surviving plays are based on an earlier English version, now lost. Whatever may be the truth of this matter, the play was widely performed throughout Europe and has regained popularity in the twentieth century, with a great many productions in Europe and America. Its structure shows a well-thought-out plan, with a much more complexly worked-out action than the typical mystery or miracle play exhibited. This action can be seen to have four distinct parts: in the first part, Everyman receives a visit from Death; in the second, he seeks companions for his journey among the values that corporal man holds dear, and is rejected; in the third, he seeks companions among more spiritual values, and is accepted; and in the fourth, even these companions finally abandon him as he actually enters the grave, a saved soul. Each of the characters in the play is personified with more than passing interest, so that, even though they represent abstractions, they have theatrical interest as human beings too. Thus, Fellowship, who will join Everyman in wine, women, and song, but will not help in time of trouble, and Cousin, who offers the excuse that he has a cramp in his toe, are all too recognizably human. Everyman, too, develops as a character throughout the play, and one feels genuine compassion and understanding by the time of his demise. The rough-hewn scheme in *Everyman*, like that in the *Second Shepherds' Play*, is far from great poetry, but does bring a special aura of primitive simplicity that adds much to the play. In short, *Everyman*, again, is a true masterpiece.

Throughout the Dark Ages there was a continuing tradition in Europe of comic entertainment in the form of jugglers, troubadours, clowns, and other such performers, and folk drama at least in a primitive form must surely have formed a part of their repertory. Still, there is no definite evidence of this activity until the twelfth or thirteenth century, after which there developed a large body of farcical drama which existed alongside the mystery, miracle, and morality plays. By far the best of these medieval farces is *The Farce of Master Pierre Pathelin*, a play probably written in Paris around 1465. It is amusing to suppose that the playwright might have been a lawyer, but in fact nothing definite is known as to who he was. That he created a comic masterpiece, however, is attested to not only by continued interest in and production of the play in the twentieth century, but also by many contemporary references to it in the fifteenth century and later. Several phrases from the dialogue crop up in other literary works and even in legal documents, and the entire play was printed (thus preserving it for the future) within a very few years after its writing—a most unusual occurrence.

The reasons for the play's success both then and now are not hard to find. The plot, the primary consideration in any farce, is very cleverly articulated, with each incident logically growing out of those which go before it. Even the courtroom scene, which at first may appear to represent a shift in focus, is connected to the earlier gulling of the cloth merchant by the latter's befuddled inability to keep the two incidents straight during the trial, and each of the play's principal scenes is so genuinely funny as to keep the laughter growing throughout the play. The characters are well thought out and developed as believable citizens of medieval France, yet they also have those comic peculiarities that farce usually employs for getting laughs out of character relationships. Pathelin is a clever rogue in the best comic tradition, his wife, Guillemette, is a nag, William Joceaume is greedy, Thibault Aignelet is a simpleton who nevertheless outwits Pathelin at the end, and the judge is a fool. These qualities do not completely describe each character, but they provide a point of departure for the comic incongruity of each. The play's original verse is rough and simple, as the translation tries to reflect, but captures the medieval spirit in much the same fashion as did the verse in the *Second Shepherds' Play* or *Everyman*. To sum up, *The Farce of Master Pierre Pathelin* is as neat and effective a farce as may be found anywhere in dramatic literature.

The medieval period in Europe, up to the Renaissance, was a period rich in theatrical activity, but short on enduring play scripts. The examples offered here cannot in that sense be accepted as typical, for the vast majority of the surviving plays are of limited or scholarly interest. In another way, however, the very excellence of these attests to the spirit of the age and to the rediscovery of theatrical art as a means of expression. Upon the foundation established by the mystery, miracle, and morality plays, as well as the rich tradition of folk farces, there was soon to be built the magnificent structure of Renaissance European drama.

N.B. The footnotes in *Pierre Pathelin* were provided by the translator.

The Second Shepherds' Play

Adapted from a translation by
Clarence Griffin Child

Characters

Coll ⎫
Gob ⎬ *Shepherds*
Daw ⎪
Mak ⎭
Gill, Mak's wife
Angel
Mary

[Enter COLL.*]* COLL. Lord, but this
   weather is cold, and I am ill
   wrapped!
Nigh dazed, were the truth told, so
   long have I napped;
My legs under me fold; my fingers are
   chapped.
With such like I don't hold, for I am all
   lapped
     In sorrow.
In storms and tempest,
Now in the east, now in the west,
Woe is him has never rest
     Midday nor morrow!

But we simple shepherds that walk on
   the moor,
In faith we're nigh at hand to be put
   out of door.
No wonder, as it doth stand, if we be
   poor,
For the best of our land lies fallow as
   the floor,
     As ye ken.

We're so burdened and banned,
Overtaxed and unmanned,
We're made tame to the hand
     Of these gentry men.

Thus they rob us of our rest, our Lady
   them harry!
These men bound to their lords' be-
   hest, they make the plough tarry;
What men say is for the best, we find
   the contrary—
Thus are husbandmen oppressed, in
   point to miscarry,
     In life.
Thus hold they us under
And from comfort sunder.
It were great wonder,
     If ever we should thrive.

For if a man may get an embroidered
   sleeve or a brooch nowadays,
Woe is him that may him grieve or a
   word in answer says!
No blame may he receive, whatever
   pride he displays;
And yet may no man believe one word
   that he says,
     Not a letter.
His daily needs are gained
By boasts and bragging feigned,
And in all he's maintained
     By men that are greater.

Proud shall come a swain as a peacock
   may go,
He must borrow my wain, my plough
   also,
Then I am full fain to grant it ere he
   go.
Thus live we in pain, anger, and woe
     By night and day!
He must have it, if he choose,
Though I should it lose,

I were better hanged than refuse,
    Or once say him nay!

It does me good as I walk thus alone
Of this world for to talk and to make
    my moan.
To my sheep will I stalk, and hearken
    anon,
There wait on a ridge, or sit on a stone,
    Full soon.
For I think, pardie,
True men if they be,
We shall have company,
    Ere it be noon. [Enter GIB.]
GIB. Ben'cite[1] and Dominus! What may
    this mean?
Why fares the world thus! The like of-
    ten we've seen!
Lord but it is spiteful and grievous, this
    weather so keen!
And the frost so hideous—it waters
    mine een!
        That's no lie!
Now in dry, now in wet,
Now in snow, now in sleet,
When my shoes freeze to my feet,
    It's not all easy!

But so far as I ken, wherever I go,
We poor wedded men suffer much
    woe,
We have sorrow once and again, it be-
    falls oft so.
Poor Capel, our hen, both to and fro
    She cackles,
But if she begins to croak,
To grumble or cluck,
Then woe be to our cock,
    For he is in the shackles!

These men that are wed have not all
    their will;
When they're hard put to it, they sigh
    mighty still;
God knows the life they are led is full
    hard and full ill,
Nor thereof in bower or bed may they
    speak their will,
        This tide.
My share I have found,
Know my lesson all round,
Woe is him that is bound,
    For he must it abide!

But now late in men's lives—such a
    marvel to me,

That I think my heart breaks such won-
    ders to see—
How that destiny drives that it should
    so be
That some men will have two wives and
    some men three
        In store.
Some are grieved that have any,
But I'll wager my penny
Woe is him that has many,
    For he feels sore!
But young men as to wooing, for God's
    sake that you bought,
Beware well of wedding, and hold well
    in thought,
"Had I known" is a thing that serves you
    nought.
Much silent sorrowing has a wedding
    home brought,
    And grief gives,
With many a sharp shower—
For thou mayest catch in an hour
What shall taste thee full sour
    As long as one lives!

For—if ever read I epistle!—I have one
    by my fire,
As sharp as a thistle, as rough as a
    briar,
She has brows like a bristle and a sour
    face by her;
If she had once wet her whistle, she
    might sing clearer and higher
        Her pater-noster;
She is as big as a whale,
She has a gallon of gall,—
By him that died for us all,
    I wish I had run till I had lost her!
COLL. Gib, look over the row! Like a
    deaf man you stand.
GIB. Yea, sluggard, the devil thy maw
    burn with his brand!
Didst see aught of Daw?
COLL. Yea, on the pasture land
I heard him blow just before; he comes
    nigh at hand
        Below there.
Stand still.
GIB. Why?
COLL. For he comes, hope I.
GIB. He'll catch us both with some lie
        Unless we beware. [Enter DAW, a boy
    employed by COLL.]
DAW. Christ's cross me speed and St.
    Nicholas!
Thereof in sooth I had need; it is worse

than it was.
Whoso hath knowledge, take heed, and
let the world pass,
You may never trust it, indeed—it's as
brittle as glass,
As it rangeth.
Never before fared this world so,
With marvels that greater grow,
Now in weal, now in woe,
And everything changeth.

There was never since Noah's flood
such floods seen,
Winds and rains so rude and storms so
keen;
Some stammered, some stood in doubt,
as I ween.
Now God turn all to good, I say as I
mean!
For ponder
How these floods all drown
Both in fields and in town,
And bear all down,
And that is a wonder!

We that walk of nights our cattle to
keep,
We see startling sights when other men
sleep. [*He catches sight of the others.*]
Yet my heart grows more light—I see
rascals a-peep.
You are two tall fellows—I will give my
sheep
A turn, below.
But my mood is ill-sent[2];
As I walk on this bent,[3]
I may lightly repent,
If I stub my toe.
Ah, Sir, God you save and my master
sweet!
A drink I crave, and somewhat to eat.

COLL. Christ's curse, my knave, thou'rt
a lazy cheat!
GIB. Lo, the boy dares to rave! Wait till
later for meat,
We have eat it.
Ill thrift on thy pate!
Though the rogue came late,
Yet is he in state
To eat, could he get it.
DAW. That such servants as I, that toil
and sweat,
Eat our bread full dry gives me reason
to fret.
While our masters sleep, we sigh, weary
and wet,
Full late we come by our dinner and
drink, yet
Soon thereto
Our dame and sire,
When we've run in the mire,
Take a nip from our hire,
And pay slow as they care to.

But hear my oath, master, since you
find fault this way,
I shall do this hereafter: work to fit my
pay;
I'll do just so much, sir, and now and
then play,
For never yet supper in my stomach lay
In the fields.
But why dispute so?
Off with staff I can go.
"Easy bargain," men say,
"But a poor return yields."
COLL.Thou wert a fool, lad, for work to
go wooing
From a man that had but little for
spending.
GIB. Peace, boy, I say! No more jan-
gling,
Or I'll make thee full sad, by the
Heaven's King,
With thy load
Of pranks! Where are our sheep, boy?
Left lorn?[4]
DAW. Sir, this same day at morn,
I them left in the corn
Ere the cock crowed.

They have pasture good; they cannot
go wrong.
COLL. That is right. By the Rood, these
nights are long!
Ere we go now, I would someone gave
us a song.
GIB. So I thought as I stood, to beguile
us along.
DAW. I agree.
COLL. The tenor I'll try.
GIB. And I the treble so high.
DAW. Then the mean shall be I.
How ye chant now, let's see! [*They
sing. Enter* MAK, *wearing a cloak.*]
MAK. Now, Lord, by thy seven names'
spell, that made both moon and stars
on high,
Full more than I can tell, thy will for
me, Lord, lack I.
I am all at odds; nought goes well; that

oft doth my temper try.
Now would God I might in heaven
dwell, for there no children cry,
    So shrill.
COLL. Who is that pipes so poor?
MAK. Would God ye knew what I en-
dure!
COLL. Lo, a man that walks on the
    moor,
    And has not all his will!
GIB. Mak, whither dost speed? What
news do you bring?
DAW. Is he come? Then take heed each
one to his thing. [*He whips* MAK's *cloak
off him.*]
MAK. What! I am a yeoman—since
there's need I should tell you—of the
King,
That self-same, indeed messenger from
a great lording,
    And the like thereby.
Fie on you! Go hence
Out of my presence!
I must have reverence,
    And you ask "who am I!"
COLL. Why dress ye up so quaint? Mak,
ye do wrong!
GIB. Would you play the saint? For that
do you long?
DAW. I know the knave can feint, the
devil him hang!
MAK. I shall make complaint; you'll be
flogged ere long,
    At a word from me—
And tell your doings, forsooth!
COLL. But, Mak, is that truth?
Now take out that southern tooth[5]
    And stick it in a turd.
GIB. Mak, the devil be in your eye, ver-
ily! to a blow
    I'd fain treat you.
DAW. Mak, know you not me? By God,
I could beat you!
MAK. God keep you all three! Me
thought I had seen you—
    I greet you,
Ye are a fair company!
COLL. Oh, now you remember, you
cheat, you!
GIB. Shrew, jokes are cheap!
When thus late a man goes,
What will folk suppose?
You've a bad name, God knows,
    For stealing of sheep!
MAK. And true as steel am I, all men
know and say,

But a sickness I feel, verily, that grips
me hard, night and day.
My belly is all awry, it is out of play—
DAW. "Seldom doth the Devil lie dead
by the way—"[6]
MAK. Therefore
Full sore am I and ill,
Though I stand stone still;
I've not eat a needle
    This month and more.
COLL. How fares thy wife, by my hood,
how fares she, ask I?
MAK. Lies asprawl, by the Rood, lo, the
fire close by,
And a house-full of home-brew she
drinks full nigh—
Ill may speed any good thing that she
will try
    Else to do!—
Eats as fast as she can,
And each year that comes to man
She brings forth a brat, and
    Some years two.

But were I now kinder, d'ye hear, and
far richer in purse,
Still were I eaten clear out of house and
home, sirs.
And she's a foul-favored dear, see her
close, by God's curse!
No one knows or may hear, I trow, of a
worse,
    Not any!
Now will ye see what I proffer?—
To give all in my coffer,
Tomorrow next to offer
    Her funeral penny.[7]
GIB. Faith, so weary and worn is there
none in this shire.
I must sleep, were I shorn of a part of
my hire.
DAW. I'm naked, cold, and forlorn, and
would fain have a fire.
COLL. I'm clean spent, for, since morn,
I've run in the mire.
    Watch thou, do!
GIB. Nay, I'll lie down hereby,
For I must sleep, truly.
DAW. As good a man's son was I,
    As any of you!
But, Mak, come lie here in between if
you please.
MAK. You'll be hindered, I fear, from
talking at ease,
    Indeed! [*They lie down, with* MAK *in
their midst to prevent him from robbing*

them. MAK *crosses himself.*]
From my top to my toe,
Manus tuas commendo,
Poncio Pilato,[8]
Christ's cross me speed! [*When the
     shepherds are asleep,* MAK *rises.*]
Now 't were time a man knew, that
     lacks what he'd fain hold,
To steal privily through then into a
     fold,
And then nimbly his work do—and be
     not too bold,
For his bargain he'd rue, if it were told
     At the ending.
Now 't were time their wrath to tell!
But he needs good counsel
That fain would fare well,
     And has but little for spending.
[*He works a spell on the shepherds.*]
But about you a circle as round as a
     moon,
Till I have done what I will, till that it
     be noon,
That ye lie stone still, until I have done;
And I shall say thereto still, a few good
     words soon
     Of might:
Over your heads my hand I lift.
Out go your eyes! Blind be your sight!
But I must make still better shift,
     If it's to be right.

Lord, how hard they sleep—that may
     ye all hear!
I never herded sheep, but I'll learn
     now, that's clear.
Though the flock be scared, yet shall I
     slip near. [*He captures a sheep.*]
Hey—hitherward creep! Now that bet-
     ters our cheer
     From sorrow.
A fat sheep, I dare say!
A good fleece, swear I may!
When I can, then I'll pay,
     But this I will borrow! [*The scene
shifts to* MAK'S *house.*]
MAK. Ho, Gill, art thou in? Get us a
     light!
GILL. Who makes such a din at this time
     of night?
I am set for to spin, I think not I might
Rise a penny to win! Curses loud on
     them light
     Trouble cause!
A busy housewife all day
To be called thus away!

No work's done, I say,
     Because of such small chores!
MAK. Open the door, good Gill. See'st
     thou not what I bring?
GILL. Draw the latch an thou will. Ah,
     come in, my sweeting!
MAK. Yea, thou need'st not care didst
     thou kill me with such long standing!
GILL. By the naked neck still thou are
     likely to swing.
MAK. Oh, get away!
I am worthy of my meat,
For at a pinch I can get
More than they that toil and sweat
     All the long day.
Thus it fell to my lot, Gill! Such luck
     came my way!
GILL. It were a foul blot to be hanged
     for it some day.
MAK. I have often escaped, Gill, as risky
     a play.
GILL. But "though long goes the pot to
     the water," men say,
     "At last
Comes it home broken."
MAK. Well know I the token,
But let it never be spoken—
     But come and help fast!

I would he were slain, I would like well
     to eat,
This twelvemonth was I not so fain to
     have some sheep's meat.
GILL. Should they come ere he's slain
     and hear the sheep bleat—
MAK. Then might I be ta'en. That were
     a cold sweat!
     The door—
Go close it!
GILL. Yes, Mak,
For if they come at thy back—
MAK. Then might I suffer from the
     whole pack.
     The devil, and more!
GILL. A good trick have I spied, since
     thou thinkest of none,
Here shall we him hide until they be
     gone.
In my cradle he'll bide—just you let me
     alone—
And I shall lie beside in childbed and
     groan.
MAK. Well said!
And I shall say that this night
A boy child saw the light.
GILL. Now that day was bright

That saw me born and bred!

This is a good device and a trick so
  vast.
Ever a woman's advice gives help at the
  last!
I know not who spies! Now go thou
  back fast!
MAK. Save I come ere they rise, there'll
  blow a cold blast! [MAK *goes back to
  where the shepherds are sleeping.*]
    I will go sleep.
Still sleeps all this company,
And I shall slip in privily
As it had never been I
    That carried off their sheep.
COLL. *Resurrex a mortruis!*⁹ Reach me a
  hand!
Judas carnas dominus! I can hardly
  stand!
My foot's asleep, by Jesus, and my
  mouth's dry as sand.
I thought we had laid us full nigh to
  England!
GIB. Yea, verily!
Lord, but I have slept well.
As fresh as an eel,
As light do I feel,
    As leaf on the tree.
DAW. *Ben'cite* be herein! So my body is
  quaking,
My heart is out of my skin with the to-
  do it's making.
Who's making all this din, so my head's
  set to aching?
To the door I'll win! Hark, you fellows,
  be waking!
    Four we were—
See ye aught of Mak now?
COLL. We were up ere thou.
GIB. Man, to God I vow,
    Not once did he stir.
DAW. Methought he was lapped in a
  wolf's skin.
COLL. So many are wrapped now—that
  is, within.
DAW. Methought with a snare, when we
  napping had been
A fat sheep he trapped, but he made
  no din.
GIB. Be still!
The dream makes thee mad,
It's a nightmare you've had.
COLL. God bring good out of bad,
    If it be his will!
GIB. Rise, Mak, for shame! Right long

dost thou lie.
MAK. Now Christ's Holy Name be with
  us for aye!
What's this, by Saint James, I can't
  move when I try.
I suppose I'm the same. Oooo, my
  neck's lain awry. [*They help him up.*]
    Enough, perdie!
Many thanks. Since yester even,
Now, by Saint Stephen,
I was plagued by a dream, 'n
    Knocked the heart of me.

I thought Gill begun to croak and
  travail full sad,
Well-nigh at the first cock, bore a
  young lad
To add to our flock. Of that I am never
  glad,
    Oh, my head!
A house full of hunger pains—
The devil knock out their brains!
Woe is him who children gains
    And yet has little bread.

I must go home, by your leave, to Gill,
  as I thought.
Prithee look in my sleeve that I steal
  naught.
I am loath you to grieve, or from you
  take aught.
DAW. Go forth—ill may'st thou thrive!
  [MAK *leaves.*]
    Now I would that we sought
    This morn,
That we had all our store.
COLL. But I will go before.
Let us meet.
GIB. Where?
DAW. At the crooked thorn. [*The scene
  shifts to* MAK'S *house.*]
MAK. Undo the door, see who's here!
  How long must I stand?
GILL. Who's making such a fuss? Now
  bad luck you attend.
MAK. Ah, Gill, what cheer? It is I, Mak,
  your husband.
GILL. Then we see here the devil in
  hand.
    Sir Guile!
Lo, he comes with a note¹⁰
As he were held by the throat.
And I cannot devote
    To my work any while.
MAK. Will ye hear the fuss she makes as
  excuse for her woes?

Naught but pleasure she takes, and
  curls up her toes.
GILL. Why, who runs, who watches,
  who comes who goes,
Who brews, who bakes, what makes me
  hoarse, d'ye suppose?
    And also,
It is sad to behold,
Now in hot, now in cold,
Full woeful is the household
    That no woman doth know![11]

But what end hast thou made with the
  shepherds, Mak?
MAK. The last word that they said when
  I turned my back
Was they'd see that they had of their
  sheep all the pack.
They'll not be pleased, I'm afraid,
  when they their sheep
    lack,
      Perdie.
But how so the game go,
They'll suspect me, whether or no,
And raise a great bellow,
    And cry out upon me.

But thou must use thy sleight.
GILL. Yea, I think it not ill.
I shall swaddle him aright in my cradle
  with skill.
Were it yet a worse plight, yet a way I'd
  find still.
I will lie down forthright. Come tuck
  me up.
MAK. That I will.
GILL. Behind!
If Coll come and his band,
They'll catch us out of hand.
MAK. But I may cry out "Stand,"
  If the sheep they find.
GILL. Hearken close till they call; they
  will come anon.
Come and make ready all, and sing
  thou alone.
Sing lullaby, thou shalt, for I must
  groan
And cry out by the wall on Mary and
  John
    Full sore.
Sing lullaby fast,
When thou hear'st them at last,
And if I don't play a shrewd cast,
    Trust me no more [*The scene shifts
  back to the shepherds.*]
DAW. Ah, Coll, good morn! Why sleep-
est thou not?
COLL. Alas, that ever I was born! We
  have a foul blot.
A fat wether have we lorn.
DAW. Marry, God forbid, say it not!
GIB. Who treats us with such scorn?
  That were a foul spot.
COLL. Some shrew.
I have searched with my dogs
All Horbury Shrogs,[12]
And of fifteen hogs[13]
    Found I all but owe ewe.
DAW. Now trust me, if you will, by Saint
  Thomas of Kent,
Either Mak or Gill their aid thereto
  lent!
COLL. Peace, man, be still! I saw when
  he went.
Thou dost slander him ill. Thou
  shouldest repent
    At once, indeed!
GIB. So may I thrive, perdie,
Should I die here where I be,
I would say it was he
    That did that same deed!
DAW. Go we thither, quick sped, and
  run on our feet,
I shall never eat bread till I know all
  complete!
COLL. Nor drink in my head till with
  him I meet.
GIB. In no place will I bed until I him
  greet,
    My brother!
One vow I will plight,
Till I see him in sight,
I will ne'er sleep one night
    Where I do another! [*They go to
  MAK's house. MAK, hearing them coming,
  begins to sing a lullaby at the top of his
  voice, while GILL groans in concert.*]
DAW. Hark the row they make! List to
  Mak there croon!
COLL. Never heard I voice break so
  clear out of tune.
Call to him.
GIB. Mak, wake there! Undo your door
  soon!
MAK. Who is that spake as if it were
  noon
    Aloft?
Who is that, I say?
DAW. [*Mocking MAK.*] Good fellows, if it
  were day—
MAK. As far as ye may,
    Kindly, speak soft;

O'er a sick woman's head in such griev-
ous throes!
I were liefer dead than she should suf-
fer such woes.
GILL. Go elsewhere, well sped. Oh, how
my pain grows!
Each footfall ye tread goes straight
through my nose
so loud, woe's me!
COLL. Tell us, Mak, if ye may,
How fare ye, I say?
MAK. But are ye in this town today?
Now how fare ye?

Ye have run in the mire and are wet
still a bit,
I will make you a fire, if ye will sit.
A nurse I would hire; can you help me
in it?
My bad luck is entire; my dream the
truth hit
In season.
I have brats, if ye knew,
Plenty more than will do,
But we must drink as we brew,
And that is but reason.

I would ye would eat ere ye go.
Methinks that ye sweat.
GIB. Nay, no help could we know in
what's drunken or eat.
MAK. Why, sir, ails you aught but good,
though?
DAW. Yea, our sheep that we get
Are stolen as they go; our loss is great.
MAK. Sirs, drink!
Had I been there
Some one had bought it sore, I swear.
COLL. Marry, some men trow that ye
were,
And that makes us think!
GIB. Mak, one and another trows it
should be ye.
DAW. Either ye or your spouse, so say
we.
MAK. Now if aught suspicion throws on
Gill or me,
Come and search our house, and then
may ye see
Who had her—
Or if I any sheep got,
Or cow to my lot.
And Gill, my wife, rose not,
Since here we laid her.

As I am true to God, here I pray

That this[14] is the first meal that I shall
eat this day.
COLL. Mak, as may I have weal, advise
thee, I say:
"He learned timely to steal that could
not say nay." [*They begin to search for
the sheep.*]
GILL. Me, my death you've dealt!
Out, ye thieves, nor come again;
Ye've come just to rob us, that's plain.
MAK. Hear ye not how she groans
amain?
Your hearts should melt!
GILL. From my child, thieves, begone.
Go nigh him not.
There's the door!
MAK. If ye knew all she's borne, your
hearts should be sore,
Ye do wrong, I you warn, thus to come
in before
A woman that has borne—but I say no
more.
GILL. Oh, my middle! I die!
I vow to God so mild
If ever I you beguiled,
That I will eat this child
That doth in this cradle lie!
MAK. Peace, woman, by God's pain, and
cry not so.
Thou dost hurt thy brain and fill me
with woe.
GIB. I trow our sheep is slain. What find
ye two, though?
Our work's all in vain. We may as well
go.
Save clothes and such matters
I can find no flesh
Hard or nesh,[15]
Salt nor fresh,
Except two empty platters.
Of any live stock but this, tame or wild,
that we see,
None as may I have bliss, smelled as
loud as he.
GILL. No, so God joy and bliss of my
child may give me!
COLL. We have aimed amiss; deceived, I
trow, were we.
GIB. Completely; each one.
Sir—Our Lady him save—
Is your child a knave?
MAK. Any lord might him have,
This child, for his son.

When he wakes, so he gripes, it's a
pleasure to see.

DAW. Good luck to the tips of his toes,
say we!
But who were his godparents, now tell
who they be?
MAK. Blest be their lips— [*Hesitates, at a
loss.*]
COLL. [*Aside.*] Hark, a lie now, trust me!
MAK. So God give them thanks,
Parkin and Gibbon Waller, I say,
And gentle John Horn; welladay,
He made all the fun and play,
    With his long shanks.
GIB. Mak, friends will we be, for we are
at one.
MAK. We! Nay, count not on me, for
amends get I none.
Farewell, all three! Glad 't will be when
ye're gone! [*The shepherds go.*]
DAW. "Fair words there may be, but
love there is none
    This year."
COLL. Gave ye the child anything?
GIB. I trow, not one farthing.
DAW. Fast back I will fling.
    Await ye me here. [DAW *goes back.
The other shepherds turn and follow him
slowly, entering while he is talking with*
MAK.]
DAW. Mak, I trust thou'lt not grieve, if I
go to thy child.
MAK. Nay, great hurt I receive; thou
hast acted full wild.
DAW. Thy bairn 'twill not grieve, little
day-star so mild.
Mak, by your leave, let me give your
child
    But six-pence. [DAK *goes to the cra-
dle, and starts to draw away the cover-
ing.*]
MAK. Nay, stop it. He sleeps!
DAW. Methinks he peeps.
MAK. When he wakens, he weeps;
    I pray you go hence!
DAW. Give me leave him to kiss, and lift
up the clout.[16]
What the devil is this? He has a long
snout!
COLL. He's birth-marked amiss. We
waste time hereabout.
GIB. "From a woof ill spun, ever comes
foul out."
    Aye, so!
He is like to our sheep!
DAW. Ho, Gib, may I peep?
COLL. I trow, "the truth will creep
Where it may not freely go."

GIB. This was a quaint gaud[17] and a far
cast.
It was a high fraud.
DAW. Yea, sirs, that was't.
Let's burn this bawd, and bind her fast.
"A false scold," by the Lord, "will hang
at the last!"
    So shalt thou!
Will ye see how they swaddle
His four feet in the middle!
Saw I never in the cradle
    A horned lad ere now!
MAK. Peace, I say! Tell ye what, this to-
do ye can spare!
It was I him begot and yon woman him
bare.
COLL. What the devil for name has he
got? Mak?
    Lo, God, Mak's heir!
GIB. Come, joke with him not. Now
may God give him care,
    I say!
GILL. A pretty child is he
As sits on a woman's knee,
A darling child, perdie,
    To make a man gay.
DAW. I know him by the ear-mark; that
is a good token.
MAK. I tell you, sirs, hark, his nose was
broken.
Then a priest told me he was by witch-
craft bespoken.
COLL. Ye deal falsely and dark; my an-
ger's awoken.
    Get a weapon. Go!
GILL. He was taken by an elf,
I saw it myself.
When the clock struck twelve,
    Was he mis-shapen so.
GIB. Ye two are at one, that's plain, in
all ye've done and said.
COLL. Since their theft they maintain,
let us leave them dead.
MAK. If I trespass again, strike off my
head!
At your will I remain.
DAW. Sirs, take my counsel instead.
    For this trespass
We'll neither curse nor wrangle in
spite,
Chide nor fight,
But have done forthright,
    And toss him in canvas. [*They toss*
MAK *in a canvas sheet. Then they move
away from* MAK's *house.*]
COLL. Lord, lo, but I am sore, like to

burst, in back and breast.
In faith, I may no more, therefore will
  I rest.
GIB. Like a sheep of seven score he
  weighed in my fist.
To sleep anywhere, therefore seemeth
  now best.
DAW. Now I you pray,
On this green let us lie.
COLL. O'er those thieves yet chafe I.
DAW. Let your anger go by.
    Come, do as I say. [*As they lie down,
an* ANGEL *appears, singing "Gloria in
Excelsis."*]
ANGEL. Rise, herdsmen gentle, attend
  ye, for now is he born
That shall rend from the Fiend what
  Adam had lorn;
That devil to end, this night is he born;
God is made your friend now on this
  morn.
    Lo! Thus doth he command:
Go to Bethlehem, see
Where he lieth so free,
In a manger full lowly
  'Twixt where twain beasts stand.
    [*The* ANGEL *disappears.*]
COLL. This was a fine voice, even as
  ever I heard.
It is a marvel, by St. Stephen, thus with
  dread to be stirred.
GIB. 'Twas of God's Son from heaven
  he these tidings averred.
All the wood for seven miles about with
  lightning
    Shone fair.
DAW. Of a Child did he tell,
In Bethlehem, mark ye well.
COLL. That this star yonder doth
  dwell—
    Let us seek him there.
GIB. Say, what was his song? How it
  went, did ye hear?
Three breves[18] to a long—
DAW. Marry, yet, to my ear
There was no crotchet[19] wrong, naught
  it lacked and full clear!
COLL. To sing it here, us among, as he
  sang it, full near,
    I know how—
GIB. Let's see how you croon!
Can you bark at the moon?
DAW. Hold your tongues, have done!
    Hark after me now! [*They sing.*]
GIB. To Bethlehem he bade that we
  should go.

I am sore afraid that we tarry too slow.
DAW. Be merry, and not sad; our song's
  of mirth, not of woe,
To be forever glad is the reward we
  shall know
    And shall choose.
COLL. Hie we thither, then, speedily,
Though we be wet and weary,
To that Child and that Lady!
    Those joys not to lose.
GIB. We find by the prophecy—let be
  your din!—
David and Isaiah, and more that I
  mind me therein,
They prophesied by clergy, that in a
  virgin,
Should God come to lie, to assuage our
  sin,
    And slake it,
Our nature, from woe.
For it was Isaiah said so:
"*Ecce virgo
    Concipiet*"[20] a child that is naked.
DAW. Full glad may we be and await
  that day
That lovesome one to see, that all
  power doth sway.
Lord, well it were with me, now and for
  aye,
Might I kneel on my knee some word
  for to say
    To that child.
But the angel said
In a crib was he laid,
He was poorly arrayed,
    Both gracious and mild.
COLL. Patriarchs that have been and
  prophets before,
They desired to have seen this child
  that is born.
They are gone full clean; that have
  they lorn.
We shall see him, I ween, ere it be
  morn,
    For token.
When I see him and feel,
I shall know full well,
It is true as steel,
    What prophets have spoken:

To so poor as we are that he would ap-
  pear,
First find and declare by his messenger.
GIB. Go we now, let us fare, the place is
  us near.
DAW. I am ready and eager to be there;

let us together with cheer
  To that bright one go.
Lord, if thy will it be,
Untaught are we all three,
Some kind of joy grant us, that we
  Thy creatures, comfort may know!
[*They enter the stable and adore the infant Saviour.*]
COLL. Hail, thou comely and clean one!
  Hail, young Child!
Hail, Maker, as I mean, from a maiden
  so mild!
Thou hast harried, I ween, the devil so
  wild;
The false beguiler of men now goes beguiled.
  Lo, he merries,
Lo, he laughs, my sweeting!
A happy meeting!
Here's my promised greeting:
  Have a bob of cherries!
GIB. Hail, sovereign Saviour, for thou
  hast us sought!
Hail, noble nursling and flower, that all
  things hast wrought!
Hail, thou, full of gracious power, that
  made all from nought!
Hail, I kneel and I cower! A bird have I
  brought
  To my bairn from far.
Hail, little tiny tot!
To lead our creed thou art begot.
I fain would share in thy lot,
  Little day-star!
DAW. Hail, darling dear one, full of
  Godhead indeed!
I pray thee be near, when I have need.
Hail, sweet is thy cheer! My heart
  would bleed
To see thee sit here in so poor a
  weed,²¹
  With no pennies.
Hail, put forth thy hand to us all;
I bring thee but a ball.
Keep it, and play with it withal,
  And go to the tennis.
MARY. The Father of Heaven this night,
  God omnipotent,
That setteth all things aright, his Son
  hath he sent.

My name he named and did light on
  me ere that he went.
I conceived him forthright through his
  might as he meant,
  And now he is born.
May he keep you from woe!
I shall pray him do so.
Tell it forth as ye go,
  And remember this morn.
COLL. Farewell, Lady, so fair to behold
With thy child on thy knee!
GIB. But he lies full cold!
Lord, 'tis well with me! Now we go, behold!
DAW. Forsooth, already it seems to be
  told
  Full oft!
COLL. What grace we have found!
GIB. Now are we won safe and sound.
DAW. Come forth; to sing are we
  bound.
  Make it ring then aloft! [*They depart singing.*]

1. Shortened form of *benedicite,* "bless you!"
2. Daw regrets his previous short temper toward the others, then in the next lines proposes a mild penance for himself.
3. A meadow or heath.
4. Lost.
5. Mak has been affecting a southern accent, but these northern shepherds consider all southerners deceitful.
6. A proverb suggesting that appearances are deceptive.
7. To pay the cost of her funeral.
8. A malapropism: "I commend your hands to Pontius Pilate."
9. Garbled, nonsensical Latin.
10. Sound.
11. That has no woman in it.
12. A thicketed area near Wakefield, where the play presumably was originally staged.
13. Sheep.
14. Pointing to the cradle.
15. Soft.
16. Cloth.
17. Shrewd trick.
18. Short notes.
19. An even shorter note.
20. "Behold, a virgin shall conceive . . ." (Isaiah 7:14).
21. Dress; clothing.

Everyman

Translated by Clarence Griffin Child

Characters

God
Everyman
Death
Good Fellowship
Kindred
Cousin
Goods
Good Deeds
Knowledge
Confession
Beauty
Strength
Discretion
Five Wits
Messenger
Angel
Doctor

Here beginneth a treatise how the High Father of Heaven sendeth Death to summon every creature to come and give an account of their lives in this world, and is in manner of a moral play.

[*The* MESSENGER *enters.*]
MESSENGER. I pray you all give your audience,
And hear this matter with reverence,
In form a moral play.
The Summoning of Everyman it is called so,
That of our lives and ending maketh show
How transitory we be every day.
This matter is wondrous precious,
But the meaning of it is more gracious
And sweet to bear away.
The story saith: Man, in the beginning
Watch well, and take good heed of the ending,
Be you never so gay!
Ye think sin in the beginning full sweet,
Which, in the end, causeth the soul to weep,
When the body lieth in clay.
Here shall you see how Fellowship and Jollity,
Both Strength, Pleasure, and Beauty,
Will fade from thee as flower in May,
For ye shall hear how our Heaven's King
Calleth Everyman to a general reckoning.
Give audience and hear what he doth say. [*The* MESSENGER *goes.*]
GOD. I perceive, here in my majesty,
How that all creatures be to me unkind,
Living, without fear, in worldly prosperity.
In spiritual vision the people be so blind,
Drowned in sin, they know me not for their God;
In worldly riches is all their mind.
They fear not my righteousness, the sharp rod.
My law that I disclosed, when I for them died,
They clean forget, and shedding of my blood red.
I hung between two it cannot be denied,
To get them life I suffered to be dead,
I healed their feet, with thorns was hurt my head.
I could do no more than I did truly.
And now I see the people do clean forsake me;
They use the seven deadly sins dam-

300

nable
In such wise that pride, covetousness,
   wrath, and lechery,
Now in this world be made commend-
   able,
And thus they leave of angels the
   heavenly company.
Every man liveth so after his own plea-
   sure,
And yet of their lives they be nothing
   sure.
The more I them forbear, I see
The worse from year to year they be;
All that live grow more evil apace;
Therefore I will, in briefest space,
From every man in person have a
   reckoning shown.
For, if I leave the people thus alone
In their way of life and wicked passions
   to be,
They will become much worse than
   beasts, verily.
Now for envy would one eat up
   another, and tarry not.
Charity is by all clean forgot.
I hoped well that every man
In my glory should make his mansion,
And thereto I made them all elect,
But now I see, like traitors abject,
They thank me not for the pleasure
   that I for them meant,
Nor yet for their being that I have
   them lent.
I proffered the people great multitude
   of mercy,
And few there be that ask it heartily.
They be so cumbered with worldly
   riches, thereto
I must needs upon them justice do,—
On every man living without fear.
Where art thou, Death, thou mighty
   messenger? [DEATH *enters.*]
DEATH. Almighty God, I am here at
   your will,
Your commandment to fulfil.
GOD. Go thou to Everyman,
And show him in my name
A pilgrimage he must on him take,
Which he in no wise may escape,
And that he bring with him a sure
   reckoning
Without delay or any tarrying.
DEATH. Lord, I will in the world go run
   over all,
And cruelly search out both great and
   small.

Every man will I beset that liveth
   beastly
Out of God's law, and doth not dread
   folly.
He that loveth riches I will strike with
   my dart
His sight to blind and him from heaven
   to part—
Except if Alms be his good friend—
In hell for to dwell, world without end.
Lo, yonder I see Everyman walking.
Full little he thinketh on my coming!
His mind is on fleshly lusts and his
   treasure,
And great pain it shall cause him to en-
   dure
Before the Lord, of Heaven the King.
Everyman, stand still! Whither art thou
   going
Thus gayly? Hast thou thy Maker for-
   got? [EVERYMAN *enters.*]
EVERYMAN. Why askest thou?
Wouldest thou know? For what?
DEATH. Yea, sir, I will show you now.
In great haste I am sent to thee
From God, out of his majesty.
EVERYMAN. What, sent to me!
DEATH. Yea, certainly.
Though thou hast forgot him here,
He thinketh on thee in the heavenly
   sphere,
As, ere we part, thou shalt know.
EVERYMAN. What desireth God of me?
DEATH. That shall I show thee.
A reckoning he will needs have
Without any longer respite.
EVERYMAN. To give a reckoning longer
   leisure I crave.
This blind matter troubleth my wit.
DEATH. Upon thee thou must take a
   long journey,
Therefore, do thou thine accounting-
   book with thee bring.
For return again thou canst not by no
   way,
And look thou be sure in thy
   reckoning,
For before God thou shalt answer, and
   show true
Thy many bad deeds and good but a
   few,
How thou hast spent thy life and in
   what wise
Before the Chief Lord of Paradise.
Get thee prepared that we may be
   upon that journey,

For well thou knowest thou shalt make
none for thee attorney.

EVERYMAN. Full unready I am such
reckoning to give.
I know thee not. What messenger art
thou?

DEATH. I am Death that no man fear,
For every man I arrest and no man
spare,
For it is God's commandment
That all to me should be obedient.

EVERYMAN. O Death, thou comest when
I had thee least in mind!
In thy power it lieth to save me yet;—
Thereto of my goods will I give thee, if
thou wilt be kind,—
Yea, a thousand pounds shalt thou
get!—
And defer this matter till another day.

DEATH. Everyman, it may not be in any
way.
I set no store by gold, silver, riches, or
such gear,
Nor by pope, emperor, king, prince, or
peer.
For, if I would receive gifts great,
All the world I might get,
But my custom is clean the contrary
way.
I give thee no respite. Come hence, nor
delay!

EVERYMAN. Alas, shall I have no longer
respite!
I may say Death giveth no warning!
To think on thee, it maketh my heart
sick,
For all unready is my book of
reckoning.
But if I might have twelve years of
waiting,
My accounting book I would make so
clear
That my reckoning I should not need
to fear.
Wherefore, Death, I pray thee, for
God's mercy,
Spare me til I be provided with a
remedy!

DEATH. It availeth thee not to cry, weep,
and pray,
But haste thee lightly, that thou mayest
be on thy journey,
And make proof of thy friends, if thou
can,
For, know thou well, time waiteth for
no man,

And in the world each living creature
Because of Adam's sin must die by nature.

EVERYMAN. Death, if I should this pil-
grimage take,
And my reckoning duly make,
Show me, for Saint Charity,
Should I not come again shortly?

DEATH. No, Everyman, if once thou art
there,
Thou mayest nevermore come here,
Trust me, verily.

EVERYMAN. O gracious God, in the high
seat celestial,
Have mercy on me in this utmost need!
Shall I no company have from this vale
terrestrial
Of mine acquaintance that way me to
lead?

DEATH. Yea, if any be so hardy
As to go with thee and bear thee com-
pany.
Haste thee that thou mayest be gone to
God's magnificence,
Thy reckoning to give before his pres-
ence.
What, thinkest thou thy life is given
thee,
And thy worldly goods also?

EVERYMAN. I had thought so, verily.

DEATH. Nay, nay, it was but lent to thee,
For, as soon as thou dost go,
Another a while shall have it and then
even so,
Go therefore as thou hast done.
Everyman, thou art mad! Thou hast
thy wits five,
And here on earth will not amend thy
life,
For suddenly I do come!

EVERYMAN. O wretched caitiff, whither
shall I flee
That I may escape this endless sorrow!
Nay, gentle Death, spare me until to-
morrow
That I may amend me
With good advisement!

DEATH. Nay, thereto I will not consent,
Nor no man respite, if I might,
But to the heart suddenly I shall smite
Without any "advisement."
And now out of thy sight I will me hie,
See that thou make thee ready speed-
ily,
For thou mayest say this is the day
Wherefrom no man living may escape

away.

EVERYMAN. Alas, I may well weep with sighs deep!

Now have I no manner of company

To help me on my journey and me to keep,

And also my writing is all unready.

What can I do that may excuse me!

I would to God I had never been begot!

To my soul a full great profit it would be,

For now I fear pains huge and great, God wot!

The time passeth—help, Lord, that all things wrought!

For, though I mourn, yet it availeth naught.

The day passeth and is almost through,

I wot not well of aught that I may do.

To whom were it best that I my plaint should make?

What if to Fellowship I thereof spake,

And what this sudden chance should mean disclosed?

For surely in him is all my trust reposed—

We have in the world so many a day

Been good friends in sport and play.

I see him yonder certainly—

I trust that he will bear me company;

Therefore to him will I speak to ease my sorrow.

Well met, good Fellowship, and a good morrow! [*Enter* FELLOWSHIP.]

FELLOWSHIP. I wish thee good morrow, Everyman, by this day!

Sir, why lookest thou so piteously?

If anything be amiss, prithee to me it say

That I may help in remedy.

EVERYMAN. Yea, good Fellowship, yea,

I am in great jeopardy!

FELLOWSHIP. My true friend, show to me your mind.

I will not forsake thee to my live's end,

In the way of good company.

EVERYMAN. That was well spoken and lovingly.

FELLOWSHIP. Sir, I must needs know your heaviness.

I have pity to see you in any distress.

If any have wronged you, revenged ye shall be,

Though I upon the ground be slain for thee,

Even should I know before that I

should die.

EVERYMAN. Verily, Fellowship, gramercy![1]

FELLOWSHIP. Tush! By thy thanks I set not a straw.

Show me your grief and say no more.

EVERYMAN. If my heart should to you unfold,

And you then were to turn your heart from me,

And no comfort would give when I had told,

Then should I ten times sorrier be.

FELLOWSHIP. Sir, I say as I will do indeed!

EVERYMAN. Then you be a good friend at need.

I have found you true heretofore.

FELLOWSHIP. And so ye shall evermore,

For, in faith, if thou goest to hell,

I will not forsake thee by the way.

EVERYMAN. Ye speak like a good friend—I believe you well.

I shall deserve it, if so I may!

FELLOWSHIP. I speak of no deserving, by this day,

For he that will say, and nothing do,

Is not worthy with good company to go.

Therefore show me the grief of your mind,

As to your friend most loving and kind.

EVERYMAN. I shall show you how it is:

Commanded I am to go a journey,

A long way hard and dangerous,

And give a strict account without delay

Before the High Judge, Adonai.[2]

Wherefore, I pray you, bear me company,

As ye have promised, on this journey.

FELLOWSHIP. That is matter, indeed!

Promise is duty—

But if I should take such a voyage on me,

I know well it should be to my pain;

Afeard also it maketh me, for certain.

But let us take counsel here as well as we can,

For your words would dismay a strong man.

EVERYMAN. Why, if I had need, ye said

Ye would never forsake me, quick nor dead,

Though it were to hell truly!

FELLOWSHIP. So I said certainly,

But such pleasant things be set aside,

the truth to say;
And also, if we took such a journey,
When should we come again?
EVERYMAN. Nay, never again till the day
    of doom.
FELLOWSHIP. In faith, then, will I not
    come there.
Who hath you these tidings brought?
EVERYMAN. Indeed, Death was with me
    here.
FELLOWSHIP. Now, by God that all hath
    bought,
If Death were the messenger,
For no man living here below
I will not that loathly journey go—
Not for the father that begat me!
EVERYMAN. Ye promised otherwise,
    pardy![3]
FELLOWSHIP. I know well I do say so,
    truly,
And still, if thou wilt eat and drink and
    make good cheer,
Or haunt of women the lusty company,
I would not forsake you while the day
    is clear,
Trust me, verily.
EVERYMAN. Yea, thereto ye would be
    ready!
To go to mirth, solace, and play,
Your mind would sooner persuaded be
Than to bear me company on my long
    journey.
FELLOWSHIP. Now, in good sooth, I
    have no will that way—
But if thou would'st murder, or any
    man kill,
In that I will help thee with a good will.
EVERYMAN. Oh, that is simple advice, in-
    deed!
Gentle Fellowship, help me in my
    necessity!
We have loved long, and now I am in
    need!
And now, gentle Fellowship, remember
    me!
FELLOWSHIP. Whether ye have loved me
    or no,
By Saint John, I will not with thee go!
EVERYMAN. Yea, I pray thee, take this
    task on thee and do so much for me,
As to bring me forward on my way for
    Saint Charity,
And comfort me till I come without the
    town.
FELLOWSHIP. Nay, if thou wouldest give
    me a new gown,

I will not a foot with thee go,
But, if thou hadst tarried, I would not
    have left thee so.
And so now, God speed thee on thy
    journey,
For from thee I will depart as fast as I
    may!
EVERYMAN. Whither away, Fellowship?
    Will you forsake me?
FELLOWSHIP. Yea, by my faith! I pray
    God take thee.
EVERYMAN. Farewell, good Fellow-
    ship,—for thee my heart is sore.
Adieu forever, I shall see thee no
    more!
FELLOWSHIP. In faith, Everyman,
    farewell now at the ending.
For you I will remember that parting is
    grieving. [FELLOWSHIP goes.]
EVERYMAN. Alack! Shall we thus part in-
    deed?
Ah, Lady, help! Lo, vouchsafing no
    more comfort,
Fellowship thus forsaketh me in my ut-
    most need.
For help in this world whither shall I
    resort?
Fellowship heretofore with me would
    merry make,
And now little heed of my sorrow doth
    he take.
It is said in prosperity men friends may
    find
Which in adversity be fully unkind.
Now whither for succor shall I flee,
Since that Fellowship hath forsaken
    me?
To my kinsmen will I truly,
Praying them to help me in my neces-
    sity.
I believe that they will do so
For "Nature will creep where it may
    not go."[4] [KINDRED and COUSIN enter.]
I will go try, for yonder I see them go.
Where be ye now, my friends and kins-
    men, lo?
KINDRED. Here we be now at your com-
    mandment.
Cousin,[5] I pray you show us your in-
    tent
In any wise and do not spare.
COUSIN. Yea, Everyman, and to us de-
    clare
If ye be disposed to go any whither,
For, wit you well, we will live and die
    together!

KINDRED. In wealth and woe we will with you hold,
For "with his own kin a man may be bold."
EVERYMAN. Gramercy, my friends and kinsmen kind!
Now shall I show you the grief of my mind.
I was commanded by a messenger
That is a High King's chief officer.
He bade me go a pilgrimage to my pain,
And I know well I shall never come again;
And I must give a reckoning straight,
For I have a great enemy that lieth for me in wait,
Who intendeth me to hinder.
KINDRED. What account is that which you must render?—
That would I know.
EVERYMAN. Of all my works I must show
How I have lived and my days have spent,
Also of evil deeds to which I have been used
In my time, since life was to me lent,
And of all virtues that I have refused.
Therefore, I pray you, go thither with me
To help to make my account, for Saint Charity!
COUSIN. What, to go thither? Is that the matter?
Nay, Everyman, I had liefer fast on bread and water
All this five year and more!
EVERYMAN. Alas, that ever my mother me bore!
For now shall I never merry be,
If that you forsake me!
KINDRED. Ah, sir, come! Ye be a merry man!
Pluck up heart and make no moan.
But one thing I warn you by Saint Anne,
As for me, ye shall go alone!
EVERYMAN. My cousin, will you not with me go?
COUSIN. No, by our Lady! I have the cramp in my toe.
Trust not to me, so God me speed,
I will deceive you in your utmost need.
KINDRED. It availeth not us to coax and court.

Ye shall have my maid, with all my heart.
She loveth to go to feasts, there to make foolish sport
And to dance, and in antics to take part.
To help you on that journey I will give her leave willingly,
If so be that you and she may agree.
EVERYMAN. Now show me the very truth within your mind—
Will you go with me or abide behind?
KINDRED. Abide behind? Yea, that I will, if I may—
Therefore farewell till another day!
EVERYMAN. How shall I be merry or glad?—
For fair promises men to me make,
But, when I have most need, they me forsake!
I am deceived—that maketh me sad!
COUSIN. Cousin Everyman, farewell now, lo!
For, verily, I will not with thee go.
Also of mine own an unready reckoning,
I have to give account of, therefore I make tarrying.
Now God keep thee, for now I go!
[KINDRED *and* COUSIN *go.*]
EVERYMAN. Ah, Jesus, is all to this come so?
Lo, "fair words make fools fain,"
They promise, and from deeds refrain.
My kinsmen promised me faithfully
For to abide by me steadfastly,
And now fast away do they flee.
Even so Fellowship promised me.
What friend were it best for me to provide?
I am losing my time longer here to abide.
Yet still in my mind a thing there is,
All my life I have loved riches.
If that my Goods now help me might,
He would make my heart full light.
To him will I speak in my sorrow this day.
My Goods and Riches, where art thou, pray? [GOODS *is disclosed hemmed in by chests and bags.*]
GOODS. Who calleth me? Everyman? Why this haste thou hast?
I lie here in corners trussed and piled so high,
And in chests I am locked so fast,

Also sacked in bags, thou mayest see
　　with thine eye,
I cannot stir; in packs, full low I lie.
What ye would have, lightly to me say.
EVERYMAN. Come hither, Goods, with
　　all the haste thou may,
For counsel straightway I must ask of
　　thee.
GOODS. Sir, if ye in this world have sor-
　　row or adversity,
That can I help you to remedy shortly.
EVERYMAN. It is another disease that
　　grieveth me;
In this world it is not, I tell thee so,
I am sent for another way to go,
To give a strict account general
Before the highest Jupiter of all.
And all my life I have had joy and
　　pleasure in thee,
Therefore I pray thee go with me,
For, peradventure, thou mayest before
　　God Almighty on high
My reckoning help to clean and purify,
For one may hear ever and anon
That "money maketh all right that is
　　wrong."
GOODS. Nay, Everyman, I sing another
　　song—
I follow no man on such voyages,
For, if I went with thee,
Thou shouldest fare much the worse
　　for me,
For, because on me thou didst set thy
　　mind,
Thy reckoning I have made blotted
　　and blind,
So that thine account thou canst not
　　make truly—
And that hast thou for the love of me.
EVERYMAN. That would be to me grief
　　full sore and sorrowing,
When I should come that fearful an-
　　swering.
Up, let us go thither together!
GOODS. Nay, not so! I am too brittle, I
　　may not endure,
I will follow no man one foot, be ye
　　sure.
EVERYMAN. Alas! I have thee loved, and
　　had great pleasure
All the days of my life in goods and
　　treasure.
GOODS. That is to thy damnation, I tell
　　thee a true thing,
For love of me is to the love everlasting
　　contrary.

But if thou hadst the while loved me
　　moderately,
In such wise as to give the poor a part
　　of me,
Then would'st thou not in this dolor
　　be,
Nor in this great sorrow and care.
EVERYMAN. Lo, now was I deceived ere
　　I was ware,
And all I may blame to misspending of
　　time.
GOODS. What, thinkest thou I am thine?
EVERYMAN. I had thought so.
GOODS. Nay, Everyman, I say no.
Just for a while I was lent to thee,
A season thou hast had me in prosper-
　　ity.
My nature it is man's soul to kill,
If I save one, a thousand I do spill.
Thinkest thou that I will follow thee?
Nay, from this world not, verily!
EVERYMAN. I had thought otherwise.
GOODS. So it is to thy soul Goods is a
　　thief,
For when thou art dead I straightway
　　devise
Another to deceive in the same wise
As I have done thee, and all to his
　　soul's grief.
EVERYMAN. O false Goods, cursed may
　　thou be!
Thou traitor to God that hast deceived
　　me,
And caught me in thy snare.
GOODS. Marry, thou broughtest thyself
　　to this care,—
Whereof I am glad!
I must needs laugh, I cannot be sad!
EVERYMAN. Ah, Goods, thou hast had
　　long my hearty love.
I gave thee that which should be the
　　Lord's above.
But wilt thou not go with me, in-
　　deed?—
I pray thee truth to say!
GOODS. No, so God me speed!
Therefore farewell, and have good-
　　day. [GOODS is hidden from view.]
EVERYMAN. Oh, to whom shall I make
　　my moan
For to go with me on that heavy jour-
　　ney!
First Fellowship, so he said, would have
　　with me gone,
His words were very pleasant and gay,
But afterwards he left me alone;

Then spake I to my kinsmen, all in despair,
And they also gave me words fair,
They lacked not fair speeches to spend,
But all forsook me in the end;
Then went I to my Goods that I loved best,
In hope to have comfort, but there had I least,
For my Goods sharply did me tell
That he bringeth many into hell.
Then of myself I was ashamed,
And so I am worthy to be blamed.
Thus may I well myself hate.
Of whom shall I now counsel take?
I think that I shall never speed.
Till I go to my Good Deeds.
But, alas! she is so weak,
That she can neither move nor speak.
Yet will I venture on her now.
My Good Deeds, where be you? [GOOD DEEDS *is shown.*]
GOOD DEEDS. Here I lie, cold in the ground.
Thy sins surely have me bound
That I cannot stir.
EVERYMAN. O Good Deeds, I stand in fear!
I must pray you for counsel,
For help now would come right well!
GOOD DEEDS. Everyman, I have understanding
That ye be summoned your account to make
Before Messias, of Jerusalem King.
If you do my counsel, that journey with you will I take.
EVERYMAN. For that I come to you my moan to make.
I pray you that ye will go with me.
GOOD DEEDS. I would full fain, but I cannot stand, verily.
EVERYMAN. Why, is there something amiss that did you befall?
GOOD DEEDS. Yea, Sir, I may thank you for all.
If in every wise ye had encouraged me,
Your book of account full ready would be.
Behold the books of your works and your deeds thereby.
Ah, see, how under foot they lie
Unto your soul's deep heaviness.
EVERYMAN. Our Lord Jesus his help vouchsafe to me,
For one letter here I cannot see.

GOOD DEEDS. There is a blind reckoning in time of distress!
EVERYMAN. Good Deeds, I pray you help me in this need,
Or else I am forever damned indeed.
Therefore help me to make reckoning
Before him, that Redeemer is of everything,
That is, and was, and shall ever be, King of All.
GOOD DEEDS. Everyman, I am sorry for your fall,
And fain would I help you, if I were able.
EVERYMAN. Good Deeds, your counsel, I pray you, give me.
GOOD DEEDS. That will I do, verily.
Though on my feet I may not go,
I have a sister that shall with you be, also,
Called Knowledge, who shall with you abide,
To help you to make that dire reckoning. [KNOWLEDGE *enters.*]
KNOWLEDGE. Everyman, I will go with thee and be thy guide,
In thy utmost need to go by thy side.
EVERYMAN. In good condition I am now in every thing,
And am wholly content with this good thing,
Thanks be to God, my creator!
GOOD DEEDS. And when he hath brought thee there,
Where thou shalt heal thee of thy smart,
Then go with thy reckoning and thy good deeds together,
For to make thee joyful at heart
Before the Holy Trinity.
EVERYMAN. My Good Deeds, gramercy!
I am well content, certainly,
With your words sweet.
KNOWLEDGE. Now go we together lovingly
To Confession, that cleansing river fair.
EVERYMAN. For joy I weep—I would we were there!
But, I pray you, give me cognition,
Where dwelleth that holy man, Confession?
KNOWLEDGE. In the House of Salvation.
We shall find him in that place,
That shall us comfort by God's grace.
[CONFESSION *enters.*]
Lo, this is Confession. Kneel down, and

ask mercy,
For he is in good favor with God Almighty.
EVERYMAN. O glorious fountain that all uncleanness doth clarify,
Wash from me the spots of vice unclean,
That on me no sin be seen!
I come with Knowledge for my redemption,
Redeemed with heartfelt and full contrition,
For I am commanded a pilgrimage to take,
And great accounts before God to make.
Now I pray you, Shrift, Mother of Salvation,
Help my good deeds because of my piteous exclamation!
CONFESSION. I know your sorrow well, Everyman,
Because with Knowledge ye come to me.
I will you comfort as well as I can,
And a precious stone will I give thee,
Called penance, voice-voider of adversity.[6]
Therewith shall your body chastened be
Through abstinence and perseverance in God's service.
Here shall you receive that scourge of me
That is penance strong, that ye must endure,
To remember thy Saviour was scourged for thee
With sharp scourges, and suffered it patiently—
So must thou ere thou escape from that painful pilgrimage.
Knowledge, do thou sustain him on this voyage,
And by that time Good Deeds will be with thee.
But in any case be sure of mercy,
For your time draweth on fast, if ye will saved be.
Ask God mercy, and he will grant it truly.
When with the scourge of penance man doth him bind,
The oil of forgiveness then shall he find. [CONFESSION goes.]
EVERYMAN. Thanked be God for his gracious work,
For now will I my penance begin.
This hath rejoiced and lightened my heart,
Though the knots be painful and hard within.
KNOWLEDGE. Everyman, see that ye your penance fulfil,
Whatever the pains ye abide full dear,
And Knowledge shall give you counsel at will,
How your account ye shall make full clear.
EVERYMAN. O eternal God, O heavenly being,
O way of righteousness, O goodly vision,
Which descended down into a virgin pure
Because he would for every man redeem
That which Adam forfeited by his disobedience—
O blessed God, elect and exalted in thy divinity
Forgive thou my grievous offence!
Here I cry thee mercy in this presence.

O spiritual treasure, O ransomer and redeemer,
Of all the world the hope and the governor,
Mirror of joy, founder of mercy,
Who illumineth heaven and earth thereby,
Hear my clamorous complaint, though late it be,
Receive my prayers, unworthy in this heavy life!
Though I be a sinner most abominable,
Yet let my name be written in Moses' table.

O Mary, pray to the Maker of everything
To vouchsafe me help at my ending,
And save me from the power of my enemy,
For Death assaileth me strongly!—
And, Lady, that I may, by means of thy prayer,
In your Son's glory as partner share,
Through the mediation of his passion I it crave.
I beseech you, help my soul to save!

Knowledge, give me the scourge of
penance;
My flesh therewith shall give acquit-
tance.
I will now begin, if God give me grace.
KNOWLEDGE. Everyman, God give you
time and space!
Thus I bequeath you into the hands of
our Saviour,
Now may you make your reckoning
sure.
EVERYMAN. In the name of the Holy
Trinity,
My body sorely punished shall be.
Take this, body, for the sin of the flesh.
As thou delightest to go gay and fresh,
And in the way of damnation thou
didst me bring,
Therefore suffer now the strokes of
punishing.
Now of penance to wade the water
clear I desire,
To save me from purgatory, that sharp
fire.
GOOD DEEDS. I thank God now I can
walk and go,
And am delivered of my sickness and
woe!
Therefore with Everyman I will go and
not spare;
His good works I will help him to de-
clare.
KNOWLEDGE. Now, Everyman, be merry
and glad,
Your Good Deeds cometh now, ye may
not be sad.
Now is your Good Deeds whole and
sound,
Going upright upon the ground. [GOOD
DEEDS *rises and walks to them.*]
EVERYMAN. My heart is light and shall
be evermore.
Now will I smite faster than I did be-
fore.
GOOD DEEDS. Everyman, pilgrim, my
special friend,
Blessed be thou without end!
For thee is prepared the eternal glory.
Now thou hast made me whole and
sound this tide,
In every hour I will by thee abide.
EVERYMAN. Welcome, my Good Deeds!
Now I hear thy voice,
I weep for sweetness of love.
KNOWLEDGE. Be no more sad, but ever
rejoice!

God seeth thy manner of life on his
throne above.
Put on this garment to thy behoof,
Which wet with the tears of your weep-
ing is,
Or else in God's presence you may it
miss,
When ye to your journey's end come
shall.
EVERYMAN. Gentle Knowledge, what do
you it call?
KNOWLEDGE. A garment of sorrow it is
by name,
From pain it will you reclaim.
Contrition it is,
That getteth forgiveness,
Passing well it doth God please.
GOOD DEEDS. Everyman, will you wear it
for your soul's ease? [EVERYMAN *puts
on the robe of contrition.*]
EVERYMAN. Now blessed be Jesu, Mary's
son,
For now have I on true contrition!
And let us go now without tarrying.
Good Deeds, have we all clear our
reckoning?
GOOD DEEDS. Yea, indeed, I have them[7]
here.
EVERYMAN. Then I trust we need not
fear.
Now, friends, let us not part in twain!
KNOWLEDGE. Nay, Everyman, that will
we not, for certain.
GOOD DEEDS. Yet must thou lead with
thee
Three persons of great might.
EVERYMAN. Who should they be?
GOOD DEEDS. Discretion and Strength
they hight.[8]
And thy Beauty may not abide behind.
KNOWLEDGE. Also ye must call to mind
Your Five Wits as your counsellors be-
side.
GOOD DEEDS. You must have them
ready at every tide.
EVERYMAN. How shall I get them
hither?
KNOWLEDGE. You must call them all to-
gether,
And they will hear you immediately.
EVERYMAN. My friends, come hither
and present be,
Discretion, Strength, my Five Wits, and
Beauty. [*They enter.*]
BEAUTY. Here at your will be we all
ready.

What will ye that we should do?

GOOD DEEDS. That ye should with
Everyman go,
And help him in his pilgrimage.
Advise you—will you with him or not,
on that voyage?

STRENGTH. We will all bring him
thither,
To help him and comfort, believe ye
me!

DISCRETION. So will we go with him all
together.

EVERYMAN. Almighty God, beloved
mayest thou be!
I give thee praise that I have hither
brought
Strength, Discretion, Beauty, Five
Wits—lack I nought—
And my Good Deeds, with Knowledge
clear,
All be in my company at my will here.
I desire no more in this my anx-
iousness.

STRENGTH. And I, Strength, will stand
by you in your distress,
Though thou wouldest in battle fight
on the ground.

FIVE WITS. And though it were through
the world round,
We will not leave you for sweet or sour.

BEAUTY. No more will I unto Death's
hour,
Whatsoever thereof befall.

DISCRETION. Everyman, advise you first
of all.
Go with a good advisement and delib-
eration.
We all give you virtuous monition
That all shall be well.

EVERYMAN. My friends, hearken what I
will tell.
I pray God reward you in his heavenly
sphere.
Now hearken all that be here,
For I will make my testament
Here before you all present.
In alms, half my goods will I give with
my hands twain,
In the way of charity with good intent,
And the other half still shall remain
In bequest to return where it ought to
be.
This I do in despite of the fiend of hell,
Out of his peril to quit me well
For ever after and this day.

KNOWLEDGE. Everyman, hearken what I

say.
Go to Priesthood, I you advise,
And receive of him in any wise
The Holy Sacrament and Unction to-
gether.
Then see ye speedily turn again hither.
We will all await you here, verily.

FIVE WITS. Yea, Everyman, haste thee
that ye may ready be.
There is no emperor, king, duke, nor
baron bold,
That from God such commission doth
hold
As he doth to the least priest in this
world consign,
For of the Blessed Sacraments, pure
and benign,
He beareth the keys, and thereof hath
the cure
For man's redemption, it is ever sure,
Which God as medicine for our souls'
gain
Gave us out of his heart with great
pain,
Here in this transitory life for thee and
me.
Of the Blessed Sacraments seven there
be,
Baptism, Confirmation, with Priest-
hood good,
And the Sacrament of God's precious
Flesh and Blood,
Marriage, the Holy Extreme Unction,
and Penance.
These seven are good to have in re-
membrance,
Gracious Sacraments of high divinity.

EVERYMAN. Fain would I receive that
holy body.
And meekly to my spiritual father will I
go.

FIVE WITS. Everyman, that is best that
ye can do.
God will you to salvation bring,
For Priesthood exceedeth every other
thing.
To us Holy Scripture they do teach,
And convert men from sin, heaven to
reach.
God hath to them more power given
Than to any angel that is in heaven.
With five words he may consecrate
God's body in flesh and blood to make,
And handleth his Maker between his
hands.
The priest bindeth and unbindeth all

bands
Both in earth and heaven.—
Thou dost administer all the Sacraments seven.
Though we should kiss thy feet, yet thereof thou worthy wert.
Thou art the surgeon that doth cure of mortal sin the hurt.
Remedy under God we find none.
Except in Priesthood alone.—
Everyman, God gave priests that dignity,
And setteth them in his stead among us to be,
Thus be they above angels in degree.
KNOWLEDGE. If priests be good, it is so surely;
But when Jesus hung on the cross with grievous smart,
There he gave out his blessed heart
That same Sacrament in grievous torment.—
He sold them not to us, that Lord omnipotent.
Therefore Saint Peter the apostle doth say
That Jesus' curse have all they
Which God their Saviour do buy or sell,
Or if they for any money do "take or tell."[9]
Sinful priests give sinners bad example in deed and word,
Their children sit by other men's fires,[10] I have heard,
And some haunt of women the company,
With life unclean as through lustful acts of lechery—
These be with sin made blind.
FIVE WITS. I trust to God no such may we find.
Therefore let us do Priesthood honor,
And follow their doctrines for our souls' succor.
We be their sheep, and they shepherds be,
By whom we all are kept in security.
Peace! for yonder I see Everyman come,
Who unto God hath made true satisfaction.
GOOD DEEDS. Methinketh it is he indeed.
EVERYMAN. Now may Jesus all of you comfort and speed!
I have received the Sacrament for my redemption,
And also mine extreme unction.
Blessed be all they that counselled me to take it!
And now, friends, let us go without longer respite.
I thank God ye would so long waiting stand.
Now set each of you on this rood[11] your hand,
And shortly follow me.
I go before where I would be.
God be our guide!
STRENGTH. Everyman, we will not from you go,
Till ye have gone this voyage long.
DISCRETION. I, Discretion, will abide by you also.
KNOWLEDGE. And though of this pilgrimage the hardships be never so strong,
No turning backward in me shall you know.
Everyman, I will be as sure by thee,
As ever I was by Judas Maccabee.[12]
EVERYMAN. Alas! I am so faint I may not stand,
My limbs under me do fold.
Friends, let us not turn again to this land,
Not for all the world's gold,
For into this cave must I creep,
And turn to the earth, and there sleep.
BEAUTY. What—into this grave! Alas! Woe is me!
EVERYMAN. Yea, there shall ye consume utterly.
BEAUTY. And what,—must I smother here?
EVERYMAN. Yea, by my faith, and never more appear!
In this world we shall live no more at all,
But in heaven before the highest lord of all.
BEAUTY. I cross out all this! Adieu, by Saint John!
I take "my tap in my lap"[13] and am gone.
EVERYMAN. What, Beauty!—whither go ye?
BEAUTY. Peace! I am deaf, I look not behind me,
Not if thou wouldest give me all the gold in thy chest. [BEAUTY *goes, followed by the others, as they speak in turn.*]

EVERYMAN. Alas! in whom may I trust!
Beauty fast away from me doth hie.
She promised with me to live and die.
STRENGTH. Everyman, I will thee also
forsake and deny,
Thy game liketh me not at all!
EVERYMAN. Why, then ye will forsake
me all!
Sweet Strength, tarry a little space.
STRENGTH. Nay, Sir, by the rood of
grace,
I haste me fast my way from thee to
take,
Though thou weep till thy heart do
break.
EVERYMAN. Ye would ever abide by me,
ye said.
STRENGTH. Yea, I have you far enough
conveyed.
Ye be old enough, I understand,
Your pilgrimage to take in hand.
I repent me that I thither came.
EVERYMAN. Strength, for displeasing
you I am to blame.
Will ye break "promise that is debt"?
STRENGTH. In faith, I care not!
Thou art but a fool to complain,
You spend your speech and waste your
brain.
Go, thrust thyself into the ground!
EVERYMAN. I had thought more sure I
should you have found,
But I see well, who trusteth in his
Strength,
She him deceiveth at length.
Both Strength and Beauty have for-
saken me,
Yet they promised me fair and lovingly.
DISCRETION. Everyman, I will after
Strength be gone—
As for me, I will leave you alone.
EVERYMAN. Why, Discretion, will ye for-
sake me!
DISCRETION. Yea, in faith, I will go from
thee,
For when Strength goeth before
I follow after, evermore.
EVERYMAN. Yet, I pray thee, for love of
the Trinity
Look in my grave once in pity of me.
DISCRETION. Nay, so nigh will I not
come, trust me well!
Now I bid you each farewell.
EVERYMAN. Oh, all things fail save God
alone—
Beauty, Strength, and Discretion!

For when Death bloweth his blast,
They all run from me full fast.
FIVE WITS. Everyman, my leave now of
thee I take.
I will follow the others, for here I thee
forsake.
EVERYMAN. Alas! then may I wail and
weep,
For I took you for my best friend.
FIVE WITS. I will thee no longer keep.
Now farewell, and here's an end!
EVERYMAN. O Jesu, help! All have forsa-
ken me.
GOOD DEEDS. Nay, Everyman, I will
abide by thee,
I will not forsake thee indeed!
Thou wilt find me a good friend at
need.
EVERYMAN. Gramercy, Good Deeds,
now may I true friends see.
They have forsaken me everyone,
I loved them better than my Good
Deeds alone.
Knowledge, will ye forsake me also?
KNOWLEDGE. Yea, Everyman, when ye
to death shall go,
But not yet, for no manner of danger.
EVERYMAN. Gramercy, Knowledge, with
all my heart!
KNOWLEDGE. Nay, yet will I not from
hence depart,
Till whereunto ye shall come, I shall
see and know.
EVERYMAN. Methinketh, alas! that I
must now go
To make my reckoning, and my debts
pay,
For I see my time is nigh spent away.
Take example, all ye that this do hear
or see,
How they that I love best do forsake
me,
Except my Good Deeds that abideth
faithfully.
GOOD DEEDS. All earthly things are but
vanity.
Beauty, Strength and Discretion do
man forsake,
Foolish friends and kinsmen that fair
spake,
All flee away save Good Deeds, and
that am I!
EVERYMAN. Have mercy on me, God
most mighty,
And stand by me, thou Mother and
Maid, holy Mary!

GOOD DEEDS. Fear not, I will speak for thee.

EVERYMAN. Here I cry God mercy!

GOOD DEEDS. Shorten our end and minish our pain,
Let us go and never come again.

EVERYMAN. Into thy hands, Lord, my soul I commend—
Receive it, Lord, that it be not lost!
As thou didst me buy, so do thou me defend,
And save me from the fiend's boast
That I may appear with that blessed host
That shall be saved at the day of doom.
In manus tuas, of mights the most,
Forever *commendo spiritum meum.*[14]
[EVERYMAN *goes into the grave.*]

KNOWLEDGE. Now that he hath suffered that we all shall endure,
The Good Deeds shall make all sure;
Now that he hath made ending,
Methinketh that I hear angels sing,
And make great joy and melody,
Where Everyman's soul shall received be! [*The* ANGEL *appears.*]

THE ANGEL. Come, excellent elect spouse to Jesu!
Here above shalt thou go,
Because of thy singular virtue.
Now thy soul from thy body is taken, lo!
Thy reckoning is crystal clear.
Now shalt thou into the heavenly sphere,
Unto which ye all shall come
That live well before the day of doom.
[*The* ANGEL *goes and the* DOCTOR *enters.*]

DOCTOR. This moral men may have in mind,—
Ye hearers, take it as of worth, both young and old,
And forsake Pride, for he deceiveth you in the end,
as ye will find,
And remember Beauty, Five Wits, Strength, and

Discretion, all told,
They all at the last do Everyman forsake
Save that his Good Deeds there doth he take.
But beware, if they be small,
Before God he hath no help at all,
None excuse for Everyman may there then be there.
Alas, how shall he then do and fare!
For after death amends may no man make,
For then Mercy and Pity do him forsake.
If his reckoning be not clear when he doth come,
God will say, *Ite, maledicti, in ignem æternum.*[15]
And he that hath his account whole and sound,
High in heaven he shall be crowned,
Unto which place God bring us all thither
That we may live, body and soul, together!
Thereto their aid vouchsafe the Trinity—
Amen, say ye, for holy Charity!
Thus endeth this moral play of Everyman.

1. From the French *grand merci*, great thanks.
2. An Old Testament name for God.
3. From the French *par Dieu*, by God.
4. A proverb suggesting that the natural blood relationship will cause Everyman's kin to aid him even when they do not wish to.
5. Employed here to mean any kinsman.
6. That which annuls adversity by means of the voice.
7. The accounting books.
8. Are called.
9. A proverbial phrase describing bribery.
10. They have fathered illegitimate children.
11. The cross Everyman carries.
12. Apocrypha, 1 Maccabees 3.
13. A proverbial phrase for a hasty departure, from a housewife snatching her "tap" (flax for spinning) from her lap in order to run.
14. "Into thy hands . . . I commend my spirit."
15. "Go, wicked ones, into eternal fire."

Pierre Pathelin
(La Farce de Maître
Pierre Pathelin)

Translated by Sharon Parsell

Characters
Pierre Pathelin, a lawyer
Guillemette, his wife
William Joceaume, a cloth merchant
Thibault Aignelet, a shepherd
The Judge

The action takes place in a small town in France during the reign of Louis XI.

Scene 1

In front of PATHELIN's *house*

PATHELIN. By the Holy Virgin! Guillemette,
What pains I've taken—
Grubbing for money
And raking it in.
And yet, we still have nothing!
Where have all my clients gone?
GUILLEMETTE. Good Lord! Enough of this
Lawyering nonsense.
Used to be everyone came 'round
To have you plead their cause.
Now they think you're burnt out
And snicker you're asleep at the gate.
PATHELIN. Ah well, if I may submit—
With all due modesty—
There's still not one better than I
At lawyering in the district,

Except perhaps the mayor.
GUILLEMETTE. Of course! He knows Latin,
And has even spent time in school.
PATHELIN. What case can't I plead,
When I put my mind to it?
I've only to crack my lawbooks—
If I may say so—and I can plead
As well as the priest chants on Sunday.
It's as if I've the learning of a Charlemagne.
GUILLEMETTE. What's it worth? Not a penny!
We're starving to death;
Our clothes are in tatters.
And if it please you, may I ask,
Where are new ones coming from?
Pauh! What good's your learning to us?
PATHELIN. Hush woman! Upon my word,
Once I've racked my brain,
You'll have all the dresses and hoods
You could want.
God willing, we'll get out of this fix.
Ah, how quickly the good times will return!
Once I put my mind to the task,
Who's as talented as I?
GUILLEMETTE. By St. James, indeed!
You're a past master at flim-flammery.
PATHELIN. By the Good Lord who caused me to be born,
As a lawyer, I *am* master.
GUILLEMETTE. Of what, I've just told you.
No one need go to school to know that.

314

PATHELIN. Who but I follows such a no-
ble calling?
GUILLEMETTE. Good Lord! Flim-flam-
mery, you mean;
There, you've got the title.
PATHELIN. Let it be said that those
Who are richly clad
Are not truly lawyers;
Enough of this chatter;
I'm going shopping.
GUILLEMETTE. Shopping?
PATHELIN. By St. John, yes!
[*Sings.*] Shopping, my sweet.
[*Speaks.*] Will it upset you
If I bargain for some cloth
Or whatever else we need around the
house?
We've nothing to wear!
GUILLEMETTE. But you haven't a penny!
How will you manage it?
PATHELIN. That, dear lady, is my secret.
If I don't come home with enough
cloth
For us both, call me a liar.
What suits you—
Tweed, cloth from Brussels?
Tell me; I must know.
GUILLEMETTE. Bring home what you
can;
Beggars can't be choosy.
PATHELIN. [*Counting on his fingers.*] For
you, two and a half yards,
And for me, three, maybe four yards.
That's it!
GUILLEMETTE. You're certainly gener-
ous!
What stooge is going to give you credit?
PATHELIN. Who? Never you mind.
I'll get credit, you'll see—
And repay it on Judgment Day;
That'll be soon enough.
GUILLEMETTE. So, my dear, we shall see.
Others will be clad before we.
PATHELIN. I'll buy grey or maybe green.
And for a waistcoat, Guillemette,
I'll need three quarters of a yard of
brown;
No, perhaps a yard.
GUILLEMETTE. Lord have mercy!
Go on.
I suppose you'll find a stooge
To buy you a drink or two.
PATHELIN. Take care! [*He leaves.*]
GUILLEMETTE. [*Alone.*] Heavens! What a
man!
Could anyone fall for such blarney?

Scene 2

In front of the cloth merchant's shop.

PATHELIN. Ah ha! Is this the shop?
Let me see; yes, by the Holy Virgin,
There's my stooge. [*He enters.*]
God be with you.
WILLIAM JOCEAUME. And also with you.
PATHELIN. What a pleasure to see you.
Tell me, how's your health?
Is life treating you well, William?
WILLIAM. Yes, indeed!
PATHELIN. Let's shake hands.
All is well?
WILLIAM. Yes, of course.
At your service.
And you?
PATHELIN. By St. Peter the Apostle!
Of course, I'm well.
At your service, dear sir.
How's business?
WILLIAM. Oh, just look.
You know, it's not
Always easy for us merchants.
PATHELIN. But business is good;
Surely it gives you a livelihood?
WILLIAM. God willing!
At least I'm still working!
PATHELIN. Ah! What a noble merchant
(Praise God)
Your father was!
It gives me great pleasure
To see that you are the spitting image
Of that noblest, wisest man.
Indeed, you are his double,
May God count his blessèd soul
Among the elect!
WILLIAM. Amen!
By God's grace,
So be it with us!
PATHELIN. My stars,
How he could foretell the future.
What a disposition he had—
Goodness incarnate.
WILLIAM. Please, sit down;
Forgive my manners.
PATHELIN. No, no. I'm fine standing.
By God, what stories I could tell!
WILLIAM. Please, be seated.
PATHELIN. [*Taking a seat.*] Gladly! Is
there a child that
Resembles his father so? Amazing!
You're him all over again—
Even the cleft in your chin—

Surely, you were cut from the same
bolt of cloth.
And who dares tell your mother
You're not your father's son?
No, not a bit of difference.
Tell me, my good man, has your
Aunt, the glorious Laurette, passed
away?
WILLIAM. Good heavens, no!
PATHELIN. Now, there's a woman!
Tall, straight and gracious!
By God's Holy Mother!
You have her carriage;
Alike as two snowmen.
No one in the county has
Such resemblances as your family.
The more I see you, by God,
It's your father all over again.
Two drops of spit couldn't be more
alike.

I've no doubt!
What a good man.
Why, he'd offer credit to a total stran-
ger.
God have mercy on him!
Pray to Jesus that the world
Resemble him more!
Then we'd surely see
Fewer people cheating each other. [*He
fingers a piece of cloth.*]
My this cloth is well made!
Goodness, it's soft and supple.
WILLIAM. I had it specially woven
From the wool of my own sheep.
PATHELIN. What? How clever you are!
Indeed, you are your father's son.
Do you never stop?
WILLIAM. What do you expect?
One must work
If one wants to live well.
PATHELIN. [*Fingering another piece of
cloth.*] This wool, is it dyed?
It's as strong as leather from Cordova.
WILLIAM. It's good grey cloth from
Rouen,
I can assure you, and tightly woven.
PATHELIN. Indeed, I'm quite taken with
it.
I certainly had no intention to buy—
By Jesus—when I came in.
I had put aside eighty gold crowns to
settle a loan.
But you're going to get twenty or thirty
of that, I can see,
Because I'm really taken with this cloth.

WILLIAM. Gold crowns? You intend to
short-change
The lender to buy this cloth?
PATHELIN. Oh yes! If I want it,
That's all the same to me.
What cloth!
The more I see it,
The more I want it.
I must have a gown from it
And one for my wife too.
WILLIAM. Fine, it's as expensive as cav-
iar.
You can have it if you want.
Ten or twenty francs at the least.
PATHELIN. What does it matter,
If it's good?
Besides, I've got a little set aside.
WILLIAM. Good heavens! By St. Peter!
Wish I were so lucky.
PATHELIN. Enough!
I like the material.
I want it.
WILLIAM. Good. You only have to say
How much you need for your gar-
ments.
I am at your service.
Take what you want,
Even if your purse is empty.
PATHELIN. How generous! Thank you.
WILLIAM. Does this blue-green please
you?
PATHELIN. First off, how much per
yard?
Here's God's penny[1] to sign our bar-
gain.
Let's do this with God's blessing.
WILLIAM. What an honest man you are.
I am obliged to you.
Do you want to know my price?
PATHELIN. Yes!
WILLIAM. Then, each yard will cost you
twenty-four pence.
PATHELIN. You jest! Twenty-four
pence! Holy Mother!
WILLIAM. That's what it cost me.
Should I charge you less. . . .
PATHELIN. Whew! That's expensive!
WILLIAM. You don't know how my over-
head has increased,
How much of the flock froze last win-
ter.
PATHELIN. Twenty pence, twenty pence.
WILLIAM. Ha! That's my final price, I
swear.
Come to the market on Saturday
And see how the price of wool has

risen.
Eight francs, I swear, for what
Four used to buy.
PATHELIN. Enough, no more talk;
I'll pay what you ask.
Measure!
WILLIAM. Please, how much shall I cut?
PATHELIN. That's easy enough to an-
swer;
What width?
WILLIAM. Tailor's width.
PATHELIN. Three yards for me, and for
her
(she's hefty, you know) two and a half.
In all six yards;
Or am I mistaken?
WILLIAM. You're lacking a half a yard
To make it six yards even.
PATHELIN. I want six yards even
Because I want a hood too.
WILLIAM. [*Pulling off a length of cloth.*]
Let's get it measured.
This piece should do.
Let's see: one, two , three, four,
Five, and six.
PATHELIN. By St. Peter's belly, man,
Just six!
WILLIAM. Shall we measure it a second
time?
PATHELIN. Why bother.
A little more, a little less!
What's it between friends?
How much all told?
WILLIAM. [*Counting on his fingers.*] Let
me see:
At two francs a yard,
That's fifteen francs for the six yards.
PATHELIN. Well done!
That makes six gold crowns.[2]
WILLIAM. Indeed, it does.
PATHELIN. Fine, my good man, credit
me.
I shall pay you at my house.
It's your choice—gold or silver.
WILLIAM. Holy Mother! It will certainly
Put me out to go all the way to your
place.
PATHELIN. Ah! As with the Evangelists,
Truth is on your side;
Indeed, it will put you out.
But why not?
Have you ever had occasion to come to
my house?
We'll seal the deal with a glass.
WILLIAM. Ah, by St. James!
There's nothing I like better

Than a drink now and then.
I'll come! You know, though, it's
Bad luck to extend credit on the first
sale.
PATHELIN. Yes, but think of getting
Gold instead of silver!
Besides, my wife is
Roasting a goose for supper.
WILLIAM. [*Aside.*] Truly, this man
mystifies me! [*Aloud.*] Let's go, old
friend;
I'll bring the cloth.
PATHELIN. Oh no, dear friend.
I'll save you the trouble
And carry it myself.
WILLIAM. That I cannot allow!
In the name of propriety,
I should carry it.
PATHELIN. [*Taking the cloth and putting it
under his arm.*] By Mary Magdalene, I
cannot tell you
How it would grieve me
To burden you so.
See, how neatly it fits under my arm?
Ah, what a time we'll have
Eating and drinking together!
WILLIAM. But, I warn you:
I must have my money
As soon as I get there.
PATHELIN. And so it shall be!
But not before you've had a good sup-
per.
It's a good thing I didn't bring my
money.
This way you'll see how well I live.
Ah, how your late father used to drop
by:
"How's it going, what's new, old boy?"
But then, not all you rich folks treat us
poor folks
so well.
WILLIAM. You, Sir, are misled;
I'm as poor as you.
PATHELIN. We shall see! Adieu!
Come along. And don't forget
I've promised you a feast.
WILLIAM. I certainly won't!
Go on and count out my gold.
PATHELIN. [*Leaving the shop.*] Of course!
I've never tricked a soul. [*To himself.*]
Gold! Pauh! I'll see him hanged first.
He struck a bargain at his price;
But he'll be paid at mine.
And to claim it,
He'll have to travel to Perpignan—
At least, or further.

WILLIAM. [*In front of his shop.*] Those
  crowns he's going to pay me
Won't see the light of day.
I'll tuck them away far from thieves.
What a fool! He paid two francs a yard
For cloth that only cost me one.

Scene 3

PATHELIN's *house.*

PATHELIN. Where is it?
GUILLEMETTE. Where's what?
PATHELIN. That old dress of yours.
GUILLEMETTE. What on earth?
What could you want with that?
PATHELIN. Nothing, nothing at all.
I have it, the cloth!
What do you say to that?
Pretty, isn't it?
GUILLEMETTE. Holy Mother!
Bless my soul!
Who did you dupe this time?
How on earth will we ever pay for it?
PATHELIN. You ask me how?
Believe me, it's been paid for.
The merchant who sold me this
Wasn't a fool, my sweet.
I'll be hanged if I didn't
Charm that crazy bastard.
Now there's a man made for cheating.
GUILLEMETTE. How much did the cloth
  cost?
PATHELIN. Nothing.
Rest assured, he's been paid.
GUILLEMETTE. You don't have a penny
  to your name!
Paid, you say?
With what?
PATHELIN. By the martyrs' blood,
Don't concern yourself about it,
  woman;
I've a penny here and there.
GUILLEMETTE. Now you've done it!
You've gone and signed a note.
What will happen when it falls due?
They'll come and seize what little
We have.
PATHELIN. I told you, woman,
It cost only a penny
For the lot of it!
GUILLEMETTE. Hail Mary!

Only a penny?
Impossible!
PATHELIN. Let me tell you,
Had I wanted more,
I could have charmed it out of him.
GUILLEMETTE. And who is this fool?
PATHELIN. William, William Joceaume.
You know the family.
GUILLEMETTE. But only a penny
  changed hands?
How did you manage that?
PATHELIN. It was done with God's
  penny
And had I wished
To swear with upraised hand,
I could have kept that too.
Now what do you think?
And that penny he has
To share with God.
When it's all over
Even that will look good to him.
He can rant and rage all he wants.
GUILLEMETTE. Tell me, how did you
  convince him
To part with this precious cloth?
PATHELIN. Holy Mother!
I chatted him up a bit
Until he begged me to take it
For nothing.
I reminded him what
A good fellow his old man was.
"Brother," I said,
"What a noble pedigree you have;
For sure, there's not a better family
  anywhere."
But let me tell you, woman,
You can't find lower than that
Around here.
"Ah," I said, "Dear William,
How you resemble your dear father
In every way."
God knows, how I polished up
His father's reputation.
"And," I said, "That wonderful man
Was always quick to sell his goods
—And with a smile—on credit.
You are his living portrait."
In fact, you could pull out the old
  shark's teeth
(And the young baboon's too for that
  matter)
Before they'd say a civil word.
So, there you have it.
I buttered him up
To the tune of six yards.
GUILLEMETTE. And what are you going

to give him?

PATHELIN. Give him? The devil for all I care.

GUILLEMETTE. It appears to me
That what we have here is
The fable of the fox and the crow.
There sat the crow way up in a tree
With a fine bit of cheese in his mouth.
Along came a fox who thought:
"Ah ha! Here's my chance!"
So he sat himself under that tree and
    started:
"My, you're a pretty one!
What a fine voice you have!"
That silly crow was so beside himself,
Hearing his voice praised, that
He opened his beak to sing.
Of course, the cheese fell to the
    ground;
Master Renard snatched it up
And gobbled it down.
That's the story, I'm sure,
Of your cloth.
You snapped it up by blarney
And cheated him by using fine words,
Just as the fox got the cheese.
That's the result of your shenanigans.

PATHELIN. Enough!
He's on his way here
To eat roast goose.
Now here's what we'll do
When he demands his money.
It's really quite simple:
I'll take to my bed
As if I were sick.
When he insists on seeing me,
Pull a long face and groan,
"Shh! Quiet please, he's been sick,
You know, for two months at least."
Then he'll say:
"That's a lie!
Why he was just in my shop."
"Please, this is hardly the time
To joke," you'll answer.
Let him go on and rage;
What more can he do?

GUILLEMETTE. Upon my word!
That's one part I can play!
But if you've missed your mark,
And the law gets after you . . .
It won't go so easy for you.

PATHELIN. Quiet!
I know what I'm doing.
It will work like a charm.

GUILLEMETTE. Pray that it does!
Remember that Saturday

You spent in the pillory
With everyone laughing at you
Because of your tomfoolery?

PATHELIN. Enough!
Let's drop all this chatter.
He's on his way;
There's no time to waste.
That cloth stays here.
I'm off to bed. [*He goes into the bedroom.*]

GUILLEMETTE. Off with you, now!

PATHELIN. Not a snicker!

GUILLEMETTE. Don't worry,
I'll cry hot tears.

PATHELIN. We'll have to be extra careful
To make sure he doesn't catch on.

Scene 4

WILLIAM's *shop.*

WILLIAM. It's time to toast the setting
    sun.
Ho! Today something special,
By St. Matthew!
Goose and a nip or two at Lawyer
    Pathelin's!
Plus, a bill to be settled.
Ah, what a way to end the day!
For once, I'm going to get filled up
Without putting out a penny.

Scene 5

PATHELIN's *house.*

WILLIAM. [*Knocking at the door.*] Ho,
    Lawyer Pathelin!

GUILLEMETTE. [*Opening the door*] Please,
    Sir, not so loud!

WILLIAM. God be with you, ma'am.

GUILLEMETTE. Shh—not so loud!

WILLIAM. Why?

GUILLEMETTE. Why?
It's good manners!

WILLIAM. Where is he?

GUILLEMETTE. [*Pointing toward the bed-
    room.*] There!
Where should he be?

WILLIAM. Who?

GUILLEMETTE. Hah!
You're joking . . .
Where is he? God bless us!
He's not budged, the poor soul,
For eleven weeks.
WILLIAM. What??
GUILLEMETTE. Allow me, if you will,
To speak louder: I know he's asleep.
He so needs his sleep.
Poor man, with what he's been
    through!
WILLIAM. Who??
GUILLEMETTE. Lawyer Pierre Pathelin.
WILLIAM. What?
Wasn't he just in my shop
Buying six yards of cloth?
GUILLEMETTE. Who? Him?
WILLIAM. Indeed,
He was just in my shop,
Not fifteen minutes ago.
By God, I've waited long enough!
No more jokes!
My money!
GUILLEMETTE. What? You must be jok-
    ing!
I'll have you know this is no laughing
    matter.
WILLIAM. Come on, my money!
You're a crazy one!
He owes me fifteen francs.
GUILLEMETTE. Ho! William!
Don't come 'round here
Playing the fool and telling tall tales.
Go tell them to your cronies;
And don't bother me with such non-
    sense.
WILLIAM. Good God!
He owes me fifteen francs!
GUILLEMETTE. [Yelling.] Good sir,
This is hardly the time for practical
    jokes!
WILLIAM. Pipe down!
You're not in a well
Or at the bottom of a cave, woman.
GUILLEMETTE. Good Lord! You're a
    lusty one!
Bellowing must be your speciality!
WILLIAM. Something strange is going on
    here!
You want me to speak lower, fine.
Discussions of this type
Are very much to my liking.
The fact is, your husband Pierre Pathe-
lin
Helped himself to six yards of my cloth
    today.

GUILLEMETTE. That nonsense again?
Something funny *is* going on.
Devil take me if I'm lying, dear sir;
But that poor man hasn't left his bed
For eleven weeks.
Enough of your stories!
You've taken leave of your senses!
Get out of here
I'm tired of listening to you.
WILLIAM. Good woman,
I implore you,
Get Lawyer Pathelin out here.
GUILLEMETTE. Surely, I've missed the
    point of this joke.
WILLIAM. Very well!
Am I not at the home of
Lawyer Pierre Pathelin?
GUILLEMETTE. Indeed, you are.
St. Matthew protect me
From such madness.
Speak softer.
WILLIAM. Devil be hanged!
I demand to see your husband!
GUILLEMETTE. God protect me!
Softer please,
I'm afraid you'll wake him.
WILLIAM. You're asking me
To speak softer, woman?
You're shrieking!
GUILLEMETTE. I am not! It's you
Who's raising this ruckus!
WILLIAM. All right, if you want an end
    to this,
Pay me.
GUILLEMETTE. Softer, now!
WILLIAM. You're the one who'll wake
    him
With all your braying,
Not I.
Just pay me, and I'll go.
GUILLEMETTE. Surely you must be
    drunk
Or out of your mind. Oh, Lord!
WILLIAM. Drunk? Me?
By St. Peter, now that's
Something new. Me, drunk.
GUILLEMETTE. Shh! Quiet.
WILLIAM. I ask, good woman,
With St. George as my witness,
For my six yards of cloth.
GUILLEMETTE. You're insane!
And to whom did you give this cloth?
WILLIAM. Why, to Lawyer Pathelin!
GUILLEMETTE. What need does he
Have of new clothing,
Poor man?

The next time he leaves his bed,
It will be feet first,
In a shroud.
WILLIAM. And all this happened just
  now,
I suppose?
I talked to him not an hour ago.
GUILLEMETTE. My your voice is loud!
Please, speak softer.
WILLIAM. You're the one who's scream-
  ing.
You've bloody well angered me.
Pay me, and I'll go.
God, each time I ask,
I come up empty.
PATHELIN. [*From his bed.*] Guillemette, a
  little rose water.
Come, fix my bed.
Lazy slut, who are you talking to?
The pitcher, a drink.
Rub my feet.
WILLIAM. I hear him.
GUILLEMETTE. Indeed.
PATHELIN. Hey, slut!
Come here, open the windows
And cover me.
Chase away those ghosties.
Marmara, carimari, carimara.
Away, away, quick!
GUILLEMETTE. [*Going to* PATHELIN.]
  What's the matter with you?
Are you out of your mind?
PATHELIN. You can't see what I feel.
There goes a black monk flying!
Catch him, get him down from there!
Cat! Cat! Look at him fly!
GUILLEMETTE. [*Turning to* WILLIAM.]
  What now?
Good lord.
Just look what you've done.
PATHELIN. Those doctors are killing me
With all those potions
They're making me drink.
And they think they're curing me.
GUILLEMETTE. Alas, you see, dear sir,
How the poor man suffers.
WILLIAM. [*Peering into the bedroom.*] Did
  he really take sick
When he came home from shopping?
GUILLEMETTE. Shopping?
WILLIAM. By St. John, indeed!
For the cloth I sold him. [*To* PATHELIN.]
  Pay me, Lawyer Pathelin!
PATHELIN. Oh! I tell you, sir,
I've only passed two little turds.
Round, black and hard as rocks they

were.
Should I take another enema?
WILLIAM. How should I know!
Fifteen francs or six gold crowns.
PATHELIN. These three little cubes,
Are they really pills?
They nearly broke my jaw.
For God's sake, don't make me take
  them.
Doctor, they make me throw up.
I've never had anything more bitter.
WILLIAM. On my father's soul,
Spit up those six gold crowns!
GUILLEMETTE. Your kind should be
  hanged.
Get out of here, William.
Devil take you!
Name of God!
PATHELIN. And my urine . . .
Does it tell you I'm not long for this
  world?
How many hours before I die?
GUILLEMETTE. Get out of here, William.
It's a sin to plague him so.
WILLIAM. Woman! By God!
Six yards of cloth now!
PATHELIN. Study my shit,
Doctor. Is it too hard?
You don't know how I strained,
to get it out.
WILLIAM. Fifteen francs, exactly.
By St. Peter in Rome.
GUILLEMETTE. Why torment this poor
  man?
How can you be so cruel?
Surely you can see
He thinks you're his doctor.
Alas! What poor Christian
Ever had such troubles?
Eleven weeks it is
Since he took to his bed.
WILLIAM. What's going on here?
He was at my shop today;
And we bargained together.
At least, that's what I thought.
I don't know what's going on.
GUILLEMETTE. By the Virgin Mary, dear
  sir,
You're out of your mind.
You're in a muddle.
Get out of here before people
Start to talk. . . .
The doctors will be here in a minute.
No matter what the neighbors think,
My conscience is clear.
WILLIAM. Damn it! I've had it!

By God, how can I believe this . . .
At least, you have a goose on the spit?
GUILLEMETTE. Now there's a pretty
    question!
Sir, that is not meat
For an invalid.
Eat your goose without such practical
    jokes.
You're certainly inventing a lot.
WILLIAM. Please, don't get upset;
I believe what I saw . . .
I swear by the Holy Sacrament . . .
Adieu. [*He leaves and returns to his shop.*]
That woman confused me
And muddled my thinking.
Surely I know my own stock.
Six yards in one piece!
Did he really take six yards?
God knows! I don't understand it.
I saw him at death's door—
Or so I thought—
And yet, he took my cloth,
Carried it off under his arm.
By St. Mary,
I don't know if I'm dreaming. . . .
How on earth did I hand over
My cloth? In a trance?
I've never given credit, never.
Did I do that?
Holy Mother, take my body and soul
If I could figure out who's crazy—
Them or me!
I can't make heads or tails of it.
PATHELIN. [*From his bed.*] Is he gone?
GUILLEMETTE. Shh! I'll say he's gone!
Raving and grumbling.
He's really in a muddle!
PATHELIN. Can I get up?
We did it!
GUILLEMETTE. He could come back.
Wait, don't move.
All is lost,
If you get up now.
PATHELIN. St. George!
He got his comeuppance!
That one who's so tightfisted.
He needs my money about as much
As a hen needs teeth.
GUILLEMETTE. Tricking that bastard
Really made my day!
We'll hear no more from him.
PATHELIN. By God! Don't laugh.
If he comes back, he'll mean business.
Indeed, he'll be back.
GUILLEMETTE. Heavens!
What will happen?
WILLIAM. [*Alone in his shop.*] Ah! By the

holy sun that shines,
I'll go back to that wretch of a lawyer
And get to the bottom of this.
Ho! God! What a leech
To live off the income of others.
By St. Peter, he has my cloth!
The liar, I'll get it back!
GUILLEMETTE. [*At her house.*] When I
    think about
The look on his face,
I can't help laughing.
PATHELIN. Quiet!
Pray God that he does nothing.
If he hears you laughing,
We'll have to run for it,
He is so hardheaded.
WILLIAM. [*To himself.*] And this sup-
    posed lawyer,
With his three lessons and three
    Psalms.[3]
He takes people for Simple Simons?
He, by God, deserves to be hanged—
Hoist on his own petard.
He has my cloth; I'm not mistaken. . . .
What a trick he played on me! [*He
    knocks on* PATHELIN'*s door.*]
Hola! Are you hiding?
GUILLEMETTE. My word! He heard me!
He looks mad!
PATHELIN. I'll pretend to be delirious.
Open up.
GUILLEMETTE. [*Opening the door.*] Lord!
    How you shout!
WILLIAM. Woman! By God! Laughing!
My money, *now!*
GUILLEMETTE. St. Mary!
You think I was laughing?
Who has suffered more than I?
He's breathing his last. What agony!
What a terrible frenzy!
He's delirious again.
He dreams, he sings, and then he bab-
    bles.
So many tongues, so much babble. . . .
There's not much time left to him.
By his soul, I don't know whether
To laugh or to cry.
WILLIAM. I don't see the need for
    either.
I'll be brief:
Give me my money!
GUILLEMETTE. That again! You're crazy!
WILLIAM. I am not used to such words
When I sell my cloth.
Do you think I'm dumb enough
To buy a pig in a poke?
PATHELIN. [*Faking delirium.*] Oyez, Oyez!

The Queen of Guitars approaches
With her twenty-four little ones
All fathered by the Abbot of Iver-
neaux.
I'm their godfather!
GUILLEMETTE. Hush, now!
Think of God the Father,
Dear one, and not guitars.
WILLIAM. What blither and blather!
Quick, I'll be paid in
Silver or gold, no matter,
For the cloth you pinched.
GUILLEMETTE. We've heard it all before,
haven't we?
WILLIAM. Believe what you will, woman.
By God, I speak the truth.
Pay up or be hanged!
I'm only asking for what I'm due.
Is that a crime?
GUILLEMETTE. Alas, how can you tor-
ment him so?
I see by your face
That you're certainly not in your right
mind.
By St. Mary the Sinner,
If I could, I'd lock you up.
You're crazy!
WILLIAM. By God! I am mad!
I'll have my money, *now!*
GUILLEMETTE. Ha! What sweet words!
Cross yourself! *Benedicite.*
Make the sign of the cross!
WILLIAM. [*To himself.*] I'll be lucky if I
see
That cloth again this year. . . .
God, what a mess!
PATHELIN. Mother of God, the
Coronade.
Oker poker Dominoker.
The sea 'tis blue o'er the waves.
Od's bod, dis ist gegangen!
Casa caressa, don't giff oop the schip!
No tickee, no shirtee!
What's money to me? [*To* WILLIAM.] Did
ya 'ear that, dear friend?
GUILLEMETTE. He had an uncle from
Limoges,
A brother of his aunt by marriage.
That was, I suppose,
A dialect from the area.
WILLIAM. He's a sly one all right,
With my cloth tucked away!
PATHELIN. Cum in, sweet laidy.
And whot's all dis crap?
To de rear march, boys!
Zum wohl! I wanna be a praist
Cha, cha, cha! Devel take ya!

Oochy koochy ole fuddy duddy.
Do praists laff
Whan dey say de mass?
GUILLEMETTE. Oh woe, oh woe!
The hour approaches
To administer the last rites.
WILLIAM. But how can he speak Flem-
ish?
Where's he from, this rascal?
GUILLEMETTE. His mother came from
Calais;
So he speaks it easily.
PATHELIN. Whare ye goin', ye cluwn?
Was fûr loosfa, Gooderman,
Erin go bragh?
Heinz, Heinz cum so lappen.
Ik sage niks dis maken,
Gilly Gilly silly solly.
Silop, Solop, gif ein dollop
Dissen, datten, ein, zwei, drei,
Mon grozs fat und trout in dem hart,
Ho! Willy nilly cumen den
Prost! Ein trink! Bitte, bitte
Connemara, maggots in den water.
Water, water, Gott im Himmel!
Ho! Willy, inky dinky,
Get Father Thomas here,
I want to make my confession.
WILLIAM. What's this?
Does he never stop?
Give me a pledge
—Or my money—
And I'll go.
GUILLEMETTE. By the Passion of Our
Lord,
You're a hard man!
What do you want?
Never have I seen such a stubborn
man.
PATHELIN. Oyez oyez!
Place yer bets! Eh, whot's bitin' me
arse?
Bed bug, flea, mosquito, or louse.
Mon dieu, the flux, the flux, St. Gar-
bot![4]
Ik speaka kin franche.
De Konig uff die raider ist appy;
'E knows who Ik seh.
Oy veh tip o' de 'at to Sin Jin!
I'll turn the other cheek.
WILLIAM. How can he carry on like this?
He's worn out!
GUILLEMETTE. His old teacher was from
Cherbourg.
Now that he's dying, it's
All coming back to him.
It's the end.

WILLIAM. Holy Mary,
What a nightmare this is!
I know I talked to him at the shop.
GUILLEMETTE. You believe that?
WILLIAM. Indeed I do.
Now I'm not so sure.
PATHELIN. 'Ark! 'Ear han arse brayin'?
Ola, Ola couzine mina!
Dee alla in dee drinka.
Punch 'n Judy dee lichta an,
Me tinks ah git de drifta.
Tutte frutti hits alla an acta
'Ouse dee Jounken.
Umpa, dumpa, poodle jumpa.
Clippty cloppa, 'ad enuf?
GUILLEMETTE. God bless you!
PATHELIN. Hic, haec, hoc, tick tock!
Digger, rigger, tigger
Inchy pinchy olla beni!
Quist qui veni vidi vinci
Minch, chinch in a clinch
'Ere's a baig 'un.
Massa, massa cum quick!
O solo mio joomp ofer dee moon.
Calle halle I spaigh.
Har car amour der Dieu!
WILLIAM. Alas! Dear God, listen to it!
He's dying! How he babbles!
Surely, the devil has him!
God, how he jabbers.
His words mean nothing.
These aren't words
A godfearing man could understand!
GUILLEMETTE. His father's mother came
　　from Brittany.
He's going to die, I know it!
The last rites!
PATHELIN. Eh! By St. Gignon, you lie!
Repent, the kingdom is at hand!
Seven 'n haight, seven 'n haight
Don't bae laite.
Go, ye bloody cur uf a cabbage
Go, ye scaimp tea's maide.
Bloody wail, I'd saiy.
God's bod, 'ouse cumin' ta tea?
Happles 'n pairs, happles 'n pairs
Whaires de bair?
St. Georgie's dragon, a tuppence.
A tip . . . Whot ham ah saiyin'?
Lawze, ye Picard ass!
"Et bona dies sit vobis,
Magister amantissime,
Pater reverendissime,
Quomodò brulis? Quae nova?
Parisiis non sunt ova.
Quid petit ille mercator?

Dicat sibi quod trufator
Ille, qui in lecto jacet,
Vult ei dare, si placet,
De ocâ ad comedendum:
Si sit bona ad edendum,
Pete sibi sine mord,"⁵
GUILLEMETTE. Lord, he's dying!
Look, he's foaming at the mouth!
Do you see how wrought up he is?
O Lord Most High, O God in Heaven!
Where's he going, my poor husband?
I'll be alone and grieving.
WILLIAM. [Aside.] I'd better leave before
　　he croaks. [To GUILLEMETTE.] I don't
　　think he'll tell you
His most important secrets with me
　　here.
Forgive me, I swear,
Because I know in my soul,
That he has my cloth. Adieu, madame.
Pray God, he'll forgive me!
GUILLEMETTE. So be it!
WILLIAM. [Alone.] By St. Mary's brood!
Am I ever mixed up;
The devil's been playing tricks on me.
Benedicite. At least,
He'll leave me alone now.
So, I lost a little cloth;
But I still have my wits!
PATHELIN. [After WILLIAM leaves.] Ah ha!
　　I did it!
He's gone, isn't he, sweet William?
God! What he's got to ponder under
　　his bonnet!
His dreams—what madness!
GUILLEMETTE. Oh, we really tricked
　　him, all right!
I was pretty good, wasn't I?
PATHELIN. By all the saints in heaven,
　　woman,
You played it to the hilt.
We certainly got enough cloth
To clothe us out of it.

Scene 6

WILLIAM's shop.

WILLIAM. [Alone.] For sure I'm the king
　　of the unlucky.
Everyone—no matter who—treats me
　　like Pathelin

And will take what little I have.
Even now, the shepherds are stealing
  my sheep.
Here's one now!
Lord knows I've always been good to
  him.
I'll fix him so quick,
He won't know what hit him.
By the Blessèd Virgin!
THIBAULT AIGNELET. God bless you day
  and night,
Good sir.
WILLIAM. There you are, you varlet,
You good-for-nothing rascal!
THIBAULT. If it please you, sir,
A strange man, dressed in the king's
  uniform,
—And not too clean at that—
Carrying the sergeant's wand[6]
Said to me . . . I don't rightly
Remember his words.
He spoke of you, good sir,
And a certain summons.
Believe me, by the Holy Virgin,
I hardly understood him.
His words tumbled out pell-mell.
Sheep, I think, and the afternoon;
All the time talking about you, good sir,
And butchers. . . .
WILLIAM. If I don't lead you by the nose
To the judge today,
I pray God that the deluge carry me
  away!
You'll no longer bludgeon my sheep,
By God, without remembering it!
You'll pay me six yards, I say,
For killing my sheep
And for ten years of robbing me blind!
THIBAULT. Don't believe everything
You hear, good sir, upon my soul. . . .
WILLIAM. And by the Blessèd Virgin to
  whom we pray,
I'll be repaid before Saturday.
My six yards. . . . I mean
That which you stole from me!
THIBAULT. What six yards?
Oh, good sir, surely, you're confused.
By St. Leu, my patron, I don't dare say
  anything to you.
WILLIAM. Get out of here!
See what kind of settlement
You get from the court!
THIBAULT. Good sir, can't we settle this
Without going to court, for God's sake?
WILLIAM. Away!
The case against you is clear.

Get out of here!
I won't settle with you;
By God, I'll settle only when the judge
  tells me.
Oh, how they all trick me;
By gad, if only I'd been on guard!
THIBAULT. Adieu, good sir. [*To himself.*]
  Then I must defend myself.

Scene 7

PATHELIN's *house.*

THIBAULT. [*Knocking at* PATHELIN's *door.*]
  Anybody home?
PATHELIN. I'll be hanged,
He's come back to kill me!
GUILLEMETTE. Oh Lord, no, blessèd St.
  George,
What will happen to us now?
THIBAULT. [*Entering.*] God bless you;
  God be with you!
PATHELIN. [*Opening the door to his bed-
  room.*] And also with you, my friend!
What is it?
THIBAULT. I'll be tried by default
If I don't appear before the judge
This afternoon, kind sir.
Please, sir, can you come along
And plead my case? I don't know how
  to do it.
And I'll pay you well,
Even if it means rags for me.
PATHELIN. Come, tell me about it.
Are you the plaintiff or the defendant?
THIBAULT. I have a case to be heard
(You'll hear me out, kind sir)
Against my boss.
For years I've tended his sheep.
By my faith, he's paid me little enough.
Do I make myself clear?
PATHELIN. Heavens yes!
To the court, that will say all.
THIBAULT. To tell the truth, kind sir,
I did beat some of them
So hard that they fell over dead.
Then I told him—so he wouldn't scold
  me—
That they'd had the pox.
"Ah ha," he said, "separate them
From the flock. Toss them away."
"Gladly," I said.

But that's not the way it happened,
Because, by St. John, I ate them.
Who knows better than I how to recog-
nize the pox?
What more can I say to you?
This went on for years;
I killed so many sheep
That he finally caught on.
And when he found out . . .
My God, how he spied on me!
(How those sheep bleated when they
were beaten!)
Then he caught me in the act.
I can't deny that.
I would like to ask you
(Don't worry, I'll pay)
To plead my case in court.
I know the law's on his side;
But you'll find a loophole, I know,
To put him in the wrong.
PATHELIN. On your word, now,
Do you have enough to pay me
If I turn the law to your advantage?
Come now, the truth.
THIBAULT. I won't pay you in francs,
But in glittering gold crowns.
PATHELIN. Then you have a good case.
It's not half so bad
As the best I've pleaded.
When I apply myself,
Ah, you should hear me discourse
After they make their case!
Listen up, I must ask you,
By all the saints in heaven,
If you're clever enough
To understand my defense?
What's your name?
THIBAULT. By St. Maur! Thibault Ai-
gnelet!
PATHELIN. Aignelet? Milk lamb,
hmmm . . .
And you cheated your master?
THIBAULT. Indeed I did.
It's possible that I ate
More than thirty sheep in three years.
PATHELIN. That's a tidy sum
For your skittles and beer.
How I'll give it to him!
Do you think he can find
Witnesses to prove his case?
That's the thing in a trial.
THIBAULT. Witnesses, oh sir!
Holy Mary and all the saints in heaven!
For every one of mine,
He'll find ten who will testify against
me.

PATHELIN. Ah ha! Now that will cer-
tainly
Ruin your case. . . . Let me think. . . .
I'll pretend I don't know you
And have never spoken with you.
THIBAULT. God, no!
PATHELIN. No, nothing to it.
Now here's what could happen:
If you speak, they'll lead you
Little by little into difficulties
And so on to confessions.
That could be very prejudicial.
God, those devils are cruel!
Here's what you'll do,
If you're called before the judge:
Don't say anything more than "Baa,"
Whatever they ask you.
And if they berate you by saying,
"Dirty vagabond, God's put you in your
place,
You scamp! How dare you mock the
king's justice!"
Say, "Baa."
"Ah! What an idiot" they'll say,
"He thinks he's talking to his sheep!"
Now, if you want to get the best of
them,
Say nothing more than "Baa."
Watch out!
THIBAULT. I understand.
I'll watch myself.
And do it up right.
You've my word on that.
PATHELIN. Watch yourself, be on guard,
Even to me; when I ask you
One thing or another, remember
Say nothing more than "Baa."
THIBAULT. Me! Oh no, by my word!
Do you think I'm a fool?
I'll say nothing more than "Baa"
To you or to anyone else.
For each word I hear,
A loud "Baa," as you've taught me,
"Baa"!
PATHELIN. Holy John! That's the way
To lead your adversary by the nose!
Now remember, I'll want my fee
As soon as it's all over.
THIBAULT. Kind sir, you think
I'd forget to pay you? Never!
Now, please be diligent on my behalf.
PATHELIN. Our Lady of Boulogne!
The judge is in court.
The gavel always goes down at six o'-
clock—
Or there abouts.

Wait 'til I go ahead; we don't want
To get there at the same time.

THIBAULT. Oh, I see: you don't want
them
To know you're my lawyer.

PATHELIN. Holy Mary! Fool,
If you don't pay me enough . . .

THIBAULT. Heavens! You've my word
on that,
Kind sir, have no doubt.

PATHELIN. [*Alone.*] Ah ha! My luck's
changing!
A nibble at last!
I'll reel him in
And pocket a crown or two for my
pains!

Scene 8

A provincial courtroom.

PATHELIN. [*To the judge.*] Sir, God give
you grace
And all your heart's desires!

JUDGE. Welcome, sir!
Put on your hat.
There, take your place.

PATHELIN. [*Retreating to a dark corner of
the courtroom.*] Thank you, your
Honor, if it please the court.
I'm only here as an observer.

JUDGE. Let's get about it.
Where's the first case to be heard?

WILLIAM. [*Appearing before the bench.*] My
lawyer's on his way.
He had something to finish up.
Your Honor, if it please you,
The case is worth the delay.

JUDGE. Ho, now! I've other things to
do.
If the other party is present,
We'll proceed without delay.
You're the plaintiff?

WILLIAM. Indeed I am.

JUDGE. Where's the defendant?
Is he present in court?

WILLIAM. Indeed, look there,
That one who says nothing.
God knows what he's thinking!

JUDGE. Since you're both present,
Let's hear the evidence.

WILLIAM. Here's what I demand, your
Honor.
It's true, by God and all charity.
That I sheltered him as a child.
And when I saw him grown,
I sent him out to tend my flock.
He was my shepherd—and a good one.
But it's just as true as you're sitting
there,
Your Honor, that he butchered my
sheep.
Without a doubt . . .

JUDGE. I hear you. [*To* WILLIAM.] You
mean you *paid* this man?

PATHELIN. Of course, how could he pretend
To hire him without paying him?

WILLIAM. [*Recognizing* PATHELIN, *who
hides his face.*] Lord, let me be wrong!
That's him without a doubt!

JUDGE. Why are you holding your hand
like that,
Lawyer Pathelin? Do you have a tooth-
ache?

PATHELIN. Indeed, my teeth are throb-
bing.
I've never felt such pain.
I don't dare raise my head.
Please, let us proceed.

JUDGE. [*To* WILLIAM.] Get on with it;
make your point.
And above all, be clear!

WILLIAM. [*Aside.*] I'm not mistaken;
It is he. [*To* PATHELIN.] By the Holy
Rood,
Was it not to you
I sold six yards of cloth, Lawyer Pathe-
lin?

JUDGE. Who said anything about cloth?

PATHELIN. He's mistaken.
He thinks he's making a point,
But he doesn't know our ways.

WILLIAM. [*Aloud.*] I'll be hanged!
He's the one that took my cloth!

PATHELIN. When is this wretched man
going
To make his case?
He intends, the oaf, to say
That his shepherd sold the wool,
As I understand it,
From which my gown is woven.
Stole it, he says, and made wool
From the fleece of his master's sheep.

WILLIAM. Curses on you!
You've my wool or I'm blind.

JUDGE. Quiet! God, how you ramble on!

Let's get back to the case,
And leave the court out of your ram-
blings.
PATHELIN. Even with this pain, I must
laugh.
He's already so mixed up
That's he's lost the thread.
We must set him straight.
JUDGE. Let's hear more about those
sheep.
WILLIAM. He pinched six yards, that's
fifteen francs.
JUDGE. Are we fools or idiots?
Where do you think you are?
PATHELIN. Good heavens! He's making
fun of you.
Just look at him.
We should, I think, examine the other
party.
JUDGE. You're right.
He's not said a word.
It appears he doesn't understand. [To
THIBAULT.] Come here! Speak!
THIBAULT. Baa!
JUDGE. What??
"Baa?" Do you take me for a goat?
Speak to me!
THIBAULT. Baa!
JUDGE. You're mocking me, you bloody
fool!
PATHELIN. What a blockhead!
He thinks he's still with his flock.
WILLIAM. [To PATHELIN.] I'll be damned,
If you're not the one
Who pinched my cloth. . . . [To the
JUDGE.] You don't know, your
Honor,
What mischief. . . .
JUDGE. Quiet! Are you crazy?
Drop this nonsense,
And get back to the case at hand.
WILLIAM. I'm sorry, your Honor, it's
under my skin;
However, I won't say another word
about it.
Another time, when it's more appropri-
ate.
It's a bitter pill to swallow. . . .
Now I'll tell you
How I gave six yards away.
Oh, excuse me, your Honor, I mean
sheep.
My shepherd, when he was with the
flock . . .
He promised me six gold crowns, if I
sold. . .

For three years my shepherd had me
convinced
That he carefully tended my flock
And did no wrong. . . .
Now he refuses to pay me or return the
cloth!
Oh! Lawyer Pathelin, indeed!
This lout here stole my fleeces
And killed healthy sheep
By beating their brains out. . . .
With my cloth under his arm
He scooted out of my shop,
Saying six gold crowns
Were waiting for me at his house. . . .
JUDGE. There's no rhyme or reason to
this.
What's all this?
First one thing, then another!
In a word, by God, I'm lost!
He rants about cloth;
Then he raves about sheep.
Higgledy, piggledy!
What's going on here??
PATHELIN. I'm quite sure that
He's withheld the poor chap's salary.
WILLIAM. [To PATHELIN.] By God! You'd
better shut up!
My cloth, as true as the mass . . .
I know where the shoe pinches,
No matter what. . . .
By the Holy Writ! There, you have it!
JUDGE. Have what?
WILLIAM. Nothing your Honor. [To him-
self.] Lord, the tricks he plays! [To the
JUDGE.] All right, I'll shut up—
If I can—and speak no more
About it, whatever happens.
JUDGE. Very well, get to the point;
And clear it all up.
PATHELIN. This shepherd can in no way
Answer to charges against him
Without a lawyer; surely, he's afraid
Or else he doesn't know how to ask.
Why don't you turn it over to me?
I'll take him on.
JUDGE. Agreed.
But remember:
There's little money in it for you.
PATHELIN. Upon my word, I'll do it for
nothing—
The love of God.
I'll question this wretch to find out
If he has any defense.
He has no chance of success
Unless I defend him. [To THIBAULT.]
Come, my friend,

What have we here?
Can you understand me?
THIBAULT. Baa!
PATHELIN. What! "Baa," again?
By God's Blood, are you crazy?
Tell me your side.
THIBAULT. Baa!
PATHELIN. "Baa?"
Are you braying to your sheep?
It's for your own good:
Do you understand me?
THIBAULT. Baa!
PATHELIN. Now answer yes or no. [*To*
  THIBAULT.] Well done, keep it up!
THIBAULT. Baa!
PATHELIN. Louder! Or you'll be in big
  trouble.
I have no doubt of that.
THIBAULT. Baa!
PATHELIN. What fool would bring this
  idiot to court?
Your honor, send him back to his flock.
He's a born idiot.
WILLIAM. An idiot!! By God!!
He's smarter than you are.
PATHELIN. [*To the* JUDGE.] Send him
  back to his flock
Without sentencing him.
What fool ever brought him to court?
WILLIAM. [*To the* JUDGE.] And you'll let
  him go
Without hearing me out?
PATHELIN. Lord, yes. He's an idiot.
Can we do otherwise?
WILLIAM. Please, your Honor, let me
Finish first and make my case.
I'm telling you the truth,
Not nonsense.
JUDGE. What a mess!
Listening to such fools!
Enough!
Court is adjourned!
WILLIAM. [*To the* JUDGE.] You're not go-
  ing to ask them to reappear?
JUDGE. Whatever for?
PATHELIN. [*To the* JUDGE.] Reappear?
  Have you ever seen
Such an idiot as my poor client?
  [*Pointing to* WILLIAM.] And this one, is
  he much better off?
They're both crazy, and brainless, to
  boot.
By St. Mary!
What featherheads!
WILLIAM. Where's the cloth you
  swindled from me,

Lawyer Pathelin?
By St. Peter and the Apostles,
That's not the act of an honest man.
PATHELIN. St. Peter damn me!
If he wasn't a fool, he's become one.
WILLIAM. [*To* PATHELIN.] How well I
  recognize your words,
Your gown, and your face.
I'm not a fool; I'm smart enough
To know what's happened to me. [*To
  the* JUDGE.] I'll explain it all to you,
  your Honor;
You've my word on that.
PATHELIN. [*To the* JUDGE.] Your Honor,
  please, shut him up! [*To* WILLIAM.]
  Have you no shame?
Hounding this poor shepherd for three
  or four
Puny sheep that aren't worth two but-
  tons?
Why such a fuss?
WILLIAM. What sheep? That old song
  again?
I'm talking to you,
To you!
You'll give it back to me.
By the Christ who comes at Christmas!
JUDGE. See here!
Have I lost my mind?
He won't stop braying!
WILLIAM. I demand . . .
PATHELIN. [*To the* JUDGE.] Can't you
  shut him up? [*To* WILLIAM.] By God,
  there's too much nonsense here.
Let's assume that he killed
Six or seven or perhaps a dozen sheep
And bloody well ate them.
That makes you angry!
Well, you were certainly warm
While he shivered to protect your
  sheep!
WILLIAM. [*To the* JUDGE.] See, your
  Honor, see!
I speak to him of cloth;
And he answers me with sheep! [*To*
  PATHELIN.] Six yards of cloth, where
  are they—
The ones you carried out under you
  arm?
Do you intend to return them?
PATHELIN. Your Honor, do you intend
To hang him for six or seven fleeces?
At least, think about it.
Don't be so hard on this sad shepherd.
Why he's almost naked as a jaybird!
WILLIAM. Look, how he twists things!

What devil made me sell my cloth
To such as he! [*To the* JUDGE.] There,
  your Honor, I demand . . .
JUDGE. [*To* WILLIAM.] Case dismissed!
I'll have you know,
It's a privilege to appear before this
  court. [*To* THIBAULT.] Ah, my fool!
  . . . Back to your sheep!
THIBAULT. Baa!
JUDGE. [*To* WILLIAM.] By the Blood of
  Our Lady,
You show what you are, sir!
WILLIAM. Your Honor, please, upon my
  soul.
I was only trying . . .
PATHELIN. Won't he ever shut up?
WILLIAM. [*To* PATHELIN.] Indeed, my
  business is with you.
You really did a job on me—
Carrying my cloth away
With your fine compliments. . . .
PATHELIN. [*To the* JUDGE.] Lord, I must
  call up all my patience;
You heard it all, your Honor.
WILLIAM. Good Lord! What cheek! [*To
  the* JUDGE.] Cheat! . . . Your Honor,
  what I mean . . .
JUDGE. What a farce!
No more! [*He gets up.*]
Praise God, I'm leaving. [*To* THIBAULT.]
  Go, my friend;
An don't ever come back for any rea-
  son.
Do you understand me?
Case dismissed!
PATHELIN. [*To* THIBAULT.] Say thank
  you.
THIBAULT. Baa!
JUDGE. [*To* THIBAULT.] I said, *go.*
It's for the best.
WILLIAM. But is it just
That he go like this?
JUDGE. Indeed it is!
I have other cases to hear.
You're too boisterous;
I've had enough of you.
Court is closed! [*To* PATHELIN.] Will you
  come dine with me, Lawyer Pathelin?
PATHELIN. Another time, perhaps. . . .
  [*The* JUDGE *leaves.*]
WILLIAM. [*To* PATHELIN.] What a thief
  you are!
Tell me: will I ever be paid?
PATHELIN. For what? Are you crazy?
Who do you think I am?
Damn it! I'd like to know

Who you've mistaken me for!
WILLIAM. Aargh!
PATHELIN. Please, sir, watch yourself.
Just who do you think I am?
WILLIAM. Do you take me for a fool?
It is you of whom I speak,
You and no one else.
I'm convinced of that.
PATHELIN. Me? No, indeed not!
Mind your tongue! [*Pointing to a spec-
  tator in the courtroom.*]
Perhaps you've mistaken me
For that idiot there.
I've the same carriage.
WILLIAM. God no!
He doesn't have your ugly face.
Didn't I see you sick in your bed this
  afternoon?
PATHELIN. What? Sick?
Indeed not!
Drop your game.
It's all clear now.
WILLIAM. You are the one! St. Peter
  damn me!
I know it now all too well.
PATHELIN. You'll stop at nothing.
I'm not who you say I am.
I've never taken any cloth from you.
I've my reputation.
WILLIAM. Ha! I saw you in your house.
By the Holy Rood, it was you!
It's useless to discuss this any longer.
It's all a muddle!
PATHELIN. By Our Lady, that's it!
Now you've got the drift of it! [WILLIAM
  leaves; PATHELIN *turns to* THIBAULT.]
Speak, Aignelet!
THIBAULT. Baa!
PATHELIN. Come here!
It went well, didn't it!
THIBAULT. Baa!
PATHELIN. Your case is dismissed.
No more "Baas"; they're of no use now.
Didn't I skin him alive?
Didn't I counsel you well?
THIBAULT. Baa!
PATHELIN. Damn it! No one can hear
  you now.
Speak up; don't be afraid!
THIBAULT. Baa!
PATHELIN. It is time for me to go.
Pay me now.
THIBAULT. Baa!
PATHELIN. Truth be told,
You played your part well—
And with a straight face.

We got away with it
Because you didn't laugh.
THIBAULT. Baa!
PATHELIN. "Baa"? No need of that!
Come on; pay me.
THIBAULT. Baa!
PATHELIN. "Baa"? Wise up!
Pay me; I must go.
THIBAULT. Baa!
PATHELIN. Listen to me, my friend;
Stop these "Baas"
And pay me!
Enough of this foolishness!
Where's my money?
THIBAULT. Baa!
PATHELIN. You're joking! [*To himself.*] Is
this all I'm going to get?
THIBAULT. Baa!
PATHELIN. Ah, you're a master of the
language!
To whom are you peddling this line?
Tell me, who is it?
No more "Baas."
My money!
THIBAULT. Baa!
PATHELIN. Is this all I'm getting?
Whom are you kidding?
Didn't you promise to pay me;
Or am I mistaken?
THIBAULT. Baa!
PATHELIN. You're making me eat crow.
[*To himself.*] Saints alive!
Surely I'm smarter than that bleating
shepherd!
The lout, he took me in!
THIBAULT. Baa!
PATHELIN. Have you nothing more to
say?
If you're doing this
To amuse yourself, say so.
Don't make me mad!
Come, it's time for supper.

THIBAULT. Baa!
PATHELIN. By St. John! You've a point!
[*To himself.*] This pup taught me a
trick or two.
Well, I consider myself
The slickest swindler for miles around,
The best among those crooks
Who give fine words as payment for
Judgment Day.
And here I am: outsmarted by a
shepherd from the fields. [*To*
THIBAULT.] By St. John! If I find the
sergeant,
I'll have him arrest you!
THIBAULT. Baa!
PATHELIN. Pauh! Baa! I'll be hanged!
Where's the sergeant, quick?
When I find him, damn it,
It's jail for you!
THIBAULT. [*Fleeing.*] If he catches me,
I'll pardon him!

1. Earnest money to seal a transaction. After a
penny was dedicated to God, the price could
neither go up nor down.
2. Prices would be discounted for payment in
gold since it was a sounder currency.
3. An indication of the theological and litur-
gical base of legal education in the Middle Ages.
4. Patron saint of dysentery.
5. Good day to you,
   Holy Father
   What are you burning? What's new?
   There are no eggs in Paris.
   What does this merchant want?
   He tells us that the joker,
   The one in bed here,
   Wants to give him, if you please
   Goose to eat;
   If it is good,
   Give it to him at once.
6. Officers of the court carried special emblems
to indicate their function.

The Doubles According to Plautus
A commedia dell'arte scenario

One form of theater which developed early in the Renaissance was so extraordinary that it is difficult to know how best to represent it in an anthology such as the present one, yet it was so influential with respect to later comedy that it can under no circumstances be omitted. The commedia dell'arte developed out of late-fifteenth- and early-sixteenth-century Italian practices in a manner that is still in dispute, flourished all over Europe in the latter half of the sixteenth century and throughout the seventeenth, then declined and disappeared in the eighteenth century.

The commedia dell'arte is chiefly characterized by the facts that it was professional (hence its name: comedy "of the profession") and that it was improvised. It was professional in that commedia dell'arte companies of some ten or more members were formed to tour first around Italy and eventually throughout Europe. These companies carried ten, twenty, or more plays in their repertory, ready to perform on a street corner, in a courtyard, or in a ducal palace. The actors spent a lifetime performing a single character (or perhaps two—a young lover early in their careers, a character role later), that character appearing in a great many different plays, encountering a variety of comic circumstances, but always maintaining the same basic qualities. The better actors working under these circumstances developed a very high level of skill, sometimes achieved a real measure of acclaim and wealth, and established a benchmark of comic excellence unsurpassed in any later theater. Thus, after many centuries of obscurity or eclipse, the theater reemerged in the Renaissance commedia dell'arte as a viable means by which artists might make a living and to which one might reasonably devote a lifetime of effort. The essentially amateur performing of mystery, miracle, and morality plays, and of medieval farces, was replaced by the splendid professionalism of the commedia dell'arte.

Even more important was the fact that these performances were improvised. A detailed scenario provided the outline of the performance, but the highly trained actors, responding to their audiences and to the cues provided by fellow actors with whom they worked daily, improvised the details of the plot and the exact dialogue in which it was performed. The nature of this improvising should not be misunderstood: actors who played the same role year after year built up a vast repertory of set speeches for virtually all occasions, of comic bits of business, of characteristic turns of phrase, and of *lazzi* (units of stage business that fill out or enrich the play) which could be called upon at will. The result was no doubt a performance full of zest that required the actor to be on his toes at every moment in order to respond to any cue thrown him, but not one which was in any ordinary sense unstructured or sloppy.

What had happened was the virtual elimination of the playwright's art in the theater. Whereas Seneca wrote closet drama in which literary mastery was everything and performance nothing, the commedia dell'arte created theater in which performance was everything and literary values were forgotten. Several hundred scenarios of typical commedia dell'arte plays have been preserved and are available for modern study, and several very successful actors, upon retirement, published books of their set speeches and *lazzi* that were of great interest to later actors and to scholars, but the scripts, the usual literary remnants by which later ages enjoy a playwright's efforts, are not available because they never existed.

What has been preserved more than any other feature of the commedia dell'arte is a memory of the characters, developed over a lifetime of playing by highly skilled actors and passed along from generation to generation for re-creation and enrichment. In many cases based on the stock comic characters of Menander, Plautus, and Terence, but greatly enriched by some two centuries of Renaissance vitality and inventiveness, the commedia dell'arte characters provide the stock repertory upon which later generations of comic playwrights have drawn. The pair of young lovers were the only characters who traditionally played without masks; others developed masks and costumes unique to their characters which could be copied by succeeding generations of actors undertaking those roles. The old man Pantalone, for example, full of sage advice and usually father of one of the lovers, was one of the favorite commedia characters, as was the other best-known old man, Graziano, the pedant doctor. Miles Gloriosus emerges in the commedia as the Captain, a braggart warrior but also a coward. Women appeared on the commedia stage for the first time in a serious, professional manner; the leading lady often used her own name, but the servant girls Columbina and Franceschina became comic portraits of enduring significance. It was the ancient "clever servant" tradition, however, that generated the richest variety in the commedia; such servants were grouped under the generic heading *zanni*, and were by all odds the comic favorites of centuries of theatergoers as well as the etymological source of the term "zany." Chief among these servants were Arlecchino (Harlequin), Pulcinella (Punch), Brighella, Scapino, and Francatrippe.

In 1618, Basilio Locatelli of Rome prepared a manuscript volume of the scenarios of commedia dell'arte plays; a second volume followed in 1622, the two volumes together containing 103 scenarios. These two volumes were discovered in the Casanatense Library in 1890, and are one of the most important sources of such material today. Locatelli did not write these "plays" himself, but gathered them from a variety of manuscript sources available to him. Evidently these included actors' notes and other actual theater records, but it is also true that a great many of the scenarios are based at least in part on plays then in existence, both classical and contemporary, for by this time a literary drama had begun to flourish in Renaissance Italy also. In fact, commedia dell'arte plays, though sometimes original, were frequently based on literary sources of all sorts; their improvised nature did not divorce them totally from their literary heritage illustrated earlier in this volume.

Locatelli's 1618 volume is the source of the scenario reprinted here. The scenario is based, of course, on Plautus's *The Menaechmi*, a play which was also to serve Shakespeare as a matrix for *The Comedy of Errors*. This particular version may well have been in the commedia repertory for generations, and can serve as an example of typical commedia work over some two centuries. A comparative reading of the scenario with Plautus's and Shakespeare's plays will reveal how two master playwrights handled this plot, but one can know only in outline how the commedia players may have handled it. No analysis here can transmute so bare an outline into a significant work of dramatic art, yet a study of it is as important to understanding the future development of European drama as is a study of Seneca's plays. The commedia dell'arte was a tremendously important Renaissance development in the history of European comedy, but it was ephemeral even beyond the sense in which theater is always temporal. As K. M. Lea has noted, "If drama is to be great and lasting it is necessary that the player and the poet should meet on honourable terms." Both have important contributions to make.

N.B. The footnotes in this scenario were written by the translator.

The Doubles
According to Plautus

Translated by K. M. Lea

Characters
Pantalone
Flavia, his daughter (*Mulier*)
Silvio, her husband (*Menaechmus*) ⎫
Captain, his brother (*Menaechmus* ⎬ *Doubles*
  the traveler*) ⎭
Zanni (*Peniculus*) servant
Burattino (*Messenio*) servant
Hortentia, courtesan (*Erotion*)
Franceschina, her maid (*Ancilla*)
Host, Coviello
Olivetta, his wife
Doctor   (*Medicus*)
    (*Cylindrus, the cook*)
    (*Porters*)[1]

The scene represents Fano.

PROPERTIES. Suits and beards to match
for the doubles; a dress, rings, a collar;
inn-sign; valise; glass of wine.

Act 1

SILVIO [*with* ZANNI] comes from the
house announcing that he is in love
with the Courtesan Hortentia and has
promised her a dress, a collar, and two
rings, but has neither money nor goods
to send her. He tells Zanni to find some
contrivance to filch the things from
Flavia his wife. Zanni tries to persuade
him to leave the Courtesan alone, but
at length with Silvio's pleading he says
that he has thought of a plan. Flavia is

to be told of a most excellent comedy
which is to be presented; when she says
that she wishes to go to it, he is to explain that he has promised to lend the
players a dress, a collar, and rings. Silvio asks what is to be said if Flavia
really wants to come; he is told to repeat that it is a promise; they have their
antics of "Yes" and "No," and knock; at
this:

FLAVIA from the house hears all this;
she refuses and does not want to see
the comedy so that she need not give
them the clothes. In the end, after Silvio's pleading she relents and tells him
to take the things and return them as
soon as possible. They have their little
scene [*azzi*] and Flavia goes into the
house leaving Silvio and Zanni delighted; they knock and at this:

HORTENTIA [*with* FRANCESCHINA] from
the house receives the dress, the collar,
and the rings from Silvio, thanking and
paying him compliments. She invites
him to dine with her and Silvio accepts.
Hortentia and Franceschina go in; Silvio and Zanni go down the street.

PANTALONE announces that he has
come in from the country in answer to
a letter sent him by his daughter Flavia.
He praises the country, and knocks to
find out what his daughter wants with
him; at this:

FLAVIA from the house hears that
Pantalone has had her letter and has
come in from the country to know what
is the matter. He is surprised that Silvio
his son-in-law should have left her
alone. Flavia grumbles about her husband for wasting their substance and

334

frequenting courtesans and taverns. Pantalone is shocked and says that something must be done. Flavia goes into the house. Pantalone says he will look for Silvio and goes down the street.

CAPTAIN [*with* BURATTINO] down the street arriving as from a journey; he says he has come from Spain where he has been since a child, and that he has a brother in Bologna, his native city. They have their by-play together and want to find a lodging; they knock; at this:

HOST from the inn has his scene with the strangers announcing the excellence of the wines and the accommodation, he calls

OLIVETTA from the inn, she caresses the strangers, takes the valise, playing about with Burattino; all go into the inn, leaving the Captain, who says he will go and explore the city, observing how beautiful both it and its surroundings are; at this:

HORTENTIA comes from the house saying that she expects Silvio for dinner; she sees the Captain and thinking it is Silvio, invites him to come and dine; not knowing the lady he thanks her for her kindness, and in the end, overcome by Hortentia's entreaties, accepts the invitation and they go into the house.

HOST [*with* OLIVETTA, BURATTINO] comes from the inn shouting at Burattino for having put about ten candles on the table and for carrying on with his wife Olivetta. They beat Burattino, who goes off down the street; they return into the house.

Act 2

CAPTAIN [*with* HORTENTIA] from the house takes his leave, paying her compliments and thanking her for the kindness which he has received. Hortentia gives him the dress, the collar, and the rings, so that he may have them altered to suit her. The Captain

takes them all, promising to do her this service. Hortentia retires, leaving him astounded at her favours; he has no idea who she may be; he knocks and at this:

HOST from the inn takes the Captain's things into his charge, after his antics the host goes in. The Captain says he will explore the city; at this:

PANTALONE comes down the street looking in vain for Silvio; seeing the Captain he takes him for his son-in-law, and scolds him for his loose living, his shocking habits, and ill treatment of Flavia. The Captain abuses him, calling him a pander and giving him the lie. He goes off down the street leaving Pantalone amazed that he should have become so insolent; at this:

SILVIO coming up the street sees Pantalone, he embraces and caresses him, welcoming his return from the country and thanking him for the warning given him. Pantalone is surprised that a few moments ago he had behaved so differently. He commends Flavia to his care; Silvio assures him of his affection and promises to cherish her. He goes off down the street, leaving Pantalone marvelling that at first he had been so brutal and afterwards so civil; at this:

CAPTAIN comes up the street furious with the people who are joking with him. Pantalone exhorts him to have some regard for his wife and his house. The Captain flies into a temper and abuses him, saying he has no wife and calling Pantalone a cuckold. He leaves Pantalone astounded, and sure that he is mad he goes off to find a doctor.

SILVIO, ZANNI come up the street remarking that it is time to go dine with Hortentia who must be waiting for them; they knock and at this:

HORTENTIA, FRANCESCHINA from the house hear that Silvio and Zanni have come to dinner. They turn Zanni away saying that Silvio has already dined there alone. Zanni goes in to find out for himself and comes out weeping, saying the plates are dirty and everything is eaten. Silvio shouts to the women that he has never been there, they take their part in the dispute, reminding him of the things that they gave him, and grumbling that this should be the only thanks that they get. Hortentia describes his behaviour after dinner and argues with him. Silvio and Zanni go off down the street in a rage, leaving Hortentia and Franceschina amazed at his behaviour and denial; at this:

CAPTAIN appears up the street, Hortentia inquires about the things which she gave him, and asks why he was angry with her. He insists that he is not angry at all, and departs to fetch the things, leaving Hortentia and Franceschina bewildered; at this:

SILVIO comes up the street on his way home; he sees Hortentia who asks him whether he has brought her possessions. They quarrel noisily, and Silvio departs in a temper, leaving Hortentia and Franceschina; to them comes

CAPTAIN up the street, Hortentia screams at him demanding her goods. The Captain speaks her fair, and says he will bring them as soon as possible. Hortentia and Franceschina leave him and go into the house; at this:

ZANNI from the street sees the Captain and takes him for his master Silvio; he demands the wages due to him. The Captain says he does not know him. Zanni astonished at this reminds him of his own wife whom he serves; at this:

FLAVIA comes out of the house and supposing it is Silvio her husband tells him to pay Zanni. The Captain jokes with her and then allows Zanni to bargain that he shall sleep with Flavia instead of having his wages. Zanni agrees and goes into the house with Flavia; the Captain goes down the street.

SILVIO comes up the street complaining of Hortentia's ill treatment and misbehaviour; at this:

BURATTINO from the street sees Silvio and takes him for the Captain, his master; he tells him to go to the innkeeper and make him hand over his goods because he has had a row with him, he is to wait for him at the sign of the Sun. [Burattino promises to do all this][2] and goes out. Silvio remains mystified, determined to follow this up; he knocks, at this:

HOST from the inn sees Silvio, and mistaking him for the Captain hands over all his possessions and makes out

the bill, which Silvio settles. The Host retires into the inn leaving Silvio amazed in possession of the goods; he knocks and at this:

ZANNI from the window complains to Silvio that his wife Flavia will not sleep with him; he demands his wages. Silvio scolds him and Zanni bets him that Flavia will support him when he says that this was the bargain; at this:

FLAVIA from the house tells Silvio to his face that he had agreed to let Zanni sleep with her instead of paying him his wages. Silvio is astounded and says it is not true. He restores his wife's property. Zanni is astonished; they have the scene of the thrashing and all go into the house.

PANTALONE, THE DOCTOR from the street say that they wish to examine Silvio, who must be mad, and cannot talk sense; at this:

SILVIO from the house invites Pantalone to dinner which is now ready. The Doctor feels his pulse which he finds steady and regular. Silvio is surprised and goes in. The Doctor takes his leave and goes down the street: Pantalone remains; to him:

CAPTAIN comes down the street and again has words with Pantalone, abusing him. Pantalone calls for

THE DOCTOR to return, he counts the Captain's pulse, mistaking him for Silvio. The Captain cudgels them both and they go off down the street.

Act 3

CAPTAIN amazed at what has happened goes to fetch his possessions; he knocks and at this:

THE HOST from the inn hearing that the Captain has called for his things tells him he has had them already. They argue and the Captain in a rage swears he will go for the justice. The Host is left dumbfounded; at this:

SILVIO comes up the street and is mistaken for the Captain by the Host, who repeats that he has had his things. Silvio acknowledges them, and after their scene [*azzi*] he departs, leaving the Host to marvel; at this:

THE CAPTAIN comes up the street and demands his things and argues. The Host protests that he has just admitted to having had them. The Captain denies it and goes off in a rage. The Host remains; at this:

SILVIO reappearing in the street is questioned by the Host concerning the things and admits he has had them; at this:

PANTALONE comes down the street to find out if Silvio is in his right mind. The Host tells him to wait there as a witness, Pantalone stands to one side and again Silvio acknowledges the goods and goes out. The Host and Pantalone are left; at this:

THE CAPTAIN comes up the street demanding his possessions from the Host with threats and abuse.[3] The Host in a fury summons Pantalone from his corner to act as a witness. The Captain goes in swearing he will have his things by force, the Host and Pantalone follow.

SILVIO comes down the street marvelling at the extraordinary events and at the recovered goods; at this:

PANTALONE comes from the inn announcing that he has locked Silvio into a room and is off to find the Doctor. He sees Silvio and is dumbfounded, supposing he is a ghost. At last he addresses him, marvelling how he could have got out of the inn. Silvio is equally taken aback: hearing a disturbance within they draw their swords; at this:

CAPTAIN [*with* HOST, OLIVETTA] comes from the inn with a drawn sword shouting that he will have his goods; all rush between them. Pantalone, at a loss to know which is his son-in-law Silvio, shows his bewilderment; at this:

ZANNI [*with* BURATTINO] from the street is unable to identify his master Silvio, and Burattino cannot tell which is the Captain. The Host does not know who gave him the goods and the garment, nor who went into the inn; all are left astounded, playing their various antics; at this:

HORTENTIA, FRANCESCHINA from the house behave in the same way, not knowing which is Silvio; they have their scene and finally call

FLAVIA from the house; she cannot recognize her husband, and tries first one and then the other. At last they discover that the Captain is Silvio's brother, and making merry he marries Hortentia and Zanni takes Franceschina.

1. In parentheses are given the corresponding characters in Plautus's play.

2. I have bracketed this direction which turns the sense of the passage and suggests that Silvio is giving orders to Burattino mistaking him for Zanni. There is no further indication that the servants are also doubles in this scenario and as a direction for the man's acquiescence to his master's orders the phrase is so common that it may well have slipped in unconsciously while Loccatelli composed or copied out this monotonously confusing plot.

3. *Con felle parole et con amorevolezza:* I have taken it that Loccatelli intended some word connected with *amaro,* "bitter," but it is impossible that *amorevolezza* is correct and that the Captain tried to coax the Host when threats failed.

The Mandrake

Niccolò Machiavelli

The essence of the Renaissance was the scholarly rediscovery of classical learning, a process which may be said to have begun in Italy before spreading all over Europe. In the theater, even while the commedia dell'arte was developing as the "professional" (and ultimately most important) contribution of Renaissance Italy to a newly awakened drama, Italian scholars were reading the ancient play scripts and writing plays in imitation of them. They worked in tragic, pastoral, and comic modes, but nowhere were they so successful as with *The Mandrake*—certainly the best play written in Renaissance Italy, and, in the opinion of some, the best play ever written by an Italian.

Despite this extraordinary achievement in playwriting, Niccolò Machiavelli is better known for other accomplishments. He was a consummate politician and a prolific writer about political matters; *The Prince* is his most significant work in this field. Born in Florence on May 3, 1469, Machiavelli came from a respectable but impoverished family which could not afford the complete classical education that had by this time become the accepted standard for promising young men. Although he was largely self-taught, Machiavelli rose at the remarkably young age of twenty-nine to an important post in the Florentine government, a post from which he soon reached out to greater and greater power and influence in Italian affairs. He traveled often throughout Europe on diplomatic missions, learning about the functioning of other governments and writing on this subject with great lucidity. After fourteen years in power, Machiavelli was the victim of a governmental change in Florence, and he found himself not only out of office but also charged with complicity in a plot to overthrow the new government. He denied these charges even under severe torture ("four turns of the rack," according to one source), and was eventually released from prison upon intervention of the pope. He retired to an embittered obscurity while still in his early forties, there to devote himself to writing and to seeking an opportunity to return to power. All of his most important literary works have their origin in this period. After the death of the Florentine prince who had dismissed Machiavelli, the latter was able again to find an important office in government, and to spend his last few years in this service. He died in Florence on June 21, 1527.

Machiavelli may have written as many as four plays, but two of these are of poor quality and their authorship has been doubted. His *La Clizia* is a somewhat better play, but is an adaptation of Plautus's *Casina*. Thus, Machiavelli's significant reputation as a playwright rests on *The Mandrake*, a play that he wrote between 1513 and 1520, that had what was probably its first production before Pope Leo X in 1520, and that was published in 1524. In 1526, for a special performance before Prince Francesco Guicciardini in Modena, Machiavelli wrote an introductory song and four songs to be sung between the acts—perhaps in imitation of the ancient tradition of a chorus. Since the songs are quite unrelated to the play itself, they have not been reprinted here.

The mandrake is a potatolike plant that is native to the Mediterranean region and that was the subject of many ancient superstitions. It is mentioned twice in the Old Testament in contexts that evoke its alleged aphrodisiac properties, and it was widely believed in medieval times to promote fertility. The root is often forked and was believed to resemble a human being; hence, there arose a superstition to the effect that, if human semen were spilled on the ground, mandrakes would grow in the spot. Other superstitions held that mandrakes could only be harvested by tying a black dog to the root by moonlight so that the tubers could be pulled up without being touched by human hands, and that when they were so uprooted they shrieked in a human manner. In fact, the root does possess both narcotic and emetic properties that may account for some of these superstitions. Machiavelli was right in line with the folk wisdom of his time, therefore, in using the mandrake as he has in the play.

The plot structure of *The Mandrake* is simplicity itself. Act 1 is exposition and the laying of the plot for Callimaco to sleep with Lucrezia. The exposition is perhaps rather too obviously handled, as Callimaco tells his servant everything that the latter certainly already knew, but at least it is efficient and to the point. Each of the next three acts consists of a central trick: act 2 is the gulling of Nicia, act 3 is the persuading of Lucrezia (by tricking her confessor into supporting the plot), and act 4 is the trick by which Callimaco is actually introduced into Lucrezia's bed. Act 5 wraps up the play by portraying the results of these tricks, and turns primarily on the dramatic irony of everyone except Nicia understanding what is really going on. To describe this plot as simple is not in any way to fault it, however. It is direct and effective, with each event clearly proceeding from the one before it in a fashion rarely matched by even the finest playwrights. Its debt to Plautus and Terence is obvious, but the striking fact is not this debt, but the play's remarkable freshness and originality—especially as compared with others of this period.

The characters also owe much to classical tradition, although again what is perhaps even more remarkable is the degree to which these traditions are transcended. Ligurio is the stock parasite, but he becomes far more believable as a cynical manipulator than simply as a grubber after a free meal. Nicia is clearly the gulled old man from New Comedy who was contemporaneously developing as Dr. Graziano in the commedia dell'arte, but Machiavelli makes of him a unique comic figure. The "young lovers" are vastly changed, for Lucrezia has no interest whatsoever in a love affair and is morally outraged at the suggestion of infidelity (yet finally decides that Nicia deserves to be cuckolded), while Callimaco is singlemindedly devoted to hopping into bed with Lucrezia, apparently irrespective of love, honor, or any other conventional value. It is in Timoteo, however, that Machiavelli has created perhaps his most interesting and original character: cynical, and yet not totally evil; money-hungry, and yet not simply greedy; jovial, but far more than a debauchee. It is especially interesting, in view of Timoteo's character, to think of that first performance of the play before the pope.

The Mandrake has frequently been attacked as an immoral play, but it would be more accurate to describe it as "amoral." Even Lucrezia's moral reservations are circumvented by arguments of practicality rather than by direct confrontation of the issues raised, and in other respects moral considerations simply never come up. It is easy to infer why Machiavelli might have seen the world in this light in view of what is known about his life at the time he was writing *The Mandrake*, but there is no reason to infer that he liked what he saw. The very cynicism with which the play world is drawn invites the ironic conclusion that the world is full of hypocrites, but does so without a lot of tedious moralizing. It is an ancient and honorable tradition of comedy to portray the world in this light; there would be nothing comic about slipping on a banana peel if one had to consider the moral responsibility of the litterer who left it there or the painful consequences upon the posterior of the one who slips. It is tempting, in view of Machiavelli's reputation as an immoral politician, to infer similar immorality in his play, but both his playwriting and his politics are better understood in the light of his ironic ability to view life rationally, but totally aside from moral considerations. That such a view of life may be incomplete in no way lessens its accuracy or its value.

The Mandrake stands as one of the comic masterpieces of Western civilization, too infrequently produced because of its alleged obscenity, but now ripe for rediscovery. It ranks alongside *Volpone* as a bitter but comically devastating exposure of human venality.

The Mandrake
(La Mandragola)

*English Version by Frederick
May and Eric Bentley*

Characters
Callimaco, a young man
Siro, a servant
Messer Nicia Calfucci, LL.D.
Ligurio, a parasite
Sostrata, a mother
Timoteo, a friar
A woman
*Lucrezia, wife of Messer Nicia, daughter of
Sostrata*

THE TIME: *Early sixteenth century.*
THE PLACE: *Florence.*

Prologue

Ladies and gentlemen, God bless you!
May Fate and Fortune long caress you!
(I thought I'd make a little fuss
Of you, so you'll be nice to *us*.)
Just sit quite still, don't make a sound,
And you will like us, I'll be bound.
The story's good we'll tell to you.
It happened here. What's more: it's
    true.
Florence we'll show you now, your
    home;
Tomorrow, maybe, Pisa, Rome,
The nicest towns you ever saw.
(Don't laugh so hard; you'll break your
    jaw.)

This right-hand door—can you all
    see?—
Belongs to a learnèd LL.D.
His erudition's vast: I'm told
He has Boethius down cold.
That dingy street is Lovers' Lane:
Those who fall there don't rise again.
If you don't leave us in the lurch
You'll see emerging from that church
A well-known friar (though I would not
Presume to say well known for what).
Next, you are all to get to know
A young man called Callimaco
Who lives in this next house by chance.
He is just back from Paris, France.
Callimaco is such a dandy
One look at him makes women randy.
This fellow loved unto perdition
A certain girl of good position
And played a little trick on her.
And who are we that should demur,
Good people, since on this our earth,
Of trickery there is no dearth?
(When you are tricked, fair ladies, see
That you are tricked as pleasantly.)
The mandrake of our title is
A plant with certain properties:
When women eat the root, their
    fate . . .
But this is to anticipate.
Our author's called . . . alas, his name
As yet is not well known to Fame.
If you should find his tale confusing,
The whole show somewhat unamusing,
He's quite a decent chap, I think,
And may well stand you to a drink.

341

He offers, though, for your delight
Well, what? An evil parasite . . .
A scholar who is not too bright . . .
A lover who is full of fight . . .
A friar whose moral sense is slight . . .
Is that sufficient for one night?
True, true, such antic jollity
Is nothing but frivolity.
This comedy is not profound.
I'm not so sure it's even sound.
Our author sends you his excuses.
He says life's hard, the world obtuse is,
And he most gladly would display
His gifts in any other way,
The only question is: who'd pay?
Attribute then to lack of money
His condescending to be funny.
Can he expect a warm reception?
If so, he'll be a rare exception.
This age to sour contempt is quicker,
To twisted smile, malignant snicker.
The virtues that did thrive of yore,
D'you think we'll see them any more?
Men won't devote their nights and days
To toil without their meed of praise:
Who on a plant would spend his pow-
   ers
Knowing that all his lovely flowers
Would by a tempest then be tossed
Or in a fog concealed and lost?
Moreover, if you have concluded
Our man's your victim, you're deluded.
No matter for what sort you take him
You cannot nudge him, push him,
   shake him,
And, as for malice, he can do
Far better at the trade than you
For in the whole of Italy
Wherever reigns, not *yes*, but *sì*,
There's not a soul he would kowtow to.
The only man he'd make a bow to
Is the only V.I.P. he knows:
A man in more expensive clothes.
Backbite him if you please, but we
Must get on with this comedy
If you are to be home by three.
Don't take the play too much to heart.
If you see a monster, do not start:
Just look right through him, and he'll
   go.
But, wait, here comes Callimaco,
Siro his servant at his side.
These two, between them, will confide
The plot to you. Pay close attention!
The play will now unfold without my
   intervention.

Act 1

Scene 1

[*Enter* CALLIMACO *and* SIRO.]

CALLIMACO. Don't go, Siro, I want to talk to you.

SIRO. I'm not going.

CALLIMACO. You must have been quite surprised by my sudden departure from Paris, and now very likely you're surprised that, having been here a month, I still haven't done anything.

SIRO. I don't deny it.

CALLIMACO. If I haven't told you already what I'm about to tell you, it's not because I don't trust you, but because it seemed best not to talk of confidential matters unless one was forced to. But now, since I shall need your help, I am going to tell you everything.

SIRO. I am your servant, and servants must never question their masters, nor pry into their affairs. But when the master volunteers information, the servant must serve him faithfully. Which is what I've done, and what I propose to do.

CALLIMACO. I know. I think you've heard me say a thousand times—but it won't hurt you to hear it the thousand and first—that when I was ten years old, my father and mother being dead, I was sent by my guardians to live in Paris, where I've been these twenty years. After ten years the Italian Wars began—as a result of King Charles's invasion of Italy, which laid waste this country—so I decided to settle in Paris and never go back to my native land. I thought I should be safer than in Italy.

SIRO. Very true.

CALLIMACO. Having sent instructions that all my possessions here, with the exception of my house, should be sold, I settled down in Paris. And I have passed the last ten years in great happiness . . .

SIRO. I know.

CALLIMACO. . . . devoting part of my time to study, part to pleasure, and part to business, and so arranging things that the three never got in each other's way. In consequence, as you know, I lived quietly, helping whoever I could, trying to injure nobody, so that, it seems to me, I came to be well thought of by everyone, be he gentleman or merchant, foreign or native, rich or poor.

SIRO. That's true, too.

CALLIMACO. But Fortune, deeming that I was *too* happy, sent to Paris a certain Cammillo Calfucci.

SIRO. I begin to guess what your trouble is.

CALLIMACO. Like the other Florentines, he was frequently invited to dine at my house, and one day, when we were gathered together, an argument started as to where the more beautiful women were to be found—Italy or France. I could have no opinion concerning Italian women—I was so little when I left the country—so Cammillo Calfucci took up the cudgels for the Italians and another Florentine defended the French. After a great deal of argument back and forth, Cammillo, in something of a temper, said that, even if Italian women in general were monsters, he had a kinswoman who could redeem her country's reputation all by herself.

SIRO. I see what you're after.

CALLIMACO. And he named Madonna Lucrezia, wife of Messer Nicia Calfucci, and so praised her beauty and sweetness of manner that he left us all amazed and aroused in me such a desire to see her that I set out for Florence, putting aside all other considerations and not bothering whether there was a war on or not. Having arrived here, I found that Madonna Lucrezia's reputation fell far short of the truth; which is quite a rare phenomenon. And I'm burning with such desire to make her mine, I hardly know what to do with myself.

SIRO. If you'd told me this when we were in Paris, I'd have known how to advise you. Now, I don't know what to say.

CALLIMACO. I'm not telling you this with a view to advice, but to get it out of my system. And so you can be ready to help when the need arises.

SIRO. I couldn't be readier. What hopes have you got?

CALLIMACO. Alas, none. Or very few. Let me explain. First, her nature is hostile to my desires. She's the quintessence of chastity. The thought of love affairs is alien to her. Then, her husband's very rich, lets himself be ruled by her in everything, and, if he's not exactly young, he's not antique either, that's clear. Again, there are no relatives or neighbors whose homes she frequents at wakes and holidays and the other pleasant occasions that young women delight in. No tradesman sets foot in her house, and she hasn't a single servant or retainer who doesn't go in fear of her. Bribery and corruption are therefore excluded.

SIRO. What are you thinking of doing, then?

CALLIMACO. No situation is so desperate that one may not continue to hope. Even if one's hopes are feeble and vain, the determination to see a thing through causes them to seem far otherwise.

SIRO. So what makes you go on hoping?

CALLIMACO. Two things. First, the simple-mindedness of Messer Nicia, who, though he holds an LL.D. from the university, is the most thick headed and foolish man in Florence. Second, his desire, and hers, to have children. Having been married for six years without getting any, and being very rich, they're dying of their desire for a family. There's a third factor: her mother. She was a bit of a baggage when she was young; but she's rich now, and I've no idea how to deal with her.

SIRO. Since that's how matters stand, have you tried anything?

CALLIMACO. Yes. In a small way.

SIRO. Tell me.

CALLIMACO. You know Ligurio, who's always coming to eat at my house? He used to be a professional matchmaker. Now he goes around cadging dinners and suppers. Being a pleasant sort of chap, he's had no trouble becoming intimate with Messer Nicia, and leading him a dance. The old boy wouldn't invite him to dinner, it's true, but he's been lending him money from time to time. As for me, I've struck up a friendship with this Ligurio, told him of my love for Madonna Lucrezia, and he's promised to help me with all he's got.

SIRO. Take care he doesn't deceive you. These parasites don't make a habit of fidelity.

CALLIMACO. True. Nonetheless, when you place yourself in someone's hands, you place yourself in someone's hands. I've promised him a large sum of money if he succeeds, and, if he fails, a dinner and a supper. I'd never eat alone in any case.

SIRO. So what has he promised to do?

CALLIMACO. He's promised to persuade Messer Nicia to take his wife to the Baths—this May.

SIRO. What good would that do you?

CALLIMACO. What good would it do me? The place may well make a different woman out of her. In haunts like that, they do nothing but throw parties and such. And I'd be taking with me all the plausible arguments I could think up, omitting no tittle of pomp and circumstance. I'd become the bosom pal of both parties, wife and husband. Who can say what will happen? One thing leads to another. Time rules all.

SIRO. I'm quite impressed.

CALLIMACO. Ligurio left me this morning saying that he'd take this matter up with Messer Nicia and would let me know the answer.

SIRO. Here they come—together.

CALLIMACO. I'll step to one side—to be on hand for a word with Ligurio when he takes leave of the old boy. Meanwhile you go home and get on with your work. If I want you for anything I'll let you know.

SIRO. Right. [*Exeunt.*]

Scene 2

[*Enter* MESSER NICIA *and* LIGURIO.]

MESSER NICIA. I think your advice is good, and I talked the matter over last night with my wife. She said she'd give me her answer today. But,

to tell the truth, I'm not over-keen.

LIGURIO. Why not?

MESSER NICIA. Because I'm in a rut and I'd like to stay in it. What's more, to have to transport wife, servants, household goods, it doesn't appeal to me. Besides, I was talking yesterday evening to some doctors. One of them said I should go to San Filippo; another said Porretta; another, Villa. What a bunch of quacks! If you ask me, the medical profession doesn't know its business.

LIGURIO. What you mentioned first must be what troubles you most: you're not accustomed to lose sight of the Cupola.

MESSER NICIA. You're mistaken. When I was younger I was a victim of Wanderlust. They never held a fair at Prato but I was there. There's not a castle in the neighborhood that I haven't visited. Better yet: I've been to Pisa and Livorno. What do you think of that?

LIGURIO. Then you must have seen the Sliding Tower of Pisa?

MESSER NICIA. You mean the Leaning Tower.

LIGURIO. The Leaning Tower, of course. And at Livorno, did you see the sea?

MESSER NICIA. You know very well I did.

LIGURIO. How much bigger is it than the Arno?

MESSER NICIA. Arno! Pooh! It's four times bigger, no, more than six; you'll make me say more than seven times in a minute. Nothing but water, water, water!

LIGURIO. Well then, I'm amazed that you, who—as the saying is—have pissed your way through so much snow, should make such a fuss about going to the Baths!

MESSER NICIA. Your mother's milk is still on your lips, my child. Do you think it's a small matter to transplant an entire household? Yet my desire for children is so strong I'm ready to do anything. But have a word or two with those M.D.s. See where *they* advise me to go. Meanwhile I'll join my wife at home. I'll see you there later. [*Exit.*]

LIGURIO. Good idea.

Scene 3

[*Enter* CALLIMACO.]

LIGURIO. Can there be a bigger fool in the whole wide world? And how Fortune has favored him! He's rich, and his beautiful wife is well bred, virtuous, and fit to rule a kingdom. It seems to me that the proverb about marriage seldom proves true—the one that runs: "God makes men, but they find their mates for themselves." For in general we see a man of parts paired off with a shrew while a prudent woman gets a half-wit for a husband. But that fellow's half-wittedness has this much to be said for it: it gives Callimaco reason to hope. And here he is. Hey, Callimaco—lying in wait for someone?

CALLIMACO. I'd seen you with our learnèd friend, and I was waiting for you to part company with him, so I could hear what you'd done.

LIGURIO. He's a fellow of small prudence and less spirit, as you know. He doesn't want to leave Florence. However, I worked on his feelings for a while, and he told me he'd do just as I said. I believe we'll be able to move him in the right direction. Whether we can complete our project is, of course, another story.

CALLIMACO. How so?

LIGURIO. Well, as you know, all sorts of people go to these Baths, and it might be that a man would come along who'd find Madonna Lucrezia as attractive as you do. He might be richer than you. He might be more charming. So there's the danger of going to all this trouble for someone else's benefit. It is also possible that, with so many competitors for her favor, she might become the harder to attain. Or that, having got used to the idea of yielding, she might yield, not to you, but to another.

CALLIMACO. You have a point. But what am I to do? Which way am I to turn? I must try something. Something tremendous or something dangerous, something harmful or something infamous, I don't care. Better to die than to live like this! If I could sleep at night, if I could eat, if I could engage in conversation, if I could find pleasure in anything at all, I should be able to await Time's verdict more patiently. Here and now I can see no remedy. If hope is not kept alive within me by some course of action, I shall assuredly die. Faced with this prospect of Death, I am resolved to fear nothing, but adopt a course of action that is bestial, cruel, and nefarious.

LIGURIO. You mustn't talk like that! You must curb such excess of passion!

CALLIMACO. Actually, by feeding my imagination on thoughts like this, I keep myself in check—as you can see. However, it is necessary for us either to proceed with our plan for sending him to the Baths or to try some other avenue, if only that I may have a little hope to feed on. And if it can't be true hope, then let it be false, so long as it provides me with thoughts that lighten my burden of troubles!

LIGURIO. You're right. I'm for doing as you say.

CALLIMACO. Though I know that men of your sort live by cheating others, I believe you. I don't propose to fear your cheating me because, if I saw you try to, I should proceed to take advantage of the fact. And you would forfeit your right to come and go in my house, and all hope of receiving what I have promised you.

LIGURIO. Don't doubt my fidelity. Even if I had no sense of my own interests, and did not hope what I hope, well, you and I are so congenial, I'm almost as desirous as you are that you should get what you want. But enough. Messer Nicia has commissioned me to find a doctor who can say which of the Baths it would be best for him to go to. Let yourself be advised by me. Tell him you've studied medicine and been practicing for some time in Paris. Simpleminded as he is, he'll believe you, and, since you're an educated man, you'll be able to treat him to a little Latin.

CALLIMACO. What good will that do us?

LIGURIO. It will enable us to send him to whichever Baths we wish, and put into operation another plan I've thought of—one that's more likely to succeed and takes less time.

CALLIMACO. What did you say?

LIGURIO. I say you're to take heart: if you put your trust in me, I'll have the whole thing finished by this time to-morrow. Even if he investigates your claim to be a doctor—and he won't—the short time at his disposal and the nature of the case will stop him get-ting anywhere. By the time he figured anything out—if he did—it'd be too late for him to frustrate our plan.

CALLIMACO. You fill me with new life. Oh, this is too fair a promise! You feed me with too much hope! How will you do it?

LIGURIO. You'll find out at the proper moment. Right now there's little enough time for action, let alone talk. Go home and wait for me. I'll hunt up our learnèd friend. And if I bring him along, take your cue from me, and make everything you say fit in.

CALLIMACO. I'll do as you say, though the hopes you raise within me may, I fear, go up in smoke. [*Exeunt.*]

Act 2

Scene 1

[*Enter* LIGURIO, MESSER NICIA, *and* SIRO.]

LIGURIO. As I say, I believe God ex-pressly sent us this man that you might have your desire. His practice in Paris was extensive and successful, and you needn't be surprised that he hasn't practiced here in Florence. The reasons are, first, that he's rich, and second, that he has to return to Paris at once.

MESSER NICIA. Well, now, brother, there's an important point: I shouldn't like him to get me into an awkward situation and then leave me in it.

LIGURIO. The only thing you have to worry about is that he might not be willing to undertake your cure. If he does take you on, he won't leave you till he's seen it through.

MESSER NICIA. That part I'll leave to you, but, as for science, once I've talked with him, *I'll* tell *you* whether he knows his stuff or not. He won't sell *me* any pig in a poke!

LIGURIO. Because you're the man I know you to be, I *want* you to talk with him. And if he doesn't impress you, for presence, learning, and La-tin, as someone you can trust like your dear old sainted mother, my name's not Ligurio.

MESSER NICIA. Well then, by the Holy Angel, so be it! And let's get going! Where does he live?

LIGURIO. On this square. That's his door right opposite.

MESSER NICIA. Good Fortune attend us!

LIGURIO. [*Knocks at the door.*] Here goes!

SIRO. [*From within.*] Who is it?

LIGURIO. Is Callimaco at home?

SIRO. Yes, he is.

MESSER NICIA. Why don't you call him *Master* Callimaco?

LIGURIO. Oh, he doesn't care about such trifles.

MESSER NICIA. Tsk, tsk, tsk. You must pay him the respect due to his pro-fession: if he takes it amiss, so much the worse for him.

Scene 2

[*Enter* CALLIMACO.]

CALLIMACO. Who is it that wants me?

MESSER NICIA. *Bona dies, domine magis-ter.*[1]

CALLIMACO. *Et vobis bona, domine doctor.*[2]

LIGURIO. What do you think?

MESSER NICIA. By the Holy Gospel, he's good!

LIGURIO. If you want me to stay, you must talk a language I understand. If not, let's part company.

CALLIMACO. What fair business brings you here?

MESSER NICIA. I wonder. I want two things that another man might run a mile to avoid. *Primo,* to give myself a lot of trouble. *Secundo,* to inflict it on someone else. I have no children, I'd like some, and to get myself into this trouble, I've come to importune you.

CALLIMACO. It will never be less than a joy to me to give pleasure to you and to all other men of merit and virtue,

nor have I practiced these many
years in Paris but for the privilege of
serving such as you.

MESSER NICIA. I appreciate that, and
should you ever need my own professional services, I would be happy
to oblige. But to return *ad rem nos-
tram.*[3] Have you thought which of the
Baths is most likely to get my wife
pregnant? I know, you see, that Ligurio here has told you—what he has
told you.

CALLIMACO. Very true. But, that we
may enable you to have your desire,
we must know the cause of your
wife's sterility. For there can be various causes. *Nam causae sterilitatis sunt:
aut in semine, aut in matrice, aut in
strumentis seminariis, aut in virga, aut in
causa extrinseca.*[4]

MESSER NICIA. This is the most worthy
man one could hope to find!

CALLIMACO. Alternatively, the sterility
might be caused by impotence in
you. If that should be the case, there
would be no remedy.

MESSER NICIA. Impotent? Me? Hoho!
Don't make me laugh! I don't believe
there's a more vigorous, virile man
than me in Florence.

CALLIMACO. Well, if that's not it, you
may rest assured we'll find a remedy.

MESSER NICIA. Would there be any
remedy other than the Baths? Because *I* don't want to go to all the in-
convenience, and my wife would be
unwilling to leave Florence.

LIGURIO. Let me answer your question
in the affirmative. Callimaco, being
circumspect, sometimes carries cir-
cumspection to excess. Didn't you tell
me you knew how to prepare certain
potions that will make a woman pregnant quite infallibly?

CALLIMACO. I did. But it has not been
my habit to communicate that fact to
strangers. They might regard me as a
charlatan.

MESSER NICIA. Don't worry about me.
I'm amazed at your abilities. There's
nothing I couldn't believe you capable of. There's nothing I wouldn't do
for you!

LIGURIO. I think you ought to see a
specimen of her water.

CALLIMACO. Undoubtedly. One could

get nowhere without it.

LIGURIO. Call Siro, tell him to go home
with Messer Nicia, pick up the specimen, and then come back. We'll wait
for him indoors.

CALLIMACO. Siro, go with him. And if
you agree, messere, you come back
too, and we'll think of a way out. [*Exit
with* LIGURIO.]

MESSER NICIA. If I agree? I shall be back
like a shot. I place more confidence
in you than Hungarians do in
swords!

Scene 3

MESSER NICIA. That master of yours is a
very distinguished man.

SIRO. Better than that, even.

MESSER NICIA. The King of France
holds him in great esteem?

SIRO. Very great.

MESSER NICIA. And for that reason, I
take it, he is glad to stay in France?

SIRO. That's my belief.

MESSER NICIA. He's quite right. The
people of this city are dirty dogs. No
appreciation of merit. If he were to
stay, no one would trouble to look at
him twice. I speak from experience.
I've given it everything, learning my
hics, haecs, and *hocs,* and, if I hadn't
got a private income, I'd be having a
thin time of it, I can tell you.

SIRO. Do you make a hundred ducats a
year?

MESSER NICIA. Go on. I don't make a
hundred *lire.* Or a hundred groats.
The fact is, if you don't spend your
time keeping up with the neighbors—such is Florence—you won't
find a dog to bark you a civil greeting. The rest of us are good for nothing but funerals and wedding break-
fasts and loafing all day on the
square. But they don't bother me. I
have no need of anybody. There are
plenty who'd be glad to change
places with me. But I shouldn't like
what I've just said to get around, or
someone might slap a fine on me or
slug me in a dark alley.

SIRO. Don't worry, messere.

MESSER NICIA. This is my house. Wait
for me here. I'll be right back. [*Exit.*]

SIRO. Go ahead.

Scene 4

SIRO. [*Alone.*] If all men of learning were like that one, the rest of us would have straw in our hair. [*Gesture indicating insanity.*] I'm quite sure that the wicked Ligurio and my mad master are leading him to his downfall. And, to tell the truth, I'd enjoy his downfall, if only we could be sure of getting away with it. Otherwise I'm risking my neck and my master is risking both his neck and his property. He's already turned himself into a doctor. I just don't know what their little plan is, or where they're heading with all this deception. But here's Messer Nicia again, specimen in hand. You can't help laughing at him, the old cuckoo.

Scene 5

[*Enter* MESSER NICIA.]

MESSER NICIA. [*To someone in the house, evidently* LUCREZIA.] Up till now I've always done everything your way. In this matter I want you to do things *my* way. If I'd thought that you and I weren't going to have children, I'd rather have married a peasant girl. Siro! Follow me. The trouble I had getting My Lady Fool to give me this specimen! That's not to say, of course, that she wants children less than I do. On the contrary! But the moment I suggest anything practical, oh, what a song and dance!

SIRO. Be patient: soft words make women do what other people want.

MESSER NICIA. Soft words! She raised the roof! Go, this instant: tell your master and Ligurio I'm here.

SIRO. Look, they're just coming out of the house.

Scene 6

[*Enter* LIGURIO *and* CALLIMACO.]

LIGURIO. [*Aside to* CALLIMACO.] Messer Nicia will be easy to persuade. The problem will be his wife. But we shall find a way to bring her round.

CALLIMACO. Have you got the specimen?

MESSER NICIA. Siro has it under his cloak.

CALLIMACO. Give it to me. Aha! Weak kidneys!

MESSER NICIA. Yes, it does look a bit turbid. Yet she only just did it.

CALLIMACO. Oh, don't let that surprise you. *Nam mulieris urinae sunt semper maiioris glossitiei et albedinis et minoris pulchritudinis quam virorum. Huius autem in caetera, causa est amplitudo canalium, mixtio eorum quae ex matrice exeunt cum urina.*[5]

MESSER NICIA. Whores of Heaven! This man gets better all the time! He thinks of everything!

CALLIMACO. I'm afraid this woman is not properly covered at night. For that reason her urine is not of the finest quality.

MESSER NICIA. She has a good quilt over her. But she spends four hours on her knees before she gets into bed, stringing off paternosters. She's as strong as a horse when it comes to standing the cold.

CALLIMACO. Well, to cut a long story short, Messer Nicia, either you trust me or you don't. Either I am to expound a sure remedy to you or I am not. For myself, I'd let you have the remedy. Only put your trust in me, and you shall have it. And if, one year from now, your wife is not holding a child in her arms, a child of her own, I will gladly pay you two thousand ducats.

MESSER NICIA. Pray tell me what this remedy is. My only wish is to honor you in everything, and to trust you more than my father-confessor.

CALLIMACO. This, then, you must know. Nothing more surely makes a woman pregnant than getting her to drink a potion made from the root of the mandrake. This is something I have tested several times. Every time, it worked. Were that not so, the Queen of France would be childless, not to mention countless other princesses of that land.

MESSER NICIA. Is it possible?

CALLIMACO. It is exactly as I say. And Fortune must love you dearly, for she has caused me to bring to Florence all the ingredients of that potion. You could have it at once.

MESSER NICIA. When would she have to take it?

CALLIMACO. This evening after supper. The moon is well disposed. There could not be a more propitious moment.

MESSER NICIA. Well, that won't be hard to arrange. Make it up in any case. I'll see that she takes it.

CALLIMACO. There's a further consideration. The first man who has to do with her after she's taken this potion will die within the week. Nothing in this world can save him.

MESSER NICIA. Blood and guts! I won't touch the filthy stuff! You can't make me run my neck into *that* kind of noose!

CALLIMACO. Be calm. There is a remedy.

MESSSER NICIA. What is it?

CALLIMACO. Arrange for someone else to sleep with her. Immediately. So that, spending the night with her, he may draw upon himself all the infection of the mandrake. After which you can lie with her without danger.

MESSER NICIA. I won't do it.

CALLIMACO. Why not?

MESSER NICIA. I don't want to make my wife a whore and myself a cuckold, that's why not.

CALLIMACO. What did you say, Messer Nicia? Is this our wise Doctor of Laws? You are not prepared to do what the King of France has done, and great lords at his court without number?

MESSER NICIA. Who on earth do you expect me to find? Who would do such a thing? If I tell him about it, he won't want to do it. If I don't tell him, I shall be guilty of treachery—which is a felony in Florence. And I don't want to get into hot water!

CALLIMACO. If that's your only trouble, I believe I can take care of it.

MESSER NICIA. How?

CALLIMACO. I'll tell you. I'll give you the potion this evening after supper. Have her drink it, then put her straight to bed. It'll be about ten o'clock. Then we'll disguise ourselves—you, Ligurio, Siro, and I—and go search the New Market, the Old Market, every street and alley. The first idle young lout that we come upon, we gag him, and, to the tune of a sound drubbing, take him into your

house—and into your bedroom—in the dark. Then we put him in the bed and tell him what to do. I don't think there'll be any problem. In the morning you send the fellow packing before daybreak. Then get your wife washed and you can take your pleasure of her without the slightest risk.

MESSER NICIA. I'll go along—since you tell me that a king and princes and lords have used this method. One request, though: let's keep this secret—on account of the felony!

CALLIMACO. Who d'you think would blab?

MESSER NICIA. There's another obstacle. A tricky one, too.

CALLIMACO. What?

MESSER NICIA. We must get my wife to agree. And I don't think she ever will.

CALLIMACO. An excellent point. Personally, I would never marry in the first place unless I knew I could get the lady to see things my way.

LIGURIO. I have it!

MESSER NICIA. What?

LIGURIO. The remedy. We make use of her father-confessor.

CALLIMACO. And who'll persuade the father-confessor?

LIGURIO. You, me, and money, Our own wickedness and that of the priests.

MESSER NICIA. I'm afraid she'll refuse to talk with her father-confessor, if only to contradict her husband.

LIGURIO. There's a remedy for that too.

CALLIMACO. Tell me.

LIGURIO. Get her mother to take her to him.

MESSER NICIA. True. She trusts her mother.

LIGURIO. And I happen to know that her mother is of our way of thinking. Well, now, time's running on, and it'll soon be evening. Callimaco, go and take a little stroll, and be sure that you're at home to receive us at eight o'clock with the potion all ready. We'll go see the mother, then call on the friar, then report back to you.

CALLIMACO [*Aside to* LIGURIO.] Hey! Don't leave me alone!

LIGURIO. You look as if your goose were cooked.

CALLIMACO. Where am *I* supposed to put myself?

LIGURIO. Here, there, everywhere. Up this street and down the next. Florence is such a big city.

CALLIMACO. I'm dead. [*Exeunt.*]

Act 3

Scene 1

[*Enter* SOSTRATA, MESSER NICIA, *and* LIGURIO.]

SOSTRATA. I have always heard it said that it is the part of the prudent man to choose the lesser of two evils. If this is the only way you can have children, you must take it—provided it in no way offends against conscience.

MESSER NICIA. That's right.

LIGURIO. You will go and see your daughter, and Messer Nicia and I will call on her confessor, Friar Timoteo. We'll tell him how things stand, so that you won't have to. Then you'll hear what *he* has to say.

SOSTRATA. Very good. You take that street there. I'll go see Lucrezia and, come what may, I'll take her to talk with Friar Timoteo. [*Exit.*]

Scene 2

MESSER NICIA. You're probably surprised, Ligurio, that we have to go all round the world to persuade my wife? You wouldn't be—if you knew the whole story.

LIGURIO. I imagine it's because all women are suspicious.

MESSER NICIA. It's not that. She used to be the sweetest person in the world, and the easiest to manage. But one of her neighbors told her that, if she made a vow to attend first Mass at the Chapel of the Servites for forty mornings in a row, she would become pregnant. She made the vow and went to the chapel about twenty times. Well, you know how it is, one

of those frisky friars started pestering her. Naturally, she refused to go back. It's a sad state of affairs when the very people who ought to be setting a good example turn out like that. Am I right?

LIGURIO. Right, by Satan!

MESSER NICIA. From that day to this she's gone around with her ears pricked like a hare. Suggest anything at all, and she kicks up a fuss.

LIGURIO. My surprise is gone. But that vow—how did she go about fulfilling it?

MESSER NICIA. She got a dispensation.

LIGURIO. Good. Now let me have twenty-five ducats if you have them. Affairs of this kind cost money. One must make friends with the friar and give him hopes of better things to come.

MESSER NICIA. Here you are, then. I'm not worried. I'll get it back in other ways.

LIGURIO. These friars are smart. Shrewd. Which stands to reason, since they know both their own sins and everyone else's. If you're not wise to their ways, you can easily get gypped, and not know how to make them do what you want. So don't spoil everything by talking to him. A man like you, who spends the whole day in his study, knows all about his books, but can't cope with mundane matters. [*Aside.*] This fellow is such a fool, I'm afraid he'll spoil everything.

MESSER NICIA. Tell me what you want me to do.

LIGURIO. Leave the talking to me. Don't say a word unless I give the signal.

MESSER NICIA. I'm happy to do as you say. What signal will you give?

LIGURIO. I shall wink—and bite my lip. No, no. Let's try something else. How long is it since you last spoke with Friar Timoteo?

MESSER NICIA. Over ten years.

LIGURIO. Good. I'll tell him that you've gone deaf and can't answer him: you needn't say a word unless we shout.

MESSER NICIA. I'll do that.

LIGURIO. And don't be upset if I say something that doesn't seem to fit. Everything contributes to the final result.

MESSER NICIA. When the time comes!

Scene 3

[*Enter* TIMOTEO *and* A WOMAN.]

TIMOTEO. If you wish to make confession, I shall accede to your wish.

THE WOMAN. Not today. Someone's expecting me. It's enough if I worked some of it out of my system just standing here. Have you said those masses to Our Lady?

TIMOTEO. Yes, madonna.

THE WOMAN. Here, take this florin. Every Monday for the next two months I want you to say the Mass for the Dead for my husband's soul. He was a terrible man, but then there's the call of the flesh. I get a bit of the old feeling whenever I think of him. Do you think he's in Purgatory?

TIMOTEO. Undoubtedly.

THE WOMAN. I'm not so sure. You know what he did to me—and not just once either. I used to complain about it to you. I got as far over in bed as I could, but he was so importunate. Ugh, Lord Above!

TIMOTEO. Don't worry. God's clemency is great. If a man lack not the will, he shall not lack the time for repentance.

THE WOMAN. Do you think the Turks will invade Italy this year?

TIMOTEO. If you don't say your prayers, yes.

THE WOMAN. Glory be! Lord preserve us from the Turks and all their deviltries! All that impaling they go in for—it scares the life out of me! But there's a woman with a piece of linen for me—in the church yonder. I must let her know I'm here. Good day.[*Exit.*]

TIMOTEO. God be with you.

Scene 4

TIMOTEO. Women are the most charitable creatures, and the most trying. The man who shuns them avoids the trials, but also goes without their services; while the man who accepts them gets both the services and the trials. Well, it's the old truth, you can't have honey without flies. What are you about, my worthy friends? Can that be Messer Nicia?

LIGURIO. You'll have to shout. He's got so deaf, he can't hear a word.

TIMOTEO. You're welcome, messere.

LIGURIO. Louder!

TIMOTEO. Welcome!!

MESSER NICIA. Pleased to see you, Father!

TIMOTEO. What are you about?

MESSER NICIA. Oh, nicely, thanks.

LIGURIO. You'd better talk to me, Father. If you want *him* to hear, you'll have to shout till the whole square resounds with it.

TIMOTEO. What do you want with me?

LIGURIO. Messer Nicia here and another worthy man—I'll tell you about *him* later—are charged with the distribution of several hundred ducats as alms.

MESSER NICIA. Blood and guts!

LIGURIO [*Aside.*] Hold your tongue, damn you. We shan't need that much. [*Aloud.*] Don't be surprised at anything he might say, Father, he can't hear a thing. Every now and again he *thinks* he hears something and replies with an irrelevant remark.

TIMOTEO. Pray continue. Let him say what he likes.

LIGURIO. I've got some of the money with me now. They've chosen you as the person to distribute it.

TIMOTEO. I'll be very glad to.

LIGURIO. But first, you must help us. A strange thing has happened to Messer Nicia. Only you *can* help us. It concerns the honor of his house.

TIMOTEO. What is it?

LIGURIO. I don't know if you've met Messer Nicia's nephew, Cammillo Calfucci?

TIMOTEO. Yes, I have.

LIGURIO. Well, a year ago, he went to Paris on business, and, as his wife was dead, he left his daughter, who was of marriageable age, in the care of a convent which shall be nameless.

TIMOTEO. What happened?

LIGURIO. What happened? Just this. As a result of the nuns' carelessness or her own featherheadedness, she now finds herself four months pregnant. If things can't very discreetly be put to rights, Messer Nicia, the nuns, the girl, Cammillo, and the house of Calfucci will all be dishonored together. Now Messer Nicia values his honor so highly and is so sensitive to scandal that—if the whole thing can be prevented from leaking out—he will give three hundred ducats for the love of God.

MESSER NICIA. There's a story for you!

LIGURIO [Aside.] Quiet! [Aloud.] And he wants to put the matter in your hands. Only you and the mother superior can set things to rights.

TIMOTEO. How?

LIGURIO. You can persuade the mother superior to give the girl a potion. To make her miscarry.

TIMOTEO. This is something that requires a little thinking over.

LIGURIO. Think over all the good that will result. You'll be preserving the honor of the convent, the girl, and all her relatives. You'll be restoring a daughter to her father. You'll be giving satisfaction to Messer Nicia here and all *his* relatives. And you'll be able to distribute alms to the tune of three hundred ducats. While, on the other hand, the only harm you do is to a piece of unborn flesh that knows neither sense nor sensation and might miscarry anyhow in any number of ways. I believe in the greatest good of the greatest number. Always do what benefits the greatest number!

TIMOTEO. So be it, in God's name! You shall have your way! May all be done for the good Lord's sake and in Holy Charity's name! Give me the name of the convent, give me the potion, and, if you agree, the money you mentioned, that we may start to do good!

LIGURIO. There's a man of God for you! Just what I expected. Here's the first installment. [Gives him money.] The convent is called. . . Oh, but wait. There's a woman in the church signaling to me. I'll be right back. Don't leave, Messer Nicia. I've a couple of things to say to this woman. [Exit.]

Scene 5

TIMOTEO. How many months gone is she?

MESSER NICIA. I'm amazed!

TIMOTEO. I said: How many months gone is she?

MESSER NICIA. God blast him where he stands!

TIMOTEO. Why?

MESSER NICIA. So that he'll get hurt, that's why!

TIMOTEO. I seem to have landed in mud right up to my neck. Of these fellows I've got to deal with, one is crazy, and the other's deaf as a post. One runs away and the other hears nothing. But if they're trying to put one over on me, I'll beat them at that game any day of the week. But look, Ligurio is back. [Enter LIGURIO.]

Scene 6

LIGURIO. Keep quiet, messere! Oh, Father, I have wonderful news!

TIMOTEO. What is it?

LIGURIO. That woman I just spoke to told me the girl has had a miscarriage.

TIMOTEO. Good! This money will go into the general fund.

LIGURIO. What did you say?

TIMOTEO. I said you've more reason than ever to distribute alms.

LIGURIO. The alms are yours for the asking. But now you'll have to do something else for Messer Nicia.

TIMOTEO. Such as what?

LIGURIO. Something less burdensome, less scandalous, more acceptable to us, more profitable to you.

TIMOTEO. What is it? I'm with you all the way. We've been growing so intimate, there's nothing I wouldn't do for you.

LIGURIO. I'll tell you all about it in church. Just the two of us. Messer Nicia will be so kind as to wait for us. We'll be back in a trice.

MESSER NICIA. As the hangman said to his victim.

TIMOTEO. Let us go. [Exit with LIGURIO.]

Scene 7

MESSER NICIA. [*Alone.*] Is it day or night? Do I wake or dream? Am I drunk? I haven't touched a drop all day and I can't make head or tail of these carryings-on. We've got something to tell Friar Timoteo, so he tells him something else. Then he wanted me to pretend to be deaf. I'd have had to stop my ears up as if there were Sirens around if I wasn't to hear the mad things he was saying. God only knows what he had in mind. I find myself twenty-five ducats the poorer, not a word has been said about my affair, and now they leave me looking like a stuffed dummy. But look, they're back. If they haven't been talking of *my* affair, they're going to catch it. [*Reenter* TIMOTEO *and* LIGURIO.]

Scene 8

TIMOTEO. Get your womenfolk to come and see me. I know what I have to do. And if only my authority prevail we shall conclude this alliance tonight.
LIGURIO. Messer Nicia, Friar Timoteo is ready to do everything we ask. It's for you to see that the ladies come and see him.
MESSER NICIA. You make a new man of me. Will it be a boy?
LIGURIO. A boy.
MESSER NICIA. I weep for sheer tenderness!
TIMOTEO. Go into the church. I'll wait for the ladies here. Keep to one side, so they don't see you. As soon as they're gone, I'll tell you what they said. [*Exit* LIGURIO *and* MESSER NICIA.]

Scene 9

TIMOTEO. [*Alone.*] I wish I knew who's being taken in by whom. This scoundrel Ligurio came with that first story just to try me out. If I hadn't consented to do what he asked, he wouldn't have told me what he's now let out and revealed their plot for nothing. That first story was neither here nor there. So I myself have been taken in! And yet the cheat is not against my interests. Messer Nicia and Callimaco are rich, and both of them, for different reasons, will have to spend some of their riches. It is fitting that the affair should be kept secret: that's as important to them as it is to me. Whatever happens, I have no regrets. It's true there are going to be difficulties. Madonna Lucrezia is a good woman and nobody's fool. But I'll get at her through her goodness. Women are pretty brainless, anyhow. A woman need only put one word after another, and she's considered a genius. In the kingdom of the blind, the one-eyed man is King. Here she comes with her mother, a real shrew who will help me make the daughter do as I want.

Scene 10

[*Enter* SOSTRATA *and* LUCREZIA.]
SOSTRATA. I believe you believe me, daughter, when I tell you that no one in the world holds your honor more dear than I, and that I would never advise you to do anything that wasn't right. As I've told you over and again, if Friar Timoteo says that something shouldn't weigh on your conscience, don't give it a thought—go ahead and do it.
LUCREZIA. I've always feared that Messer Nicia's desire to have children might cause him to make some blunder. That's why, when he talked to me about anything, I always felt suspicious and doubtful, particularly since that business at the Chapel of the Servites. But of all the things he's tried, this seems the strangest. To have to submit my body to such an outrage! To be the cause of a man's death by such an outrage! If I were the only woman left alive, and the world depended on me for the continuance of the human race, even then I don't see how I could agree to it.
SOSTRATA. There's not much *I* can say

to you, daughter. You'll be talking with the friar: see what he says, and then do as he tells you. As I tell you. As everyone that loves you tells you.

LUCREZIA. This is torture. I'm breaking out in a sweat.

Scene 11

TIMOTEO. Welcome, ladies. I know what you want to hear about: Messer Nicia has already talked to me. As a matter of fact I've been poring over my books two hours and more, studying up on the subject. My researches have yielded many things, both general and particular, that support our case.

LUCREZIA. Are you serious? You're not laughing at me?

TIMOTEO. Ah, Madonna Lucrezia, this is no laughing matter! Don't you know me better than that?

LUCREZIA. I know you, Father. But this seems to me the strangest thing ever.

TIMOTEO. I believe you, madonna: but I would not have you continue to talk so. There are many things which, at a distance, seem terrible, unbearable, strange, but which, when you come close, are found to be human, bearable, familiar. That's why they say that fear can be greater than the thing feared. This is a case in point.

LUCREZIA. I pray God it is!

TIMOTEO. To return to what I was saying before. As far as conscience is concerned, you must pay attention to this general truth: when it is a question of a certain good and a doubtful evil, one must never forego the good from fear of the evil. Here we have a certain good—that you will become pregnant—that you will win a soul for the Lord God. The uncertain evil is that whoever lies with you after you've taken the potion will die. In some cases the man does not die. But, since there's an element of doubt, it is best that Messer Nicia should not run the risk. As to the act itself, to call it a sin is mere moonshine, for it is not the body that sins, it is the will. The real sin would be to act contrary to your husband's

wishes, and you will be acting in accordance with them. It would be a sin to take pleasure in the act, but you *won't* be taking pleasure in it. Besides, what one should always think of is the end in view. What are your proper aims? To fill a seat in Paradise and to make your husband happy. Now the Bible says that the daughters of Lot, believing that they were the only surviving women in the world, consorted with their father. Their intention being good, they were not sinning.

LUCREZIA. What are you persuading me to do, Father?

SOSTRATA. Let yourself *be* persuaded, daughter. Can't you see that a childless woman has no home? Her husband dies, and she's no better than a lost dog. Everyone abandons her.

TIMOTEO. Madonna, I swear to you, by this consecrated breast, that to yield to your husband's wishes in this matter need weigh on your conscience no more than eating meat on Fridays. A little holy water will wash the sin away.

LUCREZIA. Where are you leading me, Father?

TIMOTEO. To such things as will ever cause you to pray to God on my behalf, and will bring you greater joy next year than this.

SOSTRATA. She'll do what you want. I'll put her to bed tonight myself. What are you frightened of, crybaby? I know fifty women in this city who'd thank God for the opportunity.

LUCREZIA. I consent. But I do not believe that I shall live to see tomorrow.

TIMOTEO. Have no fear, my daughter. I shall pray to God for you. I shall call upon the Archangel Raphael to be with you. Go then, make haste. Prepare yourself for this mystery. Evening is upon us.

SOSTRATA. Peace be with you, Father.

LUCREZIA. God and Our Lady help me, and keep me from harm! [*Exit* LUCREZIA *and* SOSTRATA.]

Scene 12

TIMOTEO. Oh, Ligurio, come out here!
[*Enter* LIGURIO *and* MESSER NICIA.]

LIGURIO. How is it going?

TIMOTEO. Well. They've gone home, prepared to do everything. There'll be no hitch: her mother's going to stay with her. She'll put her to bed herself.

MESSER NICIA. Is that the truth?

TIMOTEO. Oh! So you've been cured of your deafness?

LIGURIO. St. Clement has granted him that boon.

TIMOTEO. Then you must set an *ex voto* on the altar to publicize the event and enable me to share in the proceeds.

MESSER NICIA. We're getting off the subject. Will my wife make a fuss about doing what I want?

TIMOTEO. No, I tell you.

MESSER NICIA. I'm the happiest man alive.

TIMOTEO. I can well believe it. You'll soon be the father of a fine boy. Let childless men go hang!

LIGURIO. Then go to your prayers, Father. If we need anything else, we'll come for you. You, messere, go to her and keep her steadfast in this resolve. I'll go see Master Callimaco and have him send you the potion. Arrange things so that I can see you at seven o'clock and settle what's to be done at ten.

MESSER NICIA. Well said. Good-by!

TIMOTEO. God be with you. [*Exeunt.*]

Act 4

Scene 1

CALLIMACO. [*Alone.*] I'd very much like to know what those fellows have done. Shall I ever see Ligurio again? It's the eleventh hour, after all, maybe even the twelfth. What anguish I've had to suffer! What anguish I'm still suffering! It's very true that Nature and Fortune keep man's account in balance: there's nothing good befalls but that it's made up for by something bad. The more my hopes have grown, the more my fears have grown. Unhappy that I am! Can I go on living amid such afflictions? Tormented by hopes and fears like these? I am a ship rocked by opposing winds, and the nearer she gets to the harbor, the more she has to fear. Messer Nicia's simplemindedness gives me grounds for hope; the foresight and resolution of Lucrezia give me cause for fear. No respite, no peace anywhere! From time to time I try to regain my self-control. I take myself to task for my raging passion. I say to myself: "What are you doing? Are you mad? If you possess her, what then? You'll see what a mistake you've made. You'll repent all the trouble and thought that you lavished on the affair. Don't you know how little good a man discovers in the things that he desires, compared with what he thought he would discover? Look at it another way. The worst that can befall you is that you will die and go to hell. Many a man has died before you, a large number of worthy men have gone to hell, are *you* ashamed to go there? Look Fate in the face. Fly from evil—or, if you cannot fly from it, bear it like a man, don't grovel and prostrate yourself before it like a woman!" That is how I cheer myself up! But it doesn't last very long. The desire to be with her at least once comes at me from all points of the compass. It shoots through me from top to toe and changes my whole being. My legs tremble, my bowels melt, my heart is pounding fit to burst, my arms hang limp, my tongue falls mute, my eyes are dazed, my head swims. If I could only find Ligurio I'd have someone to pour out my woes to. Here he comes now—in a hurry, too. The news he brings will either grant me a few more moments of life or kill me.

Scene 2

[*Enter* LIGURIO.]

LIGURIO. I've never been more eager to find Callimaco, and I've never found it harder to find him. If it had been

bad news that I was bringing, I'd
have found him right away. I've been
to his house, out into the square,
down to the market, along the Pan-
cone degli Spini, up to the Torna-
quinci Loggia, and not found him.
These young lovers have quicksilver
under their feet, they can't stand still.
[LIGURIO *is wandering all over the
place.*]

CALLIMACO. Why do I hold back? Why
not give him a shout? He looks
rather pleased with himself. Ligurio!
Ligurio!

LIGURIO. Callimaco! Where have you
been?

CALLIMACO. What's the news?

LIGURIO. Good.

CALLIMACO. Really good?

LIGURIO. The best.

CALLIMACO. Lucrezia is willing?

LIGURIO. Yes.

CALLIMACO. Friar Timoteo did the necessary?

LIGURIO. He did.

CALLIMACO. Blessèd Friar Timoteo! I
shall pray for him all the rest of my
life!

LIGURIO. That's a good one! As if God's
Grace were for evil as well as good!
The friar will need more than
prayers.

CALLIMACO. Such as what?

LIGURIO. Money.

CALLIMACO. We'll give him some. How
much have you promised him?

LIGURIO. Three hundred ducats.

CALLIMACO. Excellent.

LIGURIO. And Messer Nicia came up
with twenty-five.

CALLIMACO. Why on . . . ?

LIGURIO. Suffice it that he did.

CALLIMACO. And what did Lucrezia's
mother do?

LIGURIO. Almost everything. The moment she knew her daughter was going to have such a pleasant night—
and without sin—she went to work
on Lucrezia, pleading, commanding,
reassuring, everything. She got her
over to Friar Timoteo's place, continuing the good work till she gave
her consent.

CALLIMACO. God, what have I done to
deserve such a boon? I could die for
joy!

LIGURIO. What sort of man *is* this?
Whether for joy or sorrow, he's determined to die! Did you get the potion ready?

CALLIMACO. Yes, I did.

LIGURIO. What'll you send him?

CALLIMACO. A glass of hippocras. Just
the thing to settle the stomach and
cheer the brain. Oh dear, oh dear, oh
dear! I am undone!

LIGURIO. What's the matter? What can
it be?

CALLIMACO. There's no remedy now.

LIGURIO. What the devil's the matter
with you?

CALLIMACO. We're getting nowhere! I'm
locked in a fiery furnace!

LIGURIO. Why? Why won't you tell me?
What's the matter? Take your hands
from your face!

CALLIMACO. Don't you remember I told
Messer Nicia that you, he, Siro, and I
would catch somebody to put in bed
with his wife?

LIGURIO. What of it?

CALLIMACO. What of it? If I'm with you,
I can't be the man that's caught! And
if I'm not with you, he'll see through
the deception!

LIGURIO. True. But can't we find a
remedy?

CALLIMACO. I don't see how.

LIGURIO. Yes, we can.

CALLIMACO. What?

LIGURIO. Let me think it over for a moment.

CALLIMACO. So that's it! If you're still at
the thinking stage, my goose *is*
cooked.

LIGURIO. I have it!

CALLIMACO. What?

LIGURIO. The friar. He's brought us this
far. He can bring us the whole way.

CALLIMACO. How?

LIGURIO. We must all wear disguises. I'll
have the friar wear a disguise, then
get him to change his voice, his features, his clothes, and then tell Messer Nicia that he's you. He'll believe
me.

CALLIMACO. I like that. But where do I
come in?

LIGURIO. I'm counting on you to put a
tattered old cloak on, then to come
round the corner of his house, lute in
hand, singing a little song.

CALLIMACO. With my face showing?

LIGURIO. Yes. If *you* wore a mask he'd smell a rat.

CALLIMACO. He'll recognize me.

LIGURIO. No, he won't. I want you to grimace, twist your face up, open your mouth, grind your teeth together. Close one eye. Go on, try it!

CALLIMACO. Like this?

LIGURIO. No.

CALLIMACO. Like *this?*

LIGURIO. Not enough.

CALLIMACO. This way?

LIGURIO. Yes, yes, keep that. And I have a false nose at home. I'd like you to stick that on.

CALLIMACO. All right. Then what?

LIGURIO. As soon as you appear at the corner, we'll be there. We'll snatch the lute from you, grab hold of you, twirl you round and round, take you into the house, put you into the bed. The rest you'll have to do for yourself.

CALLIMACO. The thing is to get there.

LIGURIO. You'll get there. But as to how you're to get there again, *you* must solve that one.

CALLIMACO. How?

LIGURIO. Possess her tonight, and, before you leave, let her know how things stand, reveal the deception. Let her see how much love you bear her, tell her you adore her. Tell her she can be your friend without loss of reputation or your foe *with* loss of reputation. It's inconceivable that she wouldn't want to co-operate. On the contrary, she won't want this night to be the only one.

CALLIMACO. Do you believe that?

LIGURIO. I'm certain of it. But don't let's waste any more time. It's eight o'clock already. Call Siro and send the potion to Messer Nicia. Then wait for me at home. I'll collect Friar Timoteo, see that he gets into disguise, and bring him back here. Then we'll dig out Messer Nicia, then do what's left to do.

CALLIMACO. That sounds good. Get going. [*Exit* LIGURIO.]

Scene 3

CALLIMACO. Hey, Siro!

SIRO. [*Entering.*] Sir?

CALLIMACO. Come here.

SIRO. Here I am.

CALLIMACO. Get the silver goblet from my bedroom closet. Cover it with a cloth. Bring it here. And be sure you don't spill the stuff on the way over.

SIRO. [*Going.*] I'll do that.

CALLIMACO. That fellow's been with me ten years now, and he's always served me faithfully. I believe I can trust him even in this affair. And, although I've not said a word to him about this deception, he's guessed what's afoot, for he's quite a rascal, and he's falling in, I see, with my plans.

SIRO. [*Returning.*] Here it is.

CALLIMACO. Good. Now go to Messer Nicia's house, and tell him this is the medicine that his wife is to take right after supper. And the sooner supper is, the better it'll work. Tell him that we'll be at the corner, in due order, at the time he's to meet us there. And hurry.

SIRO. Right.

CALLIMACO. One moment. Listen. If he wants you to wait for him, wait, and come back here with him. If he *doesn't* want you to wait, come right back as soon as you've given him this—and the message.

SIRO. Yes, sir. [*Exit.*]

Scene 4

CALLIMACO. [*Alone.*] Here I stand, waiting for Ligurio to come back with Friar Timoteo. And the man who said that waiting is the hardest part spoke true. I'm wasting away at the rate of ten pounds an hour, thinking where I am now and where I may be two hours hence and fearing lest something should happen to upset my plan. For, if anything did, this would be my last night on earth. I should either throw myself in the Arno, or hang myself, or fling myself out of the window, or stab myself on her doorstep. But isn't that Ligurio? And there's someone with him with a hunchback and a limp. That'll be the friar in disguise, I'll swear. These friars! Know one, and you know the lot! Who's the fellow that's joined them? It looks like Siro. He must have finished his errand at Messer Nicia's. It's him all right. I'll wait here for them. Then—to business!

Scene 5

[*Enter* SIRO, LIGURIO, TIMOTEO, *in disguise.*]

SIRO. Who's that you've got with you, Ligurio?

LIGURIO. A very worthy man.

SIRO. Is he lame, or shamming?

LIGURIO. Mind your own business.

SIRO. Oh, he looks like a regular scoundrel.

LIGURIO. For God's sake, be quite, you'll spoil everything! Where's Callimaco?

CALLIMACO. Here. Welcome!

LIGURIO. Oh, Callimaco, give a word of warning to this lunatic Siro. He's said a thousand crazy things already.

CALLIMACO. Listen, Siro. This evening you must do everything Ligurio says. When he tells you to do something, it is I who am telling you to do it. And everything you see, feel, hear, and smell you're to keep strictly to yourself. That's if you value my honor, my wealth, my life, and your own best interests.

SIRO. I'll do as you say.

CALLIMACO. Did you give the goblet to Messer Nicia?

SIRO. Yes, sir.

CALLIMACO. What did he say?

SIRO. That everything was now in order, and that he'd go ahead.

TIMOTEO. Is this Callimaco?

CALLIMACO. At your service. Let's agree on the terms of the transaction: you may dispose of me and mine as of yourself.

TIMOTEO. So I have heard and, believing every word of it, I have agreed to do what I should never have done for any other man in the world.

CALLIMACO. Your labor shall not be in vain.

TIMOTEO. It will be enough to possess your favor.

LIGURIO. An end to all this hanky-panky! We'll get into our disguises, Siro. Callimaco, you come with us, and make your preparations. Friar

Timoteo will wait for us here. We'll be right back and then dig out Messer Nicia.

CALLIMACO. Good idea. Let's go.

TIMOTEO. I'll wait for you. [*Exit* CALLIMACO, LIGURIO, SIRO.]

Scene 6

TIMOTEO. [*Alone.*] It's true what they say: "Bad company will lead a man to the gallows." And a man often comes to grief by being too easygoing and goodhearted, not by being too wicked. God knows, *I* never thought of doing anybody any harm. I stayed in my cell, said my office, tended my flock, until that devil Ligurio turned up, and made me dip my finger in this transgression. I then had to follow with my arm, and finally it was total immersion. I still have no idea where I'll end up. I comfort myself with this thought: when something involves a large number of people, a large number of people have to be extremely careful. But here's Ligurio with that servant. [*Enter* LIGURIO *and* SIRO, *in disguise.*]

Scene 7

TIMOTEO. Welcome back!

LIGURIO. Do we look all right?

TIMOTEO. More than all right.

LIGURIO. Only Messer Nicia is missing. Let's walk toward his house. It's after nine. Let's go.

SIRO. Who is that opening his door? Is it his servant?

LIGURIO. No, it's the man himself. Ha! Ha! Ha! [*Enter* MESSER NICIA, *in disguise.*]

SIRO. You find it funny?

LIGURIO. Who wouldn't? Just look at him—wearing some kind of jerkin that doesn't even cover his arse. And what the devil has he got on his head? It looks like one of those silly hoods that canons wear. And—lower down—a smallsword! Ha! Ha! Ha! And he's muttering God knows what under his breath. Let's stand to one side and hear his tale of woe about his wife and what she's been doing to him.

Scene 8

MESSER NICIA. [*In disguise.*] The way that loony wife of mine has been carrying on! She sent the maidservant to her mother's house and the manservant to our country house. I applaud her for that—but not for making such a fuss before she'd get into the bed. "I don't want to!" "What is it I'm to do?" "What are you making me do?" "Woe is me!" "Mother, Mother!" And if "Mother, Mother" hadn't given her a tongue-lashing, she'd never have got into that bed. I hope she catches a fever that goes from bad to worse! I like my women finicky, it's true. But not that finicky! She's made my head swim, the bird brain! Oh, these women! They drive you crazy, you tell 'em so, and they come back at you with: "What have I done now? What's eating you this time?" Oh, well. Soon—very soon now—we shall be seeing a little action around here. And I intend to see it with both hands, so to speak. I'm doing all right, aren't I? Look at me now: taller, younger, slimmer. . . . At this rate I could get me a woman without even paying for the privilege. But where have the others got to?

Scene 9

LIGURIO. Good evening, messere.
MESSER NICIA. Oooh! Hey! Oooh!
LIGURIO. Don't be afraid, it's only us.
MESSER NICIA. Oh! You're all here! If I hadn't recognized you, I'd have run you through with this sword! You're Ligurio, aren't you? And you're Siro! Hm? And the other one's your master. Eh?
LIGURIO. Yes, messere.
MESSER NICIA. Let me have a look! Oh, he's well disguised! His own mother wouldn't know him!
LIGURIO. I had him put a couple of nuts in his mouth, so nobody can recognize his voice.
MESSER NICIA. You're stupid.
LIGURIO. Why?
MESSER NICIA. Why didn't you tell me sooner? Then *I* could have put nuts

in my mouth. You know how important it is that nobody should recognize our voices!
LIGURIO. Here you are then. Put this in your mouth!
MESSER NICIA. What is it?
LIGURIO. A ball of wax.
MESSER NICIA. Give it here. . . . Ca, pu, ca, coo, co, cu, cu, spu . . . A pox take you, you murdering hound!
LIGURIO. Oh, forgive me! I must have got them mixed up.
MESSER NICIA. Ca, ca, pu, pu . . . What, what was it?
LIGURIO. Bitter aloes.
MESSER NICIA. Damn you, Ligurio! Master Callimaco, do you stand by and say nothing?
TIMOTEO. I'm very angry with Ligurio.
MESSER NICIA. You *have* disguised your voice! That's *good!*
LIGURIO. Don't let's waste any more time here. I'll take over the duties of captain and give the army the order of the day. Callimaco will take the right horn of the crescent; I'll take the left. Messer Nicia will be in between us. Siro will bring up the rear and back up any of our forces that yield ground. The password shall be St. Cuckoo.
MESSER NICIA. Who's St. Cuckoo?
LIGURIO. He's the most venerated saint in all France. Let's go. Let's prepare our ambush at this corner. Listen! I hear a lute.
MESSER NICIA. That's our man. What shall we do?
LIGURIO. We'll send a scout forward to find out who he is. On hearing his report, we decide what action to take.
MESSER NICIA. Who'll go?
LIGURIO. You go, Siro! You know what to do. Observe, study the situation, return at the double, report.
SIRO. Right.
MESSER NICIA. I hope we don't make some terrible mistake. Suppose it's a cripple or a sickly old man, we'd have to repeat the performance tomorrow night!
LIGURIO. Don't worry: Siro's a reliable fellow. And here he comes. What have you found, Siro?
SIRO. The loveliest piece of man you ever saw and still on the right side of

twenty-five! He's alone—walking along in a tattered old cloak playing a lute.

MESSER NICIA. It's a stroke of luck, if what you say is true, but be sure of what you say, it'll be your fault if anything goes wrong.

SIRO. He's just like I said.

LIGURIO. Let's wait for him to turn this corner, then pounce!

MESSER NICIA. Come over here, Master Callimaco. You *are* quiet this evening. Here he comes.

Scene 10

[*Enter* CALLIMACO, *in disguise.*]

CALLIMACO. [*Singing.*]
Since Fortune keeps me from thy bed
Mayst thou find the Devil there instead!

LIGURIO. Hold him! Tightly now! Hand over that lute!

CALLIMACO. Help! What have I done?

MESSER NICIA. You'll soon see! Put something over his head. Gag him.

LIGURIO. Twirl him around!

MESSER NICIA. Give him another twirl! And another! Now pop him into the house.

TIMOTEO. Messer Nicia, I'm going to take a rest. I've got a splitting headache. I won't come back in the morning unless you need me.

MESSER NICIA. No, of course, Master Callimaco, don't bother. We can take care of this. [*Exeunt, except* TIMOTEO.]

Scene 11

TIMOTEO. [*Alone.*] Now they're safely in the house, I'll be off to the monastery. And you, spectators, don't be impatient with us, for none of us will take time out to sleep tonight—so the action of the play won't be interrupted. I'll be saying my office. Ligurio and Siro will be having supper, since they haven't eaten all day. Messer Nicia will be pacing the floor like a cat on hot bricks till the suspense is over. And, as for Callimaco and Madonna Lucrezia, if I were he and you were she, do you think we'd sleep tonight?

Act 5

Scene 1

TIMOTEO. [*Alone.*] I've not been able to shut my eyes all night, so great was my desire to know how Callimaco and the others were getting on. While waiting I've been killing time in various ways: I said Matins, read a life of one of the Holy Fathers, went into church and relit a lamp that had gone out, changed the veil on a Madonna that works miracles. How many times have I told those friars to keep her clean! And then they're surprised that people aren't devout any more! I can remember the time when there were five hundred *ex votos*. Today there aren't twenty. It's our own fault. We haven't known how to keep up her reputation. Every evening after Compline we used to have a procession in there. We used to sing Lauds there every Saturday. We were always making vows, so there were always fresh *ex votos* on the altar. We used to comfort our confessees and get *them* to make offerings to her. Now none of this is done, and they're surprised that the life's gone out of it all! Oh, the dim-wittedness of my brothers in Christ! But I hear a rumpus in Messer Nicia's house. By my faith, there they are! They're shoving their prisoner out of the house. I'm just in time. They certainly took ages getting him out. It's daybreak already. I'll stay and listen without letting them see me.

Scene 2

[*Enter* MESSER NICIA, CALLIMACO, LIGURIO, *and* SIRO.]

MESSER NICIA. You take this side, and I'll take the other. Siro, you take him by his cloak from behind.

CALLIMACO. Don't hurt me!

LIGURIO. Don't worry! Just get moving!

MESSER NICIA. Don't let's go any further!

LIGURIO. You're right. Let's let him go. Let's give him a couple of turns, so that he won't know which house he came out of. Round with him, Siro!

SIRO. Here we go!

MESSER NICIA. One more!

SIRO. There you are!

CALLIMACO. My lute!

LIGURIO. Be off, you scoundrel! And if I ever hear you breathe a word about this, I'll slit your windpipe for you!

MESSER NICIA. He's gone. Now let's go and get these disguises off. And we must all be seen out of doors bright and early so that it shan't appear that we've been up all night.

LIGURIO. Correct.

MESSER NICIA. You and Siro, go find Master Callimaco and tell him all went well.

LIGURIO. But what can we tell him? We don't know a thing. As you know, when we got into the house we went straight down to the cellar and started drinking. You and your mother-in-law were still at grips with him when we left you. We didn't see you again till just now when you brought us to throw him out.

MESSER NICIA. That's true. Oh, I've got some fine things to tell you. My wife was in bed in the dark. Sostrata was waiting for me by the fire. I got up there with the said young fellow and, to leave nothing to chance, I took him into a small room off the big room, where the lamp casts a very faint light—he could hardly see my face.

LIGURIO. Wisely done.

MESSER NICIA. I made him undress. When he boggled, I turned on him and showed him my teeth like a dog. He couldn't get out of his clothes fast enough. Finally he was naked. He'd got quite an ugly mug. His nose was tremendous. His mouth was sort of twisted. But you never saw such fine skin. White, soft, smooth. As for the rest, don't ask.

LIGURIO. No good *talking* of that sort of stuff. You had to see it.

MESSER NICIA. You're not making fun of me? Well, since I had my hands in the dough, so to speak, I decided to go through with it, and find out if the fellow was hale and hearty. For if he had the pox, where would I be

then, hm?

LIGURIO. Oh, you're right.

MESSER NICIA. As soon as I saw he was healthy I dragged him to the bedroom, put him into bed, and, before I left, stuck in both hands to feel how things were going. I'm not a man to take a firefly for a lantern.

LIGURIO. How prudently you've managed this affair!

MESSER NICIA. Having made this checkup, I left the room, bolted the door, and went to join my mother-in-law by the fire—where we spent the whole night talking.

LIGURIO. What about?

MESSER NICIA. About how foolish Lucrezia had been, and about how much better it would have been if she'd given in without shilly-shallying. Then we talked about the baby. I felt as if I held him in my arms already, dear little chap! Then I heard it striking seven and, fearing that day might be breaking any minute, back I went to the bedroom. Now what would you say if I told you that I just couldn't wake the scoundrel up?

LIGURIO. I can well believe it.

MESSER NICIA. He'd enjoyed his anointing. Finally I got him up, called you, and we whisked him out of the house.

LIGURIO. Things *have* gone well.

MESSER NICIA. Now what will you say if I tell you I'm sorry?

LIGURIO. About what?

MESSER NICIA. About that young man. To have to die so soon! That this night should cost him so dear!

LIGURIO. That's *his* problem. Don't you have your own worries?

MESSER NICIA. You're right. But it will seem a thousand years before I see Master Callimaco and share my joy with him.

LIGURIO. He'll be out and about within the hour. But it's broad daylight now. We'll go and get these things off. What will you do?

MESSER NICIA. I'll go home too and put on my best clothes. I'll have them get my wife up and washed. Then I'll see that she goes to church to receive a blessing on this night's work. I'd like you and Callimaco to be there. And we should talk to the friar and thank and reward him for his good offices.

LIGURIO. An excellent notion. Let's do that. [*Exeunt, except* TIMOTEO.]

Scene 3

TIMOTEO. [*Alone.*] I heard what they were saying, and liked it. What a stupid fellow this Messer Nicia is! It was the conclusion they came to that pleased me most. And since they'll be coming to see me, I won't stay here, I'll wait for them in church, where my merchandise will have a greater value. But who's coming out of that house? It looks like Ligurio, and the man with him must be Callimaco. I don't want them to find me here, for the reason I just gave. After all, if they don't come and see me, there's always time for me to go and see them. [*Exit.*]

Scene 4

[*Enter* CALLIMACO *and* LIGURIO.]

CALLIMACO. As I've already told you, my dear Ligurio, I didn't begin to be happy till past three o'clock this morning, because, though I *had* had a lot of pleasure, I hadn't really enjoyed it. But then I revealed to her who I was, and made her appreciate the love I bore her, and went on to tell her how easily—because of her husband's simplemindedness—we should be able to live together in happiness without the slightest scandal. I finished by promising her than whenever it pleased God to translate her husband I should take her as my wife. She thought this over and having, among other things, tasted the difference between my performance and Nicia's, between, that is, the kisses of a young lover and those of an old husband, she said to me, after heaving several sighs:

"Since your guile, my husband's folly, the simplemindedness of my mother, and the wickedness of my father-confessor have led me to do what I should never have done of my own free will, I must judge it to be

Heaven that willed it so, and I cannot find it in myself to refuse what Heaven wishes me to accept. In consequence, I take you for my lord, my master, and my guide. You are my father, my defender, my love and sovereign good, and what my husband wanted on *one* night I want him to have forever. So make friends with him, and go to church this morning, and then come and have dinner with us. You shall come and go as you please, and we shall be able to meet at any time without arousing the least suspicion."

When I heard these words I was ravished by their sweetness. I couldn't tell her more than a fraction of what I wished to say in reply. I'm the happiest and most contented man that ever walked this earth, and if neither Death nor Time take my happiness from me, the saints themselves shall call me blessèd!

LIGURIO. I am delighted to hear of all your good fortune. Everything's worked out just as I said it would. But where do we go from here?

CALLIMACO. We walk in the direction of the church, because I promised her I'd be there. She'll be coming with her mother and Messer Nicia.

LIGURIO. I can hear their door opening. Yes, it's the ladies, and the learnèd doctor's bringing up the rear.

CALLIMACO. Let's go into the church and wait for them there. [*Exeunt.*]

Scene 5

[*Enter* MESSER NICIA, LUCREZIA, *and* SOSTRATA.]

MESSER NICIA. Lucrezia, it is my belief that we should do things in a God-fearing manner, not foolishly.

LUCREZIA. Why, what is there to do now?

MESSER NICIA. There! The answers she gives me! She's getting quite cocky!

SOSTRATA. You mustn't be so surprised: she's a little bit changed.

LUCREZIA. What are you getting at?

MESSER NICIA. I meant that it would be best for me to go on ahead and have a word with Friar Timoteo. I want to tell him to meet us at the church door, so he can confer the blessing on you. Why, this morning, it's as if you'd been reborn!

LUCREZIA. Then why don't you get moving?

MESSER NICIA. You're saucy this morning! Last night you seemed half dead!

LUCREZIA. I have you to thank, haven't I?

SOSTRATA. Go and find Friar Timoteo. But there's no need: he's just coming out of church.

MESSER NICIA. So he is.

Scene 6

[*Enter* TIMOTEO.]

TIMOTEO. Callimaco and Ligurio told me that Messer Nicia and the ladies are on the way to church, so I've come out.

MESSER NICIA. *Bona dies,* Father!

TIMOTEO. Welcome! And Heaven's blessing upon you, madonna! May God give you a fine baby boy!

LUCREZIA. May God so will it!

TIMOTEO. You may rely on that: He *will* so will it!

MESSER NICIA. Is it Ligurio and Master Callimaco that I see there in church?

TIMOTEO. Yes, messere.

MESSER NICIA. Invite them over.

TIMOTEO. Come, sirs! [*Enter* LIGURIO *and* CALLIMACO.]

CALLIMACO. God save you!

MESSER NICIA. Master Callimaco, give my wife here your hand.

CALLIMACO. Willingly.

MESSER NICIA. Lucrezia, when we have a staff to support our old age, we shall owe it to this man.

LUCREZIA. I hold him dear. May he be a good friend of the family!

MESSER NICIA. Heaven bless you! I should like him and Ligurio to come and dine with us this morning.

LUCREZIA. By all means.

MESSER NICIA. And I should like to give them the key to the downstairs room off the loggia, so that they can come and go when they like. For they have no women at home. They must live like beasts.

CALLIMACO. I accept, and I'll use it whenever the occasion arises.

TIMOTEO. Am I to have the money for the almsgiving?

MESSER NICIA. You are, *domine:* I shall be sending you some today.

LUCREZIA. Does no one remember poor old Siro?

MESSER NICIA. He only has to ask, I'm at his service. Lucrezia, how much shall I give the friar for his blessing?

LUCREZIA. Give him ten groats.

MESSER NICIA. God Almighty! [*He nearly chokes.*]

TIMOTEO. Madonna Sostrata, you seem to have taken on a new lease of life!

SOSTRATA. Who wouldn't be happy today?

TIMOTEO. Let us enter the church and say the customary prayers. After the service, go dine at your leisure. As for you, spectators, don't wait for us to come out again. The service is long, and I shall stay in church, and they'll go off home through the side door. Farewell! [*Exeunt.*]

1. Good day, Lord Teacher.
2. Good day to you, Lord Doctor.
3. To our business.
4. These are the causes of sterility: either in the semen, or in the womb, or in the distribution of the semen, or in the penis, or for an external reason.
5. For the urine of women always is of greater brightness and whiteness and of less beauty than that of men. Moreover, the reason of this is in the large size of the urinary canal and in the mixture of those fluids that come out of the canal with the urine.